EVANGELICAL Sunday School Lesson COMMENTARY

TWENTY-NINTH ANNUAL VOLUME

Based on the

Uniform Bible Lesson Series

Editorial Staff
James E. Humbertson—EDITORIAL DIRECTOR
O. W. Polen—EDITOR IN CHIEF
O. C. McCane—GENERAL DIRECTOR OF PUBLICATIONS
Hoyt E. Stone—EDITOR, YOUTH AND CHRISTIAN EDUCATION LITERATURE

Lesson Exposition Writers
Noel Brooks
Charles W. Conn
Homer G. Rhea, Jr.
Sabord Woods

Published by
PATHWAY PRESS   Cleveland, Tennessee

Lesson treatments in the *Evangelical Sunday School Lesson Commentary* for 1980-81 are based upon the outlines of the Uniform Bible Lesson Series prepared by the Evangelical Curriculum Commission (formerly the Curriculum Commission of the National Sunday School Association).

Copyright 1980

PATHWAY PRESS, Cleveland, Tennessee

ISBN: 0-87148-294-0

Printed in the United States of America

TABLE OF CONTENTS

Introduction to the 1980-81 Commentary 5
Using the 1980-81 Commentary 6
Exposition Writers 7
Golden Text Homily Writers 9
Acknowledgments 11
Lesson Cycle (1978-1985) 12

FALL QUARTER LESSONS

Introduction to Fall Quarter Lessons 13
Map 14
September 7, The Conqueror of Fear 15
September 14, The Triumph of Faith 23
September 21, An Inescapable Question 31
September 28, Our Glorified Lord 39
October 5, The Conqueror of Demons 47
October 12, The Compassionate Savior 55
October 19, The Lord of the Harvest 63
October 26, The Giver of Light 72
November 2, The Giver of Life 80
November 9, The Call to Discipleship 88
November 16, The Gift of Sight 96
November 23, Demonstrating Thankfulness 104
November 30, The Seeking Savior 112

WINTER QUARTER LESSONS

Introduction to Winter Quarter Lessons 120
Map 121
December 7, Giving That Costs 122
December 14, Welcoming Christ 128
December 21, Wise Men Worship Christ (Christmas Lesson) 134
December 28, Christ's Supreme Authority 141
January 4, Understanding the Lord's Supper 148
January 11, The Danger of Self-Sufficiency 155
January 18, The Price of Consecration 161
January 25, Tragedy of Rejecting Christ 168

February 1, Price of Redemption 174
February 8, Overcoming Doubt 180
February 15, Love, the Christian's Motivation 186
February 22, Christ, Our Triumphant Lord 193

SPRING QUARTER LESSONS

Introduction to Spring Quarter Lessons 199
Map 200
March 1, Children, a Gift From God 201
March 8, God's Call to Service 208
March 15, Way to Revival 215
March 22, Choosing a Leader 222
March 29, The Folly of Self-Will 229
April 5, God-Given Victory 236
April 12, Conquering Jealousy 243
April 19, Alive Forever (Easter Lesson) 250
April 26, Responsibilities of Friendship 257
May 3, Demonstrating True Greatness 264
May 10, Following God's Plan 271
May 17, Doing Things God's Way 278
May 24, The Consequences of Rebellion 286
May 31, The Importance of Choice 293

SUMMER QUARTER LESSONS

Introduction to Summer Quarter Lessons 300
Map 301
June 7, Anointed by the Spirit (Pentecost Sunday) 302
June 14, The Results of Choice 311
June 21, The Value of Wise Counsel 319
June 28, No Other Gods 327
July 5, Seeking God's Help 336
July 12, Courage to Champion God's Cause 345
July 19, Quest for Spiritual Power 354
July 26, Showing Concern for Others 363
August 2, Principles of Success 370
August 9, Responding to God's Call 378
August 16, Deliverance Through Prayer 387
August 23, Giving Priority to God's Word 396
August 30, Divine Discipline 405

INTRODUCING THE 1980-81 COMMENTARY

The *Evangelical Sunday School Lesson Commentary* contains in a single volume a full study of the Sunday school lessons for the months beginning with September, 1980, and running through August, 1981. The twelve months of lessons draw from both the Old Testament and New Testament in an effort to provide balance and establish relationship between these distinct but inspired writings. The lessons in this 1980-81 volume are drawn from the third year of a seven-year cycle, which will be completed in August, 1985. (The cycle is printed in full on page 12 of this volume.)

The lessons for the *Evangelical Commentary* are based on the Uniform Bible Lesson Series Outlines, prepared by the Evangelical Curriculum Commission. (The Evangelical Curriculum Commission is a member of the National Association of Evangelicals.) The lessons include studies from both the Old and New Testaments; and taken together with the other annual volumes of lessons in the cycle, they provide a valuable commentary on a wide range of biblical subjects.

The 1980-81 commentary is the work of a team of Christian scholars and writers who have developed the volume under the supervision of Pathway Press. All the major writers, introduced on the following pages, represent a team of ministers committed to a strictly evangelical interpretation of the Scriptures. The guiding theological principles of this commentary are expressed in the following statement of faith:

1. WE BELIEVE the Bible to be the inspired, the only infallible, authoritative Word of God.

2. WE BELIEVE that there is one God, eternally existing in three persons: Father, Son, and Holy Spirit.

3. WE BELIEVE in the deity of our Lord Jesus Christ, in His virgin birth, in His sinless life, in His miracles, in His vicarious and atoning death through His shed blood, in His bodily resurrection, in His ascension to the right hand of the Father, and in His personal return in power and glory.

4. WE BELIEVE that for the salvation of lost and sinful men, personal reception of the Lord Jesus Christ and regeneration by the Holy Spirit are absolutely essential.

5. WE BELIEVE in the present ministry of the Holy Spirit by whose cleansing and indwelling the Christian is enabled to live a godly life.

6. WE BELIEVE in the personal return of the Lord Jesus Christ.

7. WE BELIEVE in the resurrection of both the saved and the lost—they that are saved, unto the resurrection of life; and they that are lost, unto the resurrection of damnation.

8. WE BELIEVE in the spiritual unity of believers in our Lord Jesus Christ.

USING THE 1980-81 COMMENTARY

The *Evangelical Sunday School Lesson Commentary* for 1980-81 is presented to the reader with the hope that it will become his weekly companion through the months ahead.

Following a year of specialized study on the theme "The Year of the Bible," which introduced the seven-year cycle, it became the purpose of the following volumes of lessons to explore more fully books and subjects which were given only a survey treatment in the 1978-79 sequence of studies.

The fall quarter, entitled "Life of Christ," continues a four-quarter series of lessons on the life of the Lord Jesus which was begun in the spring of 1980. This series is based on the Gospels—Matthew, Mark, Luke, and John.

The winter quarter, entitled "Life of Christ," continues and concludes the four-quarter series of lessons on the life of the Lord Jesus.

The spring quarter, entitled "1 and 2 Samuel," is a series of lessons which recount the lives of Samuel as the last of the judges, Saul as the first king, and David as the successor to Saul and to the throne.

The summer quarter, entitled "A Nation in Transition," is a series of lessons from the Books of 1 and 2 Kings, 2 Chronicles, and Isaiah.

The lesson sequence used in this volume is prepared by the Evangelical Curriculum Commission. (The Evangelical Curriculum Commission is a member of the National Association of Evangelicals).

The specific material used in developing each lesson is written and edited under the guidance of the editorial staff of Pathway Press.

BIBLE BACKGROUND: At the opening of each week's lesson, you will see printed the Bible background. These references point out passages of Scripture that are directly related to the lesson, and it is advisable for you to read each one carefully before beginning the lesson study.

TIME and PLACE: A time and place is given for each lesson. Where there is a wide range of opinions regarding the exact time or place, the printed New Testament works of Merrill C. Tenney and Old Testament works of Samuel J. Schultz are used to provide the information.

PRINTED TEXT and CENTRAL TRUTH: The printed text is the body of Scripture designated each week for verse-by-verse study in the classroom. Drawing on the Bible background the teacher delves into this printed text, expounding its content to the students. Although the printed text contains different insights for each teacher, the central truth states the single unifying principle that the expositors attempted to clarify in each lesson.

DICTIONARY: A dictionary, which attempts to bring pronunciation and clarification to difficult words or phrases, is included with most lessons. Pronunciations are based on the phonetic system used by Field Enterprises Educational Corporation of Chicago and New York in *The World Book Encyclopedia.* Definitions are generally based on *The Pictorial Bible Dictionary,* published by Zondervan Publishing Company, Grand Rapids, Michigan.

EXPOSITION and LESSON OUTLINE: The heart of this commentary —and probably the heart of the teacher's instruction each week—is the exposition of the printed text. This exposition material is preceded by a lesson outline, which indicates how the material is to be divided for study. These lesson outlines are not exhaustive, but provide a skeleton for the teacher to amplify upon and to build around.

REVIEW and DISCUSSION QUESTIONS: Immediately following the expository material in each lesson are five review questions. These questions are designed as discussion starters, along with the discussion questions appearing throughout the expository material. The review questions also serve to restate the major bits of information in the text and may be supplemented by questions of your own drawn from the expository material.

GOLDEN TEXT HOMILY: The golden text homily for each week is a brief reflection on that single verse. As the word *homily* implies, it is a discourse or sermon on a particular point. The homily may often be used effectively to give the lesson a life-related slant.

SENTENCE SERMONS: Two or more sentence sermons—popular and pithy single-line thoughts on the central truth of the lesson—are included each week.

EVANGELISTIC APPLICATION: The evangelistic application relates the general theme of the week's lesson to the ongoing task of evangelism. The theme of the lesson (but not necessarily of the lesson text) is used to make this application. At times the emphasis of the section bears on direct evangelism of class members who may not be Christians; at other times the emphasis bears upon exhorting the class members to become more involved in evangelizing others.

ILLUMINATING THE LESSON: In this section, illustrative material is provided for the teacher to use to support the lesson at whatever point seems most appropriate.

DAILY DEVOTIONAL GUIDE: The daily devotional guides are included for the teacher to use in his own devotions throughout the week, as well as to share with members of his class.

EXPOSITION WRITERS

Writers for the expository materials for the 1980-81 volume are as follows:

The lesson expositions for the fall quarter (September, October, November) were written by the Reverend Homer G. Rhea, Jr.

The Reverend Mr. Rhea serves as

editorial administrative assistant at the Church of God Publishing House, Cleveland, Tennessee; and in conjunction with the Editor in Chief, prepares the *Church of God EVANGEL,* the official journal of the denomination. He was reared and educated in Mississippi, where he served in the pastoral ministry for over fifteen years. He is an ordained minister in the Church of God and has held positions as district overseer and member of the Mississippi State Council and the State Youth and Christian Education Board.

The Reverend Mr. Rhea is author of the Instructor's Manual to the Church Training Course *Highlights of Hebrew History* by Charles Conn. He is also a frequent contributor of articles to the *Church of God Evangel* and the *Youth and Christian Education Leadership Magazine.*

Biblical expositions for the winter quarter (December, January, February) were prepared by the Reverend Charles W. Conn (Litt.D.), president of Lee College in Cleveland, Tennessee. Before coming to Lee College in 1970, Dr. Conn spent eight years on the Executive Committee of the Church of God, including a four-year term as general overseer of the denomination. He is a well-known writer in the Evangelical church world and is the author of thirteen books published by Pathway Press. He served for ten years as editor in chief of Church of God publications, during which time he served on various boards and committees of the National Sunday School Association (NSSA), the National Association of Evangelicals (NAE), and the Evangelical Press Association (EPA).

Lesson expositions for the spring quarter (March, April, May) were written by the Reverend Noel Brooks (B.D., D.D.), former faculty member at Southwestern College, Oklahoma City, Oklahoma. Dr. Brooks is a native of England, where he pastored for thirty-eight years. He was educated in England and earned the Bachelor of Divinity (B.D.) degree from the University of London. The Reverend Dr. Brooks also holds an honorary doctorate from Holmes Theological Seminary.

Recognized for his unusual depth of biblical knowledge, Dr. Brooks is in demand as a conference speaker throughout the Pentecostal Holiness Church, of which he has been a member since 1954.

In addition to his duties as a visiting lecturer at Southwestern College and church gatherings, the Reverend Dr. Brooks writes a Sunday school adult quarterly for the Pentecostal Holiness Church and provides a regular page, entitled "The Advocate Bible School," in the *Advocate* magazine. He has also authored several books.

The lesson expositions for the summer quarter (June, July, August) were written by the Reverend Sabord Woods (Ph.D.) and the Reverend Homer G. Rhea, Jr.

Dr. Woods is associate professor of English, Lee College, Cleveland,

Tennessee. He is primarily a teacher. As an adolescent and young adult he enjoyed a successful pulpit ministry—conducting revivals, pastoring a mission while yet in high school, serving as assistant pastor and minister of music, and pastoring two churches during his early and middle twenties. However, at the same time he was completing a Bachelor of Arts Degree in English (1961) and, later, teaching at various levels in the public schools in Jesup, Georgia. In June, 1966 he completed the Master of Arts Degree in English, and in the fall of 1966 he joined the faculty of Lee College, where he is currently Associate Professor of English. In December, 1975 he received the Doctor of Philosophy Degree in English at the University of Tennessee at Knoxville. Since childhood he has taught Sunday School—juniors, teenagers, adults. Now, in writing for the *Evangelical Sunday School Commentary,* he combines the years of Bible study which have gone into personal devotions and preparation for preaching and Sunday School teaching with writing skill developed through training and performance as a professional in English.

The Reverend Mr. Rhea serves as editorial administrative assistant at the Church of God Publishing House, Cleveland, Tennessee; and in conjunction with the Editor in Chief, prepares the *Church of God EVANGEL,* the official journal of the denomination. He was reared and educated in Mississippi, where he served in the pastoral ministry for over fifteen years. He is an ordained minister in the Church of God and has held positions as district overseer and member of the Mississippi State Council and the State Youth and Christian Education Board.

The Reverend Mr. Rhea is author of the Instructor's Manual to the Church Training Course *Highlights of Hebrew History* by Charles Conn. He is also a frequent contributor of articles to the *Church of God Evangel* and the *Youth and Christian Education Leadership Magazine.*

GOLDEN TEXT HOMILY WRITERS

Terry A. Beaver
Pastor, Church of God
Bradley, Illinois

Richard Y. Bershon
Chief, Chaplain Service
V. A. Medical Center
Tomah, Wisconsin

Donald N. Bowdle, Ph.D., Th.D.,
Professor of History and Religion
Dean, Division of Religion
Lee College, Cleveland, Tennessee

Edward E. Call
Professor of Missions
Church of God School of Theology
Cleveland, Tennessee

E. C. Christenbury, Ed.D.
Associate Professor of Education
Lee College, Cleveland, Tennessee

John R. Church, Ph.D.
Winston Salem, North Carolina

Dennis Cox, Vice-President
Spiritual Affairs
Southwestern College
Oklahoma City, Oklahoma

Wayne Dehart
Pastor, Church of God
Clarksburg, West Virginia

Kenneth K. Foreman
Executive Director of Christian Education
Pentecostal Church of God
Joplin, Missouri

James A. Guynn
Pastor, Church of God
Harrisburg, Illinois

Ralph W. Harris (Retired)
Former Editor, Church School Literature
Gospel Publishing House
Springfield, Missouri

Lambert Huffman
Winona Lake, Indiana

James E. Humbertson
Editorial Director, *Evangelical Commentary*
Pathway Press
Cleveland, Tennessee

Robert Humbertson, Ph.D.,
Chairman, Department of Languages
Lee College
Cleveland, Tennessee

Leroy Imperio
Pastor, Church of God
Elkins, West Virginia

Henry H. Kinsey
Director, Stateside Military
Church of God
Cleveland, Tennessee

Idabeth McDole, D.D.
Editor, *Pentecostal Messenger*
Messenger Publishing House
Joplin, Missouri

Levy E. Moore
Chaplain and Christian Service Director
Emmanuel College
Franklin Springs, Georgia

Tom L. Murray
Assistant to the President
Southwestern College
Oklahoma City, Oklahoma

Scott T. Muse, Jr., Ph.D.
President, Southwestern College
Oklahoma City, Oklahoma

Jerry Noble
Media Coordinator
"Forward in Faith"
Cleveland, Tennessee

T. Paul Patton
Pastor, Church of God
Chattanooga, Tennessee

E. A. Pettersen
A. C. Nielsen Company
New York, New York

Garnet E. Pike
Dean, Emmanuel College School of Christian Ministries
Franklin Springs, Georgia

Wayne S. Proctor
Pastor, Church of God
Nashville, Tennessee

Jerry Puckett
Plant Superintendent
Church of God Publishing House
Cleveland, Tennessee

Homer G. Rhea, Jr.
Editorial Administrative Assistant
Church of God Publishing House
Cleveland, Tennessee

H. Edward Rowe
Christian Freedom Foundation
New York, New York

Edward E. Shoupe
Chaplain (Lieutenant Colonel)
United States Air Force
(Retired)

Philip Siggelkow
President, International Bible College
Moose Jaw, Saskatchewan, Canada

M. David Sisler, Jr.
Pastor, Church of God
New Britain, Connecticut

Jack Smith
Associate Pastor, North Cleveland
Church of God
Cleveland, Tennessee

Hoyt E. Stone
Editor, Christian Education Literature
Church of God Publishing House
Cleveland, Tennessee

Jewell Travis
Director, East Tennessee Evangelism
and Home Missions
Chattanooga, Tennessee

Laud O. Vaught, Ph.D.
President, Northwest Bible College
Minot, North Dakota

Fred H. Whisman
Cost Analyst
Church of God Publishing House
Cleveland, Tennessee

C. Wayne White
Chaplain (Captain)
United States Army
Fort Hood, Texas

Charles G. Wiley
Pastor, Church of God
Piedmont, West Virginia

Wilbur G. Williams
Former Editor, *Evangelical Commentary*
Marion, Indiana

ACKNOWLEDGMENTS

Many books, magazines, and newspapers have been used in the research that has gone into this 1980-81 *Evangelical Commentary*. A few of the major books that have been used are listed below.

Bibles
King James Version, Oxford University Press, Oxford, England
New American Standard Bible, A. J. Holman Co., Publishers, New York, New York
New English Bible (NEB), Oxford University Press, Oxford, England
New International Version (NIV), Zondervan Publishing House, Grand Rapids, Michigan

Commentaries
Clarke's Commentary, Abingdon-Cokesbury, Nashville, Tennessee
Commentaries on the Old Testament (Keil & Delitzsch) Eerdmans Publishing Co., Grand Rapids, Michigan
Ellicott's Bible Commentary, Zondervan Publishing House, Grand Rapids, Michigan
Expositions of Holy Scriptures (Alexander MacLaren), Eerdmans Publishing Co., Grand Rapids, Michigan
The Interpreter's Bible, Abingdon Press, New York, New York
The Pulpit Commentary, Eerdmans Publishing Co., Grand Rapids, Michigan
The Wesleyan Commentary, Eerdmans Publishing Co., Grand Rapids, Michigan
The Expositor's Greek Testament, Eerdmans Publishing Co., Grand Rapids, Michigan

Illustrations
Dictionary of Illustrations for Pulpit and Platform, Moody Press, Chicago, Illinois
I Quote, George W. Stewart Publishers, Inc., New York, New York
3,000 Illustrations for Christian Service, Eerdmans Publishing Co., Grand Rapids, Michigan
Knight's Master Book of New Illustrations, Eerdmans Publishing Co., Grand Rapids, Michigan
Notes and Quotes, The Warner Press, Anderson, Indiana
The Pointed Pen, Pathway Press, Cleveland, Tennessee
The Speaker's Sourcebook, Zondervan Publishing House, Grand Rapids, Michigan

General Reference Books
Harper's Bible Dictionary, Harper and Brothers Publishers, New York, New York
The International Standard Bible Encyclopedia, Eerdmans Publishing Co., Grand Rapids, Michigan
The Interpreter's Dictionary of the Bible, Abingdon Press, Nashville, Tennessee
The World Book Encyclopedia, Field Enterprises Education Corp., Chicago, Illinois
Pictorial Dictionary of the Bible, Zondervan Publishing House, Grand Rapids, Michigan
Word Pictures in the New Testament (Robertson), Broadman Press, Nashville, Tennessee

(1978-85) UNIFORM BIBLE LESSONS SERIES (1978-85)

FALL QUARTER (September, October, November)	WINTER QUARTER (December, January, February)	SPRING QUARTER (March, April, May)	SUMMER QUARTER (June, July, August)
1978 SURVEY OF THE BIBLE	1978-79 EXPLORING THE BIBLE	1979 GREAT TRUTHS OF THE BIBLE	1979 THE BIBLE AND TODAY'S ISSUES
1979 GENESIS	1979-80 EXODUS THROUGH RUTH	1980 LIFE OF CHRIST (Harmony From Gospels)	1980 LIFE OF CHRIST (Harmony From Gospels)
1980 LIFE OF CHRIST (Harmony From Gospels)	1980-81 LIFE OF CHRIST (Harmony From Gospels)	1981 1 AND 2 SAMUEL	1981 A NATION IN TRANSITION
1981 THE EARLY CHURCH (Acts 1-12)	1981-82 THE EXPANDING CHURCH (Acts 13-28)	1982 1 AND 2 THESSALONIANS	1982 THE FAMILY
1982 1 AND 2 CORINTHIANS	1982-83 ROMANS AND GALATIANS	1983 LIFE IN THE SPIRIT	1983 POETICAL BOOKS
1983 TEACHINGS OF CHRIST (Part I)	1983-84 TEACHINGS OF CHRIST (Part II)	1984 1 AND 2 PETER JAMES AND JUDE	1984 EPHESIANS, COLOSSIANS, PHILIPPIANS
1984 THE SPIRITUAL WORLD	1984-85 PASTORAL EPISTLES (Including 1, 2, and 3 John)	1985 MESSAGE OF THE OLD TESTAMENT PROPHETS	1985 THE THINGS TO COME

INTRODUCTION TO FALL QUARTER

In our seven-year cycle of lessons, four quarters are devoted to a study of the life of Christ and two quarters are devoted to the teachings of Christ. The series on the life of Christ began with the spring quarter (March, April, May) 1980 and runs through the winter quarter 1980-81. The lessons are based on the harmony of the Gospels. Each of the four Gospels possesses its own characteristics in keeping with the personality and purpose of the author. And yet when they are combined, they present a well-rounded, Spirit-inspired story of the life of Jesus.

The study of Christ's life is the most interesting and fascinating study anyone can take. To the Christian it is more than just interesting, it is an inexhaustible fountain of refreshment, and a coffer of immeasurable treasures. "The Word was made flesh, and dwelt among us, (and we beheld his glory, the glory as of the only begotten of the Father,) full of grace and truth" (John 1:14).

The eternal Christ pitched His tent of flesh and dwelt for a while among men. He was God as though He were not man. Yet He became man that He might both identify Himself with man and fully reveal the Father to men.

These lessons are certain to challenge the student to a greater love of the Word and to inspire greater devotion to the One who gave His life for the human family.

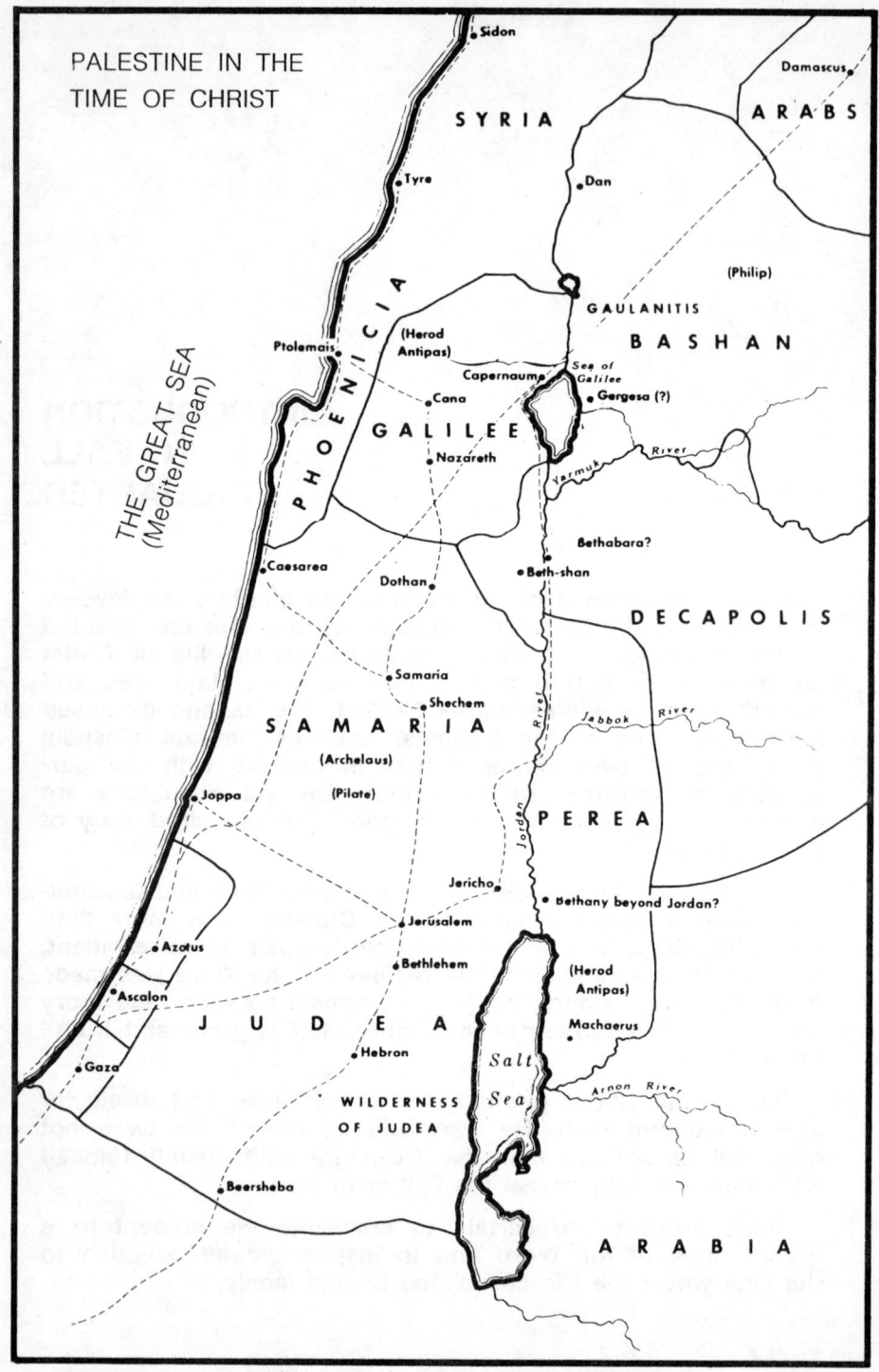

September 7, 1980

The Conqueror of Fear

Bible Background: Matthew 14:22-33; Mark 6:45-52; John 6:15-21
Supplemental References: Psalms 27:1-6; 56:1-11; 91:1-11
Time: Probably A.D. 29
Place: Sea of Galilee
Golden Text: "Jesus spake unto them, saying, Be of good cheer; it is I; be not afraid" (Matthew 14:27).
Central Truth: Christ can help us conquer fear if we look to Him in faith.
Evangelistic Emphasis: Those who seek the Savior will find deliverance from the fear of death and judgment.

PRINTED TEXT

Matthew 14:22. And straightway Jesus constrained his disciples to get into a ship, and to go before him unto the other side, while he sent the multitudes away.

23. And when he had sent the multitudes away, he went up into a mountain apart to pray: and when the evening was come, he was there alone.

24. But the ship was now in the midst of the sea, tossed with waves: for the wind was contrary.

25. And in the fourth watch of the night Jesus went unto them, walking on the sea.

26. And when the disciples saw him walking on the sea, they were troubled, saying, It is a spirit; and they cried out for fear.

27. But straightway Jesus spake unto them, saying, Be of good cheer; it is I; be not afraid.

28. And Peter answered him and said, Lord, if it be thou, bid me come unto thee on the water.

29. And he said, Come. And when Peter was come down out of the ship, he walked on the water, to go to Jesus.

30. But when he saw the wind boisterous, he was afraid; and beginning to sink, he cried, saying, Lord, save me.

31. And immediately Jesus stretched forth his hand, and caught him, and said unto him, O thou of little faith, wherefore didst thou doubt?

32. And when they were come into the ship, the wind ceased.

33. Then they that were in the ship came and worshipped him, saying, Of a truth thou art the Son of God.

DICTIONARY

constrained his disciples—Matthew 14:22—The disciples were unwilling to embark without the Lord. He, therefore, compelled them to go without Him.

fourth watch of the night—Matthew 14:25—The hours between 3 a.m. and 6 a.m.

unto the other side—Matthew 14:22—Towards Capernaum (John 6:16, 17) or Bethsaida (Mark 6:45).

LESSON OUTLINE

I. SEEKING SOLITUDE
   A. Surrounded by a Multitude
   B. Alone With God
II. EXPERIENCING FEAR
   A. The Contrary Wind
   B. The Fourth Watch
   C. The Terrified Disciples
III. ENCOURAGING WORDS
   A. The Master's Presence
   B. The Disciple's Request
   C. The Disciple's Prayer
IV. WORSHIPING CHRIST
   A. The Wind Ceased
   B. The Believers Worshiped

LESSON EXPOSITION

INTRODUCTION

The three years of Christ's earthly ministry may be divided into three time periods: the year of beginning, the year of popularity, and the year of opposition. The miracle of Jesus' walking on the water took place near the beginning of the year of opposition. The day after this mighty miracle Jesus revealed Himself as the Bread of Life. He admonished His followers that they would have to "eat my flesh, and drink my blood." By so doing, He elevated their thinking from the material to the spiritual. When they heard this, many of His disciples said, "This is an hard saying; who can hear it?" And John tells us, "From that time many of his disciples went back, and walked no more with him" (John 6:66).

This miracle took place on the Sea of Galilee. Of that majestic sea, Clarence Edward Macartney wrote in **Great Nights of the Bible:** "If you were to take the Sea of Galilee out of the Holy Land, its most pleasing physical feature would be gone. And if you were to take the Sea of Galilee out of the narratives of the four Gospels, much of their charm and beauty would be gone. On the shores of that sea Jesus wrought some of his most memorable miracles, such as the healing of the centurion's servant and the woman with the issue of blood, the raising of the daughter of Jairus, the feeding of the five thousand, the healing of the wild man of Gadara; and on two occasions he quelled the tempest on the sea."

In this account, fear and faith are contrasted. Fear fades before faith. It is no match for Christ who is the object of the disciples' faith. They learn that He is the Conqueror of fear. It is a lesson that all believers need to learn.

I. SEEKING SOLITUDE (Matthew 14:22, 23)

A. Surrounded by a Multitude (v. 22)

22. And straightway Jesus constrained his disciples to get into a ship, and to go before him unto the other side, while he sent the multitudes away.

When Herod heard of the fame of Jesus, he concluded, "This is John the Baptist; he is risen from the dead" (Matthew 14:2). Jesus heard about Herod's statement and departed into a desert place. A great multitude of people followed Him to the place. When He saw them, He was "moved with compassion toward them, and he healed their sick." That afternoon He took five loaves and two fishes and fed the "five thousand men, beside women and children" who were present. After everyone had eaten, there were twelve baskets full of fragments left over.

Seeing the miracle that Jesus performed, the men perceived that He was "that prophet that should come into the world." Jesus knew their thoughts; therefore, He knew that "they would come and take him by force, to make him a king" (John 6:15).

These men were motivated by materialism. They saw this as an opportunity to support a man whom they believed had the power to overthrow the Roman government. Against His will they would make Him king. Jesus could not let this happen. Neither could He allow His disciples to be influenced by their thinking. These first followers of Him had not yet comprehended the spiritual nature of His ministry and could have been caught up in this popular movement to make Him king. Therefore, He compelled them to get into a boat and to cross over the sea ahead of Him. He remained behind to dismiss the multitude.

John Calvin observes, "If He had permitted Himself to be now made a king, His spiritual kingdom would have been ruined, the gospel would have been stamped with everlasting infamy, and the hope of salvation would have been utterly destroyed. Modes of worship regulated according to our own fancy and honors rashly contrived by men have no other advantage than this, that they rob God of His true honor and pour upon Him nothing but reproach."

them, saying, **Be of good cheer; it is I; be not afraid.**

When the disciples saw Jesus coming to them on the water, they cried out for fear. Immediately upon hearing their cry, Jesus sought to dispel their fears. He demonstrated to them that He is the Conqueror of fear.

Jesus said unto them, "Be of good cheer," or as it is more correctly translated "take courage," or "be of good courage." This is an expression used almost exclusively by the Lord. Including this instance, He uttered these words on five separate occasions. He spoke them to the man who was sick of the palsy (Matthew 9:2); to these frightened disciples (Matthew 14:27); to His disciples just before His crucifixion (John 16:33); and to the Apostle Paul when his life was threatened (Acts 23:11). He in no way minimized the problems which each occasion presented. The sickness they faced was real sickness; the danger that confronted them was real danger; and the trials the future would bring were real trials. In no way did He suggest that it all was just in their minds. Neither did He call upon them to do something courageous. Rather He urged them to be courageous. Their problems were real; but He was with them, and as long as He was with them they had nothing to fear. "It is I—the great I AM—be not afraid."

"The abiding condition of courage is clear vision of the Lord," wrote G. Campbell Morgan. "Change the word **vision,** if you will, and say 'definite consciousness of the Lord's nearness.' Or better, cancel the preliminary words, **the vision of** and **the consciousness of,** and leave only, **the Lord Himself.** . . . All our fear and all our panic result from a dimmed vision of the Lord, a dimmed consciousness of Christ."

It is to the credit of these storm-tossed disciples that they recognized the voice of the Master. The tenderness of its tone touched their hearts and almost immediately their fears were gone. Their reaction reminds us of Mary Magdalene when she met Jesus in the garden after His resurrection. Upon first seeing Him, she mistook Him for the gardener. Immediately upon hearing His voice she recognized Him as the Lord. John records: "Jesus said to her, 'Mary.' She turned toward him and cried out in Aramaic, 'Rabboni!' (which means Teacher)"(John 20: 16, **New International Version).**

Has your walk with Him been intimate enough that you know His voice when you hear it? Of His followers Jesus said, " 'When he has brought out all his own, he goes ahead of them, and his sheep follow him because they know his voice. . . .But they will never follow a stranger; in fact, they will run away from him because they do not recognize a stranger's voice' " (John 10:4, 5, **New International Version).**

Not only did the disciples recognize the voice of the Master, but they also believed His word. He told them that they did not have anything to be afraid of, and they believed Him. The storm was still raging; the waves were still rolling; the wind was still howling, but their fears were gone.

What is your attitude toward His Word? Do you believe it? This is the key to conquering fear—to rest upon the Word of Him who is the Conqueror of fear.

B. The Disciple's Request (vv. 28, 29)

28. And Peter answered him and said, Lord, if it be thou, bid me come unto thee on the water.

29. And he said, Come. And when Peter was come down out of the ship, he walked on the water, to go to Jesus.

Recognizing the voice of his Master, Peter asks to come to Him on the water. Jesus grants his request. There is both a negative and a positive aspect to Peter's action.

It may be that Peter's thought was to outdo and outdare the other disciples. He had joined with them in their exclamation of fear when they first saw Jesus walking on the water. Now, he seeks to compensate for his doubt through this heroic act of courage and daring. He will show that his faith transcends that of any of the other disciples. It is but another form of his later statement: "Although all shall be offended, yet will not I."

Before you criticize Peter too severely, you should take inventory of your own motives in the service of Christ. Have you ever been guilty of performing your tasks in a way that others will be impressed with you? Or have you ever tried to outdo someone else? If so, aren't you "in the same boat" with Peter?

It is to Peter's credit that he had enough faith to get out of the boat and to walk on the water. How many other men have done that? Do you have that kind of faith?

It is also to Peter's credit that he wanted to be where Jesus was. His request was, "Tell me to come **to you."** The record is,

"Peter got down out of the boat and walked on the water **to Jesus.**" C. H. Spurgeon writes: "Peter did not leave the ship for the mere sake of walking the waters; but he ventured on the wave that he might come to Jesus. He sought not a promenade upon the waves, but the presence and company of his Lord. That was the one point he aimed at— to get to Jesus."

Do you long to get nearer to Jesus? Is your daily prayer, "Lord, reveal Yourself to me, reveal Yourself in me, and make me more like You." When you seek Jesus, you have your face turned in the right direction. Will you strive to serve Him and to honor Him?

C. The Disciple's Prayer (vv. 30, 31)

30. But when he saw the wind boisterous, he was afraid; and beginning to sink, he cried, saying, Lord, save me.

31. And immediately Jesus stretched forth his hand, and caught him, and said unto him, O thou of little faith, wherefore didst thou doubt?

Perhaps Peter thought that he would demonstrate before all the other disciples a courage that transcended theirs. But now, in the presence of them all, he confesses his terror and reveals the weakness, though he had thought to display the strength, of his faith.

Peter's faith failed. At the moment he took his eyes off his Lord and fixed them upon the surrounding circumstances, he began to sink. To do that is always to sink.

The believer must learn that everything in life will not come to him right side up. His experiences will range from the lowest valleys to the highest mountaintops. He will live in the tropics and at the poles. He must resolve: "These circumstances will not control me; I will learn to control them. I will learn to live from within instead of from without. I will keep my eyes on Jesus."

When Peter began to falter, Jesus saved him. Peter was safe on the water, because Christ was on the water. Though his faith was weak, he was not saved by the strength of his faith; he was saved by the strength of that gracious hand which was stretched out to catch him when he began to sink.

"Peter never finally failed," observes William Barclay, "for always in the moment of his failure he clutched at Christ. The wonderful thing about Peter is that every time he fell, he rose again; and that it must have been true that even his failures brought him closer and closer to Jesus Christ. As it has been well said, a saint is not a man who never falls; a saint is a man who gets up and goes on again every time he falls. Peter's failures only made him love Jesus Christ the more."

How do you respond to failure? Do you give up, or do you turn it over to Jesus and allow Him to turn your failure into His success?

IV. WORSHIPING CHRIST (Matthew 14:32, 33)

A. The Wind Ceased (v. 32)

32. And when they were come into the ship, the wind ceased.

After rescuing Peter from the sea, Jesus climbed into the boat with the disciples. As He did so, the wind died down. This was the second time that He calmed the sea and saved their lives.

A wealthy family in England, many years ago, took their children for a holiday in the country. Their host toured over his estate for a weekend. The children went swimming in a pool. One of the boys began to drown, and the other boys screamed for help. The son of the gardener jumped in and rescued the helpless one. Later, the grateful parents asked the gardener what they could do for the youthful hero. The gardener said his son wanted to go to college. "He wants to be a doctor," he said. The visitors shook hands on that. "We'll be glad to pay his way through," they told him.

When Winston Churchill was stricken with pneumonia after the Teheran conference, the King of England instructed that the best doctor be found to save the Prime Minister. The doctor turned out to be Dr. Fleming, the developer of penicillin. "Rarely," said Churchill to Fleming, "has one man owed his life twice to the same rescuer." It was Fleming who saved Churchill in that pool. (From **Robert G. Lee's Sourcebook of 500 Illustrations.**)

Likewise, Christ delivered the disciples from the raging sea on two different occasions. They learned that He has the power to still the storm. And this is a lesson that every believer needs to learn. The winds that bring the storms at sea are like those circumstances, events, and incidents in life which produce waves of agitation and distress in the soul. But He who quelled the tempest that night on the Sea of Galilee is able to still every storm that sweeps over the soul. When the soul is tossed by the raging sea of circumstances, the only thing to do is to call on Christ and surrender all to Him.

B. The Believers Worshiped (v. 33)

33. Then they that were in the ship came and worshipped him, saying, Of a truth thou art the Son of God.

John Calvin concludes that these words refer not only to the disciples, but also to the sailors and other passengers. If this be so, then those who had not yet declared that He was their Master, instantly acknowledged that He is the Son of God. By this term they render to Him the honor of the Messiah. At that time this lofty mystery was not generally known, how God was to be "manifest in the flesh" (1 Timothy 3:16). They had learned from the prophets that He who was to be the Redeemer would be called the Son of God. Thus they worshiped Him.

The Apostle John includes a detail of this account which Matthew does not record. "Then they were willing to take him into the boat, and immediately the boat reached the shore where they were heading" (John 6:21, **New International Version).** This additional miracle, for as such it is manifestly related, is recorded here alone. Yet all that is meant seems to be that as the storm was suddenly calmed, so the little ship—propelled by the secret power of the Lord of nature now sailing it—glided through the now unruffled waters. The disciples were so enraptured by the wonder of what had happened that they did not notice their rapid motion and found themselves at port, to their still further surprise.

Mark also adds that the disciples did not understand about the miracle of the loaves; their minds were closed (Mark 6:52). The deliverance of the disciples from the raging sea made them more sensitive to the deity of Christ than did the miraculous feeding of the five thousand with so few loaves in the wilderness. Someone has suggested that deliverance from imminent death speaks more of God's power to the humble person than the greatest works speak unto the secure. It is a blessed trouble that ends in glorifying Christ and in the increase of the knowledge of His grace.

REVIEW QUESTIONS

1. Why did Jesus send the disciples to the other side of the Sea of Galilee?
2. What time of night was it when the storm came upon the sea?
3. What was the reaction of the disciples when they saw Jesus walking on the water?
4. What unusual request did Peter make of the Lord?
5. What personal applications regarding the storms of life do you draw from this lesson?

GOLDEN TEXT HOMILY

"JESUS SPAKE UNTO THEM, SAYING, BE OF GOOD CHEER; IT IS I; BE NOT AFRAID" (Matthew 14:27).

There are many statements in the Bible about fear. The word appears hundreds of times in one way or another. The writer of Proverbs said, "The fear of the Lord is the beginning of knowledge" (Proverbs 1:7). The psalmist declared that men were to "serve the Lord with fear" (Psalm 2:11). The psalmist also said that "the fear of the Lord is the beginning of wisdom" (Psalm 111:10). Isaiah the prophet said, "The fear of the Lord is his treasure" (Isaiah 33:6). Peter admonished, "Honour all men. Love the brotherhood. Fear God" (1 Peter 2:17). The Apostle John declared that rewards were to be given to those who feared the name of the Lord (see Revelation 11:18). It would seem from this that the whole basis of the Christian expression was to be founded in a fear motive. If one confined himself to verses like these and read them from the surface only, it would appear that the only real basis for service would be that of a deep, penetrating fear of the Almighty.

The words of Jesus present quite a different note on this subject. It is Luke, when recording the statements of Jesus about seeking the Kingdom and putting it first, who quotes Jesus as also saying, "Fear not, little flock; for it is your Father's good pleasure to give you the kingdom" (Luke 12:32). It is the Apostle Paul who maintains: "Ye have not received the spirit of bondage again to fear; but ye have received the Spirit of adoption" (Romans 8:15). These statements seem to contradict each other. In many places we are told to fear God; in others we are told to fear Him not. There is no contradiction, though, if the manner in which these admonitions are given is kept in mind.

Fear has a place in religion. Jesus advised men to fear that power in the world that could destroy the souls of men (see Luke 12:5). Men without hope for the future have every right to fear the future. A man without faith is a man of fear. A man with faith in Christ really has nothing to fear. The significance of Matthew 14:27 is that in the hour of the disciples' fear, Jesus came to them. When the wind was an enemy, and when life was a struggle, Jesus was available to help. No sooner had a need arisen, than Jesus was there to help and to save.

Life often brings many winds that are contrary. We find ourselves up against these winds many times. Frequently, life is a desperate struggle with ourselves, with our circumstances, with our temptations, with our sorrows, with our decisions. However, in these times we do not have to struggle alone, for Jesus comes to us across the storms of life, with hand stretched out to save. In these times, His calm, clear voice bids us to be of good courage and not to be afraid. **—E. C. Christenbury, Ed. D., Associate Professor of Education, Lee College, Cleveland, Tennessee**

SENTENCE SERMONS

TO LIVE WITH fear and not be afraid is the final test of maturity.
—**Edward Weeks**

THERE IS MUCH in the world to make us afraid. There is much more in our faith to make us unafraid.
—**Frederick W. Cropp**

NO POWER IS strong enough to be lasting if it labors under the weight of fear.
—**Marcus Cicero**

WE CAN EASILY forgive a child who is afraid of the dark; the real tragedy of life is when men are afraid of the light.
—**Plato**

EVANGELISTIC APPLICATION

THOSE WHO SEEK THE SAVIOR WILL FIND DELIVERANCE FROM THE FEAR OF DEATH AND JUDGMENT.

Those who do not know Christ as their Savior may find the words of Hebrews 9:27 frightening: "And as it is appointed unto men once to die, but after this the judgment." The absolute certainty of death and of judgment to come is declared in this passage. All men must face that day of reckoning. Those who have not made preparation for that hour should be concerned. They must give an account of their deeds and of their rejection of Jesus Christ who willingly died for them that their sins might be forgiven.

The next verse, Hebrews 9:28, offers hope for those who will seek the Savior: "So Christ was once offered to bear the sins of many; and unto them that look for him shall he appear the second time without sin unto salvation." If the previous verse suggests fear and dread, this verse bursts forth with radiance and hope. Though death comes, its sting, which is sin, has been dealt with by the Lord. Though judgment is sure, Christ has taken that upon Himself. To those who trust in Him He offers salvation.

ILLUMINATING THE LESSON

A certain traveler upon a lonely road was set upon by bandits who robbed him of his all. They then led him into the depths of the forest. There, in darkness, they tied a rope to the limb of a great tree and bade him catch hold of the end of it. Swinging him out into the blackness of surrounding space, they told him he was hanging over the brink of a giddy precipice. The moment he let go he would be dashed to pieces on the rocks below. And then they left him. His soul was filled with horror at the awful doom impending. He clutched despairingly the end of the swinging rope. But each dreadful moment only made his fate more sure. His strength steadily failed. At last he could hold on no longer. The end had come. His clenched fingers relaxed their convulsive grip. He fell—six inches, to the solid earth at his feet! It was only a ruse of the robbers to gain time in escaping. And when he let go it was not to death, but to safety which had been waiting him through all his time of terror.

Christ is the solid rock, the foundation stone of all life. We have not to fear what will happen to us, if "underneath are the everlasting arms." All we need to do is to "let go and let God!"
—**Selected**

DAILY DEVOTIONAL GUIDE

M. Faith Conquers Fear. Psalm 27:1-6
T. Trust Overcomes Fear. Psalm 56:1-11
W. God Is Our Refuge. Psalm 91:1-11
T. God's Presence Dissolves Fear. Isaiah 43:1-7
F. Jesus Quiets Storms. Mark 6:45-52
S. Jesus Dispels Fear. John 6:15-21

September 14, 1980

The Triumph of Faith

Bible Background: Matthew 15:21-31; Mark 7:24-30
Time: A.D. 29
Place: Near the border of Tyre and Sidon, and then to the eastern shore of the Sea of Galilee
Supplemental References: 2 Kings 4:18-37; Habakkuk 3:17-19; Hebrews 11:1-6
Golden Text: "He that cometh to God must believe that he is, and that he is a rewarder of them that diligently seek him" (Hebrews 11:6).
Central Truth: Christ always honors persistent faith.
Evangelistic Emphasis: Christ always responds to those who come to Him in faith.

PRINTED TEXT

Matthew 15:21. Then Jesus went thence, and departed into the coasts of Tyre and Sidon.

22. And, behold, a woman of Canaan came out of the same coasts, and cried unto him, saying, Have mercy on me, O Lord, thou son of David; my daughter is grievously vexed with a devil.

23. But he answered her not a word. And his disciples came and besought him, saying, Send her away; for she crieth after us.

24. But he answered and said, I am not sent but unto the lost sheep of the house of Israel.

25. Then came she and worshipped him, saying, Lord, help me.

26. But he answered and said, It is not meet to take the children's bread, and cast it to dogs.

27. And she said, Truth, Lord: yet the dogs eat of the crumbs which fall from their masters' table.

28. Then Jesus answered and said unto her, O woman, great is thy faith: be it unto thee even as thou wilt. And her daughter was made whole from that very hour.

29. And Jesus departed from thence, and came nigh unto the sea of Galilee; and went up into a mountain, and sat down there.

30. And great multitudes came unto him, having with them those that were lame, blind, dumb, maimed, and many others, and cast them down at Jesus' feet; and he healed them:

31. Insomuch that the multitude wondered, when they saw the dumb to speak, the maimed to be whole, the lame to walk, and the blind to see: and they glorified the God of Israel.

DICTIONARY

Tyre (TIRE)—Matthew 15:21—Originally a rock island in the Mediterranean. About three quarters of a mile from shore, it was later connected to the mainland. In the time of Jesus, it had become one of the great commercial centers of the Mediterranean coast.

Sidon (SIGH-don)—Matthew 15:21—This town was located on the Mediterranean coast, about twenty miles north of Tyre. These cities were rivals for the leadership of Phoenicia. In

Jesus' day, Sidon was noted for its glass manufacturing. The city exported its products to all of the Roman empire.

Canaan (KAY-nan)—Matthew 15:22—That is, the area around Tyre and Sidon. The term was originally the name of the fourth son of Ham (Genesis 10:6), the progenitor of the Phoenicians and, before the conquest under Joshua, of all the peoples inhabiting the territory west of the Jordan River. Hence, this area is often called the Land of Canaan in Hebrew history.

LESSON OUTLINE

I. FAITH'S PETITION
   A. The Arrival of Jesus
   B. The Approach of the Woman
II. FAITH'S TESTING
   A. The Woman's Trial
   B. Jesus' Purpose
III. FAITH'S PERSISTENCE
   A. The Woman's Defense
   B. The Daughter's Deliverance
IV. FAITH'S REWARD
   A. The Afflicted Healed
   B. The Crowds Amazed

LESSON EXPOSITION

INTRODUCTION

Where was Christ most likely to find faith? Among the Jews? Or among the Gentiles?

Where did Elijah find faith? These are the words of Jesus: "I assure you that there were many widows in Israel in Elijah's time, when the sky was shut for three and a half years and there was a severe famine throughout the land. Yet Elijah was not sent to any of them, but to a widow in Zarephath in the region of Sidon" (Luke 4:25, 26, **New International Version**).

Where did Elisha find faith? Again Jesus says: " 'And there were many in Israel with leprosy in the time of Elisha the prophet, yet not one of them was cleansed—only Naaman the Syrian' " (Luke 4:27, **New International Version**).

Circumstances were no different in the days of Jesus. When He delivered His sermon in the synagogue in Nazareth, His message was utterly rejected. The record is as follows: "All the people in the synagogue were furious when they heard this. They got up, drove him out of the town, and took him to the brow of the hill on which the town was built, in order to throw him down the cliff. But he walked right through the crowd and went on his way" (Luke 4:28-30, **New International Version**). Concerning His rejection by the Jews, the Apostle John adds: "He came to that which was his own, but his own did not receive him. Yet to all who received him, to those who believed in his name, he gave the right to become children of God" (John 1:11, 12, **New International Version**).

Where does Christ find faith today? Does He find it among those who have served Him longest? Or is it more evident among those who are new converts? Does He find it among the old or among the young? He should find it among those seasoned saints who have served Him the longest. Their relationship with Him should have caused their faith to mature. They should be examples to young converts of what true faith is. It is sad but true that such is not always the case. Some believers never seem to develop their faith. They lose that trust in the Lord that meant so much to them initially. Their lack of faith is rebuked by the zealous faith of many young converts.

But Christ welcomes faith wherever He finds it. He delights in the strong, steadfast faith of the mature believer. He rejoices in the exuberant faith of the young convert. He honors faith because faith honors Him. Faith accepts His Word as truth and acts upon it. Christ stands behind His Word.

Today's lesson is about a woman of persistent faith. She perfectly illustrates the truth that the Lord rewards those who diligently seek Him. She is not an Israelite; she is a Syrophoenician woman. Like Elijah and Elisha, Jesus found great faith outside the borders of Israel. He responded to that faith.

I. FAITH'S PETITION (Matthew 15:21, 22)

A. The Arrival of Jesus (v. 21)

21. Then Jesus went thence, and departed into the coasts of Tyre and Sidon.

Jesus' journey into the coasts of Tyre and Sidon followed a period in which many notable miracles had been performed. He had fed the five thousand with a lad's lunch, had walked on the water, and had healed as many in the land of Gennesaret as had touched the hem of His garment.

But Jesus' journey also came at a time when His popularity was waning in Galilee. Many of His disciples had turned away, "and walked no more with him" (John 6:66). The Pharisees—already determined to kill Him—sent a delegation to push their propaganda and to make Him more unpopular with His own disciples. Jesus discussed their traditions with them. Then He instructed His disciples in what is truth rather than tradition.

Weary from all this activity and no doubt burdened that so many were unwilling to accept the truth, Jesus retired to the region of Tyre and Sidon. This was about fifty miles north of Capernaum, outside of Jewish territory, in Gentile country. It was the same area to which Elijah had been sent to the woman of Zarephath (1 Kings 17:9). Of Jesus' intentions in this land, Mark records: "He entered a house and did not want anyone to know it; yet he could not keep his presence secret" (Mark 7:24, **New International Version**).

B. The Approach of the Woman (v. 22)

22. And, behold, a woman of Canaan came out of the same coasts, and cried unto him, saying, Have mercy on me, O Lord, thou son of David; my daughter is grievously vexed with a devil.

As soon as she heard that Jesus was in her country, the Syrophoenician woman whose little daughter was possessed by an evil spirit sought Him out. She is to be commended for her approach to the Lord.

Mark tells us that she "fell at his feet." This was an act of homage and worship. It was also a display of amazing faith. Probably she had not heard much about Jesus, and perhaps she had never seen Him in person before, yet she believed and bowed herself at His feet. How does your faith compare with hers?

Then she "cried out" to Jesus. Knowing Him to be the source of her help, she sought His assistance in meeting her need. Paul encourages the believer: "Do not be anxious about anything, but in everything, by prayer and petition, with thanksgiving, present your requests to God" (Philippians 4:6. **New International Version**).

Also she revealed her need to Jesus. Her petition is specific. She had a daughter who was suffering terribly from demon possession and this is what she tells the Lord. How much of our praying is indefinite? How much of it deals in generalities? Is it any wonder that so many prayers go unanswered? We are admonished to make our requests known unto God and are assured that He will hear and answer.

Finally, she invited Jesus into the midst of her need and asked God for His help in resolving the condition. She approached Him on the basis of His mercy and acknowledged Him as Lord and Messiah. Have you made Him the Lord of your life? Have you surrendered all to Him? He must be given His rightful place in your life.

II. FAITH'S TESTING (Matthew 15:23, 24)

A. The Woman's Trial (v. 23)

23. But he answered her not a word. And his disciples came and besought him, saying, Send her away; for she crieth after us.

Why is God at times seemingly silent to the needs and petitions of His people?

This journey into Gentile country marks the only time Jesus was ever outside of Palestine and outside of Jewish territory with the exception of His trip as an infant into Egypt. Therefore, the supreme significance of this passage is that it foreshadows the going out of the gospel to the whole world; it shows us the beginning of the end of all the barriers.

Yet Jesus' response to this Syrophoenician woman raises questions about His purpose in that land. Why is it that He did not answer her when she had thrown herself at His feet, had pierced His ears with her cry, and had presented urgently the case of her child's need? Why did He respond as if He were deaf and dumb?

Perhaps two reasons may be given for Jesus' response. First, it was not His mission to minister to the Gentiles in a missionary fashion at this time. He had previously instructed His disciples, "Go not into the way of the Gentiles" (Matthew 10:5). Although He will minister to this woman's needs, His disciples must know that He was not sent to such as she.

The second reason that Jesus did not answer this woman was to test her faith. What was her faith made of? Did she have the faith, patience, and perseverance to get what she needed from Him? Lesser faith would have given up. Strong faith would only be challenged by this hurdle that stood between it and the deliverance of this child. Which category does your faith fit into—weak faith or strong faith?

The attitude of the Twelve is disappointing. It reminds us of their reaction when little children were brought to Jesus that He might place His hands on them and pray for them. The disciples rebuked those who brought them. But Jesus said: " 'Let the little children come to me, and do not hinder them, for the kingdom of heaven belongs to such as these' " (Matthew 19:14, **New International Version**).

About the Syrophoenician woman, the disciples said to Jesus, "Give this woman what she is asking for and send her on her way." Get rid of her! She is troublesome! She is a nuisance! Although they sought the Lord to meet the need of the woman's daughter, they did not seek out of compassion. They wanted the need met because they were annoyed by her crying after them. And what about your motives? Why do you want Christ to intervene in a given matter? Is it out of compassion or out of selfishness that you seek His help? An honest evaluation of motives is beneficial.

In contrast to the selfish attitude of the disciples, Jesus was moved with compassion toward this woman. Such compassion characterized His ministry. He was touched deeply by the suffering of humanity. Relieving that suffering was an integral part of His ministry. When men came to Him in need, He yearned for their deliverance.

B. Jesus' Purpose (v. 24)

24. But he answered and said, I am not sent but unto the lost sheep of the house of Israel.

The commission to reach the whole world will come later. It is Jesus' present purpose to reach the lost sheep of Israel. This work is preparatory to the larger work which will come at the time He deems appropriate. Even Paul recognized this principle of a limited objective expanded into a larger goal. He wrote: "I am not ashamed of the gospel, because it is the power of God for the salvation of everyone who believes: first for the Jew, then for the Gentile" (Romans 1:16, **New International Version**). When Paul entered a city, he went to the Jews first. Only after they rejected his message did he turn to the Gentiles. He then became the apostle to the Gentiles.

William Barclay makes an interesting observation about Jesus' purpose and this Syrophoenician woman. "But to Jesus there was a problem here. That He was moved with compassion for this woman we cannot for a moment doubt. But she was a Gentile. Not only was she a Gentile; she belonged to the old Canaanite stock, and the Canaanites were the ancestral enemies of the Jews. Even at that very time, or not so very much later, Josephus could write: 'Of the Phoenicians, the Tyrians have the most ill-feeling towards us.' If Jesus was to have any effect, He had to limit His objectives like a wise general. He had to begin with the Jews; and here was a Gentile crying for mercy. There was only one thing for Jesus to do; He must awaken true faith in the heart of this woman."

Even Christ's statement that He was sent only to the lost sheep of Israel contained some hope for this woman. She could have argued, "Lord, You did not come in search of me, but I have come in search of You." She could have reminded Him of the woman of Samaria who asked for water to drink and who was given water from the eternal springs. He even sent her away to make many others rich through the good news of redeeming grace.

Christ had the priorities of His life in order. What priorities have you set for your life? Is life a hit-or-miss affair for you or do you know where you are going? How much of your life is misdirected effort?

Once, a minister says, when he was a boy, some neighbor boys on visit found a huge, thick pasteboard box in the attic of his house. His mother, besieged by their requests, gave it to them—"to make something." That "something" they made, after spending several hours of two days and a few hours of three nights, was—what do you think?—a paper bottom boat, a few feet long and two feet wide. They took that thing to the pond with as much confidence as Robert Fulton had in his teakettle of a steamboat which struggled up the Hudson to Albany in three days. With cheers they launched their boat in the old swimming hole—believing it would, with or without cargo, "dare and defy the stormy main." But when that boat, with bubble gurgles that seemed to laugh them to scorn for their confidence in her, went to the bottom, they found that they had misdirected all their ingenuity and poorly directed all their hours of toil. How many lives are lived in the same misguided, poorly directed manner?

III. FAITH'S PERSISTENCE (Matthew 15:25-28)

A. The Woman's Defense (vv. 25-27)

**25. Then came she and worshipped him, saying, Lord, help me.
26. But he answered and said, It is not meet to take the children's bread, and cast it to dogs.
27. And she said, Truth, Lord: yet the dogs eat of the crumbs which fall from their masters' table.**

Why is it necessary in God's design for our faith to be tested?

When the Syrophoenician woman first came to Jesus, He did not answer her plea. She then turned to His disciples but they offered her no help. However, she will not be denied, so she goes back to Jesus. She came and knelt before Him and said: "Lord, help me."

There is something noble about kneeling before Jesus. By that posture, one acknowledges His lordship. It recognizes the distance between the subject and the King. This expression of honor and homage is honored of the Lord.

This woman knew that Jesus could help her. Moreover, she believed that He **would** help her. Therefore, her request was fervent. She fully trusted Him to meet her need.

How completely have you trusted your life to Christ? Do you see Him as able to meet your needs? Have you abandoned yourself to Him that He might minister to you?

This time Jesus replied to the woman's request. On the surface, His answer sounds cruel. " 'It is not right to take the children's bread and toss it to their dogs' " (Matthew 15:26, **New International Version**). A further study of the word **dogs** reveals that there was tenderness in His expression.

There are two distinct words for dogs which represent two entirely different ideas. The Hebrews had a profound hatred for the low, marauding, fierce, half-scavenger, half-wolf dog of that country. On the other hand, dogs were found in the Jewish households. They were the little dogs, the playthings of the children. The word that Christ used here was that for the little dogs. Undoubtedly He spoke to her with pity and tenderness in His voice. The tone and the look with which a thing is said make all the difference. We can be quite sure that the compassion in His eyes robbed the words of all insult and bitterness.

She was quick to acknowledge the truth of what He said. But she was just as quick to argue, "Even the dogs eat the crumbs that fall from their masters' table." She was willing to admit the charge but unwilling to forego her claim. If the dogs "eat of the crumbs," she is satisfied with crumbs. She did not expect to see her need met on the basis of any merit of her own. She depended upon the goodness of Christ's heart, not on the goodness of her cause. She relied upon the excellence of His power rather than upon the prevalence of her plea.

I don't know how much she understood of what Christ meant, but I do know that her faith was not quenched. The soul that approaches Christ in this way will overcome a thousand obstacles. Can you pray, "Lord, I will approach You, I will press through obstacles to You and throw myself at Your dear feet, knowing that he who comes to You You will in no wise cast out"? He is looking for that kind of faith.

B. The Daughter's Deliverance (v. 28)

28. Then Jesus answered and said unto her, O woman, great is thy faith: be it unto thee even as thou wilt. And her daughter was made whole from that very hour.

Jesus had a very quick eye for observing faith. If the jewel was lying in the mire, His eye caught its glitter; if there was a choice ear of wheat among the thorns, He perceived it. Weighing the woman's response, He exclaimed, "O woman, great is thy faith."

The brightest jewels are often found in the darkest places. Jesus had not found such faith, no, not in Israel, as He discovered in this poor Canaanitish woman. May we learn a lesson from this instance. Never let us speak of any area as too depraved to yield us converts, nor of any class of persons as too fallen to become believers. Let us go even to the borders of Tyre and Sidon, though the land be under a curse, for even there we may recover a jewel for the Redeemer's crown.

In spiritual things, the best plants often grow in the most barren soil. Great saints are often found in places where it seems impossible for them to exist. The Lord is able to make strong faith exist with little knowledge, little present enjoyment, and little encouragement; and strong faith in such conditions triumphs, conquers, and doubly glorifies the grace of God.

Such was the faith of this woman. She was not bred and born and educated in a way in which she was likely to become a believer, and yet she did become a believer of the first class. She had not seen the Lord before in her life, she was not like those who had associated with Him for many months: and yet, with but one view of Him, she gained this great faith. All that her faith had to rest upon was that she had heard in her own country that the Messiah of the Jews was come, and she believed that the Man of Nazareth was He, and on this she relied.

With all our advantages, with all the opportunities that we have of knowing the whole life of Christ and understanding the doctrines revealed to us in the New Testament, with many years of observation and experience, our faith ought to be much stronger than it is. This poor woman shames us when we compare her limited opportunities with her great faith.

Jesus was so delighted with the wise, prudent, and humble yet courageous manner in which she responded to His statement that He said, " 'For such a reply, you may go; the demon has left your daughter' " (Mark 7:29, **New International Version**). Thus she realized the desire of her heart. All she had to do now was to go home and find her daughter resting in a manner in which she had not rested since the demon possessed her. Jesus said to the woman, "Be it unto thee even as thou wilt." It was as if the Lord of glory surrendered at discretion to the conquering arms of a woman's faith. The Lord grant to you and me in all times of our struggling to be able thus by faith still to conquer.

This woman's faith is a challenge to all outsiders, to those who think themselves beyond hope, to those who were not brought up to attend the house of God. Such persons may take heart and find comfort in her experience. They, too, may come to Jesus Christ and trust themselves in His hands.

Her faith is also a challenge to those who feel they have been repulsed in their endeavors after salvation. Her experience says to such persons: "Yet trust in Him whose blood has not lost its efficacy, whose promise has not lost its truth, and whose arm has not lost its power to save. Cling to the Cross. If the earth sink beneath you, cling on; if storms should rage and all the floods be out and God himself seem to be against you, cling to the Cross. There is your hope."

Then, this woman's faith is a challenge to every intercessor. She was not pleading for herself; she was asking for another. She pleaded as for her own soul and her own life. Her tears brought an answer of peace. So may it be in our intercessory praying.

Finally, this woman's faith is a challenge to every mother. She was pleading for her little daughter. Maternal instinct makes the weakest strong and makes the most timid brave. Even among poor beasts and birds, how powerful is a mother's love. Why, the poor little robin which would be frightened at the approach of a footstep will sit upon its nest when the intruder comes near when her little ones are in danger. A mother's love makes her heroic for her child; and so when you are pleading with God plead as a mother's love suggests to you. What an encouragement to pray this story should be to parents (Spurgeon).

IV. FAITH'S REWARD (Matthew 15:29-31)

A. The Afflicted Healed (vv. 29, 30)

29. And Jesus departed from thence, and came nigh unto the sea of Galilee; and went up into a mountain, and sat down there.

30. And great multitudes came unto him, having with them those that were lame, blind, dumb, maimed, and many others, and cast them down at Jesus' feet; and he healed them.

Mark describes the route Jesus followed when He returned to Galilee in more detail than does Matthew. He records: "Then Jesus left the vicinity of Tyre and went through Sidon, down to the Sea of Galilee and into the region of the Decapolis" (Mark 7:31, **New International Version**).

Commenting on this passage, William Barclay says: "That was a strange way of traveling. Sidon is **north** of Tyre; the Sea of Galilee is **south** of Tyre; and the Decapolis was a confederation of ten Greek cities on the **east** of the Sea of Galilee. That is to say Jesus went **north** in order to go **south**. . . . It is clear that Jesus deliberately length-

September 14, 1980

ened out this journey to have as long as possible with His disciples before the last journey to Jerusalem. . . . This northern journey . . . took **almost six months.** We know nothing about what happened in the course of these six months; but we can be perfectly sure that they were the most important six months through which the disciples ever lived; for in them Jesus deliberately taught and instructed them, and opened their minds to the truth."

The most important moments in the life of the believer are those quiet moments when the Lord teaches him from the Word. Those moments give strength for the hard times. They prepare the soul for the storms of life. They enable the believer to handle life's conflicts.

After Jesus arrived at the Sea of Galilee, He went up into a mountain and sat down. Great multitudes came to Him bringing those who were physically afflicted, and He healed them. The lame, the blind, the dumb, and the crippled are listed as some who received deliverance at His hand. He has the power to deliver from any infirmity. Healing formed an integral part of His ministry. He continues to exercise that ministry in the Church today.

B. The Crowds Amazed (v. 31)

31. Insomuch that the multitude wondered, when they saw the dumb to speak, the maimed to be whole, the lame to walk, and the blind to see: and they glorified the God of Israel.

The miracles which Jesus wrought left the multitudes amazed. They marveled that by His power the dumb could speak, the lame could walk, the blind could see, and the crippled could be made well. Seeing all of this, they glorified the God of Israel.

A genuine miracle will glorify God. The person who receives a miracle from God should direct attention to God and not to himself. A miracle is a display of God's power. It may serve to confirm His Word. Mark records: "Then the disciples went out and preached everywhere, and the Lord worked with them and confirmed his word by the signs that accompanied it" (Mark 16:20, **New International Version).**

Job describes the magnificent power of God: "Lo, he is strong" (Job 9:19). The Hebrew word for **strong** signifies a conquering, prevailing strength and suggests the superlative degree. "He is most strong," that is, God Almighty (Genesis 17:1). And because of His almightiness, He can do whatever is feasible. No wonder the Psalmist says: "Great is the Lord, and greatly to be praised; and his greatness is unsearchable" (Psalm 145:3).

A miracle is evidence of direct communication between heaven and earth. It reveals God's concern for and intervention in the affairs of men. It calls attention to the Lord and glorifies His great name.

The unusual expression used to describe the reaction of the multitude to the miracles of Jesus is worthy of note. Matthew says that "they glorified the God of Israel." Because these miracles took place in the Decapolis, there were probably many Gentiles present. Perhaps there were more Gentiles in attendance than Jews. To the Gentile crowds these miracles were demonstrations of the power of the God of Israel.

REVIEW QUESTIONS

1. Why did the Canaanite woman come to Jesus?

2. How did Jesus explain the protest of the disciples?

3. How did the woman express her faith even after the Lord's seeming rebuff?

4. What was the double blessing the woman received from the Lord?

5. What twofold effect did Jesus' healing ministry have on the observing people?

GOLDEN TEXT HOMILY

"HE THAT COMETH TO GOD MUST BELIEVE THAT HE IS, AND THAT HE IS A REWARDER OF THEM THAT DILIGENTLY SEEK HIM" (Hebrews 11:6).

Men have lived who have pleased God. Enoch was one of them, but he was not the only one. In all ages there have been believers whose walk in life has been such that it was God's delight. It should be the aim of every one of us to please God. With the power of the Holy Ghost it is possible to please God; without that power it is impossible.

If we live so as to please the Lord, we will only be acting as we ought to act. We must please Him who has made us and who sustains our very existence. He is our God and Lord, and obedience to Him is the highest law of our being.

We learn in Revelation 4:11 that God has created all things for His pleasure. We will miss our purpose in life if we are not pleasing to God. By pleasing God we will teach transgressors God's way and sinners will be converted to Him.

Faith is absolutely essential in pleasing God. The key word in Hebrews 11:6 is "impossible." Without faith, it is impossible to please God. The writer of Hebrews does not say it is difficult, he says that it is impossible. We do not need to attempt the impossible, our failure is guaranteed. No faith—no pleasing.

Without faith there is no capacity for communion with God. Without faith man himself is not pleasing to God. Without faith there is no common ground upon which God and man can meet. Without faith all prospect of love is destroyed. By what means can we hope to please God, apart from faith in Him?

To come to God, we must believe that He is. "Must" is essential. It is the fool who has said in his heart that there is no God (see Psalms 14:1; 53:1). The devils believe and tremble (see James 2:19). You must believe that God **is** in reference to yourself—that He has to do with your life and with your living. With this faith, with this belief firmly implanted in your heart, claim the promise that God is the "rewarder of them that **diligently** seek him!"—**M. David Sisler, Pastor, Church of God, New Britain, Connecticut**

SENTENCE SERMONS

FAITH IS THE root of all blessings. Believe, and you shall be saved; believe and you must needs be satisfied; believe, and you cannot but be comforted and happy.

—Jeremy Taylor

FAITH WILL BEGET in us three things: Vision, Venture, and Victory.

—George W. Ridout

FAITH SEES THE invisible, believes the incredible, and receives the impossible.

—"**The Free Methodist**"

FAITH IS ONLY worthy of the name when it erupts into action.

—Catherine Marshall

EVANGELISTIC APPLICATION

CHRIST ALWAYS RESPONDS TO THOSE WHO COME TO HIM IN FAITH.

What is the most moving account in the Book of Revelation? Is it the great white throne? Is it the sound of many waters? Is it the sea of glass mingled with fire? Is it the fourfold hallelujah that rings out over a reconciled and conquered universe? Is it the New Jerusalem? No! In my opinion, the most moving scene is found in Revelation 3:20, "Behold, I stand at the door, and knock: if any man hear my voice, and open the door, I will come in to him, and will sup with him, and he with me."

What a portrait! There He is a weary traveler, just as you have seen Him in Holman Hunt's famous painting—the dews of night distilling upon His brow, a lantern in one hand, and knocking with the other, the head bent forward eagerly to hear if there is an answer to His knock.

The invitation to open the door and let Christ in is extended to "any man." When one comes to Him in faith, He readily responds. The person who comes to Him in faith will never be disappointed. Christ will meet his need.

ILLUMINATING THE LESSON

A famous heiress keeps her priceless collection of jewels in the vault of a large bank. One of her prize possessions is a very valuable string of pearls. It is a scientific fact that pearls lose their original luster if not worn once in a while in contact with the human body. So, once a week, a bank secretary, guarded by two plainclothesmen, wears these priceless pearls to lunch. This brief contact with the human body keeps them beautiful and in good condition.

Our faith is a lot like the pearl. It must be used in order to be useful. It must be worn out among the masses of mankind where faith and hope are needed.

—From **Quote Unquote,** compiled by Lloyd Cory; Wheaton, Illinois, Scripture Press. Used by permission.

DAILY DEVOTIONAL GUIDE

M. Faith Is Tested. 2 Kings 4:18-37
T. Faith Is Confident. Habakkuk 3:17-19
W. Faith Is Humble. Matthew 8:5-15
T. Faith Is Victorious. Mark 2:1-12
F. Faith Is Rewarded. Mark 7:24-30
S. Faith Is Indispensable. Hebrews 11:1-6

September 21, 1980

An Inescapable Question

Bible Background: Matthew 16:13-20; Mark 8:27-30; Luke 9:18-20
Time: Perhaps in autumn, A.D. 29
Place: Caesarea Philippi in northern Palestine
Supplemental References: Isaiah 28:16; Micah 5:2; 1 Corinthians 3:11; Ephesians 2:20-22; Philippians 2:11; Colossians 1:18; 1 John 4:15
Golden Text: "Thou art the Christ, the Son of the living God" (Matthew 16:16).
Central Truth: The deity of Christ is a cardinal truth of the Christian faith.
Evangelistic Emphasis: For salvation, one must accept and confess Christ as the Son of God.

PRINTED TEXT

Matthew 16:13. When Jesus came into the coasts of Caesarea Philippi, he asked his disciples, saying, Whom do men say that I the Son of man am?

14. And they said, Some say that thou art John the Baptist: some, Elias; and others, Jeremias, or one of the prophets.

15. He saith unto them, But whom say ye that I am?

16. And Simon Peter answered and said, Thou art the Christ, the Son of the living God.

17. And Jesus answered and said unto him, Blessed art thou, Simon Bar-jona: for flesh and blood hath not revealed it unto thee, but my Father which is in heaven.

18. And I say also unto thee, That thou art Peter, and upon this rock I will build my church; and the gates of hell shall not prevail against it.

19. And I will give unto thee the keys of the kingdom of heaven: and whatsoever thou shalt bind on earth shall be bound in heaven: and whatsoever thou shalt loose on earth shall be loosed in heaven.

20. Then charged he his disciples that they should tell no man that he was Jesus the Christ.

DICTIONARY

Caesarea Philippi (sez-ah-REE-ah PHIL-ah-pie)—Matthew 16:13—A city in northern Palestine was rebuilt by Herod-Philip, who called it by his own name to distinguish it from Caesarea Stratonis, the seat of the Roman government on the Mediterranean coast. The Greek name for Caesarea Philippi was Paneas, which survives in the present name of Baniyas. It was the most northerly point reached by our Lord.

Elias (ee-LYE-us)—Matthew 16:14—The old English translation of the Greek form of the word **Elijah**

Jeremias (jer-eh-MY-us)—Matthew 16:14—The old English translation of the Greek form of the word **Jeremiah**

Bar-jona (bar-JON-ah)—Matthew 16:17—That is, son of Jonah—**bar** is Aramaic for "son." The Hebrew word **Jonah** means "dove."

An Inescapable Question

LESSON OUTLINE

I. AN INESCAPABLE QUESTION
  A. The Son of Man
  B. The People's Opinion
  C. A Personal Question
II. THE ONLY ACCEPTABLE ANSWER
  A. The Christ of God
  B. A Divine Revelation
III. AN INVINCIBLE CHURCH
  A. My Church
  B. The Keys of the Kingdom
  C. The Christ

LESSON EXPOSITION

INTRODUCTION

The Mississippi River flows to the sea. This it has done for thousands of years—watering the fields, slaking the thirst of generations, carrying the ships of man's commerce. Yet no waste nor want does it show.

The rising sun, draping the mountain rim with golden curtains, has melted the snows of many winters, has renewed the verdure of many springs, has painted the flowers of many summers, has ripened the harvest of many autumns.

Yet no less light does it give for all those centuries of boundless profusion.

These are faint images of Him who goes forth conquering and to conquer.

For when judgment flames lick up that flowing stream, and the elements melt with fervent heat (2 Peter 3:10), and the light of the sun is quenched in darkness or veiled in the smoke of burning worlds, the matchless fullness of Christ will be as undiminished as ever (Robert G. Lee)!

This fullness that Dr. Lee talks about is the reflection of the divine nature of Christ. He was more than a mere man; He was both God and man. He demonstrated before men the true nature of God.

The world into which Jesus was born held a distorted view of God. The Romans and the Greeks thought of God as a vengeful, wrathful being. Jesus came to change that image and to show that God is love and mercy and tenderness.

The attitude that God is anxious to display His wrath still exists. But Christ would show us the loving-kindness of the heavenly Father.

The young lady called upon the Lord in a manner that indicated she thought He was unapproachable. She cried out to Him in a way that revealed she thought He was unwilling to forgive her. Her attitude seemed to be that He had to be persuaded to help her.

The counselor told her that God was more willing to forgive her than she was willing to be forgiven. He assured her that God was more eager to help her than she was to have His help. He then asked her to read 1 John 1:9, "If we confess our sins, he is faithful and just to forgive us our sins, and to cleanse us from all unrighteousness."

The Holy Spirit enabled her to realize that if she, being human, would do what God told her to do, that He, being divine, would do what He said He would do. A change came over her countenance and a joy came into her eyes as Christ came into her heart.

We must not forget that God is just and that He displays His wrath against sin. At the same time, we must remember that He is a God of love and great mercy. He is the God that Jesus revealed Him to be during His earthly life and ministry.

I. AN INESCAPABLE QUESTION (Matthew 16:13-15)

A. The Son of Man (v. 13)

13. When Jesus came into the coasts of Caesarea Philippi, he asked his disciples, saying, Whom do men say that I the Son of man am?

Mark indicates that this event took place while Jesus and His disciples were passing through "the towns of Caesarea, [which is called] Philippi" (Mark 8:27). Luke reveals that it happened while Jesus was praying and while no one was with Him but His disciples (see Luke 9:18). Matthew is more indefinite about the time. John Calvin observes, "All the three unquestionably relate the same narrative; and it is possible that Christ may have stopped at a certain place during that journey to pray, and that afterwards He may have put the question to His disciples."

There were two towns in the Holy Land called Caesarea. One was located in Palestine, about thirty miles north of Jaffa. Philip, the evangelist, lived here (see Acts 8:40; 21:8). Peter was sent here to minister to the Roman centurion, Cornelius (see Acts 10).

The other city—referred to in our text—was located at the base of Mount Hermon. The district in which it was located was given by Augustus to Herod the Great who built a temple of white marble in honor of the emperor. Later Philip the Tetrarch rebuilt and beautified the town, calling it Caesarea as a compliment to Augustus and adding his own name to distinguish it from the Caesarea in Palestine. Some think that on a height near Caesarea Philippi Jesus was transfigured. It was in this area that Jesus asked His disciples, " 'Who do people say the Son of Man is' " (Matthew 16:13, **New International Version)?**

Jesus refers to Himself as the Son of Man. This title is found eighty-one times in the Gospels and only one time apart from the Gospels (see Acts 7:56). With but one exception the name as found in the Gospels is used only by our Lord himself. The exception is John 12:34, and even there it is presupposed that Jesus had spoken of Himself as the Son of Man.

The term **Son of Man** was not new to the Jewish mind. Daniel used the term in chapter 7, verse 13 of his writing. This reference was interpreted by the Jews as a designation of the Messiah. Although Jesus referred to Himself as the Son of Man prior to this conversation, His predominant use of the expression came afterward.

George P. Gould offers three reasons why Jesus chose to refer to Himself frequently as the Son of Man: (1) First and foremost, it permitted the blending of the conception of the Suffering Servant with that of the Messianic King. (2) If **the Son of Man** was a title capable of being associated with suffering and death, it was a title already associated with the glorious coming of One who should have everlasting rule over a world in which the powers of evil should no more have sway. (3) If **the Son of Man**, telling of descent from heaven, spoke of a closer association with God than did any other current Messianic title, so did it speak also of close association with man—with the race.

B. The People's Opinion (v. 14)

14. And they said, Some say that thou art John the Baptist: some, Elias; and others, Jeremias, or one of the prophets.

By the messages He preached, the miracles He performed, and the life He lived, Jesus had, for nearly three years, made known to His disciples that He was the Messiah, the predicted King, the Son of God. He now asks them two questions to determine how well they have learned from His teaching. The questions are also designed to probe their thinking.

Their answer to Jesus' question "Who do people say the Son of Man is?" was very kind. They could have told Him that many regarded Him as a fanatic, an imposter, or even a glutton and a drunkard. Instead they spoke of the great respect many had for Him. Some thought He was John the Baptist, others thought He was Elijah, still others considered Him to be Jeremiah or, at least, one of the prophets. The people were divided in their opinion of Jesus.

What was there about Jesus that made some people believe He was John the Baptist?

Perhaps the characteristic about John that is most pronounced is his courage. It is reflected in the authority with which he speaks. It is seen in his bold denunciation of evil wherever he encounters it. It is revealed in his passionate plea to prepare through repentance for the coming kingdom of God. And did not Jesus minister with the same courage, boldness, and authority? Of His disciples it could later be said: "When they [the rulers and elders of the people] saw the courage of Peter and John and realized that they were unschooled, ordinary men, they were astonished and they took note that these men had been with Jesus" (Acts 4:13, **New International Version).** Does the Church exhibit this same courage today? Do you as an individual believer exhibit the courage of Christ in daily living?

What was there about Jesus that made some people believe that He was Elijah? Perhaps it was because of His miracle-working power. Elijah was noted for the many miracles that God wrought through him. So was Jesus.

William Barclay comments: "Others said that He was Elijah. In doing so, they were saying two things about Jesus. They were saying that He was as great as the greatest of the prophets, for Elijah had always been looked on as the summit and the peak and the prince of the prophetic line. They were also saying that Jesus was the forerunner of the Messiah. As Malachi wrote, the promise of God was "Behold, I will send you Elijah the prophet before the coming of the great and dreadful day of the Lord" (Malachi 4:5). To this day the Jews expect the return of Elijah before the coming of the Messiah; and to this day they leave a chair vacant for Elijah when they celebrate the Passover, for when Elijah comes, the Messiah will not be far away. So the people looked on Jesus as the herald of the Messiah and the forerunner of the direct intervention of God."

What was there about Jesus that made some of the people believe that He was Jeremiah? Perhaps some thought they caught, in the cadences of His prayers and in the stormy invective which He poured out upon hypocritical religious leaders, the voice of the prophet Jeremiah. They must have seen in this Man of Sorrows reflections of the weeping prophet.

However lofty their notions about Jesus were, they were not high enough. He was far greater than the greatest man who ever lived before Him or after Him.

C. A Personal Question (v. 15)

15. He saith unto them, But whom say ye that I am?

Now Jesus asks His disciples the second question: "Who do you say I am?" Is your concept of Me on the same level with that of the people? Have My teachings revealed to you more than they have been able to grasp? How much of My teaching have you understood?

This question "Who do **you** say I am?" is intensely personal. Each man must grapple with it by himself. One's knowledge of Christ can never be secondhand. The greatest thrill that any individual can ever experience is to come to this realization that Christ is his personal Savior. What peace and assurance that knowledge brings to the soul!

Salvation is a personal matter based upon a personal faith. No one can believe for another. Each individual must trust Christ for his own salvation.

In a church in Glasgow, there was a young theological student who served as the church missionary. Afterwards he went out as a missionary to the South Sea islands. During World War II, our newspapers carried stories of our airmen, shot down in those southern seas, managing to land on one of those islands. Instead of beating in their brains, boiling them in a pot, and devouring them, the natives treated them with great kindness and hospitality.

That change is largely due to the fact that the young missionary, John G. Paton, brought to those islands the knowledge of Christ and the Christian way of life. When he was at work translating the Scriptures into the language of those natives, John G. Paton was at a loss to discover the equivalent in their speech for the word **faith;** and without that word the translation of the Bible would be in vain. Day after day he listened to the speech of the natives, hoping that he might hit upon some expression that would represent what the Bible means by faith. But months passed and the words were still wanting, until one day a native came into his study and, throwing himself down upon a chair, exclaimed, "How good it is to lean my whole weight upon this chair!" The missionary caught at that expression, "lean my whole weight upon." There were the words for which he had been searching! There were the words for belief and faith, and never were better ones used. Saving faith in Christ is "leaning your whole weight upon Him" for salvation.

II. THE ONLY ACCEPTABLE ANSWER (Matthew 16:16, 17)

A. The Christ of God (v. 16)

16. And Simon Peter answered and said, Thou art the Christ, the Son of the living God.

There is a distinct difference between the answer of the people and the answer of the disciples as to who Jesus was. The people were divided and contradictory in their answer. Some of them thought He was John the Baptist, others considered Him to be Elijah, still others identified Him as Jeremiah, while some declared that He was at least one of the prophets. But the disciples were united in their opinion of Jesus. Peter expressed the sentiment of the group when he said, "You are the Christ, the Son of the living God." His expression is that of a man who means what he says, who values the truth he speaks, and who attaches deep importance to it. He is very definite and clear and certain in his answer. His words exalt and glorify Jesus.

Peter not only spoke for the disciples; He also spoke for believers in all ages. When he referred to Jesus as the **Christ,** the **Anointed One,** he meant the predicted Messiah, the Redeemer, the Savior of the world. His expression embraces all that is contained in our salvation. It includes both an everlasting Kingdom and an everlasting priesthood. The work of Christ is designed to reconcile us to God, to obtain for us a perfect righteousness, and to uphold and supply and enrich us with every description of blessings.

Peter also referred to Jesus as the Son of the living God. He meant all those words could signify as contrasted with the prophets and saints of all ages. Christ is a unique Being to whom we can pray, in whose unseen presence we can trust, before whom each of us can fall and exclaim, as did Thomas, "My Lord, and my God." He is the Son of the **living** God. When the attribute **living** is ascribed to God, it is for the purpose of distinguishing between Him and dead idols, who are nothing (see 1 Corinthians 8:4).

Have you made Jesus Christ, the Son of God, Lord over your life? Has He taken possession of your heart, your head, your eyes, your hands, your feet, your body, your soul, and your spirit? Does He sit supreme upon the throne of your heart? Does your life show that He rules and governs your thoughts? Does your life glorify Jesus? Are all your hopes fixed on Him? Your answer to these questions is of the utmost importance.

B. A Divine Revelation (v. 17)

17. And Jesus answered and said unto him, Blessed art thou, Simon Bar-jona: for flesh and blood hath not revealed it unto thee, but my Father which is in heaven.

A crude fisherman makes the greatest confession that man can make and shares the significance of God's greatest purpose for mankind. The religious leaders should have been aware of what was happening. Yet they were ignorant of what God was doing.

Formal education was probably considered more important in those days than it is today, and only those deeply learned in the law were considered capable of leading God's chosen people. But Jesus gathered around Him a group of men who were without formal training but whose hearts were teachable. Upon these He placed His hopes for the winning of the world to Himself. And God is still working through humble, honest, and faithful men. We should never allow ourselves to be overawed by dazzle and pretense. God is still looking for those who are consistent in service.

Peter's answer was a source of great joy to Jesus. He immediately assigned the source of Peter's knowledge to the heavenly Father. Likewise, all men who have come to perceive this truth have had their eyes opened by God that they might see His glory in Christ. Only these have learned the true meaning of happiness. Those who know Christ lack nothing that is necessary to perfect happiness. After all, we have no right to desire anything more than the eternal glory of God, and Christ puts us in possession of this.

Jesus' manner of making Himself known to His disciples was instructive. He did not tell them who He was, but He led them to make the discovery for themselves. Thus they were convinced in their own minds and were ready to share with others what they had learned. Someone has said that if a man is convinced against his will, he is unconvinced still. But when the glorious truth of the person and work of Christ shines upon the soul, one is ready to embrace it and share it. Peter had arrived at that point.

Jesus also strengthened their faith by giving them an opportunity to confess it. Once they had admitted to one another what they believed, they were reinforced in that belief. They formed a bond of unity and shared a common faith. The same bond of unity exists in each local church as well as in an entire denomination. We draw strength from the knowledge that others share our feelings and our faith. No wonder the Lord told Peter that he was entitled to a great blessing—a type of joy higher than anything the world confers. The believer derives his greatest joy from the knowledge he has of Jesus Christ and from the privilege of fellowship with other believers. Nothing the world has to offer can begin to compare with the riches of fellowship one finds in Christ Jesus.

III. AN INVINCIBLE CHURCH (Matthew 16: 18-20)

A. My Church (v. 18)

18. And I say also unto thee, That thou art Peter, and upon this rock I will build my church; and the gates of hell shall not prevail against it.

Were the keys to the kingdom given to Peter alone?

Jesus says that He will build His Church upon a rock. He means that the foundation upon which He builds is sound, secure, stable, and impregnable.

In the Old Testament, Abraham is referred to as a rock. " 'Look to the rock from which you were cut and to the quarry from which you were hewn; look to Abraham, your father'" (Isaiah 51:1, 2, **New International Version).**

Many references are made to God as a rock. The Psalmist says: "I love you, O Lord, my strength. The Lord is my rock, my fortress and my deliverer; my God is my rock, in whom I take refuge. He is my shield and the horn of my salvation, my stronghold" (Psalm 18:1, 2, **New International Version).**

Christ Jesus also is alluded to as a rock. Paul says of the children of Israel: "They all ate the same spiritual food and drank the same spiritual drink; for they drank from the spiritual rock that accompanied them, and that rock was Christ" (1 Corinthians 10:3, 4, **New International Version).** But perhaps the most beautiful reference to Christ as a rock is made by Peter: "As you come to him, the living Stone—rejected by men but chosen by God and precious to him—you also, like living stones, are being built into a spiritual house to be a holy priesthood, offering spiritual sacrifices acceptable to God through Jesus Christ. For in Scripture it says: 'See, I lay a stone in Zion, a chosen and precious cornerstone, and the one who trusts in him will never be put to shame.' Now to you who believe, this stone is precious. But to those who do not believe, 'The stone the builders rejected has become the capstone,' and, 'A stone that causes men to stumble and a rock that makes them fall.' They stumble because they disobey the message—which is also what they were destined for" (1 Peter 2:4-8, **New International Version).**

Jesus says that Peter is a rock. By nature he was but a handful of sand, which a maiden's breath can scatter to the winds; but Christ touched him and petrified him into a rock that neither earth nor hell could move. William Barclay comments: "(Peter) is not the rock on which the Church is founded; that rock is God. He is the first initial foundation stone of the whole Church. Peter was the first man on earth to discover who Jesus was; he was the first man to make the leap of faith which saw in Jesus Christ the Son of the living God. . . . And in ages to come, everyone who makes the same discovery as Peter is another and another stone added into the edifice of the Church of Christ." Paul says that the Church is "built on the foundation of the apostles and prophets, with Christ Jesus himself as the chief cornerstone" (Ephesians 2:20, **New International Version).** Peter refers to all believers as "living stones, [who] are being built into a spiritual house" (2 Peter 2:5, **New International Version).**

Further, Peter's confession, "You are the Christ, the Son of the living God," is the foundation truth upon which the Church is built. This truth must be embraced or one is not a true believer. It is the starting point on the road to Christian commitment.

So, the Church that Christ is building rests upon an unmovable foundation. Paul writes: "For no one can lay any foundation other than the one already laid, which is Jesus Christ" (1 Corinthians 3:11, **New International Version).** No force on earth or in the regions beyond can penetrate that foundation. Thanks be to God for the unsearchable provisions we have in Christ!

B. The Keys of the Kingdom (v. 19)

19. And I will give unto thee the keys of the kingdom of heaven: and whatsoever thou shalt bind on earth shall be bound in heaven: and whatsoever thou shalt loose on earth shall be loosed in heaven.

When Jesus gave the keys to the Kingdom to Peter, He was sharing with him both opportunity and responsibility. Peter was to use those keys to open the door of the Kingdom to others. He used them on the Day of Pentecost. "Those who accepted his message were baptized, and about three thousand were added to their number that day" (Acts 2:41, **New International Version).** He used the keys again in the house of Cornelius, opening to him and his household dimensions of spiritual insight and reality they had never known before. "While Peter was still speaking these words, the Holy Spirit came on all who heard the message" (Acts 10:44, **New International Version).**

The keys of the Kingdom were not given to Peter alone. Every believer is given the keys and has the opportunity to open the doors of the Kingdom to others. What are you doing to share with others about what Christ has done for you and what He can do for them?

When Jesus gave Peter the keys of the Kingdom, He charged him to make decisions that would affect all believers. What an awesome responsibility! Think of having to make decisions that will affect the souls of men for time and for eternity. His decisions about the life and practice of believers would have far-reaching consequences. Peter's activity and argument before the Council at Jerusalem indicates how seriously he accepted the responsibility Christ placed upon him.

Again, every believer has some degree of responsibility in the administration of the affairs of the Church. This responsibility should be assumed with a sense of prayerful dependence. Only as Christ who is the Head of the Church guides us can we who make up His Body make wise decisions. Knowing that He has entrusted us with the care of His Church, we should frequently fall back on Him for direction and guidance.

C. The Christ (v. 20)

20. Then charged he his disciples that they should tell no man that he was Jesus the Christ.

Having accepted Peter's confession, Jesus now instructs His disciples not to share his truth with anyone. Why? The disciples did not understand the full significance of Peter's confession nor the spiritual nature of Christ's kingdom. They still expected the overthrow of Roman tyranny as did most of those who aligned themselves with Jesus. To announce that He was the promised Messiah, the Lord of lords and King of kings, would only lead to physical disturbances and violence. Therefore, Christ ordered them to be mute about the matter.

The importance of the event we have been studying is underscored by this observation from G. Campbell Morgan: "It is, then, a remarkable fact that in His (Christ's) teaching there was no definite prediction of His personal return till Caesarea Philippi. The more carefully I study the life of the Lord, the more I am impressed with the remarkable nature of the Crisis that then occurred in His ministry. Until Peter's confession had been made, He never mentioned the Cross, the Church, nor His second coming. Everything up to that point had been preliminary and preparatory, and only after the confession had been made, 'Thou art the Christ, the Son of the living God,' did He declare His purpose of building His Church, the necessity for His cross and passion, and the certainty of His second coming."

REVIEW QUESTIONS

1. What answer did the disciples give Jesus in response to His question, "Whom do men say that I the Son of man am?"

2. What great confession did Peter make concerning the identity of Jesus?

3. What did Jesus mean by the expression "thou art Peter, and upon this rock I will build my church?"

4. What authority did Christ indicate He would give to Peter concerning the kingdom of heaven?

5. What request concerning His identity did Jesus make of the disciples in verse 20.

GOLDEN TEXT HOMILY

"THOU ART THE CHRIST, THE SON OF THE LIVING GOD" (Matthew 16:16).

Life is full of questions, but Jesus' query in Matthew 16:15 is the most important one of all. It deals with where we stand with Christ. While the question from Christ is vitally important, the answer from us is of even greater consequence. Peter answered with the only correct response, for his was an answer of faith and trust in Christ as Savior and Lord.

Notice that in Peter's answer he acknowledged that Jesus is the Christ, the Messiah prophesied throughout the Old Testament. Before Peter stood the Emissary of heaven, the Desire of all nations, Incarnate Deity. Peter acknowledged Him to be the Son of God! In so answering, the apostle represented all believers before the divine inquiry.

Peter's response was a personal acceptance of Christ as Savior. The scene is repeated millions of times as Christ presents Himself to individuals in divine love and mercy. It is more than a question to answer, it is a responsibility with eternal consequences.

During this pre-Pentecost time of his life, the Apostle Peter was fraught with human frailties, yet here we see bursting from him the height of all human wisdom and knowledge. We are made to understand this sudden wisdom when Jesus explains that it was given by the inspiration and revelation of the Father. No man can come to Jesus except the Spirit draws him.

When we make Christ the Savior and Lord of our life, He makes us a member of the eternal family of God.—**Jack Smith, Associate Pastor, North Cleveland Church of God, Cleveland, Tennessee**

SENTENCE SERMONS

CHRIST IS NOT valued at all—unless He is valued above all.

—St. Augustine

ANYTHING THAT ONE imagines of God apart from Christ is only useless thinking and vain glory.
—**Martin Luther**

NO QUESTION IS ever settled
Until it is settled right.
—**Ella Wheeler Wilcox**

EVANGELISTIC APPLICATION

FOR SALVATION, ONE MUST ACCEPT AND CONFESS CHRIST AS THE SON OF GOD.

Dr. Donald Grey Barnhouse says that many years ago he rode the streetcar home from one of the suburbs of Los Angeles late at night. There were only half a dozen passengers in the car—all men—when a young man got on the car at an intermediate stop. The new passenger paid his fare, lifted his hands and cried out, "I'm engaged to be married. My girl just said **yes.**" Everyone laughed; there was joshing and wisecracks. Love from his heart had found a response and he could not keep still about it.

Is it possible for an interchange of love between the Lord God and His creature without a great desire to acknowledge it? Is it possible to realize that Christ is the Son of God without sharing that glorious truth with others? The most beautiful discovery that the soul can make is that Jesus lives and not only that He lives but also that He lives within. What peace and joy that knowledge brings to the heart. Have you experienced that happiness? Have you accepted and confessed Christ as the Son of God?

ILLUMINATING THE LESSON

Victorinus, a great man at Rome, who had many rich heathen friends and relatives, was converted to the Christian religion. He visited a friend of his, and told him secretly that he, too, was a Christian. "I will not believe thee to be a Christian," said the other, "until I see thee openly profess it in the church." "What," said Victorinus, "do the church walls make a Christian?" But directly the answer came to his own heart: "Whosoever shall be ashamed of Me and My words, of him also shall the Son of Man be ashamed when he cometh in the glory of his Father with the holy angels."—**Augustine's "Confessions."**

DAILY DEVOTIONAL GUIDE

M. An Inescapable Question. Mark 8:27-30
T. A Personal Question. Luke 9:18-20
W. The Call to Decision. John 6:52-69
T. A Great Confession. John 11:20-27
F. Saving Faith. Acts 8:26-39
S. Our Confession. 1 John 4:1-15

September 28, 1980

Our Glorified Lord

Bible Background: Matthew 17:1-13; Mark 9:2-13; Luke 9:28-36

Time: Probably A.D. 29

Place: Near Caesarea Philippi

Supplemental References: Exodus 24:15-18; 33:12-23; John 1:14; 17:5; Acts 7:54-56; 2 Corinthians 3:18

Golden Text: "This is my beloved Son, in whom I am well pleased; hear ye him" (Matthew 17:5).

Central Truth: The Transfiguration confirmed the Person and mission of Christ.

Evangelistic Emphasis: The glorified Christ has power to attract the unconverted to himself.

PRINTED TEXT

Luke 9:28. And it came to pass about an eight days after these sayings, he took Peter and John and James, and went up into a mountain to pray.

29. And as he prayed, the fashion of his countenance was altered, and his raiment was white and glistening.

30. And, behold, there talked with him two men, which were Moses and Elias:

31. Who appeared in glory, and spake of his decease which he should accomplish at Jerusalem.

32. But Peter and they that were with him were heavy with sleep: and when they were awake, they saw his glory, and the two men that stood with him.

33. And it came to pass, as they departed from him, Peter said unto Jesus, Master, it is good for us to be here: and let us make three tabernacles; one for thee, and one for Moses, and one for Elias: not knowing what he said.

34. While he thus spake, there came a cloud, and overshadowed them: and they feared as they entered into the cloud.

35. And there came a voice out of the cloud, saying, This is my beloved Son: hear him.

36. And when the voice was past, Jesus was found alone. And they kept it close, and told no man in those days any of those things which they had seen.

DICTIONARY

into a mountain to pray—Luke 9:28—A tradition dating from the 3rd century says this was Mt. Tabor; but since this mountain would afford little privacy, it is more likely to have been Mt. Hermon, a little north of Caesarea Philippi.

Elias (ee-LYE-us)—Luke 9:30—The old English translation of the Greek form of the word **Elijah**

tabernacles—Luke 9:33—The original word means tents or booths.

LESSON OUTLINE

I. THE TRANSFIGURED CHRIST
   A. The Three Disciples
   B. The Lord of Glory
II. THE HEAVENLY VISITORS
   A. Moses and Elijah
   B. The Disciples
III. THE DIVINE VOICE
   A. Three Tabernacles
   B. A Cloud
   C. A Voice
   D. Jesus Only

LESSON EXPOSITION
INTRODUCTION

The transfiguration of Christ, while He prays on the slopes of Mount Hermon, comes soon after the incident in Caesarea Philippi. Since the Person of Christ is the focal point of both events, they are closely and vitally related. Peter's confession is that He is the Christ of God. Now the Father confirms that confession with the words: "This is my beloved Son." Then Jesus is transfigured in their presence. Charles R. Erdman remarks about the Transfiguration: "It is surely an experience quite different from that of Moses on the mountain. The face of Moses shone with a reflected light; but, in the case of Jesus, a glory from within bursts forth and irradiates his whole being, until not only his face, but his very garments are radiant with a dazzling light. Matthew has been picturing to us the career of the King. It is as if the monarch had been walking in disguise; only occasionally beneath his humble garment has been revealed a glimpse of the purple and the gold. Here, for an hour, the disguise is withdrawn and the King appears in his real majesty and in the regal splendor of his divine glory."

Glimpses of Christ's glory shone through in His character as He lived and ministered on earth. It was seen in His holiness. When we behold the sterling character of this wonderful Person, we feel like exclaiming with Isaiah: "Woe is me! for I am undone; because I am a man of unclean lips, and I dwell in the midst of a people of unclean lips: for mine eyes have seen the King, the Lord of hosts" (Isaiah 6:5). Jesus always did the things that were well-pleasing to His Father. There was no "guile found in his mouth;" and ". . . when he was reviled, [he] reviled not again; when he suffered, he threatened not; but committed himself to him that judgeth righteously" (1 Peter 2:22, 23).

Glimpses of Christ's glory were also seen in the manifestations of His love. His love extends to all mankind. There is no evidence that the rich young ruler ever accepted Christ, yet the scripture says that when Jesus looked upon him, He loved him. He loved the lost so much that He died for them. Also, He loves His own. He loves them so much that no one can ever separate them from His love (see Romans 8:37-39).

May we become more aware of the majesty of His person as we study about His transfiguration.

I. THE TRANSFIGURED CHRIST (Luke 9:28, 29)

A. The Three Disciples (v. 28)

28. And it came to pass about an eight days after these sayings, he took Peter and John and James, and went up into a mountain to pray.

Matthew and Mark say that this event took place six days after the incident at Caesarea Philippi. Luke says it happened about eight days afterward. The probability is that Luke counted both the day on which Christ spoke the words recorded, and the day on which He was transfigured.

Peter, James and John accompanied Jesus to the slopes of Mount Hermon. Why these three? Peter was bold, openhearted, enthusiastic. Maybe this experience would strengthen him in the days ahead. After all, he was to give direction to the infant church after the ascension of Christ. Of John, it is said that the Master loved him very much. His head was to lie in the bosom of the Lord, and he was to affectionately care for Jesus' mother. Also, he was to behold the Savior "in the isle that is called Patmos." Is it not fitting that he should see Him once in His glory, that he might recognize Him when He again appeared to him? James seems to have special traits of beauty about his character. His early martyr death and the fact that he was the brother of John lift him up to a very high position among the apostles of Christ.

These three apostles were chosen to behold Christ in His glory because they were afterwards to behold Him in His greatest agony. Can you imagine what their feelings might have been when they first saw Him brighter than the sun, and then when they beheld Him red as the rose with bloody sweat? I don't know which is the more beautiful picture—Christ robed in light and brighter than the sun or Christ crimsoned with His own blood, the very essence of His being poured out in agony for us. Oh, the loveliness of an agonizing Savior! I cannot compare Him in these two so strangely differing experiences; one would have needed to see Him in both to understand either of them.

The Lord probably chose these three apostles because that is the number of witnesses which the Law required for proving anything: "At the mouth of two witnesses, or three witnesses" (see Deuteronomy 17:6). The witness of Peter at Caesarea Philippi was the witness of speech; the witness on the Mount of Transfiguration was the witness of sight. Peter first declared the glory of Christ and later beheld it with his own eyes.

Jesus ascended the mountain for the purpose of prayer. Is it surprising that wonderful things happened that day? Is not prayer always a source of richness and blessing?

B. The Lord of Glory (v. 29)

29. And as he prayed, the fashion of his countenance was altered, and his raiment was white and glistening.

The glory of Christ was revealed to His disciples while He was praying. This should teach us that if we would see Christ's glory, we also must pray. If we would glow with the glory of Christ, we must be much in prayer. We are far too often like Martha, "cumbered about much serving"; we need to be more like Mary, sitting at the feet of Jesus, looking up into His dear face, and listening to His gracious words. The active life will lack power if it is not accompanied by much of the contemplative and the prayerful. There must be time spent in private prayer if there is to be true growth in grace.

In the presence of Peter, James, and John, the appearance of Christ's face changed. His face was the same as it was before, but it was now illuminated with a supernatural radiance. We can be sure that whatever glory may come to Jesus in the future His facial features will be the same, only lit up with heavenly brightness.

The Transfiguration changed nothing about the mission of Christ. Nothing was changed in His heart, in His purposes, or in His designs toward mankind. There was no swerving from the great object for which he had descended from heaven; and there was no change either in His feelings or in His manner toward the needs of humanity. In His transfigured state He talked about His decease at Jerusalem.

Jesus was transfigured in the presence of His disciples. He did not withhold His glory from them. He did not change in His attitude toward them. After the Transfiguration He spoke to His disciples in the same gentle, human, tender tones as before. He laid His hand upon them in the old-fashioned, familiar way, and said, "Arise, and be not afraid." His manner was the same as it had been when, walking upon the water, He had said to them, "It is I; be not afraid." And in His high priestly prayer, He prayed that His glory would be revealed to all believers. " 'Father, I want those you have given me to be with me where I am, and to see my glory, the glory you have given me because you loved me before the creation of the world' " (John 17:24, **New International Version).**

Not only was the face of Jesus brilliant with glory, but also in His raiment an unusual and dazzling whiteness appeared. His inner glory even shone through His garments.

II. THE HEAVENLY VISITORS (Luke 9:30-32)

A. Moses and Elijah (vv. 30, 31)

30. And, behold, there talked with him two men, which were Moses and Elias:

31. Who appeared in glory, and spake of his decease which he should accomplish at Jerusalem.

While Christ was in this transfigured state, two of the most remarkable and prominent figures in the Old Testament appeared with Him—Moses and Elijah. God gave the Law to Israel through Moses and He spoke to the people through Elijah. Moses initiated a new order of things in the world while Elijah repeated the principles upon which that order was based. Elijah lived in a time when the chosen nation had become disobedient.

This was Moses' first visit to Palestine. He had never before stood in the Promised Land. He had seen it from afar at the close of his life, but he had never entered the land. He had seen it from afar, had led the people almost to the verge of possession, and then had died in the land of Moab, receiving the high and holy honor of burial by God. He now stood in the land of Palestine. The Law had not brought him there; he was there by the infinite grace of God as manifested in the Person of His Son. Can you imagine how Moses felt?

Being in Palestine was no new experience

for Elijah. He had probably traveled all over this land founding the schools of the prophets and endeavoring to train men to carry on his work after his departure. Do you suppose he remembered that time when he thought he was the only man loyal to God in the land? What a different perspective he must have now! He knows of the many redeemed who are already in Paradise. He sees that the truth which he proclaimed is still being preached. He observes that the work of the Lord has survived all of the attacks upon it. Discouragement, abandonment, fiery trials, none of these things have been successful in stopping this mighty movement of God.

He who did not die—for the chariots and horses of fire had separated him from Elisha, and the whirlwind had caught him to the saints' abode—had returned to the earth to talk with the Lord.

These two men—Moses and Elijah—whose departure from the world had been veiled in mystery, were chosen for this mysterious return. Both men had pointed forward by symbol and prediction to the atoning work of Christ. They were, therefore, qualified to speak with Jesus intelligently concerning His coming death. They believed the promises of God about Christ's sacrifice of Himself for the redemption of all mankind.

Christ's death was the topic of conversation between Jesus and the heavenly visitors. The representative of the Law with its ordinances and its demands, and the representative of the Prophecy with its predictions about the future, stand there and bear witness that their lines of thought converge in Jesus. The finger that wrote the Law and the finger that smote and parted Jordan are each lifted to point to Him. They both stand to proclaim, "Behold the Lamb of God, the perfect Fulfiller of law, the true King of Israel." Their presence and their speech confirmed Him to be the One whom they had seen from afar.

The presence of these heavenly visitors signals that Christ is the King of life. Of these two, one had died, though mystery hung round his death and burial; the other had passed into the heavens by another gate than that of death; and here they both stand with lives undiminished by their mysterious changes. They are witnesses of an immortal life and proofs that His yet unpierced hands held the keys of life and death. He opened the gate which moves backwards to no hand but His and summoned them. They responded to Him as the King of life.

Then, these heavenly visitors represent the Old Testament believers who are still looking to the coming Deliverer. Through all the years of the past, good men had died with faith in the coming Savior. Now these two men are brought from their place of rest in the hope of learning how near their redemption is. That great crowd of holy men and women, who had died in faith, not having received the promises, anxiously awaited the report which Moses and Elijah would have for them. How they must have rejoiced at the good news that Christ intended to pay the sin debt and to set them free.

The hope of all mankind hinged on that conversation with Moses and Elijah. Those who had died trusting in the Lord waited to hear His confirmation of the plan of salvation. Those who have been born since then and who look back on that occasion rejoice that Christ expressed His determination to go to death by way of the Cross.

At the moment when Christ experienced His greatest glory upon earth, His thoughts and His conversation were turned to His hour of greatest agony and rejection.

B. The Disciples (v. 32)

32. But Peter and they that were with him were heavy with sleep: and when they were awake, they saw his glory, and the two men that stood with him.

It is difficult to imagine that the disciples were sleepy at such a moment as this. Their sleeping was probably the result of the extraordinary excitement through which they had passed. Sometimes after experiencing great mental excitement one feels physically exhausted. This appears to be what happened to the disciples on the Mount.

Interestingly, these same disciples were very sleepy at the time of Jesus' greatest glory upon earth and at the time of His great agony in the Garden of Gethsemane. They were so depressed in spirit by His sufferings, that, although they had true sympathy with Him, they fell asleep. However, it was while they were awake on each occasion that they discovered the meaning of what was happening.

The Holy Spirit is careful to record that they were fully awake when they beheld the glory of Christ. What they saw was not a dream, not a vision, not induced by a trance, but reality. They saw Jesus, Moses and Elijah.

The disciples saw Jesus in some measure as He will be in the future. Being fully awake, they saw the glory which streamed from the Savior's face and from every part of His most blessed and adorable person. I am glad to know that Jesus has a glory about Him which our opened eyes may see. His glory is such that we can see it in the time of quiet meditation, when every faculty is in full exercise, and our whole soul is in the enjoyment of the utmost degree of vigorous health. Thank God for a glory that can be seen by a man when he is fully awake, and not just in dreams and visions.

Perhaps we have a reason in this passage as to why some see so little of the glory of Christ. They are not fully awake spiritually. They are not fully committed to serve Him. Those who live to win souls for Christ, whose soul is on fire to try and carry the gospel into some place where as yet it is not known, are certain to see the glory of Christ. Those who live each day to honor Him are sure to see His glory. Those who make their work a witness by their consistent and noble manner are sure to behold the glory of the only begotten Son. It takes people who are fully awake to the cause of Christ to gain a glimpse of His glory. Have you seen the glory of the Lord?

III. THE DIVINE VOICE (Luke 9:33-36)

A. Three Tabernacles (v. 33)

33. And it came to pass, as they departed from him, Peter said unto Jesus, Master, it is good for us to be here: and let us make three tabernacles; one for thee, and one for Moses, and one for Elias: not knowing what he said.

Prior to this experience on the Mount of Transfiguration, Jesus talked to His disciples about His death at Jerusalem. They could not understand why He should have to suffer and die. Perhaps one reason for this event was to show the disciples that beyond the suffering will come the glory. There must first come the shame, but the glory will follow. Although a time of humiliation is coming; a time of triumph will follow. A Cross stands in the path Jesus must take, but beyond the Cross there is a crown.

Whatever suffering for Christ the believer encounters, there are rewards that await him in the future. Paul writes: "The Spirit himself testifies with our spirit that we are God's children. Now if we are children, then we are heirs—heirs of God and co-heirs with Christ, if indeed we share in his sufferings in order that we may also share in his glory. I consider that our present sufferings are not worth comparing with the glory that will be revealed in us" (Romans 8:16, **New International Version).**

There are some occasions when nothing should be done but to worship and glorify the Lord. At such times as that, one gains the strength needed to face the battles of life. After a period of meditation, one finds grace to serve the Lord more effectively. If we spent more time on our knees adoring Christ and seeking His favor, we would see better results in our labor for Him. He is the source of our victory.

On the Mount of Transfiguration, Peter lost his perspective. In the presence of Jesus, Moses and Elijah, he did not want to leave. Beholding the splendor of the glory of the Lord, he wanted to make provisions to stay there permanently. He lost sight of a needy world at the foot of the mountains.

One of the greatest dangers that believers face is the temptation to keep the blessings of the Lord to themselves. But the moment of glory does not exist for its own sake; it is designed to give strength for the daily ministry and to enable one to walk the way of the Cross. Its real benefit is seen in what one does after the moment of glory.

A rich experience becomes richer when it is translated into practical benefit for others. What are you doing with your close encounters with Christ? Are you keeping them to yourself or are you sharing with others?

B. A Cloud (v. 34)

34. While he thus spake, there came a cloud, and overshadowed them: and they feared as they entered into the cloud.

While Peter was expressing his wish for three tabernacles to be built, a bright cloud overshadowed him and the other disciples. For a cloud to appear on Mount Hermon was not unusual. Edersheim writes: "A strange peculiarity has been noticed about Hermon in 'the extreme rapidity of the formation of clouds upon the summit. In a few minutes a thick cap forms over the top of the mountain, and as quickly disperses, and entirely disappears.'"

I wonder what the disciples' first reaction was to the cloud that appeared on this occasion. Maybe they thought it was just an occurrence of that curious and characteristic phenomenon associated with Mount Hermon. But then the cloud took on a brightness and a mystery. A voice was heard speaking as God set His seal of approval on Jesus His Son. Perhaps at this point they realized that they were beholding the Shekinah, the glory of Almighty God.

This luminous cloud was not strange to the history of Israel. God aided the people of Israel in their deliverance from Egypt by a pillar of cloud. "And the Lord went before them by day in a pillar of a cloud, to lead them the way" (Exodus 13:21). When the Tabernacle was completed, the glory of the Lord appeared in the form of a cloud. "Then a cloud covered the tent of the congregation, and the glory of the Lord filled the tabernacle" (Exodus 40:34). When God gave the tables of the Law to Moses, He appeared in a cloud. "And the Lord descended in the cloud, and stood with him there, and proclaimed the name of the Lord" (Exodus 34:5). The cloud appeared again at the dedication of Solomon's Temple. "And it came to pass, when the priests were come out of the holy place, that the cloud filled the house of the Lord, So that the priests could not stand to minister because of the cloud: for the glory of the Lord had filled the house of the Lord" (1 Kings 8:10, 11).

When God draws near to man, it is absolutely necessary that His glory should be veiled. No man can see His face and live. That is the reason for the cloud. That was the reason for the thick veil which hung over the entrance to the most holy place. Above all, that was the reason for the body and the manhood of Jesus that the Godhead might be softened to our view. The God shines graciously through the man, and we behold the brightness of the Father's glory without being blinded thereby.

C. A Voice (v. 35)

35. And there came a voice out of the cloud, saying, This is my beloved Son: hear him.

On three separate occasions, God spoke out of heaven with an audible voice and declared that Jesus of Nazareth was the Son of God. The first statement came at the beginning of His earthly ministry. After He was baptized of John, the Spirit descended like a dove, and the voice of the Father was heard to say: " 'This is my Son, whom I love; with him I am well pleased' " (Matthew 3:17, **New International Version).**

The second heavenly utterance came when Jesus was about to send out the seventy disciples to preach the Word. The twelve had healed the sick, cast out demons, and done many mighty works. Now the laborers were to be increased and the harvest more rapidly ingathered. This witness is recorded by Matthew: " 'This is my Son, whom I love; with him I am well pleased. Listen to him' " (Matthew 17:5, **New International Version).** This is also the statement of our study text. What an impact it must have had on Peter, James and John.

The third statement came to our Lord just before His sufferings and death. They came just before He faced Gethsemane, Gabbatha (place of Pilate's judgment seat) and Golgotha. They were heard just before He was heard to cry: "My soul is exceeding sorrowful even unto death," and "My God, my God, why hast thou forsaken me?" In response to Jesus' prayer, " 'Father, glorify your name,' " the scripture says, "Then a voice came from heaven, 'I have glorified it, and will glorify it again' " (John 12:28, **New International Version).**

These divine utterances came at the beginning, near the middle, and near the end of Christ's earthly ministry. They came at a time of obedience (when He was baptized), at a time of retirement (when He went to the mountain to pray), and at a time of ministry (when He was preaching in the Temple). It is comforting to know that we too may enjoy the strengthening witness of the Spirit within. What a boost to our confidence!

D. Jesus Only (v. 36)

36. And when the voice was past, Jesus was found alone. And they kept it close, and told no man in those days any of those things which they had seen.

When the disciples heard the voice of God speaking out of the cloud, they were overcome with fear. "They fell facedown to the ground, terrified. But Jesus came and touched them. 'Get up,' he said. 'Don't be afraid.' When they looked up, they saw no one except Jesus" (Matthew 17:6, 7; **New International Version).**

The Law and the Prophets had a temporary glory that Christ alone might remain fully in view. Moses and Elijah take us beyond themselves and point us to Jesus. The scales have not fallen from our eyes until we see Jesus only.

How important it is that Jesus be given the central place in our lives. He must be supreme in our world. Our devotion must be toward Him. When He fills the whole of our vision, then is life satisfying indeed.

Only Jesus is made unto us "wisdom, and righteousness, and sanctification, and redemption" (1 Corinthians 1:30). Only Jesus is "the way, the truth, and the life," by whom we can come unto the Father (see John 14:6). Only Jesus bears the name whereby we must be saved (Acts 4:12). Only Jesus is the foundation upon which we must build (1 Corinthians 3:11). Only Jesus can render our prayers acceptable to God and effectual in their working (John 16:23, 24). Only Jesus could enter into the holy place and obtain an "eternal redemption for us" (Hebrews 9:12). Only Jesus is worthy of our eternal praise (Jude 24, 25).

REVIEW QUESTIONS

1. Name the disciples that accompanied Jesus into the mountain.
2. How was Jesus changed when He was transfigured before the disciples?
3. What was Peter's reaction of the event after the appearance of Moses and Elijah?
4. What did God say when He spoke from the cloud?
5. Why was the incident kept as a secret by the disciples?

GOLDEN TEXT HOMILY

"THIS IS MY BELOVED SON, IN WHOM I AM WELL PLEASED; HEAR YE HIM" (Matthew 17:5).

The record of the Savior's ministry as given by Matthew emphasizes His credentials. The genealogy in chapter one links Him with the royal line of David. The birth account names Him **Emmanuel**—"God with us." The Magi come seeking the newborn "King of the Jews." John the Baptist heralds the One whose kingdom is "at hand"—the One whose righteousness is such as to necessitate the urgent call to national repentance. Jesus emerges victorious in the hour of temptation. As befits a king, He delivers the great moral code on the mount. Time and again He demonstrates His power—power over the devil, over disease, over demons, even over the waves of Galilee. The inspired writer is saying, in effect, "Look! Here is proof that He is the Anointed One foreseen by the prophets! Here is your divine King, O Israel!"

But Israel's mood is one of rejection. The Pharisees ascribe His power to Satan. The scribes sneer and demand "a sign." The greater the demonstration of His credentials, the greater is the rejection. Now Jesus begins to speak of His death and resurrection of the Church which He will establish—and of His future return. The disciples are dumbfounded: "This is Messiah! This is our divine King! Can He die? If He is to go to Jerusalem and die, how can He be our King?"

At such a moment of deep puzzlement, God breaks through the wall of spiritual dullness with a striking revelation before the very eyes of the doubting disciples. In a high mountain Jesus is transfigured to radiate, temporarily, His divine glory in company with Moses and Elijah. A bright cloud overshadows the little company and the Father's voice is heard: "This is my beloved Son. . . ." The identification is unmistakable—but there is yet another word: "Hear ye him."

"Hear ye him!" The answer to all human bewilderment is found at the point of hearing Him. "Peter, James, John, don't be like the scribes and Pharisees. Don't sin the sin of unbelief. This is my own Son; Hear Him!"
—**H. Edward Rowe, Christian Freedom Foundation, New York, New York**

SENTENCE SERMONS

IF WE BECOME a partner of Christ in His work, He will become a partner with us in ours.
—**Selected**

AS BURNING CANDLES give light until they be consumed, so likewise godly Christians must be occupied in doing good so long as they shall live.
—**"The Speaker's Sourcebook"**

THE MOUNTAINTOP experiences must continue to illuminate the path of the valley.
—**Selected**

EVANGELISTIC APPLICATION

THE GLORIFIED CHRIST HAS POWER TO ATTRACT THE UNCONVERTED TO HIMSELF.

Nothing attracts with greater effectiveness than love. And there is no love comparable to the love of the glorified Christ. The radiance of His love is a magnet that draws the unconverted to Him. How could anyone refuse such boundless love?

The entire volume of divine love in its glorious resource and richness springs from the heart of Jesus. No outside factor contributes anything to its priceless values and peerless virtues. The Lord loves because the character, nature and essence of His being are love. Charles J. Rolls comments: "The fragrance of love exudes in the sweetness of His savor, is diffused in the perfume of His presence, reflects in the radiance of His righteousness, shines in the charm of His countenance, beams forth in the bounty of His beneficence, glows in the glory of His goodness and sparkles in the splendor of His superiority."

No wonder John could write: "This is love: not that we loved God, but that he loved us and sent his Son as an atoning sacrifice for our sins" (1 John 4:10, **New International Version**).

ILLUMINATING THE LESSON

We are blessed by what we sometimes call "mountaintop" experiences. At these times of spiritual elation we are lifted up into heavenly places. But it is not God's will for us to remain continuously in such places. There is work to be done; many need deliverance from the power of Satan. We must descend from the "mountain" and work for Him below.

Suddenly the disciples looked again, and Jesus was alone; Moses and Elijah had disappeared. How this reminds us that frail man is transitory, but Jesus is eternal. Let us keep our eyes upon Him, and, as the voice from the cloud commanded, "Hear Him."—**Selected**

DAILY DEVOTIONAL GUIDE

M. Vision of Christ's Glory. Daniel 7:9-14
T. The Glorified Christ. Matthew 17:1-13
W. Hearing the Father's Instructions. Mark 9: 2-13
T. Christ's Glory Revealed. John 1:1-14
F. Witnesses of Christ's Glory. 2 Peter 1:16-18
S. The Eternal Glory of Christ. Revelation 1: 12-18

October 5, 1980

The Conqueror of Demons

Bible Background: Matthew 17:14-21; Mark 9:14-29; Luke 9:37-43

Time: A.D. 29

Place: At the foot of the Mount of Transfiguration—traditionally thought to be Mount Tabor but more likely to be one of the ridges of Mount Hermon

Supplemental References: Mark 1:23-27; Luke 8:2; Acts 5:16; 19:2; Hebrews 2:14; 1 John 3:8

Golden Text: "All things are possible to him that believeth" (Mark 9:23).

Central Truth: Christ came into the world to destroy the works of the devil.

Evangelistic Emphasis: Demonic power can be broken by the power of the glorified Christ.

PRINTED TEXT

Mark 9:14. And when he came to his disciples, he saw a great multitude about them, and the scribes questioning with them.

15. And straightway all the people, when they beheld him, were greatly amazed, and running to him saluted him.

16. And he asked the scribes, What question ye with them?

17. And one of the multitude answered and said, Master, I have brought unto thee my son, which hath a dumb spirit;

18. And wheresoever he taketh him, he teareth him: and he foameth, and gnasheth with his teeth, and pineth away: and I spake to thy disciples that they should cast him out; and they could not.

19. He answereth him, and saith, O faithless generation, how long shall I be with you? how long shall I suffer you? bring him unto me.

20. And they brought him unto him: and when he saw him, straightway the spirit tare him; and he fell on the ground, and wallowed foaming.

21. And he asked his father, How long is it ago since this came unto him? And he said, Of a child.

22. And ofttimes it hath cast him into the fire, and into the waters, to destroy him: but if thou canst do any thing, have compassion on us, and help us.

23. Jesus said unto him, If thou canst believe, all things are possible to him that believeth.

24. And straightway the father of the child cried out, and said with tears, Lord, I believe; help thou mine unbelief.

25. When Jesus saw that the people came running together, he rebuked the foul spirit, saying unto him, Thou dumb and deaf spirit, I charge thee, come out of him, and enter no more into him.

26. And the spirit cried, and rent him sore, and came out of him: and he was as one dead; insomuch that many said, He is dead.

27. But Jesus took him by the hand, and lifted him up; and he arose.

28. And when he was come into the house, his disciples asked him privately, Why could not we cast him out?

29. And he said unto them, This kind can come forth by nothing, but by prayer and fasting.

DICTIONARY

scribes—Mark 9:14—Professional writers who, in Israel, become the official interpreters and teachers of the law of Moses and who served as judges in the administration of that law

saluted him—Mark 9:15—Greeted him; the equivalent of a respectful "hello"

dumb spirit—Mark 9:17—A demon who afflicted the one it possessed by rendering him unable to speak and sometimes unable to hear (v. 25)

taketh—Mark 9:18—The Greek means to seize with hostile intent; so, "wheresoever he experiences a seizure."

pineth—Mark 9:18—"Dries up" or "becomes stiff"

LESSON OUTLINE

I. POWERLESS DISCIPLES
  A. The Crowd
  B. The Father
  C. The Boy
II. OMNIPOTENT CHRIST
  A. Bring Him to Me
  B. If You Can Do Any Thing
  C. Come Out of Him
III. CONDITIONS OF SPIRITUAL POWER
  A. The Perplexity of the Disciples
  B. Prayer and Fasting

LESSON EXPOSITION

INTRODUCTION

All three of the synoptic Gospels—Matthew, Mark and Luke—place this scene of the demon-possessed boy immediately after the glorious experience on the Mount of Transfiguration. From the height of His glory manifested on earth, Jesus descended to this valley of despondency. The Mount of Transfiguration looms large in the background as Jesus stands in the valley and confronts a demon that handicaps an innocent boy.

When Jesus descended from the mountain and arrived in the valley, He found disputing scribes, a distracted father, a demon-possessed boy, and defeated disciples—what a change of scenery! A short time before, He had been talking to Moses and Elijah and listening to the voice of the Heavenly Father. He had been enveloped in the Shekinah glory of the Lord and had tenderly touched His fearful disciples bringing peace to their minds.

Now in the valley everything has changed. He comes face to face with one of the supreme examples of degradation which the New Testament records. And He proves Himself to be more than equal to the task. He silences the scribes, He comforts the father, He heals the boy, and He instructs the disciples.

By Jesus' response to this situation, He demonstrated the power of prayer. Prayer is the activity of faith. Prayer is that resting of the soul in Jesus, which rests at last in the will of God, and prompts the power of God. Here we see the exercise of prayer in its finest and truest sense. May we be instructed by its exercise.

I. POWERLESS DISCIPLES (Mark 9:14-18)

A. The Crowd (vv. 14, 15)

14. And when he came to his disciples, he saw a great multitude about them, and the scribes questioning with them.

15. And straightway all the people, when they beheld him, were greatly amazed, and running to him saluted him.

On the Mount of Transfiguration, Peter, James and John had been ministered unto. When they came down from the mountain, they were called upon to minister. The time that we spend alone with God is not for our personal benefit only. We are strengthened that we may minister strength to others. Peter's desire to stay on the mountain was a selfish desire. It indicates that he was out of touch with reality. In the real world, life is not a perpetual mountaintop experience. There are valleys through which people pass. We must minister to them in the valley or we are not fulfilling our mission in life. Jesus commends those who are sensitive to the needs of others and rewards their action in behalf of others. "Then the King will say to those on his right, 'Come, you who are blessed by my Father; take your inheritance, the kingdom prepared for you since the creation of the world. For I was hungry and you gave me something to eat, I was thirsty and you gave me something to drink, I was a stranger and you invited me in, I needed clothes and you clothed me, I was sick and you looked after me, I was in prison and you came to visit me'" (Matthew 25:34-36, **New International Version**).

When Jesus and the three disciples who were with him arrived at the foot of the mountain, they found the other disciples in an embarrassing situation. A father had brought his demon-possessed son to them that they might deliver him. They had failed in their attempts to do so. This gave the scribes—the experts in the law—an opportunity to ridicule them, and not only to ridicule them, but also to ridicule their Master.

Herein is one of the great problems every Christian faces. Our failures in the Christian life not only reflect upon us, but they also reflect upon our Lord. There is always someone who finds satisfaction in seeing a believer fall short of his profession. This same person uses that shortcoming to call into question the integrity of the entire Church and to dishonor the name of our lovely Lord. What an awesome responsibility we have as believers. We must strive to live in such a way that our life will bring honor to the Church and to the Lord. In the Sermon on the Mount, Jesus said: "'You are the salt of the earth. But if the salt loses its saltiness, how can it be made salty again? It is no longer good for anything, except to be thrown out and trampled by men. You are the light of the world. A city on a hill cannot be hidden. Neither do people light a lamp and put it under a bowl. Instead they put it on its stand, and it gives light to everyone in the house. In the same way, let your light shine before men, that they may see your good deeds and praise your Father in heaven'" (Matthew 5:13-16, **New International Version**).

When Jesus arrived at the scene, the people were surprised to see Him. They thought that He was still on the mountain. They were so involved in the discussion between the scribes and the disciples that He approached them unnoticed. When they realized that He was near, they were overwhelmed with wonder and ran to meet Him. What a difference the presence of Christ makes in any gathering!

B. The Father (vv. 16, 17)

16. And he asked the scribes, What question ye with them?

17. And one of the multitude answered and said, Master, I have brought unto thee my son, which hath a dumb spirit;

Jesus addressed the scribes and asked them what they were arguing about. There is no record of their immediate response. But the man who was responsible for the whole matter spoke. He explained that his son, his only son, was possessed by a spirit. This evil spirit had robbed him of his speech. He had brought him to the disciples in the hope that he might be healed. The disciples were unable to deliver him. Thus the scribes were arguing with them because of their failure.

Of his son, the man said to Jesus, "I brought you my son." No man could do anything more noble. The best thing that we can do for anyone is to bring them to the Lord Jesus Christ.

This man teaches us that believers have a special responsibility to the members of their own family. Parents are in a position to especially influence their children toward Christ. This father brought his son to Jesus, and in a very real sense all parents may do this. They may bring their children to Jesus by the life they live before them, by the devotions they share with them, by the prayers they pray for them, and by their direct witness to them.

This man also teaches us the value of persistence in bringing others to Christ. He could have become discouraged at the failure of the disciples to help his son. He could have listened to the arguments of the scribes and decided that his son was without hope. But he did not. As soon as Jesus arrived, the father immediately presented his case to Him. Sometimes believers are ineffective as soulwinners because they give up after their first attempt. Those who persist in their efforts to win others to Christ know the joy of ultimate victory. An undertaking of such importance should not be easily discouraged. It calls for our best effort.

Then, this man teaches us the importance of our attitude in approaching Christ. He comes to Jesus and pleads with Him for help. His heart is broken over the plight of his son. The intense weight of the burden he carries is reflected in the cry that escapes his lips. How deeply do we feel about the needs of others? How earnest is our plea in their behalf? Do we empathize with them in their need?

But also this father was bold about his approach to Jesus. He was aware that the scribes disapproved of his coming and that they disbelieved that anything good would result from it, but he came to Jesus anyhow. He knew that the disciples had failed in their attempts to deliver his son, but he came to Jesus anyhow. He was conscious that his despair would only be deepened if his mission failed, but he came to Jesus anyhow. How bold are you in approaching Jesus? Do you bring the easy cases to Him but find it harder to trust Him with the more difficult matters? There is no case too hard for Him. He desires that we show the boldness this man displayed.

C. The Boy (v. 18)

18. And wheresoever he taketh him, he teareth him: and he foameth, and gnasheth with his teeth, and pineth away: and I spake to thy disciples that they should cast him out; and they could not.

The father described his son's reaction to the demon that possessed him. He was thrown into severe convulsions; he was caused to foam at the mouth; he was made to grind his teeth; and he became very rigid in body. In addition to this, he was subject to sudden, unexpected attacks at which times he often fell into the fire and into the water. He was also deaf and speechless. All of these calamities resulted from his being demon possessed. This is not to say that all people who have these symptoms are demon possessed. But this was the case with this boy. His reactions are very instructive.

The demon had complete control over the boy. He mastered him in every way. That is what is meant by demon possession. By way of contrast, what does it mean to be God possessed, to belong to God, to be His property? That is the exact position of the believer. We are not our own, we belong to Him. Paul writes: "Do you not know that your body is a temple of the Holy Spirit, who is in you, whom you have received from God? You are not your own; you were bought at a price. Therefore honor God with your body" (1 Corinthians 6:19, 20; **New International Version**). Our lives should be totally under His control.

The father explained to Jesus that he brought his son to the disciples and that they could not help him. No doubt they were baffled and perplexed over their failure. Probably, the scribes sneered at them and thereby added to their humiliation and shame. It is encouraging to know that when we have failed miserably, Christ is always there to help us out of our dilemma. So it was with His disciples on this occasion.

II. OMNIPOTENT CHRIST (Mark 9:19-27).

A. Bring Him to Me (vv. 19, 20)

19. He answereth him, and saith, O faithless generation, how long shall I be with you? how long shall I suffer you? bring him unto me.

20. And they brought him unto him: and when he saw him, straightway the spirit tare him; and he fell on the ground, and wallowed foaming.

On other occasions the disciples had cast out demons. Once they reported to the Master, "Even the devils are subject unto us" (Luke 10:17). But this time they utterly failed. They did their best; they appear to have had some faith, or they would not have attempted the task, but their faith was not at all equal to the emergency. The scribes used this occasion to make light of the disciples and of the Master.

The rebuke which Jesus uttered was probably intended primarily for the Jews and their scribes. At the same time, He must have also had the weakness of faith of His own disciples in view. The words are the complaint of one weary of the unbelief of the masses and of the weakness of faith in even His own. How often He faced this during His ministry! How often He faces it today in the lives of unbelievers and believers.

Having made His expression of rebuke, Jesus then gave the instructions: "Bring him unto me." What the disciples could not do, Jesus will now do. And He would have us know that He is alive today to intervene in the lives of believers whenever He is needed. He is the living Lord and is fully aware of what is going on in our lives. We must never consider that He is far removed from the Church. His eyes are always upon us. We never face a struggle but that He sees us in the conflict. From the battlements of heaven Jesus looks upon the work of His Church. He is jealous for the honor of His gospel, and is as ready to intervene and win the victory now as He was then. We have but to look to our Lord. He does not sleep as did Baal of old. He is able to help; He is strong to deliver. On earth the splendor of His Godhead was veiled, but now His glory beams resplendent, and even hell confesses the majesty of His power. He lives—and He lives in the place of power. He expects us to treat Him as a living, powerful, intervening Being, and to confide in Him as such.

In obedience to the directions of Jesus, "They brought him unto him," and Jesus cast out the evil spirit and healed the poor sufferer.

How great is the power of unity! How much can be accomplished in a church when pastor and people have a common purpose and a common goal. What a beautiful spirit prevails when church members say, "While the pastor preaches, we will pray; and, more than that, we will continually remember him in our prayers, for we know that he needs them and prizes them." How beautiful when a pastor is equally committed to pray for His people. If all believers were thus alive unto God, and earnest in His service—"all at it, and always at it"—how much good might be done for the kingdom of God, the Holy Spirit blessing our labors.

B. If You Can Do Anything (vv. 21-24)

21. And he asked his father, How long is it ago since this came unto him? And he said, Of a child.

22. And ofttimes it hath cast him into the fire, and into the waters, to destroy him: but if thou canst do any thing, have compassion on us, and help us.

23. Jesus said unto him, If thou canst believe, all things are possible to him that believeth.

24. And straightway the father of the child cried out, and said with tears, Lord, I believe; help thou mine unbelief.

The father explains to Jesus that his son has been afflicted of this evil spirit from childhood. Frequently the demon cast the lad into the water or into the fire in an attempt to destroy him.

Perhaps a word should be said about this father and his attitude. He had every reason to be discouraged. First, he came looking for Jesus and found that He was on the mountain. Unable to reach Him, he turned to the disciples, but they were helpless in their attempt to deliver his son. Then he had to listen to the sneers of the scribes as they found this an opportune moment to belittle the ministry of the Lord. Yet when Jesus did appear, although this father's faith was just about shattered, he turned to Jesus for help. His plea is rather pathetic as he says to Jesus: "If you can do any thing, take pity on us and help us." How quickly he regained his lost faith when Jesus said: "What do you mean, 'If you can'? Everything is possible for him who believes." Emphatically the father replied, "I do believe." Then he added the prayer, "Help me overcome my unbelief!"

There cannot be any **if** in reference to Christ. He has the power to do anything. He is the only begotten Son of God. Even the devil himself is aware of His sonship. In the wilderness of temptation, he said, "If thou be the Son of God, command that these stones be made bread" (Matthew 4:3). But he knew in his heart that Christ was truly the Son of the Most High God. On many occasions, the demons, whom Christ cast out, cried aloud to Him, "Thou art Christ the Son of God" (see Mark 3:11; Luke 4:4). Being God's true Son, can anything be impossible to Him?

It must also be remembered that Jesus Christ is God. Can there be any **if** as to His power? What is there that God cannot do? He has made this world. He has made those millions of worlds that stud the midnight skies. But all that God has ever made, though it be far beyond our conception, is but as a speck compared with what He could make if He pleased. He has done exceedingly great marvels, such as have astounded men; but all that God has ever done is as nothing compared with what He could do if He willed to do it, for with Him all things are possible. And Jesus Christ being very God of very God, all things are possible with Him. There cannot be any **if** with the Christ of God, God's favored Son, God's equal, who is girded with omnipotence.

No, the **if** is not in Christ, it is in our lack of faith. Jesus said, "If you can believe." It is most unreasonable to expect Christ to do anything for us if we will not believe in Him. The very least thing that a great surgeon could expect of a patient would be confidence in his skill. We should not be surprised that Christ expects us to believe in Him. If we refuse Him our confidence, we should not wonder that He refuses us His power. "If you can believe."

Why is it that we cannot believe? Perhaps one reason for our lack of faith is that we measure God by ourselves. Take the matter of forgiveness for an example. We cannot think that God can forgive us because we find it so hard to forgive others. We cannot conceive that God will do it freely, from no motive but that of pure grace, because we are so mercenary. We want to be paid for what we do, and unless we can see some chance of reward, somewhere or other, we are very slow to make anything like a sacrifice. So we imagine that God is as we are. We forget the words of Scripture: "For as the heavens are higher than the earth, so are my ways higher than your ways, and my thoughts than your thoughts" (Isaiah 55:9). How wrong we are when we measure God by ourselves. We might sooner hold the ocean in the hollow of our hand or span the heavens with our fingers than, unaided by grace, get an idea of the greatness and glory of God by our own reasoning. It is because we limit the Holy One of Israel that we find the simple matter of faith so difficult. "If you can believe."

Finally it dawned on the father that the real problem was his own disbelief. Alarmed by that discovery he appealed to Christ, confessing his unbelief, and saying, "Lord, help me out of it, I beseech thee." This man believed that if Christ could help his child to get well, then He can help him to believe. There is nobody but the Lord Jesus Christ who can help us to get rid of unbelief. Jesus is worthy of being believed; He can be trusted. Let us commit ourselves into His hands and trust in His great keeping power.

C. Come Out of Him (vv. 25-27)

25. When Jesus saw that the people came running together, he rebuked the foul spirit, saying unto him, Thou dumb and deaf spirit, I charge thee, come out of him, and enter no more into him.

26. And the spirit cried, and rent him sore, and came out of him: and he was as one dead; insomuch that many said, He is dead.

27. But Jesus took him by the hand, and lifted him up; and he arose.

The time for confrontation had come. The evil spirit had mastered this boy since he was a child; now he would meet One who would master him. It was with great reluctance that he approached Jesus. He shrieked and threw the lad into convulsions before he came out of him. The boy looked so much like a corpse that many of the people said, "He's dead." But Jesus took him by the hand and lifted him to his feet, and he stood up. What a different person he became. He was no longer agitated, but calm and serene. For the first time since childhood, he knew the meaning of peace.

When the youth came to Christ, Satan threw him into convulsions. This is typical of Satan's attack on the souls of those who come to Christ to seek light and life through Him. He has a multitude of devices, for he is cunning and crafty, and he has various ways of accomplishing his ends. He may suggest to the seeker that the whole business of Christianity is based on falsehood. Or he may point the person to all the passages of Scripture that sound an ominous note and tell him that those scriptures apply to them. He may suggest that the individual has committed a sin that is a sin unto death. Or he may seek to convince him that he has committed the unpardonable sin. Satan never relates the words of Jesus when He said that "he who comes to Me, I will in no wise cast him out" (see John 6:37). He never speaks of the limitless bounds of God's free grace. No, he leaves the soul to grope without hope in a world of darkness and despair.

There is a reason why Satan puts up such a fight when a soul turns toward Christ. He does not want to lose what has been in his possession. "No king will willingly lose his subjects," said Apollyon to Christian when he stretched himself across the road, "and I swear that thou shalt go no farther; here will I spill thy soul." Satan will not stand by and see his empire thinned or his family diminished without putting up a fight. But there is good news for the seeking soul and there is good news for the believer. The Word of God admonishes: "Resist the devil, and he will flee from you" (James 4:7). Even though he may cast you to the ground, even though you may fall many times, you can always rise up again. The grace of the Lord is there to withstand the forces of evil. The victory is yours in Christ Jesus.

Another thing about Satan's approach to the soul is that he disguises himself. He appears as an angel of light. He never shows the dark and crafty side of his character. For this reason, the seeker must be very careful of the voices he hears. He must be able to detect the voice of Satan. When he has discovered that it is Satan who is speaking, he has frustrated the aims of the enemy. Satan can no longer take advantage of him. He may then with confidence turn to Christ who will bring defeat to the devil.

As surely as Jesus defeated the demon who possessed this lad, He will stop the forces of evil that assail your life if you trust in Him. Satan wants nothing to do with Gethsemane; he wants no part of Gabbatha; he wants no portion of Golgotha. When he is reminded of the blood of Jesus, he trembles.

He knows that Jesus is the way and that he cannot retain those who find the way. He knows that Jesus is the truth and that as such, Jesus exposes him for what he is. He knows that Jesus is the life and that those who come to Christ are spared the destruction and despair and death of the devil.

III. CONDITIONS OF SPIRITUAL POWER (Mark 9:28, 29)

A. The Perplexity of the Disciples (v. 28)

28. And when he was come into the house, his disciples asked him privately, Why could not we cast him out?

I suppose that the disciples wondered if the power which they once possessed had been taken from them. They did not understand why they could not deliver the demon-possessed boy. Christ attributes their lack of ability to their lack of faith. He then repeats and illustrates more largely the statement which He had previously made, that nothing is impossible to faith.

Matthew records a portion of Jesus' conversation which Mark does not include. "He replied, 'Because you have so little faith. I tell you the truth, if you have faith as small as a mustard seed, you can say to this mountain, "Move from here to there" and it will move. Nothing will be impossible for you' " (Matthew 17:20, **New International Version**). On another occasion Luke records another conversation between Jesus and the disciples: "The apostles said to the Lord, 'Increase our faith!' He replied, 'If you have faith as small as a mustard seed, you can say to this mulberry tree, "Be uprooted and planted in the sea," and it will obey you' " (Luke 17:5, 6; **New International Version**).

When faith reigns, the believer desires only that which the Lord promises to give. If we trust in Him, He will never forsake us. We must keep the door of our heart open to receive His grace.

B. Prayer and Fasting (v. 29)

29. And he said unto them, This kind can come forth by nothing, but by prayer and fasting.

The call to prayer and fasting signals a special need. John Calvin observes, "When He says that this kind of devil cannot be cast out in any other way than by prayer and fasting, he means that, when Satan has taken deep root in any one, and had been confirmed by long possession, or when he rages with unbridled fury, the victory is difficult and painful, and therefore the contest must be maintained with all our might. (Our Lord's call to prayer and fasting is designed) to stimulate the earnestness of prayer."

REVIEW QUESTIONS

1. When Jesus came upon the disciples, who was questioning them?
2. How did the man's son react under the influence of the demon?
3. What was the reaction of Jesus when He was told that His disciples were ineffective against the demon?
4. How did Jesus help the man to manifest faith?
5. Why were the disciples ineffective against the demon?

GOLDEN TEXT HOMILY

"ALL THINGS ARE POSSIBLE TO HIM THAT BELIEVETH" (Mark 9:23).

Sounds simple, doesn't it? Everything is possible; nothing is impossible. And such a simple requirement—only believe.

What is the problem then? Obviously, some people get hardly anything—let alone everything! There must be a clue which has eluded us.

The secret is in remembering who said it. This is not the back-slapping, arm-around-the-shoulder effort of a friend to console you. This is not a whistle-in-the-dark, keep-up-your-courage sort of thing.

Remember who is speaking—Jesus, the great Friend, before whom no power of evil can stand. It is the focus of our faith that counts. Let us give our attention not to the problem, nor to our great need for an answer, but to the One who is able to turn the impossible into the possible.—**Ralph W. Harris (Retired), Former Editor of Church School Literature, Gospel Publishing House, Springfield, Missouri**

SENTENCE SERMONS

THE CRY of some modern theologians that "God is dead," proves very much that the devil is alive.

—**"The Gospel Call"**

POWER WITH MEN proceeds from power with God.

—**"The Speaker's Sourcebook"**

THINKING WE HAVE some power of our own prevents our taking all power from Christ.

—**Selected**

CHRIST CAME INTO the world to destroy the works of the devil.
—Selected

EVANGELISTIC APPLICATION

DEMONIC POWER CAN BE BROKEN BY THE POWER OF THE GLORIFIED CHRIST.

There is a decided difference between the power of Christ and the power of demons. Demons are powerful. They have demonstrated their power many times and in many ways. The hopeless state of the boy in today's lesson is a striking example of how demons can master an individual. The sons of Sceva —false prophets—discovered that they were no match for demons. Though they came in the name of Jesus and in the name of Paul, they were helpless before the attack of the demon-possessed man.

But demons are not all-powerful; Christ is. There are no limitations on His power. And the demons know this. They know that whatever He commands them to do, they must do. They know that eventually He will confine them to a place of eternal torture. Therefore they fear and tremble in His presence. There is no lack of faith on their part. They believe that He is everything He claims to be and everything the Word declares Him to be. The brighter His glory shines, the darker their hope becomes.

ILLUMINATING THE LESSON

David Livingstone relates that he was once under the paw of a lion, from the recesses of the forest. The great beast was on him, and pinned him to the ground. He felt the breath of the lion soothing him to sleep. There was something in the breath that brought a dimness over the eyes, and a soothing to the spirit; and the bloody fangs of the lion that were getting ready to devour him were prefaced by this blindfolding by the very presence of the beast of prey. The devil causes a similar unconsciousness. I believe that positively there is an influence from the presence of the devil in a temptation.—**John Robertson**

DAILY DEVOTIONAL GUIDE

M. Deliverance From Demon Possession. Matthew 8:28-34

T. A Merciful Deliverance. Matthew 17:14-21

W. Christ's Authority Over Demons. Mark 1:23-27, 34

T. Healing Ministry of Believers. Acts 5:12-16; 19:12

F. Power Over Unclean Spirits. Luke 9:37-43

S. Satan's Defeat. Hebrews 2:14, 15; 1 John 3:8

October 12, 1980

The Compassionate Savior

Bible Background: John 8:1-11
Time: Probably October A.D. 29
Place: Jerusalem, Mount of Olives
Supplemental References: 2 Samuel 11:1 through 12:23; Psalms 32:1-11; 51:1-19; Matthew 5:27-32
Golden Text: "Jesus said unto her, Neither do I condemn thee: go, and sin no more" (John 8:11).
Central Truth: Christ has the authority and demonstrates the willingness to forgive any sin.
Evangelistic Emphasis: Christ has not come to condemn us but to deliver us from our sins.

PRINTED TEXT

John 8:1. Jesus went unto the mount of Olives.

2. And early in the morning he came again into the temple, and all the people came unto him; and he sat down, and taught them.

3. And the scribes and Pharisees brought unto him a woman taken in adultery; and when they had set her in the midst,

4. They say unto him, Master, this woman was taken in adultery, in the very act.

5. Now Moses in the law commanded us, that such should be stoned: but what sayest thou?

6. This they said, tempting him, that they might have to accuse him. But Jesus stooped down, and with his finger wrote on the ground, as though he heard them not.

7. So when they continued asking him, he lifted up himself, and said unto them, He that is without sin among you, let him first cast a stone at her.

8. And again he stooped down, and wrote on the ground.

9. And they which heard it, being convicted by their own conscience, went out one by one, beginning at the eldest, even unto the last: and Jesus was left alone, and the woman standing in the midst.

10. When Jesus had lifted up himself, and saw none but the woman, he said unto her, Woman, where are those thine accusers? hath no man condemned thee?

11. She said, No man, Lord. And Jesus said unto her, Neither do I condemn thee: go, and sin no more.

DICTIONARY

mount of Olives—John 8:1—The ridge of hills east of Jerusalem; it means "the mount where the olives grow." It is a limestone ridge, more than a mile in length, running in a general direction north and south, covering the whole eastern side of the city of Jerusalem.

scribes and Pharisees (FAIR-ah-sees)—John 8:3—A religious party, or school of the Jews, in the time of Christ, so called from an Aramaic form of a Hebrew word meaning "separated." Their theology was conservative, holding to the supernatural, the law of Moses, and the tradition of the elders.

The Compassionate Savior

Master—John 8:4—The translation of a Greek word; it means "teacher."

LESSON OUTLINE

I. CONDEMNED UNDER THE LAW
  A. Jesus Teaching
  B. The Woman Accused
  C. The Trap
II. CHALLENGED BY THE LORD
  A. The Lord's Answer
  B. The Lord Waits
  C. The Accusers Leave
III. CHANGED BY GRACE
  A. Jesus' Question
  B. Jesus' Challenge

LESSON EXPOSITION

INTRODUCTION

Perhaps the greatest joy a man can experience is the joy of forgiveness. By the same token, the greatest misery one can know is the misery of unforgiven sins. Somebody wrote, "The stag followed by hungry hounds with open mouths is far more happy than the woman who is pursued by her sins; the bird taken in the fowler's net and laboring to escape is far more happy than she who has woven about herself a web of deception; yon eagle beating against the brass bars is far happier than the woman whose sin stares at her from dark rooms at midnight; and the wild animal caught and suffering in the jaws of a steel trap is far happier than he that carries a guilty conscience in his bosom."

There is only One who can forgive us of our sin and who can rid us of our sin. That One is God in Christ about whom this was written: " 'He committed no sin, and no deceit was found in his mouth.' When they hurled their insults at him, he did not retaliate; when he suffered, he made no threats. Instead, he entrusted himself to him who judges justly. He himself bore our sins in his body on the tree, so that we might die to sins and live for righteousness; by his wounds you have been healed" (1 Peter 2:22-24, **New International Version**). Peter penned these words. Surely, if anyone knew the forgiveness of sins, he did. He denied the name of Christ deliberately and openly. Yet after his repentance and bitter tears, God forgave him and used him mightily in His service.

There is great beauty in divine forgiveness. You can describe God's merciful forgiveness of our sins as the lifting of a crushing burden, as the protection from deserved wrath, as the release from a justly incurred debt, as the liberation from prison, as the restoration to health after disease has wrought havoc in the human body. No joy can be like the joy of the forgiven when God, who alone can forgive, forgives transgression and covers sin. What peace and contentment He brings to the soul!

I. CONDEMNED UNDER THE LAW (John 8: 1-6)

A. Jesus Teaching (vv. 1-3)

1. Jesus went unto the mount of Olives.

2. And early in the morning he came again into the temple, and all the people came unto him; and he sat down, and taught them.

3. And the scribes and Pharisees brought unto him a woman taken in adultery; and when they had set her in the midst, . . .

The last verse of chapter 7 and the first verse of chapter 8 should be read together: "Then each went to his own home. But Jesus went to the Mount of Olives" (John 7:53; 8:1, **New International Version**).

Christ's friends and enemies departed to their own houses. Jesus spent the night in the open air watching and praying on the mount of Olives. This resting policy of our Lord reminds us again of His extreme poverty. Foxes, though they were but worthy to be exterminated, had holes in which they could hide. The birds of the air, though many ruthlessly sought to destroy them, had nests wherein they could rest. But the Son of Man had nowhere to lay His head.

The fact that Jesus had no house to go to suggests the forgetfulness and unkindness of His friends. You would think that His friends would have been anxious to entertain this Prince of prophets; that it would have been their greatest joy to have Him in their home.

On the other hand, it may be that they invited Him to their house and He declined the invitation. This may have been a time when He felt the need to be alone with the Father. There may have been matters which He needed to discuss and which He could discuss with no one but the Father. So, He retired to the mount of Olives to be alone.

I find this observation by Charles H. Spurgeon

October 12, 1980

very interesting: "Perhaps I shall startle and surprise you when I say that Jesus Christ did exactly what His disciples and the other people did. They went to their own houses, and He went to His own house. They went home, and He went home. They sought ease, and He sought ease. They sought counsel, and He sought counsel. They sought sympathy, and He sought sympathy. They sought refreshment, and He sought refreshment. The mount of Olives was, to all intents and purposes, Christ's home. It was there that He met with His Father. It was there that He cast off the cares of the day. It was there that He cried to heaven for wisdom. And it was there that, made strong by fresh contact with His Father, He girt on His golden armor to go forth once more fully protected from all the arrows of the evil one. Beloved brethren and sisters in Christ, that season of prayer upon the mount of Olives was to Jesus what our going to our houses and to our loved ones is to us. Yes, the cold mountain was His home."

After spending the night alone with His Father on the mount of Olives, the next morning Jesus appeared again in the temple court. All the people gathered around Him, and He sat down to teach them.

It is always interesting to notice a man's estimate of the value of the things he says himself. The greatest human teachers have always been reticent as to the ultimate authority of their teaching. They have always admitted that there is room for interpretation, for question, for further investigation. That note is entirely absent from the teaching of Christ. There is no apology. He never said, "It is natural therefore to suppose; it may probably be; or consult the authorities." The Gospels give us a glimpse of Jesus' view of His teaching.

" 'I tell you the truth, whoever hears my word and believes him who sent me has eternal life and will not be condemned; he has crossed over from death to life' " (John 5:24, **New International Version**).

" 'Therefore everyone who hears these words of mine and puts them into practice is like a wise man who built his house on the rock. The rain came down, the streams rose, and the winds blew and beat against that house; yet it did not fall, because it had its foundation on the rock. But everyone who hears these words of mine and does not put them into practice is like a foolish man who build his house on sand. The rain came down, the streams rose, and the winds blew and beat against that house, and it fell with a great crash' " (Matthew 7:24-27, **New International Version).**

" 'If anyone is ashamed of me and my words in this adulterous and sinful generation, the Son of Man will be ashamed of him when he comes in his Father's glory with the holy angels' " (Mark 8:38, **New International Version).**

" 'As for the person who hears my words but does not keep them, I do not judge him. For I did not come to judge the world, but to save it. There is a judge for the one who rejects me and does not accept my words; that very word which I spoke will condemn him at the last day' " (John 12:47, 48; **New International Version).**

" 'Heaven and earth will pass away, but my words will never pass away' " (Luke 21:33, **New International Version).**

On this verse from Luke's Gospel, G. Campbell Morgan comments: "My memory goes back nine-and-thirty years to a morning when I received one of the earliest and profoundest impressions of my life. It was created by that poet-preacher, Thomas Jones. I was a boy in Walter's Road Church in Swansea, and I remember the occasion as though it were but yesterday. He gave out the text, 'Heaven and earth shall pass away, but My **words** shall not pass away,' and then in his own inimitable way he began, leaning on his pulpit, 'And who is this young man that says this? Is not this the carpenter?' Then he led us on, and I saw the Lord that morning, and I have never forgotten from that day to this the tremendous importance of this statement. That impression comes back through the years to me now, with the accumulated testimony of any measure of attention I have been able to give to the teaching of Christ, and I believe the tremendous declaration that His word is the central and final authority. 'Heaven and earth shall pass away, but My **words** shall not pass away.' "

In the temple court as Jesus sat down to teach the people, suddenly there was a shocking disturbance. A crowd of men interrupted our Lord's teaching and thrust a woman at His feet. These were "scribes and Pharisees" who had "brought unto him a woman taken in adultery." They showed no regard for our Lord's teaching. They came and interrupted Him not out of regard for the woman or for justice, but with a desire to trap Him. They hoped to present Him with an impossible dilemma.

B. The Woman Accused (vv. 4, 5)

4. They say unto him, Master, this woman was taken in adultery, in the very act.
5. Now Moses in the law commanded us, that such should be stoned: but what sayest thou?

The religious leaders who brought this woman to Jesus were wrong in their approach and in their attitude. Whatever this woman had done, and however guilty she was, they had no legal right to drag her into the public gaze. With the same brutal indelicacy, they told her story; as they said she had been "taken in the very act." These were the religious and moral leaders, the custodians of morality, publicizing her sin to the crowd.

Then they raised their question. Moses commanded to stone such women. Now what does Jesus say? They supposed that they had presented to Him an unsolvable enigma.

A woman had been taken in the act of adultery, and the Law required that she should be put to death. Of this there is no room for doubt. " 'If there is a man who commits adultery with another man's wife, one who commits adultery with his friend's wife, the adulterer and the adulteress shall surely be put to death' " (Leviticus 20:10, **New American Standard Bible**). " 'If a man is found lying with a married woman, then both of them shall die, the man who lay with the woman, and the woman; thus you shall purge the evil from Israel' " (Deuteronomy 22:22, **New American Standard Bible**).

In the eyes of the Jewish law adultery was one of the three gravest sins. The rabbis said: "Every Jew must die before he will commit idolatry, murder, or adultery." According to William Barclay, the **Mishnah,** that is, the Jewish codified law, states that the penalty for adultery is strangulation, and even the method of strangulation is laid down. "The man is to be enclosed in dung up to his knees, and a soft towel set within a rough towel is to be placed around his neck (in order that no mark may be made, for the punishment is God's punishment). Then one man draws in one direction and another in the other direction, until he be dead." The **Mishnah** reiterates that death by stoning is the penalty for a girl who is betrothed and who then commits adultery. (Read Deuteronomy 22:23, 24.)

In pronouncing this adulterous woman forgiven, Jesus was not disregarding the Law nor was He condoning adultery. He expressed His views about both subjects in the Sermon on the Mount. " 'Do not think that I have come to abolish the Law or the Prophets; I have not come to abolish them but to fulfill them. I tell you the truth, until heaven and earth disappear, not the smallest letter, not the least stroke of a pen, will by any means disappear from the Law until everything is accomplished. Anyone who breaks one of the least of these commandments and teaches others to do the same will be called least in the kingdom of heaven, but whoever practices and teaches these commands will be called great in the kingdom of heaven. For I tell you that unless your righteousness surpasses that of the Pharisees and the teachers of the law, you will certainly not enter the kingdom of heaven' " (Matthew 5: 17-20, **New International Version**).

" 'You have heard that it was said, "Do not commit adultery." But I tell you that anyone who looks at a woman lustfully has already committed adultery with her in his heart. If your right eye causes you to sin, gouge it out and throw it away. It is better for you to lose one part of your body than for your whole body to be thrown into hell. And if your right hand causes you to sin, cut it off and throw it away. It is better for you to lose one part of your body than for your whole body to go into hell. It has been said, "Anyone who divorces his wife must give her a certificate of divorce." But I tell you that anyone who divorces his wife, except for marital unfaithfulness, causes her to commit adultery, and anyone who marries a woman so divorced commits adultery' " (Matthew 5:27-32, **New International Version**).

C. The Trap

6. This they said, tempting him, that they might have to accuse him. But Jesus stooped down, and with his finger wrote on the ground, as though he heard them not.

John is careful to explain the motive behind the ruler's bringing this woman to Jesus. They were trying to trap Him in an awkward situation that they might have a basis for accusing Him. They saw Him in a dilemma that put Him in conflict with the Roman authorities, or with the law of Moses, or with His own principles of love and forgiveness.

Roman law said that life must not be taken except with Roman authority. Moses said she was to be put to death. What would He say about this? If He said that she was to go free, He would be contradicting the Mosaic law. If He said she was to be put to death, He would be involving Himself with the Roman authorities. Also, if He said she was to be put to death, He would lose forever the name He had gained for love and for mercy. Never again would He be called the friend of sinners. He would lose the love and devotion of the great mass of the ordinary people. That was the trap in which the scribes and Pharisees sought to entrap Jesus. But Jesus turned their attack in such a way that it recoiled against themselves.

The situation presented in this incident represents a universal problem. That problem was how justice and mercy could be harmonized. This passage teaches us that God has found a way whereby His banished ones may be restored, how sinners may find fellowship with Him. Human wisdom could never have found an answer to such a problem.

II. CHALLENGED BY THE LORD (John 8:7-9)

A. The Lord's Answer (v. 7)

7. So when they continued asking him, he lifted up himself, and said unto them, He that is without sin among you, let him first cast a stone at her.

Some persons use the words of verse 7 to argue against capital punishment. Should they be so used?

In response to the accusations of the religious rulers, Jesus stooped down and began to write on the ground. Exactly what He wrote is merely a matter of conjecture. This pause before His reply may have been due to the shame which He felt, not only for the woman but also for her accusers. Charles R. Erdman writes: "Some have thought that He wrote, as suggested by a verse from Jeremiah, the word **apostate,** intimating how far from God were the very men who claimed to be acting in the place of God and in His service. Others have thought that Jesus wrote the words which He uttered: 'He that is without sin among you, let him first cast a stone.' " I agree with the observation Arthur W. Pink makes about the persistence of the accusers: "It is evident that our Lord's enemies mistook His silence for embarrassment. They no more grasped the force of His action of writing on the ground than did Belshazzar understand the writing of that same hand on the walls of his palace. Emboldened by His silence and satisfied that they had Him cornered, they continued to press their question upon Him. O the persistency of evildoers! How often they put to shame our **lack** of perseverance and importunity."

When the accusers kept on questioning Jesus, He straightened up and said to them, " 'If any one of you is without sin, let him be the first to throw a stone at her' " (John 8:7, **New International Version).** G. Campbell Morgan said, "That sentence put me out of the stone-throwing business for the rest of my life!"

B. The Lord Waits (v. 8)

8. And again he stooped down, and wrote on the ground.

After Jesus dropped this bombshell, He stooped down again and continued to write on the ground. What an impact His utterance had on His hearers. If these Pharisees were to be self-appointed executors of divine justice, then they should be like God in the purity of their lives. They may not have been guilty of the particular sin in question, although possibly our Lord referred to the fact that impure thoughts are sinful as well as impure deeds; but they were guilty of sin. Evidently no one in that group felt morally qualified when tested by the standard Jesus proposed. He thus upheld the law of Moses, but He convicted the proud accusers of being themselves worthy of condemnation. The defeat was manifest; the Pharisees withdrew.

Jesus teaches us that only the man who himself is without fault has the right to express judgment on the fault of others. He said, " 'Do not judge, or you too will be judged. For in the same way you judge others, you will be judged, and with the measure you use, it will be measured to you. Why do you look at the speck of sawdust in your brother's eye and pay no attention to the plank in your own eye? How can you say to your brother, "Let me take the speck out of your eye," when all the time there is a plank in your own eye? You hypocrite, first take the plank out of your own eye, and then you will see clearly to remove the speck from your brother's eye' " (Matthew 7:1-5, **New International Version).**

William Barclay comments: "One of the commonest faults in life is that so many of us demand standards from others that we never even try to fulfill ourselves; so many of us condemn faults in others which are glaringly obvious in our own lives. Many a parent punishes and rebukes a child for that which he time and again does himself; many a church member criticizes another for faults of which he himself is at least as guilty."

C. The Accusers Leave (v. 9)

9. And they which heard it, being convicted by their own conscience, went out one by one, beginning at the eldest, even unto the last: and Jesus was left alone, and the woman standing in the midst.

The words of Jesus struck the conscience of the men who had accused this woman. As each took personal inventory, he realized that he was not qualified to cast the first stone. One by one they departed until all of them were gone. The older ones left first. It appears that they had devised the plan, and the younger ones were just following them, even to the last.

What a victory for grace! Moments before, these men were ranting, raving, and demanding the death penalty for the woman caught in the act of adultery. On another occasion, these same men—self-righteous Pharisees—would have boasted of their fastings, their tithes, and their prayers. Now their moral and spiritual depravity is apparent to them and their mouths are shut. Jesus had not uttered a word against the Law; He had in nowise condoned the woman's sin. Yet His enemies were baffled in their own minds, their evil design defeated; and so they departed.

Is this not a picture of how the wicked will act in the day of their judgment? Now, they may proclaim their self-righteousness and talk about the injustice of eternal punishment. But then, when the light of God flashes upon them and their guilt and ruin are fully exposed, they shall, like these Pharisees, be speechless.

The sadness of this picture is heightened by the fact that these men turned away from Jesus. Conscious of their own sinfulness, they should have cast themselves at His feet. Instead they walked away from Him. One is reminded of the rich, young ruler who came to Jesus seeking help. Unwilling to pay the price involved—following Jesus—he turned away with sadness in his heart. There is no other way to leave Christ but in grief.

These religious rulers had challenged Jesus from the Law. He met them on their own ground and vanquished them by the Law. Now, only the woman remains in His presence.

III. CHANGED BY GRACE (John 8:10, 11)

A. Jesus' Question (v. 10)

10. When Jesus had lifted up himself, and saw none but the woman, he said unto her, Woman, where are those thine accusers? hath no man condemned thee?

Now that her accusers are gone, Jesus straightens Himself up and, for the first time, addresses the woman. One can almost feel His sympathy for her, not because of her sin, but because of the shameful treatment she had received at the hands of the religious leaders. His question to her is, "Woman, where are they? Has no one condemned you?"

Barclay observes: "The basic difference between Jesus and the scribes and Pharisees was that they wished to condemn; He wished to forgive. If we read between the lines of this story, it is quite clear that these scribes and Pharisees wished to stone this woman to death, and they were going to take pleasure in doing so. They knew the thrill of exercising power to condemn; Jesus knew the thrill of exercising power to forgive. Jesus regarded the sinner with pity, born of love; the scribes and Pharisees regarded the sinner with disgust, born of self-righteousness."

The Law required two witnesses before its sentence could be executed. Those witnesses must assist in the carrying out of the sentence. " 'A single witness shall not rise up against a man on account of any iniquity or any sin which he has committed; on the evidence of two or three witnesses a matter shall be confirmed' " (Deuteronomy 19:15, **New American Standard Bible).** " 'The hand of the witnesses shall be first against him to put him to death, and afterward the hand of all the people. So you shall purge the evil from your midst.' " (Deuteronomy 17:7, **New American Standard Bible).**

This woman had only been indicted, and not a single witness was left to testify against her. Thus the Law was powerless to touch her. The way was clear for Christ to act in "grace and truth." Mercy flowed out to her, yet not at the expense of justice. The grace of God never conflicts with His law, but, on the contrary, it upholds its authority. What a display of the divine glory of the Lord Jesus!

B. Jesus' Challenge (v. 11)

11. She said, No man, Lord. And Jesus said unto her, Neither do I condemn thee: go, and sin no more.

Perhaps there is not a more beautiful expression in the Scripture than the Lord's declaration to this adulterous woman: " 'Then neither do I condemn you'. . . . 'Go now and leave your life of sin' " (John 8:11, **New International Version**).

Jesus saw the potential for good in this woman's life and gave her another chance. He looked beyond her past and her failure and encouraged her to be what she could be. How encouraging it is to have someone believe in you. Can you imagine how Peter must have felt when Jesus told him, "You are Simon, a reed; but you shall be Peter, a rock." It must have made him want to stretch himself to be all that he was capable of being.

When parents or friends see your capacity to achieve and encourage you to reach for higher goals, that gives you an incentive to try harder. But how much more incentive do you have when the Lord of glory believes in you and challenges you to a higher level of living?

The only way that this woman—or yourself—can overcome sin and lead a life that is pleasing to the Lord is through Jesus Christ. In His power and strength you can do all things. What the Lord said to Joshua He also says to you, "Have I not commanded you? Be strong and courageous! Do not tremble or be dismayed, for the Lord your God is with you wherever you go" (Joshua 1:9, **New American Standard Bible**). You have every right to echo the words of Paul: "I can do everything through him who gives me strength" (Philippians 4:13, **New International Version**).

Behind the tenderness of Jesus' words to this woman is also a note of warning. She had a choice to make. Would she go back to her old life or would she start a new life in Him? The eternal destiny of each individual depends upon the choice to accept Jesus or to reject Him. It appears that she heeded His warning and began to walk in His way. What will your choice be?

REVIEW QUESTIONS

1. What was Jesus doing in the Temple when confronted with the adulterous woman?
2. What two religious groups had shared in the accusation against the sinful woman?
3. What was the real reason in their coming to Jesus with this case?
4. What reasoning did the accusers give for suggesting that the woman be stoned?
5. How did Jesus respond to their charge?

GOLDEN TEXT HOMILY

"JESUS SAID UNTO HER, NEITHER DO I CONDEMN THEE: GO, AND SIN NO MORE" (John 8:11).

"For God sent not his Son into the world to condemn the world; but that the world through him might be saved" (John 3:17). They mockingly called Him master, but knew not the Lord nor His nature, for God is Love and love is forgiveness.

From the beginning, there has been an accuser—Satan accused God. Satan stands today as our accuser, but as believers we are justified by Jesus' grace and by His finished work at Calvary. God in His divine wisdom realized our frailty and weakness, and knowing the letter of the law killeth (see 2 Corinthians 3:6), He sent His Son to give to us eternal life.

As believers, we too must show forth the image of God's attitude, "Neither do I condemn thee," for these words were one day spoken to every born-again believer. Can we do less for others than that which Christ did for us? For we, like the woman, deserved death, but He showed mercy and we became heirs and joint heirs with Him. In the presence of mercy, Christ admonishes us still, "Go, and sin no more."—**Henry H. Kinsey, Director, State Side Military, Church of God, Cleveland, Tennessee**

SENTENCE SERMONS

CHRIST HAS THE AUTHORITY and demonstrates the willingness to forgive any sin.
—**Selected**

AS THE SICK man is the slave of his disease, so the sinner is the slave of his sin; and unless intervention breaks the power of sin, the sinner is doomed.
—**Merrill C. Tenney**

WE HAVE TO CARE what happens to people before we can attempt to help them.
—**Rolla O. Swisher**

JESUS NEVER WEPT for himself, but He did weep for others.
—**"Notes and Quotes"**

EVANGELISTIC APPLICATION

CHRIST HAS NOT COME TO CONDEMN US BUT TO DELIVER US FROM OUR SINS.

While talking to Nicodemus, Jesus set forth

His purpose for coming into the world: "For God so loved the world that he gave his one and only Son, that whoever believes in him shall not perish but have eternal life. For God did not send his Son into the world to condemn the world, but to save the world through him. Whoever believes in him is not condemned, but whoever does not believe stands condemned already because he has not believed in the name of God's one and only Son" (John 3:16-18, **New International Version**).

Jesus came into the world to show men what God is like. Many people of His day had a distorted view of God. They pictured Him as being a God of revenge, wrath, and anger. Jesus demonstrated that God is a Father who loves and cares for His creatures. He revealed to men the mercy and compassion of God. It is still His purpose to deliver from sin and to instill peace in the heart. He stands with outstretched arms to welcome all who will come to Him.

ILLUMINATING THE LESSON

There was a Scotchman who formerly had been a notable character, a prize fighter and gambler. Changed by the grace of God, he became a mighty soul-winner, and in one series of services, his ministry was being greatly blessed. Just before he arose to speak at one service, someone sent an envelope to the platform. On opening it, he found it contained a long list of sins and crimes that he had committed in that very city.

At first he felt that he must run away; but, stepping boldly to the front of the platform, he said, "Friends, I am accused of crimes and sins committed in this very city. I will read them to you." One by one he read the charges; and, at the conclusion of each, he said, "I am guilty." When he had finished the whole list, he paused for a moment and then said, "You ask how I dare come to you and speak of righteousness and truth, with a list of crimes like this against my name? I will tell you: 'This is a faithful saying, and worthy of all acceptation, that Christ Jesus came into the world to save sinners, of whom I am chief.'"—**"Moody Church News"**

DAILY DEVOTIONAL GUIDE

M. Promise of Blessing. Deuteronomy 30:1-10
T. The Blessing of Forgiveness. Psalm 32:1-11
W. Prayer for Cleansing. Psalm 51:1-12
T. Prayer for Mercy. Psalm 86:11-17
F. Compassion for the Needy. Matthew 20:29-34
S. Compassion for the Bereaved. Luke 7:11-17

October 19, 1980

The Lord of the Harvest

Bible Background: Matthew 8:18-22; 11:20-27; 13:16, 17; Luke 9:57 through 10:24

Time: Probably late A.D. 28 or early A.D. 29

Place: Several Galilean cities which are not identified

Supplemental References: Ezekiel 3:16-27; Matthew 13:1-9, 18-23; 1 Corinthians 3:1-9

Golden Text: "The harvest truly is great, but the labourers are few: pray ye therefore the Lord of the harvest, that he would send forth labourers into his harvest" (Luke 10:2).

Central Truth: Christ commissions His followers to proclaim the message of the gospel everywhere.

Evangelistic Emphasis: Those who accept the gospel message can rejoice because their names are written in heaven.

PRINTED TEXT

Luke 10:1. After these things the Lord appointed other seventy also, and sent them two and two before his face into every city and place, whither he himself would come.

2. Therefore said he unto them, The harvest truly is great, but the labourers are few: pray ye therefore the Lord of the harvest, that he would send forth labourers into his harvest.

3. Go your ways: behold, I send you forth as lambs among wolves.

4. Carry neither purse, nor scrip, nor shoes: and salute no man by the way.

5. And into whatsoever house ye enter, first say, Peace be to this house.

6. And if the son of peace be there, your peace shall rest upon it: if not, it shall turn to you again.

7. And in the same house remain, eating and drinking such things as they give: for the labourer is worthy of his hire. Go not from house to house.

8. And into whatsoever city ye enter, and they receive you, eat such things as are set before you:

9. And heal the sick that are therein, and say unto them, The kingdom of God is come nigh unto you.

10. But into whatsoever city ye enter, and they receive you not, go your ways out into the streets of the same, and say,

11. Even the very dust of your city, which cleaveth on us, we do wipe off against you: notwithstanding be ye sure of this, that the kingdom of God is come nigh unto you.

12. But I say unto you, that it shall be more tolerable in that day for Sodom, than for that city.

17. And the seventy returned again with joy, saying, Lord, even the devils are subject unto us through thy name.

18. And he said unto them, I beheld Satan as lightning fall from heaven.

19. Behold, I give unto you power to tread on serpents and scorpions, and over all the power of the enemy: and nothing shall by any means hurt you.

20. Notwithstanding in this rejoice not, that the spirits are subject unto you; but rather rejoice, because your names are written in heaven.

DICTIONARY

purse—Luke 10:4—An "Oriental girdle made of crude leather or woven camel's hair worn around the waist. Sometimes these 'girdles' were finely tooled and contained 'slots' in which gold and silver coins could be kept. If the 'girdle' was made of cloth, then the money was placed within the folds themselves."

scrip—Luke 10:4—A small bag for carrying food or small articles

Sodom—Luke 10:12—An Old Testament city located in the central plains. It was destroyed by fire and brimstone because of its exceedingly sinful population.

LESSON OUTLINE

I. WEAK EXCUSES
   A. The Hasty Commitment
   B. The Reluctant Disciple
   C. The Straight Furrow

II. WISE INSTRUCTIONS
   A. The Seventy
   B. The Salutation
   C. The Rejection
   D. The Judgment

III. WONDERFUL RESULTS
   A. The Disciples Rejoice
   B. The Savior Rejoices
   C. The Disciples' Privilege

LESSON EXPOSITION

INTRODUCTION

This lesson brings us to a period of expansion in the work of the Kingdom. Jesus commissions seventy disciples in addition to the Twelve. He instructs them as to their mission and manner in sharing the good news. They return to Him overjoyed because of the results God has given them.

Here is an account of God working through men. It is a perfect picture of the proper combination of humility and humanity. The humility is to let God be God, acknowledging that He alone can give sight to the blind and life to the dead. The humanity is to be ourselves as He has made us, not suppressing our personal individuality, but exercising our God-given gifts and offering ourselves to God as instruments of righteousness in His hand. I wonder if anything is more needed for the Christian mission in the modern age than this healthy fusion of humility and humanity in our reliance on the power of the Holy Spirit. Men who will go forth with this vision will discover what the Spirit is saying through the Word to the churches.

I. WEAK EXCUSES (Luke 9:57-62)

A. The Hasty Commitment (vv. 57, 58)

(Luke 9:57, 58 is not included in the printed text.)

It is easy to make a commitment that one cannot keep. Simon Peter did in the last days before the crucifixion of Christ. He boasted that he would be faithful to Christ even if all the other disciples forsook Him. And yet he was the one who denied any association with Jesus at the crucial moment of Jesus' trial.

The man in this text offers to go with Jesus wherever He goes. Jesus cautions him to stop and count the cost before he makes such a commitment. Following Christ is not all glamorous and attractive. There are deprivations and difficulties involved.

Jesus never tried to con anyone into the kingdom of God or into His service. He always leveled with individuals about what their involvement meant. He never induced anyone to serve Him through false pretenses. He pointed out the good and the bad and allowed individuals to decide on the basis of what was best for them. He relied upon the Holy Spirit to attract men to the kingdom of God.

B. The Reluctant Disciple (vv. 59, 60)

(Luke 9:59, 60 is not included in the printed text.)

We are not to suppose that this man's father was already dead. If that be the case, then the words of Jesus have a very harsh sound. It is more likely that this was a delaying tactic. The man knew that he should follow Jesus, but he was not ready to do so.

There are times when one must choose the priorities of his life. Will first place be given to the realm of the natural or to the realm of the spiritual? Will one's relatives be put before one's Lord? This is essentially the decision this man had to make. When the choice is between the natural and the spiritual, the direction of Jesus is always: "But seek first his kingdom and his righteousness" (Matthew 6:33, **New International Version**).

There may be a reason why one cannot immediately fulfill a call or a commission. When this is the case, the Lord understands. But if one is offering an excuse only to keep from doing the Lord's bidding, this is unacceptable to Him. He requires that one make haste to obey Him and to become active in His service.

C. The Straight Furrow (vv. 61, 62)

(Luke 9:61, 62 is not included in the printed text.)

When the Honorable John C. Stennis was conducting his first campaign for the United States Senate, he promised the people of Mississippi that if they sent him to Washington, D. C., he would always "plow a straight furrow." Respected by his colleagues as a man of impeccable character and esteemed by his constituents as a statesman, he has always kept that promise.

Senator Stennis has "plowed a straight furrow" because he has followed high moral principles in his public and private life. He has not looked back to the low and expedient paths. In this he is a worthy example of living life on a high plane.

No plowman ever plowed a straight furrow looking back over his shoulder. The watchword, for the believer is not, "backwards!" but, "forwards!" Genuine progress made in any area of life is the result of a single purpose. Benjamin Disraeli said, "The secret of success is constancy to purpose." The man who looks back or turns aside from his purpose is sure to fail. Such persons are not equipped to represent Christ.

II. WISE INSTRUCTIONS (Luke 10:1-16)

A. The Seventy (vv. 1-4)

1. After these things the Lord appointed other seventy also, and sent them two and two before his face into every city and place, whither he himself would come.

2. Therefore said he unto them, The harvest truly is great, but the labourers are few: pray ye therefore the Lord of the harvest, that he would send forth labourers into his harvest.

3. Go your ways: behold, I send you forth as lambs among wolves.

4. Carry neither purse, nor scrip, nor shoes: and salute no man by the way.

Discuss the practical values of witnesses going out by twos.

In addition to the Twelve, Jesus now chooses seventy other disciples to assist Him in His work. The number **seventy** is significant to the Jews. When Moses needed assistance in leading and directing the children of Israel during their wilderness wanderings, he selected seventy men. "The Lord therefore said to Moses, 'Gather for Me seventy men from the elders of Israel, whom you know to be the elders of the people and their officers and bring them to the tent of meeting, and let them take their stand there with you. Then I will come down and speak with you there, and I will take of the Spirit who is upon you, and will put Him upon them; and they shall bear the burden of the people with you, so that you shall not bear it all alone.' . . . So Moses went out and told the people the words of the Lord. Also, he gathered seventy men of the elders of the people, and stationed them around the tent. Then the Lord came down in the cloud and spoke to him; and He took of the Spirit who was upon him and placed Him upon the seventy elders. And it came about that when the Spirit rested upon them, they prophesied. But they did not do it again" (Numbers 11:16, 17, 24, 25; **New American Standard Bible).**

Also, there were seventy members of the Sanhedrin, the supreme council of the Jews. And seventy was believed to be the number of nations in the world. So, the Jews would identify with this selection of seventy men to assist Jesus in His ministry.

This was to be the last intensive campaign in the public ministry of Jesus. He intended to visit a great many places, and He had selected the places. They were on the other side of Jordan, a neglected area. To these selected cities He sent the seventy men, two by two; thirty-five teams to cover the ground in preparation for His coming. These men were not involved in an effort to promote themselves; their one aim was to prepare the people to hear Jesus. We will do well to emulate them. Our mission is to share Jesus. We will have His blessing only so long as He has a central place in our lives and ministry. Always, He must increase and we must decrease.

Jesus told these disciples that the harvest field in which they were to work was very great and the laborers were few. Therefore, He urged them to earnestly pray that the Lord of the harvest would send forth more laborers into the field. This is a prayer which all believers may offer earnestly and at all times. We never reach the place that all areas of service in the Kingdom work are filled. There is always need for laborers to hasten the progress of the Lord's work.

How sensitive are we to the opportunities around us for doing the Lord's work? The abilities God has given us can be used in our everyday living in a way that will glorify His name. The consistency of our daily walk is a witness for the Lord. Through the testimony of our lips we can share with others the good news of God's grace.

Jesus warned these disciples that as they went forth they could expect to meet with dangers. "I send you forth as lambs in the midst of wolves."

It is interesting to observe the sense of urgency with which Jesus instructed these disciples to prosecute their mission. They were to take no money with them, no wallet in which to carry food, no change of shoes with which to rest their weary feet. Furthermore, they were to spend no time bowing and scraping as Orientals often do when they meet a stranger. They were to salute no man on the way. They must journey as men who are impelled by one supreme motive. By these instructions, our Lord indicated the urgency of His work. Our time in service must be well spent.

Those who are involved in the Lord's service should learn to live loosely to the things of this world. Once Dr. Johnson, after seeing through a great castle and its policies, remarked grimly, "These are the things which make it difficult to die." We must never be caught up with the lesser things in life while the greater things are calling for our attention. The things of the Lord must always come first.

B. The Salutation (vv. 5-7)

5. And into whatsoever house ye enter, first say, Peace be to this house.

6. And if the son of peace be there, your peace shall rest upon it: if not, it shall turn to you again.

7. And in the same house remain, eating and drinking such things as they give: for the labourer is worthy of his hire. Go not from house to house.

Although the seventy were to waste no time with salutations on the highway, they were, upon entering a home, to be most courteous to their host. They were to hail him with the well-known salutation, "Peace be to this house."

Peace is one of the great words of Jesus. It was spoken by the angels when they appeared to the shepherds of Bethlehem, saying, " 'Glory to God in the highest, and on earth peace to men on whom his favor rests' " (Luke 2:14, **New International Version**). It was Christ's word of assurance to His disciples in view of their immediate separation: " 'I have told you these things, so that in me you may have peace' " (John 16:33, **New International Version**). Again, it is found in His utterance as He stood weeping over Jerusalem: " 'If you, even you, had only known on this day what would bring you peace—but now it is hidden from your eyes' " (Luke 19:42, **New International Version**). It is one of the final words of comfort which Christ left with His disciples: " 'Peace I leave with you; my peace I give you. I do not give to you as the world gives. Do not let your hearts be troubled and do not be afraid' " (John 14:27, **New International Version**). It was used also by the disciples in their salutations and benedictions: "Grace, mercy and peace from God the Father and Christ Jesus our Lord" (1 Timothy 1:2, **New International Version**).

As these disciples entered a home, they were to offer the peace which the gospel can give, but if rejected, they were to believe that their very message would return to them with added force. Thus our Lord signified that no word spoken for His sake is really wasted. Sometimes we say that kindness and good works are wasted on certain people. But kindness and good works are never wasted. If we do a good deed for someone and he refuses our kindness or proves unworthy of it, then the blessing intended for him returns to bless us. It is never wasted.

Paul wrote: "Let us not become weary in doing good, for at the proper time we will reap a harvest if we do not give up. Therefore, as we have opportunity, let us do good to all people, especially to those who belong to the family of believers" (Galatians 6:9, 10; **New International Version**).

The seventy were to remain in the same house, eating and drinking without complaint whatever was set before them. They were to set a beautiful example of courtesy and appreciation. And they were to do this with the realization that such hospitality was their due, if they rendered useful service in return. "The laborer is worthy of his hire."

Some do not see the work of a minister as labor, but Christ does. At the time when Charles Darwin was engaged in compiling his epoch-making work on the **Origin of Species**, he used to stand hour after hour in his greenhouse observing his plants. He was suffering in health at the time. His faithful, old domestic servant, who was concerned about him, confided to Mrs. Darwin that she thought the "master would be a good deal better if he could find something to do." This is exactly the concept that some have of the ministry. They cannot discern what labor it is.

C. The Rejection (vv. 8-12)

8. And into whatsoever city ye enter, and they receive you, eat such things as are set before you:

9. And heal the sick that are therein, and say unto them, The kingdom of God is come nigh unto you.

10. But into whatsoever city ye enter, and they receive you not, go your ways out into the streets of the same, and say,

11. Even the very dust of your city, which cleaveth on us, we do wipe off against you: notwithstanding be ye sure of this, that the kingdom of God is come nigh unto you.

12. But I say unto you, that it shall be more tolerable in that day for Sodom, than for that city.

Are there modern day examples of cities, peoples or nations rejecting the messengers of God?

The ministry of preparing the way for another, of being a forerunner is not a very glamorous work. And yet if our priorities are right, whatever work we do for God is important. When service to God and man becomes more important than money or any other personal gain, we are in a frame of mind in which the Lord can use us.

Several years ago, a discouraged young doctor in the East of London, one of the modern successors of Luke, the beloved physician, was visited by his aged father. His father came up from a farm in the country to check on his son.

"Well," he said, "how are you getting along?"

"I am not doing well at all," was the disheartened answer. "I am not doing a thing."

The old man's countenance fell, but he spoke of courage, patience, and perseverance. Later in the day, he went with his son to the charity ward of the hospital where his son had an unsalaried position and where he spent an hour or more every day.

The father sat by, a silent but intensely interested spectator, while twenty-five poor unfortunates received help. The doctor forgot his visitor while he bent his skilled energies to this task. Hardly had the door closed on the last patient when the old man burst out—"I thought you told me you were not doing anything," he thundered. "Not doing anything! Why, if I had helped twenty-five people in a month as much as you have done in one morning, I would thank God that my life counted for something."

"There isn't any money in it, though," explained the son, somewhat abashed at his father's vehemence.

"Money!" the old man shouted still more scornfully. "Money! What is money in comparison with being of use to your fellowmen? Never mind about money. You go right along at this work every day. I'll go back to the farm and gladly earn money enough to support you as long as I live. Yes, and I will sleep sound every night with the thought that I have helped you to help your fellowmen."

Where are your priorities in life? What is really important to you? How much value do you place on serving others? Do you make the most of opportunities to be helpful?

The seventy were to continue in the home which received them, content with what was given, offering relief to those in distress and using every opportunity to proclaim the message of grace.

The deportment of the disciples in the home in which they were staying was most important. They were to accept the food offered to them. In this as in all other things, they were to be moderate (see Philippians 4:5).

They were also to minister to the needs of the people—heal the sick. They were to do as Christ had done, give a visible proof of the benefit of the gospel. In this way they would attract men to its spiritual blessedness by means of its temporal effects. Believers can do this work of the disciples by alleviating sickness, by visiting, by caring, by seeking out the needy and helping them. Miracles are the great bell of the universe, to call attention to the Lord. They demonstrate His love and care. They also reveal the greatness of His power.

Not every city or home they entered would receive them gracefully. Some would refuse to accept their message. From these they were to turn away and shake off the dust on their feet. This was an Oriental symbol which intimated that they had no connection with the enemies of Christ.

The gospel message is never given a universal reception. There are always some who refuse to accept its gracious offer. Alphonse Karr heard a gardener ask his master permission to sleep in the stable in the future. He said that there was no possibility of sleeping in the chamber behind the greenhouse because the nightingales kept up a noise all the night. Upon hearing this story Spurgeon commented: "The sweetest sounds are but an annoyance to those who have no musical ear. Doubtless the music of heaven would have no charm to carnal minds. Certainly the joyful sound of the gospel is unappreciated so long as men's ears remain uncircumcised."

D. The Judgment (vv. 13-16)

(Luke 10:13-16 is not included in the printed text.)

Jesus addresses Himself to those cities which have rejected Him. He declares that it will be more tolerable for Tyre and Sidon in the Day of Judgment than for the cities of Israel. Even these heathen cities would have repented if they had seen the evidence of divine power which Jesus had manifested in Israel. Jesus was stating the abiding principle that unusual opportunities involve unusual responsibilities. He was also declaring that rejection of His disciples was rejection of Him and that rejection of Him was rejection of God the Father—a matter not to be taken lightly.

William Barclay very aptly observes that "one of the towns on which woe is pronounced is Chorazin. It is implied that Jesus did many mighty works there. In the gospel history as we have it, Chorazin is never even mentioned, and we do not know one thing that Jesus did or one word that Jesus spoke there. Nothing could show so vividly how much we do not know about the life of Jesus. The gospels are not biographies; they are only sketches of the life of Jesus (see John 21:25)."

III. WONDERFUL RESULTS (Luke 10:17-24)
A. The Disciples Rejoice (vv. 17-20)

**17. And the seventy returned again with joy, saying, Lord, even the devils are subject unto us through thy name.
18. And he said unto them, I beheld Satan as lightning fall from heaven.
19. Behold, I give unto you power to tread on serpents and scorpions, and over all the power of the enemy: and nothing shall by any means hurt you.
20. Notwithstanding in this rejoice not, that the spirits are subject unto you; but rather rejoice, because your names are written in heaven.**

When the seventy disciples returned to Jesus, they were ecstatic with joy. They proudly announced that "even the demons submit to us in your name." They were overjoyed by the great success the Lord had granted to them.

G. Campbell Morgan comments: "It is significant that when they came back, they reported to Him. I sometimes think that one of the things that has hindered Christian work has been reports made in public meetings and printed. It would be a great thing if we reported only to Jesus. That was true, also, of the Twelve. We should like to know more about those cities they visited; the names of them, and the sizes of the congregations, and the number of the sons of peace they found, and the centers where they did their best work. But why do we hanker after such particulars? Our passion for statistics is self-centered, of the flesh and not of the Spirit."

Jesus responds to the report of these disciples by announcing Satan's defeat. He says that the overthrow of these messengers of Satan reminds Him of the ultimate defeat of the Prince of darkness and of all the forces of evil. It is just a matter of time for the believer until complete victory belongs to him. Satan is already an eternally defeated foe. There may be a slight delay before he is put away, but the fact of his confinement is certain. As believers, we should hold our heads high and remember always that we are on the winning side. We may not win every skirmish or even every battle, but we will win the war. Jesus is our Captain.

Of Jesus' defeat of Satan Paul writes: "And having disarmed the powers and authorities, he made a public spectacle of them, triumphing over them by the cross" (Colossians 2:15, **New International Version).** John adds: "He who does what is sinful is of the devil, because the devil has been sinning from the beginning. The reason the Son of God appeared was to destroy the devil's work" (1 John 3: 8, **New International Version).**

Jesus also assures the seventy that He is giving them power over all that might oppose or might threaten to destroy them. Although in our own strength we are helpless to defeat the forces of evil, in the strength of Christ we are victors.

When the Lord assures these disciples that He has given them power over all the power of the enemy, He does not mean that they will not be confronted by the evil forces. He knows that just as the sun rises on the evil and the good, so the agents of darkness assail the just as well as the unjust. But He would have believers live surrounded by such an atmosphere that none of the assaults of Satan can really hurt them.

Believers find this kind of protection when they put their trust in God. What comfort to know that we serve a God who is rich, who will clothe and feed us as He does the lilies. He cares for us more than for the sparrows, not one of which perishes without His notice. His power is much greater than the power of the enemy.

Jesus reminded the seventy that the most important thing in their lives was that their names were written in heaven. No matter how much joy they experienced through the exercise of God's power in their lives, the thing that really mattered was that they were numbered among those whose eternal destiny will be in the presence of Christ.

It might well be claimed that the discovery of the use of chloroform saved the world more pain than any other single medical discovery. Once someone asked Sir James Simpson, its discoverer, "What do you regard as your greatest discovery?" The questioner naturally expected the answer, "The discovery of chloroform." But Simpson answered, "My greatest discovery was when I discovered that Jesus Christ is my Savior." Even the greatest man can only say in the presence of God,

"Nothing in my hand I bring,
Simply to Thy Cross I cling;
Naked, come to Thee for dress;
Helpless, look to Thee for grace;
Foul, I to the fountain fly;
Wash me, Savior, or I die."

B. The Savior Rejoices (vv. 21, 22)

(Luke 10:21, 22 is not included in the printed text.)

At this point, Jesus shares in the joy of His followers. He thanks the Father for what He was accomplishing through these humble messengers. He recognizes the results which they enjoyed as a manifestation of divine power. Then Jesus makes a striking claim which indicates that He is not only the ideal Man but that He is also the Son of God who alone can reveal the Father to men. This is a vital part of His mission.

C. The Disciples' Privilege (vv. 23, 24)

(Luke 10:23, 24 is not included in the printed text.)

Finally, Jesus congratulates the disciples upon their great privilege. Many before them, including prophets and kings, desired to see the things which they were seeing as His servants and as instruments of His power.

Who can describe the joy which comes to those who serve the Lord? What greater privilege can a person know than to reveal Christ to another person? It is a wonderful thing to know that Jesus uses believers for such glorious achievements as winning others to Himself. This principle is as real today as it was in Jesus' day. The joy which the seventy had can be ours also.

REVIEW QUESTIONS

1. For what purpose did Jesus appoint the Seventy?

2. How did Jesus describe the position of the Seventy in the world?

3. What did Jesus say the Seventy were to do in the event that they were not received in a city?

4. What report did the Seventy have when they returned from the mission?

5. Why did Jesus tell the Seventy that they should rejoice?

GOLDEN TEXT HOMILY

"THE HARVEST TRULY IS GREAT, BUT THE LABOURERS ARE FEW: PRAY YE THEREFORE THE LORD OF THE HARVEST, THAT HE WOULD SEND FORTH LABOURERS INTO HIS HARVEST" (Luke 10:2).

As we look into the Scriptures, we see in the life of Jesus that He often used events in nature to illustrate spiritual truth. He used sayings such as "Behold, a sower went forth to sow" (Matthew 13:3). Also, "Verily, verily, I say unto you, Except a corn of wheat fall into the ground and die, it abideth alone" (John 12:24). Even our text reveals the thinking of a man who understood the production of the land and knew about harvesting.

What is a harvest but the cutting of the mature grain from the dead stalks of summer's growth and gathering the life-bearing seed into barns? Our Lord, of course, was not speaking of the fruit of the earth; but rather of the souls of men, which is the most valuable product of all.

The time of the harvest is now. Jesus implied urgency when He said, "Say not ye, There are yet four months, and then cometh harvest? behold, I say unto you, Lift up your eyes, and look on the fields; for they are white already to harvest" (John 4:35). As the world population expands, the abundance of the harvest becomes astounding.

While Jesus was speaking to the seventy, He brought to their attention the ever-present problem, "But the labourers are few." Even though God has always done great things with small numbers, there is still the need of dedicated workers. This kind of dedication is revealed in the words of Frederick W. Robertson, "It is not the possession of extraordinary gifts that makes extraordinary usefulness, but the dedication of what we have to the service of God." In God's harvest, the need for dedicated workers is met through prayer.

Trench said, "Prayer is not the overcoming of God's reluctance, it is the laying hold of His highest willingness." It seems that the success of the growth of God's Church depends a great deal upon the fervent prayer of His people. Prayer, like faith, however, must be accompanied by work. "Pray ye therefore the Lord of the harvest, that he would send forth labourers." To pray and yet be unwilling to submit to the yoke of Christ in personal involvement would be only half of what God expects of us. If we abide in the Lord we will bring forth fruit. "If ye abide in me, and my words abide in you, ye shall ask what ye will, and it shall be done unto you" (John 15:7).

It is obvious that the abundance of the harvest before the Church today will require power beyond the mere norm, not only power of action and energy but power of authority as well. Where can we find such power but in the Lord of the harvest? Christ has already commissioned us, for He said, "Go ye into all the world, and preach the gospel to every creature" (Mark 16:15). The people we meet daily are part of this world Jesus was talking about, and therefore they are part of the harvest. As Christians, we are God's workmen and have entered into His harvest.

In the recent past, there was a song called "Harvest Home" which many farm workers sang as they brought in the last load from the harvest field. There will come a time when the harvest will be finished, and with it our last opportunity to share in the greatest harvest of all.

Let us attune our ears to the voice of the Lord of the harvest, our minds to His purpose, and our hands to the reaping. Because in so doing souls shall be saved, and there will not be the cry of many as in the days of Jeremiah the prophet, "The harvest is past, the summer is ended, and we are not saved" (Jeremiah 8:20).—**James A. Guynn, Pastor, Harrisburg, Illinois**

SENTENCE SERMONS

SERVE WITHOUT EXPECTING or demanding gratitude, for when you do you cease to deserve it.
—**"Notes and Quotes"**

OUR WORLD BEGINS at the church doorsteps, and leads towards the street.
—**Selected**

MANY MEN ARE go-getters when the going is easy and the getting is good, but there are few when the going gets tough and the getting is uncertain.
—**Charles W. Conn**

"TODAY" IS THE TIME when idlers delay, when fools prattle, when the fearful shudder, but when the courageous advance and the wise grasp opportunities.
—**"Notes and Quotes"**

EVANGELISTIC APPLICATION

THOSE WHO ACCEPT THE GOSPEL MESSAGE CAN REJOICE BECAUSE THEIR NAMES ARE WRITTEN IN HEAVEN.

There are many benefits to those who live a Christian life. Some of those blessings are realized in this life; some of them are received in the life to come. Believers enjoy a peace that those outside of Christ cannot know. They can be at peace with God, with others, and with themselves. Since they know peace even amid turbulant circumstances, their peace defies understanding.

Then, the life of a Christian is dominated by love. This love transcends anything that can be known outside of Christ. It enables the believer to live on a higher level than is other-

October 19, 1980

wise possible. Its beauty is indescribable.

Beyond these present benefits, the person who accepts the gospel message inherits eternal life through Christ Jesus. This means that he will lead a rich and rewarding life throughout all eternity. Such a prospect is something worth rejoicing about. May we lift our voices in praise to our God.

ILLUMINATING THE LESSON

A man once rose in one of Mr. Moody's meetings and gave his experience. "I have been for five years on the Mount of Transfiguration." "How many souls did you lead to Christ last year?" was the sharp question that came from Mr. Moody, in an instant. "Well, I don't know," was the astonished reply. "Have you led any?" persisted Mr. Moody. "I don't know that I have," answered the man. "Well," said Mr. Moody, "we don't want that kind of mountaintop experience. When a man gets so high that he can't reach down and save poor sinners, there is something wrong." —**"The Sunday School Chronicle"**

DAILY DEVOTIONAL GUIDE

M. Called to Serve. Exodus 3:1-12

T. Be Courageous! Joshua 1:1-9

W. Answering the Call. 1 Samuel 3:1-20

T. Declare God's Word! Ezekiel 2: 1 through 3:3

F. Called to Be Witnesses. Luke 24:36-49

S. A Ministry of Reconciliation. 2 Corinthians 5:11-21

October 26, 1980

The Giver of Light

Bible Background: John 9:1-41
Time: Probably late fall A.D. 29
Place: Jerusalem
Supplemental References: Isaiah 35:1-10; 42:1-8; Luke 4:18
Golden Text: "I am the light of the world: he that followeth me shall not walk in darkness, but shall have the light of life" (John 8:12).
Central Truth: Christ heals to relieve suffering and to glorify God.
Evangelistic Emphasis: Christ gives spiritual sight to all who express faith in Him.

PRINTED TEXT

John 9:1. And as Jesus passed by, he saw a man which was blind from his birth.

2. And his disciples asked him, saying, Master, who did sin, this man, or his parents, that he was born blind?

3. Jesus answered, Neither hath this man sinned, nor his parents: but that the works of God should be made manifest in him.

4. I must work the works of him that sent me, while it is day: the night cometh, when no man can work.

5. As long as I am in the world, I am the light of the world.

6. When he had thus spoken, he spat on the ground, and made clay of the spittle, and he anointed the eyes of the blind man with the clay.

7. And said unto him, Go, wash in the pool of Siloam, (which is by interpretation, Sent.) He went his way therefore, and washed, and came seeing.

8. The neighbours therefore, and they which before had seen him that he was blind, said, Is not this he that sat and begged?

9. Some said, This is he: others said, He is like him: but he said, I am he.

10. Therefore said they unto him, How were thine eyes opened?

11. He answered and said, A man that is called Jesus made clay, and anointed mine eyes, and said unto me, Go to the pool of Siloam, and wash: and I went and washed, and I received sight.

12. Then said they unto him, Where is he? He said, I know not.

13. They brought to the Pharisees him that aforetime was blind.

14. And it was the sabbath day when Jesus made the clay, and opened his eyes.

15. Then again the Pharisees also asked him how he had received his sight. He said unto them, He put clay upon mine eyes, and I washed, and do see.

16. Therefore said some of the Pharisees, This man is not of God, because he keepeth not the sabbath day. Others said, How can a man that is a sinner do such miracles? And there was a division among them.

17. They say unto the blind man again, What sayest thou of him, that he hath opened thine eyes? He said, He is a prophet.

DICTIONARY

the pool of Siloam (sigh-LOW-am)—John 9:7-11—From the Hebrew word meaning "sent" or "outflow," referred to in Nehemiah 3:15 as "the pool of Siloah by the king's garden." This pool was fifty feet long, twenty feet deep, and twenty feet wide, lying at the mouth of the Tyropean Valley. Water was drawn from it for the temple.

the sabbath day—John 9:14, 16—The Hebrew word for Sabbath means "rest" and refers here to the seventh day of the week, a divine institution mentioned in Genesis 2:3; Exodus 16:23-29; 20:11; 31:17. Man was to leave off his secular labors and keep the day holy to the Lord.

LESSON OUTLINE
I. RELIEVING PHYSICAL SUFFERING
  A. The Blind Man
  B. The Light of the World
  C. The Blind Man Obeys
  D. The Neighbors
II. ANSWERING CRITICS
  A. The Pharisees
  B. The Parents
  C. The Testimony
III. WORSHIPING THE LORD
  A. The Worshiper
  B. The Judgment

LESSON EXPOSITION
INTRODUCTION

Every miracle—healing or otherwise—that Jesus performed was for a purpose. Not every miracle He wrought is recorded, but those that are recorded are recorded for a purpose. John writes: "Jesus did many other miraculous signs in the presence of his disciples, which are not recorded in this book. But these are written that you may believe that Jesus is the Christ, the Son of God, and that by believing you may have life in his name" (John 20:30, 31, **New International Version).** John concludes his Gospel by saying: "Jesus did many other things as well. If every one of them were written down, I suppose that even the whole world would not have room for the books that would be written" (John 21:25, **New International Version).**

Jesus' reason for healing the man born blind was that God might be glorified. That was the ultimate objective behind every miracle He performed and behind everything He did. To glorify God is still His purpose in dealing with men. This should be the motivation behind the efforts of all believers. Anything else is second best.

I. RELIEVING PHYSICAL SUFFERING (John 9:1-12)

A. The Blind Man (vv. 1, 2)

1. And as Jesus passed by, he saw a man which was blind from his birth.

2. And his disciples asked him, saying, Master, who did sin, this man, or his parents, that he was born blind?

There is a division of opinion as to exactly when this incident occurred. Some scholars are of the persuasion that this event immediately follows the happenings of the preceding chapter. In that chapter Jesus encountered serious opposition while visiting the temple. As Jesus left the temple, immediately following the controversy, He met the blind man. Others see this as a completely fresh scene, altogether removed from that setting. They conclude that Jesus would not have attracted attention to Himself immediately after the incident in the temple. John simply says, "As he went along, he saw a man blind from birth" **(New International Version).** He does not specify the time or the place.

This is the only person, the record of whose deliverance is recorded in the Gospels, of whom it is said that he had borne his affliction from birth. Two people are referred to in **Acts** who were afflicted from birth: the lame man at the Beautiful Gate of the temple (Acts 3:2) and the impotent man at Lystra (Acts 14:8).

Apparently the man was well known. At least the disciples seemed to know a lot about him. Perhaps he had been seen frequently at the temple gate or elsewhere begging alms. Being aware of his circumstances, they posed a question that was on the minds of many people. They wanted to know why he was blind. Was it because he had sinned? Or was it the result of the sin of his parents?

Inherent in this question is the idea that suffering is the result of sin. But how could sin be traced to the man if he was born blind? In the minds of the Jews this was possible. Some of them actually believed in prenatal sin. They believed that a man could begin to sin while he was still in his mother's womb. Other Jews accepted the Greek idea of the preexistence of the soul. They believed that when the soul entered the body it was already good or bad.

The idea that children may reap the consequences of their parents' sin is set forth in the Old Testament. " 'You shall not worship them (idols) or serve them; for I, the Lord your God, am a jealous God, visiting the iniquity of the fathers on the children, on the third and the fourth generation of those who hate Me' " (Exodus 20:5, **New American Standard Bible**).

B. The Light of the World (vv. 3-5)

3. Jesus answered, Neither hath this man sinned, nor his parents: but that the works of God should be made manifest in him.

4. I must work the works of him that sent me, while it is day: the night cometh, when no man can work.

5. As long as I am in the world, I am the light of the world.

Jesus answers His disciples by saying that this man's blindness was not the result of sin on the part of the man or on the part of his parents. His reply was in direct contradiction to the commonly held belief among Jews that illness always came because of sin in the victim's life.

As a general proposition, it is certainly true that human suffering is the result of human sin. We suffer because we are a fallen race, and we are a fallen race because we and our forebears have been disobedient to the will of God. But it is not true that every particular ailment can be traced back to somebody's particular sin. Jesus made it plain that this man's blindness was not the result of any specific sin. It was an opportunity God had placed in men's pathway whereby they might see His power and mercy operating on a miraculous scale.

Manford George Gutzke writes: "Some years ago I stayed overnight in a home that had been saddened by the tragic death of the only son. He had been a member of the air force. Having completed his term of duty, he was ready to come home and was waiting at the military base for transportation. He went for a plane ride with a friend, just to pass the time. That plane crashed, and the young man who had gone through years of military service without injury was killed. His parents were crushed. He was their only son, and when I visited in their home a year later, the heaviness of their grief was still with them. After some hesitation the mother asked me a natural question: 'Did our son lose his life because of something that we did? Is this because of something his father did, or did I do something wrong?' With this story in John in my mind I was so glad to be able to answer her, 'No, no, no!' "

Jesus indicated to His disciples that He was constrained to do the work of God. He used the words **I must.** This was His mission in the world. And so it is our mission. Whatever else we do with our lives, our first responsibility is to be involved in God's work. Only in this way can we fulfill His will for our lives. This does not mean that everyone is to enter some so-called "full-time" ministry. It does mean that we should conduct ourselves in such a way that whatever we are doing, it is a ministry.

Jesus also recognized that there was a limited time to do the work He had to do. He is the eternal Son of God, but He had only a certain amount of time to accomplish His earthly ministry. Every believer should realize that he has only a limited amount of time to work. We sometimes live as though we have forever to do what we are going to do for the Lord. We need to determine what we can do for the Lord in the time that we have and then set out to do it.

And, then, in the presence of this man who had never seen the light of day, Jesus said a very significant thing. He said that He was the Light of the world. Can you imagine the hope this expression must have created in this man's heart.

C. The Blind Man Obeys (vv. 6, 7)

6. When he had thus spoken, he spat on the ground, and made clay of the spittle, and he anointed the eyes of the blind man with the clay,

7. And said unto him, Go, wash in the pool of Siloam, (which is by interpretation, Sent.) He went his way therefore, and washed, and came seeing.

What Jesus does now seems strange to us, but it did not seem strange at all to the people of His day. "He spit on the ground, made some mud with the saliva, and put it on the man's eyes" **(New International Version).** In that day spittle, and especially the spittle of some distinguished person, was believed to possess certain curative qualities. Spittle was looked upon at that time as being remedial.

Barclay makes an interesting suggestion: "The fact is that Jesus took the methods and the customs of his time and used them. He was a wise physician. He had to gain the confidence of his patient. It was not that Jesus believed in these things, but He kindled expectation by doing what the patient would expect a doctor to do. After all, to this day the efficacy of any medicine or treatment depends at least as much on the patient's faith in it as in the treatment or the drug itself."

G. Campbell Morgan also observes that "this was an occasion when He (Jesus) made use of means. The particular value of the means I do not pretend to know.... Whether our Lord was accommodating His method for the sake of those around Him at the time, I cannot say. Sometimes He removed disability without any means. At other times He used means. That illuminated the whole region in which we discuss healing. Without means or with means, it is always God who heals. He did not explain."

After Jesus put the spittle on the man's eyes, He then sent him to wash his eyes in the pool of Siloam. This pool was one of the great landmarks of Jerusalem. In simple obedience the man went and washed and came back seeing.

The blind man's action is very beautiful. He did not stop to reason and ask questions, but he promptly did what he was told to do. As John Trapp puts it, "He obeyed Christ blindly. He looked not upon Siloam with Syrian eyes as Naaman did upon Jordan; but passing by the unlikelihood of a cure by such means, he believed and did as he was bidden, without hesitation." What a lesson for all believers!

D. The Neighbors (vv. 8-12)

8. The neighbours therefore, and they which before had seen him that he was blind, said, Is not this he that sat and begged?

9. Some said, This is he: others said, He is like him: but he said, I am he.

10. Therefore said they unto him, How were thine eyes opened?

11. He answered and said, A man that is called Jesus made clay, and anointed mine eyes, and said unto me, Go to the pool of Siloam, and wash: and I went and washed, and received sight.

12. Then said they unto him, Where is he? He said, I know not.

There can be no question about the fact that the blind man experienced a miracle of God. Those who knew him engaged in much discussion about his deliverance. Two groups of people were present: his neighbors who knew him well and those who had seen him frequently begging for alms at the temple gate. His neighbors who knew him best of all declared, "This is he." Others who had seen him begging for alms day after day said, "He is like him." They were not convinced that this was the same man they had seen frequently as a blind man. But the blind man himself declared, "I am he."

Then the inquirers asked him how he had received his sight. He was at a loss to tell them how the miracle was wrought. In effect what he said was, "A man named Jesus made clay, put it on my eyes, and told me to go wash in the pool of Siloam. Well, I went and washed, and I received my sight." Are we not just as baffled at times when we consider the great things God has done for us?

Then, those questioning the blind man asked, "How did you receive your sight?" Honestly and sincerely he answered, "A man named Jesus put some clay on my eyes and told me to go wash in the pool of Siloam. I obeyed Him, and received my sight." Though the steps leading up to the miracle were given by the healed man, he was unable to tell how the actual miracle took place. It is impossible for anyone to explain a miracle.

Obedience played an important part in the blind man's deliverance. It is certain that he would not have received his healing had he not obeyed the Lord. His healing was directly connected to his obedience.

One of the finest tributes ever paid to a devoted animal is told in a story by Archibald Rutledge. By chance he came upon a Negro turpentine worker, whose faithful dog had died a few moments earlier in a great forest fire because he would not desert his master's dinner pail which he had been told to watch. With tears on his face the old Negro said, "I always had to be careful what I told him to do because I knew he would do it." Of how many of us, I wonder, could the Lord say such a thing? Love of God makes us obedient unto Him. What He asks, we give. Where He sends us, we go. While He leads, we follow. Love is not cautious; it is ever brave and generous. It makes us willing to do whatever He tells us to do.

Jesus expressed the importance of obedience and His disapproval of disobedience in the parable of the two sons. " 'What do you think? There was a man who had two sons. He went to the first and said, "Son, go and work today in the vineyard." "I will not," he answered, but later he changed his mind and went. Then the father went to the other son and said the same thing. He answered, "I will, sir," but he did not go. Which of the two did what his father wanted?' 'The first,' they answered. Jesus said to them, 'I tell you the truth, the tax collectors and the prostitutes are entering the kingdom of God ahead of you. For John came to you to show you the way of righteousness, and you did not believe him, but the tax collectors and the prostitutes did. And even after you saw this, you did not repent and believe him' " (Matthew 21:28-32, **New International Version**).

Peter learned the value of obedience. He had been on an unsuccessful fishing expedition. This professional fisherman came to shore with his nets empty and his spirits sagging. Then Jesus told him to do something that must have seemed preposterous to him. He told Peter to go back out on the same lake and cast his nets on the other side of the boat. And Peter obeyed. He didn't believe, but he obeyed. Don't accuse Peter of having faith on this occasion; don't accuse him of expecting to catch a single fish. It was not faith, but obedience that Christ rewarded that day. When Peter obeyed the Lord, he caught more fish than he could handle. What a beautiful lesson for all of us in the power and blessedness of obedience.

II. ANSWERING CRITICS (John 9:13-34)
A. The Pharisees (vv. 13-17)

13. They brought to the Pharisees him that aforetime was blind.

14. And it was the sabbath day when Jesus made the clay, and opened his eyes.

15. Then again the Pharisees also asked him how he had received his sight. He said unto them, He put clay upon mine eyes, and I washed, and do see.

16. Therefore said some of the Pharisees, This man is not of God, because he keepeth not the sabbath day. Others said, How can a man that is a sinner do such miracles? And there was a division among them.

17. They say unto the blind man again, What sayest thou of him, that he hath opened thine eyes? He said, He is a prophet.

These neighbors and observers of the blind man brought him to the Pharisees. They took note that he was healed on the Sabbath. So these self-righteous Pharisees began to inquire as to how it came about. The man who had been blind told them that Jesus put mud on his eyes; that he washed his eyes, and now he can see. This information produced an eruption of indignation among the Pharisees. It did not matter that a miracle had been performed. It was of no consequence that a man who had been born blind could now see. All they could see was that a miracle had been performed on the Sabbath. In the eyes of these fanatics this was a dreadful and awful thing. In their opinion anything that involved as much effort as this miracle undoubtedly should not be performed on the sacred Sabbath. To them, an institution was more important than a man; a custom meant more to them than human welfare did.

William Barclay points out that Jesus had broken the Sabbath law, as the scribes had worked it out, in three different ways: (1) By making clay He had been guilty of working on the Sabbath day. (2) It was forbidden to heal on the Sabbath. (3) It was quite definitely laid down in the law in regard to the Sabbath and healing that: "As to fasting spittle, it is not lawful to put it so much as upon the eyelids."

The scribes had worked out a system that forbade the least amount of work on the Sabbath. "A man may not fill a dish with oil and put it beside a lamp and put the end of the wick in it." "If a man extinguishes a lamp on the Sabbath to spare the lamp or the oil or the wick, he is culpable." "A man may not go out on the Sabbath with sandals shod with nails." (The weight of the nails would have constituted a burden, and to carry a burden was to break the Sabbath.) They did not allow a man to cut his fingernails or pull out a hair of his head or his beard. So you can easily see that to do something like make mud would be regarded as a violation of the law.

Also, medical attention was forbidden on the Sabbath unless a life was in actual danger. And even then all that could be done was something that would keep the person from getting worse. Obviously the blind man was not about to die, so Jesus' act was a deliberate violation of the Sabbath rules drawn up by the scribes.

The Pharisees used this occasion to make accusations against Jesus. He was a Sabbath-breaker—or so they claimed. John tells us that seven times Jesus healed on the Sabbath. Was this a courageous defiance by our Lord? Or was it His desire to show that the Sabbath is one of God's merciful provisions? Was He seeking to demonstrate that the Sabbath is to be a season when God's mercy is made manifest?

The Pilgrim Fathers, according to the old hymn, left England, first for Holland, and then for America, for "freedom to worship God." But freedom to have a **day** of rest and worship was one of the chief motives of their migration. King James had decreed that Sunday was a day for sports, and issued his **Sports Book.** The Pilgrim Fathers desired to build their families, and their civilization, upon another basis. Hence they came to America. From the very beginning, in all the colonies, observation of the Sabbath was part of the law of the land. There is no doubt, either, that their observance of this day made a mighty contribution to the moral stamina and spiritual well-being of the nation, as well as to its material and economic prosperity. The Sabbath gave the people a chance to know the Bible, the fountain whence have flowed the noblest streams of influence in the religion, education, and politics of the nation.

Man is a seven-day machine, designed so by the Great Artificer. The greatest blessing ever conferred upon man as a toiler and a laborer is the Sabbath. Henry George said, "Moses was the first labor reformer, and the Sabbath was his chief labor reform." An all-wise God who understands the needs of the human body has set aside one day as a day of rest, relaxation, restoration, and reverence.

After listening to the opinions of the blind man's neighbors and observers, the Pharisees turned to him and asked his opinion. "You're the one He healed. It is your eyes that are open. What do you think of this man?" Without any hesitation he replied, "He is a prophet."

In the Old Testament a prophet was often tested by the signs he could produce. Moses guaranteed to Pharaoh that he really was God's messenger by the signs and wonders which he performed (see Exodus 4:1-17). Elijah proved that he was the prophet of the real God by doing things the prophets of Baal could not do (see 1 Kings 18). No doubt this man's thoughts were running on these things when he said that in his opinion Jesus was a prophet.

Another thing, this man was surely aware of the teaching of the law about Sabbath-breaking. He must have known that the Pharisees would interpret Jesus' action as a violation of the law. And yet he boldly declared, "He is a prophet."

Does the Lord sometimes allow critics to question our spiritual experience as a test of our faith?

B. The Parents (vv. 18-23)

(John 9:18-23 is not included in the printed text.)

Unwilling to accept the conclusions of the blind man's neighbors or to accept the explanation of the man himself, the Pharisees call in his parents. They asked them if he was blind from birth, and if so, how it was that he could see now. The parents acknowledged that he was their son and that he had been blind from birth, but they refused to explain the method of his deliverance. They knew that if they confessed faith in Jesus, the threat of excommunication hung over them. "If any man did confess that he (Jesus) was Christ, he should be put out of the synagogue." For fear that they would be excommunicated, they did not acknowledge that Jesus had wrought this miracle. They referred the Pharisees to the man himself. "He is of age; ask him what happened."

The silence of the blind man's parents stemmed from their fear that if they were put out of the synagogue, they would be separated from God.

C. The Testimony (vv. 24-34)

(John 9:24-34 is not included in the printed text.)

Unable to get a satisfactory answer from the blind man's parents, the Pharisees call upon him again. They seek to intimidate him by implying that he is not giving glory to God and by calling Jesus a sinner. The blind man's answer is a classic. " 'Whether he is a sinner or not, I don't know. One thing I do know. I was blind but now I see!' " (John 9:25, **New International Version).**

"I was blind but now I see" is the testimony every believer can give. He may not understand all about his conversion. His knowledge of the Scripture may be limited. He may not have the answer to many theological questions. But one thing he knows: I was lost, but now I am found; I was blind, but now I see; I was dead in sin, but now I am alive in Christ. Anybody can tell somebody else, this is what Christ did for me, and what He did for me He will do for you.

The Pharisees, then, hurled insults at the man. They said to him, " 'You were steeped in sin at birth; how dare you lecture us!' " (John 9:34, **New International Version**). And then they threw him out.

III. WORSHIPING THE LORD (John 9:35-41)

A. The Worshiper (vv. 35-38)

(John 9:35-38 is not included in the printed text.)

The man born blind made a strong defense for Jesus against the Pharisees before he was fully aware of who Jesus was. He recognized Him as a prophet, but he did not know that He was the Son of God.

Jesus heard about what happened to the man born blind, how the Pharisees had thrown him out. So He found him and asked him, " 'Do you believe in the Son of Man?' " (John 9:35, **New International Version**). The man responded by acknowledging that he did not know who the Son of Man was. He wanted to believe in Him, so he asked Jesus to tell him who he is. Jesus said, " 'You have now seen him; in fact, he is the one speaking with you' " (John 9:37, **New International Version**). At that, the man exclaimed: " 'Lord, I believe,' " and he worshiped Jesus.

When Jesus heard about the loyalty and faithfulness of this blind man, he sought him out to help him. No devotion given to the Lord is ever in vain. He always honors those who honor Him. He brought the blind man into a richer and deeper relationship to Himself. May we always show Him this same kind of loyalty.

B. The Judgment (vv. 39-41)

(John 9:39-41 is not included in the printed text.)

There are approximately fourteen million people in the world who cannot see. Some have been made blind by injuries. Most of them, however, were born blind.

But the blindest people of all are the people who have eyes but will not see. It is amazing how many shut their eyes tight and refuse to look facts in the face. If a person is born blind, that is bad; but if a person has two good eyes and will not use them, that is unforgivable. That is the position in which the Pharisees found themselves.

Jesus announced to the Pharisees that He came into the world for judgment. Whenever a man comes face to face with Jesus, he has to make a decision about Him. By that decision, he either turns away from God or takes a step toward God. In this case, the Pharisees moved away from God. And Jesus told them that they were responsible for their own actions. Their condemnation lay in the fact that they knew so much, and they claimed to see so well, and yet they failed to recognize God's Son when He came.

REVIEW QUESTIONS

1. What, in your thinking, prompted the disciples to ask the question: "Who did sin, this man, or his parents, that he was born blind?"

2. What does the explanation "that the works of God should be manifest in him" imply?

3. What unusual approach did Christ make in order to bring healing to the blind man?

4. What reactions did the neighbors have when they saw the blind man healed?

5. What was the attitude of the Pharisees concerning the healing?

GOLDEN TEXT HOMILY

"I AM THE LIGHT OF THE WORLD: HE THAT FOLLOWETH ME SHALL NOT WALK IN DARKNESS, BUT SHALL HAVE THE LIGHT OF LIFE" (John 8:12).

The Gospel according to John relates several important discourses of Jesus during His early and later Galilean ministries. The "light of the world" teaching was given at the joyous Feast of Tabernacles (see John 7:2, 8, 11), which Josephus called the holiest and greatest Jewish festival (see **Antiquities** 8:4: 1) superior in the popular mind even to Passover and Pentecost. The Feast of Tabernacles commemorated God's providential provision during Israel's wilderness trek from Egypt to Canaan.

According to John 8:20, Jesus was now teaching in "the treasury," located in the Court of the Women, the most public part of the Temple yet adjacent to the chamber where the Sanhedrin met. Great golden candelabra were lit on each of the eight nights of the feast in recollection of God's guiding ancient Israel with the pillar of fire by night (see Numbers 9:15, 16). He had used the emblem of water earlier in the feast (see John 7:37, 38; Numbers 20:7-13; 1 Corinthians 10:4) as a background against which to offer the discourse on His being the complete and spiritual fulfillment of the temporary quenching of thirst in the wilderness. Water and light have continued to represent the effects of Jesus' person and ministry.

"Ye are the light of the world" (Matthew 5: 14). How humbling, yet how instructive it is to observe that Jesus has designated His own as lights in the world as He himself is the Light of the world! Our light is not our own, but we reflect the light of Him who is inherently the "brightness [radiation] of his [the Father's] glory, and the express image [impress] of his person" (Hebrews 1:3). Just as Jesus by His coming dispels the darkness of sin both in the world at large and in the lives of individuals who trust Him, so the believer's mission is to let his light "so shine before men, that they may see your good works, and glorify your Father which is in heaven" (Matthew 5:16).

Light and mission: this is the essence of our experience and of our responsibility.—**Donald N. Bowdle, Ph.D., Th.D., Professor of History and Religion, Dean of the Division of Religion, Lee College, Cleveland, Tennessee**

SENTENCE SERMONS

POOR EYES LIMIT your sight; poor vision limits your deeds.

—**Franklin Field**

CHRIST HEALS TO RELIEVE suffering. The relieved sufferer's healing glorifies God.

—**Selected**

VISION IS OF GOD. A vision comes in advance of any work well done.

—**Katherine Logan**

MANY WHO HAVE 20/20 vision see less than some who are blind in both eyes.

—**Selected**

EVANGELISTIC APPLICATION

CHRIST GIVES SPIRITUAL SIGHT TO ALL WHO EXPRESS FAITH IN HIM.

There is a vivid contrast between physical blindness in the man born blind and spiritual blindness in the Pharisees. Jesus healed the blind man because he obeyed the Lord and did the things Jesus asked him to do. But even Jesus himself could not heal the spiritual blindness of the Pharisees. And why not? For the simple reason that they did not admit their blindness.

Jesus can change a man's mind if a man is willing to have his mind changed. If he is willing to see the light, God will show him the light. But as long as a man calls light darkness and darkness light, good evil and evil good, then even Jesus Christ, the Son of God, cannot help him.

Where do you find yourself in this matter? If you have not accepted Christ as your Savior, do you recognize your need of Him? Are you willing for Him to open your spiritually blinded eyes? He is eager and ready to help you. He can open the eyes of your soul to new and beautiful surroundings. He can enable you to see purposes and possibilities you have never seen before.

ILLUMINATING THE LESSON

The age of miracles is past,
   I hear the skeptic say;
How little does he understand
   Christ's miracles today.
His great and marv'lous works go on.
   How do I know, my friend?
He wrought His miracles in me,
   His wonders never end.

Did Jesus make the blind to see?
   My sight He has restored.
He caused the dumb to speak, you say?
   My lips now praise the Lord.
He also made the deaf to hear?
   But my ears too were sealed,
I could not hear His gentle voice
   'Til by His love He healed.

—**Lena Traas**

From **The New Speaker's Sourcebook,** by Eleanor Doan; Grand Rapids; Zondervan Publishing Co. Used by permission.

DAILY DEVOTIONAL GUIDE

M. Look to the Lord! Psalm 121:1-8

T. The Creator Gives Light. Isaiah 42:5-12

W. Woe to Blind Guides. Matthew 23:16-24

T. The Light of the Body. Luke 11:33-36

F. The Light of the Gospel. 2 Corinthians 4: 1-6

S. Walking in the Light. Ephesians 5:8-21

November 2, 1980

The Giver of Life

Bible Background: John 11:1-46

Time: Probably January or February A.D. 29

Place: Bethany

Supplemental References: 1 Kings 17:8-24; Mark 5:21-24, 35-43; Luke 7:11-16; Acts 9:36-43

Golden Text: "I am the resurrection, and the life: he that believeth in me, though he were dead, yet shall he live" (John 11:25).

Central Truth: Because Christ is the Resurrection and the Life, all who believe in Him inherit eternal life.

Evangelistic Emphasis: Christ has the power to raise a person from death in sin to new life in God.

PRINTED TEXT

John 11:30. Now Jesus was not yet come into the town, but was in that place where Martha met him.

31. The Jews then which were with her in the house, and comforted her, when they saw Mary, that she rose up hastily and went out, followed her, saying, She goeth unto the grave to weep there.

32. Then when Mary was come where Jesus was, and saw him, she fell down at his feet, saying unto him, Lord, if thou hadst been here, my brother had not died.

33. When Jesus therefore saw her weeping, and the Jews also weeping which came with her, he groaned in the spirit, and was troubled,

34. And said, Where have ye laid him? They said unto him, Lord, come and see.

35. Jesus wept.

36. Then said the Jews, Behold how he loved him!

37. And some of them said, Could not this man, which opened the eyes of the blind, have caused that even this man should not have died?

38. Jesus therefore again groaning in himself cometh to the grave. It was a cave, and a stone lay upon it.

39. Jesus said, Take ye away the stone. Martha, the sister of him that was dead, saith unto him, Lord, by this time he stinketh: for he hath been dead four days.

40. Jesus saith unto her, Said I not unto thee, that, if thou wouldest believe, thou shouldest see the glory of God?

41. Then they took away the stone from the place where the dead was laid. And Jesus lifted up his eyes, and said, Father, I thank thee that thou hast heard me.

42. And I knew that thou hearest me always: but because of the people which stand by I said it, that they may believe that thou hast sent me.

43. And when he thus had spoken, he cried with a loud voice, Lazarus, come forth.

44. And he that was dead came forth, bound hand and foot with graveclothes: and his face was bound about with a napkin. Jesus said unto them, Loose him, and let him go.

November 2, 1980

DICTIONARY

not yet come into the town—John 11:30—Refers to Bethany, the hometown of Mary and Martha. It is located about two miles southeast of Jerusalem.

Lazarus (LAHZ-ah-rus)—John 11:43—The brother of Martha and Mary. The name is an abbreviated Greek form of **Eleazor** meaning "God is my help."

graveclothes—John 11:44—A Greek word used only here in the entire New Testament; it refers to the bandages which kept the sheet and spices around the body.

LESSON OUTLINE

I. THE FACT OF DEATH
  A. Lazarus Sick
  B. Lazarus Asleep
II. THE HOPE OF RESURRECTION
  A. The Comforting Crowd
  B. Martha's Confession
III. THE SORROW OF SEPARATION
  A. Mary's Response
  B. Jesus Deeply Moved
  C. Jesus Wept
IV. THE WORD OF AUTHORITY
  A. The Glory of God
  B. Jesus' Prayer
  C. Lazarus Raised
  D. Many Believed

LESSON EXPOSITION

INTRODUCTION

The story of Lazarus is a story of hope. Every believer can identify with that hope. Though Lazarus was dead, Jesus restored him to life. This action is significant to the believer both in the realm of the physical and in the realm of the spiritual.

The Bible teaches that every individual who has not accepted Christ is spiritually dead. But Jesus has the power to quicken a dead soul and to bring it to life. He is the Resurrection and the Life. Every person who turns to Him in repentance and in faith experiences new life in Him.

The Bible also teaches that there is to be a restoration of physical life through Christ. Every believer is to receive a glorified body. The spiritual life which one receives is eternal life. Though a believer may pass through the phase of physical death, he will not remain in that state. At the time of the Resurrection, he will receive a glorified body and in that body he will live eternally.

I. THE FACT OF DEATH (John 11:1-16)

A. Lazarus Sick (vv. 1-6)

(John 11:1-6 is not included in the printed text.)

In this passage we are introduced to three people who played an important part in the life of Jesus. Lazarus, Mary, and Martha were friends of Jesus and they were friends to Jesus. Jesus loved them and they loved Him. It seems that Jesus spent considerable time in their home in Bethany. On one occasion Mary demonstrated her affection for the Master by anointing Him with precious perfume. So it is not surprising that when Lazarus became seriously ill, the two sisters sent word to Jesus about his condition. What is surprising—on the surface at least—is Jesus' reaction when He heard the news. Although He loved them, He did not go immediately to them.

Jesus' reaction is explained in His words upon hearing the news of Lazarus' sickness: "When he heard this, Jesus said, 'This sickness will not end in death. No, it is for God's glory so that God's Son may be glorified through it'" (John 11:4, **New International Version).**

B. Lazarus Asleep (vv. 7-16)

(John 11:7-16 is not included in the printed text.)

When Jesus announced to His disciples that He was going back to Judea, they were concerned. They reminded Him of the danger He had faced there earlier when some tried to stone Him. Jesus replied that there were twelve hours of daylight in a day and that the man who walks by day will not stumble. The implication is that Christ's time to face death will not come prematurely. The lesson for the believer is that if a man chooses to serve God, then that man's day will not end before God wishes it to end.

Jesus then tells the disciples that Lazarus is asleep and that He is going to wake him up. They did not understand that Jesus meant Lazarus was dead. They said that if he was asleep, then, he would soon be better. Christ explained that He meant Lazarus was dead. When He said to them, "Let us go to him," Thomas responds by saying to the rest of the disciples, "Let us also go, that we may die with him."

II. THE HOPE OF RESURRECTION (John 11:17-27)

A. The Comforting Crowd (vv. 17-19)

(John 11:17-19 is not included in the printed text.)

When Jesus arrived at the house of Martha and Mary, He discovered that Lazarus had been in the tomb for four days. He also found many Jews at their house. They had come to comfort them in the loss of their brother.

Barclay comments: "So when Jesus found a crowd in the house at Bethany, He found what anyone would expect to find in a Jewish house of mourning. To the Jew it was a sacred duty to come to express loving sympathy with the sorrowing friends and relations of one who had died. . . . Visits of sympathy to the sick and to the sorrowing were an essential part of Jewish religion. A certain Rabbi expounded the text in Deuteronomy 13:4: 'Ye shall walk after the Lord your God.' He said that text commands us to imitate the things which God is depicted as doing in Scripture. God clothes the naked (Genesis 3:21); God visited the sick (Genesis 18:1). God comforted the mourners (Genesis 25:11); God buried the dead (Deuteronomy 35:6). And in all these things we imitate the actions of God. . . . It would be to a household filled and crowded with sympathizers that Jesus that day came."

B. Martha's Confession (vv. 20-27)

(John 11:20-27 is not included in the printed text.)

When Martha heard that Jesus was coming, she went out to meet Him. This was in keeping with her character as a person of action. She expressed to Jesus her disappointment. In effect she is saying, "If You had come when we sent word to You about Lazarus, he would not have died." Then on the heels of those words, she declares unshakable faith in Christ, "But I know, that even now, God will give You whatever You ask" **(paraphrased).**

Jesus assured Martha that Lazarus would be raised from the dead. She thought that He was talking about the future Resurrection. But "Jesus said to her, 'I am the resurrection and the life. He who believes in me will live, even though he dies; and whoever lives and believes in me will never die. Do you believe this?' " (John 11:25, **New International Version).** Every believer can cry, "Yes, Lord, I believe that You are the present Resurrection and the Life. I have been quickened by Your resurrection power; I have received Your life."

Martha makes one of the most beautiful and powerful confessions in Scripture. " 'Yes, Lord,' she told him, 'I believe that you are the Christ, the Son of God, who was to come into the world' " (John 11:27, **New International Version).**

III. THE SORROW OF SEPARATION (John 11:28-37)

A. Mary's Response (vv. 28-31)

(John 11:28, 29 is not included in the printed text.)

30. Now Jesus was not yet come into the town, but was in that place where Martha met him.

31. The Jews then which were with her in the house, and comforted her, when they saw Mary, that she rose up hastily and went out, followed her, saying, She goeth unto the grave to weep there.

Having met the Master, Martha goes back and tells Mary the good news that Jesus has come. Mary is more retiring in nature than is Martha; but when she hears that Jesus is asking for her, she arises quickly and goes to Him. Those in the house with her followed. They think that she is going to the tomb of Lazarus.

Martha took Mary aside and told her privately that Jesus was calling for her. There were two reasons for this secrecy. First, she did not want to cause excitement and direct the attention of Jesus' enemies to Him. This is why Jesus had not yet come into the village of Bethany. Bethany was less than two miles from Jerusalem. Many of the Jews from Jerusalem would be there. Among those were some who disliked Christ. So this precaution was taken to prevent any danger coming to Him.

The second reason for the secrecy was to give Mary the chance of a private talk with Jesus. How much she needed to be alone with Him. What comfort He could bring to her in this troubled moment.

Jesus is always near when He is needed. That is perhaps the most important thing a believer can know. One of the most interesting of London's ancient cemeteries is Bunhill Fields. There rests the dust of Charles Wesley, Isaac Watts, and Daniel Defoe, the author of **Robinson Crusoe**. The cemetery is sometimes spoken of as the "Westminster Abbey of Nonconformity." Directly across from this ancient graveyard is the chapel of John Wesley, the house in which he lived and died, and the monument which has been reared to his memory. Just before his death on March 2, 1791, John Wesley opened his eyes and exclaimed in a strong, clear voice, "The best of all is, God is with us!" Yes, best of all, and last of all, God is with us.

On this occasion, Jesus called for Mary; Mary did not call for Him. His call was timed perfectly. Mary needed His help at this moment, and it was at that precise time that He called. The late Dr. J. H. Jowett said that he was once in a most pitiful perplexity, and he consulted Dr. Berry of Wolverhampton. "What would you do if you were in my place?" he entreated.

"I don't know, Dr. Jowett. I am not there, and you are not there yet. When do you have to act?"

"On Friday," Dr. Jowett replied.

"Then," answered Dr. Berry, "you will find your way perfectly clear on Friday. The Lord will not fail you."

And sure enough, on Friday all was plain. Give God time, and even when the knife flashes in the air the ram will be seen caught in the thicket. Give God time, and even when Pharaoh's host is on Israel's heels, a path through the waters will be suddenly opened. Give God time, and when the bed of the brook is dry, Elijah shall hear the guiding voice. At the exact time that we need God's help, He is there to minister to our needs.

Mary had an important part in having her needs met. She responded immediately to Jesus' call. She did not question or hesitate in any way. How quick are we to respond to the Master's call? Our reaction is important to receiving His blessing.

B. Jesus Deeply Moved (vv. 32-34)

32. Then when Mary was come where Jesus was, and saw him, she fell down at his feet, saying unto him, Lord, if thou hadst been here, my brother had not died.

33. When Jesus therefore saw her weeping, and the Jews also weeping which came with her, he groaned in the spirit, and was troubled,

34. And said, Where have ye laid him? They said unto him, Lord, come and see.

Mary's initial reaction to Jesus was the same as Martha's. She implied that if He had heeded their call and had come to Lazarus that he would not have died. When Jesus saw how distraught Mary was, as were her friends, He was touched deeply. He inquired about Lazarus' burial place and was taken to it.

As Mary approached Jesus, she assumed an attitude of worship. She fell at His feet. Her expression carries a note of disappointment, but it also reveals reverence. "Lord, if **only** you had been here, Lazarus would not be dead." What faith in His power and presence! What hope resting in His sufficiency!

The Jews have a legend that when Abraham started on his journeys he saw the stars in the heavens and said, "I will worship the stars." But before long the stars set. Then Abraham saw the constellations—the Pleiades and the rest of them—and he said, "I will worship the constellations." But the constellations also set. Then Abraham saw the moon sailing high in the heavens and he said, "I will worship the moon." But the moon also vanished when her season was over. Then Abraham saw the sun in all his majesty, coming out of his chamber like a bridegroom and rejoicing as a strong man to run a race. But when the day was spent, he saw the sun sink on the western horizon. Stars, constellations, moon, and sun—all were unworthy of his worship, for all had set and all had disappeared. Then Abraham said, "I will worship God, for He abides forever."

God alone is worthy of our worship. Whatever else we worship—ambition, money, appetite, beauty, affections, friends—all of them, one by one, like the heavenly bodies, set and disappear. But God remains. Jesus Christ remains. He is the same yesterday, today, and forever. We must give Him first place in our lives. We must give Him our devotion, our strength, and our love. Like Mary, let us fall at His feet and worship Him. He is worthy of all our praise and all our adoration.

When Jesus perceived the depth of sorrow and anguish which Mary felt, He was "deeply moved and troubled." Rieu translates it: "He gave way to such distress of spirit as made His body tremble." Barclay says "that such deep emotion seized Jesus that an involuntary groan was wrung from His heart."

He adds, "Jesus showed us a God whose very heart is wrung with anguish in the anguish of His people, a God who in the most literal way is afflicted in our afflictions. . . . The greatest thing that Jesus did for us was to bring us the news of a God who cares."

What a difference it makes in our lives when we understand that God cares for us. During World War II when the Germans blitzed England, an old lady in London refused to move from the house where she had lived for twenty years, to a safer place. Her explanation was this: "I says my prayers to God every night and I goes to sleep. There's no need for us both to keep awake." Yes, we serve a God who cares. In sorrow, in danger, or in any other circumstance, God identifies with us.

C. Jesus Wept (vv. 35-37)

35. Jesus wept.

36. Then said the Jews, Behold how he loved him!

37. And some of them said, Could not this man, which opened the eyes of the blind, have caused that even this man should not have died?

Why did Jesus weep at the grave when He knew what He was about to do?

"Jesus wept." Literally, "Jesus shed tears." There were two other instances when our Lord wept. When He beheld the city of Jerusalem, before His public entry, He wept. Luke records: "As he approached Jerusalem and saw the city, he wept over it and said, 'If you, even you, had only known on this day what would bring you peace—but now it is hidden from your eyes'" (Luke 19:41, 42, **New International Version).** The other occasion of His weeping was in the garden of Gethsemane. Matthew records: "'My Father, if it is possible, may this cup be taken from me. Yet not as I will, but as you will'" (Matthew 26:39, **New International Version).** The writer of Hebrews comments on this scene: "During the days of Jesus' life on earth, he offered up prayers and petitions with loud cries and tears to the one who could save him from death, and he was heard because of his reverent submission" (Hebrews 5:7, **New International Version).**

There are various reasons suggested as to why Jesus wept at the tomb of Lazarus. Some conclude that it was at the thought of bringing Lazarus back from the glories of heaven into a sinful world. Others are of the opinion that it was because of the unbelief of the Jews. They think that the display of tears and wailing of the Jewish visitors to Bethany was sheer hypocrisy. Most, however, believe that He wept to assure all believers of every generation that He feels the weight of our sorrows and recognizes the anxiety prompted by life's burdens.

There is nothing wrong in weeping. Christ, who hungered, thirsted, slept, walked, and became indignant, also wept. Paul tells us in Romans 12:15 to "rejoice with those who rejoice; mourn with those who mourn" **(New International Version).**

The Jews observed Jesus' weeping. They responded. "Behold how He loved him!" J. C. Ryle has declared, "That of all the graces, love is the one which most arrests the attention and influences the opinion of the world." On this occasion our Lord's audience saw in Him the trait that brought Jesus from heaven to earth and that which would soon take Him to the Cross. Paul writes: "You see, at just the right time, when we were still powerless, Christ died for the ungodly. Very rarely will anyone die for a righteous man, though for a good man someone might possibly dare to die. But God demonstrates his own love for us in this: While we were still sinners, Christ died for us" (Romans 5:6-8, **New International Version).** This is supreme love. God's love for sinful men.

But some of the Jews were cynical. They said, "If this man opened the eyes of the blind man, why couldn't He keep this man from dying?" In other words, "If He is one with God as He declares, why did He not prove it and prevent Lazarus from dying?" In spite of all the evidences God gives for belief, there are some who will harden their hearts. Our Lord had already said to others of like nature, "'You diligently study the Scriptures because you think that by them you possess eternal life. These are the Scriptures that testify about me, yet you refuse to come to me to have life'" (John 5:39, 40; **New International Version).**

IV. THE WORD OF AUTHORITY (John 11: 38-46)

A. The Glory of God (vv. 38-40)

38. Jesus therefore again groaning in himself cometh to the grave. It was a cave, and a stone lay upon it.

39. Jesus said, Take ye away the stone. Martha, the sister of him that was dead, saith unto him, Lord, by this time he stinketh: for he hath been dead four days.

40. Jesus saith unto her, Said I not unto thee, that, if thou wouldest believe, thou shouldest see the glory of God?

To get this picture right we must have in our minds a picture of the usual Palestinian tomb. The tombs were either natural caves or caves hewn out in the rock. They consisted of an entrance in which the bier was first laid. Beyond the entrance there was a cave, usually about six feet long, nine feet wide, and ten feet high. In such a tomb there were usually eight shelves cut in the rock, three on each side and two on the wall facing the entrance; and on these shelves the bodies were laid. The bodies were wrapped in a linen garment, but the hands and feet were swathed in bandagelike wrappings, and the head was wrapped in a towel. The tomb had no door; but in front of the opening there ran a groove in which there was set a great stone like a cartwheel. The stone was rolled across the entrance so that the cave was sealed (Barclay).

As Jesus approached the tomb of Lazarus, He was again deeply troubled within. Regaining His composure, He said to those around Him, "Take away the stone." Martha objected saying that Lazarus had been dead for four days and that by this time there would be a bad odor. But Jesus explained to her that she was about to see the glory of God.

In performing a miracle, Jesus used both human and divine means. As if to teach us that God will not do for us what we can do for ourselves, He employed the human factors to the limit of their capacity. The first thing He did when He arrived at the tomb of Lazarus was to instruct the men who were present to roll away the stone from the mouth of the tomb. Jesus could have commanded the stone to roll away, and by a miracle it would have been done. Or He could have called for an angel to roll it away and an angel would have come and performed the deed. Instead, He called upon men to do what men could in this case. Men could not raise Lazarus from the dead, but they could roll away the stone. They could not raise Lazarus from the dead, but they could remove the graveclothes. What a beautiful example of how God works!

When the stone was removed from the mouth of the tomb, those present smelled the stench of death. No one could deny that Lazarus was indeed dead. Likewise, nobody could question the fact that Jesus had performed a notable miracle when He raised Lazarus from the dead. How careful the Lord is in His work to see that God gets the glory for all that He does. We should exercise the same care.

There is a valuable spiritual lesson for us in this story. We have to remove the stone from the door of the tomb before we know the glory and power of Christ. Whatever is blocking His blessings must be rolled away. It may be our prejudices, our lack of self-control, our love of earthly things. All these things must be gotten rid of.

Another thing, before we can deal with sin as we should, we must recognize it for what it is. We need to understand that while we are in sin, we are in death. Sin is not something pleasant and desirable; it is death. The stench of its death needs to fill our nostrils as it filled the nostrils of those clustered around the tomb. Only then do we appreciate the infamy of sin and the love, life, and power of Christ.

B. Jesus' Prayer (vv. 41, 42)

41. Then they took away the stone from the place where the dead was laid. And Jesus lifted up his eyes, and said, Father, I thank thee that thou hast heard me.

42. And I knew that thou hearest me always: but because of the people which stand by I said it, that they may believe that thou hast sent me.

In His prayer at the tomb of Lazarus, Jesus is again careful to see to it that God is glorified in what He is doing. He thanks the Father for the assurance He has that God has already heard His prayer. This indicates that He had been holding communion with His Father all the way through. Where was He when He gained this assurance? Was He given the assurance that Lazarus would be raised from the dead while He was still in the land where He first received the message that Lazarus was sick? His conversation with His disciples then indicates that He had been given such assurance. If Jesus knew already that God was going to raise Lazarus, why did He pray at the tomb? Was it because He needed to pray, or was it for someone else's benefit?

Jesus answers that question. He was thinking about His hearers when He prayed. He wanted to be sure that they understood that this miracle was from God. His prayer may be paraphrased: "Father,

I am not surprised, I thank You. You hear Me always; but because of the multitude which stands around I said it that they may believe that You did send Me."

Jesus was about to perform a miracle, but He was doing it in fellowship with God; and He took this means of making the multitude face that fact. Throughout His ministry, He emphasized His cooperation with the Father. He did nothing by Himself; He always worked together with the Father. This was Peter's understanding of the way Christ worked. He said, "God anointed Jesus of Nazareth with the Holy Spirit and power, and . . . he went around doing good and healing all who were under the power of the devil, because God was with him" (Acts 10:38, **New International Version**).

C. Lazarus Raised (vv. 43, 44)

43. And when he thus had spoken, he cried with a loud voice, Lazarus, come forth.

44. And he that was dead came forth, bound hand and foot with graveclothes: and his face was bound about with a napkin. Jesus saith unto them, Loose him, and let him go.

In the presence of the Jews who were there to comfort Martha and Mary, Jesus called for Lazarus to come out of the grave. The dead man responded by coming forth while still wrapped in his graveclothes. Jesus then instructed those around Him to remove the graveclothes. Again, we have a mixture of the divine and the human at work.

The resurrection of Lazarus is one of the most significant miracles recorded in the Gospel of John or in all of the Bible. Miracles, as recorded in the Bible and especially in the four Gospels, not only show the **power** of God who is able to do these things, but also reveal the **plan** of God as these great things are accomplished.

The various miracles Jesus did do not show anything in particular about His patience, His meekness, or His humility. They reveal the power of God! They show what God can do, what He will do, and His control over the forces of nature.

The believer who studies this miracle of the raising of Lazarus from the grave will be challenged to know more about God and about the will of God as He chooses to work in and through His people. The possibilities for answer to prayer are tremendous. What could be more incredible than for God to raise a man from the dead who had been in the grave for four days? The actual fact of the matter is that what God will do for any man or woman is incredible to the natural heart of any human being (Gutzke).

D. Many Believed (vv. 45, 46)

(John 11:45, 46 is not included in the printed text.)

The response to this miracle which Jesus had performed was varied. Many of the Jews who were present believed. They were convinced that Jesus is the Messiah, and they put their faith in Him. Some of the others, however, were less charitable. They went to the Pharisees and told them what Jesus had done.

Jesus received a mixed response to His ministry. Not everyone who heard Him accepted His message. Some did; others did not. The same thing is true in the ministry of every believer. Some will believe; others will not.

REVIEW QUESTIONS

1. How did Jesus interpret the serious illness of Lazarus?

2. Why did Jesus delay His going to Bethany when He heard of Lazarus' illness?

3. How did Jesus express His feelings about the death of Lazarus?

4. How did Jesus preface His miracle of raising Lazarus?

5. What types of responses were manifested as a result of the raising of Lazarus from the dead?

GOLDEN TEXT HOMILY

"I AM THE RESURRECTION, AND THE LIFE: HE THAT BELIEVETH IN ME, THOUGH HE WERE DEAD, YET SHALL HE LIVE" (John 11:25).

There are many kinds of death. Many people experience a living death long before their last breath is drawn and long before their eyelids close for the last time.

The Bible speaks of people being "dead in trespasses and sins" (Ephesians 2:1), suggesting that it is possible to be physically alive, and yet be dead in a spiritual sense.

Just as surely as God will one day resurrect the dead, He will also resurrect those who are dead in trespasses and sins. We do not need to wait for this kind of resurrection, however. It is a resurrection that is occurring every day all over the globe. People dead in sin are being brought alive by the grace of God that comes to them through faith in Jesus Christ.

Today's golden text is one of those scriptural references that has a double meaning. Christ promises two resurrections for those who believe in Him: first, there is a resurrection from sin and guilt into the New Birth; and then, for those who die as Christians, there will one day be a literal resurrection from the grave unto life eternal.

—Selected

SENTENCE SERMONS

MAN CAN TAKE life but he cannot give it back.

—Selected

LIFE IS REAL! Life is earnest!
And the grave is not its goal.

—Henry Wadsworth Longfellow

THE TRUEST END of life is to know the life that never ends.

—William Penn

CHRIST HAS THE POWER to raise a person from death in sin to new life in God.

—Selected

EVANGELISTIC APPLICATION

CHRIST HAS THE POWER TO RAISE A PERSON FROM DEATH IN SIN TO NEW LIFE IN GOD.

In the first chapter of Ephesians, Paul sets forth the glory of God's redemptive work. He tells of the wonder of the Lord's purpose of pure love for the universe through the Church. His imagination was kindled at the thought of the length, the breadth, the height of the divine operation. Its length is seen in an eternal purpose slowly worked out through the ages. Its breadth is reflected in the fact that it is to extend over the whole universe. Its height is manifested in that it is to carry men up to no lower point than the throne of Christ in heavenly places.

In the second chapter, Paul draws attention to what may be called a fourth dimension of the divine operation—its depth. How wonderfully low God stooped in order to reach the point to which man had sunk! What a contrast between the life men lived before they knew Christ and were found in Him, and the life believers know in Jesus. It is the difference between life and death. Paul writes: "But because of his great love for us, God, who is rich in mercy, made us alive with Christ even when we were dead in transgressions—it is by grace you have been saved" (Ephesians 2:4, 5; **New International Version).**

ILLUMINATING THE LESSON

Robert Louis Stevenson tells the story of a ship at sea in time of storm. The passengers were in great distress. After a while one of them, against orders, went up on deck and made his way to the pilot.

The seaman was at his post of duty at the wheel and when he saw the man was greatly frightened he gave him a reassuring smile. Then the passenger turned and went back to the other passengers and said, "I have seen the pilot and he smiled, 'All is well.'"

When our small boat of life is storm-tossed and our hearts are fearful, we may push through the storm to our Pilot who is standing at the wheel, and when we see His face we shall know that all is well.

—**Selected**

DAILY DEVOTIONAL GUIDE

M. The Creator of Life. Genesis 1:20-31
T. Restoration to Life. 1 Kings 17:17-24
W. Responding to a Call for Help. Mark 5: 21-24, 35-43
T. The Abundant Life. John 10:7-18
F. The Gift of Eternal Life. Romans 5:15-21
S. The Only Source of Life. 1 John 5:1-12

November 9, 1980

The Call to Discipleship

Bible Background: Matthew 19:16 through 20:16; Mark 10:17-31; Luke 18:18-30
Time: Probably A.D. 29
Place: Perea, the region in Palestine immediately east of the Jordan, and near the border of Judea.
Supplemental References: 1 Timothy 6:6-10, 17-19; 2 Timothy 2:19-22
Golden Text: "If any man will come after me, let him deny himself, and take up his cross, and follow me" (Matthew 16:24).
Central Truth: What the Christian gives up in coming to God has no comparison with what he receives.
Evangelistic Emphasis: Nothing should keep us from coming to God on His terms.

PRINTED TEXT

Mark 10:17. And when he was gone forth into the way, there came one running, and kneeled to him, and asked him, Good Master, what shall I do that I may inherit eternal life?

18. And Jesus said unto him, Why callest thou me good? there is none good but one, that is, God.

19. Thou knowest the commandments, Do not commit adultery, Do not kill, Do not steal, Do not bear false witness, Defraud not, Honour thy father and mother.

20. And he answered and said unto him, Master, all these have I observed from my youth.

21. Then Jesus beholding him loved him, and said unto him, One thing thou lackest: go thy way, sell whatsoever thou hast, and give to the poor, and thou shalt have treasure in heaven: and come, take up the cross, and follow me.

22. And he was sad at that saying, and went away grieved: for he had great possessions.

23. And Jesus looked round about, and saith unto his disciples, How hardly shall they that have riches enter into the kingdom of God!

24. And the disciples were astonished at his words. But Jesus answereth again, and saith unto them, Children, how hard is it for them that trust in riches to enter into the kingdom of God!

25. It is easier for a camel to go through the eye of a needle, than for a rich man to enter into the kingdom of God.

26. And they were astonished out of measure, saying among themselves, Who then can be saved?

27. And Jesus looking upon them saith, With men it is impossible, but not with God: for with God all things are possible.

28. Then Peter began to say unto him, Lo, we have left all, and have followed thee.

29. And Jesus answered and said, Verily I say unto you, There is no man that hath left house, or brethren, or sisters, or father, or mother, or wife, or children, or lands, for my sake, and the gospel's,

30. But he shall receive an hundredfold now in this time, houses, and brethren, and sisters, and mothers, and children, and lands, with persecutions; and in the world to come eternal life.

31. But many that are first shall be last; and the last first.

November 9, 1980

LESSON OUTLINE

I. REQUEST CONCERNING ETERNAL LIFE
   A. The Rich Young Ruler
   B. The Good Teacher
   C. The Sad Conclusion
II. RESPONSIBILITIES OF DISCIPLESHIP
   A. The Eye of a Needle
   B. All Things Are Possible
III. REWARDS OF DISCIPLESHIP
   A. The Worthwhile Sacrifice
   B. The Last Shall Be First

LESSON EXPOSITION

INTRODUCTION

The man described as a rich young ruler had much to offer the kingdom of God. He was a young man; therefore, he had the rest of his life to offer. His life had not been spent; his best days were yet to be. At this stage in his life he had the opportunity to say, "Lord, take my life and guide my steps, lead me in the way You would have me go." So, he could offer himself and his life to the Lord.

Also, he was a rich man. There is no indication that he acquired his riches in a deceitful way. Apparently he was an honest, hardworking man of high moral principles, a keeper of the law. Certainly, the kingdom of God needs men who are honest and who are willing to work. Then, being a wealthy man, he had his riches to offer the kingdom of God. Now, no man can purchase his salvation with any amount of money, but progress and growth in the Lord's work sometimes requires money. He could have been helpful in this respect.

Finally, he was a ruler. This means that he was a man of considerable influence. When he spoke, people listened. He could have offered his influence to the kingdom of God. Perhaps many other persons would have been attracted to Christ because of his decision to follow the Lord.

Every individual has something to offer the kingdom of God. Whatever the person's gift or talent or ability may be, it can enhance the Lord's work. Unquestionably, everyone has influence. This is especially true of parents. But everyone either at work, or at play, or at school, or at home influences others. A life committed to Christ may influence others to make that same commitment.

Peggy was a high school senior who attended the same church I attended. She had moved to my hometown from another state. She sat behind me in a general business class. One day she told me, "I'm the kind of person who models her life after someone else. When I lived in another state, I modeled my life after a person there, but that person failed me. After moving here, I began to model my life after a person here, but that person failed me too."

I said, "Well, Peggy, who are you modeling your life after now?"

She replied, "You."

I had no idea that she was watching my life. My first reaction was to think, **Lord, have I done or said anything that would make Peggy think less of Christ?**

Who is watching your life? What influence are you having on them?

I. REQUEST CONCERNING ETERNAL LIFE
   (Mark 10:17-22)

A. The Rich Young Ruler (v. 17)

17. And when he was gone forth into the way, there came one running, and kneeled to him, and asked him, Good Master, what shall I do that I may inherit eternal life?

The rich young ruler is to be commended for the things he did as recorded in this verse. First, he came to Jesus. The most noble thing any man can do is to come to Jesus. Solomon shows how foolhardy it is for anyone to refuse to come to the Lord. "Because I called, and you refused; I stretched out my hand, and no one paid attention; and you neglected all my counsel, and did not want my reproof; I will even laugh at your calamity; I will mock when your dread comes, when your dread comes on like a storm, and your calamity comes on like a whirlwind, when distress and anguish come on you. Then they will call on me, but I will not answer; they will seek me diligently, but they shall not find me, because they hated knowledge, and did not choose the fear of the Lord" (Proverbs 1:24-29, **New American Standard Bible).**

Second, the rich young ruler came running to Jesus. If there is anything we need to get in a hurry about, it is our soul's salvation. How foolish it is to make careful plans and preparations for this life, and to neglect the future life.

Also, he kneeled to Jesus. Now, remember,

he was the ruler, and Jesus was the peasant. By all the standards of his day, Jesus should have been kneeling to him. Not only did he kneel to Jesus, but he did so in broad open daylight. Unashamedly, so that everyone could see, he gives this allegiance to the Lord. By his action, he acknowledges that Jesus is Master. Have you gone even as far in your allegiance to the Lord? Have you gone farther to publicly confess your faith and trust in Him?

Then the rich young ruler realized that salvation is a personal matter. He asked, "What must I do to inherit eternal life?" He realized that he had to do something; that no one else could do it for him. Salvation cannot be inherited, or taught; it is a personal matter between the soul and the Savior. No one can make that decision for you, you must choose for yourself. You alone can determine this direction for your life.

The rich young ruler was wrong in that he thought he could inherit eternal life. Perhaps he thought that he could use his money or his influence and thereby gain eternal life. But it cannot be so. That life when it comes, comes from God alone, and it comes in His way. Paul wrote: "For it is by grace you have been saved, through faith—and this not from yourselves, it is the gift of God—not by works, so that no one can boast. For we are God's workmanship, created in Christ Jesus to do good works, which God prepared in advance for us to do" (Ephesians 2:8-10, **New International Version**).

B. The Good Teacher (vv. 18-20)

18. And Jesus said unto him, Why callest thou me good? there is none good but one, that is God.

19. Thou knowest the commandments, Do not commit adultery, Do not kill, Do not steal, Do not bear false witness, Defraud not, Honour thy father and mother.

20. And he answered and said unto him, Master, all these have I observed from my youth.

The rich young ruler refers to Jesus as a "good teacher." Immediately, Jesus asked him why he referred to Him as good when that attribute in its noblest sense can only be applied to God. Jesus was not denying that He was good, or that He was God. But He was putting the man's statement in proper perspective. He did not view Christ as God; he saw Him as a human teacher, yet he attributed goodness which belongs only to God to Him. So Jesus is saying to him, "Let's get this matter straight. Don't call Me good unless you acknowledge that I am God. If you regard me as God, then, you can call Me good." What is He to you? Is He God? Is He good?

Then, Jesus listed some of the Ten Commandments and reminded him that he must observe them. His reaction is, " 'All these I have kept since I was a boy' " (v. 20, **New International Version**). What a clear testimony that morality and good works will not bring eternal life. Apparently, this man had lived a respectable, honorable life. But these things will not save. Only faith in the shed blood of Jesus will redeem.

The chief business of a believer is to follow Jesus. All his life may be summed up in that expression. He has Christ in him; Christ gives him new life from day to day. The very way in which that life expends its force is in the following of Christ. Every believer should so follow Him as to gain a reputation as one who walks close to Him. There are some in heaven of whom it is written, "They follow the Lamb wherever he goes" (Revelation 14:4, **New International Version**). Of Caleb, it was said that he followed the Lord fully. Every believer should strive to put his foot down in the very footprints of his crucified Lord. If you are a disciple of Jesus, your chief business is to follow Jesus. It is not by good works that we gain eternal life; it is by following our lovely Lord.

C. The Sad Conclusion (vv. 21, 22)

21. Then Jesus beholding him loved him, and said unto him, One thing thou lackest: go thy way, sell whatsoever thou hast, and give to the poor, and thou shalt have treasure in heaven: and come, take up the cross, and follow me.

22. And he was sad at that saying, and went away grieved: for he had great possessions.

What is involved in bearing one's cross and following Christ? Does the involvement vary with each individual?

It is significant to note that Jesus beholding the rich young ruler loved him. I think this was in a special way, not just the general love the Son of God would have for men everywhere. Evidently the young man was genuinely sincere.

Jesus told him that he must get rid of the things he was trusting in, and then come to Him that he might have life. He was trusting in his possessions; others are trusting in church membership, or water baptism, or tithing. Although every believer should be an active church member, should be baptized, and should tithe, none of these things will save him. For salvation, he must come to Christ, and Christ alone.

This story ends on a sad note. This rich young ruler walked away from all the promise there was for him in Christ. All the good things he had done—coming to Jesus, running to Jesus, kneeling to Jesus—were to no avail now. All that a person has to do to be lost is to turn away from Jesus. He does not have to murder anyone or to live a vile, wicked life; all he has to do is refuse to accept Christ as his Savior.

The young man went away grieved. There is no other way to walk away from Jesus. When a person turns his back on Christ, he is heading for sorrow, sadness, grief, heartache, and ultimately doom and despair. What a sad finish to an otherwise inspiring story.

II. RESPONSIBILITIES OF DISCIPLESHIP (Mark 10:23-27)

A. The Eye of a Needle (vv. 23-25)

23. And Jesus looked round about, and saith unto his disciples, How hardly shall they that have riches enter into the kingdom of God!
24. And the disciples were astonished at his words. But Jesus answereth again, and saith unto them, Children, how hard is it for them that trust in riches to enter into the kingdom of God!
25. It is easier for a camel to go through the eye of a needle, than for a rich man to enter into the kingdom of God.

The rich young ruler came to Jesus in search of eternal life. He had observed the rituals and ceremonies connected with religion in his day, but something was missing in his life. Jesus told him that He was the Giver of eternal life. If he would get rid of what he was trusting in—his possessions—and come to Jesus, he could have eternal life. Now Jesus tells His disciples that eternal life belongs to those who enter the kingdom of God. He is, therefore, telling them that He is the door by which men enter the Kingdom. Peter, who heard Christ's statement that day, confirmed this conclusion in his own statement before the Sanhedrin. Speaking of Jesus he said, " 'Salvation is found in no one else; for there is no other name under heaven given to men by which we must be saved' " (Acts 4:12, **New International Version).**

Jesus explained to the disciples that it is difficult for a rich man to enter the kingdom of God. They were astonished by that statement. This thought was the exact opposite of popular Jewish concepts about riches. They believed that prosperity was a sign of God's favor, and that therefore prosperity was evidence of a man's goodness. If a man was rich and prosperous, they believed that God must have honored and blessed him. Wealth was the proof of excellence of character and of favor with God. So, the disciples were shocked at the words of Jesus. To help them understand, Jesus repeated His statement but added, "It is difficult for those who trust in riches to enter the kingdom of God."

Prosperity may indeed be the result of the blessing of God upon the individual, but not necessarily so. There are many who have never named the name of Christ who are wealthy. Some of these have gained their riches through deceitful and dishonest means. To believe that every believer is going to prosper just because he is a believer is to ignore the plight of the vast majority of believers, particularly those outside the United States. On the other hand, poverty is not necessarily a sign that one is devoid of the blessings of God. I need only mention the circumstances that surrounded the life of Jesus. By all earthly standards, His entire life was poverty ridden. He can empathize with the poor. Are we going to say that He did not have the blessings of God on His life?

Perhaps we need to rethink our whole idea about riches. After all, what is true wealth? What are the things that have lasting value? What is really important in life? A hill shepherd's wife wrote a most interesting letter to a newspaper some time ago. Her children had been brought up in the loneliness of the hills. They were simple and unsophisticated. Then her husband got a position in a town and the children who had been brought up in the hills were introduced to the town. They changed and they changed very considerably—and they changed for the worse. The last paragraph of her letter reads like this—"Which is preferable for a child's upbringing—a lack of worldliness, but with better manners and sincere and simple thoughts, or worldliness, and its present-day habit of knowing the price of everything and the true value of nothing?"

Jesus further explained what He meant about the difficulty of a rich man entering the kingdom of God by using an illustration. He said, " 'It is easier for a camel to go through the eye of a needle than for a rich man to enter the kingdom of God' " (v. 25, **New International Version).** Some commentators have concluded that Jesus is referring to a small gate in the wall when He employs the phrase "the eye of the needle." The cities in those days were walled around to keep out bandits and hostile forces. There was always a big gate for the caravans to go through. People riding camels and coming in processions would go through that big gate in the wall. At sunrise it would be opened but at sundown that gate was closed. There was beside the big gate a small gate which might be called the pedestrian gate. Persons traveling on foot passed through this gate. Although small, this gate could accommodate a camel; but it would be a tight squeeze. It would appear that this gate was lower than the height of a camel and narrow. A camel could squeeze through if all his baggage was unloaded and he would get on his knees. Then he could squirm through the gate. Thus we have a picture of a rich man divesting himself of trust in his riches, and humbly coming to Christ for redemption.

Other biblical scholars conclude that Jesus was simply trying to show His disciples that riches, which human beings universally want more than anything else on earth, are spiritually dangerous. They point out that Jesus liked to employ hyperbole in His teachings. He often used the most extreme examples to illustrate a truth—the building beam sticking out of a man's eye compared with a splinter; the camel trying to get through the eye of a needle representing a rich man trying to get into heaven. The evil is not in riches themselves but in the trust that men put in these riches. And the disposition to trust in them is so overwhelming that most people succumb. Thus we understand the Lord's statement, "How hard it is for them that trust in riches to enter into the kingdom of God!"

B. All Things Are Possible (vv. 26, 27)

26. And they were astonished out of measure, saying among themselves, Who then can be saved?

27. And Jesus looking upon them saith, **With men it is impossible, but not with God: for with God all things are possible.**

In what sense are earthly riches a hindrance to Christian discipleship?

The disciples conclude that if what Jesus is saying is true then salvation is well nigh impossible for anyone. Jesus confirms their fears by telling them that if salvation depended on a man's own efforts then no one would ever be saved. It would not be possible. He explains that salvation is the gift of God with whom all things are possible. The man who trusts in himself will never experience redemption. The man who trusts in God will know the joys of eternal salvation.

But salvation becomes impossible for God to perform if a man is unwilling to trust in Christ. At Tunbridge, England, there is a monument erected to the memory of a group of gypsies. Gipsy Smith, the noted evangelist, tells us the meaning of that monument: Thirty gypsies, workers in the fields of hops, were driving rapidly and carelessly, singing and laughing, across a bridge over the Medway, when the wagon crashed into the railing and wagon, horses, and gypsies were thrown into the river.

One young gypsy seized a horse drifting downstream and, mounting him, watched earnestly and anxiously for his mother. At length he saw her and laid hold upon her; but she struggled in such a way that he was not able to save her. When the gypsies were being buried in the churchyard, the boy who had tried in vain to save his mother knelt down in the trench containing the coffins of those who had perished, and cried out, "Mother! Mother! I tried to save you; I did all a man could do, but you would not let me!"

So Jesus said on one occasion, " 'You refuse to come to me to have life' " (John 5:40, **New International Version).** Christ himself cannot save us unless we are willing to be saved.

One of the things we need to learn is that salvation is of God. D. L. Moody told: "An old man got up in one of our meetings and said, 'I have been forty-two years learning three things.' I pricked up my ears at that. I thought if I could find out in three minutes what a man had taken forty-two years to learn, I should like to do it. The first thing he said he had learned was that he could do nothing toward his own salvation. 'Well,' I said to myself, 'that is worth learning.' The second thing he found out was that God did not require him to do anything. Well, that was worth finding out, too. And the third thing was that the Lord Jesus Christ had done it all, that salvation was finished, and that all he had to do was **take** it. Dear friends, let us learn this lesson. Let us give up struggling and striving, and accept salvation at once."

The secret to salvation is trust in Christ and in Christ alone. When a soul renounces all else, salvation is certain. Let us fix our gaze on Christ.

III. REWARDS OF DISCIPLESHIP (Mark 10: 28-31)

A. The Worthwhile Sacrifice (vv. 28-30)

28. Then Peter began to say unto him, Lo, we have left all, and have followed thee.

29. And Jesus answered and said, Verily I say unto you, There is no man that hath left house, or brethren, or sisters, or father, or mother, or wife, or children, or lands, for my sake, and the gospel's,

30. But he shall receive an hundredfold now in this time, houses, and brethren, and sisters, and mothers, and children, and lands, with persecutions; and in the world to come eternal life.

As was usually the case, Peter became the spokesman in response to what he had seen and heard. He saw the rich young ruler as he refused to part with his possessions and therefore rejected Christ's invitation to follow Him. So, Peter sees an opportunity to parade his own goodness before the Lord. He says, "Jesus, look at us. We have done exactly what this man refused to do. We have left everything to follow you." How easy it is for us to draw a contrast between ourselves and those who are weaker than we are. How sad that we sometimes seek to enhance our own image at the expense of someone else. It should not be that way.

Jesus sees merit in what Peter has said, but adds a word of warning. He assures Peter that anyone who gives up the things that are precious to him—home, brother, sister, mother, children and fields—will receive a hundred times as much in this present age and in the age to come, eternal life. So the call to Christianity is not a call to give up something and to receive nothing in return. For everything that is surrendered for the glory of God, the believer is compensated many fold in some form.

There are present benefits which come to the believer. And then, over and above this, the believer is given eternal life in the world to come. There is no life on earth that offers so much as does the Christian life. What an encouragement this is to believers to share with others the true meaning of Christianity.

To this glowing statement Jesus added the words: "and persecutions." The benefits which come to believers are more than material blessings; they are of a higher nature. I see in this the sheer honesty of Jesus. Things are not always going to be rosy for His followers. In the midst of all the blessings, there will be difficult moments. It is misleading and Jesus never intended for us to think that there would never be any sickness, or heartaches, or trouble for the believer. These things are a part of life. What Jesus does tell us is that we can rise above the circumstances which life brings our way. He teaches us that we can live victoriously in the midst of adverse surroundings. But He never tried to con anyone into following Him. Rather, He sought to challenge men to take up His cause. So He said, "There are rewards in serving Me, but there will also be problems. I want you to understand that and to be big enough to face what life brings."

Jesus also wanted His disciples to know that every sheet that is not balanced and every account that is not settled in this life will be in the life to come. He has forever to repay us for any sacrifice we make for Him. At the same time, we need constantly to remind ourselves that no sacrifice we have ever made can ever be compared to the sacrifice that Christ made for us.

In fairness to the disciples of Christ, a word should be said about their selflessness. They did leave all else to follow Him. They saw the cause which He represented as more important than anything else. For that we commend them.

There is need in the church today for a spirit of unselfishness. We need the spirit John Hancock displayed during the Revolutionary War. John Hancock, who in many ways was a vain, pompous, and somewhat ridiculous figure, nevertheless showed himself during the Revolution to be a truly patriotic citizen. He was very rich, owning more real estate in Boston than any other man. When the issue between Washington and the British, who were occupying Boston, was touch and go, Hancock pleaded with Washington to put the torch to the city—this city in which he owned a vast fortune in properties and on which, of course, at that time there was no insurance.

John Hancock, with all his ridiculous pomposity, showed himself to be a man of great heart and sacrificial spirit. He was willing to sacrifice all that he had in the interest of the cause he served. How deep is our commitment to Christ? Is our attitude one of unselfishness? Have we put everything in Christ's hands?

B. The Last Shall Be First (v. 31)

31. But many that are first shall be last; and the last first.

It is clear that, in his own eyes, Peter feels that he has done something worthy of note. On that basis he drew a contrast between the rich young ruler and himself. The young man had refused to part with his possessions or to accept Christ; Peter had left everything and followed Jesus. But the Lord warns him against any self-confident pride. Many who have the opportunity of being nearest to Christ in this present life may not receive the greatest rewards. Men will be judged according to their faithfulness.

Barclay very succinctly says, "What Jesus was saying was, 'The final standard of judgment is with God. Many a man may stand well in the judgment of the world, but the judgment of God may well upset the world's judgment. Still more—many a man may stand well in his own judgment, and find that God's evaluation of him is very different.' It is a warning against all pride. It is a warning that the ultimate judgments belong to God who alone knows the motive of men's hearts. It is a warning that the judgments of heaven may well upset the reputations of earth."

REVIEW QUESTIONS

1. What admirable qualities did the rich young ruler possess?
2. What was his one great lack?
3. What was Jesus' attitude toward the rich young ruler?
4. What lesson did Jesus share with His disciples as a result of this incident?
5. What rewards did the Lord promise for true discipleship?

GOLDEN TEXT HOMILY

"IF ANY MAN WILL COME AFTER ME, LET HIM DENY HIMSELF, AND TAKE UP HIS CROSS, AND FOLLOW ME" (Matthew 16:24).

It is important for us to frequently review the requirements of discipleship. They are stated clearly in the text: deny self, take up the cross, follow Christ.

We must renounce, forego, or postpone any pleasure, profit, or interest which may conflict with Christ's will for our lives. Self-denial is not carelessness about one's life, health, or family. It is not bodily abuse in any respect. It is simply the surrender of our will to Christ.

The counterpart of Christian self-denial is the giving of one's life to God. Self-denial is a self-surrender, which by **de**throning self, **en**thrones Christ.

Self-denial, then, is the first step in Christian discipleship. The second step is taking up the cross.

As Christ bore His own cross to His own crucifixion, so His followers must bear their cross to their crucifixion. The great crucified leader is followed by an immense throng of crucified followers. They are crucified symbolically in all of their sufferings of mind and body in behalf of Christ and the truth.

The third step in Christian discipleship is to follow Christ wherever He may lead. Wilfred T. Grenfell, medical missionary to Labrador, at age fifty-four, wrote: "Feeble and devious as my own footsteps have been since my decision to follow Jesus Christ, I believe more than ever that this is the only real adventure in life. No step in life do I even compare with that one in permanent satisfaction." The adventure of following Christ is a supreme effort to pattern our life after the life of Christ. May we follow Him all the days of our life. May we never think of turning back or failing Him for even one day.

We have accepted the challenge of Christian discipleship. We have dedicated ourselves to following in Christ's steps. To the Lord Jesus Christ we will be true regardless of what the future holds. We have forsaken all to follow Jesus.—**Robert Humbertson, Ph.D., Chairman, Department of Languages, Lee College, Cleveland, Tennessee.**

SENTENCE SERMONS

MANY CANNOT enjoy the abundant life because of the abundance of things.
—**Selected**

IT IS IMPOSSIBLE to be loyal to Christ unless He is given first place.
—**Selected**

WE GROW RICH by depositing the Word of God in our hearts.
—**Wilbur Smith**

NO MAN, NO MATTER what may be his background can rise to the stature of spiritual manhood who has not found it nobler to serve somebody else than to serve himself.
—"Speaker's Sourcebook"

EVANGELISTIC APPLICATION

NOTHING SHOULD KEEP US FROM COMING TO GOD ON HIS TERMS.

An Oriental king once summoned into his presence his three sons and set before them three sealed urns—one of gold, the other of amber, and the third of clay. The king bade his eldest son to choose among these three urns that which appeared to him to contain the greatest treasures. The eldest son chose the vessel of gold, on which was written the word **Empire.** He opened it and found it full of blood. The second chose the vase of amber, whereon was written the word **Glory;** and when he opened it, he found it full of ashes of men who had made a great name in the world. The third son chose the vessel of clay, and on the bottom of this vessel was inscribed the name of **God.** The wise men at the King's court voted that the third vessel weighed the most, because a single letter of the name of God weighed more than all the rest of the universe.

Likewise, God's terms of salvation are the only terms which offer any hope for the soul. All else is utterly worthless.

ILLUMINATING THE LESSON

A distinguished man lay on his deathbed, when a great mark of distinction and honor was brought to him. Turning a cold glance on the treasure he would once have clutched with an eager grasp, he said with a sigh, "Alas! this is a very fine thing in this country; but I am going to a country where it will be of no use to me."
—Selected

A London merchant wrote down these four rules for his own guidance, and embodied them in his practice for fifty years. "If rich, be not too joyful in having, tok solicitous in keeping, too anxious in increasing, nor too sorrowful in losing." The Lord gave him wealth, and he used it well.
—Selected

DAILY DEVOTIONAL GUIDE

M. God Provides Strength. Isaiah 40:27-31

T. Discipleship Calls for Obedience. Matthew 19:16-22

W. Discipleship Brings Blessings. Matthew 19:27-30

T. The Importance of Priorities. Luke 18:22-27

F. Obedience Brings Contentment. 1 Timothy 6:6-10

S. Spiritually Qualified Workmen. 2 Timothy 2:14-26

November 16, 1980

The Gift of Sight

Bible Background: Matthew 20:29-34; Mark 10:46-52; Luke 18:35-43

Time: Probably in A.D. 30

Place: Jericho

Supplemental References: Psalm 103:1-3; 2 Corinthians 4:3-6

Golden Text: "Jesus said unto him, Go thy way; thy faith hath made thee whole. And immediately he received his sight, and followed Jesus in the way" (Mark 10:52).

Central Truth: A positive attitude of faith in God opens the door to receive His blessings.

Evangelistic Emphasis: God will hear the sincere, believing cry of a person's heart.

PRINTED TEXT

Mark 10:46. And they came to Jericho: and as he went out of Jericho with his disciples and a great number of people, blind Bartimaeus, the son of Timaeus, sat by the highway side begging.

47. And when he heard that it was Jesus of Nazareth, he began to cry out, and say, Jesus, thou son of David, have mercy on me.

48. And many charged him that he should hold his peace: but he cried the more a great deal, Thou son of David, have mercy on me.

49. And Jesus stood still, and commanded him to be called. And they called the blind man, saying unto him, Be of good comfort, rise; he calleth thee.

50. And he, casting away his garment, rose, and came to Jesus.

51. And Jesus answered and said unto him, What wilt thou that I should do unto thee? The blind man said unto him, Lord, that I might receive my sight.

52. And Jesus said unto him, Go thy way; thy faith hath made thee whole. And immediately he received his sight, and followed Jesus in the way.

DICTIONARY

Jericho (JER-ih-ko)—Mark 10:46—A word meaning "place of fragrance" or "moon city." It is the name of an ancient town in the wide plain north of the Dead Sea where the Jordan valley broadens between the Moab mountains and the mountains of Judah.

Bartimaeus (bar-tih-MAY-us)—Mark 10:46—Apparently a hybrid name combining the Aramaic word **bar** (son of) with the Greek word **timaios** (honorable). Mark's accompanying phrase, "the son of Timaeus," simply explains the Aramaic prefix for his Roman readers.

of Nazareth (NAZ-ah-reth)—Mark 10:47—Literally, "the Nazarene." The name **Jesus** was a common one, and a man's hometown was often used to distinguish him from other men of the same name. Nazareth was located on the most southern of the ranges of lower Galilee.

November 16, 1980

LESSON OUTLINE
I. CALLING ON THE LORD
  A. Bartimaeus
  B. Jesus of Nazareth
II. A DIVINE RESPONSE
  A. The Crowd
  B. Jesus Calls
III. RECEIVING WHOLENESS
  A. Bartimaeus Comes
  B. Bartimaeus' Need
  C. Bartimaeus Healed

LESSON EXPOSITION

INTRODUCTION

Faith is an essential element of life. It is an attribute which we exercise everyday. Its worth and importance are measured by its object. For example, I have been late to work because I had faith in a watch that had stopped. There was nothing wrong with my faith. I arrived late simply because I put my faith in an object that was not worthy of my faith.

Have you ever tried skating on ice? You can have great faith in ice and go right through it. On the other hand, you can have little faith in thick ice and be perfectly safe.

It isn't the volume of faith that matters; it's the object of our faith that's important.

The writer of Hebrews defines faith thus: "Now faith is being sure of what we hope for and certain of what we do not see" (Hebrews 11:1, **New International Version**). Faith apprehends as real fact, what is not revealed to the senses. It rests on the fact, acts upon it, and is upheld by it in the face of all that seems to contradict it. One translation says that faith is "the confirmation, the title-deed of the things we do not see, the conviction of their reality—faith perceiving as real fact what is not revealed to the senses." Thus faith gives us the right to claim our possessions. Faith enables the believer to grasp the blessings of God as reality even before they are visible. Abraham, therefore, by faith saw the day of Christ and rejoiced, and the saints under the Old Testament saw the King in His beauty.

The faith the writer of Hebrews is talking about has God as its object. To believe God is to rely upon His Word. It is to have unhesitating assurance of the truth of His Book. On the surface, the Word may seem to be unsupported by any other evidence, yet the saint believes. He relies upon and has an unfaltering confidence of the fulfillment of God's promises, even though everything seen seems against fulfillment.

Paul exercised such faith in the midst of a storm when all physical evidence pointed to utter disaster. To his fellow passengers he said, "'But now I urge you to keep up your courage, because not one of you will be lost; only the ship will be destroyed. Last night an angel of the God whose I am and whom I serve stood beside me and said, "Do not be afraid, Paul. You must stand trial before Caesar; and God has graciously given you the lives of all who sail with you." So keep up your courage, men, for **I have faith in God** that it will happen just as he told me'" (Acts 27:22-25, **New International Version**).

So, faith is "taking God at His word." It is not trust without evidence. It is belief based on the very best of evidence, the word of Him who cannot lie. Believing God and believing in God are inseparable. When we believe God we trust His Word; when we believe in God we trust Himself. When we believe God we fix our eyes on what He has said; when we believe in God we fix our eyes upon what He is, upon His person, upon Himself.

I. CALLING ON THE LORD (Mark 10:46, 47)

A. Bartimaeus (v. 46)

46. And they came to Jericho: and as he went out of Jericho with his disciples and a great number of people, blind Bartimaeus, the son of Timaeus, sat by the highway side begging.

On His way to Jerusalem for the Passover, Jesus passed through Jericho, a city which was about fifteen miles from Jerusalem. As Jesus made His way down the main road which ran through Jericho, He was surrounded by many people. This was not an unusual sight. Anytime that a distinguished Rabbi or teacher was on such a journey, it was the custom that he be surrounded by a crowd of people. These disciples and learners listened to him as he taught while he walked. That was one of the commonest ways of teaching. Also, the law required that every male Jew over twelve years of age who lived within fifteen miles of Jerusalem must attend the Passover. It was not possible for everyone to go. Those who could not go lined the streets of the towns and villages through which the Passover pilgrims passed to bid them Godspeed on their way.

William Barclay adds: "So then the streets of Jericho would be lined with people, and there would be even more than usual, for there would be many eager and curious to catch a glimpse of this audacious young Galilean who had pitted Himself against the assembled might of orthodoxy."

Another thing about Jericho is that many priests lived there. Over 20,000 priests, and as many Levites, served the Temple. Since they all could not serve at the same time, they were divided into twenty-six courses and served by rotation. When they were not on actual Temple duty, many of these priests and Levites resided in Jericho.

Again Barclay comments: "There must have been many of them in that crowd that day. At the Passover all were on duty for all were needed. It was one of the rare occasions when all did serve. But many would not have started yet. They would be doubly eager to see this rebel who was about to invade Jerusalem. And there would be many cold, black, and hostile eyes in that crowd that day, because it was clear that if Jesus was right the whole Temple worship was one vast irrelevancy."

As Jesus approached the northern gate of the city, a blind man named Bartimaeus heard the crowd coming, inquired about the person attracting this attention, and cried out to Jesus for help. What a scene! There is the picture of pitiful need: "a blind beggar," poor and helpless because blind, with none to sympathize and none to aid. Then, there is the majestic form of the Master passing near, but passing for the last time, able to heal, if only He can be reached. Can you imagine the anxiety Bartimaeus must have felt at this moment? Can you sense the hope which must have risen within him? This was a once-in-a-lifetime opportunity for him. He must not let it pass him by. Our hope for Bartimaeus is kindled because we know the nature of this Man of Galilee.

B. Jesus of Nazareth (v. 47)

47. And when he heard that it was Jesus of Nazareth, he began to cry out, and say, Jesus, thou son of David, have mercy on me.

Why do you think Bartimaeus was so sure Jesus could help him?

We are not told how much Bartimaeus knew about Jesus. The words of his appeal tell us something about his understanding. He called Him Jesus and he must have known that the Hebrew equivalent of this name is **Joshua,** which means "Jehovah the Savior" or "Jehovah will save."

Whatever Bartimaeus understood about this name, we know, as Charles J. Rolls said, "As a name, **Jesus** is more grandly honored and more grievously hated, more acclaimed and more accused than any other. We find it imprinted over six hundred times on the pages of the four Gospels, and it is the most charming, consoling, comforting name by which our beloved Savior is known."

He adds, "The One who bears this designation of delightful dignity is the fairest Flower in the fragrant garden of virtue, the rarest Treasure in the palatial mansion of truth, the greatest Gift amid the riches of eternal glory, the loveliest Legacy in the lasting heritage of life, the brightest Ray in the brilliant beams of ineffable light, the purest Pleasure in the peerless delights of perennial peace, and the choicest Companion in the celestial courts of communal love."

By the use of the title **Son of David,** Bartimaeus indicates that he has a restricted understanding of who Jesus was. **Son of David** is a Messianic title. It has in it all the thought of a conquering Messiah, a king of David's line who would lead Israel to national greatness. That represents a very limited view of who Jesus was. We know Him to be much more than a national hero. We know Him as the Savior of the world.

Whatever may have been lacking in his understanding about Jesus, it is evident that Bartimaeus had faith in Him. By his action, he shows his confidence in Christ. He fully expected to gain his sight through the healing touch of the Lord. That is what faith in Christ is all about. Whether one comes to Him for care, for healing, for sight, for help, for the healing of another, for pardon, for power, Christ can be trusted to do what is best for the individual. What He is relied upon for, that will He do.

A ruler of the synagogue asked Jesus to come and heal his daughter who was at the point of death. On the way, a woman who had been subject to bleeding for twelve years came up behind Him and touched the edge of His cloak. Her touch was an act of faith. Jesus perceived that faith and said to her, "Your faith has healed you." Immediately the woman received her healing. Jesus continued on to the ruler's house where He was told that the child was dead. He went into the room where she was, took her by the hand, and she got up. Thus we are given examples of the power of faith in Jesus Christ. How great is our need to rely upon Him more. He has not changed.

II. A DIVINE RESPONSE (Mark 10:48, 49)

A. The Crowd (v. 48)

48. And many charged him that he should hold his peace: but he cried the more a great deal, Thou son of David, have mercy on me.

Are there any in this day that attempt to discourage people from calling out to God for help?

Those who were traveling with Jesus were embarrassed and offended by the commotion created by this blind man who was trying to get Jesus' attention. Although they attempted to silence him, Bartimaeus was determined to receive the help which the Lord could offer him.

His attitude says something for the character of Bartimaeus. He could not be stopped in his effort to meet the Lord. He was unalterably determined to confront Jesus with his world of darkness that he might escape into a world of light, life, and love. It is that kind of determined faith that receives from the Lord.

The attitude of those surrounding Jesus indicates the vast gap between them and the Lord when it comes to the needs of men. To them, the blind man was a nuisance; to Him, he was a man of great need. To them, Bartimaeus was a nobody; to Him, he was an eternal soul of infinite worth. Occasionally, we should examine our attitude in the light of the attitude of Christ. Are we walking in His footsteps, are we following His example, are we thinking His thoughts? How much richer our lives will be when they are conformed to the image of Christ. He desires to express Himself through us. Are we giving Him the opportunity to do so?

Bartimaeus discovered that the exercise of His faith required overcoming the obstacles that stood in his way. And yet, that is the very character of faith. It is manifested by our bringing to Jesus our need and surmounting all the obstacles that lie between us and Him.

On one occasion Jesus was ministering in Capernaum. When the people heard that He was there, they gathered in such numbers that the room was completely full. People were even gathered outside the door. Some men brought a paralytic to Jesus. The four men who were carrying him could not get him to Jesus because of the crowd. But their faith in Jesus was such that they were determined to get the man to Him. They refused to let this obstacle stand between them and the Lord.

They climbed on top of the house and made an opening in the roof above Jesus. Then they lowered the mat that the paralyzed man was lying on. When Jesus saw the exercise of faith in this measure, He healed the man immediately. It seems that when faith is tested and comes through the test victoriously, the rewards of faith are even greater.

Standing the test of faith is a lifelong venture. The writer of Hebrews says, "Remember those earlier days after you had received the light, when you stood your ground in a great contest in the face of suffering. Sometimes you were publicly exposed to insult and persecution; at other times you stood side by side with those who were so treated. You sympathized with those in prison and joyfully accepted the confiscation of your property, because you knew that you yourselves had better and lasting possessions. So do not throw away your confidence; it will be richly rewarded. You need to persevere so that when you have done the will of God, you will receive what He has promised. For in just a very little while, 'He who is coming will come and will not delay. But my righteous one will live by faith. And if he shrinks back, I will not be pleased with him.' But we are not of those who shrink back and are destroyed, but of those who believe and are saved" (Hebrews 10:32-39, **New International Version).**

B. Jesus Calls (v. 49)

49. And Jesus stood still, and commanded him to be called. And they call the blind man, saying unto him, Be of good comfort, rise; he calleth thee.

The ears of Jesus are sensitive to the cries of those who are in need. When He heard the cry of the blind man, He stopped. The people encouraged Bartimaeus to cheer up because Jesus was calling for him.

The Christ who heard the cry of Bartimaeus still hears the prayers of those who call upon Him. One of life's greatest privileges is to be able to come to Him in prayer having the absolute assurance that He will hear and answer. Nothing gives more meaning to the Christian life than does the privilege of prayer.

A medical missionary captured by bandits in China, informed that he was to be shot ten minutes' distance away, tells how a terrible fear and helplessness came over him at the thought of such a death so far away from his native country, from his friends and his family. But he had strength enough to pray. This was his prayer: "My Lord God, have mercy on me, and give me strength for this trial. Take away all fear, and if I have to die, let me die like a man." Instantly, he said, his terrible fear began to disappear. By the time he had reached the gorge where he was to be shot, he felt perfectly calm and unafraid. At the last moment, however, the bandits relented and his life was spared. In the days which followed, full of danger and suffering, the memory of this experience was cherished more and more. "My own will had failed in the most critical moment of my life. But the knowledge that I could depend on a power greater than my own, one that had not failed me in that crisis, sustained me in a wonderful way to the very end of my captivity. What ingratitude it would be in me not to proclaim this power."

Perhaps we need a renewed faith in the power of prayer. Jesus said, " 'Therefore I tell you, whatever you ask for in prayer, believe that you have received it, and it will be yours' " (Mark 11:24, **New International Version).** Bartimaeus gives us a beautiful example of the truth of this passage. He firmly expected Jesus to hear his cry. This expectation is seen in his persistence. This expectation is rewarded when the people tell him that Jesus is calling for him.

III. RECEIVING WHOLENESS (Mark 10:50-52)

A. Bartimaeus Comes (v. 50)

50. And he, casting away his garment, rose, and came to Jesus.

When Bartimaeus heard that Jesus was calling for him, he cast aside his cloak, leaped to his feet, and came to Him.

The Jews wore two principal garments, an interior and an exterior. The interior was called a coat or a tunic. It was made commonly of linen and encircled the whole body, extending down to the knees. It was extended to the knee and had long or short sleeves. Over this was commonly worn an outer garment called a cloak or a mantle. It was made nearly square, of different sizes, five or six cubits long and as many broad, was wrapped around the body, and was thrown off when labor was performed.

When Bartimaeus heard that Jesus was calling for him, he threw off this outer garment. He was filled with joy at the prospect of being healed and so he cast aside his cloak that he might run to Jesus without impediment.

Here we have the perfect response of faith. God honors that faith that acts promptly and in exact obedience to the instructions of the Lord. Such faith comes simply because He calls, though it may know what the outcome of its obedience will be. Bartimaeus was still blind when he cast aside his cloak. He was still blind when he leaped to his feet. He was still blind when he came in haste to Jesus. That is faith!

That is the kind of faith that Abraham exhibited. "By faith Abraham, when called to go to a place he would later receive as his inheritance, obeyed and went, even though he did not know where he was going. . . . By faith Abraham, when God tested him, offered Isaac as a sacrifice. He who had received the promises was about to sacrifice his one and only son, even though God had said to him, 'It is through Isaac that your offspring will be reckoned' " (Hebrews 11:8, 17, 18; **(New International Version).**

Bartimaeus' faith was centered in the right person. The shuffling of feet must have sounded like all the residents of the city were passing through the gate. But when the blind man leaped to his feet, he went in search of Jesus. He did not look for priests, for friends, for family; his only interest was to come to Jesus.

B. Bartimaeus' Need (v. 51)

51. And Jesus answered and said unto him, What wilt thou that I should do unto thee? The blind man said unto him, Lord, that I might receive my sight.

Bartimaeus knew exactly what he wanted from the Lord. When Jesus asked him what he wanted Him to do for him, he responded directly and immediately, "I want to see."

Our Lord always yielded to those who knew what they wanted and who persisted in obtaining it. All the baser forces in the world could not turn Him aside from His course; but the importunate prayer of a beggar or a Syrophoenician woman could get anything from Him. Persistency never failed to open the floodgates of His power. This man had learned the secret of success, whether in heavenly things or in earthly things. He cried for the one thing that he wanted until he got it.

It is as true now of the risen Christ as of the Jesus of Palestine long ago—that He is to be won only by the importunate. The Light of the world comes to all. But He thrusts Himself on none. As in the case of the disciples on the Emmaus road, when He has been in our presence long enough for us to get to know Him, He makes as though He would go farther. We must then constrain Him to abide with us or He will pass on.

In looking at Holman Hunt's great picture, "The Light of the World," did you ever happen to observe the feet rather than the face of the Savior? If so, you would notice that they are not turned towards the door but towards the roadway. If Christ does not get admission, if there is no response from behind that sealed portal at which He is knocking, not the clenched fist but with gentle, half-open hand, Christ will pass on.

What a friend we have in prayer! What a protector! And how little use we make of it! When the Atlantic cable was laid in 1850, there were great celebrations and rejoicings on both sides of the Atlantic. But what is the Atlantic cable, with the messages of war and peace, of nations in commotion and sore travail, which flash across it, compared with the heavenly cable of prayer. By that cable the tempted and tried man communicates with the God of heaven and receives messages and messengers of encouragement from heaven just as Jacob did at Bethel when he saw a ladder set up on earth, the top of which reached to heaven and the angels of God ascending and descending.

We cannot overstate the importance of prayer. When General U. S. Grant was fighting his last campaign with cancer at Mount McGregor, General O. O. Howard, who had honestly won the title "The Christian Soldier," came to call on him. He spoke to Grant for a time about some of the battles and campaigns of the war in which both men had played so illustrious a part. Grant listened for a time and then, interrupting him, said,

"Howard, tell me what you know about prayer." Face to face with death and the unknown, the question of prayer was of greater interest to the dying soldier than the reminiscences of his battles.

C. Bartimaeus Healed (v. 52)

52. And Jesus said unto him, Go thy way; thy faith hath made thee whole. And immediately he received his sight, and followed Jesus in the way.

As soon as Bartimaeus came to Jesus and confessed his need, Jesus declared him healed. "Go," He said, "your faith has healed you."

Here is a vivid example of the results of faith. The exercise of faith still brings deliverance. God had provided for us and offers to us physical healing and strength in Jesus Christ. Matthew records: "When evening came, many who were demon-possessed were brought to him, and he drove out the spirits with a word and healed all the sick. This was to fulfill what was spoken through the prophet Isaiah: 'He took up our infirmities and carried our diseases' " (Matthew 8:16, 17; **New International Version).** We appropriate this healing to ourselves by faith. We miss it by our lack of faith. Mark says of Jesus in Nazareth: "He could not do any miracles there, except lay his hands on a few sick people and heal them. And he was amazed at their lack of faith" (Mark 6:5, 6; **New International Version).**

This story vividly demonstrates that Jesus never leaves a man as He finds him. The last glimpse we have of Bartimaeus is a very happy one. It shows him no longer stationary, no longer unable to move without some friendly hand to guide him. It shows him following Jesus. Sight has brought freedom and activity; it has brought joy and exultation. Shortly after this incident comes the triumphal entry into Jerusalem. The people spread palm branches and their own garments on the road that Jesus may pass over them on His colt. They cry out, "Hosanna to the son of David. Blessed is he that cometh in the name of the Lord." May we not believe that Bartimaeus was one of that joyful band who sang around Jesus their chorus of love and praise?

What can you say for yourself? Has Jesus made a difference in your life? Have things changed since you met Him? Do you know anyone who has had an encounter with Christ and who has not been changed by the experience?

We will all do well to catch the spirit of Bartimaeus. He may have been a beggar by the wayside, but he was a man of gratitude. Having had his sight restored, he followed Jesus. He did not go his own way and do his own thing after his need was supplied. He began with need, went on to gratitude, and finished with loyalty—and this is a perfect summary of the stages of discipleship.

Jesus is looking for people who want more from Him than just the meeting of their physical needs. He is looking for a people who will follow Him after their deliverance. The witness of a believer to the saving power or the healing power of Christ in their own lives is one of the most effective means of winning others to the Lord.

REVIEW QUESTIONS

1. Where was Jesus at the time of the healing of Bartimaeus?
2. What is significant about the way Bartimaeus addressed Jesus?
3. What was the reaction of the crowd to the cries Bartimaeus made in his effort to be heard?
4. How did Bartimaeus exemplify true prayer?
5. Aside from the lesson on faith what applications do you draw from this incident?

GOLDEN TEXT HOMILY

"JESUS SAID UNTO HIM, GO THY WAY; THY FAITH HATH MADE THEE WHOLE. AND IMMEDIATELY HE RECEIVED HIS SIGHT, AND FOLLOWED JESUS IN THE WAY" (Mark 10:52).

Faith in the life of the individual commands the attention of God. This lonely beggar sitting by the highway heard that Jesus of Nazareth was passing by within the crowd. Learning that it was Jesus who was passing by, the beggar began to cry aloud in a language no one else had used as yet, "Jesus, thou son of David, have mercy" (v. 47). The many who charged him to hold his peace may have regarded his cries as a nuisance. But this blind man's faith directed him past the crowd and noise to Christ. So many times the "crowd" would hinder, but faith touched the Savior and, "Jesus stood still, and commanded him to be called" (v. 49). When our faith is rooted in Christ, nothing can keep us from getting the attention of our heavenly Father.

This is a most illuminating story. In it we also see the conditions for the miracle. There is the persistence of Bartimaeus. Nothing would stop his clamor to come face-to-face with Jesus. His response to the call of Jesus was immediate and eager, so eager that he cast off his hindering cloak to run to Jesus the more quickly. Nothing must hinder our coming to the Master to receive. Bartimaeus knew precisely what he wanted—his sight. It is expected when we come to God that we be specific in our request to Him. In the end there is the precious touch.

Bartimaeus may have been a beggar by the wayside, but he was a man of gratitude. In the end, it brought his complete healing and approval of the Master who said, "Go thy way; thy faith hath made thee whole."—**T. Paul Patton, Pastor, Chattanooga, Tennessee**

SENTENCE SERMONS

MAN'S EXTREMITY IS God's opportunity. Extremities are a warrant for importunities. A man at his wit's end does not have to be at his faith's end.
—**Matthew Henry**

TO HEAR GOD speak once makes it all the more reason to listen a whole lifetime.
—**C. C. Woods**

A POSITIVE ATTITUDE of faith in God opens the door to receive His blessings.
—**Selected**

CIRCUMSTANCES ARE NEVER unfavorable when God is on our side.
—**"Notes and Quotes"**

EVANGELISTIC APPLICATION

GOD WILL HEAR THE SINCERE, BELIEVING CRY OF A PERSON'S HEART.

When Simon Peter attempted to walk on the water, his faith failed him. But when he cried out to the Lord in a brief, simple prayer, the Lord heard the cry of his heart. The publican felt unworthy even to lift his face toward heaven. He expressed in a few words the deep burden of his soul, and Christ responded to his plaintive plea. Bartimaeus, crying out of the midst of a world of darkness, wanting the scales of blackness removed from his eyes, simply prayed, "Lord, I want to see." But that simple prayer arose from the deepest recesses of his soul. Christ saw his faith and his sincerity; He felt the weight of his burden; and He granted him deliverance. Each of these persons had this in common: they came to Christ in sincerity and in faith;

they uttered the desperate desire of their soul; and each of them had their needs met. Christ will hear the prayer of anyone who comes to Him in the same spirit and with the same attitude that these came.

ILLUMINATING THE LESSON

A father promised his seven-year old son a pocket watch the next time he went to town. Days before he got the watch the little fellow wore a shoestring tied to one of his belt loops. When he was asked "Why the shoestring," he replied, "That's for the watch Dad is going to bring from town."

DAILY DEVOTIONAL GUIDE

M. Healing Through Prayer. 2 Kings 20:1-7
T. God Provides Complete Healing. Psalm 103:1-5
W. Provision for Healing. Isaiah 53:1-12
T. Persistence in Prayer. Matthew 20:29-34
F. Cry for Help. Luke 18:35-43
S. Receiving Sight. Acts 9:10-19

November 23, 1980

Demonstrating Thankfulness

Bible Background: Luke 17:11-19

Time: Probably late in A.D. 29

Place: On the border between Galilee and Samaria

Supplemental References: 2 Kings 7:3-11; Psalms 26:1-7; 95:1-6; Philippians 4:4-7

Golden Text: "I will praise the name of God with a song, and will magnify him with thanksgiving" (Psalm 69:30).

Central Truth: It pleases the Lord when His people express thankfulness to Him.

Evangelistic Emphasis: God blesses all men but can save only those who respond to Him.

PRINTED TEXT

Luke 17:11. And it came to pass, as he went to Jerusalem, that he passed through the midst of Samaria and Galilee.

12. And as he entered into a certain village, there met him ten men that were lepers, which stood afar off:

13. And they lifted up their voices, and said, Jesus, Master, have mercy on us.

14. And when he saw them, he said unto them, Go shew yourselves unto the priests. And it came to pass, that, as they went, they were cleansed.

15. And one of them, when he saw that he was healed, turned back, and with a loud voice glorified God,

16. And fell down on his face at his feet, giving him thanks: and he was a Samaritan.

17. And Jesus answering said, Were there not ten cleansed? but where are the nine?

18. There are not found that returned to give glory to God, save this stranger.

19. And he said unto him, Arise, go thy way: thy faith hath made thee whole.

DICTIONARY

Samaria—(suh-MAIR-ee-uh)—Luke 17:11—In New Testament times the province or region between Judea on the south and Galilee on the north; bounded by Perea and Decapolis on the east and northeast, with Phoenicia on the northwest, and the Mediterranean Sea on the west

Galilee—(GAL-uh-lee)—Luke 17:11—The northern of the three mail provinces of Palestine west of the Jordan, extending about sixty miles from north to south and thirty miles from east to west. It was the scene of a considerable part of Jesus' ministry.

lepers—Luke 17:12—The biblical leprosy was a whiteness (Exodus 4:6) that disfigured its victim but did not disable him. It is described in Leviticus as a white spot (spreading or disappearing, sometimes with a reddish base) or as raw spots.

November 23, 1980

LESSON OUTLINE
I. CRYING FOR MERCY
  A. The Journey to Jerusalem
  B. The Ten Lepers
II. RESPONDING TO NEED
  A. Cry for Mercy
  B. Command to Go
III. EXPRESSING GRATITUDE
  A. The Grateful Samaritan
  B. The Ungrateful Jews
  C. The Pronouncement

LESSON EXPOSITION

INTRODUCTION

Thanksgiving is one area of Christian discipleship that has been neglected. Once a year we remind ourselves of our responsibility to show gratitude. Other than that very little is said about the subject. Yet the Bible speaks frequently of praise and thanksgiving. The Psalms in particular are filled with exhortations to express gratitude. In Psalm 107 the Psalmist burst forth four times with the cry: "Oh that men would praise the Lord for his goodness, and for his wonderful works to the children of men."

The Lord's dealings with us make thanksgiving and praise on our part the only fitting thing. As we reflect upon the wondrous goodness of God to men we ought to pause and show gratitude to Him. At the same time, we should be appalled at the little thought and strength and time that men give to thanksgiving. This is true even of the average Christian. Oh, that we would stir ourselves to show our Lord our love and gratitude for Him! He justly merits the highest praise and worthiest worship we can possibly render.

The Psalmist says it best: "It is good to give thanks to the Lord, And to sing praises to Thy name, O Most High; To declare Thy lovingkindness in the morning, And Thy faithfulness by night. . . . For Thou, O Lord, hast made me glad by what Thou hast done, I will sing for joy at the works of Thy hands" (Psalm 92:1, 2, 4; **New American Standard Bible).**

Thanksgiving is more than a privilege. It is that, but it is also a responsibility. To fail to thank the Lord for His blessings is just as distinct and definite disobedience to God's commands as to steal or to murder. To the Ephesians, Paul said: "But among you there must not be even a hint of sexual immorality, or of any kind of impurity, or of greed, because these are improper for God's holy people. Nor should there be obscenity, foolish talk or coarse joking, which are out of place, but rather thanksgiving" (Ephesians 5:3, 4; **New International Version).** To the Thessalonians he said: "Be joyful always; pray continually; give thanks in all circumstances, for this is God's will for you in Christ Jesus" (1 Thessalonians 5:16-18, **New International Version).**

Today's lesson speaks of one person who expressed gratitude to the Lord for His blessings upon his life and of nine others who did not.

I. CRYING FOR MERCY (Luke 17:11, 12)

A. The Journey to Jerusalem (v. 11)

11. And it came to pass, as he went to Jerusalem, that he passed through the midst of Samaria and Galilee.

In the first ten verses of the seventeenth chapter of Luke, we have the account of the last stage in Luke's wonderful story of a Sabbath afternoon in Peraea. Having rebuked the Pharisees for their scoffing, our Lord turned again to His disciples. In these verses we have His teaching on four distinct matters. The subjects He included were offences, forgiveness, faith and service.

In Luke's narrative, considered from the standpoint of the historical or chronological sequence, there is a gap between verses 10 and 11 in chapter 17. There is no doubt that our Lord was in Peraea when the message came to Him that Lazarus was sick; it was there that He tarried; and thence He went and raised Lazarus from the dead. The story is found in John 11. In that same chapter we find that after He had raised Lazarus, He traveled north to Ephraim, where He tarried, for how long we are not told, but for some time apparently, in quietness, with His disciples.

The story as we have it here in Luke takes up at that point, and we find Him traveling still further north than Ephraim, on the border line between Samaria and Galilee. That does not mean that He went into Samaria. It does not mean that He went into Galilee. He had already left Galilee, not to go back, until after His cross and resurrection. The opening phrase of this verse, "As they were on the way to Jerusalem," does not mean that at that time He was on His actual way to the city. Verse 51 of chapter 9 marks the breaking point between Caesarea Philippi and the final six months in the ministry of Jesus:

"As the time approached for him to be taken up to heaven, Jesus resolutely set out for Jerusalem" **(New International Version).** That was six months before the Cross, during which time He was moving resolutely towards the ultimate. That is the fact which Luke had in mind when, at this point, he wrote: "It came to pass, as they were on their way to Jerusalem." In the next chapter, 18, at verse 31, we read, "Jesus took the Twelve aside and told them, 'We are going up to Jerusalem' " **(New International Version).** That is the record of the beginning of the final journey to Jerusalem (Morgan).

B. The Ten Lepers (v. 12)

12. And as he entered into a certain village, there met him ten men that were lepers, which stood afar off.

Leprosy has always been the scourge of the eastern countries. Every village in Christ's day had its leprous outcasts, who lived on the dung heaps, ostracized from society. There were no charitable institutions to take care of these unfortunate souls in their dire need. They were left to perish in their agony of body and soul, despised and rejected.

Although the Jews had no dealing with the Samaritans, in this group of lepers there was at least one Samaritan. William Barclay observes: "Here is an example of one great law of life. A common misfortune had broken down the racial and the national barriers. In the common tragedy of their leprosy they had forgotten that they were Jews and Samaritans and remembered only that they were men in need. It is said that if a flood surges over a piece of country, and the wild animals congregate on some little bit of higher ground, you will see standing together animals who are natural enemies and who, at any other time, would have done their best to kill each other. Surely one of the things which should draw all men together is their common need of God."

The ten lepers who met Jesus as He entered the village stood afar off. This they were required to do by the law. " 'As for the leper who has the infection, his clothes shall be torn, and the hair of his head shall be uncovered, and he shall cover his mustache and cry "Unclean! Unclean!" He shall remain unclean all the days during which he has the infection; he is unclean. He shall live alone; his dwelling shall be outside the camp' " (Leviticus 13: 45, 46; **New American Standard Bible).** The exact distance at which a leper should stand is not stated. At least one authority declared that when the wind was blowing from the leper to the healthy person, the leper should stand at least fifty yards away. What a vivid illustration of the utter isolation in which lepers lived.

These ten lepers may represent the abounding fruit of sin, for they were all afflicted. Jesus represents the abundance of divine power to meet this need, for they were all cleansed. The Lord's tenderness toward outcasts, His attention to prayers from a distance, and His regard for the ceremonial law so long as it was in force, are each set forth in this passage. The story is very instructive.

II. RESPONDING TO NEED (Luke 17:13, 14)
A. Cry for Mercy (v. 13)

13. And they lifted up their voices, and said, Jesus, Master, have mercy on us.

Although these ten lepers were outcasts, they were nevertheless men of wisdom. Their wisdom is seen in that they turned to Jesus in their hour of need. They had heard through some means about His miracle-working power. Perhaps they had heard of other lepers whom He had cleansed. With their croaking, weak voices they cried as best they could, "Jesus, Master, have mercy on us."

Did these lepers really believe that Jesus could heal them? Did they know by what power He performed His miracles? Did they know who Jesus really was? All these questions, and many others, we might ask. But not Jesus! They cried to Jesus in sheer desperation —a last chance, so to speak. And Jesus heard them.

In this heart-rending plea for mercy we hear all humanity crying to God for deliverance from the ravages of sin. We, too, were outcasts in our state of sin. We, too, needed the cleansing power of Christ to make us whole and set us in right relation again with God and with our fellowmen. Our salvation did not depend on our knowledge or understanding of the doctrines of the church. We were saved by throwing ourselves completely and utterly on the love of God as revealed in Jesus Christ.

Many millions of people in our world today can give this testimony: "I came to Jesus full of sin, guilty and lost, with a hard heart and a heavy spirit; and I looked to Him, trusting Him alone to save me; and He has saved me. He has changed my nature, He has blotted out my sin, and He has made me love Him, and love all that is good and true and generous, for His sake."

Consider who this Christ is in whom we have placed our trust. He is God, "very God of very God." He is perfect man, and He has taken perfect manhood upon Himself for our sakes. He has lived a perfect life. He has died "the just for the unjust, to bring us to God"; and God has accepted the sacrifice of His dear Son. He is risen from the dead, and has gone into heaven, and sits now at the right hand of God, and will shortly come. What a Savior! What wisdom that turns to Him for help! He is the never-failing One. No one ever looked to Him in faith and came away disappointed.

B. Command to Go (v. 14)

14. And when he saw them, he said unto them, Go shew yourselves unto the priests. And it came to pass, that, as they went, they were cleansed.

Jesus required these ten lepers to perform an act of faith in Him. They were to do so before they had the slightest evidence in themselves He had wrought a good work upon them. They had not yet begun to feel their foul blood cleansed. The horrible dryness of leprosy had not yielded to healthy perspiration. Yet they were to go toward the house in which the priest lived to be examined by him and to be pronounced clean. They were to exhibit faith in Christ's power to heal them by going to show themselves healed. But as yet they were in the same condition as before. They were to start to the place where they should be examined by the priest, believing that Jesus had healed them, or would heal them, though, as yet, they had no internal evidence whatever that their flesh should become as that of a little child.

The lesson that Jesus is teaching us in this story is that faith obeys Him. Whatever He instructs the individual to do, that he willingly does. This does not mean that He requires everyone to declare his healing before there is evidence of it. That is what He required to the ten lepers, but it is not necessarily what He expects from others. Some of those who came to Him He healed instantly. Others He instructed to do certain things, such as, wash in the pool of Siloam. The important thing always is that the subject do what the Master asks. We should not come to Him with preconceived notions about how He is going to deal with us. He is sovereign. He can handle our case anyway He pleases. It is our place to be yielded to Him and to be obedient to His directions. He may choose to minister to us in a way altogether different from the way He ministers to someone else. May we learn to follow Him.

Whatsoever is one of the most precious words in the Bible. In using it God gives us, in many passages, a sweeping assurance. But the word also has challenging obligations. In the fifteenth chapter of John, Jesus told His disciples that if they abide in Him and His words abide in them they can ask **whatsoever** they will and it will be theirs. A few verses later He tells them that they are His friends if they do **whatsoever** He commands. These two **whatsoevers** must be taken together. We have no right to ask the Lord whatsoever we will unless we are doing whatsoever He commands. When we fulfill the first, He will fulfill the second.

III. EXPRESSING GRATITUDE (Luke 17:15-19)

A. The Grateful Samaritan (vv. 15, 16)

15. And one of them, when he saw that he was healed, turned back, and with a loud voice glorified God,

16. And fell down on his face at his feet, giving him thanks: and he was a Samaritan.

The combination of faith and obedience brought healing to the ten lepers. Jesus told them to go and show themselves to the priests. As they were on their way, they were cleansed. Jesus could just as well have performed the miracle when they were in His presence, but He chose to test their faith. The amazing miracle took place as they obeyed Him.

When one of the lepers realized that he was healed, he came back to Jesus, praising God in a loud voice. The weak cry for help had been changed into a strong voice of praise.

Think of how this leper must have felt. His body had been racked with pain. His features had been marred and disfigured as the treacherous disease ate away at his bones and flesh. Now, instead of decaying, raw flesh, he had clean, new skin. There was no more pain, and the stench and filth with which he had continuously lived were gone forever.

Can you imagine the mental and spiritual anguish this leper had suffered? What could be worse than utter loneliness and desolation? He had been cut off completely from family and friends and social fellowship. But, now he could again enter into the stream of life. He could be reunited with his family and friends. He would no longer bear the stigma, "unclean," which had cut him off from others. All barriers were gone, and he was free to go wherever he desired.

Is it surprising that we hear him praising the Lord with a loud voice. The joy and happiness which he felt must have known no bounds. How sweet are the sounds of praise!

Mrs. Charles E. Cowman tells of a missionary in China who was living a defeated life. Everything seemed to be touched with sadness and although he prayed and prayed for months for victory over depression and discouragement, his life remained the same. He determined to leave his work and go to an interior station and pray till victory came. He reached the place and was entertained in the home of a fellow missionary. On the wall hung a motto with these words, "Try Thanksgiving." The words gripped his heart and he thought within himself, "Have I been praying all this time and not praising?" He stopped and began to praise and was so uplifted that he returned immediately to his flock to tell them that praise changes things.

Ten lepers had faith that Jesus could heal them, but only one had grace to thank Him after he was healed. The others went on their way; he returned and threw himself at Jesus' feet and thanked Him. Interestingly enough, this leper was a Samaritan. Apparently he was not plagued with the disease that afflicted the minds of the Jews. They felt that they were a privileged people. In their minds, what they received they deserved to receive because of who they were. But the Samaritan humbly recognized his own unworthiness and displayed a spirit of love and gratitude. With which of the two do you more closely identify —the Jews or the Samaritan?

As Spurgeon observes, there are more who receive benefits than ever give praise for them. Ten persons healed, one person glorifying God; ten persons healed of leprosy, mark you, and only one person kneeling down at Jesus' feet, and thanking Him for it. If for this surpassing benefit, which might have made the dumb to sing, men only thank the Lord in proportion of one to nine, what shall I say of what we call the everyday blessings of life. Life, health, eyesight, hearing, family love, fellowship of friends; and yet is there one man in nine that praises God for these? We do not praise the Lord fitly, proportionately, intensely. We receive a continent of mercies, and only return an island of praise. He gives us blessings new every morning, and fresh every evening, great is His faithfulness; and yet we let the years roll round, and seldom observe a day of praise. Sad is it to see God all goodness, and man all ingratitude! The tribe who receives benefits may say, "My name is legion"; but those who praise God are so few that a child may write them.

I would also submit to you that the number of those who pray is greater than the number of those who praise. For these ten men who were lepers all prayed. But when it came to magnifying and praising God, only one of them took up the note. One would have thought that all who prayed would praise, but it is not so. There have been cases where a whole ship's crew in time of storm has prayed, and yet none of that crew has sung the praise of God when the storm has become calm. Multitudes of people pray when they are sick and near to dying; but when they get better, their praises grow sick unto death. It is too sadly true that more pray than praise!

B. The Ungrateful Jews (vv. 17, 18)

17. And Jesus answering said, Were there not ten cleansed? but where are the nine?

18. There are not found that returned to give glory to God, save this stranger.

Is it reasonable to believe that a greater manifestation of gratitude to God would aid in trying to cure the ills of society?

Jesus inquires about the nine Jews who were cleansed but who did not return to offer thanks. Their situation is interesting.

As long as their plight was the same as that of the Samaritan, they associated with him. But as soon as they were cleansed, they would seem to have separated themselves from him. It was as if now that they were saved from being outcasts, they could no longer associate together. Are we not guilty of adopting the same attitude? We express love for a native in a foreign land, but neglect to minister to our neighbor.

H. E. Fosdick tells the following story which I share with you in his own words. "Some time ago I heard a group of children sitting on the street curb and singing a missionary hymn:

The little black baby that rolls in
the sand,
In a country far over the sea,
Is my African brother, and Jesus
loves him
Just as He loves you and me.

"At first I was amused to hear them singing there. Then I fell to meditating on how easy was the problem presented to them so long as the little black baby was rolling in the sand in a country far over the sea. They did not have to deal with him individually. If they helped him at all, they did it in general and at long range through a great organization. But what a difference when our 'African brother' no longer rolls in the sand in a country far over the sea, but moves into our neighborhood."

Not only did the nine lepers disassociate themselves from the Samaritan, but they also put their religious observance above their gratitude. They were more interested in seeing the priest than in praising God for the miracle they had experienced. They were more concerned about being declared fit to return to society than they were in worshiping the God who made them fit. How quickly we forget. In many ways we are as guilty as were the nine lepers. Have we never been more interested in the gift than in the Giver? Have we never put more stock in the healing than in the Healer? We need to take a look at our priorities. We need to reevaluate the things that really matter to us. In short, we need to put God first in our lives.

Inasmuch as only one man—and he a foreigner—returned to give thanks to the Lord, perhaps we can learn something about true thanksgiving. Genuine praise is marked by individuality. The Samaritan did not take his cue from the other nine. He did not wait until they turned back to praise before he did so. No, he acted on his own. He felt a personal need to express the gratitude of his heart. Gratitude is a very personal thing. Nobody else can express for me what I feel. Each believer has a personal responsibility to render thanks to the Lord.

Another characteristic of true thankfulness is promptness. This man returned immediately to give praise to God. What a lesson we can learn here! What grand designs some of us have formed of future service for God! What small results have followed! It is better to lay one brick today than to propose to build a palace next year. Magnify our Lord in the present for present salvation. Why should praise be kept waiting at the door even for a night? The manna came fresh in the morning; so let our praises rise to the Lord. Someone has said, "He praises twice who praises at once; but he who does not praise at once praises never."

Genuine gratitude is spiritual in nature. The healed man reasoned: the first thing I ought to do is to go back, and bear witness to the people, glorifying God in the midst of them all, and falling down at Christ's feet. So he went first to Jesus. In him the spiritual overrode the ceremonial. He felt that his main duty was to adore in person the divine person who had delivered him from his disease. Let us go first to Jesus. Let us in spirit bow before Him. Let us pine to get to Jesus himself, and tell Him how much we love Him.

C. The Pronouncement (v. 19)

19. And he said unto him, Arise, go thy way: thy faith hath made thee whole.
There was for the healed Samaritan a glad word of blessed assurance and promise. Jesus declared him whole. His faith had resulted not only in his physical well-being, but in complete wholeness. In His statement, Jesus called attention to the means of the cure, namely, faith in Himself. In so doing, He is nurturing that germ of new life into fuller trust in His divine person. He also indicates that the faith which first had secured the healing of the body and which was manifested in the man's return and his gratitude now secured for him the salvation of his soul.

Looking back upon this story, we are reminded that gratitude is often found where it is least expected. Who would have thought that the despised Samaritan would have been the one out of the ten who would render praise to God? Sometimes the most unlikely ones around us surprise us with their expressions of love for the Lord. From this account, we also discover that praise is always pleasing to our Lord. How His heart rejoices when His people praise Him! We further learn from this experience that thanksgiving is the certain condition of further blessedness and joy. What a challenge to be a people of faith and gratitude!

REVIEW QUESTIONS

1. What geographical area was Jesus in when He confronted the ten lepers?

2. How did Jesus respond to the lepers' plea for mercy?

3. How did Jesus react to the ingratitude manifested by the nine lepers who did not return?

4. How did Jesus respond to the gratitude expressed by the Samaritan?

5. What practical applications do you draw from this lesson?

GOLDEN TEXT HOMILY

"I WILL PRAISE THE NAME OF GOD WITH A SONG, AND WILL MAGNIFY HIM WITH THANKSGIVING" (Psalm 69:30).

The sixty-ninth Psalm might well be classified as a "case history" in the representative life of mankind on earth. It seems to have the encompassment of all the extremities of earthly life. The ins and outs, ups and downs, highs and lows, triumphs and defeats, joys and sorrows. Through all these crises, the psalmist, like any ordinary godly person, arrives at the end victoriously.

There are three periods of importance in this psalm: (1) the time of desperation, (2) the time of recognition of his foolishness and sin, and (3) the time of praise.

The psalmist, David, begins with a desperate cry for salvation from his vacillating condition. He felt that circumstances were moving him from one extreme to another. Listen to his plaintive cry:

1. "Save me, O God; for the waters are come in unto my soul" (v. 1).

2. "I sink in deep mire, where there is no standing" (v. 2).

3. "I am come into deep waters" (v. 2).

4. "The floods overflow me" (v. 2).

This is, of course, an analogical situation. David was not actually in those situations physically; however, he was very much in them mentally. His mental attitude was near to the point of paranoia. The strong possibility exists that his problems were brought about by a spiritual deficiency in his life. His imagination seems to be enlarging as he moves on with time. Not only does he see waters flooding his life; he also visualizes enemies exceeding in number more than the hairs on his head (v. 4). His fears, his hallucinations have contorted his entire personality. His voice quivers as he cries out, "I am weary of my crying: my throat is dried: mine eyes fail while I wait for my God" (v. 3).

David then enters the second period of his crises. This is his recognition of his foolishness in permitting these circumstances to overwhelm him. He suddenly realizes these are satanical attacks which moved him into these positions of despair. Thus he begins his climb by first realizing his deliverance will come through faith in God rather than faith in his own ability. He prepares himself for a series of praises to Jehovah for the victory he expects to come at any moment.

The third and final period is his triumph. A time of victory for himself and those around him who might be observing his plight. It is his feeling that when he begins his praises, others will follow. Listen to the golden text verse: "I will praise the name of God with a song, and will magnify him with thanksgiving." The humble, he cries, shall see this and be glad; the poor shall praise and be heard by God. The inhabitants of heaven shall praise Him, the seas and everything therein shall praise Him.

God, he exclaims, will save Zion, and His people will inherit it when the battles of life are ended. The enemies of the righteous shall be destroyed. Then shall the righteous shine forth as the sun in the kingdom of their Father.—**Wayne S. Proctor, Pastor, Nashville, Tennessee**

SENTENCE SERMONS

THE WORSHIP MOST acceptable to God comes from a thankful and cheerful heart.
—**Plutarch**

LET THE MAN who would be grateful think of repaying a kindness, even while receiving it.
—**Seneca**

PRIDE SLAYS THANKSGIVING, but an humble mind is the soil out of which thanks naturally grows.
—**Henry Ward Beecher**

A PROUD MAN is seldom a grateful man, but he never thinks he gets as much as he deserves.
—**Henry Ward Beecher**

EVANGELISTIC APPLICATION

GOD BLESSES ALL MEN BUT CAN SAVE ONLY THOSE WHO RESPOND TO HIM.

When one considers the extent of the richness of God's blessings to all mankind, it increases the wonder that more people do not render devotion to Him. He is our Creator. He has given us life and health and strength. For what we have and what we are, we are indebted to Him. No phase of our life is untouched by His hand. And this He does for us

November 23, 1980

even before we surrender our lives to Him. While we were yet sinners, God blessed our lives in numerous ways. His goodness is designed to lead us to repentance.

Not only is God our Creator, but He desires to be our Savior. At Calvary, Jesus Christ, God's Son, paid our sin debt. We did nothing to deserve this treatment. All our lives we were in rebellion against God. Yet out of His great love for us, He made the supreme sacrifice. The work, however, that He has done for mankind is of no avail to the individual unless that person responds to Him. Christ stands with outstretched arms to welcome all who will receive His love.

ILLUMINATING THE LESSON

As an elderly lady with arthritis sat by her window watching the traffic go by, she said, "I don't know what I'd do without it."

Later on she was moved to a room in the rear where she could no longer see the traffic from her window. She commented, "I like this better. The sweetest children play in the back yard next door."

At last she was moved to the slums of the city. To a friend she said, "Come and see my beautiful view—my beautiful view of the sky."

BUT WHERE ARE THE NINE?

I meant to go back, but you may guess
I was filled with amazement I cannot express
To think that after those horrible years,
That passion of loathing and passion of fears,
By sores unendurable—eaten, defiled—
My flesh was as smooth as the flesh of a child.
I was drunken with joy; I was crazy with glee;
I scarcely could walk and I scarcely could see,
For the dazzle of sunshine where all had been black; . . .
But I meant to go back—oh, I meant to go back!
I had thought to return, when my people came out.
There were tears of rejoicing and laughter and shout;
They embraced me—for years I had not known a kiss;
Ah, the pressure of lip is an exquisite bliss!
They crowded around me, they filled the whole place;
They looked at my feet and my hands and my face;
My children were there, my glorious wife,
And all the forgotten allurements of life.
My cup was so full I seemed nothing to lack!
But I meant to go back—Oh, I meant to go back!
—Author unknown

DAILY DEVOTIONAL GUIDE

M. A Wise Decision. 2 Kings 7:7-11
T. A Voice of Thanksgiving. Psalm 26:1-7
W. Approaching God With Thankfulness. Psalm 95:1-6
T. A Song of Thanksgiving. Psalm 118:1-14
F. Cause for Thanksgiving. 2 Corinthians 9:6-15
S. Prayer and Thanksgiving. Philippians 4:4-9

November 30, 1980

The Seeking Savior

Bible Background: Luke 19:1-10
Time: Probably late in A.D. 29
Place: Jericho, about fifteen miles east of Jerusalem
Supplemental References: John 3:14-17; Acts 10:30-35; 2 Corinthians 5:14-17; Colossians 3:12-17; Hebrews 2:1-3
Golden Text: "For the Son of man is come to seek and to save that which was lost" (Luke 19:10).
Central Truth: God will make a way for the one who perseveres in following Him.
Evangelistic Emphasis: God will remove all obstacles to salvation and blessing for those who earnestly seek Him.

PRINTED TEXT

Luke 19:1. And Jesus entered and passed through Jericho.

2. And, behold, there was a man named Zacchaeus, which was the chief among the publicans, and he was rich.

3. And he sought to see Jesus who he was; and could not for the press, because he was little of stature.

4. And he ran before, and climbed up into a sycomore tree to see him: for he was to pass that way.

5. And when Jesus came to the place, he looked up, and saw him, and said unto him, Zacchaeus, make haste, and come down; for to day I must abide at thy house.

6. And he made haste, and came down, and received him joyfully.

7. And when they saw it, they all murmured, saying, That he was gone to be guest with a man that is a sinner.

8. And Zacchaeus stood, and said unto the Lord; Behold, Lord, the half of my goods I give to the poor; and if I have taken any thing from any man by false accusation, I restore him fourfold.

9. And Jesus said unto him, This day is salvation come to this house, forsomuch as he also is a son of Abraham.

10. For the Son of man is come to seek and to save that which was lost.

DICTIONARY

Jericho—Luke 19:1—Possibly "place of fragrance" or "moon city." Jericho was an ancient city about fifteen miles east of Jerusalem in the wide plain where the Jordan valley broadens between the Moab mountains and the western precipices. Its history is important both from the Old and New Testaments (see Joshua 3:16).

Zacchaeus (zak-KEY-us)—Luke 19:2—The Greek form of the Hebrew **Zaccai**, meaning "the just" or "pure"; a rich Jew and chief officer of the tax or tribute collectors, residing in Jericho.

publicans—Luke 19:2—A word derived from the Latin **publicanus**. A publican was a collector of tool and tribute, a tax collector.

press—Luke 19:3—Crowd of people

November 30, 1980

LESSON OUTLINE
I. HINDRANCES TO MEETING CHRIST
  A. Jesus in Jericho
  B. The Chief Tax Collector
  C. A Short Man
II. OVERCOMING OBSTACLES
  A. The Command
  B. The Response
  C. The Obedience
III. RESPONDING TO CHRIST
  A. Restitution
  B. Salvation
  C. Redemption

LESSON EXPOSITION

INTRODUCTION

In order to see Jesus, Zacchaeus was willing to take certain risks. He was at the top of his profession—the chief tax collector. As such, he was the most hated man in his community. For him to appear in public, and especially in a crowd, was dangerous. There were many in that crowd who would welcome an opportunity to inflict harm upon him. Apparently Zacchaeus considered the chances he was taking and regarded them worth the risk that he might see Jesus.

Zacchaeus faced other problems as well. Being a short man, the crowd obscured his vision. Although Jesus was nearby, he could not see Him because those around him were taller than he. Still, he would not be stopped; he must see Jesus. So he ran on ahead of the crowd and climbed up into a fig-mulberry tree. A traveler describes the tree as being like "the English oak, and its shade is most pleasing. It is consequently a favorite wayside tree. . . . It is very easy to climb, with its short trunk and its wide lateral branches forking out in all directions."

Zacchaeus met the Lord because of his perseverance. He would not be denied this opportunity to have a face-to-face encounter with Christ. He could have been discouraged easily by the hissing of the crowd or the limitations of his stature. But he refused to be turned aside from his quest to see Jesus.

Any man who perseveres in his search for the Lord will find Him. Nicodemus found Him. Even though he came to Jesus under the cover of darkness and the meeting place was a rooftop in Jerusalem, he found Him. Out of that conversation came a commitment that enabled Nicodemus to identify himself with Christ when others were denying or forsaking Him. Perseverance pays off in the quest for salvation. It also pays in the search for success in Christian living. Jesus said, " 'Because of the increase of wickedness, the love of most will grow cold, but he who stands firm to the end will be saved' " (Matthew 24:12, 13; **New International Version**).

I. HINDRANCES TO MEETING CHRIST (Luke 19:1-3)

A. Jesus in Jericho (v. 1)

1. And Jesus entered and passed through Jericho.

To have Jesus and Jericho appear in the same sentence is something of a paradox. Jesus stands for everything that is good and wholesome; Jericho stands for all that is bad and undesirable. At that time, the city was largely peopled by Roman tax gatherers and by priests of Jerusalem. It was an evil place. The highway between Jericho and Jerusalem was not safe. Our Lord's parable of the Good Samaritan had recognized that. Jericho was a city which had been cursed, and no one would suspect that anyone would come out of it to be saved. We might as well expect converts from the vilest cities of our day, as from Jericho in those days.

Why, then, did Jesus pass through Jericho on His way to Jerusalem? He was on His way to the Cross. He need not have gone through Jericho. There were other ways, but He chose this direction. The only incident recorded is this story of Zacchaeus, and I have no doubt that the reason of His going was the finding of this man.

Two important facts emerge from this account. First, it does not matter where one comes from; it may be from one of the wickedest settlements, one of the worst ghettos; but if that person turns to Christ, he can be saved. The Savior's reach is to all mankind. He did not die for the wealthy or the middle class alone. He died also for the poor and the outcast. Wherever there is a man on earth who needs a Savior, Christ died for him. Some of the wealthiest people who have ever lived have been committed to Christ. Some of the poorest the earth has ever produced have also marched under His banner. So, it is not surprising that Jesus is in Jericho, a most unlikely place, in search of a tax collector, a most unlikely person, to present to him the plan of salvation.

Second, Jesus' action underscores the importance of one person. In going out of His way to find Zacchaeus, He brings hope to all of us. Cannot every believer testify that in one way or another, Jesus went out of His way to find him?

B. The Chief Tax Collector (v. 2)

2. And, behold, there was a man named Zacchaeus, which was the chief among the publicans, and he was rich.

Are there occupations which contribute to acts of dishonesty?

Zacchaeus was a Jew who was a discredit to his race. He was an evil Jew who used extortion as a vehicle in which he rode to riches. He did not hesitate in practicing fraud to fatten his purse. He used trickery to enlarge his treasures of money. As a Roman tax collector, he would stoop to all sorts of wickedness and stop at no righteous barrier to get money, to have money, and to hoard money.

For a Jew to become a publican meant disfranchisement and social ostracism. He was regarded as a henchman for Rome. Such conduct took on the appearance of treason. So Jericho treated Zacchaeus as a contagious person. He was deeply despised, a man held in deep disrepute. His very name brought a hiss to the mouths of the people.

In the Gospels two words travel in company—**publican** and **sinner**. And when the Pharisees wished to speak contemptuously of Jesus, they accused Him of friendship with publicans and sinners.

Not only was Zacchaeus a publican, but he was also the chief among the publicans. Shrewdest thief among thieves! Crookedest crook of all the crooks! He was the chief publican—the polluted river among smaller streams of pollution that defiled the community. Zacchaeus was a great sinner indeed—a sinner who did "evil with both hands earnestly" (Micah 7:3). Sin had wrought its folly, devastation, and the death in his life. His heart had grown hard under the daily practice and hourly belief that a man's life consists in the abundance of things which he possesses. Sin had made his soul grow lean while his pocketbook grew fat. Covetousness and greed did inhabit his blood.

Zacchaeus was rich. He had many servants and an abundance of money. He had a fine house, fine foods aplenty, and orchards and fields. But yet, he was poor. He had good clothes, but he had a bad heart beneath the clothes. With all he fed his stomach, he let his soul starve. He had an evil conscience. He could not live with himself. Being covetous, he was guilty of idolatry. Loving money much, he loved God little, if at all, and regarded not the distress of man.

C. A Short Man (v. 3)

3. And he sought to see Jesus who he was; and could not for the press, because he was little of stature.

Zacchaeus was little of stature—physically. He was what we would call a runt. He wore a small hat. He wore small shoes or sandals. He wore small clothes. By all measuring rods he was not tall. Randy Newman's song "Short People" fits him perfectly. The signature of physical littleness was written all over him. But he was more truly and tragically little in spiritual force, in moral sympathy, in tenderheartedness, in gracious generosity, in square dealing. The reservoir of his life held and ran only polluted water. Chief! Rich! Little! That describes Zacchaeus when we consider the publican, when we think of money matters, when we look at his physical stature.

It is interesting that this man who was so wrapped up in himself turned his attention to another, even Jesus. I suppose that he was at his tax collector's booth when he looked down the street and saw a large crowd gathered. Someone must have told him that the man who claimed to be the Messiah, the Christ, had come to town. He had heard enough about this man that he wanted to investigate matters for himself. So he left his booth wanting to see Jesus, who He was. He came to the multitude crowded around Jesus. But, being small of stature, he could not see Him for the crowd. Maybe some of those in the crowd hissed at him or pushed him about with their elbows or deliberately stepped upon his feet. No doubt, Satan, the enemy of men's souls, tried to get him to believe that Jesus was just a weak-minded enthusiast and fanatic. Anyway, Zacchaeus "wanted to see Jesus who he was"—and was willing to lose money to learn more about Him. However, He could not get to Jesus for the press, the crowd of people.

For all his faults, his quest to see Jesus was a noble venture for Zacchaeus. It is always a move in the right direction when one turns toward Christ.

November 30, 1980

II. OVERCOMING OBSTACLES (Luke 19:4-7)

A. The Command (vv. 4, 5)

4. And he ran before, and climbed up into a sycomore tree to see him: for he was to pass that way.

5. And when Jesus came to the place, he looked up, and saw him, and said unto him, Zacchaeus, make haste, and come down; for to day I must abide at thy house.

Zacchaeus was determined to see Jesus. He would not allow difficulties to distract him from his purpose. He would not let obstacles defeat him. He meant to see Jesus. He went to see Jesus. He spent time to see Jesus. It would have been very easy for him to justify himself in giving up on this project. He could have reasoned that he was too short, that the effort was too frustrating, that it was just no use for him to persist in trying to see Jesus. He would not, however, make his first effort to see Jesus his only effort and his last effort to see Him. He was little of stature, but a little man can run. He was a physical runt, but a runt can climb. So down the road he ran, and up the sycamore tree he climbed. Then down the road from among the tree's branches he looked—hoping to see Jesus.

It is probable that Zacchaeus was not alone in that tree. The boys of old time were no doubt just like the boys of the present age. They, too, were perched on the boughs of the tree to look at Jesus as He passed along. So here is this old man sitting among the branches of the tree with the boys. With anxiety he is peeping down to see which is Christ, for He is dressed just like those around Him. He has a coat like that of a common peasant, made of one piece from top to bottom; and Zacchaeus can scarcely distinguish Him. However, before he has caught a sight of Jesus, Christ has fixed His eye upon him, and standing under the tree, He looks up and calls Zacchaeus by name, telling him to come down from the tree.

Jesus' call to Zacchaeus was a personal call. Had He looked up into the tree and said, "Come down," all the boys perched on the limbs would have come down. Instead He pesonalized His call, "Zacchaeus, make haste and come down." God does not call His people in groups, but in units of one. At the tomb of Lazarus, Jesus did not call for all the dead to come forth, He called only for Lazarus. In the resurrection garden, He personalized His plea: "Jesus saith unto her, Mary; and she turned and said unto him, Rabboni, which is to say, Master" (John 20: 16, **paraphrased).** When Jesus saw Peter and Andrew fishing by the lake, He singled them out and said, "Follow me." When He saw Matthew sitting at the table at the receipt of customs, He said to him directly, "Arise, and follow me," and Matthew did so. When the Holy Spirit comes home to a man, God's arrow goes into his heart. It does not graze his helmet or make some little mark upon his armor; but it penetrates between the joints of the harness, entering the marrow of the soul. Was not God's call to you a personal call? Did not the Spirit strive with you personally?

Jesus' call to Zacchaeus was a call for immediate action. How many people seem to view the need of the soul as less than urgent! Men make haste to lay up treasures on earth not realizing that treasures in heaven are the greatest treasures. Others make haste to write their names on the scrolls of fame, make haste to dance to the music of self-indulgence, make haste to chase the short-lived butterflies of pleasure, make haste to care for the body, but give little heed to the needs of the soul. Jesus reminds us: " 'Do not be afraid of those who kill the body but cannot kill the soul. Rather, be afraid of the one who can destroy both soul and body in hell' " (Matthew 10:28, **New International Version).** How we need to make haste to emphasize the things that matter most in time and in eternity, in life and in death.

Zacchaeus is called upon to humble himself, to come down. But if he obeys, he will be greatly rewarded. Jesus will go home with him and will abide in his house.

B. The Response (v. 6)

6. And he made haste, and came down, and received him joyfully.

Zacchaeus obeyed the Lord's command and with haste came down from the tree to receive Jesus. Zacchaeus came down from earth's tree to receive Jesus who came down from heaven's throne. At the foot of the sycamore tree they stood—a seeking sinner and a seeking Savior—face to face, eye to eye, hand to hand, soul to soul. Here stands the most unlikely person in Jericho to receive Christ into his house. Is it not true that the person we consider least likely to recieve the Savior is sometimes the first one to accept Him?

It is important to note that Zacchaeus received Christ. He did not receive a creed, an ordinance, or a doctrine; he received a person. He received Christ as his guest, and he entertained Him. Will you so receive Christ—giving Him your heart, your love, yourself—letting Him come and find meat and drink for His love within your soul? Zacchaeus received Christ as his Lord. He proved this by his actions. He was ready to give to the poor and to make restoration where he had wronged anyone. By your actions also you demonstrate that you have made Christ your Lord and Master. Zacchaeus also admitted Christ as his Savior. If you do not accept Him in His character as Savior, you reject Him altogether. He cannot be separated from the merit of His blood and the love of His heart toward guilty sinners. The Christ of reality "is come to seek and to save that which was lost." He must be received by us in that character if He is to be received at all.

Zacchaeus received Christ joyfully. Think what joy there ought to be in the heart that receives Christ into it. First of all, what an honor it is! Frail creatures that we are, the Lord of glory comes and dwells in us. Why, this is an honor even the angels do not know. Next, when Jesus comes into the heart, He comes to put away all sin. Whenever Christ is received, all the guilt of the past is blotted out and gone, never to be remembered anymore. When you receive Christ, you receive full remission of all your sin; every transgression goes into complete oblivion. Also, when you receive Christ, you receive the fountain of inward purity, the wellspring of cleansing which shall overflow unto ultimate perfection.

C   The Obedience (v. 7)

7. And when they saw it, they all murmured, saying, That he was gone to be guest with a man that is a sinner.

Can you imagine how the faces of the multitude changed when Jesus said that He was going to stay at Zacchaeus' house? They thought Christ to be the holiest and best of men and were ready to make Him a king. But He said, "Today I must stay at your house." Perhaps there were some Jews present who had been to that house. They had been summoned in the name of justice. Their conception of it was something like what a fly would have for a spider's web after he had once escaped from it. There were others who had lost nearly all their property; and the idea they had of walking in there was like walking into a den of lions. Among themselves they must have asked, "Is this holy Man going into such a den as that, where we have been robbed and ill-treated? It is bad enough for Jesus to speak to him up in the tree, but the very idea of going into his house!" They all murmured at His going to be "a guest with a man who was a sinner."

Even some of His disciples thought that His action was very imprudent. They thought that it might injure His character and that He might offend the people. They reasoned that it would have been much better if He had chosen to visit this man at night, like Nicodemus, and give him an audience when nobody saw Him. In their opinion, to publicly acknowledge such a man was the most imprudent act He could commit.

So, why did Jesus encounter Zacchaeus publicly? What the Jews did not understand and what His own disciples did not fully grasp was that Jesus was motivated by love. He was not going to Zacchaeus' house because he deserved His presence or merited such a visit; He was going out of love for an eternal soul. Jesus was fully aware of all the evil that had been dispensed from that house. He was fully conscious of the unpopular nature of such a visit. And yet He was drawn to this house out of love for the soul of this man. Wasn't that why He visited your house? What have you ever done that would merit a call from such a regal guest? Was it not love that drew Him to you and caused Him to bring new life into your home?

III. RESPONDING TO CHRIST (Luke 19:8-10)

A. Restitution (v. 8)

8. And Zacchaeus stood, and said unto the Lord; Behold, Lord, the half of my goods I give to the poor; and if I have taken any thing from any man by false accusation, I restore him fourfold.

To what extent should a convert go to rectify dishonest acts of the past?

Perhaps the presence of an unexpected guest caused a flutter at the house of Zacchaeus. Maybe Mrs. Zacchaeus was upset by the unannounced entrance of so dignified a guest. There may have been frantic efforts to "tidy up" the house before He entered.

I am certain of this, the servants never ministered to a greater guest. This self-invited guest talked of something more important than political matters, financial success, tax gathering, social favor, and fine furnishings. As Jesus fed His body on Zacchaeus' bread, He fed the soul of Zacchaeus on the bread of heaven—causing him to hunger and thirst after righteousness. When it was time for Jesus to go, Zacchaeus stood and said something to Him. Jesus listened with great joy to every word he spoke. Every word was as music in the Master's ears.

First, Zacchaeus said that he was going to give half of his goods to the poor. Can you imagine that? All that we have seen in this man so far is greed. And now he stands to tell the Lord that he is going to give to the poor that which he has so eagerly gathered to himself. And he spoke with determination. There is a touch in the original language which does not come out in the English. The word translated "stood" shows a man with tense muscles and set jaws, taking a deep breath as he turns to a new life. Jesus had touched Zacchaeus' experience and touched it hard enough to reach his bank account. When a man begins immediately to talk about using his money for the good of others, who can doubt the genuineness of his conversion?

Second, Zacchaeus said that he was going to repay fourfold any amount he had taken falsely. The extreme penalty exacted by Hebrew law for theft was fourfold restitution—that is, the criminal was compelled to restore to the plaintiff four times the value of the stolen goods. No one had accused Zacchaeus of theft. Upon his own motion he pleaded guilty. He was his own judge and imposed his own sentence. And the sentence was 400 percent —the extreme penalty reserved for the worst sort of villain. Then, after he had made amends, Zacchaeus was to give half of his residue to the poor.

The rich, young ruler went away from Jesus sorrowfully. Zacchaeus went the Jesus way happily. At one leap, Zacchaeus scaled higher heights than all the years of prayer-mumbling and tithing had secured for the rulers of Israel. He was so far above them that a telescope would not have discovered the mountain upon whose summit he sat.

B. Salvation (v. 9)

9. And Jesus said unto him, This day is salvation come to this house, forsomuch as he also is a son of Abraham.

All of us have days in our lives that are special. Birthdays, anniversaries, and days of special consequence we mark on our calendar to remember. But there is one day that should stand above all other days in importance to us. It is the day when we met Jesus; the day when salvation came to our house. That day had arrived for Zacchaeus. It was the happiest day of his life. Is that how you regard the day of your conversion?

Salvation came to Zacchaeus immediately. This great work was wrought in his soul in a single moment. How typical this is of how salvation comes to every believer. Its working in a man may not only be performed this day, this hour, or this quarter of an hour, but this minute, or even this second.

It was obvious to Zacchaeus, to Jesus, and to those who were present that a change had come into his life. There is no way that a man can be saved and not be aware of the great change that has been worked in him. God the Holy Spirit is willing and waiting to give the full assurance of faith and of understanding to those who seek it at His hands.

Although Zacchaeus was aware that salvation had come to his heart, it is doubtful that he fully understood all that meant to him. While he enjoyed the thrill of the new birth, he probably did not feel the full impact of the blessings that would come to him as he continued in service for Christ. One of the benefits of the Christian life is the constant discovery of new blessings. Each day brings new joy and satisfaction.

Christ's statement gives every indication that the members of Zacchaeus' household also believed. They were not converted on the basis of his faith, only he was. But they could have and probably did believe for themselves. His wife, his children, his servants—all committed to Christ, all beginning a new venture together.

C. Redemption (v. 10)

10. For the Son of man is come to seek and to save that which was lost.

What a gracious mission Christ undertook. It was a mission of pure mercy, and indescribable love. Our Lord Jesus Christ did not come into the world to seek His own honor, but He came to seek and to save the lost. He did not come to get anything for Himself, but He came to give everything to those who are lost. There was no law, except His own love, to compel Christ to come to save sinners. They had no claim on Him. When He resolved to come, it was an act of matchless mercy. If

He had not chosen to come, He would still have been the ever-blessed Son of the Highest, enshrined in glory everlasting though every one of us had perished. His coming was infinite goodness, returning good for evil, coming down to our lost estate, and determining, by superabundant affection, to save us from it.

Let us never forget that Jesus came to save the lost—not to save the good and the excellent. What pictures that word **lost** brings to the mind!—a lost ship with waves beating it, the crew leaving it, and the darkness enveloping it; a lost child unable to find its way home, crying bitterly; a lost man with chart and compass gone, character weakened, will impaired, and all ahead of him hopelessness and despair; a lost woman with everything which makes life worth living gone. The lost—these are they that Christ came in search of; these are thay that He seeks to save.

Jesus came to this world a seeking Savior. From His first infant step to His last step in manhood, when He fainted beneath the weight of the Cross, He was seeking the lost. He has been doing so ever since. He seeks by means of a mother's prayers, a father's influence, a preacher's sermon, a verse of Scripture, a strain of sweet music, and in many other ways.

REVIEW QUESTIONS

1. What kind of a man was Zacchaeus?

2. How did Zacchaeus give evidence of his being a recipient of salvation?

3. How did the people react to Jesus' being a guest of Zacchaeus?

4. What assurance did Zacchaeus get from the Lord?

5. What applications do you draw from today's lesson?

GOLDEN TEXT HOMILY

"FOR THE SON OF MAN IS COME TO SEEK AND TO SAVE THAT WHICH WAS LOST" (Luke 19:10).

One of the most powerful impressions Augustine's **Confessions** leaves on the mind is that even more than he was seeking God, God was seeking him. It is this which gives to the **Confessions,** from one point of view the most subjective of books, so true an objectivity. At almost every stage in the narrative he pauses to emphasize this.

The unseen hand of God sometimes guides us even though we are unaware of His guidance. What seems at first to be a matter of chance often proves to be the providence of God in our life. But the most vivid evidence of divine intervention in the world of humanity is in the person of God's Son, Jesus Christ. The Son of Man came into this world for the sole purpose of seeking and saving that which was lost. Even before the lost could begin seeking the Lord, He was seeking them.

Only in Christ can we have that which was lost in the fall of man restored. But through Christ the restoration of that which was lost is total and complete.—**Homer G. Rhea, Jr., Editorial Administrative Assistant, Church of God Publishing House, Cleveland, Tennessee**

SENTENCE SERMONS

SALVATION MAY COME quietly, but we cannot remain quiet about it.
—**Selected**

THE RECOGNITION OF SIN is the beginning of salvation.
—**Martin Luther**

THE BLOCK OF GRANITE, which was an obstacle in the path of the weak, becomes a stepping-stone in the path of the strong.
—**Thomas Carlyle**

GOD WILL MAKE a way for the one who perseveres in following Him.
—**Selected**

EVANGELISTIC APPLICATION

GOD WILL REMOVE ALL OBSTACLES TO SALVATION AND BLESSING FOR THOSE WHO EARNESTLY SEEK HIM.

Two people in or near Jericho have found Christ. For one of them, Bartimaeus, He opened up a world of sight; for the other, Zacchaeus, He opened up a world of light. Both of them came to Christ in spite of the obstacles they faced. Bartimaeus was not stopped by his blindness nor by the opposition of the crowd; Zacchaeus did not let his shortness nor the hostility of the people keep him from Jesus. No matter what the nature of an obstacle may be, it cannot keep one away from Christ if that person is determined to meet Him.

The great need is for sinners to obey Christ's command and to make haste to come to Him for salvation. Every obstacle can be overcome and peace can be found by the seeking soul. What could make a more beautiful picture than a seeking sinner and a seeking Savior. The search is not a one-way experience. The Savior desires the conversion of the sinner. He demonstrated His desire by giving His life for the lost. The least the sinner can do is to yield to His grace that He may give to him newness of life.

ILLUMINATING THE LESSON

J. P. Bosovich, manager of a Robert Hall clothing store in Grand Rapids, Michigan was surprised when he opened a letter and found a check for payment for two sweaters which a woman had stolen. He was even more surprised when the woman gave her name and address in an Ohio town, and offered to send more money if she had not sent enough. "This is the first time I've had this happen to me since I've been in the clothing business," said Bosovich. The woman concluded her letter by saying: "The Lord has saved me and has made me a new person."

—**Walter B. Knight**

DAILY DEVOTIONAL GUIDE

M. God Is Our Salvation. Isaiah 12:1-6
T. Believing Brings Eternal Life. John 3:1-15
W. The Father's Love. John 3:16-21
T. Salvation Offered to Everyone. Acts 10:30-35
F. Developing Christian Graces. Colossians 3:12-17
S. Our Great Salvation. Hebrews 7:23-28

INTRODUCTION TO WINTER QUARTER

The lessons for the winter quarter (December, January, February) continue and conclude a study of the life of Christ that was begun with the spring quarter 1980. Based on the Gospels of Matthew, Mark, Luke, and John the series of studies acquaints us with incidents in the earthly life of our lovely Lord.

One would expect that a person so important as that of the Lord Jesus Christ would have had many volumes written about Him in His time. He was observed by thousands of persons as He walked among men and did marvelous deeds. As a matter of fact, the amount of information concerning Him is comparatively meager. Aside from the four Gospels, and a few scattered allusions in the Epistles, history is almost silent concerning the greatest life that ever lived.

Perhaps it is because there is such precious little information about Jesus that we return again and again to the Gospels to glean what new insights one might gain from a study of these chapters. For the thirsting soul desiring to know more about Jesus, these lessons will be refreshing and filling.

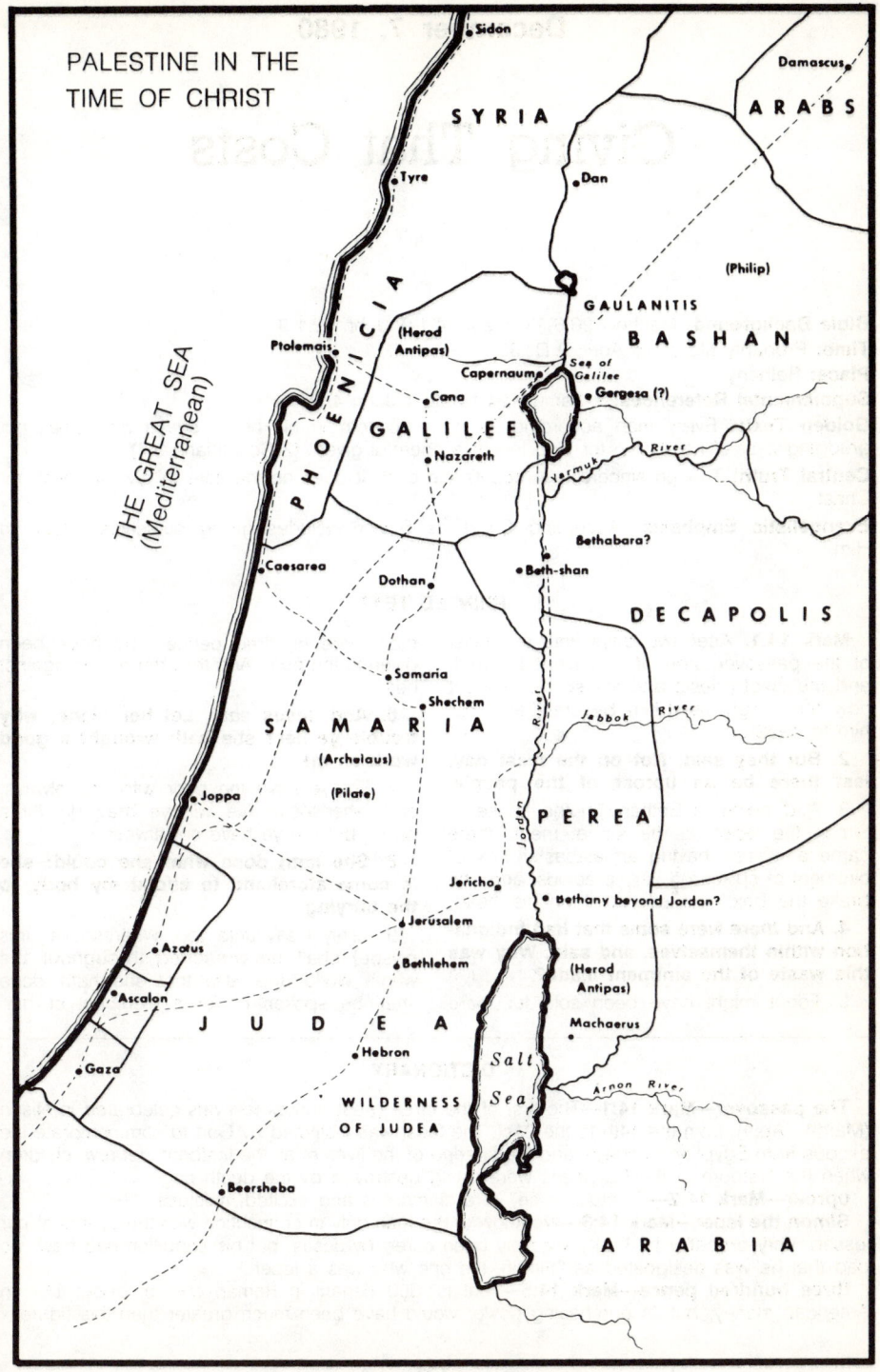

Used by permission of Gospel Publishing House.

December 7, 1980

Giving That Costs

Bible Background: Matthew 26:6-13; Mark 14:1-9; John 12:1-9
Time: Probably March or April, A.D. 30
Place: Bethany
Supplemental References: 2 Samuel 24:18-25; 1 John 4:16-19
Golden Text: "Every man according as he purposeth in his heart, so let him give; not grudgingly, or of necessity: for God loveth a cheerful giver" (2 Corinthians 9:7).
Central Truth: Though sincere love counts the cost, it does not hesitate to give its best for Christ.
Evangelistic Emphasis: Accepting Christ as Savior includes giving ourselves totally to Him.

PRINTED TEXT

Mark 14:1. After two days was the feast of the passover, and of unleavened bread: and the chief priests and the scribes sought how they might take him by craft, and put him to death.

2. But they said, Not on the feast day, lest there be an uproar of the people.

3. And being in Bethany in the house of Simon the leper, as he sat at meat, there came a woman having an alabaster box of ointment of spikenard very precious; and she brake the box, and poured it on his head.

4. And there were some that had indignation within themselves, and said, Why was this waste of the ointment made?

5. For it might have been sold for more than three hundred pence, and have been given to the poor. And they murmured against her.

6. And Jesus said, Let her alone; why trouble ye her? she hath wrought a good work on me.

7. For ye have the poor with you always, and whensoever ye will ye may do them good: but me ye have not always.

8. She hath done what she could: she is come aforehand to anoint my body to the burying.

9. Verily I say unto you, Wheresoever this gospel shall be preached throughout the whole world, this also that she hath done shall be spoken of for a memorial of her.

DICTIONARY

The passover—Mark 14:1—The first of the three great annual festivals celebrated in Nisan (March—April), from the 14th to the 21st. The feast was instituted by God to commemorate the exodus from Egyptian bondage and the sparing of the lives of all the firstborn Hebrew children when the firstborn of the Egyptians were being destroyed by the death angel.

uproar—Mark 14:2—"Tumult, noise" of a clamorous and excited multitude.

Simon the leper—Mark 14:3—We know of the man only in connection with the events of our lesson. Very probably he had previously been cured by Jesus, but his condition had been so bad that he was designated as "Simon, the one who was a leper."

three hundred pence—Mark 14:5—That is, 300 denarii in Roman coin or about $54 in American money, but its purchasing power would have been much greater than this figure.

December 7, 1980

LESSON OUTLINE
I. LOVE-MOTIVATED GIVING
II. MISUNDERSTOOD VALUES
III. RECOGNITION OF LOVING SERVICE

LESSON EXPOSITION

INTRODUCTION

The life of Christ is central in any study of the Bible. All things that happened before the life of Christ were directed toward that event. All things that occurred afterwards were a reflection of it. The purpose of all Scripture was either to prepare man for the advent of Christ or to interpret the advent for man.

Of the four accounts of Christ's life, the Gospel according to Mark is the earliest and most primitive. It is generally believed that the Gospel according to Mark represents the views of Simon Peter, which were recorded by Mark. It is also generally believed that Mark's Gospel is the earliest of all accounts of the life of Christ; the other three accounts—Matthew, Luke, John—apparently were written and distributed later. All of this makes a study of the life of Christ in the Gospel according to Mark of great value to us. We are able to see in it the earliest and most succinct account of the life of our Lord. Very likely we are able to see His life through the eyes of His most prominent apostle, Simon Peter.

The event related in this lesson occurred as Jesus neared the end of His earthly life. Hostility against Him among the Jews had reached its height and the web of betrayal was already at work. Yet in this account we see the compassion and the concern of Jesus as He came into contact with those in need. Aware as He was of the criticism of the Jews, He nonetheless extended His mercy and love to those that other men despised. This was the very essence of His life on earth, the purpose for which He came to live among men.

I. LOVE-MOTIVATED GIVING (Mark 14:1-3)

1. After two days was the feast of the passover, and of unleavened bread: and the chief priests and the scribes sought how they might take him by craft, and put him to death.

The events described here occurred during Jesus' last days in Jerusalem. He had gone to Jerusalem to observe the Passover, but He would never leave again. There He would be betrayed and crucified.

The feast of the Passover had been instituted in Egypt and was commemorated in remembrance of the avenging angel's passing over the houses of the Israelites when he slew the firstborn of the Egyptians (see Exodus 12:1-27). The feast of the Passover lasted one day and was followed by seven days of unleavened bread. This commemorated the fact that the Jews had to leave Egypt in such haste that they ate unleavened bread, or flat loaves without the rising agent of leaven in them. The Passover was one of the most sacred of all Jewish holy days.

The chief priests and scribes conspired during this time of national religious observance to put Jesus to death. They were too blind and too prejudiced to know that the Passover they so religiously observed was but a foreshadow of Jesus himself. They worshiped the day and conspired to kill its purpose.

2. But they said, Not on the feast day, lest there be an uproar of the people.

The chief priests and scribes recognized the religious devotion of the people. They did not wish to arrest Jesus during the sacred season, for they feared the people might be aroused against them for violating the solemn time. There is no indication that the leaders were conscientious regarding the Passover and days of unleavened bread—only that they did not wish to arouse the hostility of then people. The only restraining influence on them was this fear; it does not seem that any fear of the Lord was in them. It is equally true today that the only restraint some leaders know is fear of losing their position or their popularity; they are not motivated by conscience or by a wholesome fear of God. When such men are religious men, as these were, the state of mankind is all the worse.

3. And being in Bethany in the house of Simon the leper, as he sat at meat, there came a woman having an alabaster box of ointment of spikenard very precious; and she brake the box, and poured it on his head.

Jesus was in Bethany, a small town about two miles from Jerusalem, at the time of these events. He was a guest in the home of a man named Simon, who is identified here as a leper. It is not likely that Simon was still afflicted with leprosy at the time of this lesson, but it is much more likely that he had once had leprosy and was now cured. Since the name Simon was so common among the Jews, the words **the leper** were probably used as a manner of identifying which Simon was being discussed. If he had been a leper at the time Jesus was in his house, the Lord would no doubt have healed him then. Certainly others would not have been around him, for lepers were unclean, unable to have contact with other persons.

As Jesus was having a meal with Simon and the gathered company, a woman made her way to Him and anointed Him as described here. She brought ointment in an alabaster box, opened it, and poured it upon Christ's head. Alabaster is a form of glasslike stone, frequently carved into vases, vials, and other containers. It is still widely used in the Holy Land. It was not the alabaster box that was precious, however, rather it was the ointment that the box contained. Spikenard was a fragrant essence from a plant by that name. When it is said here that she broke the box, we are not to understand that she crushed the container, but simply that she broke it open. Very likely the "breaking" of the alabaster box was a simple matter of opening it.

As was the custom in Palestine, those who ate at the table lay on couches beside it. They did not sit upright at a table in the way we do. They reclined at the side of the table as they ate. This would have caused Jesus' head to be low enough that the woman might easily pour the ointment upon Him.

II. MISUNDERSTOOD VALUES (Mark 14:4, 5)

4. And there were some that had indignation within themselves, and said, Why was this waste of the ointment made?

What is the proper attitude to have toward those who give of their very meager means to wealthy preachers and churches?

This question and criticism arose among the disciples. Two reasons indicate that it was Judas Iscariot who raised the objection, or spoke for the body of disciples. First, Judas is mentioned in verse 10, which follows the Lord's explanation of the event. Second, it was Judas who raised an objection on a similar occasion in the home of Mary, Martha, and Lazarus (John 12:1-8).

It is interesting that there were two similar incidents in the last days of the Lord. The incident recorded by John occurred six days before the Passover, and the account in Mark's Gospel happened only two days before the Passover. John's account occurred in the home of Lazarus; this incident happened in the home of Simon the leper. In John's account it was Mary who anointed the feet of Jesus; in this account an unnamed woman anointed His head. Both incidents happened in the town of Bethany; both involved a meal function; and both involved the use of precious ointment, which was questioned by certain disciples. However, some scholars believe the two accounts refer to the same incident.

5. For it might have been sold for more than three hundred pence, and have been given to the poor. And they murmured against her.

The criticism was against the woman who anointed the head of Jesus. It was stated that she could have sold the ointment and contributed its price to the poor. This was definitely contrived reasoning to cover the criticism. Three hundred pennyworth of charity to the poor would not make a dent into the need; once it was used the poor still would be equally poor. Such a meager offering could have done little to relieve the great distress of poverty. On the other hand, there was but one Lord and Savior. Use of the ointment to anoint His head was an act of worship which was both appropriate and everlasting. Jesus would speak effectively in the defense of the woman, but it is interesting that such insincere arguments are used by those who resist sincere acts of worship by others.

The same thing happens today when critics complain about the use of our means in the worship of the Lord. There are still some who talk much about charitable work instead of worshipful acts. It is true that the poor need to be blessed by the bounty of the rich. It is equally true that the best and most enduring way to benefit the poor is to spread the worship of Christ upon the earth.

III. RECOGNITION OF LOVING SERVICE (Mark 14:6-9)

6. And Jesus said, Let her alone; why trouble ye her? she hath wrought a good work on me.

Jesus rebuked the critical disciples and observed to them that the woman was acting in the divine will. Her act of worship had been an act of faith, and the Lord accepted the sincerity of her sacrifice. The three hundred pennyworth of ointment she poured upon His head was but a sacrifice of worship and adoration.

Her work was a good work because it was performed in worship of the Lord.

Her work was good work because it set an example of devotion and sacrifice.

Her work was a good work because her boldness was an example of faith and courage.

Her work was a good work because of its prophetic implications, even though the woman may not have been aware of them.

When we follow the impulses of our heart in matters of faith and devotion, we may frequently do things that are of greater importance and significance than we imagine. If the woman had been so hesitant and withdrawn that she failed to obey the impulse of her heart, she would have missed a great blessing, and all who have followed her would have missed a great example. She allowed her heart to direct her and thereby glorified the Lord.

7. For ye have the poor with you always, and whensoever ye will ye may do them good: but me ye have not always.

If those who had mentioned charity for the poor were sincere, they would have opportunity enough to demonstrate that concern. The poor have been on earth from the beginning of time and shall remain until the end of time. No device of man has been able to eliminate the misfortune of poverty. The Lord does not criticize, but rather demands concern and provision for the poor.

At this point, however, He pointed out the insincerity of the argument that the ointment should have been used for the poor. He was facing the Cross, and His earthly life would soon be over. Whatever act of worship was to be done toward Him must be done soon, for He would be taken away. The woman's act of faith had therefore been appropriate and opportune. The disciples could not have used the money to feed the poor with an explanation that they would sacrifice in worship to the Lord later. He would soon depart from them, and they would miss their opportunity forever. What was to be done toward Him must be done quickly, but the opportunity to relieve the poverty of the poor would remain forever.

8. She hath done what she could: she is come aforehand to anoint my body to the burying.

Without being aware of what she had done, the woman had prophetically pointed to the death and burial of Jesus. At death, persons of distinction were thoroughly anointed and wrapped in aromatic shrouds to inhibit the decay of their bodies. The pungent and pleasant smells of the ointment would counteract the offensive odors of the dead body. This was the common practice at the time of Jesus, so He stated here that the woman's act had been predictive of His imminent death.

In the same way the three Wise Men had brought gifts of prophetic significance when He was born; theirs had been the gifts given to a king, to a god, and for a person's burial. Naturally, the Wise Men were not aware of the prophetic significance of their gifts—they were simply giving items of great value. In the same way, this woman did not grasp the significance of what she had done—she simply performed an act of worship because of her gratitude to the Lord.

9. Verily I say unto you, Wheresoever this gospel shall be preached throughout the whole world, this also that she hath done shall be spoken of for a memorial of her.

Without mentioning her name, the Lord declared that the woman's act would forever be mentioned in tribute to her. It is altogether possible that many others had an impulse to that which the woman did, but timidity and uncertainty caused them to hold back. This woman obeyed the urgings of her heart and thereby secured for herself a permanent place in the record of the faithful.

The Lord implied here that His gospel would be preached throughout the whole world, emphasizing that this act of devotion would in all places be mentioned as an example of good works. The woman's act became a part of Holy Writ, and two thousand years later we are still reading about the generous and sincere devotion she manifested.

In the same way, many persons who have obeyed the impulses of their heart have been used of God, have advanced the cause of Christ, have blessed thousands of their fellowmen, and have secured for themselves a perpetual memorial. The Lord gave no praise to those who wanted to do good but held back because of fear or timidity; He praised only those who in faith obeyed the urgings of their heart. The same is true today. There is no praise to those who have a desire to do good but fail to act upon that desire; praise belongs to those who have both the desire to do good and the courage to act upon that desire. Those are the people the Lord can use.

REVIEW QUESTIONS

1. Why were the chief priests and scribes reluctant to take Jesus by craft and put him to death during the Feast of the Passover?
2. What made the woman's gift a true gift of love?
3. Discuss the response of Jesus to the gift of the woman.
4. Why was Judas disturbed about the anointing of Jesus with the precious ointment?
5. What motive prompted Judas to betray Jesus?

GOLDEN TEXT HOMILY

"EVERY MAN ACCORDING AS HE PURPOSETH IN HIS HEART, SO LET HIM GIVE; NOT GRUDGINGLY, OR OF NECESSITY: FOR GOD LOVETH A CHEERFUL GIVER" (2 Corinthians 9:7).

He who sows sparingly shall reap sparingly; and he who sows bountifully shall reap also bountifully. Every man according as he has purposed in his heart. Let him give, not grudgingly or because it is of a necessity: God loves a person who finds it a joy to give unto the Lord and His work. God is able to make all grace abound unto you so that you will have at all times a sufficiency of things.

He has given abroad and He has given to the poor. He that gives seed to the sower also gives bread for your food, multiplying what you have sown or given to increase the fruits of your righteousness. Being persons of plenty, being enriched in things, should cause us to be thankful to God. Through the love of God for the saints, we supply the needs of the saints. Because of our charitable giving with cheerfulness, the saints glorify God for our obedience unto the gospel of God (see 2 Corinthians 9:6-15).

They exalt your liberal distribution unto them and unto all men. They pray for you because of the exceeding grace of God within you, giving God glory for His unspeakable gift in proving the sincerity of your love.

He was rich, yet He became poor for our sake, showing His charity in giving abundantly of Himself that we might be supplied with necessities of our spiritual lives. Paul said in 2 Corinthians 8:12 that if there be a willingness of mind and a readiness of our will, then there would be a performance also. God did not intend for some of His saints to be burdened while others were eased. If we possess much we should share with others. And if we have little gathered, we shall have no lack. God has put into out hearts the cost of giving to others cheerfully, for the necessity of the saints (see Corinthians 8:8-15).—**Leroy Imperio, Pastor, Elkins, West Virginia**

SENTENCE SERMONS

IT WILL COST me to be loyal to Christ—but it will also pay.
—**Anonymous**

I HAVE HELD many things in my hands and lost them all; but whatever I have placed in God's hands, that I still possess.
—**Martin Luther**

THOUGH SINCERE LOVE counts the cost, it does not hesitate to give its best to Christ.
—**Selected**

LOVES SACRIFICES ALL things to bless the thing it loves.
—**Edward George Bulwer-Lytton**

EVANGELISTIC APPLICATION

ACCEPTING CHRIST AS SAVIOR INCLUDES GIVING OURSELVES TOTALLY TO HIM.

DOES YOUR GIFT REPRESENT YOU?

It happened one time after a pastor had made an appeal in a church for a great and worthy cause, that a certain woman, a member of the church, came to him and handed him a check for $50, asking at the same time if her gift was satisfactory. The pastor immediately replied, "If it represents you." There was a moment of soul-searching thought and she asked to have the check returned to her. She left with it and a day or two later she returned, handing the pastor a check for $5,000 and again asking the same question, "Is my gift satisfactory?" The pastor gave the same answer as before, "If it represents you." As before, a truth seemed to be driving deeply. Later in the week she came again with a check. This time it was for $50,000. As she placed it in the pastor's hand she said, "After earnest, prayerful thought, I have come to the conclusion that this gift does represent me and I am happy to give it." Perhaps in this light the words **as God hath prospered him** from 1 Corinthians 16:2 may take on new meaning.

—John Allen Lavendar
from **Stewardship Illustrations**

ILLUMINATING THE LESSON

A widow woman turned in a pledge card

during a mission service stating that she would give ten dollars per month for missions. When her pastor saw the card, he came to the speaker and said the lady must have made a mistake. She had really meant to give ten dollars annually. The speaker told the pastor to ask the lady what she really meant. The pastor discovered, to his surprise, that the lady did mean to give ten dollars per month. The pastor knew what he had pledged. He could not understand how a woman with so little could do so much. He was measuring sacrifice by what he was doing and did not want to believe that a poor woman would give so much. Our love to Christ is not shown by what we claim to be; it is shown by our giving—sacrificially.

DAILY DEVOTIONAL GUIDE

M. Offerings Needed. Exodus 35:4-19

T. Responding Willingly. Exodus 36:1-7

W. Paying Our Way. 1 Chronicles 21:18-27

T. The Value of Gifts. Mark 12:41-44

F. The Greatest Gift. John 3:14-21

S. Pattern for Giving. 2 Corinthians 9:1-15

December 14, 1980

Welcoming Christ

Bible Background: Psalm 118:1-29; Matthew 21:1-11; Mark 11:1-11; Luke 19:28-44; John 12:12-19
Time: Probably April, A.D. 30
Place: Jerusalem
Supplemental References: 1 Samuel 10:20-27; 2 Samuel 19:9-40; Revelation 3:20-22
Golden Text: "Blessed be the King that cometh in the name of the Lord" (Luke 19:38).
Central Truth: Life is triumphant when we welcome Christ as King of our life.
Evangelistic Emphasis: Every person needs to welcome Christ as Savior and Lord of his life.

PRINTED TEXT

Psalm 118:19. Open to me the gates of righteousness: I will go into them, and I will praise the Lord:

20. This gate of the Lord, into which the righteous shall enter.

21. I will praise thee: for thou hast heard me, and art become my salvation.

22. The stone which the builders refused is become the head stone of the corner.

23. This is the Lord's doing; it is marvellous in our eyes.

24. This is the day which the Lord hath made; we will rejoice and be glad in it.

25. Save now, I beseech thee, O Lord: O Lord, I beseech thee, send now prosperity.

26. Blessed be he that cometh in the name of the Lord: we have blessed you out of the house of the Lord.

27. God is the Lord, which hath shewed us light: bind the sacrifice with cords, even unto the horns of the altar.

28. Thou art my God, and I will praise thee: thou art my God, I will exalt thee.

29. O give thanks unto the Lord; for he is good: for his mercy endureth for ever.

John 12:12. On the next day much people that were come to the feast, when they heard that Jesus was coming to Jerusalem,

13. Took branches of palm trees, and went forth to meet him, and cried, Hosanna: Blessed is the King of Israel that cometh in the name of the Lord.

14. And Jesus, when he had found a young ass, sat thereon; as it is written,

15. Fear not, daughter of Sion: behold, thy King cometh, sitting on an ass's colt.

16. These things understood not his disciples at the first: but when Jesus was glorified, then remembered they that these things were written of him, and that they had done these things unto him.

17. The people therefore that was with him when he called Lazarus out of his grave, and raised him from the dead, bare record.

18. For this cause the people also met him, for that they heard that he had done this miracle.

19. The Pharisees therefore said among themselves, Perceive ye how ye prevail nothing? behold, the world is gone after him.

DICTIONARY

Hosanna—John 12:13—A translation from the Hebrew which means "save we pray" and quoted from Psalm 118:25

December 14, 1980

Lazarus—John 12:17—The brother of Martha and Mary who lived in Bethany
Pharisees (FAIR-uh-sees)—John 12:19—One of the three prominent societies of Judaism at the time of Christ. Of the three—Pharisees, Sadducees, and Essenes—the Pharisees were by far the most influential.

LESSON OUTLINE
I. CHRIST, WORTHY OF PRAISE
II. CHRIST, FULFILLMENT OF PROPHECY
III. CHRIST, KNOWN FOR HIS POWER

LESSON EXPOSITION
INTRODUCTION

During His last visit to the Jerusalem area, Christ spent several days in the small town of Bethany, about two miles away. We have the record that during His days in Bethany He attended two social functions (meals at the house of Lazarus and of Simon the leper), at each of which a woman anointed Him in an act of worship. The two incidents were similar, but different. In Lazarus' house, it was Mary who anointed His feet. In Simon's house, an unnamed woman anointed His head. The result of the two incidents was much the same, with criticism by the apostles and an explanation by Jesus. In each of the two instances He pointed out that He had been anointed for the time of His death.

In this lesson we see Him make the short journey from Bethany into Jerusalem. It is the final stage of His journey toward the Cross. Opposition to Him had reached its peak among the Jewish leaders, and the seeds of conspiracy had already been sown in the heart of Judas. The people of Israel loved Jesus and worshiped Him, as this lesson reveals. They brought great praise to Him and worshiped Him as their king.

I. CHRIST, WORTHY OF PRAISE (John 12:12, 13)

12. On the next day much people that were come to the feast, when they heard that Jesus was coming to Jerusalem,

The day following His visit in Bethany, Jesus and His disciples made the short journey to Jerusalem. The Holy City was filled with people because of the Passover feast. Each year Jews came to Jerusalem from all parts of the world to celebrate the feast. It was one of the holiest times of the Jewish year and multitudes came for the celebration. It was, in fact, customary for Jews to come to Jerusalem for the celebration of all holy days, such as the Feast of Pentecost (Acts 2:5-11).

13. Took branches of palm trees, and went forth to meet him, and cried, Hosanna: Blessed is the King of Israel that cometh in the name of the Lord.

The fame of Jesus had gone throughout Palestine, where most of the Jews had heard of Him and His wondrous works. Jews from other parts of the world no doubt heard about Him when they came into the Holy City. Now word raced through the city that Jesus was coming into Jerusalem. The people broke palm branches from trees that grew plentifully in Jerusalem and waved the fronds in joy and greetings. Jesus came around the slope of the Mount of Olives, where He would cross the Kidron Valley and make the ascent into Jerusalem.

The people hailed Jesus with the word **Hosanna**, which means "I entreat you to save me" or "I ask you for salvation." They declared Him to be the king of Israel, One who had come in the name of the Lord. This means that they fully accepted Him to be the Messiah of God. The Messiah would be king, and He would come in the name of the Father.

The joyous declaration that Jesus was king of Israel, the One sent of the Father, did not escape the attention of the Pharisees and other enemies of Christ. The jubilant crowds were not intimidated by the enmity and disbelief of their religious leaders, for they recognized Christ to be of a higher identity and authority than any of their Jewish leaders. Adam Clarke says: "Both the words and actions of the people prove that they acknowledged Christ as their king, and looked to Him for deliverance. How easily might He have assumed the sovereignty at this time, had He been so disposed." With such enthusiastic acceptance, Jesus could easily have claimed His Kingship at that time. The people would have supported Him in gaining the throne.

II. CHRIST, FULFILLMENT OF PROPHECY
(Psalm 118:19, 20; John 12:14-16)

Psalm 118:19. Open to me the gates of righteousness: I will go into them, and I will praise the Lord:

20. This gate of the Lord, into which the righteous shall enter.

This Psalm is clearly one of the Messianic Psalms, those that speak in a prophetic way about the Messiah. It should be read in its entirety, for it speaks unmistakably about Christ and His human experience.

Verses 10-13 speak about the opposition that He would face. Unbelievers of all lands surrounded Him like bees in their multitude and anger. Yet the Lord would attain final and complete victory. The result would be triumphal entry through the gates of righteousness. The gates mentioned in these verses refer to the gates of Jerusalem, the Holy City, even the gate of the Temple itself.

The Lord would enter the city in righteousness. The Jews had expected their Messiah to come with great military and political power, with which He would expel all of Israel's enemies from the land. Yet when the Messiah did come, He came in peace and righteousness, to establish a spiritual kingdom.

Verse 22 says, "The stone which the builders refused is become the head stone of the corner." Israel as a nation rejected the Messiah, who is the chief cornerstone of all salvation. The word **Hosanna** is actually a prayer for salvation. The people of the land received the Messiah as is described in this lesson, but the national leaders rejected Him and thereby suffered great loss.

John 12:14. And Jesus, when he had found a young ass, sat thereon; as it is written,

While John simply tells us that Jesus found a young ass and sat thereon, Matthew 21 tells us the circumstances by which Jesus came to have the lowly beast of burden. He sent two of his disciples into the village of Bethphage and told them where they would find an ass and her colt tied. The disciples were instructed to "loose them and bring them unto me." In the event someone should ask them what they were doing they should say, "The Lord hath need of them," whereupon the owner would send the beast to Him. It is obvious that Jesus knew the whereabouts of the ass and her colt. The entire act was a fulfillment of prophecy.

The Lord entered Jerusalem riding upon an ass as a manifestation of His humility and peace. The Jews had expected their Messiah to come riding a mount of war, going forth to battle, vanquishing all foes. Their image of Him was one of military might, leading the forces of Israel in combat against all who opposed the Hebrew people. Instead, He would enter the Holy City riding upon a lowly and common beast of labor.

15. Fear not, daughter of Sion: behold, thy King cometh, sitting upon an ass's colt.

The quotation here is from Zechariah 9:9, which says, "Rejoice greatly, O daughter of Zion; shout, O daughter of Jerusalem: behold, thy King cometh unto thee: he is just, and having salvation; lowly, and riding upon an ass, and upon a colt the foal of an ass."

In his commentary on the Gospel of John, Alvah Hovey says: "The freedom with which the inspired writers of the New Testament treat the text of the Old Testament—sometimes quoting it with verbal accuracy, sometimes condensing two clauses into one, sometimes changing the tense of a verb to bring out more clearly its prophetic pertinency, and sometimes giving an implied thought for the one expressed—is by no means inconsistent with the highest reverence for the divine authority of that volume. This they uniformly show by the manner in which they refer to the ancient Scriptures. And so far as we can judge, they never attribute to an Old Testament writer any thought foreign to his language, or, indeed, any thought that is not fairly implied in his language. In this passage, it appears that the expression 'fear not' is substituted for 'rejoice.' "

16. These things understood not his disciples at the first: but when Jesus was glorified, then remembered they that these things were written of him, and that they had done these things unto him.

Even though they were witness to them, the disciples did not grasp the significance of the events they saw that day. The enthusiasm and the jubilation of the people no doubt overwhelmed them, and they were impressed with the great reception their Lord received. It would take some time, however, for them to grasp the full significance of what happened on that day.

It is not at all unusual for a person to become so absorbed in the events of the moment that he fails to grasp their significance at the time. How often today we look back upon things that happened to us, or around us, and realize only now how important the events really were.

Regarding still another event, Jesus would say, "What I do thou knowest not now; but thou shalt know hereafter" (John 13:7).

There were numerous things about the final

days of Jesus that the disciples could not understand. After His death and resurrection, however, they would meditate upon these things and understand their meaning. We have similar statements in other places: "When therefore he was risen from the dead, his disciples remembered that he had said this unto them; and they believed the scripture, and the word which Jesus had said" (John 2:22).

The revelation of Jesus Christ, and the full impact of His life upon the earth, was too great for any human being to comprehend immediately. Today, we have had nearly two thousand years to consider the events of His life, and we have heard all of our lives how He was the Son of God, the King of Israel, Messiah, our Lord and Master. Many of the things that occurred while He was alive, however, were too wonderful, too different, too strange for His disciples to comprehend instantly. Full understanding would come to them in later days as they meditated upon the things they had witnessed.

III. CHRIST, KNOWN FOR HIS POWER (John 12:17-19)

17. The people therefore that was with him when he called Lazarus out of his grave, and raised him from the dead, bare record.

There were some present who had witnessed all that Jesus did from the time He raised Lazarus from the dead. That event in Bethany (John 11:45) had gained the attention of the entire region. Everywhere Jesus went He was noted as the one who had restored Lazarus to life. The implication of this verse is that many of the things recorded here—the praise and worship, the shouts of Hosanna, the welcome as a king, the acceptance as the Messiah—were related to the raising of Lazarus from the dead. The words "bare record" mean that the people had continually borne witness to the great miracle of raising the dead. It means that there was an ongoing, unending process of praise and witness that stemmed from that event.

18. For this cause the people also met him, for that they heard that he had done this miracle.

Since the raising of Lazarus attracted so much attention, why doesn't the Lord manifest His power by such miracles today?

The people of the region had not failed to let the visitors in Jerusalem know what a great miracle Jesus had performed. They no doubt let the people know that they had been witness to the great and undeniable demonstration of divine power. The result was dramatic and electric: the people met Jesus with rejoicing, beseeching Him for salvation. If He had the power to raise the dead to life again, then He had the power to set their twisted lives straight, and to give them fullness of life. Their hosannas were very real, for in the mouths of the many witnesses, Jesus was recognized to be the power of God. He was the King of Israel, He was the One that cometh in the name of the Lord.

The excitement and faith that had been generated by the raising of Lazarus can be seen in such statements as these: "But some of them went their ways to the Pharisees, and told them what things Jesus had done" (John 11:46). "Much people of the Jews therefore knew that he was there: and they came not for Jesus' sake only, but that they might see Lazarus also, whom he had raised from the dead" (John 12:9). Nothing that had ever happened in the region seems to have excited such enthusiasm and faith as had the raising of Lazarus.

19. The Pharisees therefore said among themselves, Perceive ye how ye prevail nothing? behold, the world is gone after him.

The Pharisees became resigned to the fact that in the eyes of the people Jesus was Lord and God. The Pharisees did not accept Him as such, but they admitted that He now had such loyalty and acceptance with the people. Nothing they could do now could stop this broad acceptance and worship. The only alternative would be to put Jesus to death. The Pharisees had somehow come to this conclusion at the time He raised Lazarus from the dead. "Then gathered the chief priests and the Pharisees a council, and said, What do we? for this man doeth many miracles" (John 11:47). "Then from that day forth they took counsel together for to put him to death" (John 11:53).

Because they were experienced men, the Pharisees knew that moderate efforts would no longer be enough to stop Jesus. If He had demonstrated the power to raise the dead to life again, then He himself must be put to death.

It is ironic and tragic that Jesus should be

received in Jerusalem on this occasion with such mixed emotions. The people of Israel received him with rejoicing, calling upon Him for salvation, while the religious leaders received Him with suspicion and enmity. One group would make Jesus King, the other would put Him to death. "He came unto his own, and his own received him not. But as many as received him, to them gave he power to become the sons of God, even to them that believe on his name" (John 1:11, 12).

REVIEW QUESTIONS

1. What is the meaning of the word "Hosanna?"
2. What mental attitude did Christ manifest by riding into Jerusalem on an ass?
3. At what point in the ministry of Christ did the chief priests and Pharisees determine to put Him to death?
4. How do you account for the mixed attitudes about Jesus when He rode into Jerusalem?
5. What prophecies concerning Christ were fulfilled in the events recorded in today's lesson?

GOLDEN TEXT HOMILY

"BLESSED BE THE KING THAT COMETH IN THE NAME OF THE LORD" (Luke 19:38).

The use of the word **king** in this place is perhaps more literal than the way in which we use the word in our worship today. The people lining the streets of Jerusalem were well acquainted with the concept of a king as ruler and master. Today we have a somewhat more abstract approach to the word. In this day we are more comfortable with presidents, prime ministers, premiers, and chairmen of boards than with kings.

The people of Israel, being under the harsh occupational rule of the Roman armies, knew that it was impossible for one of their number to call himself a king on the basis of governmental or political power. That would have been suicidal. The Romans were firmly in control, and no man could declare himself a king with political authority.

But Jesus did not come as a king exercising political authority. He came as a king in the name of the Lord! His claim to kingship was a spiritual claim, grounded in His godship, not in the might of arms or the cunning of political intrigue. He was a king not by virtue of earthly parentage, but by virtue of His divine nature and origin.

Blessed be Jesus Christ, King and Master, "the King that cometh in the name of the Lord"!

—Selected

SENTENCE SERMONS

WHAT THE SUNSHINE is to the flower, the Lord Jesus is to my soul; and I welcome Him.

—**Alfred Lord Tennyson**

LIFE IS TRIUMPHANT when we welcome Christ as King of our life.

—Selected

JESUS CHRIST IS a friend to sinners, but is welcomed as companion only by the godly.

—**"Speaker's Sourcebook"**

EVANGELISTIC APPLICATION

EVERY PERSON NEEDS TO WELCOME CHRIST AS SAVIOR AND LORD OF HIS LIFE.

When Jesus entered Jerusalem on that Palm Sunday, He entered it as God's Messiah. That was the meaning of the pageantry of that tumultuous hour, and He openly accepted the tribute. Most of the pilgrims who acclaimed Jesus with their hosannas were no doubt provincials, His own countrymen from Galilee in the north—an entirely different crowd from the city rabble which was to cry "Crucify Him" before the week was over. It must not be forgotten that even after the tide of popular sentiment had begun to set against Him, and indeed up to the very last, there were thousands of people to whom Jesus remained a friend and a hero—people whom He had healed of bodily diseases, families whose tangled homelife He had straightened out, men and women for whom spiritually He had made all things new. They brought their tribute to Him now. Amid the shouts of the welcoming throng the King rode toward His capital. "Blessed is he that cometh in the name of the Lord!"

By this act Jesus declared Himself. No longer, as at the beginning of His ministry, did He withdraw from the plaudits of the crowd. No longer, as in Galilean days, did He hold back the secret of his royal dignity from all save the initiated few. Ringing in His mind were the words of one of the great prophets of His people, words which often from His boyhood days He had pondered—"Rejoice greatly, O daughter of Zion; shout, O daughter of Jerusalem: behold, thy King cometh unto thee" (Zechariah 9:9). At last the old seer's dream had come true. Not forever should the throne of David stand vacant. By His action on that Palm Sunday, Jesus said in a way more plain than words, "Behold your King!"

—James S. Stewart, **The Life and Teaching of Jesus Christ**

ILLUMINATING THE LESSON

A train of cars was passing swiftly down the steep grade of the Alleghany Mountains, when the engineer discovered a little girl and her baby brother playing on the track just ahead. At this crisis, the girl discovered a niche in the side of the rock, into which she thrust the baby, and pressed herself; saying, as she did so, "Cling close to the rock, Johnny; cling close to the rock." The train thundered by, and they escaped unharmed. So amid the perils of life may the sinner hide in the "Rock of Ages."

All hail the power of Jesus' name!
Let angels prostrate fall;
Bring forth the royal diadem,
And crown Him Lord of all.
Let every kindred, every tribe
On this terrestrial ball,
To Him all majesty ascribe
And crown Him Lord of all.

—**Edward Perronet**

DAILY DEVOTIONAL GUIDE

M. Welcoming a Victor. 1 Samuel 18:1-7

T. Accepting a Leader. 2 Samuel 19:9-17

W. Receiving the Savior. Psalm 118:19-24

T. Praising the Redeemer. Psalm 118:5-29

F. Helping the Needy. Matthew 25:34-40

S. Loving the Stranger. 3 John 1:5-8

December 21, 1980

Wise Men Worship Christ

(Christmas)

Bible Background: Matthew 2:1-23
Time: Scholars differ on the time of the birth of Jesus, but it is generally considered to have been 4 or 5 B. C.
Place: Bethlehem
Supplemental References: Isaiah 9:1-7; Jeremiah 31:15; Hosea 11:1; Micah 5:1-15
Golden Text: "When they were come into the house, they saw the young child with Mary his mother, and fell down, and worshipped him" (Matthew 2:11).
Central Truth: It is a mark of wisdom when men seek a better understanding of God's revelation in Christ Jesus.
Evangelistic Emphasis: To turn to Christ and love and worship Him is true wisdom.

PRINTED TEXT

Matthew 2:1. Now when Jesus was born in Bethlehem of Judaea in the days of Herod the king, behold, there came wise men from the east to Jerusalem,

2. Saying, Where is he that is born King of the Jews? for we have seen his star in the east, and are come to worship him.

3. When Herod the king had heard these things, he was troubled, and all Jerusalem with him.

4. And when he had gathered all the chief priests and scribes of the people together, he demanded of them where Christ should be born.

5. And they said unto him, In Bethlehem of Judaea: for thus it is written by the prophet,

6. And thou Bethlehem, in the land of Juda, art not the least among the princes of Juda: for out of thee shall come a Governor, that shall rule my people Israel.

7. Then Herod, when he had privily called the wise men, enquired of them diligently what time the star appeared.

8. And he sent them to Bethlehem, and said, Go and search diligently for the young child; and when ye have found him, bring me word again, that I may come and worship him also.

9. When they had heard the king, they departed; and, lo, the star, which they saw in the east, went before them, till it came and stood over where the young child was.

10. When they saw the star, they rejoiced with exceeding great joy.

11. And when they were come into the house, they saw the young child with Mary his mother, and fell down, and worshipped him: and when they had opened their treasures, they presented unto him gifts; gold, and frankincense, and myrrh.

12. And being warned of God in a dream that they should not return to Herod, they departed into their own country another way.

DICTIONARY

Bethlehem (BETH-la-hem)—Matthew 2:1—In Hebrew it means "House of bread." Located about five miles south of Jerusalem, Bethlehem is one of the oldest towns in the Holy

December 21, 1980 135

Land and is mentioned many times in the Bible (Genesis 35:19, 20; Ruth 1:16-22; 1 Samuel 16:4, 5, 12, 13; 2 Samuel 23:14-17; Micah 5:2; Luke 2:10, 11).

Judaea (jew-DEE-uh)—Matthew 2:1—A territorial division of Palestine known in the Old Testament as Judah; that section of the nation Israel which remained loyal to the Davidic dynasty. In Jesus' day, it was the third district, west of the Jordan and south of Samaria.

Herod the king—Matthew 2:1—He was the son of Antipater, the Idumaean, and was known as Herod the Great. He was king over all Palestine from 37 B. C. to 4 B. C.

wise men—Matthew 2:1—A translation of the Greek word **magi,** it probably refers to the astrologers and students of the stars of the East. Since the Jews were scattered throughout Arabia, Persia, Media, and Chaldea at this time, these Magi perhaps learned of the predicted King from these dispersed Jews and their literature. Our word **magician** is derived from the Greek word **magi.**

chief priests—Matthew 2:4—Probably those who served in the office of high priest, as well as the heads of the courses into which the priests were divided

scribes—Matthew 2:4—The transcribers and teachers of the Law. Together with the chief priests and elders, the representatives of the scribes constituted the Sanhedrin. Most of them belonged to the party of the Pharisees and were the "wise men" among them.

frankincense—Matthew 2:11—The fragrant gum of a tree (Song of Solomon 3:6) grown on the limestone rocks of South Africa and Somaliland and used for making incense for burning in temples and for other ceremonial purposes

myrrh—Matthew 2:11—A fragrant substance produced from a tree grown in Arabia that is used for various purposes, including anointing of the priesthood, purification of women, anointing of the body, and embalming of the dead

---

LESSON OUTLINE

I. SEEKING GOD'S SON
II. WORSHIPING GOD'S SON
III. FOLLOWING GOD'S PLAN

LESSON EXPOSITION

INTRODUCTION

There are two rather detailed accounts of the birth of Jesus, one recorded by Matthew and the other by Luke. Mark and John make almost no mention of His birth. Neither is there any mention of the Savior's birth in the writings of Paul. In fact, no special note of His birth was made by the earliest Christians; the emphasis was almost entirely upon His death. Several hundred years would pass before His birth would be regarded as a point of spiritual and historical importance.

The two accounts of Christ's birth differ in many ways. For instance, the genealogy in Matthew seems to trace the earthly ancestry through Joseph, the earthly father of Jesus. The genealogy in Luke seems to follow the Davidic line through Mary, the mother of Jesus. In Matthew, the account of the birth places great emphasis on Joseph, whereas the Lucan account emphasizes Mary's role in the birth. Matthew emphasizes the religious implications of the birth as it has to do with the nation Israel and the throne of David. Luke's account is much more personal and mystical, with elaborate details on the feelings and circumstances of Mary. Naturally, both accounts are accurate and need to be read with equal acceptance and understanding. It requires attention to both accounts for the Holy Spirit to communicate to our mind the broad significance of Christ's birth on earth.

In this lesson, we look at the birth of Christ through the account of Matthew. God used the apostle and former tax collector to give a very insightful record of the most important birth the world has ever seen. Matthew's account takes into consideration the legal and official circumstances attached to the Holy Birth.

I. SEEKING GOD'S SON (Matthew 2:1-8)

1. Now when Jesus was born in Bethlehem of Judaea in the days of Herod the king, behold, there came wise men from the east to Jerusalem,

At the time of Jesus' birth, Bethlehem was a small town about five miles south of Jerusalem. It lay in the hill country of Judea, where shepherding was the principal occupation. It was in the vicinity of Bethlehem that Ruth and Boaz had met, and this was also the area from which the great King David had come. It was therefore very appropriate that Jesus should be born there. The word **Bethlehem** means "the house of bread," an appropriate name for the place where the True Bread from heaven was born into the world.

At the time of Jesus' birth, a man known in history as Herod the Great ruled over the land of Israel. Herod was not of the line of David, or even a Jew, but rather, he was an Idumaean. Herod's father, Antipater, had been made king of Israel as a political favor of the Roman government. The entire Herodian line of kings proved to be cruel and conniving; Herod the Great had much political ability, but he was cruel and self-seeking. He ruled over Israel for thirty-seven years. Jesus was born during the last years of his reign.

2. Saying, Where is he that is born King of the Jews? for we have seen his star in the east, and are come to worship him.

The Wise Men, or Magi, those who made a scientific study of stars and the heavenly bodies, came from their eastern country in search of One who had been born King of Jews. We are not told the names of the countries from whence they came, nor are we told by what process they interpreted the meaning of the stars. Adam Clarke says, "The Jews believed that there were prophets in the kingdom of Saba and Arabia, who were of the posterity of Abraham by Keturah; and that they taught in the name of God, that they had received in tradition from the mouth of Abraham. That many Jews were mixed with this people there is little doubt; and that these eastern Magi or philosophers or astrologers or whatever else they were might have been originally of that class there is room to believe. These, knowing the promise of the Messiah, were now, probably, like other believing Jews, waiting for the consolation of Israel."

It is generally believed that these eastern Wise Men had seen either a meteor, a nova (new star), or the conjunction of several stars so that it looked in brilliance and position like one great star. However, the Wise Men correctly interpreted the sign as indicating that the Jewish Messiah had been born.

3. When Herod the king had heard these things, he was troubled, and all Jerusalem with him.

It was with good reason that Herod became troubled by the questions of the Wise Men. He was an Idumaean and had no actual claim to the throne on which he sat. He was a usurper; the appearance of a true claim to the throne would inevitably bring about his deposition or loss of authority.

4. And when he had gathered all the chief priests and scribes of the people together, he demanded of them where Christ should be born.

In desperation, Herod called together all the chief priests and scribes of the Jewish people. This included the high priest presently serving, all former high priests still living, and all the deputy priests presently serving or who had ever filled such an office. This would have been quite an assembly of the most learned scholars in the Jewish nation.

Because of his own fear, and in response to a twisted plot in his wicked brain, Herod desired to know one thing: where was the Jewish Messiah, or Christ, to be born? He sat improperly and unjustly upon his throne and realized that the appearance of a messiah might well create such upheaval that he would be dethroned. It seems that Herod was well acquainted with the Jewish anticipation that the Messiah would come. Upon hearing the words of the Wise Men, he had only one terrifying question: Where would the Christ be born?

5. And they said unto him, In Bethlehem of Judaea: for thus it is written by the prophet,

6. And thou Bethlehem, in the land of Juda, art not the least among the princes of Juda: for out of thee shall come a Governor, that shall rule my people Israel.

The Jewish scholars were able to answer Herod's question without hesitation: In Bethlehem of Judea. It was a well-known prophecy and an understood truth that the Messiah would be born in Bethlehem. The scholars cited the words of Micah 5:2 to the disturbed king: "But thou, Beth-lehem Ephratah, though thou be little among the thousands of Judah, yet out of thee shall he come forth unto me that is to be ruler in Israel; whose goings forth have been from of old, from everlasting."

It is completely understandable that the Wise Men should have come to Jerusalem. From verse 9 we can assume that the star would have led them to Bethlehem without this stop in Jerusalem. Yet if the infant was to be King of Israel, it should be assumed that He was born in the royal household in Jerusalem. While the Wise Men knew about the Jewish expectation and correctly read the sign in the heavens, they would have no way of knowing that He was born in a small hamlet in Judah. The fact was that long ago God had ordained that His Son, a governor and ruler for Israel, should be born in one of the least likely villages of the nation. Bethlehem was important, as we have already pointed out, but it was not prominent and prestigious.

7. Then Herod, when he had privily called the wise men, enquired of them diligently what time the star appeared.

This verse reveals that Herod was no doubt showing a brave face to the religious leaders and to the public. It is altogether likely that he seemed unconcerned, or even reverential, before the people. His concern and fear surface here, however, when he calls the Wise Men for a private conference. He did not wish to show any public concern or distress, yet subsequent events proved him to be in a violent panic.

Herod sought to know when the star had appeared to the Wise Men. Use of the word "diligently" indicates that he probed them closely and interrogated them at length. He no doubt checked out every aspect of their story in an effort to find out when the star had appeared. If he could learn that, he would know approximately what age the child should be.

Certainly these events did not happen at the very time of Christ's birth; many facts indicate that they occurred somewhat later, as much as two years after the actual birth. Jesus had been born in a stable, but the family was in a house when the Wise Men arrived. He had been presented in the Temple forty days after His birth (Luke 2:22), and it seems that the family had made a brief journey to Nazareth (Luke 2:39). The Wise Men arrived after the initial events of the birth had been completed and after Joseph seems to have made Bethlehem his home.

8. And he sent them to Bethlehem, and said, Go and search diligently for the young child; and when ye have found him, bring me word again, that I may come and worship him also.

How can a genuine believer be distinguished from a hypocrite?

Herod pretended that he would like to worship the child and urged the Wise Men to let him know when they had found Him. From verse 12 we conclude that the Wise Men were not aware of the character of Herod, nor were they aware of his evil reason for wanting to know the identity of the child. This realization would come to them later in a dream.

Verse 13 states that Herod would seek for the young child in an effort to destroy Him. In verse 16, we learn that Herod actually had all male children two years old and under put to death. He was an exceedingly wicked man who had already had numerous persons who were a threat to his throne put to death, including his own sons. Herod is said to have had ten wives and numerous children. He had his eldest son put to death only five days before his own death. He had his second wife put to death and treated other members of the family with extreme cruelty. The slaughter of the male children in the region of Bethlehem would have been but a small matter to him, and yet, one so wicked pretended that he wished to find the child and worship Him.

II. WORSHIPING GOD'S SON (Matthew 2:9-11)

9. When they had heard the king, they departed; and, lo, the star, which they saw in the east, went before them, till it came and stood over where the young child was.

God still leads searching souls to Christ. Discuss some of the providential ways by which men have come to learn of Jesus.

With the king's hypocrisy still in their ears, the Wise Men proceeded the short distance to Bethlehem, less than ten miles from Jerusalem. It was customary for such travelers to journey at night, being guided by the stars. It appears in this instance, however, that the men traveled at night because they were dismissed at that time from the presence of King Herod. As they approached Bethlehem, they suddenly saw the same star they had seen in the East. Now it was over Bethlehem, over the very house where the young child was. It is often assumed that the star was a meteor sweeping close to the earth; certainly it was something of the sort in order to indicate the place where Jesus was.

It is clear that the star had not remained in the sight of the Wise Men during their long journey. It had appeared to them in their eastern countries to launch them on their journey, and now it appeared again as they completed the journey. The journey probably had taken a very long time without the star being in constant sight. It was probably for that reason that the Wise Men went first into Jerusalem instead of into Bethlehem. Now in Bethlehem, they saw the star once again and knew that they had reached their destination.

10. When they saw the star, they rejoiced with exceeding great joy.

The Wise Men were overwhelmed with joyous emotion when the star reappeared to them. After having experienced the events in Jerusalem, they were now overjoyed to see the confirmation of their original reading of the star. They were also happy to know the precise location of the newborn King of Israel.

11. And when they were come into the house, they saw the young child with Mary his mother, and fell down, and worshipped him: and when they had opened their treasures, they presented unto him gifts; gold, and frankincense, and myrrh.

The Wise Men did not find the Messiah in the palace in Jerusalem, but rather, they found Him in a common house in Bethlehem. His parents were not a king and a queen; they were common folk of the Jews. Note here that Joseph is not mentioned, not because he was absent, but because people generally see infants with their mother. Joseph is mentioned prominently in verses 13, 19, and the following verses.

It is commonly believed that the Wise Men themselves were royalty. (Legend has given them the names of Gaspar, Melchior, and Balthazar. This is purely legend, however, and we have only as much identity as is found in the Scripture.) Certainly the gifts they brought to the Christ Child were royal in nature, gifts that royalty would give. Gold was a gift for a king, frankincense a gift for deity, and myrrh also a gift for deity, but with a foretoken of death. This gives the gifts a very definite prophetic suggestion. One writer, quoted by Adam Clarke, has stated this truth very clearly: "Some will have these gifts to be emblematic of the divinity, regal office, and manhood of Christ. 'They offered Him incense as their God; gold as their King; and myrrh as united to a human body, subject to suffering and death.' " It should be further observed that they offered Christ gifts that were both highly esteemed and precious among themselves.

What became of these gifts is never intimated in Scripture. Clearly the Lord did not still possess the gifts when He became a man, and yet it is impossible to believe that Joseph and Mary would have made use of them selfishly or carelessly. It can only be conjectured that the gifts supplied the means whereby Jesus, Mary, and Joseph would live while they were in exile in Egypt.

III. FOLLOWING GOD'S PLAN
(Matthew 2:12-23)

12. And being warned of God in a dream that they should not return to Herod, they departed into their own country another way.

Herod thought that he could put the infant Messiah to death. He did not take into account the providential watchcare of God; he did not know with whom he was dealing. God revealed to the Wise Men that they should shun Herod and return to the East in a way different from that which they had come. They should not even pass through Jerusalem. He who had sent His Son to the earth now executed a providential plan to preserve His Son's life and permit His work.

Verses 13-23 relate how the Lord directed Joseph to take Jesus and Mary into Egypt and to remain there until it would be safe to leave. In a violent outbreak of evil, Herod would seek to destroy the child and would thereby destroy many others. Joseph arose in the night and began his long journey to Egypt.

In Egypt there was a large settlement of Jews to which Joseph very likely went. As has been mentioned, the gifts given to Joseph, Mary, and Jesus by the Wise Men would have provided for their subsistence while in Egypt. Many innocent infants were slaughtered by Herod, but God spared the life of Christ. It has been suggested that these infants were the first martyrs for Christ; each gave his life because of Him.

When Herod died, Joseph was directed to return to Israel. Because Joseph feared the new king, Archelaus, who would be as cruel as his father Herod, Joseph declined to remain in Judea. He instead went farther north to Nazareth in Galilee. In Nazareth, where Joseph and Mary had lived earlier, Jesus would live in safety and do the work for which He was born.

REVIEW QUESTIONS

1. What prompted the journey of the Wise Men?

2. How did Herod react to news of the birth of Christ?

3. What course of action did Herod pursue when he found out about the birth of Christ?

4. Why was Herod so interested in the

exact time when the star appeared?
5. Why did the Wise Men return another way?

GOLDEN TEXT HOMILY

"WHEN THEY WERE COME INTO THE HOUSE, THEY SAW THE YOUNG CHILD WITH MARY HIS MOTHER, AND FELL DOWN, AND WORSHIPPED HIM" (Matthew 2:11).

Christmas is for families. "I'll Be Home for Christmas" is the song on our lips. It is for ordinary folks. A birth (a common human experience) into a family (the most common institution) gives this season of the year special meaning. A house, a baby, a mother—common things make Christmas significant. It is a time of the year when families are magnetically drawn together. Hearts are set aglow. Gifts are exchanged, joys are expressed, and peace is proclaimed. The reason—God's supreme revelation of Himself is given in the Christ Child. God has broken into the commonness of life. This is how God comes to us all.

The Christmas story centers around personalities—the Christ Child, Mary, Joseph, shepherds, innkeeper, Wise Men, and Herod. The personalities who missed Christmas—the innkeeper and Herod—did not recognize the visitation from God. It came when least expected—in their daily activities. Common tasks, humdrum labors, worldly ambitions, and daily commerce clouded the expectations and crowded out participation.

What a contrast with righteous Simeon, the one who lived in eager and constant anticipation of seeing the Christ Child. All of his hopes centered in the Child's coming. One day while serving in the Temple, as was his custom, the Christ Child came. Simeon burst forth in praise and worship when he saw Him.

> Mine eyes have seen thy salvation, Which thou hast prepared before the face of all people; A light to lighten the Gentiles, and the glory of thy people Israel (Luke 2:30-32).

Shepherds, wise and devout men still recognize God coming to us in the daily occurrences of life. The mundane and ordinary are transformed into ultimate significance and meaning. To bow and worship Him is still the only proper response. They join in the anthem, "O come let us adore Him, Christ the Lord," for He alone is worthy.—**Garnet E. Pike, dean, Emmanuel College School of Christian Ministries, Franklin Springs, Georgia**

SENTENCE SERMONS

WHEN MEN SEEK a better understanding of God's revelation in Christ, it is a mark of wisdom.
—**Selected**

IF YOU HITCH your wagon to a star, be sure it is the star of Bethlehem.
—**Anonymous**

THE REAL CHRISTMAS is found not in gaily wrapped packages, but in a Christ-loving heart.
—**Wilbur G. Williams**

THE COMING OF CHRIST by way of a Bethlehem manger seems strange and stunning. But when we take Him out of the manger and invite Him into our hearts, then the meaning unfolds.
—**C. Neil Strait**

EVANGELISTIC APPLICATION

TO TURN TO CHRIST AND LOVE AND WORSHIP HIM IS TRUE WISDOM.

According to ancient tradition, the Three Wise Men were three kings, differing the one from the other as sharply and as strikingly as any three individuals could possibly do.

Gaspar, the youthful King of Tarshish, set out on his quest hoping that the star would lead him to a king. The world, he felt, wanted a master, a sovereign, a ruler, a lord. And, longing for such a lord, Gaspar took with him a tribute of gold, a royal gift.

Balthazar, the mature King of Chaldea, hoped that the star would lead him to a god. Thirsting for a god as the hart thirsts for the waterbrooks, longing for a god as blind men long for light, Balthazar answered the challenge of the star. He took with him a tribute of incense—frankincense with which to worship.

And Melchior, the aged King of Nubia, longed for a Savior. Hoping fervently that the star might lead him to a savior—a savior who he instinctively felt must of necessity be a sufferer—he took with him his gift of myrrh.

And so they came to Bethlehem. When they saw that the star had but led them to a baby in a woman's arms, all three were at first overwhelmed with chagrin and dismay. But as they sat and pondered this strange happening they heard Mary, after the fashion of mothers, singing to her child. And all three listened.

"My soul doth magnify the Lord!" she said.

"The Lord!" exclaimed Gaspar. "Then I have found my Sovereign, my Monarch, my King, my Lord!" And he offered his gold. But Mary sang on.

"And my spirit hath rejoiced in God . . . " she continued. "In God!" cried Balthazar, his face lighting up. "Then I have found Him—the God for whom my spirit hungered!" And he presented his incense to the babe. But Mary had not yet finished her song.

"My soul doth magnify the Lord and my spirit hath rejoiced in God my Savior!" "My Savior!" echoed Melchior, "My Savior!" And he offered his vase of myrrh.

And so Gaspar found in Jesus the King of his desire; Balthazar found in Jesus the God he had so passionately sought; Melchior found in Jesus the Savior for whom his very soul was aching.

Every man finds in Jesus exactly what he needs most. That is the essence of His Christmas story; and that is the essence of the everlasting gospel.

—F. W. Boreham MY CHRISTMAS BOOK

ILLUMINATING THE LESSON

Two women were having a happy time at a very elaborate luncheon in a downtown hotel. When asked what the occasion was, one said, "It's the baby's birthday." "But where is the baby?" asked the inquirer. "Oh," said the mother, "you don't think I'd bring him, do you? Why he doesn't know anything about it."

Many celebrate Christmas but leave out Christ.

—Carl C. Williams

Love divine, all love excelling,
  Joy of heav'n to earth come down!
Fix in us Thy humble dwelling;
  All Thy faithful mercies crown.
Jesus, Thou art all compassion,
  Pure unbounded love Thou art;
Visit us with Thy salvation;
  Enter every trusting heart.

—John Wesley.

DAILY DEVOTIONAL GUIDE

M. Beginning With Wisdom. Proverbs 1:1-9
T. Seeking the Lord. Isaiah 55:1-7
W. Thanking God for His Gift. Luke 2:8-20
T. Accepting God's Message. Luke 1:26-38
F. Bearing Witness to Christ. John 1:1-14
S. Inquiring About Christ. John 12:12-30

December 28, 1980

Christ's Supreme Authority

Bible Background: Matthew 21:12-27; Mark 11:12-33; Luke 19:45-20:8
Time: A.D. 30
Place: Jerusalem and its vicinity
Supplemental References: Matthew 28:18; John 2:13-22; Acts 10:36-38
Golden Text: "Jesus came and spake unto them, saying, All power is given unto me in heaven and in earth" (Matthew 28:18).
Central Truth: Christ is Master over man and nature.
Evangelistic Emphasis: Christ demonstrates His authority over sin by forgiving transgressions and bringing salvation.

PRINTED TEXT

Mark 11:12. And on the morrow, when they were come from Bethany, he was hungry:

13. And seeing a fig tree afar off having leaves, he came, if haply he might find any thing thereon: and when he came to it, he found nothing but leaves; for the time of figs was not yet.

14. And Jesus answered and said unto it, No man eat fruit of thee hereafter for ever. And his disciples heard it.

15. And they come to Jerusalem: and Jesus went into the temple, and began to cast out them that sold and bought in the temple, and overthrew the tables of the moneychangers, and the seats of them that sold doves;

16. And would not suffer that any man should carry any vessel through the temple.

17. And he taught, saying unto them, Is is not written, My house shall be called of all nations the house of prayer? but ye have made it a den of thieves.

18. And the scribes and chief priests heard it, and sought how they might destroy him: for they feared him, because all the people was astonished at his doctrine.

19. And when even was come, he went out of the city.

20. And in the morning, as they passed by, they saw the fig tree dried up from the roots.

21. And Peter calling to remembrance saith unto him, Master, behold, the fig tree which thou cursedst is withered away.

22. And Jesus answering saith unto them, Have faith in God.

23. For verily I say unto you, That whosoever shall say unto this mountain, Be thou removed, and be thou cast into the sea; and shall not doubt in his heart, but shall believe that those things which he saith shall come to pass; he shall have whatsoever he saith.

24. Therefore I say unto you, What things soever ye desire, when ye pray, believe that ye receive them, and ye shall have them.

25. And when ye stand praying, forgive, if ye have ought against any: that your Father also which is in heaven may forgive you your trespasses.

26. But if ye do not forgive, neither will your Father which is in heaven forgive your trespasses.

DICTIONARY

Bethany (BETH-ah-knee)—Mark 11:12—The name of a village situated on the eastern slope of Mount Olivet, about two miles from Jerusalem. It was the home of Martha, Mary, and Lazarus. The name comes from the Hebrew word which means either "house of the poor man" or "house of misery."

if haply—Mark 11:13—"Whether" or "perhaps"

temple—Mark 11:15—The part of the Temple involved was the outermost enclosure, called the Court of the Gentiles, into which even non-Jews could be admitted.

would not suffer—Mark 11:16—"Would not allow" or "would not permit"

LESSON OUTLINE
 I. CHRIST HAS AUTHORITY OVER NATURE
 II. CHRIST HAS POWER OVER MEN
 III. CHRIST ANSWERS PRAYER
 IV. CHRIST CONFOUNDS ADVERSARIES

LESSON EXPOSITION
INTRODUCTION

The events of this lesson follow Christ's triumphal entry into Jerusalem. Mutitudes who had gathered in Jerusalem for the Passover received the Lord joyously because of the great works He had done. The raising of Lazarus from the dead was the major cause for His great popularity. If Jesus could raise the dead to life again, the people reasoned, He could also provide salvation for them. They had therefore greeted Him with the word **Hosanna**, a plea for His protection and grace.

Just as Jesus asserted His authority over death with the raising of Lazarus, so He continued to assert His authority in Jerusalem in other ways. First, He asserted power over nature and then He asserted His moral authority over the disobedience of men. At the time of this lesson Jesus was nearing the end of His life on earth. He would never leave Jerusalem again, but would be crucified within a week after these events.

I. CHRIST HAS AUTHORITY OVER NATURE
  (Mark 11:12-14)

12. And on the morrow, when they were come from Bethany, he was hungry:

Because Bethany was only about two miles from Jerusalem, Jesus generally stayed at night in Bethany, where His friends, Lazarus, Mary and Martha lived, and came back into Jerusalem during the day. Verse 11 states that Jesus returned to Bethany with His twelve apostles following His triumphal entry into Jerusalem. Now, on the day following, Jesus is again walking from Bethany to Jerusalem, the twelve apostles with Him. He was hungry and used His hunger as an occasion for teaching a great moral lesson.

13. And seeing a fig tree afar off having leaves, he came, if haply he might find any thing thereon: and when he came to it, he found nothing but leaves; for the time of figs was not yet.

From the pathway where He walked, Jesus saw a flowering fig tree in the distance. The tree was filled with leaves, even though it was not yet the season to bear figs. Yet, leaves and figs were always borne at the same time. The sight of the leaves on the tree therefore indicated that the tree should have fruit upon it. Jesus and His disciples went to the tree so they might eat some figs, but the tree had no fruit upon it. The hypocrisy of the tree was that it proclaimed by the bearing of leaves that it also had figs—even though the fruit was out of season. Being about March, it was time for the trees to begin to bud. This particular tree, however, gave the appearance of having already budded and of now being full fruited. Jesus and the disciples were disappointed to discover that no fruit was there. The signals given by the tree were false; it made a claim which it did not fulfil.

14. And Jesus answered and said unto it, No man eat fruit of thee hereafter for ever. And his disciples heard it.

Jesus passed an audible judgment upon the fig tree, declaring that it should henceforth be barren. The statement "and His disciples heard it" actually sums up the purpose of the curse. Jesus did not sentence the fig tree to barrenness in a fit of spite, but rather to be an example to the disciples. It has also become an example to us that we should be fruitful and productive in the work of the Lord. Later in the week, at the Last Supper, Jesus would say very much the same to His disciples: "Every branch in me that beareth not fruit he taketh away: and every branch that beareth fruit, he purgeth it, that it may bring forth more fruit . . . If a man abide not in me, he is cast forth as a branch, and is withered; and men gather them, and cast them into the fire

December 28, 1980

and they are burned . . . Herein is my Father glorified, that ye bear much fruit; so shall ye be my disciples" (John 15:2, 6, 8).

It must be borne in mind that the fig tree had proclaimed by bearing leaves that it also had fruit on it. The tree was not doing what it claimed to be doing, and it was not doing what it was created to do. Jesus used this incident as a symbol of righteous indignation with hypocrisy and of displeasure with unfruitfulness. Men and nations alike are apt to receive the same judgment for the same sins.

II. CHRIST HAS POWER OVER MEN (Mark 11:15-19)

15. And they come to Jerusalem: and Jesus went into the temple, and began to cast out them that sold and bought in the temple, and overthrew the tables of the moneychangers, and the seats of them that sold doves;

Later in the day Jesus went into the Temple in Jerusalem, where He became indignant at the sight He saw. The court of the Temple was filled with money changers and merchants, those who sought to make personal gain from the worship of the Lord.

These money changers were both greedy and dishonest. They sold for exorbitant prices the doves that were required for Jewish worship. When worshipers entered the Temple with their sacrifices, these would be declared imperfect, thereby unfit for sacrifice. The money changers would then offer to sell to the worshipers doves suitable for sacrifice. Naturally the prive would be very high. Then the money changers would sell the very same doves they had rejected as being unworthy to later worshipers who would come by.

Once again, Jesus turned His indignation toward hypocrisy and deceit. The guilt of the money changers was much like the guilt of the fig tree. Israel's claims were great and beautiful, but the merchandise in the Temple did not live up to those claims.

16. And would not suffer that any man should carry any vessel through the temple.

Other things were sold than the doves mentioned in verse 15. Some had turned the Temple into a place of buying and selling. What had once been done as a convenience to the people had now become a practice of greed and extortion.

17. And he taught, saying unto them, Is it not written, My house shall be called of all nations the house of prayer? but ye have made it a den of thieves.

What aspects of human life and behavior pose the most serious threat to proper reverence for the house of God in today's world?

As it had been with the fig tree, Jesus did not overturn the tables of merchandise in a fit of selfish anger; He did so in order to teach a lesson and to establish the holiness of God. The Jewish people and their house of worship were known among all nations for their worship of God. Jewish pilgrims and proselytes came from all nations to worship in Jerusalem. When they arrived at the holy place, they did not find prayer, devotion, and brotherhood, but rather deceit, lying, and cheating. Those who had traveled from far parts of the world were compelled to buy sacrifices that had been manipulated in the manner already mentioned. The sincere and unknowing worshipers were treated no better than if they had wandered into a den of thieves.

How can reverence for God's house best be expressed and promoted?

18. And the scribes and chief priests heard it, and sought how they might destroy him: for they feared him, because all the people was astonished at his doctrine.

When the religious leaders saw what Jesus did, and with what authority He did it, they intensified their efforts to put Him to death. His life was a rebuke to their lives and His authority a rebuke to their authority. He exposed the sin of their hearts and without hesitation repudiated their evil acts. As long as Jesus lived He would be condemnation in their conscience. He really lived the life that they merely claimed to live; He really had the authority they merely claimed to have; He really had the power they merely claimed to have; He really held the faith and the convictions they merely claimed to hold. Moreover, He was rapidly gaining the acceptance and devotion of the people that the religious leaders wished to have. They saw their own popularity eroding away as Jesus continued His work. The very fact that He was alive filled them with fear, and such fear rapidly turns to hate.

19. And when even was come, he went out of the city.

Once again, Jesus and His disciples left Jerusalem at the close of the day and returned to Bethany for the night. Jesus no doubt found great comfort in spending the evenings privately with those who loved and cared for Him. The events of the day must have been very tiring, and the burden of His soul must have been very heavy, but He found relaxation and spiritual repair in the company of friends who loved Him.

III. CHRIST ANSWERS PRAYER
    (Mark 11:20-26)

20. And in the morning, as they passed by, they saw the fig tree dried up from the roots.

As He customarily did when He was in Jerusalem, Jesus left Bethany in the early morning and walked the two miles into Jerusalem. On this morning He and His disciples saw a strange sight: the fig tree that had been so full of leaves the day before was now dried up and withered away. What had yesterday given such leafy promise of bearing fruit was now drooped and dry and sterile.

21. And Peter calling to remembrance saith unto him, Master, behold, the fig tree which thou cursedst is withered away.

Peter gave voice to the astonishment of the Twelve. This was customary for him, for Peter was the natural leader of the group. He frequently was the one to speak for the entire group. (See Matthew 16:15, 16, where Jesus asked the Twelve a question and Peter answered for them.) Peter here made an association between the fact that Jesus had cursed the fig tree yesterday and that it was now dried up and withered. The disciples did not miss the point that the tree had died as a consequence of the Lord's curse.

22. And Jesus answering saith unto them, Have faith in God.

Note that it was Peter who spoke in verse 21, and yet this verse says Jesus answered "them." Peter frequently gave voice to the Twelve, and thereby gained much teaching and spiritual insight for the entire group. Peter may have been impulsive in some of his actions and statements, but the entire body of disciples generally profited by his bold nature.

The Lord used the occasion of the fig tree to teach His disciples an important lesson. They had already seen the end of a fruitless life and the divine displeasure with false claims. Now He would teach them further regarding the power of faith in the spiritual life. They had seen the result of divine judgment, and now they would learn of the authority they would have to learn of the authority that passes such judgment.

23. For verily I say unto you, That whosoever shall say unto this mountain, Be thou removed, and be thou cast into the sea; and shall not doubt in his heart, but shall believe that those things which he saith shall come to pass; he shall have whatsoever he saith.

The authority of God is extended over all creation, over the affairs of man and of nature. Jesus had exercised His authority on a fig tree in the field and on the mercenaries in the Temple. Here He used the most extreme example to show His disciples how great is the power of faith. His example is clearly hypothetical, yet it is very effective. The most extreme physical feat imaginable would be the removing of a mountain from one place to another. Yet the Lord uses such a figure in His lesson.

There is not a single instance in all of Scripture where a mountain was actually removed from one place to another. No prophet, no apostle, and not even the Lord Himself ever performed such a feat. Very clearly, then, He was not advocating that His followers endeavor to move mountains physically from one place to another. And yet, He said, this is a possible consequence of absolute faith.

Obviously the use of the word "mountain" here refers to massive difficulties of various sorts. Human life is beset with mountains of doubt, of trouble, of sin, and of physical need. Faith in God will vanquish all these mountains and cast them into the sea of submission and defeat. The figure of a mountain is used in order to emphasize the magnitude of the difficulty. Nothing is too difficult for the man who has faith in God and who asserts that faith with the authority of a holy life.

24. Therefore I say unto you, What things soever ye desire, when ye pray, believe that ye receive them, and ye shall have them.

Specifically, the Lord instructed His disciples that they could have the desires of their heart if they would only believe. What a righteous heart can comprehend and spiritually desire, faith in God can perform. Naturally this teaching comes with conditions. There is the condition that the desire is in keeping with the Word and will of God. If we desire something that is contrary to these, then there is no promise that we shall receive them. There is also the condition that our desires must be worthwhile rather than whimsical. Some people are unable to distinguish desires from notions. People frequently get notions of things they would like and then change their minds regarding them almost immediately. A true desire is an earnest and proper yearning for something of great good.

Next, there is the condition of desiring that which is worthwhile. There is no promise that God will give us our purely selfish desires any more than He was willing to turn the stones into bread so that He might personally eat. He never used the power of God for selfish benefit, and He would certainly not permit this for us.

Finally, there is the condition of desiring what is superior. Frequently our desires conflict with each other, one eliminating the other. This is the case when we desire something immediately and yet something different ultimately. God frequently has to deny our immediate desires in order to grant our ultimate desires.

With these factors in mind, we must hold to the promise of God, realizing that He will give us whatsoever we desire when we pray in faith. This is an absolute promise of God, as we pray desiring what is best for us.

25. And when ye stand praying, forgive, if ye have ought against any: that your Father also which is in heaven may forgive you your trespasses.

The answers to our prayers are linked with our forgiveness of those who offend us. This relates directly to the Lord's promise to give us the desires of our heart. We cannot hold enmity and malice in our hearts and still exercise pure faith and holy desires. The opposing elements simply will not mix. We must be as willing to forgive those who wrong us as the Lord has been willing to forgive us. This points up to us how interwoven our lives are. We are not to live selfishly or pray selfishly. Just as we cannot stand without the love of God, so we should not stand without love for our fellowman.

26. But if ye do not forgive, neither will your Father which is in heaven forgive your trespasses.

The efficacy of our praying is bound up in our readiness to forgive our fellowman. God will not measure blessings to us if we measure resentment and malice toward our fellowmen. No man who refuses to forgive others has any right to expect the Lord to forgive him. An unforgiving heart cannot be forgiven; and a forgiven heart will also be a forgiving heart. No man can reach for forgiveness in one direction while withholding his hand from forgiveness in the other. This was the sin of the Jewish leaders, and in a way it was the sin of the fig tree. The priests expected to receive good things from God while dealing in evil toward their fellowman. The fig tree expected to enjoy the blessings of sunshine and rain without providing the benefit of fruit to man. In each instance they expected to be receivers without being givers, they expected blessings without blessing. These things make us guilty in the work of the Lord, for the Christian way is to give to others as we receive from the Lord.

IV. CHRIST CONFOUNDS ADVERSARIES
   (Mark 11:27-33)

For the third day Jesus went into Jerusalem on the week of Passover. On this occasion the chief priests, scribes and elders accosted him with the question, "By what authority doest thou these things? and who gave thee this authority to do these things?" (v. 28). They had long been seething with indignation toward the Lord as they watched Him speak and act with authority. They were afraid of Him; they hated Him and sought to put Him to silence.

As Jesus often did, He answered their question with another question. He asked them, "The baptism of John, was it from heaven, or of men?" (v. 30). This confounded the Jewish leaders because they dared not answer at all. If they replied, "From heaven," they would stand condemned for having not accepted John. Their own words would be their condemnation. If they should say, "Of men," then they would incur the indignation of the people, who had recognized John as a prophet. Any answer the leaders might give would be harmful to them and to their influence with the people. No doubt they conferred among themselves about how they should answer. Jesus had boxed them into a corner, however, and they could not answer at all. Having declined to give Him an answer to His question, they certainly could not expect Him to give an answer to theirs. Jesus put them to silence and caused them frustration and confusion. His power over them was as dramatic as His power over the fig tree and over the money changers.

REVIEW QUESTIONS

1. What did Jesus observe about the fig tree that caused Him to think it might have fruit on it?

2. Why were people carrying vessels through the Temple precincts?

3. What attitude did Jesus have regarding the use of the Temple?

4. What reaction did the scribes and chief priests have to the Temple-cleansing act by Jesus?

5. What conditions did Jesus place on the exercise of faith's authority?

GOLDEN TEXT HOMILY

"JESUS CAME AND SPAKE UNTO THEM, SAYING, ALL POWER IS GIVEN UNTO ME IN HEAVEN AND IN EARTH" (Matthew 28:18).

Christ had all power and authority before His crucifixion, death, and resurrection. Christ performed miracles, turned water into wine, fed five thousand, chose His disciples, and gave them power over the enemy. Although Christ had all power and authority, He never worked independent of His Father, but always in the will and plan of God the Father.

I believe Christ was telling His disciples that nothing had changed since His death and resurrection. He was still head and founder of the Kingdom and His Church that would be established on Pentecost.

He had already sent His disciples out two by two, also the Seventy. He had given them power to heal the sick, to cast out devils, and to preach the kingdom of God.

Christ was recommending His disciples to carry out the order already given prior to His death and resurrection.

Christ, being head and founder of the Kingdom and His Church, had the only authority to give the formula for water baptism, "in the name of the Father, and of the Son, and of the Holy Ghost," and to issue the Great Commission to go into all the world and preach and teach His Word.—**Charles G. Wiley, Pastor, Piedmont, West Virginia**

SENTENCE SERMONS

NATURE IS BUT a name for an effect whose cause is God.

—**William Cowper**

JESUS CHRIST the condescension of divinity and the exaltation of humanity.

—**Phillips Brooks**

REVERENCE FOR THE things of God, including His house, must be taught as well as caught.

—**H. C. Garner**

OUR ADVERSARIES ARE no match for the Christ of Calvary.

—**Anonymous**

EVANGELISTIC APPLICATION

CHRIST DEMONSTRATES HIS AUTHORITY OVER SIN BY FORGIVING TRANSGRESSIONS AND BRINGING SALVATION.

MONEY CHANGERS IN THE TEMPLE

This phrase, taken from the act of our Lord recorded in Matthew 21:12, is usually taken to describe something deplorable, the sordid, the profaning of religion by commercialism. But in the highest sense, each Christian can be a "money changer." When a person brings money to be used in furthering the program and purposes of Christ, money becomes changed into life. Money can be changed into health and life in a hospital down the street or across the sea; it can be changed into a college where a young person finds what is needful for real living. It is changed into food as the Church meets physical need in all parts of the earth. By its right use, money is the alchemy by which human life and energy are transported from one place to another. Hence, "the offering of an upright man enriches the altar, and its fragrance reaches the Most High" (Ecclesiasticus 35:5, 6).

By our money we can talk in many languages to proclaim the gospel; by our money we can heal the sick, give sight to the blind, care for the fatherless, teach the ignorant and feed the hungry. Hence it becomes the "open sesame" to a glorious ministry.

You—yes, you— can be a money changer in the temple!

—**Gordon W. Mattice**—from **Stewardship Illustrations**

ILLUMINATING THE LESSON

Sosomenes relates, that when the holy family reached the term of their journey, and approached the city of Heliopolis, in their flight into Egypt, a tree which grew before the gates of the city, and was regarded with great veneration as the seat of a god, bowed down its branches at the approach of the infant Christ. Likewise it is related (not in legends merely, but by grave, religious authorities),

December 28, 1980

idols of the Egyptians fell with their faces to the earth. I have seen pictures of the flight into Egypt, in which broken idols lay by the wayside.

—M. Jameson

DAILY DEVOTIONAL GUIDE

M. Christ Teaches With Authority. Matthew 7:21-29

T. Christ Declares His Authority. Matthew 28: 8-18

W. Christ Acts With Authority. Mark 1:21-28

T. Christ Judges With Authority. John 5:19-27

F. Christ's Authority on Earth. Ephesians 1: 15-23

S. Christ's Authority in Heaven. 1 Peter 3: 18-4:5

January 4, 1981

Understanding the Lord's Supper

Bible Background: Matthew 26:17-30; Mark 14:12-25; Luke 22:7-20; John 13:21-30

Time: Probably A.D. 30

Place: Jerusalem

Supplemental References: Exodus 12:1-14; 1 Corinthians 11:23-34

Golden Text: "This is my blood of the new testament, which is shed for many for the remission of sins" (Matthew 26:28).

Central Truth: The Lord's Supper helps us remember the meaning of Christ's death and the promise of His second coming.

Evangelistic Emphasis: The Lord's Supper is a continuing reminder that Christ died for the sins of all mankind.

PRINTED TEXT

Matthew 26:17. Now the first day of the feast of unleavened bread the disciples came to Jesus, saying unto him, Where wilt thou that we prepare for thee to eat the passover?

18. And he said, Go into the city to such a man, and say unto him, The Master saith, My time is at hand; I will keep the passover at thy house with my disciples.

19. And the disciples did as Jesus had appointed them; and they made ready the passover.

20. Now when the even was come, he sat down with the twelve.

21. And as they did eat, he said, Verily I say unto you, that one of you shall betray me.

22. And they were exceeding sorrowful, and began every one of them to say unto him, Lord, is it I?

23. And he answered and said, He that dippeth his hand with me in the dish, the same shall betray me.

24. The Son of man goeth as it is written of him: but woe unto that man by whom the Son of man is betrayed! it had been good for that man if he had not been born.

25. Then Judas, which betrayed him, answered and said, Master, is it I? He said unto him, Thou hast said.

26. And as they were eating, Jesus took bread, and blessed it, and brake it, and gave it to the disciples, and said, Take, eat; this is my body.

27. And he took the cup, and gave thanks, and gave it to them, saying, Drink ye all of it;

28. For this is my blood of the new testament, which is shed for many for the remission of sins.

29. But I say unto you, I will not drink henceforth of this fruit of the vine, until that day when I drink it new with you in my Father's kingdom.

30. And when they had sung an hymn, they went out into the mount of Olives.

DICTIONARY

first day of the feast of unleavened bread—Matthew 26:17—The Feast of Unleavened Bread began on the day after the Passover and lasted seven days.
Judas—Matthew 26:25—Judas Iscariot, the betrayer of Jesus

LESSON OUTLINE

I. PREPARATION FOR THE LORD'S SUPPER
II. OBSERVING THE LORD'S SUPPER
III. BLESSINGS OF THE LORD'S SUPPER

LESSON EXPOSITION

INTRODUCTION

The events leading to the crucifixion of Christ happened with rapidity during His final week on earth. All that happened was of great significance, and a great deal of attention is given to these events in the four Gospels.

Jesus had a final supper with His disciples on the night before His crucifixion. This Last Supper was recorded by all four Gospels, one of the few events in the life of Christ to be recorded by all four. Generally, the Synoptic Gospels (Matthew, Mark, and Luke) recorded the same events, while John recorded things that they did not mention. The only events to be recorded by all four Gospels were the triumphal entry, the Last Supper, the arrest, trial and crucifixion of Jesus, and the Resurrection.

The account of the Lord's last Passover Feast with His disciples is of great importance to us. Its importance is of two sorts: it gives us an intimate glimpse of the Lord and His final communication with His disciples, and it also relates the institution of what Christians call the Lord's Supper.

The final evening Jesus spent with the Twelve was regarded to be so important that all four Gospels give considerable detail about the events of the evening. Five chapters of the Gospel of John are devoted to what Jesus said to His disciples on that last night. For one event to be given so much attention, we must conclude that this was one of the most important events of the life of Christ.

I. PREPARATION FOR THE LORD'S SUPPER
(Matthew 26:17-19)

17. Now the first day of the feast of unleavened bread the disciples came to Jesus, saying unto him, Where wilt thou that we prepare for thee to eat the passover?

Unleavened bread was associated with the Passover because it had been eaten by the earliest Jews preceding their flight from Egypt. One of the most solemn events of the Jewish year was the celebration of the Passover, with the eating of unleavened bread as one of its most prominent features. Observance of these times and feasts was very important to the Jews, thus these times and feasts were followed faithfully. The disciples therefore wondered to the Lord where He would wish to have the Passover dinner.

Within the precincts of Jerusalem itself, there was no place where Jesus could feel as free and as at home as He did in Bethany, in the home of Lazarus. Yet He did have some friends in Jerusalem. The Jews of Jerusalem helped to make provision for the multitude of pilgrims that came to the city for the Passover. It is said that any pilgrim could request of a resident the use of a room for observing the Passover, and that request would be granted without charge. Jewish scholars say that a man might go forth before the Passover and request the use of any unoccupied room. This was granted without murmur or reluctance. The host would also provide the utensils for the Passover.

18. And he said, Go into the city to such a man, and say unto him, The Master saith, My time is at hand; I will keep the passover at thy house with my disciples.

We get a much more complete picture of the securing of the Passover room in Luke 22:8-12. It was Peter and John who went into the city to secure the room, probably from a particular man well known to Jesus and the disciples. There is no indication that he was a stranger, nor is there a clear statement of his identity.

The message of the Lord was that His time was at hand. The meaning of this is that the time had come for Him to be crucified. The Lord was aware that He was now facing the end, but it is not likely that either the disciples or the one from whom they secured the Passover room could have known exactly what He meant. Such a term as "My time is at hand" was frequently used to indicate some decisive moment in a person's life.

From the time that Jesus was born into the earth, He had been headed for the Cross. This was a constant timetable in His mind, a timetable to which He made constant reference as he spoke with His disciples. There is no indication, however, that they ever fully grasped the significance of His words. The disciples may have known and feared that He would be put to death, but their knowledge was vague and incomplete. Only the Lord could comprehend His death, with its suffering and significance.

19. And the disciples did as Jesus had appointed them; and they made ready the passover.

Peter and John (Luke 22:8) did as the Lord instructed them. The role of a disciple was to follow the instructions of his Master. Disciples carried out the instructions of their Teacher, not because they were servants, but because they were pupils. The very word **disciple** means "a learner." One of the methods of learning was the following of instruction. Peter and John prepared for the Passover precisely as the Lord instructed them. This means that they provided the lamb and bitter herbs that would be eaten, along with unleavened bread and the sacramental wine.

II. OBSERVING THE LORD'S SUPPER (Matthew 26:20-27)

20. Now when the even was come, he sat down with the twelve.

We are told in Mark 14:15 that this last Passover was eaten in a large upper room. Even now, visitors to Jerusalem are shown such a room, but there is no likelihood that it really is the room where Jesus and His disciples ate. It does show a typical room in the upper part of a Jewish house. The room where Jesus and His disciples ate was certainly a guest room in the upper part of the owner's home. It was a room large enough for the entire group.

21. And as they did eat, he said, Verily I say unto you, that one of you shall betray me.

As Jesus and the disciples partook of the Passover, He revealed to them that one of their number would be the cause of His death. From verse 15 we know that Judas had already betrayed Jesus to His enemies; he had already made an agreement to deliver the Lord into their hands. Jesus chose the intimate moment of sharing the Passover dinner with His disciples to reveal to the body that one of their number was a traitor. He did not speak in an accusing or condemning voice, but He matter of factly stated the fact of betrayal. Knowing all things, Jesus had known from the beginning that He would be betrayed; He knew at what moment Judas had made covenant with the chief priests. It was no new or surprising thing to Him that Judas had betrayed Him, but we can well imagine the surprise and shock that His words brought to the disciples themselves.

22. And they were exceeding sorrowful, and began every one of them to say unto him, Lord, is it I?

News that one of them would betray the Lord had the immediate effect of self-examination. It is very interesting that not one of the disciples began to accuse another. Instead of looking at one another with suspicion, they looked at the Lord earnestly and began to ask, "Lord, is it I?" Naturally it was only the eleven innocent disciples who engaged in this self-examination. Judas himself feigned an attitude of sorrow. He would later ask the Lord if he was the person, but he would ask then only to ascertain whether or not the Lord was aware of his guilt (v. 25). The eleven innocent men conscientiously sought to examine themselves for possible guilt. This is an appropriate reaction to the disclosure of sin.

23. And he answered and said, He that dippeth his hand with me in the dish, the same shall betray me.

As the Jews ate their Passover Feast, they dipped the unleavened bread in the juice of bitter herbs. Containers of this juice were placed at various places on the table so that every person eating would be near to one. Several people dipped in the same dish. This bread dipped into the juice was called a sop (John 13:26). Judas sat either beside the Lord or across the table from Him, for it is evident that they dipped in the same vessel of bitter herb juice.

24. The Son of man goeth as it is written of him: but woe unto that man by whom the Son of man is betrayed! it had been good for that man if he had not been born.

Jesus assured the disciples that He must depart this life as it had been written of Him, particularly in such scriptures as Psalm 22, Isaiah 53, and Daniel 9:26. The death of Jesus was inevitable, but this did not lessen the guilt of the one who caused that death. Neither the guilt nor the punishment of Judas would be diminished by the fact that Christ's death had been prophesied.

The eternal torment of Judas would be so great that it would have been better for him never to have been born. The same can be said of any soul that is lost in hell, but Judas must forever know that it was he who brought about the death of the Lord. This would add not only to his guilt but also to his suffering.

25. Then Judas, which betrayed him, answered and said, Master, is it I? He said unto him, Thou hast said.

Discuss the action of Judas in his question, "Is it I?" Is it possible that Judas did not know who the betrayer would be?

It was only after the Lord had narrowed the identification of the traitor and mentioned his ultimate doom that Judas spoke up. It is interesting to note that the other eleven disciples used the term "Lord" when they addressed Jesus (v. 22). Judas used the term "Master." There is a difference in the two. The term **lord** means "an owner, a sovereign," and this term is the most intimate and exalted term that can be used. The term **master** means "teacher, Rabbi, one who instructs." Both terms are appropriate to Jesus, for He is both Lord and Master, our sovereign and our teacher. Many other instructors, though, were called master, such as Plato, Aristotle, Hillel, Gamaliel, and others. The term **lord,** on the other hand, is so exalted and august that it was used only in cases of extreme deference.

At this point, Judas desired to know if he was known to be the traitor. The reply of Jesus, "Thou hast said," was a common way of saying, "Yes, it is true."

26. And as they were eating, Jesus took bread, and blessed it, and brake it, and gave it to the disciples, and said, Take, eat; this is my body.

This verse marks the institution of what we call the Lord's Supper. The Passover meal was ended, and a new sacrament was begun. It should be noted that this event was of such importance that the Apostle Paul recorded it in 1 Corinthians 11, the only time in his epistles that Paul directly quoted the words of Jesus Christ.

The same bread that had been used for the Passover Feast was now given a new meaning and significance. Breaking the bread and distributing it to His disciples, the Lord called it His body. Naturally He meant that the bread symbolized His body, which was broken for them (1 Corinthians 11:24; Luke 22:19). Just as the unleavened bread had for centuries symbolized Israel's deliverance from Egypt, so hereafter it would symbolize the Christian's deliverance from sin through the sacrifice of Jesus Christ.

The fact that the Lord blessed the bread means simply that He gave thanks for it. This was not like the giving of thanks that we usually do before eating, but it was rather an acknowledgment or recognition of the divine purposes of the bread. The Lord made the bread to represent Himself, the Bread of Life, of which we all must partake. He broke the bread to signify the way in which His body would be broken, or given, by crucifixion (Luke 22:19).

27. And he took the cup, and gave thanks, and gave it to them, saying, Drink ye all of it.

As He had done with the bread, Christ then took the cup from which the group had drunk at the Passover and incorporated it into the sacrament of the Lord's Supper. As He had with the bread, He gave thanks for the cup and instructed all of His disciples to drink from it. The word "all" used here refers to all of the disciples, not all of the wine in the cup. The emphasis is that all of the Lord's followers must drink of His cup and share in that which it represents. Just as we all must partake of Christ's death, so should we all partake of the cup that represents that death. Jesus, the True Vine, made the fruit of the vine the symbol of His sacrificial blood.

III. BLESSINGS OF THE LORD'S SUPPER
(Matthew 26:28-30)

28. For this is my blood of the new testament, which is shed for many for the remission of sins.

The cup of the sacrament is specifically called the blood that Jesus was to shed. In the taking of this sacrament, we eat unleavened bread in remembrance of His broken body; we drink of the cup as a symbol of His spilled blood. With the institution of this sacrament, Jesus referred to the new covenant then being established. As the Passover had represented the old covenant (called Old Testament), so the Lord's Supper is a sacrament of the New Testament (or new covenant) which He established for His followers.

The Passover, observed for hundreds of years by the Jews, had been a type, or symbol, of the blood of Jesus which was to be shed. All over Jerusalem on the day of the Passover there were Jews partaking of the Passover Feast without knowing that He who fulfilled the Passover was about to give His life for them. On the night that the Jews escaped from Egypt, they were protected from the avenging angel by the sprinkling of a lamb's blood on their doorposts. This was a type of the blood of Christ. Now the true Lamb of God was about to give His blood for the remission of the sins of all who would believe on Him.

29. But I say unto you, I will not drink henceforth of this fruit of the vine, until that day when I drink it new with you in my Father's kingdom.

With the institution of this sacrament, Jesus told His disciples that the next time He drank with them it would be of a new wine in His Father's kingdom. "That is, I shall no more drink of the produce of the vine with you; but shall drink **new** wine—wine of a widely different nature from this—a wine which the kingdom of God alone can afford," paraphrases Adam Clarke. This was to emphasize to the disciples that His life on earth was over. The fulfillment of His earthly course was complete. Hereafter He would not share earthly things with His disciples, for His life on earth was at an end, but they would share heavenly things.

30. And when they had sung an hymn, they went out into the mount of Olives.

The events in the Upper Room were concluded with the singing of a hymn. It was customary at the observance of the Passover for the Jews to sing a song of six parts as an act of great worship. The parts which made up the song were Psalms 113, 114, 115, 116, 117, and 118. This particular song was sung because it recounted to the Jews the great elements of Jewish faith: (1) Israel's deliverance from Egypt, (2) the parting of the Red Sea, (3) the giving of the Law, (4) the resurrection of the dead, and (5) the coming of the Messiah. The Lord sang these songs with His disciples, and He then began His final steps toward the Cross. The time had come for Him to make the supreme sacrifice of His life for the salvation of man.

REVIEW QUESTIONS

1. Discuss the arrangements the disciples and Jesus made in order to partake of the Feast of the Passover.

2. What was the apparent attitude of Jesus toward Judas during the Passover supper?

3. What is the significance of commemorating the Lord's Supper as Christians do today?

4. What promise did Jesus give the disciples regarding the next time He would partake of the fruit of the vine?

5. Where did Jesus and His disciples go immediately after they had sung a hymn and concluded the Feast of the Passover?

GOLDEN TEXT HOMILY

"THIS IS MY BLOOD OF THE NEW TESTAMENT, WHICH IS SHED FOR MANY FOR THE REMISSION OF SINS" (Matthew 26:28).

This text becomes meaningful as we examine the context of verses 26-29. The key phrase is "my blood of the new testament [covenant]." The Hebrew translation is **berith** and means "to cut covenant."

The term **covenant** might be explained by the meaning of our marriage vows in a much earlier generation. A covenant is kept until death with no provision made for breakage.

In Greek there are two words that are translated as covenant: **suntheke** and **diatheke**. In **suntheke** two equal persons cut covenant and exchange assets and vows of protection and so forth. In **diatheke** a superior person provides all the elements of covenant for the other person.

The covenant between Jonathan and David would be typical of **suntheke,** but when David offered covenant rights to Jonathan's destitute, crippled son, Mephibosheth, it would be an example of **diatheke.** Mephibosheth had everything to gain and David had the power to give.

This word **diatheke** is used to signify Christ's covenant with us.

A covenant agreement has seven steps.

1. The garments are exchanged indicating that we are giving our wealth or assets away to each other. In the Old Covenant God did not give things to Abraham but said, "I am thy [your] . . . reward" (Genesis 15:1).

In the New Covenant, Christ does not simply give clothes; He gives Himself. In Galatians 3:27, Paul spoke of putting on Christ. We put off the old man and put on Christ.

2. The belts that hold the weapons of warfare are exchanged, indicating that all of our power of protection would be used to fight for the other person.

In God's covenant with Abraham, we do not see God giving things but as always He gives Himself stating, "I am thy [your] shield" (Genesis 15:1).

In the New Covenant Christ promises to be with us and to give us "power to tread on serpents and scorpions, and over all the power of the enemy: and nothing shall by any means hurt you" (Luke 10:19).

3. The steps of covenant cutting continue as an animal is slain. (Only in covenant is an animal equally divided into two parts.) The two who are cutting covenant move between the pieces, indicating that their promises to fulfill the terms of the covenant are unto death. An earlier generation repeated the words, "May I become as this dead animal if I fail to do my part."

As was stated earlier, the covenant God makes is **diatheke**, indicating that all of the giving is on God's part. This is shown clearly with Abraham's covenant. God indicates that Abraham is no more capable of fulfilling the terms of covenant than the human race is today. Genesis 15:12, 17 tells us, "When the sun was going down, a deep sleep fell upon Abram; and, lo, an horror of great darkness fell upon him. . . . And it came to pass, that, when the sun went down, and it was dark, behold a smoking furnace, and a burning lamp that passed between those pieces." Two things moved between the animal pieces. Most commentators agree that the burning torch and the smoking furnace represent deity, but most important we know that Abraham did not walk between the pieces. Abraham prepared the animals, but when it came time to fulfill the covenant requirements, it was impossible for sinful man to take part. A divine substitute for Abraham had to be found.

Thus it is in the New Covenant, Christ came as the divine descendant of Abraham and He did not symbolically walk between the walls of death. He actually embraced death and became at the same time the perfect sacrifice.

4. The palm of the hand or wrist was cut and blood was mingled when covenant was cut. The shaking of hands today dates back to this custom as does the raising of the right hand in court when an oath is taken. (At one time the uplifted hand would have revealed droplets of blood to the witnesses.) Abraham and his descendants followed this custom by circumcision. "And ye shall circumcise the flesh of your foreskin; and it shall be a token of the covenant betwixt me and you" (Genesis 17:11).

In the New Covenant our hearts are circumcised. "Now I say that Jesus Christ was a minister of the circumcision for the truth of God, to confirm the promises made unto the fathers" (Romans 15:8). Christ did not symbolically shed His blood but in actuality gave His very life's blood to establish the New Covenant.

5. Names are exchanged as a seal of covenant. If I made a covenant with John Smith, my name would become Edward Smith Call while his would become John Call Smith.

The Hebrew name for God is an unpronounceable **Ha**. When the Old Covenant was cut, Abram's name received this sound and became Abra**ha**m; his wife became no longer Sarai, but Sar**ah**; and God in turn was thereafter called the God of Abraham. As each preceding generation came into covenant experiences, God became the God of Isaac and of Jacob.

In the New Covenant the divine Son of God became the Son of man and we embrace the name Christian.

6. Cutting covenant is always memorialized with a meal in which the sacrifice is eaten. The Lord's Supper commemorates this meal. Christ being not only our substitute but also the sacrifice in the covenant cutting, says, "Take, eat; **this is my body**. And he took the cup, and gave thanks, and gave it to them, saying, Drink ye all of it; For **this is my blood** of the new testament [covenant]" (Matthew 26:26-28).

7. Finally the Old Covenant concerned not only Abraham, but also his descendants. The Hebrew boy as he reached the age of accountability went through a public ceremony in which he committed himself to the laws of the Old Covenant.

We today have the privilege of accepting the sacrificial death of Christ for our atonement and entering into the New Covenant.

The Old Covenant was but a foreshadow of the reality that the New Covenant fulfills.
—Edward E. Call, professor of Missions, Church of God Graduate School of Theology, Cleveland, Tennessee

SENTENCE SERMONS

THAT CHRIST DIED for the sins of all mankind is our continuing reminder through the Lord's Supper.

—Selected

THE LORD'S SUPPER helps us remember the meaning of Christ's death and the promise

of His second coming.
—**Selected**

THE LORD'S SUPPER is the most important part of Christian worship, and earth's nearest approach to heaven.
—**Andrew W. Blackwood**

BREAD OF THE WORLD, in mercy broken,
Wine of the soul in mercy shed,
By whom the words of life were spoken,
And in whose death our sins are dead.
Look on the hearts by sorrow broken,
Look on the tears by sinners shed;
And be Thy feast to us the token
That by Thy grace our souls are fed.
—**Reginald Heber's Hymn**

EVANGELISTIC APPLICATION

THE LORD'S SUPPER IS A CONTINUING REMINDER THAT CHRIST DIED FOR THE SINS OF ALL MANKIND.

UPPER ROOM: FURNISHED

In the midst of a prayer meeting service in a large downtown church, with several hundred people present, a timid little woman arose to speak. It was in the midst of the Lenten season and the pastor had asked a rather simple but searching question: "Suppose you had the chance to be some one person associated with those last days of Jesus in Jerusalem, whom would you choose to be?" The woman was trying to reply to that question.

"There are a lot of people in the passion story whose place I could never fill," she said. "I could not carry my Master's cross as Simon of Cyrene did. Nor could I have followed Him out to the garden as some of the others did. But I could make ready for Him the best room in my house, where He might eat the Last Supper with His disciples. I could promise Him that it would be made ready to His satisfaction." She was that kind of person.

Someone had to make ready a room and furnish it. There is no record of any such thing in the Scripture, but it is easy to imagine some housewife telling her Christian friends, years afterward, how the Lord had come to their home that night and had eaten that last solemn meal under her roof. She never wrote a Gospel nor became a martyr, nor did she hold an office in the church; but she could provide a furnished room!

A great deal of the service of the kingdom of God (and the Church) must be rendered by those who never get their names into the papers, are never publicly commended, and are never elected as a delegate. But there is need for a furnished upper room, and some devoted heart furnishes it without thought of publicity or commendation. In the eternal records of God the name is inscribed, and after it the notation clearly written: "Well done, thou good and faithful steward."—**Roy L. Smith from "Steward Illustrations"**

ILLUMINATING THE LESSON

S. S. Lappin, in "Where the Long Trail Begins," tells an interesting story about the pioneer days of his family and a little one in his home.

"What I remember best is that once, in the autumn, when learning to walk, the baby pressed his hand into the soft clay with which the cracks of our house had been filled. When spring came again, he had gone from us, but all through that summer and till autumn came again, there was a little handprint in the hardened clay. My mother's vision was very defective, and sometimes that summer when we were alone at the house, I saw her go to that print in the clay and run her sensitive fingertips along its outline."

So, in the Lord's Supper, we come that we may place our hands in the imprint of the Master's hand, that we may see that they are pierced for us.

DAILY DEVOTIONAL GUIDE

M. Remembering God's Plan of Redemption. Exodus 12:1-14
T. Honoring Jesus. Matthew 26:6-13
W. Plotting Against Jesus. Luke 22:1-6
T. Preparing for the Lord's Supper. Luke 22:7-13
F. Recognizing Deceit. John 13:21-30
S. Explaining the Lord's Supper. 1 Corinthians 11:23-34

January 11, 1981

The Danger of Self-Sufficiency

Bible Background: Matthew 26:31-35, 69-75

Time: A.D. 30

Place: Jerusalem

Supplemental References: Genesis 12:10-20; Mark 14:26-31, 66-72; Luke 22:31-38, 56-62; John 18:16, 17; 1 Corinthians 10:1-15; 1 Peter 5:8-10

Golden Text: "Wherefore let him that thinketh he standeth take heed lest he fall" (1 Corinthians 10:12).

Central Truth: In times of pressure, depending on self instead of Christ results in failure.

Evangelistic Emphasis: Depending on one's own ability brings failure in witnessing for Christ.

PRINTED TEXT

Matthew 26:31. Then saith Jesus unto them, All ye shall be offended because of me this night: for it is written, I will smite the shepherd, and the sheep of the flock shall be scattered abroad.

32. But after I am risen again, I will go before you into Galilee.

33. Peter answered and said unto him, Though all men shall be offended because of thee, yet will I never be offended.

34. Jesus said unto him, Verily I say unto thee, That this night, before the cock crow, thou shalt deny me thrice.

35. Peter said unto him, Though I should die with thee, yet will I not deny thee. Likewise also said all the disciples.

69. Now Peter sat without in the palace: and a damsel came unto him, saying, Thou also wast with Jesus of Galilee.

70. But he denied before them all, saying, I know not what thou sayest.

71. And when he was gone out into the porch, another maid saw him, and said unto them that were there, This fellow was also with Jesus of Nazareth.

72. And again he denied with an oath, I do not know the man.

73. And after a while came unto him they that stood by, and said to Peter, Surely thou also art one of them; for thy speech bewrayeth thee.

74. Then began he to curse and to swear, saying, I know not the man. And immediately the cock crew.

75. And Peter remembered the word of Jesus, which said unto him, Before the cock crow, thou shalt deny me thrice. And he went out, and wept bitterly.

DICTIONARY

Galilee (GAL-uh-lee)—Matthew 26:32—The northernmost of the three main provinces of Palestine west of the Jordan. It was the scene of a considerable part of Jesus' ministry.

Nazareth (NAZ-uh-reth)—Matthew 26:71—A town in lower Galilee, the hometown of Mary and Joseph

LESSON OUTLINE
I. THE FOLLY OF SELF-SUFFICIENCY
II. THE TRAGEDY OF DENIAL
III. THE WISDOM OF REPENTANCE

LESSON EXPOSITION

INTRODUCTION

Jesus chose men to do His work in building the church. This was necessary, for nothing can communicate with men as well as other men. Neither angels nor supernatural signs can take the place of men in the work of the Lord. Yet, the use of men in the Lord's work presents the possibility of failure. Men are mortal, subject to failure, misunderstanding, and loss. As long as men are mortal they have the possibility of imperfection and ruin. The only security from failure is in the Lord Jesus Christ himself. That is one reason why He has chosen men to work for Him: they must work in His strength and His grace, rather than in their own.

This lesson concerns a man of great promise and ability who failed momentarily to lean on the Lord as he should. In so doing, even the great Simon Peter failed in his courage and confidence. He suffered a lapse of faith that brought injury to the Christian cause, hurt to himself, and disappointment to his fellows. When any Christian fails in his stand for Christ he hurts far more than himself, and the damage he does long outlives the period of his failure.

I. THE FOLLY OF SELF-SUFFICIENCY (Matthew 26:31-35)

31. Then saith Jesus unto them, All ye shall be offended because of me this night: for it is written, I will smite the shepherd, and the sheep of the flock shall be scattered abroad.

A materialistic minded world along with a humanistic philosophy are influences that cause men to entertain a self-sufficient concept. What can the church do to correct this pattern of thinking?

The dialogue recorded in verses 31-35 apparently occurred as Jesus and His disciples walked from the Upper Room to the Garden of Gethsemane on the side of the Mount of Olives. During the Lord's Last Supper with His disciples, Jesus had revealed that one of His disciples would betray Him. This would be Judas Iscariot, who left the supper before Jesus and the other eleven (John 13:30). The eleven disciples did not know that Judas would betray Jesus; they thought he had left the supper early because he was the treasurer of the group and needed to make arrangements concerning the feast (John 13:28, 29).

Then Jesus and the eleven walked through the night from the Upper Room across the Valley Kidron to the Garden of Gethsemane. Jesus stated that all of their lives would be dramatically touched on that night; He, the Shepherd, would be smitten and they, the flock, would be scattered abroad. This was a prophecy of Zechariah 13:7. The meaning is that, because Jesus would be crucified, His disciples would be shaken in faith and confidence, driven back from the boldness and courage they now had. The sense of the word **offend** here is "to drive back."

32. But after I am risen again, I will go before you into Galilee.

To encourage their confidence, Jesus gave the assertion that He would rise again. He would rise from the dead and precede His disciples into Galilee. His work had begun in the northern province of Galilee, and to that province He would return after His crucifixion and resurrection. It is doubtful that the disciples grasped the full meaning of His words at this time but they would remember them during the sorrowful days that lay ahead of them. While they were grieving that the Shepherd had been smitten and the sheep scattered, they would remember that the Shepherd had promised to lead them back to Galilee.

33. Peter answered and said unto him, Though all men shall be offended because of thee, yet will I never be offended.

The presumption of Peter came through strongly. He was always quick to act and to react. Here, however, his presumption smacks of towering self-esteem. He asserts that all other men may be driven back from the Lord but that he is so strong he shall stand. How little did he know, and how much he had to learn. Adam Clarke has said, "The presumptuous person imagines he can do everything, and can do nothing; thinks he can excel all, and excels in nothing; promises everything, and performs nothing. The humble man acts a quite contrary part. There is nothing we know so little of as ourselves—nothing we see less of than our own weakness and poverty. The strength of pride is only for a moment. Peter, though vainly confident, was

January 11, 1981

certainly sincere—he had never been put to a sore trial, and did not know his own strength. Had this resolution of his been formed in the strength of God, he would have been enabled to maintain it against earth and hell."

Paul had a better way of expressing confidence and courage when he said, "I can do all things through Christ which strengtheneth me" (Philippians 4:13). It was also Paul who said, "Most gladly therefore will I rather glory in my infirmities, that the power of Christ may rest upon me. . . . for when I am weak, then am I strong" (2 Corinthians 12:9, 10).

34. Jesus said unto him, Verily I say unto thee, That this night, before the cock crow, thou shalt deny me thrice.

Jesus replied to Peter's presumption in a very positive way. The words "Verily I say unto thee" suggest that He spoke solemnly and emphatically. It was already night and darkness lay across the city. "It was night," John 13:30 says; Matthew 26:31 adds, "this night." This was to emphasize that before the coming of day Peter would betray the Lord three times. This underscores how quickly he who had boasted would stumble and fall back from following the Lord. Not only would Peter deny the Lord once, but he would deny Him three times. Peter's failure would be so great that he would disavow any knowledge of, or connection with, Jesus.

35. Peter said unto him, Though I should die with thee, yet will I not deny thee. Likewise also said all the disciples.

Peter responded with a second assurance that he would never deny the Lord. Once again he made the assertion in his own determination rather than in the strength the Lord might give him. Peter's assurance that he would die with Jesus before denying Him is important. This particular point will have a great part in Peter's denial that will follow.

It was Peter's nature to be bold and assertive. It is easy for those who have this nature to trust in their own strength and resolution, to take pride in never taking no for an answer, in being headstrong in their activities and attitudes, in being forthright and unequivocal. Yet this very nature frequently leads to trouble because it is often based in pride and exaggerated self-esteem. Those who have this presumptuous nature are not accustomed to rebuff and defeat, and therefore collapse when they are finally confronted with it. A milder and meeker man is often stronger in reality than a man of unwarranted self-confidence and presumptuous self-assurance.

It is interesting to note that the energetic and emphatic exchange between Jesus and Peter evoked from the other disciples an assurance that neither would they ever deny the Lord. Subsequent events of the evening indicate that their assurance was based upon a greater humility than had been Peter's.

II. THE TRAGEDY OF DENIAL (Matthew 26: 69-74)

69. Now Peter sat without in the palace: and a damsel came unto him, saying, Thou also wast with Jesus of Galilee.

In the Garden of Gethsemane Jesus gave Himself to earnest prayer while the apostles prayed less intensely nearby. They frequently fell asleep (vv. 40, 43, 45). Eventually Judas arrived with a multitude of religious leaders who were intent upon putting Jesus to death (v. 47). When the mob attempted to take Jesus by force, Peter tried to defend the Lord with a sword and injured the servant of the high priest (v. 51). In the stress of the critical moment Jesus rebuked Peter and instructed him to "put up again thy sword into his place: for all they that take the sword shall perish with the sword" (v. 52).

Then Jesus was led away to Caiaphas, the high priest, for trial. Peter, having been rebuffed by the Lord, followed afar off. It is very likely that he was offended by the rebuke of Jesus and thereby conditioned for what would happen next.

While Jesus was in the inner part of Caiaphas' house, Peter sat in the courtyard of the palace bewildered and confused by the events of the evening. A serving girl passed through the courtyard, which was an enclosed part of the palace, and observed that Peter was a part of the company of Jesus. This was a golden opportunity for Peter to assert the truth of what she said, but the boldness and impetuosity were now gone. Instead of stoutly affirming that he was with Jesus, Peter was so subdued and intimidated that he missed his chance to live up to his earlier bravado.

70. But he denied before them all, saying, I know not what thou sayest.

What are the steps generally taken by one who has been a believer to that of denying Christ?

In verse 58 Peter followed the Lord afar off instead of taking his place beside Him. Now in verse 70 he actually comes to a verbal denial. It was a mild form, "I know not what thou sayest," but it was a denial nonetheless. Spiritual defection is not achieved in one great act; it generally comes upon a person by degrees. Peter answered the maiden loudly enough for all present in the courtyard to hear his words. It was a clear effort to disassociate himself from Jesus.

71. And when he was gone out into the porch, another maid saw him, and said unto them that were there, This fellow was also with Jesus of Nazareth.

A second serving girl came to Peter when he moved to another part of the house and identified him to all the people present. Whereas the first maiden had spoken directly to Peter, this second one spoke to the gathered people regarding Peter. The people gathered were aware that Jesus had been apprehended in the Garden of Gethsemane. This damsel observed to them that, "This fellow was also with Jesus of Nazareth." Once again, Peter was given the opportunity to attest his friendship with, and loyalty to, Jesus. Even at this point he still could have recovered his earlier intentions by frankly acknowledging that he was one of Jesus' men. There seems to have been no desire to bring charges against the followers of Jesus or to cause them harm, so it is by no means certain that Peter would have been hazarding his life.

72. And again he denied with an oath, I do not know the man.

Peter's first denial of Jesus had been rather indirect, but then he became much more emphatic in the denial. He lied with an oath, "I do not know the man." Peter told the lie and added the oath to make it believable.

What could account for Peter's strange behavior on that night, so soon after he had declared his allegiance to Christ? Where is the man who assured Jesus that he would die with Him but would never betray Him? The only conceivable reason is that he had been chagrined and offended when Jesus rebuked him for endeavoring to use the sword. At that moment Peter really would have died with the Lord, for he was certainly no swordsman and would have been defeated in any swordplay. Under the pressure of the arrest and being carried away by the mob, Jesus had no time to explain to Peter or to soothe his offended feelings. Peter could only feel that he had done everything possible to defend Jesus and had been rebuked for his efforts.

That is just the point of the whole affair. True faith in Christ would have accepted His words with confidence and acceptance. Whether or not he understood, Peter's loyalty and love should have known that whatever Jesus did was for the best. This is the basis of true love and dependence, when we know that whatever another does is somehow for our benefit. Even when we do not understand all the circumstances, true love makes us certain that if we did know the circumstances we would agree with the action. That is Paul's meaning when he says, "Charity [love] suffereth long . . . is not easily provoked . . . believeth all things" (1 Corinthians 13:4, 5, 7).

73. And after a while came unto him they that stood by, and said to Peter, Surely thou also art one of them; for thy speech bewrayeth thee.

The crowd that had overheard the exchange between Peter and the two serving girls had been watching him and listening to him closely. They observed that his accent was different from that of Jerusalem. In Israel, as in other nations of the world, dialects differed from one part of the country to another. By listening to Peter speak, the people could tell that he was from Galilee, just as a drawling accent often reveals that an American is from the South. Neither Peter's lie nor his oath convinced the bystanders of what he said. The word **bewray** has long since been dropped from modern English usage. It was a stronger word than the present word **betray** and meant "to accuse." Those who pressed upon Peter said that not only had the two damsels accused him but that his dialect accused him also.

74. Then began he to curse and to swear, saying, I know not the man. And immediately the cock crew.

In verse 70 Peter made an indirect denial of Christ. In verse 72 he made an explicit denial and added an oath. In this verse he made a more vehement denial and added cursing and swearing. The meaning here is that he swore by God's name that he had no part with Jesus. In so short a time the disciple who declared his steadfastness had sunk to the very bottom.

The betrayal of Judas and the denial of Peter were comparable. Both men stood guilty and would have been lost because of their deeds. The difference was that Judas betrayed the Lord deliberately and with forethought. His was a cold and calculated betrayal. Peter's denial was on the spur of the moment while he was nursing an imagined grievance. There was no premeditation in his sin. This does not lessen the gravity of what he did or make him any less guilty, but only explains why he may have done it. At this point it must be emphasized that the two men stood equally guilty for what they had done. The consequence for each man would be determined by what happened later.

Peter was jarred to his senses by the crowing of a cock. In the dark hours of the early morning he heard a cock crow to mark the approach of dawn. The rooster's natural activity became the instrument by which God brought the fallen apostle to his senses. In the same way today He uses commonplace events and ordinary things to remind us of His claims upon us. The most ordinary incident may be God's way of saving us from catastrophe or directing us into truth.

III. THE WISDOM OF REPENTANCE (Matthew 26:75)

75. And Peter remembered the word of Jesus, which said unto him, Before the cock crow, thou shalt deny me thrice. And he went out, and wept bitterly.

Upon hearing the cock crow, Peter recalled everything Jesus had said to him earlier in the evening. We can only imagine with what shock it must have come upon the self-proclaimed strong man that he had actually denied his Lord. His self-assurance crumbled and he was struck with his own vanity. From another Gospel we receive the additional fact that Jesus turned and looked at Peter about the time of this third denial (Luke 22:61). Apparently Jesus was led from one section of the house to another and passed through the room where Peter stood with the accusing mob. Unable to speak to Peter, Jesus could only turn and look at him. That look, however, was louder than any words He could have said. Peter was broken in spirit and began to weep bitterly.

It is not stated where Peter went and "wept bitterly," but one opinion is that he returned to the Garden of Gethsemane. That would have been the logical place for him to go, for that is where Jesus had been praying earlier in the night. That is where Peter had fallen asleep when the Lord asked the disciples to pray; that is where Jesus had been arrested and Peter had endeavored to defend Him with a sword. Where he went is not important, but the fact that he went is important. By repenting of his sin he was restored to his Lord and to the company of disciples.

Judas hanged himself instead of repenting (Matthew 27:4, 5) and was lost forever. Without repentance, Peter too would have been lost forever. The fact that he wept bitterly implies the intensity with which he must have prayed and repented of the terrible deed he had done. The Lord accepted this repentance and Peter was restored to his place. It is noteworthy that every list of the twelve apostles in Holy Scripture puts the name of Simon Peter first.

REVIEW QUESTIONS

1. What admonition did Jesus give His disciples concerning the events that awaited Him?

2. What was Peter's attitude about his ability to avoid denial of the Lord?

3. What response did Jesus give to Peter's bold statement?

4. List the steps that transpired in Peter's denial of the Lord.

5. In what way was Peter's denial of the Lord similar to the betrayal of Judas? In what way was the denial much different?

GOLDEN TEXT HOMILY

"WHEREFORE LET HIM THAT THINKETH HE STANDETH TAKE HEED LEST HE FALL" (1 Corinthians 10:12).

All through the Bible, both Old and New Testament, we find very earnest warnings to Christian people against the danger of giving way to temptation and going back into the world. God and the inspired writers realized that this vile world is not a friend to grace. It requires just as much effort on our part to keep saved as it does to get saved. St. Paul was constantly exhorting and warning those to whom he wrote against the danger of falling from grace. In verse 27 of chapter 9, Paul has told us that he himself keeps his own body under subjection lest after having preached the gospel to others he himself should become a castaway. He then gives to us the historic record of how the children of Israel, after they had been delivered from bondage, turned from God and had judgment visited upon them. They ate of that spiritual meat and did drink of that spiritual drink, for they drank of that Rock which was Christ, and yet God rejected them. He points out to us

that these things are given as an example of how God deals with people that reject Him and turn into sin. Then he gives to us the solemn warning of the text, "Wherefore let him that thinketh he standeth take heed lest he fall." Many people today need to take this warning to heart and walk close to God.
—**John R. Church, Ph.D., Winston Salem, North Carolina**

SENTENCE SERMONS

DEPENDING ON SELF instead of Christ during times of pressure results in failure.
—**Selected**

ONE MAY BE HUMBLE out of pride.
—**Michel Eyquem de Montaigne**

GOD RESISTETH THE PROUD, and giveth grace to the humble.
—**1 Peter 5:5**

IT IS FUN to believe in yourself, but don't be too easily convinced.
—**T. Harry Thompson**

ILLUMINATING THE LESSON

There never was a saint yet that grew proud of his fine feathers, but what the Lord plucked them out by and by; there never yet was an angel that had pride in his heart, but he lost his wings, and fell into Gehenna, as Satan and those fallen angels did; and there shall never be a saint who indulges self-conceit and pride and self-confidence, but the Lord will spoil his glories, and trample his honors in the mire, and make him cry out yet again, "Lord, have mercy upon me," less than the least of all saints, and the "very chief of sinners."
—**Spurgeon**

EVANGELISTIC APPLICATION

DEPENDING ON ONE'S OWN ABILITY BRINGS FAILURE IN WITNESSING FOR CHRIST.

NIBBLING THEMSELVES AWAY

An old shepherd once said, "There is nothing vicious about a sheep. He does not go off storming into the desert, nor does he climb some mountainside out of sheer wickedness. Instead, he just nibbles himself away. He gets so much interested in the tuft of grass that is just ahead of his nose that he eats himself off the trail before he knows it."

The number of actually wicked people in the world is probably not large. They get into the headlines and attract a great deal of attention, but they are a very small minority of the total population. The vast majority of those who get into serious trouble—those who get lost—are people who "just nibble themselves" off the trail.

They become so interested in that little extra profit, that additional sale, a few more votes, an extra convenience or two for the home, one more record broken, that they lose their sense of proportion. They allow trifles to blind them to the magnificences of life.

A young theological student and his wife, who set out for the seminary without sufficient funds to pay their first year's expenses, became so engrossed in earning "a little extra" that they skimped their schoolwork. The next year, in order to make up some work, they both took additional courses and worked even a little more on the outside. When the strain became acute they became irritable with one another, each confiding in a friend that he did not believe the other appreciated him. Before the end of the year their home was in serious jeopardy and serious damage had been done to their spiritual life. This was reflected in an unhappy experience in their first church and, eventually, a divorce. They had nibbled themselves away.

The prophet says that most of us—all of us, in fact—go astray at least to some extent by this method. Beginning with a minor compromise, we go on to greater indiscretions. Rebelling against God in little things, we begin defying Him in the basic matter. The tufts of grass just ahead of our noses seem so seductive.—Roy L. Smith, from **Stewardship Illustrations**

DAILY DEVOTIONAL GUIDE

M. Flee Dishonesty. Genesis 12:10-20
T. Accept Christ as Lord. John 6:63-71
W. Abide in Christ. John 15:1-8
T. Beware of False Security. 1 Corinthians 10:1-12
F. Commit All to Christ. 1 Peter 5:1-7
S. Permit Christ to Lead. 1 Peter 5:8-11

January 18, 1981

The Price of Consecration

Bible Background: Matthew 26:36-56; Mark 14:32-46; Luke 22:39-48; John 18:1-11
Time: A.D. 30
Place: Mount of Olives
Supplemental Reference: Psalm 41:5-9
Golden Text: "O my Father, if it be possible, let this cup pass from me: nevertheless not as I will, but as thou wilt" (Matthew 26:39).
Central Truth: Jesus consecrated Himself for our sake; we should consecrate ourselves for His sake.
Evangelistic Emphasis: Repenting of our sins and surrendering our will to Christ is the only way to fulfill God's purpose for our lives.

PRINTED TEXT

Matthew 26:36. Then cometh Jesus with them unto a place called Gethsemane, and saith unto the disciples, Sit ye here, while I go and pray yonder.

37. And he took with him Peter and the two sons of Zebedee, and began to be sorrowful and very heavy.

38. Then saith he unto them, My soul is exceeding sorrowful, even unto death: tarry ye here, and watch with me.

39. And he went a little farther, and fell on his face, and prayed, saying, O my Father, if it be possible, let this cup pass from me: nevertheless not as I will, but as thou wilt.

40. And he cometh unto the disciples, and findeth them asleep, and saith unto Peter, What, could ye not watch with me one hour?

41. Watch and pray, that ye enter not into temptation: the spirit indeed is willing, but the flesh is weak.

42. He went away again the second time, and prayed, saying, O my Father, if this cup may not pass away from me, except I drink it, thy will be done.

43. And he came and found them asleep again: for their eyes were heavy.

44. And he left them, and went away again, and prayed the third time, saying the same words.

45. Then cometh he to his disciples, and saith unto them, Sleep on now, and take your rest: behold, the hour is at hand, and the Son of man is betrayed into the hands of sinners.

46. Rise, let us be going: behold, he is at hand that doth betray me.

47. And while he yet spake, lo, Judas, one of the twelve, came, and with him a great multitude with swords and staves, from the chief priests and elders of the people.

48. Now he that betrayed him gave them a sign, saying, Whomsoever I shall kiss, that same is he: hold him fast.

49. And forthwith he came to Jesus, and said, Hail, master; and kissed him.

50. And Jesus said unto him, Friend, wherefore art thou come? Then came they, and laid hands on Jesus, and took him.

DICTIONARY

Gethsemane (geth-SEM-uh-nee)—Matthew 26:36—From the Aramaic for "oil press"; the place of Jesus' agony and arrest

Zebedee (ZEB-uh-dee)—Matthew 26:37—A fisherman on the Sea of Galilee, the father of James and John. He was the husband of Salome and possibly lived in the vicinity of Bethsaida.

chief priests and elders—Matthew 26:47—The smaller synagogues had but one official, while the larger ones had several elders (Luke 7:3) which formed a local tribunal or committee of management. The **chief** or **ruler** had the responsibility of controlling the synagogue services, deciding on the reader and maintaining order.

LESSON OUTLINE

I. BE WATCHFUL
II. PRAY FERVENTLY
III. FACE OPPOSITION COURAGEOUSLY

LESSON EXPOSITION

INTRODUCTION

The events of this lesson occurred concurrently with those of last week's lesson. In this lesson we study the events between Peter's presumptuous assurance that he would never deny the Lord and the time after Jesus' arrest when he did deny Him. In our study of Peter's denial, the focus was upon the human frailty and failure of an apostle, a mortal man. In this, we look at the human dread of Jesus Christ, who was both God and man. More than any other time in His life, Jesus revealed His human side along with His divine side as He faced the human sorrow of dying.

Jesus was born into the world to give His life as a sacrifice for the sins of men. He was aware of this destiny all of His days. As the Son of God, He never hesitated or shrank from fulfilling His purpose. At this point, however, His death was imminent, not something that He knew would happen in the future. It was now upon Him, and this would be His last night before offering His life as a sacrifice for mankind.

The purpose of the Incarnation was that Jesus might live on earth in human flesh, feeling the pain, the sorrows, and the weaknesses of mankind. During His life He had known weariness, hunger, loneliness, rejection, misunderstanding, and all the host of trials that come to mankind. It was a different matter to face death, which would involve enough pain to tear life from the human body. Jesus had to face this in all its pain and terror, else He would not have the human experience that comes at last to all men. At this time of greatest distress, Jesus needed to be alone so He could pray and reconcile Himself to this final hour. He wanted His disciples to be close to Him, but He did not want them to share in the agonies of prayer and resolve that belonged to Him.

I. BE WATCHFUL (Matthew 26:36-38)

36. Then cometh Jesus with them unto a place called Gethsemane, and saith unto the disciples, Sit ye here, while I go and pray yonder.

Gethsemane was a garden of olive trees at the base of the Mount of Olives. The word **gethsemane** means "oil press or olive press." This was an appropriate name for the place where Jesus went to pray on this particular night. His heart was pressed and heavy with the burdens of the world.

He instructed eight of His disciples to remain at a particular part of the garden while He went deeper into it to pray.

37. And he took with him Peter and the two sons of Zebedee, and began to be sorrowful and very heavy.

As frequently happened, Peter, James, and John went a little farther with the Lord than did the others. These three had formed a type of inner circle around the Lord. This was not because He had partiality toward them, but it was because they so constantly sought for His company. They took advantage of every opportunity to be at His side, to question Him more closely about His teachings, and to be more intimately involved with His affairs.

The deeper into the garden Jesus went, the deeper His burden became. In the presence of the three disciples, He became crushed with the burden that was upon Him. He revealed to them what extreme anguish and heaviness lay upon His heart. There was at least a degree of comfort in having three friends so intimate that He could share the extremity of His burden with them.

38. Then saith he unto them, My soul is exceeding sorrowful, even unto death: tarry ye here, and watch with me.

Jesus said to the three disciples words to this effect: "My soul is so burdened that I shall die if I do not get relief; stay here close to Me and pray."

The great sorrow of Jesus was not merely His dread of dying: the burden of the sins of the world began to descend upon Him. He had become the Lamb of God, carrying the weight of a world filled with guilt. His burden was far greater than a broken heart, far greater than any burden that a natural man could ever bear. He had now become the sin offering of the world.

II. PRAY FERVENTLY (Matthew 26:39-45)

39. And he went a little farther, and fell on his face, and prayed, saying, O my Father, if it be possible, let this cup pass from me: nevertheless not as I will, but as thou wilt.

This is one of the most poignant verses in all the Word of God. Here we see Jesus going a little farther than His disciples before He literally staggered under His burden and fell on His face praying for relief. He appealed to His Father to allow the cup of suffering to pass from Him, to take away the necessity of such pain, to lift the requirement of death. Even as He sought surcease from His suffering, Jesus yielded Himself to the will of the Father. He earnestly desired to be spared from the necessity of so cruel a death as awaited Him, yet He would do it if there was no other way.

The pressure upon Him was so great that Luke adds, "There appeared an angel unto him from heaven, strengthening him" (Luke 22:43). The Father could not, and did not, lighten the burden that was upon Him, but He did send a heavenly messenger to succor Him and give Him strength. Luke also adds the fact that, "His sweat was as it were great drops of blood falling down to the ground" (v. 44). Much has been written about how the capillaries burst within His body and caused His sweat to have a tinge of blood. The scripture does not say that His sweat became blood, but that it fell "as it were" great drops of blood. This is a graphic description of the agony the Lord bore in His soul. How long He prayed at this time is indicated by the words of Jesus in Matthew 26:40, but no amount of time could measure the gravity of sorrow that lay in His heart.

40. And he cometh unto the disciples, and findeth them asleep, and saith unto Peter, What, could ye not watch with me one hour?

During the course of His anguished praying, the Lord came to Peter, James, and John for help in prayer. During the hour that He had been in such travail, they were overcome with weariness and fell asleep. This does not indicate that they did not care about His burden, but it means only that they did not share the great heaviness He felt. The heaviness and sorrow He felt was His alone, unshared by any companion and unexperienced by any mortal.

His words were directed to Peter, no doubt, because it had been Peter who made such a strong assertion that he would die with the Lord before he would deny Him (vv. 33, 35).

41. Watch and pray, that ye enter not into temptation: the spirit indeed is willing, but the flesh is weak.

Still directing His words toward Peter, Jesus reminded the disciples of the weakness of the flesh even when the spirit seems bold and courageous. The exhortation to "watch and pray" means that we must be on guard against undetected and unintentional sins. Christians must live with their guards raised against intrusions of disobedience, of pride, of negligence, of indulgence, and of other temptations that beset us all.

Discuss the apparent ease by which the disciples drifted into sleep even though their friend and Lord was experiencing a struggle.

---

42. He went away again the second time, and prayed, saying, O my Father, if this cup may not pass away from me, except I drink it, thy will be done.

With His disciples now aroused and rejoining Him in prayer, Jesus returned to His private spot and resumed His agony in prayer. Once again, He appealed to the Father to remove the cup of suffering and death from Him if it were possible. Nevertheless, if the salvation of man required such a bitter sacrifice, then He was ready to make it. The human side of Jesus dreaded the pain of dying as much as any other man, but the divine side stood ready to endure any suffering that might secure the salvation of the world. This mixture of human suffering and divine purpose shows the incarnation of Jesus as nothing else can.

During the prayer, He became completely reconciled to the fact that He must drink the bitter cup of death, and He was able to say, "Thy will be done." Jesus knew He would have to die, but He first had to go through human submission on His way to that destiny. If He had not faced such human dread of death, then He could not share with us when we humans dread the face of death. It was necessary for Him to share in our dying in order to accomplish our redemption.

43. And he came and found them asleep again: for their eyes were heavy.

The second time Jesus came to His disciples, He again found them asleep. It had been a very long and arduous day and they could not keep their eyes open. They were dead on their feet and could not stay awake. Jesus felt such pain that He could not find sleep; but His pain and distress had to be borne alone. He had to drink the bitter dregs of death from the cup that had been given Him, and there was no one who could share the cup with Him. His heart was heavier than His eyes, but the eyes of the disciples were heavier than their hearts. That was the difference between His divinity and their humanity.

44. And he left them, and went away again, and prayed the third time, saying the same words.

For the third time, Jesus left the disciples and prayed alone. He still appealed to the Father to remove from Him the terrible pain and heaviness in His heart. He prayed for the Father to remove from Him the necessity of the sacrificial death that awaited Him.

It must be understood that no other death the world has ever seen has equalled the death of Jesus. There may have been other horrible ways of dying, more prolonged periods of dying, and more dramatic instances of death; but Jesus is the only person ever to die with the full burden of guilty mankind upon His heart. Jesus was our sin offering, and the judgment, the pain, the death, that belongs to us rested that night upon Him. He himself bore our sins and carried them with Him to the Cross (1 Peter 2:24). As one man, He carried the collective guilt of the entire human race, and no one shared this burden with Him.

The fact that Jesus prayed three times coincides with the three times Paul prayed in 2 Corinthians 12:8. It also coincides with the Lord's direction to the church, "That in the mouth of two or three witnesses every word may be established" (Matthew 18:16). By praying three times, the Lord exhausted every appeal, and the Father gave a threefold affirmation that the sacrifice of Christ alone could atone for the sins of the world.

45. Then cometh he to his disciples, and saith unto them, Sleep on now, and take your rest: behold, the hour is at hand, and the Son of man is betrayed into the hands of sinners.

With His praying now completed, Jesus came back to His disciples with these words of resignation and warning. The disciples had missed their opportunity to bear their Lord up in prayer in His heaviest hour. Human weakness had overcome spiritual urgency. Nevertheless, Jesus alone had gained the victory and stood now ready for the ultimate sacrifice. He alone had secured the final affirmation of the Father and could die without further reluctance or dread.

As Jesus concluded His praying, three disciples slept nearby. Eight disciples slept a bit farther away, and the twelfth was on his way into the garden with Gentiles ("sinners," v. 45) who would arrest the Lord and put Him to death. The hour for which Jesus had come into the world had now come. The Lamb of God had to be offered up for the sins of the world.

III. FACE OPPOSITION COURAGEOUSLY (Matthew 26:46-50)

46. Rise, let us be going: behold, he is at hand that doth betray me.

Christ's intention was to meet Judas and the Jewish leaders when they came. This would demonstrate that He was giving up His life, because He could have taken flight if He had wished to save Himself. It would also reveal to Judas that He had known about the wicked scheme and that Judas' betrayal was no secret to Him.

47. And while he yet spake, lo, Judas, one of the twelve, came, and with him a great multitude with swords and staves, from the chief priests and elders of the people.

In order to mark more completely the great extent to which Judas had fallen, it is mentioned here that he was one of the Twelve. He who had sat at the Passover with Jesus, who had listened to His instructions, who had observed His cures and good works, who had seen His love for the poor and the suffering, and who had lived the life of spotless holiness, was now the vile agent to bring about his Lord's arrest and death. He who had seen his Lord's hands stretched out to heal the sick and to raise the dead would now see his Lord betrayed by his own hand, and taken away by the rough hands of Roman soldiers. The depth to which Judas had fallen had now exceeded that which the righteous mind can comprehend. Not only had he premeditated his vile deed and covenanted with the Lord's enemies to do it, he also literally was come to carry out the abominable deed.

Judas led a mob of evildoers with him. The chief priests and elders had sent with the former apostle the necessary Roman cohort and an assorted group to overwhelm the Lord. The comparison of the mob and the company of disciples with whom he had formerly traveled should have struck Judas with the wretched nature of his betrayal. It did not, however, and he followed his dastardly course through to the end.

48. Now he that betrayed him gave them a sign, saying, Whomsoever I shall kiss, that same is he: hold him fast.

The multitude of soldiers and hangers-on would probably not be able to tell Jesus from those who might be with Him. So that they might know which He was, Judas had agreed that he would point Him out with a kiss. What a terrible travesty on that tender gesture which betokens love and affection. A pointed finger would not suffice for his apostate mind; a verbal greeting would have been too detached and remote; he would signify which of the men was Jesus by planting on Him a brotherly kiss. The hypocrisy of this act staggers the imagination, for a kiss was traditionally given and received as a token of love. It signified brotherhood, fellowship, and unity of heart and purpose. Yet Judas dared to put a blight upon this gentlest of all tokens of love—a kiss.

49. And forthwith he came to Jesus, and said, Hail, master; and kissed him.

Judas approached the Lord and addressed Him in friendship. He called Him Master instead of Lord, just as he had done earlier in the evening at the Last Supper. This term meant only "Rabbi or teacher"; a more exalted term would have been Lord.

The statement that Judas kissed Jesus implies that he did so with tenderness and affection. With this gesture, he pretended to Christ that he loved Him with pure affection, and yet he knew that by that very kiss Jesus would be identified to His enemies, who would seize Him roughly and ultimately put Him to death. There could be no greater hypocrisy than this, no greater betrayal of life's strongest emotion, love. The person whom Judas betrayed and the sign by which the fallen apostle sealed that betrayal are combined in the most sinister and hypocritical act perpetrated by a human being.

50. And Jesus said unto him, Friend, wherefore art thou come? Then came they, and laid hands on Jesus, and took him.

Jesus called Judas "Friend," which underscored the magnitude of the person Judas had betrayed. It was the demonstration that He bore no malice toward the former disciple and regarded him only with compassion. The question "Wherefore art thou come?" was not asked for information—Jesus knew that already—but in order that Judas himself might regard the answer in his own heart. It was as if the Lord wished to break in upon the consciousness of Judas with a realization of how vile his deed actually was. It was as if the Lord had said, "Friend, do you really know what you are doing?"

In John 18:4-8 we receive important additional details concerning events of this moment. Those soldiers who first approached Jesus were struck to the ground by supernatural power when first they endeavored to lay hands upon Him. Jesus then asked them to let His disciples go, and He then submitted Himself to their seizure. He might be arrested and put to death, but only because He submitted Himself to that destiny. Because He was obedient even to death, mankind has hope for life today.

REVIEW QUESTIONS

1. Name the three disciples that accompanied Jesus into the inner Garden of Gethsemane. Why did He select these three?

2. What admonition did Jesus give the three disciples when He returned and found them asleep?

3. Discuss the meaning of the statement "Sleep on now and take your rest," in conjunction with an immediate follow-up with the words, "Rise, let us be going."

4. What sign did Judas use to identify Jesus to those who came to take Him?

5. What practical applications for your personal life do you draw from this lesson?

GOLDEN TEXT HOMILY

"O MY FATHER, IF IT BE POSSIBLE, LET

THIS CUP PASS FROM ME: NEVERTHELESS NOT AS I WILL, BUT AS THOU WILT" (Matthew 26:39).

The time was near at hand when the sins of all mankind would be borne on the sacred shoulders of the Son of God. The scripture states, "The Lord hath laid on him the iniquity of us all" (Isaiah 53:6). Soon the perfect sacrifice, the spotless Lamb of God, would pay the redemption price for humanity. He who knew no sin was made sin on our behalf (see 2 Corinthians 5:21). The burden was heavy. The price was high. The cup was bitter.

As a man, Christ felt terribly alone. In this time of awful anguish He cried out to His Father, "If it be possible." He was saying that if there were any way by which man could be saved and God be glorified—if there were any other method of redemption—let it be.

It was not merely the thought of bodily pain, though that would be long and excessive; there were other elements which made His sorrow like no other sorrow. He thought of the grievous wickedness that brought about His death, the treachery of Judas, the desertion of His friends, the denial of Peter, the unjust condemnation brought against Him by the rulers of the chosen nation—such considerations formed one ingredient in the bitter cup from which He had to drink. It is the cry of humanity, yet conditioned by perfect submission.

In this prayer are shown the two wills of Christ—the human and the divine. The natural inclination to somehow escape from this ignominy and torture is overborne by entire submission to a higher divine purpose. The will of the Father, and not the flesh, must be accomplished above all. In order to be obedient Christ had to suffer. This obedience of Christ to the perfect will of the Father brought salvation to all men everywhere.

The natural inclination of our own human nature is to shun shame or suffering and to take the path of least resistance. The affluence of our society has thus conditioned us. Contrary to this trend, the highest goal of the true disciple is to be like his master. The believer must know his master well enough to know His perfect will, and love Him enough to do His will—whatever the cost. To know and do the will of God is the way to real purpose and lasting peace.—**Jerry Noble, Media Coordinator, "Forward in Faith," Cleveland, Tennessee**

SENTENCE SERMONS

PRAYER IS A MEANS of applying divine power to human circumstances.
—**"Notes and Quotes"**

COURAGE DOES NOT look at the size or power of the enemy, but at the necessity of victory.
—**Selected**

GIVE ME TEN MEN fully consecrated to Christ, and I will shake any city for God.
—**D. L. Moody**

CONSECRATION IS HANDING God a blank sheet to fill in with your name signed at the bottom.
—**"Notes and Quotes"**

EVANGELISTIC APPLICATION

REPENTING OF OUR SINS AND SURRENDERING OUR WILL TO CHRIST IS THE ONLY WAY TO FULFILL GOD'S PURPOSE FOR OUR LIVES.

THE IMPULSE TO PRAY

One can hardly imagine that there is any person in the world who does not, for one reason or another, feel like praying. The impulse to pray is as natural as breathing. On some occasion you are struck by the mystery of life. You ask yourself: "What is the meaning of life? Why am I here? What may I hope for?" At such a time you feel like praying in the hope, perhaps, that the mystery and meaning of life will be made clear.

Or one day you suddenly realize that you have been greatly misunderstood in something you have said or done. Your motives were pure, your intentions honest, and your heart set in the right direction. But folk unwittingly misjudged you and blamed you unjustly. In that hour you want to pray.

Or you have made a great mistake. You were faulty in your judgment. You look back upon the error with regret. You wish you could undo it, and you pray that the same blunder will not be made again. You want to pray, this time for forgiveness.

Or perhaps some unusual happiness has descended upon you. Some glad surprise has greeted you on your pathway. You feel as though you were a debtor to God and to all the world. Your heart sings, your voice rings with merriment, and you are thankful. Again prayer seems the proper expression.

Or in another situation life seems to pall on you. You have been enjoying the feast with few worries and obstacles. But one cannot live forever like that. You want to do something for somebody, and you look up for some guiding hand. You pray for a wider field of endeavor.

Eventually you find yourself in the presence of death. Death previously had come to others, but never touched you. But now the grievous event has happened. A loved one is taken. The light goes out in your sky. You wonder why; you are not prepared; and so you pray out of your distress.
—**Frederick Keller Stamm,** from **Worship Resources**

ILLUMINATING THE LESSON

The old Greek story says that Achilles, the great hero of the Trojan war, was dipped while he was yet a child in the waters of the Styx by his mother, Thetis, in order to make him invulnerable. And the result of that plunge was that every part of Achilles' body was proof against wounds with the exception of the heel by which his mother held him, and which had not been submerged in the waters. For many years, as a result, Achilles escaped unhurt, but at last the poisoned arrow of the Trojan Paris found the weak spot and inflicted the death wound there. So sin and temptation attack us where we are weakest. They appeal to our inclinations, our passions, our lusts; they find out the weak spot.

—**J. D. Jones**

DAILY DEVOTIONAL GUIDE

M. Delighting in God's Will. Psalm 40:1-8
T. Facing Our Destiny. Matthew 16:21-28
W. Surrendering to God's Will. Mark 8:34-38
T. Serving in God's Kingdom. Mark 10:35-45
F. Suffering Brings Perfection. Hebrews 2:5-10
S. Fulfilling the Will of God. Hebrews 10:7-18

January 25, 1981

Tragedy of Rejecting Christ

Bible Background: Matthew 26:57-68; Mark 14:53—15:15; John 18:12-14, 19-38
Time: A.D. 30
Place: Jerusalem
Supplemental References: Psalm 69:6-20; Luke 18:18-27; 2 Timothy 4:10
Golden Text: "He came unto his own, and his own received him not" (John 1:11).
Central Truth: When men come face-to-face with Christ, they must either receive Him or reject Him.
Evangelistic Emphasis: Man makes a tragic decision when he decides to reject Christ rather than to receive Him.

PRINTED TEXT

Matthew 26:57. And they that had laid hold on Jesus led him away to Caiaphas the high priest, where the scribes and the elders were assembled.

58. But Peter followed him afar off unto the high priest's palace, and went in, and sat with the servants, to see the end.

59. Now the chief priests, and elders, and all the council, sought false witness against Jesus, to put him to death;

60. But found none: yea, though many false witnesses came, yet found they none. At the last came two false witnesses,

61. And said, This fellow said, I am able to destroy the temple of God, and to build it in three days.

62. And the high priest arose, and said unto him, Answerest thou nothing? what is it which these witness against thee?

63. But Jesus held his peace. And the high priest answered and said unto him, I adjure thee by the living God, that thou tell us whether thou be the Christ, the Son of God.

64. Jesus saith unto him, Thou hast said: nevertheless I say unto you, Hereafter shall ye see the Son of man sitting on the right hand of power, and coming in the clouds of heaven.

65. Then the high priest rent his clothes, saying, He hath spoken blasphemy; what further need have we of witnesses? behold, now ye have heard his blasphemy.

66. What think ye? They answered and said, He is guilty of death.

67. Then did they spit in his face, and buffeted him; and others smote him with the palms of their hands,

68. Saying, Prophesy unto us, thou Christ, Who is he that smote thee?

Mark 15:2. And Pilate asked him, Art thou the King of the Jews? And he answering said unto him, Thou sayest it.

3. And the chief priests accused him of many things: but he answered nothing.

4. And Pilate asked him again, saying, Answerst thou nothing? behold how many things they witness against thee.

5. But Jesus yet answered nothing; so that Pilate marvelled.

DICTIONARY

Caiaphas (KAY-uh-fus)—Matthew 26:57—High priest of the Jews from A.D. 14 to A.D. 38, before whom Jesus was condemned

January 25, 1981

chief priests and elders—Matthew 26:59—The smaller synagogues had but one official, whereas the larger ones had several elders (Luke 7:3), which formed a local tribunal committee of management. The **chief** or **ruler** had the responsibility of controlling the synagogue services, deciding on the reader, and maintaining order.

LESSON OUTLINE
I. ENEMIES OF CHRIST ACCUSE HIM
II. ENEMIES OF CHRIST PERSECUTE HIM
III. ENEMIES OF CHRIST REJECT HIM

LESSON EXPOSITION

INTRODUCTION

Between the agony of Gethsemane and the suffering on Calvary, Jesus was subjected to an unfair and illegal trial by both the Jews and the Romans. During this ordeal He was altogether alone, without friend or supporter to encourage or defend Him. Following His arrest in Gethsemane, "all the disciples forsook him, and fled" (Matthew 26:56). This was the Lord's hour of total rejection, when His enemies passed Him from one tribunal to another, each adding to His harassment and grief. If it was Jesus' hour of total rejection, then it was the hour of triumph for the powers of darkness (Luke 22:53).

Jesus did not have to suffer alone, yet of His own accord He did so. When He was arrested in Gethsemane He asked the soldiers to let His disciples go their way (John 18:8). He also emphasized to Peter at the time of His arrest that if He wished to do so he could "pray to my Father, and he shall presently give me more than twelve legions of angels" (Matthew 26:53). He did not beckon for the angels, rather He appealed for the freedom of his disciples and so He suffered all alone. It was one of the dark hours of human history.

I. ENEMIES OF CHRIST ACCUSE HIM
(Matthew. 26:57-64)

57. And they that had laid hold on Jesus led him away to Caiaphas the high priest, where the scribes and elders were assembled.

According to John 18:13, Jesus was first taken to Annas, former high priest and the father-in-law of Caiaphas. This was done as a courtesy to Annas and not for an actual hearing. From there Jesus was led to the palace of Caiaphas where the Jewish leaders were already assembled for the trial. Naturally this would be nothing more than a mock trial, for the Jewish leaders attitude regarding Jesus had been settled long before this.

58. But Peter followed him afar off unto the high priest's palace, and went in, and sat with the servants, to see the end.

What should be our attitude toward Peter for his action?

In an earlier lesson we considered in detail Peter's activities on this evening. The apostle at first attempted to defend Jesus with a sword, but Jesus instructed him to put the sword away (v. 52). Apparently stung at having his defense of Jesus rejected, the apostle now followed afar off and mingled with the high priest's servants. He dared not follow close at hand lest he himself be endangered. Inside the palace Peter stood with the servants warming himself at a fire (John 18:18). At this time he was a man of torn emotions, so eager to see what would become of Jesus that he at least followed Him afar off; but too weak to really take his place at Jesus' side.

59. Now the chief priests, and elders, and all the council, sought false witness against Jesus, to put him to death;

60. But found none: yea, though many false witnesses came, yet found they none. At the last came two false witnesses,

Lacking any real charges against Him, Jesus' antagonists had to drum up false charges against Him. The Sanhedrin Council had to go through the formality of the trial and give the appearance of despensing justice. Yet there was neither a true trial nor the slightest bit of justice. The council had already determined that Jesus must be put to death. His popularity had grown so that He was considered a threat to the Jewish religious system.

Men had to be found who were willing to swear a lie against Jesus, showing Him to be a blasphemer, one worthy of death. Condemning a person with false testimony is a tricky business: there must be enough truth in what is said to make the accusation seem plausible. An outright lie would be detected for what it was, and would ultimately prove its perpetrators to be liars. The council therefore listened to many false witnesses in search of some accusation close enough to the truth that it would condemn Jesus. Furthermore, it was necessary to find two witnesses who said the same thing. Although this was a mock trial, it had to have the appearance of being a proper and just act of jurisprudence.

At last two false witnesses came foreward who did agree on one point that could be twisted as an accusation against Jesus. It appears from the abundance of false witnesses that came forward that there were many who habitually gave false testimony for the rewards it brought to them (see Acts 6:11-13).

61. And said, This fellow said, I am able to destroy the temple of God, and to build it in three days.

The two false witnesses related the words of Jesus in John 2:19-21: "Destroy this temple, and in three days I will raise it up. Then said the Jews, Forty and six years was this temple in building, and wilt thou rear it up in three days? But he spake of the temple of his body."

This was a deliberate twisting of the Lord's words, inferring that Jesus threatened to demolish the temple of God. There is no way that either the false witnesses or the council could believe that Jesus either intended to or had any desire to destroy the Temple. Yet the purpose of this hearing was to make Him seem to be a destructive revolutionary. In the end this would be the Jewish insinuation to the Roman ruler, Pilate. And yet the false witness was a contradiction to its own purpose, for it included the words, "and to build it in three days." These were not the words of destruction, but of building and restoration. When Jesus spoke the words the entire emphasis, as it was understood by the Jews, regarded building the Temple in three days, not destroying it (John 2:20).

62. And the high priest arose, and said unto him, Answerest thou nothing? what is it which these witness against thee?

It was a frivolous, almost unbelievable charge to bring against Jesus. For the Sanhedrin to entertain such a charge with any degree of seriousness was proof that they had already determined to find Him guilty. Knowing this, Jesus remained silent. The high priest found it desirable, perhaps necessary, for Jesus to defend Himself. So he urged Him to reply to the false witness.

63. But Jesus held his peace. And the high priest answered and said unto him, I adjure thee by the living God, that thou tell us whether thou be the Christ, the Son of God.

Under the accusation of the false witnesses and the remonstrance of Caiaphas Jesus still maintained silence. Frustrated by the silence, Caiaphas railed out at Jesus, adjuring Him in the name of God to reply whether or not He was Christ. This was a solemn adjuration, one that invoked the name of God. Jesus, who had resolutely declined to answer the frivolous charges brought against Him, could not remain silent when adjured in the name of God to witness whether or not He was the Christ, the Son of God. This was a different matter and He would no longer remain silent.

64. Jesus saith unto him, Thou hast said: nevertheless I say unto you, Hereafter shall ye see the Son of man sitting on the right hand of power, and coming in the clouds of heaven.

Why was it necessary for Christ to answer the question of His Messiahship, in view of the fact that He had not answered other charges?

The reply of Jesus, "Thou hast said," was a customary way of asserting the truth of what had been asked. His reply meant, "I am the Christ, the Son of God." This was a positive assertion of His divine identity. Then Jesus went on to say that very shortly the Jewish nation would have ample proof of who He was. Caiaphas and the Jewish people would one day stand in judgment before Christ. It was as if Jesus said: "I may stand in your judgment hall today, but the day will come that you will be judged of Me."

II. ENEMIES OF CHRIST PERSECUTE HIM
   (Matthew 26:65-68)

65. Then the high priest rent his clothes, saying, He hath spoken blasphemy; what further need have we of witnesses? behold, now ye have heard his blasphemy.

These words of Jesus almost drove Caiaphas mad. At the implied threat of judgment, the high priest tore his clothing and exclaimed to the gathered council that there was no further need of any witnesses. Jesus' implication that He would one day sit in judgment on them was so blasphemous in the high priest's ears that he was ready to pass judgment on Christ without further ado.

Jesus should have been subdued, intimidated and cowering in the presence of the august Sanhedrin Council. Instead of that, He had dared to suggest that His power was greater than theirs, that His judgment was more enduring than theirs, and that they would one day answer to Him.

66. What think ye? They answered and said, He is guilty of death.

In his rage Caiaphas turned to the Sanhedrin and asked the elders of Israel what they thought. The unanimous answer was that the trial had proceeded far enough: Jesus should immediately be put to death. Still, the travesty of Jewish justice was not complete; His accusers, prosecutors and judges had all been the same. They had asked for a statement, and upon receiving it they rejected it with a sentence of death. Jesus had known from the beginning that they would judge Him to be worthy of death. The conclusion of the matter was precisely what He had known from the beginning it would be. At no time during the sad affair was Jesus surprised by anything that was said or done.

67. Then did they spit in his face, and buffeted him; and others smote him with the palms of their hands,

The normally distinguished body of Jewish elders seemed to lose grip on themselves as they became enraged and volatile. They began to spit in Jesus' face, punch Him with their fists, and slap Him with their hands. The august Sanhedrin became so distraught at the suggestion that they would one day be judged that they became madmen. The Jews were a very emotional people, but they seldom lost control of themselves so completely. Christ and His followers had this effect on them because the Christian message was a rebuke to their pretenses.

Recounting a similar incident in the trial of Stephen, Acts 7:54 notes: "When they heard these things, they were cut to the heart, and they gnashed on him with their teeth." Then Stephen said words almost the same as the words of Christ: "Behold, I see the heavens opened, and the Son of man standing on the right hand of God" (v. 56). In response to these words of Stephen, the Jewish leaders "cried out with a loud voice, and stopped their ears, and ran upon him with one accord, and cast him out of the city, and stoned him" (vv. 57, 58). On occasion the Jewish leaders could be so overcome with anger that they lost all dignity, all emotional control, and behaved like madmen.

68. Saying, Prophesy unto us, thou Christ, Who is he that smote thee?

The Sanhedrin, men who were reputed to be grave and sober, wise and just, behaved with unimaginable violence and petulance. They made ridicule of Christ and implied what He had never claimed. In their rage the priests and elders blindfolded Jesus and ordered their servants to strike Him (Mark 14:65). Needless to say, Christ knew who had delivered each slap. He could easily have told the men who delivered each blow that struck Him. The poor, deluded Jewish rulers did not even know that they were fulfilling an ancient prophecy even when they taunted Jesus by commanding Him to prophesy: "I gave my back to the smiters, and my cheeks to them that plucked off the hair; I hid not my face from shame and spitting" (Isaiah 50:6).

III. ENEMIES OF CHRIST REJECT HIM (Mark 15:1-15)

1. And straightway in the morning the chief priests held a consultation with the elders and scribes and the whole council, and bound Jesus, and carried him away, and delivered him to Pilate.

2. And Pilate asked him, Art thou the King of the Jews? And he answering said unto him, Thou sayest it.

Having tried Jesus themselves, the chief priests consulted with all the other leaders to determine what must be done with Him. They had held their trial during the night, and now it was morning. It was contrary to Roman law for the Jews to pass the death penalty on, or to execute, anyone. Only the Romans who occupied the land could give capital judgment or punishment. Although they despised the Romans' presence, the Jewish leaders must have welcomed the chance to persuade the Romans to put Jesus to death for them.

When the Jews brought Jesus before him, Pilate, the Roman ruler, asked Christ if He were indeed the king of the Jews. Jesus answered the Romans as He had answered Caiaphas, by asserting that what had been said was true. He could not deny this truth before Pilate any more than He could deny it before Caiaphas.

3. And the chief priests accused him of many things: but he answered nothing.

The Jews began to pour out their accusations against Jesus. Once again He reverted to silence, just as He had done when being tried before the Sanhedrin. He replied when something about His sacred identity and relationship with the Father was questioned, but He made no reply to the specious charges that were brought against Him. These were so frivolous that they should speak for themselves to anyone with common reason.

4. And Pilate asked him again, saying, Answerst thou nothing? behold how many things they witness against thee.

The trial before Pilate was a repetition of that before Caiaphas. The procurator urged Jesus to reply to the many charges brought against Him. There is reason to believe that Pilate was a fairly just man, but that he was completely puzzled by the strange Jewish matters. He was a weakling in that he would cater to the wishes of the Jews, and Jesus obviously knew this. There was no point in His replying to the charges, for Jesus already knew that in the end Pilate would rather have Him put to death than to incur the displeasure of the Jewish leaders.

5. But Jesus yet answered nothing; so that Pilate marvelled.

The fact that Pilate marvelled at the silence of Jesus may mean that he recognized something different in Him. Pilate regarded the Jewish people as a rabble, a people marked by constant quarreling and bickering among themselves. Yet here was a man of such composure and demeanor that He stood out from the crowd. He remained silent, yet He seemed not to fear to answer. His silence was not the result of cowardice but of composure and calm resignation. Pilate had never before seen such a man, and he could not help but marvel at the calm attitude Jesus maintained.

6. Now at that feast he released unto them one prisoner, whomsoever they desired.

7. And there was one named Barabbas, which lay bound with them that had made insurrection with him, who had committed murder in the insurrection.

8. And the multitude crying aloud began to desire him to do as he had ever done unto them.

9. But Pilate answered them, saying, Will ye that I release unto you the King of the Jews?

10. For he knew that the chief priests had delivered him for envy.

11. But the chief priests moved the people, that he should rather release Barabbas unto them.

12. And Pilate answered and said again unto them, What will ye then that I shall do unto him whom ye call the King of the Jews?

13. And they cried out again, Crucify him.

14. Then Pilate said unto them, Why, what evil hath he done? And they cried out the more exceedingly, Crucify him.

15. And so Pilate, willing to content the people, released Barabbas unto them, and delivered Jesus, when he had scourged him, to be crucified.

It is possible that Pilate came close to setting Jesus free. Certainly the charges brought against Him were unfounded. He definitely endeavored to set Jesus free according the his custom of setting one prisoner free at the Passover feast. Pilate carried out this yearly custom of releasing a prisoner in order to gain the support and appreciation of the Jewish people. Here, he endeavored to assure the release of Jesus by making the choice between a hardened criminal (a murderer named Barabbas) and Jesus. Twice he called Jesus the king of the Jews.

The chief priests stirred up the crowd and encouraged them to demand the release of Barabbas instead of Jesus. The lackeys of the Jewish leaders set up a cry that Pilate should crucify Jesus, and this cry soon became a tumult. It is altogether possible that some of those who had shouted Hosanna when Jesus entered Jerusalem a few days earlier were among those who now shouted, Crucify Him —so fickle is the nature of man and so determined was the devil that Jesus be put to death.

Pilate had his one great chance to be a strong and just individual. He knew that trumped-up charges had been brought against Jesus, who had done nothing worthy of punishment, let alone death. This was a great opportunity for Pilate to be strong, just and good. He did not do that, however, but reached in the end for the favor of the Jewish leaders. To him Jesus was just one more Jew whom other Jews wanted killed. Pilate would rather have Jesus die, unjust as it was, than to have the Jewish leaders turn against him. Ultimately, "Pilate, willing to content the people, released Barabbas unto them, and delivered Jesus, when he had scourged him, to be crucified" (Mark 15:15).

January 25, 1981

REVIEW QUESTIONS
1. What was the basis of Peter's downfall as it relates to the incident recorded in this lesson?
2. What was illegal about the Sanhedrin trial?
3. Why, do you think, Jesus did not object to the injustice of the trial?
4. What was the symbolic action of the priest to be when he heard blasphemy?
5. Discuss Christ as the Lamb of God and how His sacrifice fulfills Old Testament law.

GOLDEN TEXT HOMILY
"HE CAME UNTO HIS OWN, AND HIS OWN RECEIVED HIM NOT" (John 1:11).

At a glance our Golden Text seems to present a totally negative statement: He was not received by His own. At a closer look we see our text has some positive aspects which gleam like diamonds. Note that those He came to were His own. This statement, with a multitude of other scriptures, declares to us the fact that He is the Jewish Messiah. The verse following our Golden Text (John 1:12) tells us that as many as received Him to them He gave power to become the sons of God. This declares Him to be not only the Jewish Messiah, but also the Son of God and the Savior of the world. The first two words of our Golden Text, "He came," are aglow with the fact that Christ, the Messiah and Savior, came in the flesh. The words "He came" are ablaze with the truth of the Incarnation. Although He came some did not receive Him. Scripture replies to this rejection in Romans 3:3, 4: "For what if some did not believe? shall their unbelief make the faith of God without effect? God forbid: yea, let God be true, but every man a liar."

Some reject Him. Some receive Him. When men come face to face with Him, they must either receive Him or reject Him. History has revealed, and eternity will reveal the tragedy of rejecting Christ.—**Terry A. Beaver, Pastor Bradley, Illinois**

SENTENCE SERMONS
WHEN MEN COME face-to-face with Christ, they must either receive Him or reject Him.
—**Selected**

THE STRANGE THING about Jesus is that you can never get away from Him.
—**Japanese Student**

IF CHRIST IS the wisdom of God and the power of God in the experience of those who trust and love Him, there needs no further argument of His divinity.
—**Henry Ward Beecher**

JESUS CANNOT BE our Savior unless He is first our Lord.
—**Hugh C. Burr**

EVANGELISTIC APPLICATION
MAN MAKES A TRAGIC DECISION WHEN HE DECIDES TO REJECT CHRIST RATHER THAN TO RECEIVE HIM.

The Captain of our Salvation—our leader! Oh, how men fight under a great leader! When some Wellington, or some Sherman, or some Grant comes to the front, how men's hearts go out in courage, and how they say, "Now, it is worth our while to be soldiers!" With what alacrity they obey him, going where they are sent, and doing what they are commanded to do! And they are inspired by the thought that they will be participators of his glory—for what the army does that is noble glorifies the general, and what the general does that is noble glorifies the lowest soldier in the army.

Now our Captain has been made perfect through suffering. He knows every experience to which we are liable, having passed through the various phases of earthly life; and now He has risen to the source of power above, to the headquarters of men in this warring condition, where He sits at the right hand of God; and He is our Leader.—**Henry Ward Beecher**

ILLUMINATING THE LESSON
A distinguished artist lately, speaking to some students on artistic composition, declared it to be a wrong thing pictorially to have a picture of woodland or forest without showing a path leading out of it. When the true artist paints a landscape he invariably gives some suggestion of a path which can carry the eye out of the picture. Otherwise the tangle of trees and undergrowth would suffocate us, or the wide, trackless spaces dismay us. So God ever provides a Way of escape for His children.

DAILY DEVOTIONAL GUIDE
M. Christ, Our Substitute. Isaiah 53:1-6
T. Christ, Our Submissive Savior. Isaiah 53: 7-12
W. Christ Frees Condemned Men. Mark 15: 7-15
T. Wicked Men Persecute Christ. Luke 4:20-31
F. Unbelievers Doubt Christ. Luke 20:1-7
S. Christ Answers Questioning Men. Luke 20: 19-26

February 1, 1981

Price of Redemption

Bible Background: Matthew 27:32-61; Mark 15:21-47; Luke 23:26-56; John 19:17-42
Time: A.D. 30
Place: Golgotha, near the city of Jerusalem
Supplemental References: Psalm 22:1-31; Philippians 2:1-17; Hebrews 2:9-18
Golden Text: "Christ died for our sins according to the scriptures" (1 Corinthians 15:3).
Central Truth: Christ purchased redemption for us by dying in our place.
Evangelistic Emphasis: By His vicarious death on the Cross, Christ purchased redemption for all.

PRINTED TEXT

Matthew 27:33. And when they were come unto a place called Golgotha, that is to say, a place of a skull,

34. **They gave him vinegar to drink mingled with gall: and when he had tasted thereof, he would not drink.**

35. And they crucified him, and parted his garments, casting lots: that it might be fulfilled which was spoken by the prophet, They parted my garments among them, and upon my vesture did they cast lots.

36. **And sitting down they watched him there;**

37. And set up over his head his accusation written, THIS IS JESUS THE KING OF THE JEWS.

38. **Then were there two thieves crucified with him, one on the right hand, and another on the left.**

39. And they that passed by reviled him, wagging their heads,

40. **And saying, Thou that destroyest the temple, and buildest it in three days, save thyself. If thou be the Son of God, come down from the cross.**

41. Likewise also the chief priests mocking him, with the scribes and elders, said,

42. **He saved others; himself he cannot save. If he be the King of Israel, let him now come down from the cross, and we will believe him.**

43. He trusted in God; let him deliver him now, if he will have him: for he said, I am the Son of God.

44. **The thieves also, which were crucified with him, cast the same in his teeth.**

45. Now from the sixth hour there was darkness over all the land unto the ninth hour.

46. **And about the ninth hour Jesus cried with a loud voice, saying, Eli, Eli, lama sabachthani? that is to say, My God, my God, why hast thou forsaken me?**

47. Some of them that stood there, when they heard that, said, This man calleth for Elias.

48. **And straightway one of them ran, and took a spunge, and filled it with vinegar, and put it on a reed, and gave him to drink.**

49. The rest said, Let be, let us see whether Elias will come to save him.

50. **Jesus, when he had cried again with a loud voice, yielded up the ghost.**

DICTIONARY

Golgotha (GOL-gah-thuh)—Matthew 27:33—From the Hebrew **gulgoleth**, meaning "a skull"

February 1, 1981

and probably so called from the shape of the particular hill. It is located near the city of Jerusalem.

scribes and elders—Matthew 27:41—Scribes were a class of learned Jewish men who made the systematic study of the law and its exposition their professional occupation. Elders were the older men of the community who made the decisions.

LESSON OUTLINE
I. SUBMITTING TO CRUELTY
II. ENDURING RIDICULE
III. YIELDING TO DEATH

LESSON EXPOSITION
INTRODUCTION

The pain Christ suffered even before He reached the Cross is immeasurable and unimaginable. He suffered betrayal at the hands of one of His friends; denial by a second of His apostles; the crushing weight of the world's sins; an illegal and unwarranted arrest while He was in prayer; a mock trial before His enemies; a parade of false witnesses who spoke against Him; and humiliating treatment by the Roman soldiers. After a night of such treatment, Jesus naturally was weak and in pain as He approached the hour of actual death.

Following the trial by the Jews, Jesus had been delivered into the hands of the Romans. He was scourged by them, which means that He was whipped with a great leather whip which could actually kill a man. The scourge tore and cut the flesh, leaving it in ragged ribbons. Then the soldiers stripped the clothing from Jesus and placed a scarlet robe around Him; this in mockery because it was said that He was a king. The soldiers twisted branches of thorns into a circle and pressed this upon His head like a crown. They bowed before Him and mocked Him, calling Him king of the Jews.

The rough and brutish soldiers were merely having fun in their brutal way. They certainly had nothing against Jesus. They were simply making sport at His painful expense. They spit upon Him and slapped Him across the head with such treatment as would have been unkind and inhumane toward even a beast. Jesus suffered all of this in silence as a part of the full price of death He had to pay. Only after these humiliations were over was Jesus led away to be crucified.

I. SUBMITTING TO CRUELTY (Matthew 27: 33-38).

33. And when they were come unto a place called Golgotha, that is to say, a place of a skull,

From the Roman judgment hall, Christ was taken to a small hill outside Jerusalem called Golgotha. The meaning of the word is "a place of the skull," so named, say many, because the hill, with caves in its side, has the appearance of a skull. Others believe that it was called Golgotha because it was used as a place of execution. Very likely it gained the name for both reasons.

As was customary in such executions, Jesus was compelled to carry His cross from the judgment hall to the place of execution. Actually He carried only the shorter horizontal beam that would be fastened to the longer vertical beam after they arrived at the place of crucifixion. Three of the Gospels tell us that Simon, a man of Cyrene, was compelled to bear the cross for Christ (Matthew 27:32; Mark 15:21; Luke 23:26), because, according to an early and well-established tradition, Jesus collapsed under the weight of the cross.

34. They gave him vinegar to drink mingled with gall: and when he had tasted thereof, he would not drink.

As their one humane gesture toward the condemned, the Romans gave the victims a stupefying drink to help deaden their awareness of the excruciating pain to follow. This drink was compounded from vinegar, gall, wine, and myrrh (Mark 15:23). In reality, the vinegar and wine were the same thing, for the word **vinegar** literally means "sour wine." Jesus refused to drink the vile-tasting concoction and chose rather to feel the full pain of dying.

35. And they crucified him, and parted his garments, casting lots: that it might be fulfilled which was spoken by the prophet, They parted my garments among them, and upon by vesture did they cast lots.

Do you feel there would be overt public reactions to such cruel treatment in most parts of the world today? In America?

Crucifixion literally means "execution upon a cross." It was a form of execution practiced by the Romans, borrowed from the Assyrians. The two most prominent forms of the cross were in the form of an

X, upon which the victim was spread-eagled, and in the form of a **T**, sometimes with an upper bar to which was nailed an identifying superscription. The fact that such a superscription was nailed above the head of Jesus (v. 37) indicates that He was crucified on the latter form of cross. The victim was either tied or nailed to the cross. Thomas' statement about touching the nail prints in Jesus' hands (John 20:25) proves that Jesus was nailed to the Cross.

The pain of hanging upon the Cross with spikes piercing the hands was torturous. Because of the numerous circumstances of pain in crucifixion, it was regarded as one of the most terrifying forms of death. The fact that the Roman soldiers who crucified Him could gamble for His clothing while He suffered shows the degree of their callousness and lack of feeling. They were more interested in who might get His clothing, a kind of spoils to those who performed the grisly deed of execution, than they were in the fact that another human being was suffering unbearable pain.

36. And sitting down they watched him there;

37. And set up over his head his accusation written, THIS IS JESUS THE KING OF THE JEWS.

It was the responsibility of the soldiers to watch the victim until he died. This would prevent anyone from coming to his aid by taking the victim from the cross or by killing him instantly. The death had to be a slow expiration from the tortures of the cross.

Frequently a statement was nailed to the cross identifying the victim and giving the reason for his execution. The superscription Pilate had placed on Jesus' Cross indicates that he had some misgivings about the execution of Jesus. The Jews insisted that Pilate should alter the superscription and state that Jesus **claimed** to be the king of the Jews (John 19:21). Pilate refused to budge on that point and let the superscription remain as it was. The superscription was written in three languages—Hebrew, Greek, and Latin (John 19:20)—so people of all three languages could read it.

38. Then were there two thieves crucified with him, one on the right hand, and another on the left.

Two thieves (called "malefactors," or evildoers, in Luke 23:33) were crucified with Jesus. Probably intentionally, His death was given greater prominence by placing Him between the two. In so doing, the executioners unwittingly fulfilled another prophecy concerning the crucifixion of Christ. "He hath poured out his soul unto death: and he was numbered with the transgressors; and he bare the sin of many, and made intercession for the transgressors" (Isaiah 53:12).

II. ENDURING RIDICULE (Matthew 27:39-46)

39. And they that passed by reviled him, wagging their heads,

40. And saying, Thou that destroyest the temple, and buildest it in three days, save thyself. If thou be the Son of God, come down from the cross.

Many people were in Jerusalem who had not known of the great work of Jesus but had only heard of His reputation. They knew that Jesus of Nazareth was called the Son of God, but they knew little else about Him. As these passed by the Cross and saw Jesus hanging there, blood-covered, in great pain, and—so they thought—completely helpless, they ridiculed Him without mercy. Their most telling ridicule was quoting what the false witnesses had said about Him: that He could build up the Temple in three days. Little did they know that Jesus would do exactly that by rising again on the third day. They heaped ridicule upon Him by distorting what He had said; but He would fulfill His words in a way that they could not understand.

They called upon Jesus to come down from the Cross if He was the Son of God. That is the one thing He could not do, for the Son of God was born to die on the Cross. If He had come down from the Cross, which, naturally, He had the power to do, then He would not have been the Son of God. It was therefore necessary that He remain on the Cross. Poor ignorant men could not grasp the profound truth: it was because He was the Son of God that He could not come down from the Cross. He remained upon the Cross not because He lacked the power to come down, but because He had the power to remain upon it. This is one of the great paradoxes of Christ's divinity.

41. Likewise also the chief priests mocking him, with the scribes and elders, said,

42. He saved others; himself he cannot save. If he be the King of Israel, let him now come down from the cross, and we will believe him.

The Jewish leaders mocked and ridiculed Jesus in the same way as the passersby. Indeed, it is altogether likely that it was the Jewish leaders who instigated the ridicule from the passersby. The point that we have stated in the previous verse is equally true concerning this. The power that would have allowed Him to come off of the Cross if He so willed was also the power that held Him on it.

Note how the passersby and the religious leaders summed up every claim concerning Jesus and treated it with contempt. They quoted the distorted words about the Temple; they mentioned His being the Son of God; they referred to the King of Israel; and they referred to the fact that He had spent His life saving others. Every holy and righteous fact about His life was paraded before Him in open contempt. All of these accusations were stated to Him in order to increase His suffering and the agony of His dying.

43. He trusted in God; let him deliver him now, if he will have him: for he said, I am the Son of God.

Now His revilers struck at the very heart of Christ's life on earth, His firm trust in God. Their ridicule now turned against God the Father, for the religious leaders in effect denied that God would deliver Him or would have anything to do with Him. The ridicule denied any relationship between Jesus and the Father; it made any suggestion of such a relationship a blasphemy and a lie. This was the ultimate ridicule, the basis of injury. It said that Jesus' trust in God was vain, for God had nothing to do with Jesus. Not only was His claim of sonship denied, but so was the fact of friendship and dedication.

44. The thieves also, which were crucified with him, cast the same in his teeth.

The final straw in the ridicule was when the two evildoers also ridiculed Him. The picture is almost beyond belief: the men who were dying with the same agonies as He found relief from their suffering by heaping abuse upon the Lord. Another account of the Crucifixion clarifies the point that it was only one of the evildoers who abused Christ in this way (Luke 23:39). The second malefactor rebuked his companion and turned to Christ with a prayer (vv. 40-42). The understanding attitude of the penitent thief inescapably gave the Lord a measure of comfort in His dying hour. He saw even in dying the benefit and fruit of His sacrifice.

45. Now from the sixth hour there was darkness over all the land unto the ninth hour.

A supernatural shroud of darkness covered the scene in protest against the evil of mankind. The darkness covered the land of Judea as a dramatic statement that heaven was ashamed of what had happened on earth. The darkness was not like night, but more like a solemn gloom of a densely cloudy day. If it had been darkness like night, the people could not have watched Jesus die and the entire Crucifixion procedures would have been interrupted. It was not interrupted, but was allowed to continue to its bitter end. Yet the darkness was severe enough to be a dramatic lesson to the leaders who caused the death of Christ.

Concerning the time of day mentioned here, Adam Clarke notes: "It has been before observed, that the Jews divided their night into four watches of three hours each. They also divided the day into four general parts. The first began at sunrise; the second, three hours after; the third, at midday; the fourth, three hours after, and continued till sunset. Christ having been nailed to the Cross a little after midday, John 19:14-17, and having expired about three o'clock, Mark 15:33, the whole business of the Crucifixion was finished within the space of this third division of the day, which Mark calls the third hour."

In other words, the sixth hour, noon, to the ninth hour, 3 p.m., comprised the third section of the day. Another and more widely accepted explanation is that Jesus was crucified about 9 a.m. (the third hour), the darkness came about noon (the sixth hour), and Jesus died at 3 p.m. (the ninth hour).

46. And about the ninth hour Jesus cried with a loud voice, saying, Eli, Eli, lama sabachthani? that is to say, My God, my God, why hast thou forsaken me?

As He actually died, Jesus cried out in the Aramaic tongue as is recorded here. The Father therefore permitted Jesus a final human emotion, a feeling that He was deserted. Desertion is one of the greatest pains that comes to a human being. In the intense suffering, with the great strain on Christ's mind and heart, He felt all alone. Of course the Father had not deserted Him in the ultimate sense of the word, although He had deserted Him to the full extent of human suffering. Jesus was not forsaken by the Father's sovereign grace, or by His watchcare, or by His direction and approval. Yet He felt deserted and forgotten, without relief or comfort, without any mitigation of pain, and without anyone to share His darkest hour.

III. YIELDING TO DEATH (Matthew 27:47-50)

47. Some of them that stood there, when

they heard that, said, This man calleth for Elias.

Because of the weakened condition of the Lord, and because of His resort to the Aramaic vernacular, the people did not understand Him clearly. They felt that Jesus was calling upon Elias for deliverance. Also, many of the Jews in Jerusalem for the Passover had come from various parts of the world, did not understand the Aramaic language at all, and were confused by the similarity of sounds. His cry was further confused by the fact that prophecies concerning Elijah were prominent concerning the coming of the Messiah. The observers would have concluded that in His delirium Jesus cried out for Elijah to help Him.

48. And straightway one of them ran, and took a spunge, and filled it with vinegar, and put it on a reed, and gave him to drink.

The action here resulted from sympathy. One of the observers soaked a sponge with vinegar, or sour wine, and lifted it on a reed to the Lord's mouth. The effect of this bitter liquid on His lips would have cleared His mind and alleviated His suffering. The act was one of mercy by one willing to do all that he could.

49. The rest said, Let be, let us see whether Elias will come to save him.

Others among the onlookers viewed even this act of mercy with derision and contempt. They maintained that Jesus had cried for Elijah to help Him, which of course He had not. One of the onlookers offered assistance to the dying man, but Elijah had no part with Him. This was ridicule and contempt taken to its ultimate point. Jesus was virtually dead at this time, and still they wagged their tongues at Him as if He were the vilest, most deranged of men. The devil heaped pain and contempt upon Him to the very last gasp of His life. He felt the full onslaught of dying, which now included the emotion of being alone and a final twisting of His words to something He had not said. Jesus would die knowing that the men He had come to earth to redeem had endeavored to torment Him until the last breath of life was gone.

50. Jesus, when he had cried again with a loud voice, yielded up the ghost.

With a final cry of "It is finished" (John 19:30) Jesus "yielded up the ghost." This is a graphic way of saying that He died. To give up the ghost means that life passed from Him. In this instance, however, it means much more. The fact that He yielded up the ghost underscores the fact that He gave His life voluntarily for the redemption of men. He was not killed because He had not power to prevent His death. He did not die unwillingly. He himself said in John 10:17, 18: "I lay down my life, that I might take it again. No man taketh it from me, but I lay it down, of myself. I have power to lay it down, and I have power to take it again."

REVIEW QUESTIONS

1. Describe the place where Jesus was taken for crucifixion.
2. For what purpose was the vinegar mingled with gall, given to Jesus?
3. What writing was on the sign placed on the cross over the head of Jesus?
4. What reactions to the crucifixion did those who passed by manifest?
5. Describe the phenomenon in nature that occurred between the sixth and ninth hours.

GOLDEN TEXT HOMILY

"CHRIST DIED FOR OUR SINS ACCORDING TO THE SCRIPTURES" (1 Corinthians 15:3).

Christianity is not based on human reasoning or religious creeds, but it is based on the Word of God. It is in the Scripture where we find the real meaning and purpose for the death of Christ. We know that Christ died for the sins of the whole world, but the Scripture goes much further, in explaining why it was necessary that Jesus gave His life for us.

Throughout the Scripture there is a law that God pronounced upon sin from Adam to our present generation. This law is absolute and there can be no alternative or alteration. This law states, "Without [the] shedding of blood [there] is no remission [of sins]" (Hebrews 9:22). As we study the Scripture we realize the truth of this law. In the Old Testament, animals were brought to the altar of sacrifice, their blood was shed, before man could be forgiven of his sin. However, this was only a foreshadow of the greatest sacrificial death in history.

The amazing thing about Jesus' sacrifice was that it was not for Himself but for you and me. Christ paid the price for the sins of the whole world. There was nothing else that would suffice, for only death could satisfy the law of God. In reality, God poured His wrath for sin upon His own Son, that you and I, by our faith in Him, may go free. Isaiah gave us the heart of this truth when he declared that God shall make His (Christ's) soul an offering for sin (see Isaiah 53:10-12). To understand this is to understand the atonement.

As a result of the atonement, the only way a person may be redeemed is by his faith in Christ, who became our substitute. By our faith in Him, our penalty has been paid and we are counted righteous in the sight of God.

When Christ prayed in the Garden of Gethsemane, and succumbed completely to the will of God, He knew there was no other way that man could be redeemed. What a tragedy to reject Christ, who purchased redemption for us by dying in our place. What a Savior, what love, for what the Law of God demanded, His love provided according to the Scriptures.—**Jerry Puckett, Plant Superintendent, Church of God Publishing House, Cleveland, Tennessee**

SENTENCE SERMONS

THE CROSS IS the center of the world's history; the incarnation of Christ and the crucifixion of our Lord are the pivot round which all events of the ages revolve.
—**Alexander MacLaren**

O, CROSS OF my bleeding Lord, may I meditate on thee more. May I feel thee more, may I resolve to know nothing but thee.
—**Charles Fuller**

CHRIST'S VICARIOUS DEATH was deficient for none; sufficient for all; efficient only for those who believe.
—**Walter Brown Knight**

CHRIST DID NOT die on a velvet cross; nor has He any to offer.
—**Wilbur G. Williams**

EVANGELISTIC APPLICATION

BY HIS VICARIOUS DEATH ON THE CROSS, CHRIST PURCHASED REDEMPTION FOR ALL.

THE SIGN OF THE CROSS

"For the preaching of the cross is to them that perish foolishness; but unto us which are saved it is the power of God" (1 Corinthians 1:18).

How varied are the views men have of the Cross! To many, it is but an ornament to be worn about the neck. To the architect it is a symbol, adorning churches. To the scholar it is a goad, driving him on in intellectual pursuits. To the preacher it is a sermon, filling the need of the hour—and of eternity. To the skeptic it is a superstition, clouding men's souls. To the Communist it is a narcotic, benumbing men's minds, an opiate of the people. To the Roman it was an instrument of execution, obnoxious and hated. To Constantine it was a sign in which to conquer, turning defeat into victory. To Paul it was a symbol of glory, pointing the way to heaven. To Mary it was a memory of agony, piercing her soul. To the Sanhedrin it was a token of victory, imaginary and short lived. To the motley mob on Golgotha it was a holiday, carnal and cursed. To one thief it was the door to perdition, horrible and eternal. To the other it was the gate to Paradise, wondrous beyond work of men or angels. To Christ it was a bier and a throne, paradox of time, predestined to eternity. To multiplied millions of storm-tossed souls it is an anchor, offering a haven of rest.
—**Herschel H. Hobbs,** From **Worship Resources**

ILLUMINATING THE LESSON

Out on one of the great sheepranges of the Northwest of America, a shepherd was left in a very lonely station in charge of a large flock of sheep. He lived in a little cottage which was fitted up with the necessary comforts for all seasons of the year. There was no other house anywhere near. This man, Hans Neilson, lived there with only his dog Shep for company. After he had lived out there for two years there came a dreadfully severe winter. The sheepsheds were old, and the shelter for the sheep was poor. New sheds were to be built in the following spring. It was hard work for Hans, but he succeeded in saving all his sheep until the last and most violent blizzard of all. The wind blew and the snow fell for three days. After it was over, help was sent from headquarters to see how Hans had fared. They found his dead body near the sheepfolds, and his dog standing on guard by his master. The sheep were all alive and well, and it was quite clear to the men that Hans had been trying to place additional protection at the broken places in the old sheds when his brave battle ceased and he was overcome by the intense cold. He might have saved his life by neglecting the sheep, but he had literally given his life for his sheep.
—**J. Learnmount**

DAILY DEVOTIONAL GUIDE

M. Suffering. Psalm 22:11-18

T. Humiliation. Mark 15:24-32

W. Rejection. Mark 15:33-37

T. Compassion. Luke 23:27-38

F. Submission. Luke 23:44-49

S. Atonement. John 19:28-37

February 8, 1981

Overcoming Doubt

Bible Background: Mark 16:1-20; Luke 24:1-35; John 20:19-31
Time: A.D. 30
Place: Jerusalem
Supplemental References: Job 19:25-27; 1 Corinthians 15:1-58; Colossians 3:1-7
Golden Text: "We walk by faith, not by sight" (2 Corinthians 5:7).
Central Truth: A constant faith in Christ's presence and power gives victory over doubt.
Evangelistic Emphasis: The saving power of the Lord is able to lift the sinner from doubt to a living faith in Christ.

PRINTED TEXT

John 20:19. Then the same day at evening, being the first day of the week, when the doors were shut where the disciples were assembled for fear of the Jews, came Jesus and stood in the midst, and saith unto them, Peace be unto you.

20. And when he had so said, he shewed unto them his hands and his side. Then were the disciples glad, when they saw the Lord.

21. Then said Jesus to them again, Peace be unto you: as my Father hath sent me, even so send I you.

22. And when he had said this, he breathed on them, and saith unto them, Receive ye the Holy Ghost:

23. Whose soever sins ye remit, they are remitted unto them; and whose soever sins ye retain, they are retained.

24. But Thomas, one of the twelve, called Didymus, was not with them when Jesus came.

25. The other disciples therefore said unto him, We have seen the Lord. But he said unto them, Except I shall see in his hands the print of the nails, and put my finger into the print of the nails, and thrust my hand into his side, I will not believe.

26. And after eight days again his disciples were within, and Thomas with them: then came Jesus, the doors being shut, and stood in the midst, and said, Peace be unto you.

27. Then saith he to Thomas, Reach hither thy finger, and behold my hands; and reach hither thy hand, and thrust it into my side: and be not faithless, but believing.

28. And Thomas answered and said unto him, My Lord and my God.

29. Jesus saith unto him, Thomas, because thou hast seen me, thou hast believed: blessed are they that have not seen, and yet have believed.

30. And many other signs truly did Jesus in the presence of his disciples, which are not written in this book:

31. But these are written, that ye might believe that Jesus is the Christ, the Son of God; and that believing ye might have life through his name.

DICTIONARY

the Jews—John 20:19—An expression common in John and referring to the hierarchy and the official representatives of the nation

remit—John 20:23—A verb derived from the Latin meaning "to send back," and used in the sense "to forgive"

Thomas—John 20:24—An Aramaic word meaning "twin," also called **Didymus,** its Greek equivalent. His call to the apostleship is recorded in Matthew 10:3; Mark 3:18; Luke 6:15. He is also mentioned in John 11:16; 14:5.

signs—John 20:30—The translation of the characteristic Greek word used by John for miracles, with emphasis on the spiritual value of the miracle rather than on the word itself

LESSON OUTLINE

I. ESTABLISHING PROOF
II. RESOLVING DOUBT
III. ACCEPTING EVIDENCE

LESSON EXPOSITION

INTRODUCTION

The period immediately following Christ's crucifixion was a time of great sorrow and doubt for the disciples. It was completely beyond their ability to grasp the reason for His death or the reality of His resurrection. They had inevitably built a great expectation upon His immediately establishing the kingdom of God upon the earth. Then, to see Him put to death and buried was a matter so grave and overwhelming that they could not handle it emotionally. To them it was as if their world had ended. For about three years, Christ had been the center of their world, the one great fact upon which all others hung. When He was taken away from them, they did not know how to sort out all the pieces.

Added to their confused state of mind was a feeling of guilt because they had been unable to assist Him in time of need. In fact, they had withdrawn lest their own lives be put in jeopardy. The three days that Jesus was in the tomb must have been days of unparalleled blackness and bleakness for them. Their minds were filled with questions they could not answer, and they were tortured by the memory of a particularly violent death.

Then came the Resurrection. First, Mary Magdalene and other women found the tomb empty (Mark 16:1; Luke 24:1; John 20:1) and hastened to tell Peter and the disciples. Peter and John rushed to the tomb and found it empty. They were unable to comprehend what had happened (John 20:9) and left the tomb with even greater bewilderment. Later in the day, Mary Magdalene actually saw the risen Christ and communicated with Him. She related her experience to the disciples, but still they could not comprehend the glorious thing that had happened. The clouds were still too thick in their minds for the sunshine to break through.

I. ESTABLISHING PROOF (John 20:19-23)

19. Then the same day at evening, being the first day of the week, when the doors were shut where the disciples were assembled for fear of the Jews, came Jesus and stood in the midst, and saith unto them, Peace be unto you.

The disciples banded themselves together in hiding because they feared that the Jews might seek to put them to death. It does not appear that their fears were well founded, for no such malevolent design is indicated. Yet it is understandable that the disciples would be afraid, for the Jews had indeed caused Christ to be put to death. They feared that their close association with Him might make them the next target for the Jewish wrath.

The events described here occurred during the evening of the day Christ was raised from the dead. It was the first day of the week, our Sunday, and the disciples were gathered to pray. Their minds were confused because of the reports they had heard during the day. They did not know what to make of these. Evidently the door was shut and barricaded so that no one could break in upon the disciples.

Then came Jesus and stood in the midst of His followers. It is not specifically stated, but it is implied, that Jesus entered the room by a miracle. In both verse 19 and verse 26, it is emphasized that the doors were shut tight. It does not seem that such a point would be made of this fact except to establish a miraculous entry by Christ.

Imagine the scene when Jesus suddenly appeared before His disciples with a customary greeting. Such a majestic sight must have overwhelmed them. They were bereft because of the death of Jesus, and here He stood alive among them.

20. And when he had so said, he shewed unto them his hands and his side. Then were the disciples glad, when they saw the Lord.

To fully establish His identity, Jesus immediately showed His disciples the wounds in His hands and side. The marks of the nails in His hands and the wound where the spear entered His side were proof positive that this was their Lord who had been crucified and for whom they had grieved these three days. The exposure of these wounds would more fully convince the disciples that He had died and been resurrected. The statement, "Then were the disciples glad when they saw the Lord," indicates that it required a bit of time for them to take in the awe and the wonder of that moment. They did not simply see Jesus and begin to rejoice that He had appeared. Their first reaction would have been one of incredulity, a questioning of their own eyes and ears. They did not allow themselves to be prematurely gladdened by His appearance. When He showed them the prints in His hands and side, they were convinced that He was not an apparition, a product of their imagination, and they surrendered themselves to the emotion of gladness.

21. Then said Jesus to them again, Peace be unto you: as my Father hath sent me, even so send I you.

A second time Jesus gave the Jewish salutation of peace, which He also did in verse 26. To this day Jews greet one another with the word, **Shalom,** which means "peace."

Jesus marked the end of His earthly ministry and the beginning of the disciples' ministry. He declared to the disciples that as He had been sent into the world, so He would send them forth. They would possess the same purpose, hold the same authority, and have the same responsibility of reaching the unsaved that He had possessed. His disciples would be a continuation of His ministry. That is the purpose of the church today: to be an extension of His work, an amplification of His voice, and a continuation of His Spirit upon the earth.

22. And when he had said this, he breathed on them, and saith unto them, Receive ye the Holy Ghost.

In what sense were the disciples responsible for receiving the Holy Spirit from Christ's breathing upon them?

Jesus' breathing upon the disciples was a highly symbolic act. When God created Adam and breathed into his nostrils the breath of life, Adam became a living soul, that is, a natural man. Now Jesus duplicated that act to intimate to His disciples that they were new men, possessed of a new life, a life spiritual rather than natural.

They were now ready to receive the Holy Ghost, an impartation of power for divine service. With newness of life, they lacked only an infilling of the Holy Spirit for the work to which He would send them. Through His inspiration He would send them forth into the world to complete His work. He breathed upon them so that they might breathe newness of life upon others as they declared His Word. Inasmuch as Jesus could not continue with His disciples during the course of their ministry, they would receive the Holy Ghost, who would remain with them forever (John 14:16, 17).

23. Whose soever sins ye remit, they are remitted unto them; and whose soever sins ye retain, they are retained.

This statement by Christ has caused considerable misunderstanding, as if Jesus gave the apostles power to forgive the sins of men. If they had such power as that, they would have been able to bestow the New Birth upon men. That is by no means the meaning of this statement. God alone is able to forgive sins in this manner. It was by accepting the preaching of the disciples that men were led to salvation through the remission of sins; it was by the rejection of that preaching that some had their sins retained. The apostles were vested with the power of the gospel, which by accepting, some were reconciled to God; and by rejection, some came into condemnation. The faithful preaching of the apostles would to a great extent determine these destinies.

II. RESOLVING DOUBT (John 20:24-29)

24. But Thomas, one of the twelve, called Didymus, was not with them when Jesus came.

25. The other disciples therefore said unto him, We have seen the Lord. But he said unto them, Except I shall see in his hands the print of the nails, and put my finger into the print of the nails, and thrust my hand into his side, I will not believe.

The reason for Thomas's absence during the first appearance of the Lord is never explained. It was he who lost a great blessing by being absent. When the ten apostles related to him that they had seen the Lord, he responded with disbelief. It is quite possible that they mentioned the nailprints in order to confirm that they had truly seen the risen Lord. Thomas could not accept the witness of ten of his brethren and insisted that he would not believe until he personally could see the prints in Christ's hands. And then, as if to underscore his reluctance to believe, he added that he must even put his finger into the nailprints before he could accept the fact. Even though the ten had not been able to believe until they saw the nailprints (v. 20), Thomas's obstinate unbelief was unreasonable. Because of it he has forever earned the title of "doubting Thomas."

His skepticism might have been warranted if the other ten disciples had believed without proof and demonstrated ignorant belief. They were reliable witnesses because they had required the necessary proof. Apparently, however, Thomas maintained his attitude of unbelief for a full week.

26. And after eight days again his disciples were within, and Thomas with them: then came Jesus, the doors being shut, and stood in the midst, and said, Peace be unto you.

It appears that the first day of the week had become the regular meeting day of the apostles. Once again, they gathered in their room and tightly closed the doors about them. This time Thomas was present, probably determined not to be absent again. As He had done the previous week, Jesus suddenly appeared to the assembled group.

27. Then saith he to Thomas, Reach hither thy finger, and behold my hands; and reach hither thy hand, and thrust it into my side: and be not faithless, but believing.

It is noteworthy that Jesus did not chide with Thomas but rather invited the doubting apostle to do what he had declared he must do before believing. With this gesture, Jesus showed what compassion He had for His troubled disciple. If a touch of the nail marks were required to bring faith and peace to Thomas's mind, then Jesus invited him to do so. Jesus' words furthermore demonstrated to Thomas and the others that He was fully aware of the conversation they had earlier had. Even though He had not been seen, He had been present with them in spirit and love and understanding.

There was a touch of rebuke in the words of the Lord when He admonished Thomas to "be not faithless, but believing." And yet His admonition was one that equally pertains to every person who knows Jesus Christ. The Christian life consists in large part of believing the unbelievable, that is, by maintaining spiritual faith in matters the natural mind cannot comprehend.

28. And Thomas answered and said unto him, My Lord and my God.

It is interesting to note that he who had so stoutly maintained that he would not believe until he had the confirmation of touch apparently did not follow through with his contention. There is no indication at all that Thomas actually touched the wounds of the Lord. Instead, he was so overwhelmed by the sight and the words of his Lord that he burst into an exclamation of adoration.

It is unfortunate that some have taken advantage of this scripture to deny the Trinity. They maintain that Thomas recognized in Christ the totality of God. This theory, first set forth in early Christian days by Arius, maintains that Father, Son, and Holy Spirit are three manifestations of the same person; that Jesus is but another name for Jehovah. Those who hold this error are unable to see the compound nature of the term "God." God was One, consisting of Father, the Son of God, the Messiah, the One who had come to earth from the Father above, and Spirit. Thomas, with his doubts resolved, recognized and proclaimed Christ to be the Lord—whose disciple he was —and God, worthy of all worship and adoration. By being the first to give the title of God to Jesus, Thomas was able to make amends for his former doubts and contentions.

29. Jesus saith unto him, Thomas, because thou hast seen me, thou hast believed: blessed are they that have not seen, and yet have believed.

What is there about the doubt Thomas manifested that deserves criticism as well as commendation?

Unfortunate as it was, the doubt of Thomas gave rise to a great statement of teaching. If Thomas found blessing by believing what he saw, then how much more will men be blessed who are able to believe even when they have not seen. Jesus never revealed Himself to unbelievers; He revealed Himself to His followers only. He never made an appearance to Pilate, or Caiaphas, or Annas, or Barabbas, or any other unbeliever. He could have appeared to these in order to prove to them the validity of what He claimed, but He never forced faith in this manner. He appeared only to those who already believed in Him, and thereby confirmed their faith.

Following a short period when the disciples were able to see Him, Christ would return to heaven and be seen on earth no more. The great multitudes that were to believe on Him would do so without ever seeing Him. In only a few instances, such as when He appeared to Paul on the road to Damascus, was Jesus ever seen. And yet millions have believed on Him and triumphed for Him without ever having seen Him. What a blessing it is to be among those who have received Him and believed Him without ever having seen Him.

The Lord did not leave so much as a photograph so we could know what was His physical appearance. We can only gather a few hints from Scripture, but these provide very little by which to create an undeniably authentic likeness. Thousands of artists have depicted Him as they imagined Him to be, and there have been hoaxes that claimed to be authentic likenesses, but the truth remains that all Christians today believe steadfastly in One whom they have never seen in person or by image. What a great testament of faith this is. It is a testament to the greatness of Christ and the faithfulness of His followers.

III. ACCEPTING EVIDENCE (John 20:30, 31)

30. And many other signs truly did Jesus in the presence of his disciples, which are not written in this book.

Only a few signs are mentioned in this passage: the fact that He appeared twice to His disciples, even though the doors were shut fast, and the showing of His nailprints. Yet John states that there were "many other signs" that Jesus gave to His disciples. Since these are not mentioned in Holy Scripture, we must conclude that they were not necessary, or even beneficial, to anyone other than the disciples themselves. It was they who must pick up the lines that had fallen unto them and carry on in His name. It was they who would have to go out into a totally non-Christian world. It was they who would have to lay the foundation for Christianity in every land. It is therefore possible that they needed many signs to sustain them in the difficult days ahead. We live in a world that is well acquainted with Christianity, whether or not we can call it a Christian world, and we have numerous signs that the disciples did not have. We have the writings that they left, combined now into a New Testament; we have the example of their steadfastness, even unto death; we have the historical assurance that Jesus is with His followers in every place and every circumstance. All these are evidences and signs as surely as any that He might reveal to the eleven men who must carry on in His name.

31. But these are written, that ye might believe that Jesus is the Christ, the Son of God; and that believing ye might have life through his name.

The few signs that are recorded in Scripture have been given for a purpose, to aid in our faith that Jesus is the Christ, the Son of God. Luke says in Acts 1:3, "To whom also he shewed himself alive after his passion by many infallible proofs, being seen of them forty days, and speaking of the things pertaining to the kingdom of God." It is interesting that both John and Luke used the word **many** to signify the multitude of signs that Jesus gave His disciples. We are given only enough to assist us in faith and to confirm our faith in Him. The greatest of all evidences is the reality of Christ living in our hearts.

REVIEW QUESTIONS

1. How did the disciples react to the appearance of the resurrected Christ?

2. How did Jesus greet His disciples and what special blessing did He give them?

3. How did Jesus appeal to Thomas for his faith?

4. How did Thomas respond when he felt of the nailprints and wounded side of Jesus?

5. Discuss the place of doubt and skepticism as it relates to the Christian's role in society.

GOLDEN TEXT HOMILY

"WE WALK BY FAITH, NOT BY SIGHT" (2 Corinthians 5:7).

The writer of Judges 6:13, 15 lets us know that doubting is human. The preceding verses tell us of the oppression of the Israelites under the Midianites. The verses also tell us of the appearance of an angel to Gideon. The angel said to him: "The Lord is with thee, thou mighty man of valour" (Judges 6:12). Gideon replied to the angel in these words: "If the Lord be with us, why then is all this befallen us? and where be all his miracles which our fathers told us of, saying, Did not the Lord bring us up from Egypt? but now the Lord

February 8, 1981

hath forsaken us, and delivered us into the hands of the Midianites" (Judges 6:13).

Perhaps we have heard similar expressions of doubt in our day. People may say, "If the Lord is with us, why has this tragedy come our way?" It is human to doubt. Gideon doubted, but God helped him to overcome his doubt and used him to lead the Israelites to a great victory over the Midianites (see Judges 6-8). God also will help us to overcome our doubts. Sometimes He will give us signs of His presence and power. We see proof before our very eyes. But at other times God expects us to walk by faith. We should not expect Him to perform miracle after miracle just to keep us from doubting. He has performed many miracles and will perform many more, so let us be satisfied; let us not doubt. He is the Almighty God. He loves us and has great things in store for us. May our faith in Him become greater and greater for He is worthy of our complete trust.—**Selected**

SENTENCE SERMONS

HE THAT HAS LOST faith, what has he left to live on.
—**Roger Bacon**

NEVER DOUBT IN darkness what God has told you in the light.
—**V. Raymond Edman**

FAITH IS MORE than thinking something is true. Faith is thinking something is true to the extent that we act on it.
—**W. T. Purkiser**

TO SEEK PROOF is to admit doubt, and to obtain proof is to render faith superfluous.
—**A. W. Tozer**

EVANGELISTIC APPLICATION

THE SAVING POWER OF THE LORD IS ABLE TO LIFT THE SINNER FROM DOUBT TO A LIVING FAITH IN CHRIST.

The choice between hate and love is considered by Studdert-Kennedy with these words: "The crucified Christ is looking down upon us with death in His bleeding hands and feet, but life is the light of His burning eyes, and demanding from us all—every individual man and woman—a choice between glory or force and wrath and fear . . . He will not go away. I do not believe He will let us alone. He is going to drive us to a decision with His wounded hands. He will not let us have His world for a playground, a battlefield, a factory, or an empire any longer; we must give it to Him. We must give it to Him—or else there will be darkness over all the earth from the sixth hour until the ninth—and that may be a thousand years."—**Charles L. Wallis**—From *A Treasury of Sermon Illustrations*

ILLUMINATING THE LESSON

An Irish nobleman whose tenants owed him a great deal of money gave notice that on a particular day all debts would be canceled for those who came to his mansion and presented a statement of their accounts. Only two persons showed up. The others disbelieved the announcement; so their debts were not forgiven.

The Lord offers forgiveness to all. He has announced it in the Bible. Do not doubt it.
—**"Notes and Quotes"**

DAILY DEVOTIONAL GUIDE

M. Dealing With Doubt. Luke 24:17-27
T. Believing for Salvation. Acts 16:25-34
W. Sharing With Confidence. Acts 22:6-15
T. Reviewing the Evidence. 1 Corinthians 15:1-8
F. Believing for the Future. 1 Thessalonians 4:13-18
S. Believing With Sobriety. Titus 2:11-15

February 15, 1981

Love, the Christian's Motivation

Bible Background: John 21:1-25
Time: Probably April, A.D. 30
Place: At Sea of Tiberias in Galilee
Supplemental References: Exodus 16:14-32; Deuteronomy 11:1-25; Luke 5:1-11; 2 Corinthians 5:9-16
Golden Text: "Lovest thou me more than these?" (John 21:15).
Central Truth: The depth of our love for Christ affects the quality of our service for Him.
Evangelistic Emphasis: Love for Christ will send men out to reach the lost.

PRINTED TEXT

John 21:5. Then Jesus saith unto them, Children, have ye any meat? They answered him, No.

6. And he said unto them, Cast the net on the right side of the ship, and ye shall find. They cast therefore, and now they were not able to draw it for the multitude of fishes.

7. Therefore that disciple whom Jesus loved saith unto Peter, It is the Lord. Now when Simon Peter heard that it was the Lord, he girt his fisher's coat unto him, (for he was naked,) and did cast himself into the sea.

8. And the other disciples came in a little ship; (for they were not far from land, but as it were two hundred cubits,) dragging the net with fishes.

9. As soon then as they were come to land, they saw a fire of coals there, and fish laid thereon, and bread.

10. Jesus saith unto them, Bring of the fish which ye have now caught.

11. Simon Peter went up, and drew the net to land full of great fishes, an hundred and fifty and three: and for all there were so many, yet was not the net broken.

12. Jesus saith unto them, Come and dine. And none of the disciples durst ask him, Who art thou? knowing that it was the Lord.

13. Jesus then cometh, and taketh bread, and giveth them, and fish likewise.

14. This is now the third time that Jesus shewed himself to his disciples, after that he was risen from the dead.

15. So when they had dined, Jesus saith to Simon Peter, Simon, son of Jonas, lovest thou me more than these? He saith unto him, Yea, Lord; thou knowest that I love thee. He saith unto him, Feed my lambs.

16. He saith to him again the second time, Simon, son of Jonas, lovest thou me? He saith unto him, Yea, Lord; thou knowest that I love thee. He saith unto him, Feed my sheep.

17. He saith unto him the third time, Simon, son of Jonas, lovest thou me? Peter was grieved because he said unto him the third time, Lovest thou me? And he said unto him, Lord, thou knowest all things; thou knowest that I love thee. Jesus saith unto him, Feed my sheep.

DICTIONARY

the sea of Tiberias (tie-BEER-re-us)—John 21:1—So named by Herod Antipas, the builder of the town on its shore, as a compliment to the reigning Emperor. It is also known as

February 15, 1981

the Sea of Galilee (John 6:1) because it is located in Galilee, and the "lake of Gennesareth" (Luke 5:1) because of the extended plain adjoining the lake. The lake is about sixty miles north of Jerusalem; is from eighty to one hundred-and-sixty-feet deep; contains an abundance of fish; and is fed by the River Jordan's flowing from the north. Its waters are blue and sweet.

Nathanael (na-THAN-yell)—John 21:2—From the Hebrew meaning "God has given." A disciple of Jesus commonly identified with Bartholomew.

Cana of Galilee—John 21:2—So named to distinguish it from Cana of Asher (Joshua 19:28). It was a town probably five or six miles north of Nazareth in the uplands west of the lake.

Zebedee—John 21:2—The father of James and John, and the husband of Salome. He was a Galilean fisherman, living probably either at or near Bethsaida.

naked—John 21:7—This means that he was stripped of the upper garment to the waist for work.

two hundred cubits—John 21:8—About one hundred yards, a cubit being about eighteen inches.

LESSON OUTLINE

I. GIVING GUIDANCE
II. DEMONSTRATING CONCERN
III. EMPHASIZING LOVE

LESSON EXPOSITION

INTRODUCTION

Today's lesson concerns another of Christ's post-resurrection appearances, called Christophanies. Jesus made ten such appearances during the forty days between His resurrection and ascension. This was the seventh time the risen Christ was seen during the period, the first since His appearance to the disciples in Jerusalem with Thomas present (see last week's lesson).

During the course of the Last Supper before the Crucifixion, Jesus promised, "After I am risen again, I will go before you into Galilee" (Matthew 26:32). On the day of His resurrection, He made a similar promise in Jerusalem: "Go tell my brethren that they go into Galilee, and there shall they see me" (Matthew 28:10). There was something very special about Galilee in the ministry of Christ, for it was there that His ministry began. Most of His disciples, the exception being Judas Iscariot, were from Galilee. He himself had grown up in Nazareth, one of the cities of Galilee. Many scenes of His early ministry had been on the Sea of Galilee, called here the Sea of Tiberias. Those were two of the several names by which that small but important body of water was known.

Following the two appearances of Jesus to His disciples in Jerusalem, the apostles went on to Galilee. Especially mentioned were Peter, Thomas, Nathanael (or Bartholomew), James, and John. In Galilee, Peter announced to the disciples that he planned to resume fishing. He was a fisherman by trade, with a wife and a family, and by this time he was no doubt in need of income. Since he and some of the others had left their fishing business to follow Jesus, they had been supported by contributions from individuals (Luke 8:3), and those sources had not been sufficient since the Crucifixion. So when Peter said, "I go a fishing," he did not mean for sport or recreation, but for a livelihood. Since his life had been so dramatically altered, he had to resort to the only way he knew to support his family.

The disciples set sail with Peter and spent the night fishing on the Sea of Tiberias. As the morning came they were still without fish, having caught nothing through the night. In the early light of the morning, Jesus stood on the seashore and watched His disciples in their fruitless labor. From their boat they were able to see the figure standing on the shore, but they could not see clearly enough to recognize Jesus.

I. GIVING GUIDANCE (John 21:5-8)

5. Then Jesus saith unto them, Children, have ye any meat? They answered him, No.

Jesus called across the water and asked if the men had caught any food. He addressed them in a familiar and affectionate way: "Children." It was in no wise a term of condescension, but rather one of tender affection. The word "meat" indicated anything that is eaten, and not necessarily the flesh of fish or animal. We use the word **meal** in a similar fashion; we "enjoy a meal," "serve a meal," "eat a meal," and so forth. Jesus used the word "meat" in referring to food generally in John 4:32-34. The disciples, probably feeling that He was someone wanting to buy fish of them, replied that they had none available.

6. And he said unto them, Cast the net on the right side of the ship, and ye shall find. They cast therefore, and now they were not able to draw it for the multitude of fishes.

Do you think Jesus was using this incident to speak to the evangelistic ministry the disciples would soon be involved with? Why?

Jesus instructed the disciples to let their net down on the right side of the ship and they would find a great multitude of fishes. Jesus had given similar directions to Peter and the others during the early days of His ministry (see Luke 5:4-6), these having the same amazing results as are recorded here. The great multitude of fishes not only provided immediate benefit to the needy disciples; it was also a sign for their future work. Jesus originally called the disciples to become fishers of men (Matthew 4:19), and this great catch symbolized for them the multitude of souls that they would win in the service of the Lord.

7. Therefore that disciple whom Jesus loved saith unto Peter, It is the Lord. Now when Simon Peter heard that it was the Lord, he girt his fisher's coat unto him, (for he was naked,) and did cast himself into the sea.

Here we have a typical view of both Peter and John. We see the character of each man come out in its individual way. There was something about the voice of Christ, and particularly the instructions He gave the disciples, that caused John to recognize Him. John did not immediately act upon the recognition, but he told Peter that the figure on the shore was Jesus. Then Peter acted in a typical way by throwing a coat around himself, leaping into the sea, and hastening toward the Lord. John was sensitive and keenly attuned to the Lord; Peter was bold and impetuous, one who acted instantly upon his knowledge and impulses.

The two had acted together in characteristic fashion on the day of the Resurrection when they ran to the empty tomb (John 20:

2-8). The two men were close and affectionate colleagues in the work of the Lord, yet no two men have ever been more different than were Peter and John.

The fact that Peter leaped into the sea tells something about the character of the man. He probably did so in order to bring the ship to shore as quickly as possible. We are not to conclude that he had been totally naked, but only that he was not wearing all of the usual attire. He had probably stripped down to a simple breechcloth in order to do his work more conveniently. Upon learning that Jesus was on the shore, Peter quickly put on his fisher's coat and leaped into the water so he could help drag the ship to land. The fact that they were relatively close to shore (v. 8) and the fact that Peter drew in the net of fishes (v. 11) indicate that this was the case.

8. And the other disciples came in a little ship; (for they were not far from land, but as it were two hundred cubits,) dragging the net with fishes.

Peter and John seem to have been on the larger fishing vessel, while the other disciples were in a smaller vessel adjacent to it. The net was probably lowered between the two vessels.

II. DEMONSTRATING CONCERN (John 21: 9-14)

9. As soon then as they were come to land, they saw a fire of coals there, and fish laid thereon, and bread.

The weary disciples discovered that Jesus had a fire of coal ready, with fish and bread prepared to eat. Obviously this food was provided by a miracle, such as when He multiplied the loaves and fishes. There is no reason to suspect that the Lord had fished in the waters of the sea or that He had brought bread from a town for this purpose. Nor is there any reason to believe that He built the fire whereon the food lay. It is much more in keeping with the nature of the incident to recognize that the Lord provided the food by His power.

If it is true that Jesus provided the food by a miracle, this was the third such incident in the course of His earthly record. In the first instance He had fed five thousand men with five loaves and two small fishes (John 6:9-11). The second incident occurred when He fed four thousand men with seven loaves and a few little fishes (Matthew 15:32-38).

It should be noted that Jesus never performed a miracle to satisfy His own hunger or needs. He frequently worked miracles for the benefit of others, but never for Himself. One of the great beauties of this lesson is that the resurrected Christ had the welfare of His disciples foremost in His mind. He cared very much about what would become of them. Not only did Jesus wish to satisfy their physical needs, He also provided them a living example of the bread of life and the harvest of souls.

10. Jesus saith unto them, Bring of the fish which ye have now caught.

As yet, the fish that had been caught had not been brought to the land, but they were still in the net lying in the water offshore. Peter had probably brought one end of the net toward the shore and the other disciples had brought in the other. Now Jesus asked that the fish be brought to land.

The same is true in the matter of fishing for men. It is not enough to go through the motions as fishers of men; we must ultimately bring in the harvest of souls. The object of the fishermen was not simply to get their catch inside their net, but to bring it to land.

11. Simon Peter went up, and drew the net to land full of great fishes, an hundred and fifty and three: and for all there were so many, yet was not the net broken.

It is noteworthy that someone took time to count the number of fish that had been caught. It was a joyful, emotional scene with the disciples coming to shore to be with the Lord, and yet there was such stewardship and accountability that the fish were counted. The point is made that there were one hundred and fifty-three large fishes. The fish were large in size as well as many in number.

It should be observed that great attention was given to such accounting. For instance, we know that there were five loaves and two fishes that fed five thousand, with twelve baskets of fragments being picked up (John 6:13). We know that there were seven loaves to feed four thousand, with seven baskets of fragments being recovered (Matthew 15:37). We know that Jesus appeared once to five hundred disciples (1 Corinthians 15:6) and that there were one hundred and twenty gathered in an upper room (Acts 1:15). The point here is that we have the example of accountability toward the Lord's heritage. The Scripture was never tedious about it, but it was regarded as a part of good stewardship.

12. Jesus saith unto them, Come and dine. And none of the disciples durst ask him, Who art thou? knowing that it was the Lord.

Why were the disciples afraid to ask Jesus about His identity?

The disciples had toiled all night and they were no doubt hungry. With love, the Lord had provided food and nourishment for them. In the early light of morning, He and they partook of the fish and bread that He had provided.

It should be noted that there was always a difference in the exchanges between Jesus and His disciples following His resurrection. During the course of His ministry they had conversed freely, even vigorously, about points they did not understand, but following the Resurrection, they always regarded Him with reverential awe. Apparently they ate solemnly at this time, none daring to ask even obvious questions. The full impact of Christ's divinity had broken in upon their consciousness. Furthermore, there seems to have been some difference in His visage following His resurrection. Enough so, for instance, that Mary Magdalene momentarily mistook Him for a gardener when she first saw Him (John 20:15); two disciples on the road to Emmaus did not recognize Him (Luke 24:16-31); and the disciples did not immediately recognize Him when He appeared at this time (v. 4). Jesus was the same, yet there was enough change that the disciples never had interchanges with Him as with a man, but they maintained a proper awe and reverence of His deity.

13. Jesus then cometh, and taketh bread, and giveth them, and fish likewise.

Jesus served His disciples the bread and fish He had provided for them. We learn from Luke 24:43 that Jesus also ate in His resurrected form, so it is to be assumed that He shared this meal with His disciples. Breaking bread together has always symbolized closeness and fellowship. The word **companionship** literally means "with bread," from two root terms: **com**—with, and **panis**—bread. Much emphasis was given among the early Christians to the practice of eating together. One such meal, of course, is the highly symbolic Lord's Supper when believers break bread and share the cup together. There was also in the early days a love feast, called **Agape**, when Christians regularly shared an actual meal together.

14. This is now the third time that Jesus shewed himself to his disciples, after that he was risen from the dead.

This was the third time the risen Christ appeared to His disciples as a group. The first was when He appeared to the ten (John 20:19); the second when He appeared to all eleven, including Thomas (John 20:26); and now to seven (John 21:2). In other portions of Scripture, we also learn that He appeared individually to Peter (Luke 24:34), to James (1 Corinthians 15:7), and again to all eleven apostles before He ascended into heaven (Mark 16:1-20). As was noted in the introduction to this lesson we have the record of about ten appearances by Christ in His resurrected form. It is altogether possible that there were more that were never recorded.

III. EMPHASIZING LOVE (John 21:15-19)

15. So when they had dined, Jesus saith to Simon Peter, Simon, son of Jonas, lovest thou me more than these? He saith unto him, Yea, Lord; thou knowest that I love thee. He saith unto him, Feed my lambs.

Following their meal, Jesus turned His attention to Simon Peter and to a reconciliation of Peter's denial of Him on the night He was arrested. This does not mean that Peter was not forgiven until now, only that he is here given an opportunity to repair and wash away his great spiritual failure. Because Peter had three times denied the Lord, he is here called upon three times to affirm his loyalty to Christ. In each instance he is also given instructions regarding his ministry for Christ.

Jesus asked if Peter loved Him more than the other disciples because, on the night of the Last Supper, Peter had declared that even if all others should fail Him, he would yet remain true. Already, Peter had demonstrated his love by the way he raced to the empty tomb and was the first to enter it, and by the way he plunged into the cold waters of the Sea of Galilee to pull the boat quickly to shore. These were actions beyond what the others did, but the Lord here gave him a chance to make verbal affirmation of that great affection.

16. He saith to him again the second time, Simon, son of Jonas, lovest thou me? He saith unto him, Yea, Lord; thou knowest that I love thee. He saith unto him, Feed my sheep.

By His repetitive question, the Lord underscored that the three denials were now erased and set into the past. This opportunity for a threefold affirmation of his love would also do much to restore Peter's self-respect and self-image.

Note that in verse 15 Jesus said, "Feed my lambs," and here He says, "Feed my sheep." This shows progression and maturity as the church will grow.

17. He saith unto him the third time, Simon, son of Jonas, lovest thou me? Peter was grieved because he said unto him the third time, Lovest thou me? And he said unto him, Lord, thou knowest all things; thou knowest that I love thee. Jesus saith unto him, Feed my sheep.

The third time Jesus asked His question, Peter was grieved and felt that the Lord might be holding something against him. When Peter made his presumptuous statement of self-confidence at the Last Supper, Jesus had revealed something that Peter himself did not know (John 13:37, 38). Peter feared here that Jesus might yet see something in his life that he himself could not see.

Jesus set that possibility aside and instructed Peter a third time to feed His sheep. The lambs of verse 15 were the new converts of the early church. The sheep of this verse represent the experienced Christians, whom Peter is to feed and direct. This was a great compliment to Peter and established his prominence in the apostolic body.

18. Verily, verily, I say unto thee, When thou wast young, thou girdedst thyself, and walkedst whither thou wouldest: but when thou shalt be old, thou shalt stretch forth thy hands, and another shall gird thee, and carry thee whither thou wouldest not.

19. This spake he, signifying by what death he should glorify God. And when he had spoken this, he saith unto him, Follow me.

The Lord looked into the future regarding Peter and declared to him details about his old age and death. When Peter was a young man, he had been able to take care of himself, but when he was grown old another would take him where he would not wish to go. The meaning of this is that Peter would one day be apprehended and executed much as the Lord had been. The words, "Follow me," meant that Peter would follow Jesus in death as he had followed Him in life.

In verses 20-23 Peter raised the question about the Apostle John. If Peter would die a martyr's death, what was to become of John? Jesus replied that the issue was of no matter to Peter, even if John should remain alive until Jesus returned to earth. In other words, Peter was told not to concern himself with the affairs of John, but he was simply to follow Christ personally.

According to ancient tradition, Peter did indeed follow Christ even in death. The story is told that the apostle was crucified in Rome, asking to be fastened to the cross with his head downward because he was not worthy to die as the Lord had died. Despite his denial of Christ, Peter did love Jesus and spent a lifetime demonstrating that fact. If the legend is true, Peter demonstrated that love one final time at his death.

REVIEW QUESTIONS

1. Under what circumstances did the Risen Lord reveal Himself in this lesson?
2. Who recognized the Lord first?
3. What reaction did Peter have when he realized that it was the Lord who had been conversing with them?
4. What happened as a result of the disciples' obedience?
5. What practical applications do you draw from this lesson?

GOLDEN TEXT HOMILY

"LOVEST THOU ME MORE THAN THESE?" (John 21:15).

There has been much speculation about what the Lord meant when He referred to "these." Many have thought He meant the fish the disciples had caught that day. Others have felt that by "these" Christ was referring to the other disciples. Whatever Jesus meant, however, seems to be the matter of comparatives to which He calls Peter's attention.

Without much imagination, there are many material things, people, and situations that come to mind that could be **these**—things that today would overshadow our love for Christ. Bringing the application right up to date and not worrying about what the Lord had in mind for Peter, we can readily see in our own life the substantial array of things that could take the place of Christ in our love.

Today's competitive and affluent world has a tremendous hold on our attention and on our devotion. Much of what captures and dominates our life is wholly legitimate. To rule them out of our life would be very wrong. But to please God, we must place them all in a planned sequence of priorities and keep first things first. No doubt this is what the Lord is talking about.

First and foremost, however, in the plan of God, is His desire to have our supreme and undying devotion and love. After all, was not His love paramount over all loves? Was not the gift of salvation through His blood and His death on the Cross a product of His wonderful love? Consequently, our love for Him must take precedence over all else in our life. Otherwise, God's will and plan for our life cannot be fully realized.—**E. A. Pettersen, A. C. Nielsen Company, New York, New York**

SENTENCE SERMONS

THE DEPTH OF our love for Christ affects the quality of our service for Him.
—**Selected**

GOD HAS GIVEN us a will to choose His will.
—**Henrietta C. Mears**

DIFFICULTIES ARE GOD'S errands; and when we are sent upon them, we should esteem it a proof of God's confidence and as a compliment from Him.
—**Henry Ward Beecher**

THE SERVICE WE render for others is really the rent we pay for our room on this earth.
—**Wilfred Grenfell**

EVERY GREAT PERSON has first learned how to obey, whom to obey, and when to obey.
—**William A. Ward**

EVANGELISTIC APPLICATION

LOVE FOR CHRIST WILL SEND MEN OUT TO REACH THE LOST.

INTERPRETING GOD'S WILL

God locks up His best blessings but gives to every man a key wherewith to open the lock. One man takes his key, and goes up to the lock, and tries to unlock it; but his key will not fit; it will not go in because it is PRIDE that he has been trying to unlock with. Another man says, "Let me try my key." He takes VANITY; but he finds that vanity will not unlock the door. Another man comes up with the key of willful SELFISHNESS. His key is three times as big as the keyhole and he can't get in. They all fail to unlock the door,

and they go away. By and by another man comes. He puts his key to the lock; it slides in; there is not a ward that it does not touch; the bolt slides back without a sound, and the door swings open. He knows the secret. He comes in the spirit of LOVE, obedience, and resignation, and to him God's will is revealed.
—**Henry Ward Beecher**

ILLUMINATING THE LESSON

As a group of college students toured the slums of a city, one of the girls, seeing a little girl playing in the dirt, asked a guide, "Why doesn't her mother clean her up?" "Madam," he replied, "that girl's mother probably loves her, but she doesn't hate dirt. You hate dirt, but you don't love her enough to go down there and clean her up. Until hate for dirt and love for that child are in the same person, that little girl is likely to remain as she is."

Until hate for sin and love for the sinner gets in a person, he will do little about the plight of the lost.

—**"Notes and Quotes"**

DAILY DEVOTIONAL GUIDE

M. Testing Our Love. Luke 14:25-27
T. Loving Without Pretense. Romans 12:1-9
W. Excelling in Love. 1 Corinthians 13:1-13
T. Comprehending Christ's Love. Ephesians 3:14-21
F. Loving One Another. 1 John 3:1-11
S. Being Perfected by Love. 1 John 4:7-16

February 22, 1981

Christ, Our Triumphant Lord

Bible Background: Acts 1:1-11
Time: Between Christ's resurrection and ascension, A.D. 30
Place: An assembly room in Jerusalem
Supplemental References: Psalm 24:1-10; Mark 16:19, 20; Luke 24:49-53
Golden Text: "Every tongue should confess that Jesus Christ is Lord, to the glory of God the Father" (Philippians 2:11).
Central Truth: Our ascended and soon-coming Lord has promised power for service.
Evangelistic Emphasis: Christ provides power for those who obey His command to go and spread the gospel.

PRINTED TEXT

Acts 1:1. The former treatise have I made, O Theophilus, of all that Jesus began both to do and teach,

2. Until the day in which he was taken up, after that he through the Holy Ghost had given commandments unto the apostles whom he had chosen:

3. To whom also he shewed himself alive after his passion by many infallible proofs, being seen of them forty days, and speaking of the things pertaining to the kingdom of God:

4. And, being assembled together with them, commanded them that they should not depart from Jerusalem, but wait for the promise of the Father, which, saith he, ye have heard of me.

5. For John truly baptized with water; but ye shall be baptized with the Holy Ghost not many days hence.

6. When they therefore were come together, they asked of him, saying, Lord, wilt thou at this time restore again the kingdom to Israel?

7. And he said unto them, It is not for you to know the times or the seasons, which the Father hath put in his own power.

8. But ye shall receive power, after that the Holy Ghost is come upon you: and ye shall be witnesses unto me both in Jerusalem, and in all Judaea, and in Samaria, and unto the uttermost part of the earth.

9. And when he had spoken these things, while they beheld, he was taken up; and a cloud received him out of their sight.

10. And while they looked stedfastly toward heaven as he went up, behold, two men stood by them in white apparel;

11. Which also said, Ye men of Galilee, why stand ye gazing up into heaven? this same Jesus, which is taken up from you into heaven, shall so come in like manner as ye have seen him go into heaven.

DICTIONARY

former treatise—Acts 1:1—Luke here refers to the third Gospel which bears his name.

Theophilus (thee-AHF-ih-lus)—Acts 1:1—A personal friend of Luke's; a man of considerable importance. The name **Theophilus** means "a friend of God."

many infallible proofs—Acts 1:3—Post-Resurrection proofs that our Lord was alive

LESSON OUTLINE

I. OUR LORD
II. OUR PROMISE
III. OUR HOPE

LESSON EXPOSITION

INTRODUCTION

The Book of Acts is a continuing record of the great supernatural events that began with the advent of Christ. In the Gospel of Luke we read of "all that Jesus began both to do and teach" (Acts 1:1). The Book of Acts is also written by Luke and is a continuation of his Gospel. As the Gospel of Luke records what Jesus began to do, Acts records what He continued to do through His apostles. We see Jesus everywhere in Acts. He so constantly manifests Himself through the lives and deeds of His followers that miracles are as commonplace in Acts as they were in the Gospels.

It should be emphasized that Luke and Acts are by the same author, written to give a full background of the Christian faith. In the few years following the Crucifixion, there had come to be a great deal of curiosity about how the Christian faith had begun. For this reason Luke, a Greek physician, wrote this extensive account of Christian beginnings.

In the first chapter of Acts we see the joint, the seam, by which the two pieces (Luke and Acts) are held together. We see Jesus transfer His ministry into the hands of His disciples. It is an important chapter for many reasons. Not the least of these reasons is the fact that we catch the final glimpse of Jesus on earth. We see His departure from friends He loved and we see them pick up the slack reins and begin to do the work that He had called them to do. On His last night with His disciples, Jesus had said that He was the vine and they were the branches (John 15:1-8). Here we see Jesus and the Eleven in this fruitful relationship. In a beautiful way we see the Lord yield into the hands of trusted men the responsibility of pressing His kingdom into the world, of being on earth what He would be if it were possible for Him to remain.

I. OUR LORD (Acts 1:1-3)

1. The former treatise have I made, O Theophilus, of all that Jesus began both to do and teach.

The Book of Acts was written by Luke, who also wrote the Gospel that bears his name. Luke and Acts were written as a two-part record of the beginning of the Christian movement. Since both books are addressed to a person named Theophilus (Luke 1:3; Acts 1:1), it appears that Luke did his work under the sponsorship of a person by that name. It was a custom in those days for a writer to inscribe his work in this manner either to a wealthy person who financed it or to a noble person who desired it. Since the Luke inscription uses the term "most excellent Theophilus," a term used for nobility, it is altogether likely that Theophilus was a Roman nobleman or magistrate who desired greater knowledge of how the Christian movement began. The name Theophilus is interesting because it comes from Greek words that mean "friend of God."

2. Until the day in which he was taken up, after that he through the Holy Ghost had given commandments unto the apostles whom he had chosen:

In the Gospel of Luke we read of "all that Jesus began both to do and teach," and in the Book of Acts we read of how the apostles, through the Holy Ghost, continued the Lord's work and spread His message throughout the world. There is a strong similarity between the last chapter of Luke and the first chapter of Acts. Because Acts is a sequel to Luke, this overlap is a bridge that joins the two parts together. More than that, both sections underscore the cardinal factors of the Christian faith and the ministry of the Church. The great event in both chapters is the ascension of Christ. Until the day He was taken up, Jesus continued to give final instructions to the apostles He had chosen. Then, with the Ascension, He terminated His life on earth and the apostles were left on their own.

3. To whom also he shewed himself alive after his passion by many infallible proofs, being seen of them forty days, and speaking of the things pertaining to the kingdom of God:

Christ did not ascend into heaven immediately after His crucifixion and resurrection (called "his passion" in this verse), but He remained on earth for forty days giving His disciples final instructions concerning the kingdom of God. The numerous appearances of Christ following His crucifixion are called "infallible proofs." This means that His appearances were facts that cannot be denied or doubted; they were absolutely true, with no chance of error. Each appearance proved that Christ had risen from the dead. The fact of the Resurrection was the foundation of the disciples' faith, and this faith was essential to their continuing ministry for Christ. Knowledge that He was master over death, that He was alive forevermore, transformed the apostles into men of courage and heralds of hope. The appearance of Christ so thoroughly confirmed the deity of Christ that there is not the slightest indication of later doubt in any of those who beheld Him.

II. OUR PROMISE (Acts 1:4-8)

4. And, being assembled together with them, commanded them that they should not depart from Jerusalem, but wait for the promise of the Father, which, saith he, ye have heard of me.

Why is waiting one of the best yet one of the hardest of all Christian disciplines?

Related to the ascension of Christ was His promise of the Holy Spirit. Several times on the evening before His crucifixion, Jesus emphasized that the Holy Spirit would come to the disciples after His departure from them (John 14:16-26; 15:26; 16:7-17). The outpouring of the Holy Spirit would enable the apostles to carry on the work of Jesus. Jesus, therefore, commanded His disciples not to depart from Jerusalem but to remain there until they had received the fulfillment of this great promise.

5. For John truly baptized with water; but ye shall be baptized with the Holy Ghost not many days hence.

Why is it essential that both baptisms continue to be emphasized today?

Jesus compared the spiritual baptism the disciples would receive with the baptism in water they had already received from John the Baptist. Several of the apostles of Christ had formerly been disciples of John and were therefore well acquainted with his baptism. The import of Jesus' words here is that they would soon be baptized with the Holy Spirit as definitely as they had earlier been baptized by John.

This statement is also a response to John's words in Matthew 3:11: "I indeed baptize you with water unto repentance: but he that cometh after me is mightier than I, whose shoes I am not worthy to bear: he shall baptize you with the Holy Ghost, and with fire."

6. When they therefore were come together, they asked of him, saying, Lord, wilt thou at this time restore again the kingdom to Israel?

While Jesus was alive, the apostles could never quite understand why He did not immediately set up His kingdom on earth (Luke 19:11). They wanted the Kingdom then and there. Their expectation reflected the universal Jewish expectation that the Messiah would come and immediately establish His kingdom on the earth. They expected Him to come in wrath and vengeance to drive their enemies from their land and establish the throne of David in peace and prosperity.

Hopes for the Kingdom to be set up immediately were killed when Jesus was crucified, but they were rekindled when He was resurrected (Luke 24:21). As long as Jesus was with the disciples, they could not grasp the fact that His kingdom was not of this world.

7. And he said unto them, It is not for you to know the times or the seasons, which the Father hath put in his own power.

Jesus explained to His disciples, as He had done at earlier times, that the Kingdom should not yet be restored to Israel. Only God could know the times and seasons of His plan; these were matters too deep for the understanding of human beings.

Some authorities believe that there is a difference in the two words, **times** and **seasons**. The word **times** refers to periods of time, while **seasons** refers to opportunity and fitness. (This is clearly the meaning of the words in 1 Thessalonians 5:1 and 2 Timothy 4:2.) The meaning of this statement is that God alone knows the period when His kingdom will be set up or even when it will be appropriate for it to be established.

In a similar way, He alone knows the times and seasons of our experience. God alone knows what is best for us and when it is best. If we were left to our devices we would make chaos of our lives. We would miss God's ultimate blessings by clutching prematurely to our own desires. It is all too common for men to confuse things that are temporal with things that are eternal, things that are passing with things that are permanent, things that are trivial with things that are significant.

8. But ye shall receive power, after that the Holy Ghost is come upon you: and ye shall be witnesses unto me both in Jerusalem, and in all Judaea, and in Samaria, and unto the uttermost part of the earth.

Although the disciples could not know the time when the Kingdom would be established, they would be given spiritual power for helping to establish it. As soon as they received this infilling of power through the Holy Ghost, they would become witnesses of Christ in Jerusalem, Judea, Samaria and to the farthest part of the earth.

It is very appropriate that the city of Jerusalem would hear the gospel first. Since the time of David, this old city had been the spiritual center of Jewish faith. It had been witnessed to prophets, priests, and kings throughout the long history of Israel. Jerusalem was the heartthrob of Jewish life (it still is) and therefore deserved to be the site of the Spirit infilling. As Jerusalem had been the center of Jewish life, so should it be the fountainhead of Christian witness.

From Jerusalem the apostles were to spread the Christian witness throughout Judea, which was the land of the Jews, and into Samaria, where the people were blood brothers of the Jews. All of these places were in Palestine, on the eastern side of the Mediterranean Sea. From Palestine the gospel would be carried throughout the world. At that time it meant only the Roman world.

The disciples could not possibly have grasped the magnitude of what Jesus said. Countries that were not even in existence at that time (such as those of Western Europe, North America, and South America) would be most receptive and responsive to the good news.

The promise of the Holy Ghost is important for many reasons. Chief among these, the Holy Ghost would be with the apostles in the place of Christ (John 14:16; 16:7). The Holy Ghost would comfort, teach, and guide the apostles as Jesus had done when He was with them. Of equal importance, the Holy Ghost would provide the power by which they would do the works of the Lord (John 14: 12). There is no human way they could do the works of Christ without special spiritual empowerment.

III. OUR HOPE (Acts 1:9-11)

9. And when he had spoken these things, while they beheld, he was taken up; and a cloud received him out of their sight.

After teaching the disciples about the Holy Ghost, Jesus led the Eleven to Bethany on the eastern slope of the Mount of Olives. There He lifted up His hands and blessed them immediately before His ascension (Luke 24:50, 51). Even as He blessed them He ascended into heaven, enveloped in a cloud that took Him out of their sight.

The ascension of Jesus equaled His birth in its splendor and majesty. Having completed His admonition concerning the Holy Ghost, Jesus was taken up into the sky and enveloped in a cloud which hid Him from the view of His awestruck disciples. The cloud that received Him was no ordinary cloud, but the Shekinah which was often associated with the presence of God (see Exodus 13:21; 40:34; 1 Kings 8:10; 1 Corinthians 10:1, 2; Matthew 24:30; Revelation 1:7). This heavenly cloud covered the Lord of heaven as He returned to His eternal, celestial domain.

10. And while they looked stedfastly toward heaven as he went up, behold, two men stood by them in white apparel;

It is easy to imagine what emotion the disciples felt as they beheld the Lord's ascension. There was certainly awe and wonder, with a touch of sadness at the thought that He was gone from them. There must have been a tremor of joy and excitement, for the spectacle surpassed anything ever seen by men upon the earth.

Two men, angels of the Lord, appeared to the apostles and comforted their hearts. The Eleven were looking steadfastly into the sky when they suddenly became aware of the presence of the angels. It was not strange to them that angels should appear thus, for the appearance of angels was nothing in comparison to the glorious spectacle they had just observed.

11. Which also said, Ye men of Galilee, why stand ye gazing up into heaven? this same Jesus, which is taken up from you into heaven, shall so come in like manner as ye have seen him go into heaven.

The angels had a message for the apostles. Contrary to what they might imagine, Jesus had not left them forever; He would come again.

The ascension of Jesus is of twofold significance. First of all, it signifies the reality of heaven and the fact that Jesus and His mission are heavenly. No matter how we look at this glorious event, we see heaven. The Ascension puts the unfading stamp of heaven upon all subsequent work the disciples might do for Jesus. Our life is no mere earthly life, for all that we are and all that we do in Him comes from, and returns to, heaven. The Christian life is heaven born, heaven sent, heavenly in its purpose, and heavenly in its conclusion.

Second, the ascension of Jesus gave testimony to His second coming. As surely as He went away, He shall "in like manner" return to the earth. Everything about His departure from the earth affirms that He shall return "in the clouds of heaven with power and great glory" (Matthew 24:30). This great event was a crucial point of Christian history. It was the Ascension that finally confirmed Christ as the Son of God and established the hope of the disciples for the future. With the Ascension, the work of Christ, who was divine, became the responsibility of men who were intensely human.

In the life of Christ, heaven and earth were united for all time to those who will receive it.

REVIEW QUESTIONS

1. Who was Theophilus?
2. Why was Luke writing his treatise for his friend Theophilus?
3. How did Jesus answer the disciples question about the kingdom?
4. Where were the disciples to take their witness for Christ?
5. What was the message of the angels to the disciples?

GOLDEN TEXT HOMILY

"EVERY TONGUE SHOULD CONFESS THAT JESUS CHRIST IS LORD, TO THE GLORY OF GOD THE FATHER" (Philippians 2:11).

The Holy Spirit of truth is working in the lives of Christians, teaching them that Jesus Christ is Lord to the glory of God.

Jesus told His disciples that He was truth and that He would send the Holy Spirit of truth who would be a teacher to them. In order for someone to be taught they first must be teachable.

There was so much for the disciples to learn. Jesus had worked with them and taught them much. But He knew that there was still more for them to know. This would be the work of the Holy Spirit after Jesus left. When He, the Spirit of truth, came and baptized the 120, He began immediately to assume His role as teacher to teachable people. When Peter stood and preached on the Day of Pentecost, he saw truth as never before, because now he was able to understand his earlier statement confessing that Jesus was the Christ, the Son of God. The Holy Spirit of truth was helping Peter to see the truth, and Peter knew and was able to confess that Jesus Christ was Lord to the glory of God the Father. This has happened thousands and thousands of times since that day. The Holy Spirit of truth has helped people to experience the freedom that the truth brings. As Jesus said, "Ye shall know the truth, and the truth shall make you free. . . . If the Son therefore shall make you free, ye shall be free indeed" (John 8:32, 36). When people are freed by the truth and continue in the truth, then they are able to confess that Jesus Christ is Lord to the glory of God the Father. They are able to live in the reality of that great truth every day and thus bring glory to God every day they live.—**Levy E. Moore, Chaplain and Christian Service Director, Emmanuel College, Franklin Springs, Georgia**

SENTENCE SERMONS

CHRIST PROVIDES POWER for those who obey His command to go and spread the gospel.
—**Selected**

CHRISTIANITY IS not the truth on ice, but the truth on fire.
—**Wilbur G. Williams**

WE CANNOT GO in power until we have tarried for power.
—**Selected**

CHRISTIANITY IS EITHER relevant all the time or useless anytime. It is not just a phase of life; it is life itself.
—**Richard Halverson**

EVANGELISTIC APPLICATION

CHRIST PROVIDES POWER FOR THOSE WHO OBEY HIS COMMAND TO GO AND SPREAD THE GOSPEL.

SERMONS ON JUDGMENT

It was the preaching of Jonathan Edwards on the theme of judgment that led to the Great Awakening in New England during the first half of the eighteenth century.

"If sin, then, were already cursed by God, why should not the preacher be free to curse what God had cursed? Why should he be more restrained when speaking of sinful men than when speaking of sin in the abstract?"

Jonathan Edwards began to put that principle into practice. He preached that men were lost, that judgment was ahead, and that hell was waiting. In his historic sermon, "Sinners in the Hands of An Angry God," he pictured them as being held over the pit of hell as a man might hold a spider over a fire, and he pleaded with them to turn before it was too late. People trembled and cried out in fear. Within a few years, the whole of New England had been shaken from indifference and worldliness, and the lives of thousands were transformed.—**J. Vernon Jacobs,** From **450 True Stories from Church History**

ILLUMINATING THE LESSON

W. P. Nicholson, an Irish evangelist, went for special electrical treatment to a practitioner in Edinburgh. He was asked to sit in a chair, while the doctor sat down and began to read the daily paper. After waiting some time Mr. Nicholson asked that the treatment might begin. "You are being treated now," was the answer. He said he felt nothing at all. Then the physician took a board with several electric lamps on it, and placed it against his breast. Instantly the lamps glowed with light. The doctor said, "Mr. Nicholson, there is enough power passing through your body to run the tram car on the street. You do not feel it because you are insulated." Mr. Nicholson said afterward, when narrating this experience: "My friends, you may have all the power of almighty God passing through you, and yet be unconscious of it because there is no special call for its use. But let the need come, and the power will be manifested, for it is there."

—**"Alliance Weekly"**

Our word **strength** comes from a word signifying twisted together. "The Lord is the strength of my life." "God is the strength of my heart." Then my life is twisted together with the Lord. God and my soul are two strands twisted together with one that is infinite, the weakest shall not fail.

—**"Gospel Herald"**

DAILY DEVOTIONAL GUIDE

M. Our Victorious Lord. Mark 16:12-20
T. Power From on High. Luke 24:45-53
W. Christ, Our Spiritual Bread. John 6:53-63
T. Fellowship in Christ. Acts 2:42-47
F. Prayer for Boldness. Acts 4:23-31
S. Our Exalted Lord. Ephesians 1:15-23

INTRODUCTION TO SPRING QUARTER

The month of March begins the spring quarter of studies and marks a departure from the New Testament lessons on the life of Christ which has occupied our thoughts for the last four quarters.

The lessons for the spring quarter (March, April, May) are presented under the theme "1 and 2 Samuel." In a general way, the combined books recount the lives of Samuel as the last of the judges, Saul as the first king, and David as the successor to Saul and to the throne.

The lives of these three great leaders are intriguing studies in the development of men as they relate their life to God. The entire range of success and failure, dedication and recklessness, reward and punishment is brought into focus.

In our studies we will find that the leaders, though anointed of the Lord, were very human. They were subject to temptation and to failure, as is every person in the human family.

By a trustful and obedient walk with our Lord, may we find the important truths that are revealed in this quarter of studies. And by knowing the truth may we avoid being trapped by temptation or inclined toward failure.

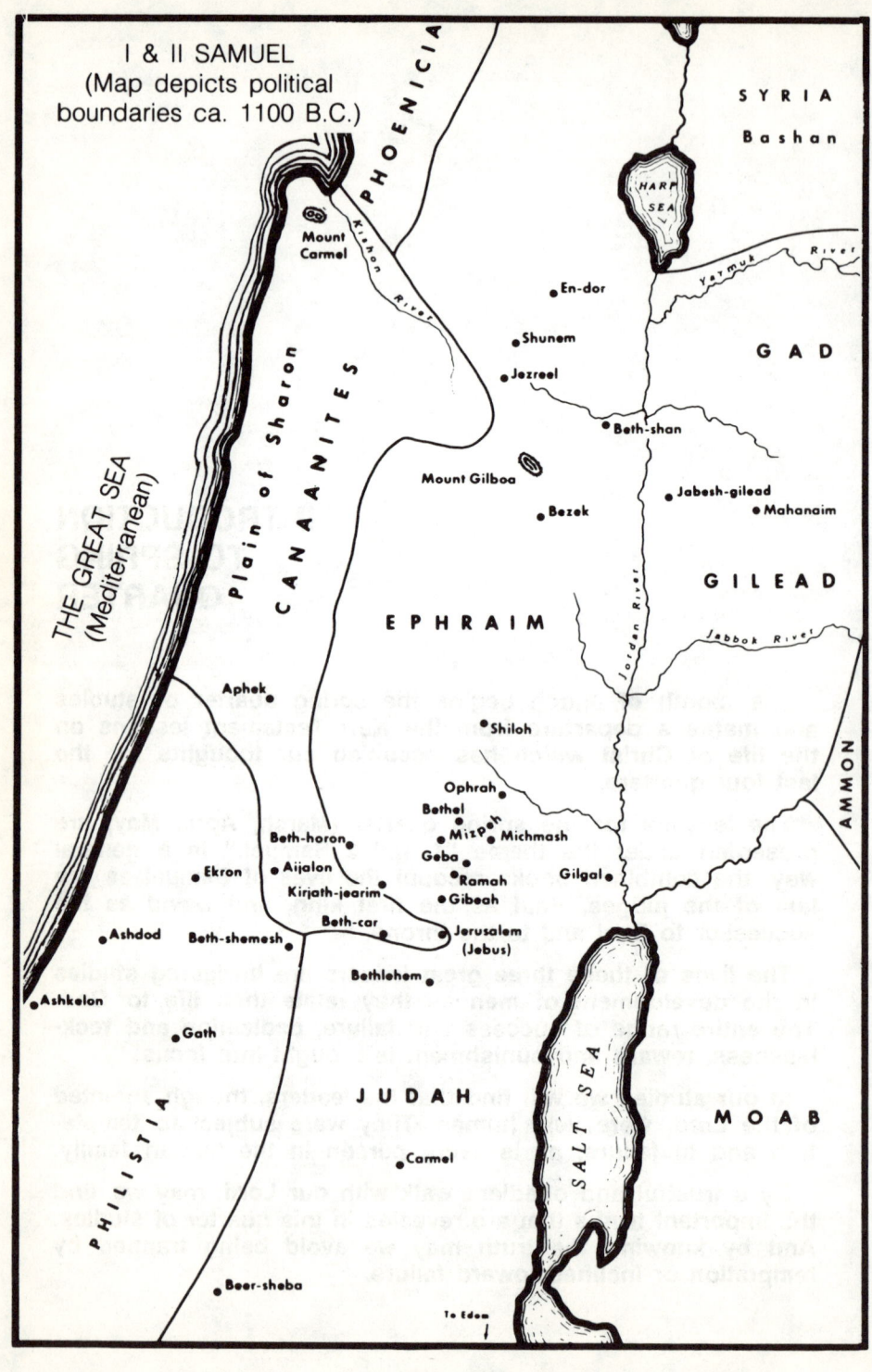

March 1, 1981

Children, a Gift From God

Bible Background: 1 Samuel 1:1—2:11
Time: About 1080 B.C.
Place: Ramathaim (or Ramah, 1 Samuel 1:19), probably a short distance north of Jerusalem; Shiloh, about ten miles north of Bethel on the road to Shechem
Supplemental References: Judges 13:2-7; Psalm 127:3-5; Luke 1:5-13
Golden Text: "Children are an heritage of the Lord" (Psalm 127:3).
Central Truth: As a heritage of the Lord, children are both a blessing and a responsibility.
Evangelistic Emphasis: Evangelism should begin in the home.

PRINTED TEXT

1 Samuel 1:19. And they rose up in the morning early, and worshipped before the Lord, and returned, and came to their house to Ramah: and Elkanah knew Hannah his wife; and the Lord remembered her.

20. Wherefore it came to pass, when the time was come about after Hannah had conceived, that she bare a son, and called his name Samuel, saying, Because I have asked him of the Lord.

21. And the man Elkanah, and all his house, went up to offer unto the Lord the yearly sacrifice, and his vow.

22. But Hannah went not up; for she said unto her husband, I will not go up until the child be weaned, and then I will bring him, that he may appear before the Lord, and there abide for ever.

23. And Elkanah her husband said unto her, Do what seemeth thee good; tarry until thou have weaned him; only the Lord establish his word. So the woman abode, and gave her son suck until she weaned him.

24. And when she had weaned him, she took him up with her, with three bullocks, and one ephah of flour, and a bottle of wine, and brought him unto the house of the Lord in Shiloh: and the child was young.

25. And they slew a bullock, and brought the child to Eli.

26. And she said, Oh my lord, as thy soul liveth, my lord, I am the woman that stood by thee here, praying unto the Lord.

27. For this child I prayed; and the Lord hath given me my petition which I asked of him:

28. Therefore also I have lent him to the Lord; as long as he liveth he shall be lent to the Lord. And he worshipped the Lord there.

2:1. And Hannah prayed, and said, My heart rejoiceth in the Lord, mine horn is exalted in the Lord: my mouth is enlarged over mine enemies; because I rejoice in thy salvation.

2. There is none holy as the Lord: for there is none beside thee: neither is there any rock like our God.

DICTIONARY

Elkanah (EL-can-nah)—1 Samuel 1:19, 21, 23—The husband of Hannah and father of Samuel, an Ephrathite who made an annual pilgrimage to Shiloh to worship. The name means "whom God has acquired."

Children, a Gift From God

Hannah (HAN-nah)—1 Samuel 1:19, 22; 2:1—Meaning "favor" or "grace," the mother of Samuel

Samuel (SAM-you-el)—1 Samuel 1:20—A Hebrew word meaning simply "name of God," but by play on letters is understood to signify "ask of God"

ephah (EE-fah)—1 Samuel 1:24—A measure of Egyptian origin, in common use among the Hebrews, and containing about three pecks and three pints

Eli (EE-lye)—1 Samuel 1:25—("High," i.e., "God is high"), the high priest in the early part of the eleventh century B.C., serving in the Tabernacle at Shiloh

LESSON OUTLINE

I. PARENTAL LOVE
   A. Overcoming Humiliation
   B. Overcoming Misunderstanding
   C. Overcoming Inability
II. PARENTAL CARE
   A. The Weaning Process
   B. The Consecration Crisis
III. PARENTAL PRAISE
   A. Hannah's Victory
   B. Hannah's Prophecy

LESSON EXPOSITION

INTRODUCTION

During our Spring Quarter of lessons we shall cover a large amount of biblical territory. The two Books of Samuel were originally one book of the Hebrew canon (they were divided by the group of Alexandrian Jewish scholars who translated the Hebrew Old Testament into Greek in the third century B.C.). The fifty-five chapters span approximately one century, from the birth of Samuel almost to the death of King David. In our lessons, as in the biblical material, three characters occupy the forefront of the stage—Samuel, the last judge of Israel; Saul, the first king of Israel; and David, Israel's great empire builder. Our first four lessons focus on Samuel, beginning in lesson one with his remarkable mother and miraculous birth.

The historical background to the birth of Samuel is described in the Book of Judges, especially the concluding chapters. To this may be added the portrait of the house of Eli, Samuel's predecessor in the judgeship, which is given in 1 Samuel 2:12-36. It is evident that Samuel was born and raised during one of the most depraved periods of Old Testament history. It was a time of **anarchy** (Judges 21:25); of **apostasy** (1 Samuel 2: 12-17, 22-25); and of **apathy** (represented by senile old Eli).

Yet against this black background two of the most lovely portraits of the Bible are painted: that of Naomi, Ruth, and Boaz (see the Book of Ruth), and that of Hannah (our present lesson). What a challenge to us who likewise live in a time of anarchy, apostasy, and apathy.

I. PARENTAL LOVE (1 Samuel 1:9-23)

A. Overcoming Humiliation (vv. 9-11)

We must not take much time to discuss Samuel's genealogy (v. 1), except to point out that according to 1 Chronicles 6:22-38 he was descended from the Kohathite branch of the tribe of Levi, though the Book of 1 Samuel does not state this. The phrase **an Ephrathite** (v. 1) is better rendered "an Ephraimite" as in the **New English Bible.** This does not mean that the family of Elkanah was descended from Ephraim, but, as D. F. Payne points out, "must refer to geographical location, not ancestry" **(New Bible Commentary Revised).**

Elkanah, though a Levite, lived in a state of bigamy. Though there are indications in the Old Testament that polygamy was tolerated and practiced, it must not be assumed that this was extensive. As John Mauchline points out, "The phrase 'a man and his wife' is found quite commonly in the Old Testament, and may well mean that for a man to have one wife was the common practice and only those who both desired and could afford it had more" **(New Century Bible, 1 and 2 Samuel).** Moreover, Jesus clearly showed that monogamy was the divine order from creation. Therefore, both polygamy and homosexual "marriages" contravene that order.

The sad picture of domestic strife in Elkanah's household, as with other biblical cases of polygamous families, is itself an indictment of polygamy.

What other examples of polygamous families in Scripture harmonize with the story of Elkanah? Is plurality of wives practiced today? What evil results are known?

Hannah's barrenness was a terrible humiliation for her, as with any Hebrew woman. E. M. Blaiklock points out that to a Hebrew woman of true faith and piety there would be the added disappointment that she would feel excluded from the messianic promise of Genesis 3:15. "She could never become the ancestress of the One who should 'bruise the serpent's head' " **(Bible Characters, Elkanah to David).** Moreover, her psychological suffering was deepened by "the other woman," Peninnah, Elkanah's other wife. "Hannah's rival used to torment her and humiliate her because she had no children. Year after year this happened when they went up to the house of the Lord" (vv. 6, 7, **New English Bible**). Why the woman blessed with children should ill-treat the woman considered to be under a divine curse is not stated, but there must have been some deep emotional disturbance in Peninnah's heart to motivate her. Blaiklock suggests that Peninnah was "an insecure woman tortured by jealousy." He adds, "Jealousy is the fear or realization of another's superiority, and Peninnah paid her rival the unsolicited compliment, but in entertaining the deadly visitant in her heart, she ruined her peace, and preyed upon herself." The special attention and honor shown to Hannah by her husband when he gave her "a worthy portion" (v. 5), or "a double portion" **(New International Version),** seems to imply that Elkanah held Hannah in very special regard. This caused, or maybe fed, the jealous spirit of Peninnah.

Though Hannah was crushed by her situation, probably over several years, she eventually triumphed over her tragedy, conquered her curse, and moved out from underneath her burden to pray through for **a son**. Not merely a **child**, but a **son**. Why a son? Surely such a woman could be satisfied with either a boy or a girl? The special emphasis is highly significant. For one thing, her eye was upon Genesis 3:15 and its promise of the Messiah. For another, she could not be unaware of the decadence of her nation and its great need of a deliverer, and—in view of her pledge to dedicate her son to God—she may have conceived the noble purpose of working with God to produce such a man.

Hannah's vow (v. 11) implies that she had the law of the Nazarite in mind (see Numbers 6:1-8). What meaning does this law have for Christians?

B. Overcoming Misunderstanding (vv. 12-18)

In her sufferings Hannah had dealings with two men (Elkanah and Eli), both of whom added to her grief through their crass misunderstanding of her feelings.

Though Elkanah was a religious man, indeed a Levite, he appears to have been little concerned about the conflict of his wives or the sufferings of Hannah. He appeared to imagine that her longing for a baby could be appeased by the gift of a large steak, and he had the unspeakable dullness to say, "Why is thy heart grieved? am not I better to thee than ten sons?" (v. 8). Blaiklock sums up Elkanah as "a harmless man, in short, notable for neither good nor ill, but more for good than ill, quietly pleased with himself, and with small concern for the deeper implications of religion." His insensitiveness to his wife's natural longings and religious ideals and visions deepened Hannah's sufferings.

Hannah also suffered through the misunderstanding of the high priest, Eli, now very old and decrepit. We shall look at Eli again in a later lesson and view him in a better light, but the point to note here is his astonishing obtuseness. When he saw Hannah in a passion of silent prayer, he assumed she was drunk! Could a prominent religious leader have made a more terrible mistake?

But Hannah's determined love swept aside the misunderstanding of both Elkanah and Eli. She set her sails to the contrary winds which blew from both quarters, and she prayed through to the throne of God for a son. We do not know what reply she gave to Elkanah, but her quiet, dignified answer to the charge of drunkenness is as noble a speech as ever a woman uttered (vv. 15, 16). It is to the credit of the old priest that he acknowledged and rectified his error (v. 17).

C. Overcoming Inability (vv. 19-23)

19. And they rose up in the morning early, and worshipped before the Lord, and returned, and came to their house to Ramah: and Elkanah knew Hannah his wife; and the Lord remembered her.

20. Wherefore it came to pass, when the time was come about after Hannah had conceived, that she bare a son, and called his name Samuel, saying, Because I have asked him of the Lord.

Like Sarah before her, and Elizabeth and Mary after her, Hannah discovered that nothing is too hard for the Lord (see Genesis 18:14). "With God nothing shall be impossible" (Luke 1:37). Few of us would question this as a **general truth**. It is its application to our particular situation which stumbles us. Yet it was in regard to particular situations that the above statements were made, and it was in regard to particular situations that Jesus said, "And . . . ask in prayer, believing, [and] ye shall receive" (Matthew 21:22). Hannah certainly exemplifies this spirit of believing prayer. By it she appropriated the omnipotence of God for natural inability, and, like Sarah before her, "received strength to conceive seed" (Hebrews 11:11). It should be noted, however, that Hannah's believing prayer was inspired by right motives, by what Jeremy Taylor and John Wesley called "purity of intention." It cannot be too strongly emphasized that our prayers for God's interventions need this motivation.

21. And the man Elkanah, and all his house, went up to offer unto the Lord the yearly sacrifice, and his vow.

22. But Hannah went not up; for she said unto her husband, I will not go up until the child be weaned, and then I will bring him, that he may appear before the Lord, and there abide for ever.

23. And Elkanah her husband said unto her, Do what seemeth thee good; tarry until thou have weaned him; only the Lord establish his word. So the woman abode, and gave her son suck until she weaned him.

In due time Hannah's son was born, and she called his name **Samuel**. The reason given is, "Because I have asked him of the Lord" (v. 20). Scholars point out that the name Samuel does not literally mean "asked of the Lord," but "heard of God" (Keil and Delitzsch, **A Commentary on the Old Testament, The Books of Samuel**). Hannah thus called her son **Samuel** because he was the answer to her prayers.

When Elkanah was preparing to attend the feast of the Lord, again Hannah announced that she would not accompany him "until the child was weaned." Her motive for this is then clearly stated: "Then I will bring him, that he may appear before the Lord, and there abide for ever" (v. 22). This was in fulfillment of her vow and in harmony with her master purpose (v. 11). It was scarcely possible for a tiny, helpless baby to be left in the sanctuary at Shiloh. Hence her promise.

Some Christians claim not only that God can do anything, but also that He is **willing** to do anything in answer to believing prayer. Is this strictly true or are there other conditions?

II. PARENTAL CARE (1 Samuel 1:24-28)

A. The Weaning Process (vv. 23, 24)

Though Hannah's heroic and sublime purpose was to give Samuel to the Lord and to place him in the charge of Eli at Shiloh for religious training, she realized that she had a more immediate responsibility, that of weaning her son. Among the ancient Hebrews, as still in Oriental society, this was a longer process than in the Western world. An example of this is seen in 2 Maccabees 7 in the story of the terrible martyrdom of seven brothers and their mother by the infamous Antiochus Epiphanes. Speaking to her youngest son the mother says, "I carried you nine months in my womb, and **nursed you for three years**" (v. 27). It is generally assumed that this was the common period for weaning a child. So for Samuel.

It is highly significant that though Hannah's mind was filled with a passionate desire to "lend her son to the Lord," she nevertheless kept him under the care and protection of her mother love for the first three years. Indeed, as Matthew Henry points out, she would do this even more lovingly because "he was devoted to God, and for Him she nursed her son."

There is a telling lesson for Christian parents here, a twofold lesson: (a) Having promised our children to the Lord, we ought to love them and care for them not only out of our natural affection for them, but also with multiplied assiduousness because they are "the Lord's." Like Hannah, we ought to "nurse them for Him." (b) We ought not, however, to imagine that because we have promised our children to God, we can opt out of personal attention to their needs by dumping them in church and Sunday school where they can be trained by proxy. Our children must have our **personal attention**, and there is no substitute for this.

In a recent article in **Christianity Today** (May 25, 1979), the psychiatrist Armand M. Nicholi II claims, "If any one factor influences the character development and emotional stability of an individual, it is the quality of the relationship he or she experiences as a child with **both** parents. Conversely, if people suffering from severe nonorganic emotional illness have one experience in common, it is the absence of a parent through death, divorce, a time-demanding job, or for other reasons. A parent's inaccessibility, either physically, emotionally, or both, can profoundly influence a child's emotional health." Nicholi further makes this startling statement: "A study in a small United States community shows that the average time per day fathers spend with their very young sons is about thirty-seven seconds."

How should we evaluate Elkanah's attitude to his wife's holy purpose?

B. The Consecration Crisis (vv. 24-28)

24. And when she had weaned him, she took him up with her, with three bullocks, and one ephah of flour, and a bottle of wine, and brought him unto the house of the Lord in Shiloh: and the child was young.

25. And they slew a bullock, and brought the child to Eli.

Hannah kept her son under her personal care for three years. She must have done for him much more than is literally implied by the term "wean." As W. J. Deane says, "His physical needs were supplied by her watchful tenderness; his spiritual training was not neglected. In his infant soul were sown the seeds of holy thoughts; from the dawn of reason his mind was turned to the Lord, whose gift he was; the child of prayer was early taught to commune with God **(Samuel and Saul: Their Lives and Times).**

If Elkanah did not take an active part in this, at least he acquiesced in it (v. 23). And all the time the crisis moment was drawing nearer when the mother would give her child to the Lord **forever.**

Let us not glide lightly over the statement, "I will bring him [to Shiloh], that he may appear before the Lord, and there abide for ever" (v. 22). It is to be feared that when many Christian parents dedicate their children to God at a church service they do not entertain the thought for a single moment that they will ever be called upon to part with them in the future in any literal sense. They are hoping, perhaps, that the child will grow up to be a Christian, at least "a good boy" or "a good girl." Who among us can really empathize with Hannah? Her holy purpose was to take her three-year-old boy to the house of the Lord at Shiloh, and leave him there **forever** that he might be trained for the service of God. Throughout his entire childhood and teen years she was to see him only once a year (see 1 Samuel 2:19). Perhaps the nearest analogy for our understanding would be the dedication of a teenager to a Roman Catholic convent or monastery.

26. And she said, Oh my lord, as thy soul liveth, my lord, I am the woman that stood by thee here, praying unto the Lord.

27. For this child I prayed; and the Lord hath given me my petition which I asked of him:

28. Therefore also I have lent him to the Lord; as long as he liveth he shall be lent to the Lord. And he worshipped the Lord there.

The presentation of Samuel to the Lord at Shiloh demanded two great qualities in the mother: (a) **A spirit of sacrifice.** There was a cross in her dedication. Indeed, that cross is at the heart of all dedication. Surely Hannah fulfilled the spirit of Luke 14:26 to the utmost extent. (b) **A spirit of faith.** She could not have been unaware of the grave moral dangers to which her son would be exposed at Shiloh (see 1 Samuel 2:12-17, 22). But she was prepared to entrust Samuel to God in such a place.

The motivation of Hannah's dedication explains her sacrifice and faith. She wanted a son who would be a servant of the Lord more than she wanted a son. Indeed, she wanted a son who would become a servant of the Lord. How rarely do our **Christian** fathers and mothers have this profound and sublime quality of motivation!

"This vow of Hannah, does it seem strange to us and unnatural, a piece of needless self-sacrifice, the act of a bigoted and hardhearted mother?" (W. J. Deane). Discuss the wisdom and the ethics of Hannah's vow.

III. PARENTAL PRAISE (1 Samuel 2:1-11)

A. Hannah's Victory (v. 1)

1. And Hannah prayed, and said, My heart rejoiceth in the Lord, mine horn is exalted in the Lord: my mouth is enlarged over

mine enemies; because I rejoice in thy salvation.

The chapter division here is out of place. Hannah's prayer is a direct continuation of the consecration crisis at Shiloh. It is in striking contrast with her prayer of four years before (1 Samuel 1:12, 13). That was silent though passionate, and a prayer of desperate supplication. This was vocal, and a paeon of praise and victory, a song of rejoicing for answered prayer. When she says "Mine horn is exalted in the Lord," she is speaking metaphorically of her rising up out of weakness and inability to a place of strength. As Keil and Delitzsch say, "The horn is the symbol of strength, and is taken from oxen whose strength is in their horns: Deuteronomy 33:17; Psalm 75:5, etc." (p. 30).

One might think that her parting forever with her three-year-old son would have broken her down in grief and tears. On the contrary, she felt that the presentation of her son to God after such a miracle of answered prayer was a thing to shout about and sing about in victory. Her spiritual discernment and sublime purposefulness completely transformed what ordinarily would be a bitter grief.

Many great Christians (David Livingstone, for example) have counted their sacrifices for God as precious privileges.

B. Hannah's Prophecy (vv. 2-11)

2. There is none holy as the Lord: for there is none beside thee: neither is there any rock like our God.

Though some critical modern commentators tend to deny the authenticity of the rest of Hannah's prayer, and to treat it as a later composition, the older commentators, such as Keil and Delitzsch (no less scholarly!) reject this view, and treat it as an inspired prophecy from the lips of Hannah. Why not? It is in harmony with the great Christian prophetic songs recorded by Luke (chapters 1 and 2), and is, as Keil and Delitzsch say, "a song of praise of a prophetic and Messianic character."

List the features of the character of God in Hannah's prayer.

REVIEW QUESTIONS

1. Why did Hannah give the name of "Samuel" to her son?

2. Why did Hannah choose not to go with her husband to offer the yearly sacrifice?

3. When Hannah finally went to the House of the Lord, what did she take with her besides Samuel?

4. For how long was Hannah planning to give Samuel to the Lord?

5. What was the nature of the prayer Hannah prayed after lending Samuel to the Lord?

GOLDEN TEXT HOMILY

"CHILDREN ARE AN HERITAGE OF THE LORD" (Psalm 127:3).

"Children are manifestly the free gift of God. Therefore, they are man's reward. The picture presented is of the Hebrew man in mid-life, at rest in his country home, with his sturdy sons around him; his wife is still young; her fair daughters are like cornices sculptured as decorations for a palace" (Isaac Taylor).

Children are a heritage of the Lord and as such they reward a man in what they themselves are. A man has no pleasure in life that can equal his joy in his children, who bear his image and in miniature reproduce himself. Their ways, their talk, their innocence, their unfolding, their very frailties, are a perpetual interest, relief, and pleasure.

Children reward a man in what they become. For a man lives over again in the success of his children. He is proud of their well-grown, healthy body; of their developed and cultured mind; of their honorable and useful position in the kingdom of God and in the business world. A man never feels to have lived in vain when he leaves a respectable and well-ordered family behind him.

Children reward a man in what they do for him. This is especially in the psalmist's mind. The good man whom God has blessed with children has a fortune laid up against old age and infirmity safer by far than shares in joint-stock companies. His every need will be safely met by the response child-love will make to all his sacrifices in days gone by.

"Ah! What would the world be to us if the children were no more? We should dread the desert behind us worse than the dark before" (Henry Wadsworth Longfellow). Children indeed are a poor man's riches and are as flowers in a bouquet.—**Jewell Travis, Director, East Tennessee Evangelism and Home Missions**

SENTENCE SERMONS

AS A HERITAGE of the Lord, children are

March 1, 1981

both a blessing and a responsibility.
—**Selected**

AS EACH ONE wishes his children to be, so they are.
—**Terrence**

INSTEAD OF BRINGING their children up, many parents let them down.
—**John Andrew Holmes**

I THINK IT must be somewhere written that the virtues of mothers shall be visited on their children, as well as the sins of their fathers.
—**Charles Dickens**

EVANGELISTIC APPLICATION

EVANGELISM SHOULD BEGIN IN THE HOME.

The Lord "raiseth up the poor out of the dust, and lifteth up the beggar from the dunghill, to set them among princes, and to make them inherit the throne of glory." How vividly the **King James Version** of this stanza of Hannah's prayer pictures the saving grace of God in the experience of sinful man. This is exactly what salvation is—a raising up from spiritual poverty and beggary to spiritual nobility and kingship—"from rags to riches" in the truest meaning of the well-worn phrase.

One of the great stories of the Bible which illustrates this sublime truth is that of the lifting up of Mephibosheth, the lame and forgotten son of Jonathan, by the victorious David. What a miserable and helpless person he was! He described himself as "a dead dog" (2 Samuel 9:8). He was utterly without a future and a hope. Yet David graciously called him to his capital, gave him recognition and security, and generously invited him to sit regularly at the king's table for the royal banquets.

The Greater David, our Lord Jesus Christ, has done all of this—and infinitely more!—for millions of spiritual Mephibosheths, and even for you and for me!

ILLUMINATING THE LESSON

After one of the terrible battles of the Civil War, a dying Confederate soldier asked to see the chaplain. When the chaplain arrived, he supposed the young man would wish him to beseech God for his recovery; but it was very different. First the soldier asked him to cut off a lock of his hair for his mother, and then he asked him to kneel down and thank God. "What for?" asked the surprised chaplain. "For giving me such a mother. Thank God that I am a Christian. And thank God for giving me grace to die with. And thank God for the Home He has promised me over there." And so the chaplain knelt down by the dying man, and in his prayer he had not a single petition to offer, but only praise and gratitude.—**"Christian Herald"**

DAILY DEVOTIONAL GUIDE

M. Faithful Parents. Genesis 17:15-22
T. God's Concern for the Underprivileged. Genesis 21:14-21
W. Responsibility for God's Heritage. Deuteronomy 6:4-9
T. A Considerate Husband. 1 Samuel 1:1-8
F. Jesus' Concern for Children. Mark 10:13-16
S. Praise for a Promised Child. Luke 1:5-13

March 8, 1981

God's Call to Service

Bible Background: 1 Samuel 3:1-21
Time: About 1070 B.C.
Place: The Tabernacle at Shiloh, about ten miles north of Bethel on the road to Shechem
Supplemental References: Jeremiah 1:1-19; Galatians 1:11-17
Golden Text: "Speak, Lord; for thy servant heareth" (1 Samuel 3:9).
Central Truth: Though God does not call everyone in the same way, He does call each of us to service for Him.
Evangelistic Emphasis: Those who live in obedience to God's Word will be ready to hear the Lord's call to service.

PRINTED TEXT

1 Samuel 3:1. And the child Samuel ministered unto the Lord before Eli. And the word of the Lord was precious in those days; there was no open vision.

2. And it came to pass at that time, when Eli was laid down in his place, and his eyes began to wax dim, that he could not see;

3. And ere the lamp of God went out in the temple of the Lord, where the ark of God was, and Samuel was laid down to sleep;

4. That the Lord called Samuel: and he answered, Here am I.

5. And he ran unto Eli, and said, Here am I; for thou calledst me. And he said, I called not; lie down again. And he went and lay down.

6. And the Lord called yet again, Samuel. And Samuel arose and went to Eli, and said, Here am I; for thou didst call me. And he answered, I called not, my son; lie down again.

7. Now Samuel did not yet know the Lord, neither was the word of the Lord yet revealed unto him.

8. And the Lord called Samuel again the third time. And he arose and went to Eli, and said, Here am I; for thou didst call me. And Eli perceived that the Lord had called the child.

9. Therefore Eli said unto Samuel, Go, lie down: and it shall be, if he call thee, that thou shalt say, Speak, Lord; for thy servant heareth. So Samuel went and lay down in his place.

10. And the Lord came, and stood, and called as at other times, Samuel, Samuel. Then Samuel answered, Speak; for thy servant heareth.

16. Then Eli called Samuel, and said, Samuel, my son. And he answered, Here am I.

17. And he said, What is the thing that the Lord hath said unto thee? I pray thee hide it not from me: God do so to thee, and more also, if thou hide any thing from me of all the things that he said unto thee.

18. And Samuel told him every whit, and hid nothing from him. And he said, It is the Lord: let him do what seemeth him good.

19. And Samuel grew, and the Lord was with him, and did let none of his words fall to the ground.

20. And all Israel from Dan even to Beersheba knew that Samuel was established to be a prophet of the Lord.

DICTIONARY

Samuel (SAM-you-el)—1 Samuel 3:1—A Hebrew word meaning simply "name of God" but often understood to mean "asked of God"
Eli (EE-lye)—1 Samuel 3:1—The high priest in the early part of the eleventh century B.C., serving the Tabernacle at Shiloh
Dan to Beer-sheba—1 Samuel 3:20—A saying to indicate the whole land; similar to "from Maine to California"

LESSON OUTLINE

I. MINISTERING TO THE LORD
   A. The Silence of God
   B. Samuel's Youthful Ministry
II. LISTENING TO THE LORD
   A. The Prophetic Call
   B. The Prophetic Message
III. OBEYING THE LORD
   A. Immediate Response
   B. Further Development

LESSON EXPOSITION

INTRODUCTION

In our lesson sequence we are bypassing the second half of the second chapter of 1 Samuel. This is not because it is unimportant. Indeed it is extremely important for two reasons: (a) It takes the lid off the national sin and shame at the time of Samuel's birth and childhood. (b) In contrast it gives brief but vivid pictures of the developing Samuel, like bits of film superimposed upon another film. Before proceeding to our lesson we should take a brief look at both.

1. **The Evil Situation.** In the Book of Judges it is the **nation** which is portrayed as evil, with the leadership usually (though not invariably) the counteraction to it. Here, in the early chapters of Samuel, it is the leadership itself which has failed. The acting high priests, Hophni and Phinehas, had wholly commercialized their office and corrupted their morals until religion itself was a national scandal. Their father Eli, the high priest and judge proper, was physically feeble and morally a coward, doing almost nothing to counteract the conduct of his wicked sons and representatives. As E. M. Blaiklock says, "He was passive in days which demanded action, silent in days which called for speech, a weakling in days which cried for strength, and mild when God's name called for passionate defense" **(Bible Characters: Elkanah to David).**

2. **The Light of Hope.** In those very times of evil, Hannah had prayed through for a son whom she dedicated to the Lord that he might be God's man for that hour. In the second chapter we are given three glimpses of the growing boy: (a) "But Samuel ministered before the Lord, being a child" (v. 18). Surely this is one of the glorious "buts" of the Bible. (b) "And the child Samuel grew before the Lord" (v. 21—carefully note the last three words). (c) "And the child Samuel grew on" (v. 26).

No doubt many (like Hannah and Ruth) were praying in Israel. Samuel was God's answer on the way. A deliverer was growing up in the nation and, like a lily in the mud of a pond, growing up at the very center of the nation's corruption, yet untouched and uninfected by it.

I. MINISTERING TO THE LORD (1 Samuel 3:1-3)

A. The Silence of God (v. 1)

1. And the child Samuel ministered unto the Lord before Eli. And the word of the Lord was precious in those days; there was no open vision.

To the modern reader the **King James Version** does not adequately communicate the meaning of the original. "The word of the Lord was precious in those days," is better rendered as in the **New English Bible**: "The word of the Lord was seldom heard." This does not refer to a mere preaching or teaching ministry, but to the prophetic ministry. "The 'word of the Lord' is the word of God announced by prophets" (Keil and Delitzsch, **A Commentary on the Old Testament, The Books of Samuel).** This is also implied by the statement, "there was no open vision," better rendered, "there were not many visions" **(New International Version).** In the words of H.D.M. Spence, "**The word of the Lord** is the will of the Lord announced by a prophet, seer, or man of God. Between the days of Deborah and the nameless man of God who came with the awful message to Eli (2:27-36), no inspired voice seems to have spoken to the chosen people. The 'open vision' refers to such manifestations of the divinity as were vouchsafed to Abraham, Moses, Joshua, and Manoah, and in this chapter to Samuel" (**Ellicott Bible Commentary, Vol. 2**). The cause of the rarity of prophetic word and vision was no doubt the moral corruption and spiritual insensitivity of the nation and leadership. Keil and Delitzsch comment, "As a revelation from God presupposed susceptibility on the part of men, the unbelief and disobedience of the people might restrain the fulfillment of this and all similar promises, and God might even withdraw His word to punish the idolatrous nation" (p. 48). See also Micah 3:5-7.

Thus religion during the infancy of Samuel consisted almost entirely of priestly ritual. Week after week, month after month, year after year, the priests at Shiloh went through the motions of their sacerdotal ritual (which, let us note, had been divinely given!). Yet, however scriptural and profound in significance a religious ritual may be, it is inadequate either as a channel of divine communication to men or as a medium of human worship. **It is only one side of the penny!** Religion must be prophetic as well as priestly. It needs prophetic light and fire.

Samuel Chadwick, in **The Way to Pentecost**, draws a contrast between the cold-water baptism of Apollos and the fiery baptism of Paul and his associates. There is, of course, a place for both in New Testament Christianity. Unfortunately, it is easy to retain the water when we lose the fire; to keep up the ritual when the fire has gone out. Merely priestly religion is inadequate. We need prophetic religion, especially the prophetic fire and the prophetic vision and the authentic prophetic message.

In Samuel's boyhood, prophetic vision was almost wholly dead. Nothing was left but the ritualistic motions, which were far from valueless, yet which alone were inadequate, insufficient, and incomplete. Has it not often been so in the history of the Church? But then, so often, has come revival and renewal!

What comparable examples of religious deadness followed by revival and renewal have been witnessed in Christian history?

B. Samuel's Youthful Ministry (vv. 2, 3)

2. And it came to pass at that time, when Eli was laid down in his place, and his eyes began to wax dim, that he could not see;

3. And ere the lamp of God went out in the temple of the Lord, where the ark of God was, and Samuel was laid down to sleep;

Almost from the beginning of Samuel's stay at Shiloh, Eli had involved the boy in the work of the sanctuary in some capacity. Of course his assignments would be suited to his years (1 Samuel 1:28; 2:11, 18). For his official duties he wore "a linen ephod" as did the priests. "The ephod was a shoulder-dress, no doubt resembling the high priest's in shape: see Exodus 28:6-8" (Keil and Delitzsch). Also he wore "a little coat," which was made by his mother and renewed year by year. "The little robe was for more general purposes" (Payne, **New Bible Commentary Revised**).

Samuel had now been several years at Shiloh. Josephus, no doubt recording Jewish tradition, says that the incident described in chapter 3 took place when he was twelve years old **(Antiquities of the Jews, 5:10:4)**. The nature of Samuel's work at this time may have some bearing on this opinion, for, as Dr. Blaiklock points out "he was strong enough to open the temple doors (v. 15) and intelligent enough to deliver a detailed message" (p. 25). Twelve, therefore, seems a reasonable guess for his age—the same age as Jesus in Luke's account of His boyhood (Luke 2:41-52).

Some have concluded that Samuel's ministry was also to light "the lamp of God" (v. 3). If this was an ordinary lamp as Payne thinks, no objection could be raised to this opinion. However, the expression "lamp of God" is striking, and may probably refer, as Keil and Delitzsch say, "to the light of the candlestick in the tabernacle, the seven lamps of which were put up and lighted every evening, and burned through the night till all the oil was consumed: see Exodus 30:8; Leviticus 24:2; 2 Chronicles 13:11." It is questionable whether such an important task would be delegated to a boy of twelve.

Blaikie has a suggestive and challenging comment on the youthful Samuel: "His entire devotion to God's service, so beautiful in one of such tender years, is the sign of a character well adapted to become the medium of God's habitual communications with His people" (**Expositor's Bible, First Book of**

Samuel). Perhaps the lesson to be learned for adults is that when we see evidences of dedication to God in our children and young people, we should provide them with opportunities of service suited to their years and abilities.

"The child is father of the man" (Wordsworth). Show how this proved to be so in the case of Samuel.

II. LISTENING TO THE LORD (1 Samuel 3: 4-14)

A. The Prophetic Call (vv. 4-10)

4. That the Lord called Samuel: and he answered, Here am I.

5. And he ran unto Eli, and said, Here am I; for thou calledst me. And he said, I called not; lie down again. And he went and lay down.

6. And the Lord called yet again, Samuel. And Samuel arose and went to Eli, and said, Here am I; for thou didst call me. And he answered, I called not, my son; lie down again.

We are not to understand that Samuel, or any of the priests, lived and slept within the sanctuary itself. "Samuel neither slept in the holy place by the side of the candlestick and table of shewbread, nor in the most holy place in front of the ark of the covenant, but in the court, where cells were built for the priests and Levites to live in when serving at the sanctuary" (Keil and Delitzsch). It seems feasible, as in the case of the later Temple of Solomon, that rooms were provided not only for storage of offerings and tithes, but probably also to give accommodation to the priests and Levites (compare 1 Kings 6:5-10, and see drawings in the **New Bible Dictionary**). Samuel apparently slept in a separate room from Eli (v. 5).

One night, before the lamp had extinguished itself as the supply of oil ran out, the Lord broke through into the young Samuel's consciousness with His Word.

7. Now Samuel did not yet know the Lord, neither was the word of the Lord yet revealed unto him.

We must not misunderstand this verse. It cannot mean that Samuel was ignorant of the Lord in an intellectual sense, or that he had no conscious trust in Him. We are told that he was both a **worshiper** and a **minister** of the Lord (1:28; 2:11, 18) and that he was "in favour both with the Lord, and also with men" (2:26). The statement, no doubt refers to the prophetic call. His situation was somewhat like that of a young Christian who is regenerated and sanctified but not yet conscious of his call to the ministry.

As in the case of Jeremiah (1:4-10) and Isaiah (6:1-8), and the apostles of Christ, and not infrequently in Christian history, **a young man** was about to **see a vision** and receive the Spirit of prophecy.

8. And the Lord called Samuel again the third time. And he arose and went to Eli, and said, Here am I; for thou didst call me. And Eli perceived that the Lord had called the child.

How did the Lord speak to Samuel? It sounded like an ordinary human voice, otherwise the boy would not have confused it with the voice of Eli. Yet we must not conclude that it actually was an audible voice, otherwise others, probably sleeping in the same room or in nearby rooms, could have heard it. In all likelihood it was a mystical experience and the sound, as well as the words, was heard only by the boy himself.

9. Therefore Eli said unto Samuel, Go, lie down: and it shall be, if he call thee, that thou shalt say, Speak, Lord; for thy servant heareth. So Samuel went and lay down in his place.

10. And the Lord came, and stood, and called as at other times, Samuel, Samuel. Then Samuel answered, Speak; for thy servant heareth.

The greatest thing—perhaps the only great thing—which Eli did for Samuel was to teach him how to recognize the voice of God, and how to respond to it. This pathetic old man, whose whole life might so easily have been a total failure and total blank, is thus redeemed from ignominy by the fact that he helped a boy to open up to God and find his lifework as one of the greatest servants of God the world has ever known. Parents, teachers, preachers, if you and I could do this one wonderful thing for only one child, we should not have lived in vain.

Some people give the impression that God is constantly talking to them in an audible manner. Is this credible? Or scriptural? How do we really hear the voice of God today?

B. The Prophetic Message (vv. 11-14)

It should be noted that at first Samuel heard only a voice calling his name. This happened three times (vv. 4, 6, 8). On the fourth occasion, however, something more wonderful happened: "The Lord came, and stood, and called" (v. 10). This implies more than a vision—it was a theophany, an appearance of Jehovah similar to those granted to the patriarchs, Moses and Joshua. The Shekinah Glory which resided in the most holy place moved out and appeared in Samuel's room. What a sublime privilege for a twelve-year-old boy!

When Samuel was ready to hear, he was given a prophetic message which filled him with fear, and which God said would send a shock of horror through the nation when fulfillment came (v. 11). The specific thing which would create this shocking sensation is not stated. Its fulfillment is narrated in chapter 4. Spence writes: "The calamity which is here referred to was the capture of the Ark of the Covenant . . . that the sacred symbol of the presence and protection of the invisible King should be allowed to fall into the hands of the uncircumcised Philistines, the heredity foes of the chosen race, was a calamity unparalleled in their annals."

"In that day" the judgment previously announced upon the house of Eli would also come to pass (see 2:27-36). We have not been able to examine that prophecy of "a man of God" who, during Samuel's infancy, had spoken a divine message which predicted the downfall of Eli's household, and also contained messianic elements (this passage is discussed by Keil and Delitzsch). In the several years succeeding the delivery of that message Eli had done nothing to curb the wickedness of his sons. Blaikie suggests that, "If Eli had bestirred himself then, and banished the young men from Shiloh, and if the young men in their affliction and humiliation had repented of their wickedness, the threatened doom might have been averted" **(Expositor's Bible, The First Book of Samuel).**

There is a searching message here for us all—especially for parents, magistrates, church leaders, and all in positions of authority. If through our softness and indulgence we condone the evils of those under our care, failing to act in admonition and discipline, we shall be held accountable before God. This was Eli's sin. In those days parenthood carried more weight than it does in our modern culture. Eli could have exercised greater parental discipline. He failed to do so. He could have corrected his sons, and saved the nation, perhaps even the boys themselves. His softness with them brought ruin on them and the nation. Now it had brought ruin upon himself.

There is much of this softness in our age. In a striking book, **The Cult of Softness,** Arnold Lunn and Garth Lean have shown that this is a basic weakness in our western culture, especially in church and government.

"They had committed the sin unto death, and no offering or sacrifice could prevent this" (Adam Clarke, linking 1 Samuel 3:14 with 1 John 5:16). Explain.

III. OBEYING THE LORD (1 Samuel 3:15-20)

A. Immediate Response (vv. 15-18)

Samuel learned, even though but a youth, and with his very first "word from the Lord," that there is a cross in prophethood. There is inevitable hurt to oneself in being a communicator of the divine Word. He experienced the temptation, which comes to every true preacher and teacher, to hide the divine message or at least to tone it down—in a word, to shirk the offense of the cross (see Galatians 5:7; 6:12).

16. Then Eli called Samuel, and said, Samuel, my son. And he answered, Here am I.

17. And he said, What is the thing that the Lord hath said unto thee? I pray thee hide it not from me: God do so to thee, and more also, if thou hide any thing from me of all the things that he said unto thee.

18. And Samuel told him every whit, and hid nothing from him. And he said, It is the Lord: let him do what seemeth him good.

Here two further good qualities of old Eli are revealed. First, he helped Samuel to overcome his temptation, and to bravely reveal the Word of the Lord which had come to him. Second, he accepted that Word with humility.

B. Further Development (vv. 19, 20)

19. And Samuel grew, and the Lord was with him, and did let none of his words fall to the ground.

20. And all Israel from Dan even to Beer-

sheba knew that Samuel was established to be a prophet of the Lord.

Samuel had overcome, with the help of Eli, his first temptation of the devil—to hide the truth! It is an ever-recurring temptation in the life of God's servants. And the higher he goes in office, and the greater his rewards, the stronger the temptation becomes. Even in His dying hours, Jesus was tempted to "come down from the cross" (Matthew 27:40).

The Lord honored Samuel's obedience with further prophetic disclosures and communications. **And all his prophecies were fulfilled!** This is the meaning of the statement, "The Lord . . . did let none of his words fall to the ground" (v. 19). These further prophecies have not been preserved, but they established Samuel in his teens and twenties to be the authentic voice of God in Israel.

Three factors shaped the young Samuel: (a) his mother's influence, (b) the **good** things at Shiloh, (c) the Spirit of God. Evaluate them and discuss their modern equivalents.

REVIEW QUESTIONS

1. What was the physical condition of Eli at the time of today's lesson?
2. How did Samuel respond to the Lord's first three calls?
3. What was the reason for Samuel's failure to recognize the voice of God?
4. In what ways did Eli instruct Samuel regarding the calls to him during the night?
5. How did Samuel's reputation increase after the initial revelation from God?

GOLDEN TEXT HOMILY

"SPEAK, LORD; FOR THY SERVANT HEARETH" (1 Samuel 3:9).

Many often become confused when others talk of hearing God speak to them. Lacking the keen spiritual discernment that comes only through experience and close fellowship, they are puzzled at such a possibility.

Seeking to communicate with the other world, to find direction for the future, many resort to spirit mediums, fortune-tellers, or palmists.

What a paradox! People refuse to become Christians because they do not want to think about the future, to plan ahead, to consider the end result of their daily sins. Yet because their hearts cry out to warn them of impending punishment, they go to these emissaries of evil instead of to Him who "knoweth all things."

How important to be taught early in life to discern when the voice of God is speaking, to know when that voice is pronouncing our name, to realize a message is about to be given! How important too to be able to respond, "Speak, Lord; for thy servant heareth."—**Wilbur G. Williams, Former Editor, the Evangelical Commentary,** Marion, Indiana

SENTENCE SERMONS

WE ARE BORN subjects and to obey God is perfect liberty. He that does this shall be free, safe, and happy.
—Seneca

THE SECRET OF success in life is for a man to be ready for his opportunity when it comes.
—Benjamin Disraeli

GOD DOES NOT call everyone in the same way, but He does call each of us to service for Him.
—Selected

GOD'S CALL TO service is unconditional, and His grace for the task unlimited.
—Selected

EVANGELISTIC APPLICATION

THOSE WHO LIVE IN OBEDIENCE TO GOD'S WORD WILL BE READY TO HEAR THE LORD'S CALL TO SERVICE.

The story is told of an Episcopalian minister in England who, as his custom was, went to the village school to catechize the children. As he questioned the pupils he eventually came to a certain lad, but before he could begin his questions the teacher intervened to say, "Don't bother with him! He's a dunce and a fool!"

The minister was greatly embarrassed at the public humiliation of the child, who was very obviously hurt. At the end of the class period he stood at the door as the pupils filed out. When "the dunce and fool" came by the minister placed his hand upon his head and spoke a few words of comfort and encouragement.

That boy, that "dunce and fool," was Adam Clarke, who grew up to master many languages and become one of the greatest of Wesleyan theologians and expositors.

Which would you rather be—the teacher whose biting words could damn the boy, or the minister whose words of comfort and encouragement saved him?

ILLUMINATING THE LESSON

The following beautiful tradition about Moses is handed down to posterity:—He led the flock of his father-in-law. One day while he was contemplating his flock in the desert, he saw a lamb leave the herd, and run further and further away. The tender shepherd not only followed it with his eyes, but went after it. The lamb quickened his step, hopped over hill, sprang over ditches, hastening through valley and plain; the shepherd unweariedly followed its track. At last the lamb stopped by a spring at which it eagerly quenched its thirst. Moses hastened to the spot, looked sadly at the drinking lamb, and said: "it was thirst, then, my poor beast, which tormented thee, and drove thee from me, and I didn't understand; now thou art faint and weary from the long, hard way, thy powers are exhausted; how then couldst thou return to thy comrades?" After the lamb had quenched his thirst and seemed undecided what course to take Moses lifted it to his shoulder, and, bending under the heavy burden, strode back to the flock. Then he heard the voice of God calling to him, saying: "Thou hast a tender heart for my creatures, thou art a kind, gentle shepherd to the flocks of man—thou art now called to feed the flocks of God."—**"Jewish Messenger"**

DAILY DEVOTIONAL GUIDE

M. Hearing God Through the Miraculous. Exodus 3:1-10

T. Hearing God When Danger Threatens. Judges 6:11-18

W. Hearing God in Times of Grief. Isaiah 6:1-8

T. Hearing God When Disaster Strikes. Jeremiah 1:1-10

F. Hearing God Speak in Daily Life. Amos 7:10-17

S. Christ's Call to Service. Matthew 28:16-20

March 15, 1981

Way to Revival

Bible Background: 1 Samuel 4:1—7:17
Time: About 1050 to 1030 B.C.
Place: Kirjath-jearim, a town on the border between Judah and Benjamin; Mizpeh; Beth-car; Eben-ezer, located between Mizpeh and Shen (1 Samuel 7:12)
Supplemental References: 2 Samuel 6:11-19; 2 Chronicles 7:14; 19:4-10; Jeremiah 7:1-16; John 3:16-19; Acts 2:32-47; 17:22-29; Revelation 3:1-22
Golden Text: "Hitherto hath the Lord helped us" (1 Samuel 7:12).
Central Truth: Our faith is misplaced unless it is centered in God and His Word.
Evangelistic Emphasis: Spiritual life is the reward for all who follow God's plan of redemption.

PRINTED TEXT

1 Samuel 7:3. And Samuel spake unto all the house of Israel, saying, If ye do return unto the Lord with all your hearts, then put away the strange gods and Ashtaroth from among you, and prepare your hearts unto the Lord, and serve him only: and he will deliver you out of the hand of the Philistines.

4. Then the children of Israel did put away Baalim and Ashtaroth, and served the Lord only.

5. And Samuel said, Gather all Israel to Mizpeh, and I will pray for you unto the Lord.

6. And they gathered together to Mizpeh, and drew water, and poured it out before the Lord, and fasted on that day, and said there, We have sinned against the Lord. And Samuel judged the children of Israel in Mizpeh.

7. And when the Philistines heard that the children of Israel were gathered together to Mizpeh, the lords of the Philistines went up against Israel. And when the children of Israel heard it, they were afraid of the Philistines.

8. And the children of Israel said to Samuel, Cease not to cry unto the Lord our God for us, that he will save us out of the hand of the Philistines.

9. And Samuel took a sucking lamb, and offered it for a burnt-offering wholly unto the Lord: and Samuel cried unto the Lord for Israel; and the Lord heard him.

10. And as Samuel was offering up the burnt-offering, the Philistines drew near to battle against Israel: but the Lord thundered with a great thunder on that day upon the Philistines, and discomfited them; and they were smitten before Israel.

11 And the men of Israel went out of Mizpeh, and pursued the Philistines, and smote them, until they came under Beth-car.

12. Then Samuel took a stone, and set it between Mizpeh and Shen, and called the name of it Eben-ezer, saying, Hitherto hath the Lord helped us.

13. So the Philistines were subdued, and they came no more into the coast of Israel: and the hand of the Lord was against the Philistines all the days of Samuel.

DICTIONARY

Ashtaroth (ASH-tah-roth)—1 Samuel 7:3, 4—A Canaanite goddess. The name is cognate with Babylonian **Ishtar**, the goddess of sensual love, maternity, and fertility. She was believed to be the wife of Baal.

Baalim—1 Samuel 7:4—The plural of Baal, this is a general term including not images of Baal but various concepts of the god.

Eben-ezer (eb-en-EE-zer)—1 Samuel 7:12—A Hebrew word meaning "stone of help," it was a stone set up by Samuel after a signal defeat over the Philistines, as a memorial of the help received on the occasion from the Lord.

LESSON OUTLINE

I. MISPLACED FAITH
II. MISUSED BLESSING
III. RESTORED BLESSING
IV. TRIUMPH OF FAITH

LESSON EXPOSITION

INTRODUCTION

As a prelude to our study there are two things to take note of.

First, the opening statement of chapter 4 really belongs to the final verse of chapter 3. Placed together it reads, "For the Lord revealed himself to Samuel in Shiloh by the word of the Lord. And the word of Samuel came to all Israel." The word **now** in 4:1 begins a new subject. This is clearly shown in the **New English Bible**.

Second, the Philistines are now reintroduced into the biblical history. They were last heard of in the story of Samson (Judges chapters 13-16). From now until the reign of David they are seen as a powerful and formidable force, bent on extending their empire over the whole of Palestine. In fact when the first Book of Samuel ends, and Samuel and King Saul are dead, it looks as if the ascendancy of the Philistines is complete, and Israel is doomed. The fact that they left their name as a permanent imprint on the land (**Palestine** is derived from **Philistine**) shows how strong their impact was.

The Philistines were of Gentile origin (see Genesis 10:14), from the area of the Aegean Sea. After failing to conquer the Egyptians they had settled in the area of southwest Palestine now known as the Gaza Strip, where they built up a strong confederacy of five city-states. Archaeologists have shown that the Philistines learned the use of the smelting of copper and iron from the Hittites and thus became far superior to the Israelites in military weapons and agricultural implements (see 1 Samuel 13:19, 20). They were also united in contrast to Israel's disunity. Indeed,

Israel had only one source of strength, namely, **their religion**. And, as our previous two lessons have shown, at this time they had become terribly debased and weak in this very thing. Israel's one hope under God was the young prophet Samuel.

For study of this subject, see C. F. Pfeiffer, **Old Testament History**; R. K. Harrison, **Old Testament Times**; M. F. Unger, **Archaeology and the Old Testament**.

I. MISPLACED FAITH (1 Samuel 4:1-22)

As noted in our introduction, nothing had been heard of the Philistines in the biblical record since Samson's crushing blow to their leaders and warriors in the hour of his death. But a whole generation (at least) had passed by. Now they were strong again and ready to begin what they planned to be their conquest of Canaan.

Their first move was an act of aggression across the border with Israel. Eben-ezer and Aphek were most probably in the Plain of Sharon north of the Gaza Strip. The **New Oxford Annotated Bible** suggests that "the strategy of the Philistines was to drive up the coast, then down the Plain of Esdraelon to the Jordon River, thus cutting communication between the parts of Israel north and south of the plain" (p. 335). In the very first engagement with Israel, the Philistines secured a victory (v. 2).

Dismayed at their defeat the elders of Israel asked the question: "Wherefore hath the Lord smitten us to day before the Philistines?" (v. 3). The form of the question should be noted. They looked upon their defeat as "an act of God." Modern Christians are more likely to blame the devil!

It was a sensible question. Unfortunately they came up with the wrong answer and a totally inadequate solution. As Blaikie says, the notion that the tide could be turned by bringing out the sacred Ark from the sanctuary at Shiloh to lead the Israelite armies against the Philistine aggressor seemed "a brilliant idea." The Ark had formerly led the tribes through the wilderness and had given them many victories (Numbers 10:35). It had led them through the Jordan (Joshua 3:6-17), and around the walls of Jericho (Joshua 6:6-11). Here was the answer to their dilemma! How often has a weak and failing church had a brilliant idea for success which even seemed to have biblical authority and historical precedent!

Yet their "brilliant idea" led them to total defeat and disaster. The Ark itself was captured. Hophni and Phinehas were killed, possibly as they stood by the Ark. Thirty thousand Israelites were slain. And when old Eli received the news, he fell off his chair from the shock and broke his neck, while his daughter-in-law died in premature child birth. How frequently our "brilliant ideas" for church success have led only to failure!

It is now our turn to ask "**Why**?" What had gone wrong? Three things at least, things which powerfully speak to the church of all time.

1. **There was no spirit of repentance in leaders or nation.**

They vainly imagined that they could use God in their national interests. Both nations and churches are often guilty of this folly. But God is not maneuverable. He does not jump when we pull a string. He responds only to true repentance.

2. **There was no turning to the Lord for His direction and guidance.**

The Israelites did not seek God for **His** solution. They concocted their own solution, their own **methodology,** and assumed that the Lord was honor-bound to go along with it. Not even the prophet Samuel is mentioned! What a portrait of so much twentieth-century ecclesiastical planning and promotion. We concoct our schemes first, basing them on accepted worldly methodologies, and then hunt up the Bible for supporting texts and examples.

3. **They confused true religion with superstition.**

They imagined that the sacred Ark was itself God, or at least that the presence and power of God was automatically and inevitably inherent in it: "Let us fetch the ark . . . that . . . **it** may save us" (v. 3). They were about to learn the bitter truth that though the Ark had been ordained by the Lord to symbolize His presence and power,

it was only a material object unless the Lord chose to work with it.

Edersheim calls the attitude of Israel in this matter "religiousness rather than religion" **(Old Testament Bible History).** Perhaps we may use the term **superstition.**

It is possible for living faith in God to degenerate into a superstitious faith. This is not far from magic and fetish. People who have little vital faith in the living Lord and His Holy Word often cling with a pathetic credulity to those things which, even though they may be originally ordained of God, are useless unless the Lord works with them.

To come up with a new gimmick for revival, even if we can quote chapter and verse for it, is the modern equivalent of carrying the Ark of the Lord into battle—and just as foolish.

Note the naming of Eli's grandson, **Ichabod.** Does this have a meaning and a message for our days? Illustrate.

II. MISUSED BLESSING (1 Samuel 5:1-12)

Though the Samuel narrative does not say so, other passages of Scripture indicate that the Philistines did not immediately return to their cities, but went to Shiloh, which lay 40 miles east of Eben-ezer and 40 miles north of Jerusalem, and utterly destroyed it (Psalm 78: 60-64; Jeremiah 7:12; 26:9). Archaeology has shown that Shiloh must have been totally destroyed at this time. The evidence shows that Shiloh was occupied from the thirteenth to the eleventh centuries B.C., but not from 1050 to 300 B.C. The date 1050 B.C. coincides with the period of the early chapters of Samuel (see J. P. Free, **Archaeology and Bible History).**

Afterwards the Philistines returned home in triumph with the captured Ark. The question emerges, Why did they not destroy the Ark? As the story unfolds we see that in spite of the trouble it caused them they did not destroy it. Again, the answer must be, **superstition.** The common people of the Philistines were not less superstitious than the Israelites. They actually thought the Ark was a **god** (see 4:7). They imagined that they had actually captured the Hebrews' God. This would mean (to them) that they could now augment the power which their god, Dagon, the god of vegetation, gave to them. With the power residing in the Ark, they would have double power. Others have suggested that in placing the Ark side by side with Dagon in the temple at Ashdod, they hoped that Dagon would somehow destroy it.

In this event the reverse happened. It was Dagon who was mutilated and nearly destroyed. On two separate nights strange events happened in their temple. On the first night Dagon fell off his pedestal, and was found lying facedown before the Ark, as if in an act of worship. There is something amusing in the picture of a god who could not get up on his feet again after he had fallen down, but had to be lifted up by human hands (see also Isaiah's ironic picture in Isaiah 46). On the next night something worse happened. Dagon was discovered with his head and hands cut off, as if supernaturally executed and mutilated.

Disaster was now to come upon the Philistine people. A severe illness began to afflict them, which the **King James Version** specifies as "emerods," and which the **New International Version** calls "tumors." The Septuagint Greek Version adds, "And rats (or **mice**) appeared in their land, and death and destruction were throughout the city." Because of this plague of rodents, some scholars are of the opinion that the sickness was bubonic plague which is spread by rats and mice, and characterized by swollen lymph glands in the groin (see v. 9).

In their superstition the Ashdodites dared not destroy the Hebrew Ark but tried to transfer the responsibility to other cities (vv. 8-12). But wherever the Ark was sent disease and death followed. It was, of course, not the Ark itself, but the Lord of Hosts, Jehovah of the Hebrews, who was at work. He had withdrawn His power in Israel in order to teach His own covenant people a lesson. Now He put forth His power destructively in Philistia in order to teach the Philistines a lesson.

Who is to say that the living God does not work like this today? In order to teach a backsliding church a lesson He withholds His power. In order to teach the godless world a lesson He puts forth His power in tribulation disasters. And, as the days darken, we are likely to see more of both kinds of divine judgment.

God is alive and well in our world! Name some happenings which indicate this.

III. RESTORED BLESSING (1 Samuel 6:1-21)

For seven months the Philistines endured the judgment of the Lord upon their country. It seems they were loathe to dispose of this captured god! Matthew Henry makes the practical comment that, "Sinners lengthen out their own miseries by obstinately refusing to part with their sins." Eventually, however, they decided that they must get rid of the terrible Ark of the Lord, and the Philistine leaders consulted their priests and diviners (that is, those who give guidance by occultic methods). Three matters deserve comment.

First (vv. 1-5), the Philistines were advised to send the Ark out of the country toward Israel, and to send a trespass offering with it. The offering would be ten small images of gold, in the shape of "emerods" and "mice." W. J. Deane writes, "The peculiar nature of this offering was in some respects analogous to a custom widely spread among heathen nations, and adopted in the Christian Church (he means the Medieval Roman Church), and practiced unto this day. The custom was this: to dedicate in a temple an offering which represents or expressed a particular mercy received in answer to prayer" **(Samuel and Saul: Their Lives and Times).** Mauchline, however, thinks that "they were at once a confession that the tumors and the mice from which they had suffered had been sent by Jehovah, and a supplication in symbolic form that the cause of their suffering might be removed" **(New Century Bible, 1 and 2 Samuel).**

Second (vv. 7-9), the Ark was to be placed on a new cart pulled by two milk cows which were to be separated from their young. If the cows went straight over the border to Israel it would be proof that Jehovah really was the agent behind the strange things which had been happening (that is, it was supernatural). But if they wandered or went around in circles looking for their calves, it would be obvious that the whole thing was a natural coincidence. In the event, the cows were impelled straight over the border, leaving the Philistines with final proof that "God had been among them of a truth."

Third (vv. 13-21), Beth-shemesh, toward which the cows headed, was just inside Israelite territory. When the Beth-shemites saw the Philistine cows pulling the cart containing their sacred Ark they were carried away with joy and excitement. At once they held a religious ceremony, offering sacrifices of thanksgiving to the Lord. However, they made a foolish and tragic blunder. Forgetting the instruction of the Mosaic Law which forbade anyone to gaze upon the sacred Ark (see Numbers 4:5, 19, 20), they "looked into the ark of the Lord" (v. 19). In consequence of their folly a severe judgment fell upon them, and they became as eager as the Philistines to dispose of the Ark.

This sequel has a lesson for all Christians in regard to the things of God. In the words of Blaikie, we must "combine reverence with intimacy in our dealings with God." Pentecostal Christians especially need this warning. In our joy and delight at the spiritual blessings which have been restored to us it is easy for liberty to turn into levity, and even to license. There are limits to liberty. We have a proper place in the presence of God. We can never meet as **equals**. God is still God—creator, king, redeemer, father, judge. We must never forget the distance between us, even though we have been "brought nigh."

See 1 Corinthians 11:27-34. This is one equivalent of "looking into the ark." What other examples can you think of?

IV. TRIUMPH OF FAITH (1 Samuel 7:1-17)

The sacred Ark was taken to a place a few miles north of Beth-shemesh by the name of Kirjath-jearim (v. 1). There it was to remain until reclaimed by King David for his new capital, Jerusalem (see 2 Samuel 6). The statement in v. 2, "it was twenty years," refers not to this entire period, but only to the first twenty years of it during the early manhood of Samuel.

During this twenty-year period Samuel continued to exercise his prophetic ministry in Israel, as described in 3:19-21. The Shiloh sanctuary had been destroyed, the priesthood virtually annihilated (Psalm 78:59-64), though it reappeared again during the reign of Saul (see 1 Samuel 14:3; 21:1-9; 22:9-23). It seems that during these twenty years Samuel was functioning as priest as well as prophet.

Samuel's ministry began to bear fruit. This is expressed in the statement, "and all the house of Israel lamented after the Lord" (v. 2). The time was ripe for a religious revival and reformation.

3. And Samuel spake unto all the house of Israel, saying, If ye do return unto the Lord with all your hearts, then put away the strange gods and Ashtaroth from among you, and prepare your hearts unto the Lord, and serve him only: and he will deliver you out of the hand of the Philistines.

4. Then the children of Israel did put away Baalim and Ashtaroth, and served the Lord only.

It is evident from these verses that Israelitish religion during this period had become syncretistic, that is, a mixture of the true national religion with the corrupt nature worship of Canaan. This kind of thing has repeatedly occurred throughout history. It is alive today on the mission fields, and even in our Western churches.

5. And Samuel said, Gather all Israel to Mizpeh, and I will pray for you unto the Lord.

6. And they gathered together to Mizpeh, and drew water, and poured it out before the Lord, and fasted on that day, and said there, We have sinned against the Lord. And Samuel judged the children of Israel in Mizpeh.

When the time was ripe, Samuel called the nation to Mizpeh, a high peak a few miles north of Jerusalem, for a great ceremony of repentance. The unusual rite of pouring out water before the Lord probably dramatized the pouring out of prayers of repentance for the nation's sins.

Here is the pattern for true revival. It cannot be **planned** or **promoted**, like a business enterprise or a carnival. It must be preceded by true repentance and prayer.

Let us note, too, that this day Samuel initiated a new ministry, that of **judge**, or political leader of the nation under God (in the succession of Eli and his predecessors).

7. And when the Philistines heard that the children of Israel were gathered together to Mizpeh, the lords of the Philistines went up against Israel. And when the children of Israel heard it, they were afraid of the Philistines.

8. And the children of Israel said to Samuel, Cease not to cry unto the Lord our God for us, that he will save us out of the hand of the Philistines.

When the Philistines heard of the great gathering at Mizpeh they were greatly alarmed and at once massed their armies for an attack before the Israelites could mobilize. The Israelites were panic-stricken and called upon Samuel to intercede on their behalf.

Here was Samuel's greatest test so far. Was the Lord with this man who had ably proved himself as prophet and priest? Was he also a true charismatic judge?

9. And Samuel took a sucking lamb, and offered it for a burnt-offering wholly unto the Lord: and Samuel cried unto the Lord for Israel; and the Lord heard him.

10. And as Samuel was offering up the burnt-offering, the Philistines drew near to battle against Israel: but the Lord thundered with a great thunder on that day upon the Philistines, and discomfited them; and they were smitten before Israel.

11. And the men of Israel went out of Mizpeh, and pursued the Philistines, and smote them, until they came under Beth-car.

12. Then Samuel took a stone, and set it between Mizpeh and Shen, and called the name of it Eben-ezer, saying, Hitherto hath the Lord helped us.

What a contrast there is between Samuel's action here and the action taken by the Israelites twenty years before (1 Samuel 4)! He relied wholly upon truly spiritual means, the offering of a whole burnt-offering (symbol of complete consecration) and earnest prayer. "And the Lord heard him" (v. 9). Here is the secret of effective ministry for God: earnest prayer from a fully consecrated life (see James 5:16). "The Lord thundered with a great thunder" (v. 10). How truly it has been said, "Prayer moves the arm that moves the world."

It is noteworthy that Samuel gave all glory to God. The memorial which he erected, which he called Eben-ezer, meaning "the stone of help," was his way of declaring "Hitherto hath the Lord helped us."

13. So the Philistines were subdued, and they came no more into the coast of Israel: and the hand of the Lord was against the Philistines all the days of Samuel.

Throughout the whole life of Samuel the Philistines were subdued. Once again they had witnessed the power of the Hebrews' God, and came to respect and fear Samuel His prophet as they respected and feared the sacred Ark.

Do you think it is possible for a religious revival to produce the kind of respect and fear of the power of God in the ungodly world as happened in Philistia during the days of Samuel? Can you think of examples?

REVIEW QUESTIONS

1. What evidence of repentance did Samuel demand of the Israelites?

2. What procedure was followed in Israel's mass meeting at Mizpeh?

3. What ritual did Samuel perform before praying his intercessory prayer?

4. What force of nature did God use in defeating the Philistines?

5. How did Samuel commemorate this great victory?

GOLDEN TEXT HOMILY

"HITHERTO HATH THE LORD HELPED US" (1 Samuel 7:12).

The stone set up by Samuel between Mizpeh and Shen was called Ebenezer, which means "the stone of help." The purpose of the stone was to perpetuate the memory of the victory granted by the Lord to Israel over the Philistines in answer to Samuel's prayer.

Samuel wanted Israel to always remember that the source of their victory over their enemies was not of their own might, but in God. Where they saw the stone, they were to remember, "Hitherto hath the Lord helped us." This truth was resounded time and again throughout God's Word.

David, a great warrior and king, commanded mighty armies of fighting men, yet time and again he acknowledged that the source of his strength and victory was in the Lord. When David spoke to King Saul concerning Goliath, the Philistine who was intimidating the armies and people of God, he said, "The Lord that delivered me out of the paw of the lion, and out of the paw of the bear, he will deliver me out of the hand of this Philistine" (1 Samuel 17:37).

In the New Testament, Jesus is called "the living stone" (1 Peter 2:4). Not only did Jesus die and was buried, but God raised Him up and set Him at His right hand in the heavenly places. Jesus is there now—far above all principality, and power, and might, and dominion, and every name that is named, not only in this world, but also in that which is to come.

Christ is God's living stone, set at His right hand as a reminder to us that "hitherto hath the Lord helped us." In Hebrews 12:2, men and women of faith are instructed to look "unto Jesus the author and finisher of our faith." When we face trials, tests, temptations, we need to look unto Him. He reminds us that God has helped us in the past and is still our help today.—**Kenneth K. Foreman, Executive Director of Christian Education, Pentecostal Church of God, Joplin, Missouri**

SENTENCE SERMONS

OUR FAITH IS misplaced unless it is centered in God and His Word.
—**Selected**

OUR GOD HAS boundless resources. The only limit is in us. Our asking, our thinking, our praying are too small. Our expectations are too limited.
—**A. B. Simpson**

PRAYER IS NOT overcoming God's reluctance; it is laying hold of His highest willingness.
—**Archbishop Richard C. Trench**

REVIVALS DEMAND THE UNUSUAL, and the unusual does not come with usual effort.
—**"Notes and Quotes"**

EVANGELISTIC APPLICATION

SPIRITUAL LIFE IS THE REWARD FOR ALL WHO FOLLOW GOD'S PLAN OF REDEMPTION.

"The way of transgressors is hard" (Proverbs 13:15). The "broad" way "leadeth to destruction" (Matthew 7:13). In the beginning it does not seem to be so. There are pleasures in sin for a season (Hebrews 11:25). If this were not so, not as many would follow the broad way, for it is pleasure appeal which figures so largely in sinning.

However, ultimately sin leads to disaster and death. "The end thereof are the ways of death" (Proverbs 14:12). "The wages of sin is death" (Romans 6:23). This fact is both exemplified and illustrated by wine. "Look not thou upon the wine when it is red, when it giveth his colour in the cup, when it moveth itself aright. **At the last** it biteth like a serpent, and stingeth like an adder" (Proverbs 23:31, 32).

The judgments which fell upon those who misused the Ark of the Lord in the early stories of Samuel portray this truth powerfully. Israelite leaders, priests, and armies; Philistine lords and people; Beth-shemite worshipers—all alike sinned against the Ark of God. The end result was death and destruction.

ILLUMINATING THE LESSON

The great revival under Jonathan Edwards, in the eighteenth century, began with his famous call to prayer. The marvelous work of grace among the Indians under Brainerd had its origin in the days and nights that Brainerd spent before God in prayer for an enduement of power from on high for his work. A most remarkable and widespread display of God's reviving power was that which broke out at Rochester, N. Y., under the labors of Charles Finney. It not only spread through New England but to Great Britian as well. Mr. Finney attributed the power of this work to the spirit of prayer that prevailed. The great revival of 1859 in the United States began in prayer and was carried on by prayer more than anything else. "Most revivals," writes Dr. Cuyler, "have humble beginnings, and the fire starts in a few warm hearts. Never despise the day of small things. During my own long ministry nearly every work of grace had a small beginning . . . a humble meeting in a private home . . . a group gathered for Bible study by Mr. Moody in our mission chapel . . . a meeting of young people in my home."—**"Alliance Weekly"**

DAILY DEVOTIONAL GUIDE

M. Misplaced Faith. 1 Samuel 4:1-19
T. A Lesson in Believing. 1 Samuel 4:10-22
W. Treatment of Holy Things. 1 Samuel 5:1-12
T. Correcting Mistakes. 1 Samuel 6:1-21
F. Justified by Faith. Romans 5:1-8
S. The Source of Victory. 1 John 5:1-12

March 22, 1981

Choosing a Leader

Bible Background: 1 Samuel 8:1—12:25
Time: Probably around 1020 B.C.
Place: Mizpeh, Gibeah, and Ramah especially
Supplemental References: 1 Kings 1:32-39; Romans 13:1-7
Golden Text: "God is the judge: he putteth down one, and setteth up another" (Psalm 75:7).
Central Truth: We need to exercise godly wisdom in choosing our civic and spiritual leaders.
Evangelistic Emphasis: Proper leadership helps to make the church effective in its evangelistic efforts.

PRINTED TEXT

1 Samuel 10:17. And Samuel called the people together unto the Lord to Mizpeh;

18. And said unto the children of Israel, Thus saith the Lord God of Israel, I brought up Israel out of Egypt, and delivered you out of the hand of the Egyptians, and out of the hand of all kingdoms, and of them that oppressed you:

19. And ye have this day rejected your God, who himself saved you out of all your adversities and your tribulations; and ye have said unto him, Nay, but set a king over us. Now therefore present yourselves before the Lord by your tribes, and by your thousands.

20. And when Samuel had caused all the tribes of Israel to come near, the tribe of Benjamin was taken.

21. When he had caused the tribe of Benjamin to come near by their families, the family of Matri was taken, and Saul the son of Kish was taken: and when they sought him, he could not be found.

22. Therefore they enquired of the Lord further, if the man should yet come thither. And the Lord answered, Behold, he hath hid himself among the stuff.

23. And they ran and fetched him thence: and when he stood among the people, he was higher than any of the people from his shoulders and upward.

24. And Samuel said to all the people, See ye him whom the Lord hath chosen, that there is none like him among all the people? And all the people shouted, and said, God save the king.

25. Then Samuel told the people the manner of the kingdom, and wrote it in a book, and laid it up before the Lord. And Samuel sent all the people away, every man to his house.

26. And Saul also went home to Gibeah; and there went with him a band of men, whose hearts God had touched.

DICTIONARY

Mizpeh (MIZ-peh)—1 Samuel 10:17—This name means "watchtower," a town probably located a short distance north of Jerusalem.

March 22, 1981

Matri (MAY-try)—1 Samuel 10:21—One of the main clans of the Benjamite tribe
Saul—1 Samuel 10:21—The Hebrew word means "ask for."
Kish—1 Samuel 10:21—The Hebrew word means "a bow."
the stuff—1 Samuel 10:22—This expression refers to "the baggage" or "carriage" brought along by the Israelites.

LESSON OUTLINE

I. REFUSING GOD'S PLAN
   A. The Demand for a King
   B. The Divine Direction
II. REVEALING THE CHOICE
   A. Divine Providence
   B. Divine Purpose
III. ANOINTING A LEADER
   A. A Private Anointing
   B. A Public Appointment

LESSON EXPOSITION

INTRODUCTION

In our previous lesson, comment was withheld from the last three verses of 1 Samuel 7. A glance at these verses is necessary before we proceed to our present lesson. They summarize Samuel's new role of judge over Israel which he had assumed at the great Mizpeh renewal and triumph over the Philistines (1 Samuel 7:6). For twenty years, Samuel had been prophet and priest to the nation. At Mizpeh he became judge (or charismatic political leader). He continued to exercise this role until he was "old" (8:1; 12:2). In this capacity he was the first "circuit rider," traveling around the nation year by year and concentrating upon four centers of administration, Ramah (his home), Bethel, Gilgal and Mizpeh. How long he did this we are not told, but possibly for a quarter of a century. It is at the end of this period that our lesson begins.

We should also note that though our Bible Background covers five whole chapters (8-12) our study outline deals with only three chapters (8, 9, 10). It is important to understand that our lesson leaves the story of the change from judgeship to kingship unfinished. Specifically, we do not go on to study the actual **crowning** of Israel's first king. We study only the events leading up to it, and the **private** anointing of Saul by Samuel for his office.

I. REFUSING GOD'S PLAN (1 Samuel 8:1-22)
A. The Demand for a King (vv. 1-8)

Israel's demand for a king was rooted in two causes, one of them more to the surface, the other deeper down.

1. **The Surface Cause** (vv. 1-5). It might be more correct to put this in the plural, for the elders of Israel gave two reasons for the demand for a change of constitution from judgeship to monarchy.

(a) "Behold, thou art old, and thy sons walk not in thy ways" (v. 5). Samuel's two sons bore highly religious names—Joel, meaning "Jehovah is God" and Abijah, meaning "Jehovah a Father." Spence comments, "The names of these sons are especially significant of the holy atmosphere their father lived in." **(Ellicott's Bible Commentary, Vol. 2).**

Do **our** children's names reveal anything about our faith and character?

In his old age, Samuel appointed his two sons as assistants. It seems that his circuit-riding system of government was proving too strenuous for him in advancing years. Unfortunately, the sons did not have their father's qualities. They treated their high office as a money-making job rather than a sacred vocation, and commercialized it to the point of bribery.

We do not know whether Samuel's sons were unfit for sacred office prior to their appointment (if so Samuel carries blame for appointing them), or whether they were corrupted by their appointment. The latter is highly probable. It is notorious that "power corrupts" and that appointment to high office becomes a great temptation to line one's own pockets while one has the opportunity.

In any case Samuel made a mistake which is quite common in the church. He did not honor the divine principle of being called of God and of being anointed for service. In the judgeship these two principles were basic. Matthew Henry comments, "Those who have the most grace themselves cannot give grace to their children." Holiness does not run in the blood, and neither does Holy-Ghost power. Samuel's mistake lay in appointing to office two men who did not have the character or the charisma for the position. Are we not often equally remiss in the church?

The growing inability of Samuel and the unsuitability of his sons provoked a national crisis. D. F. Payne writes, "We can well understand the elders' demand, from a political point of view. Stability was what Israel lacked, as the vicissitudes depicted in Judges show. The tribal elders connected this with the lack of stable leadership. Philistine pressure, of course, lay behind their demand" **(New Bible Commentary Revised).**

(b) "Make us a king to judge us like all the nations" (v. 5). John Mauchline says that this aspect of the elders' request is of special interest for it points to the intertwining of faith and culture. The Israelites could not live in isolation from their environment. "They lived among other peoples and were inevitably subject to cultural influences. These were particularly attractive when they came from a prosperous people which had arrived at a more highly developed culture than they themselves had" **(New Century Bible, 1 and 2 Samuel).** The impact of heathen culture upon Israel is seen constantly in the Old Testament, leading repeatedly to syncretism and compromise, followed by divine chastening. This is why they clamoured for a king. They wanted to be like their heathen neighbors in this respect. There was a glory and a power in monarchy which their type of government did not possess. This could only disturb Samuel. The last thing a discerning prophet could wish for was that "the holy nation" should become "like all the nations."

Blaikie applies the thought to those Christians who begin to lust after "conformity to the world," especially in regard to pleasure and luxurious, extravagant ways of living: "You wish to be like the nations. You forget that your very glory is to be unlike them. Your glory is that you are a chosen generation, a holy nation, a royal priesthood, a peculiar people, your bodies temples of the Holy Ghost, your souls united to the Lord Jesus Christ" **(Expositor's Bible, The First Book of Samuel).**

In what ways has the modern church become "like all the nations?"

---

2. **The Deeper Cause** (vv. 6-8). Samuel's immediate reaction to the demand for a king was one of intense displeasure (v. 6). Blaiklock thinks that this reveals "a corner of basic pride" in Samuel **(Bible Characters: Elkanah to David).** He resented the implications because the demand for change reflected upon himself. This is not certain, however. His displeasure may have been due to his concern at the phrase "like all the nations." To his mind this could only be a downward path. The fact that his displeasure drove him to his knees in prayer suggests that his displeasure was spiritually motivated.

The answer to his prayer must have surprised him—as it frequently does us all. As a result of his prayer, Samuel learned what the Lord felt about the situation. He was able to see the deeper cause of the demand. It was in keeping with the soul of the nation from the days of Moses. Repeatedly they had rebelled against God's rule, even in Moses' time and often throughout the judgeship. It had not been mere rejection of Moses nor of the various judges, but rejection of the Lord himself.

B. The Divine Direction (vv. 9-22)

To his further surprise Samuel was told to "hearken unto the voice of the people" (vv. 7, 9). F. F. Bruce writes, "A hereditary monarchy introduced a principle which was bound to change the character of civil rule in Israel. Hitherto they had been ruled by charismatic judges raised up by God from this tribe or that in His sovereign good pleasure; the hereditary principle meant that their rulers in the future would not necessarily have the special endowments which had marked Samuel and his predecessors, but would more probably resemble the kings of Israel's neighbors" **(Israel and the Nations).** Why then did the Lord direct Samuel to go along with it? For three reasons at least: (1) The kind of **rule** which He seeks among men is that which is freely accepted and obeyed. There is a sense in which the rule of God is sovereign, eternal, and changeless. Yet there is another sense in which His subjects accept that rule and freely obey it. (2) Another reason is indicated by Hosea 13:11: "I gave thee a king in mine anger." In other words, the kingship was a divine judgment upon Israel. He gave them what they demanded. In Pauline language, "He gave them up" to the evils of monarchy (see Romans 1:24, 26, 28). This is one way in which the wrath of God works. (3) A third reason is suggested by Blaikie: the people had proven themselves unworthy of theocracy. Therefore God withdrew it (p. 115).

Before "giving them up" to monarchy, however, Samuel was instructed to "shew them the manner of the king that shall reign over them" (v. 9). He proceeded to do so (vv. 10-18). Mauchline describes it as "a thumbnail sketch of a king and his demands on his people—centralized government and administration, oppressive evils at home and the game of power politics among neighboring peoples, issuing in compulsory military service and labor corps duties and a heavy burden of taxation in kind." No doubt the picture was drawn from neighboring monarchies. It should be said, too, that the change from monarchy to a republic or a military dictatorship merely carries over these from monarchical government.

In spite of the harsh picture the people were adamant (vv. 19-22). "Nay, but we will have a king over us!"

We know that the judgeship was not perfect (compare Samson and Eli). In what ways, however, was it preferable to monarchy?

II. REVEALING THE CHOICE (1 Samuel 9:1-27)

A. Divine Providence (vv. 1-14)

We are not told how long the people waited for further action on the part of Samuel. But already there was a man of the tribe of Benjamin who was designed by God to be Israel's first king (vv. 1, 2). This man, Saul, was in his thirties at least (this is evident from the fact that when he had been king for two years, his son Jonathan was a soldier, 13:2). He was physically powerful and handsome, and "a man of standing" (v. 1, **New International Version**). In short, he had the natural qualities to be a leader of men.

How this man was brought to the attention of Samuel is one of the many great stories of divine Providence narrated in Scripture. By an apparently natural chain of events—the loss of his father's asses and a frustrating search for them—Saul is blindly led to his destiny.

Matthew Henry describes this story as "a great event from small occurrences." What is the lesson for our own lives?

This is one of the wonderful ways of God with human lives. There is a remarkable interweaving of ordinary happenings with divine design. The hand of God was in the loss of the animals and also in the frustrating search for them. By this loss and frustration God was directing Saul toward Samuel's home. What a message for all who have to endure loss and frustration! The Lord may be at work in it all for our good! Certainly He is at work for our spiritual and eternal good (see Romans 8:28).

The decisive point is reached when Saul's unnamed servant suggests that they seek the help of "a man of God" who lived in that area. This, of course, was Samuel.

B. Divine Purpose (vv. 15-27)

God had already prepared Samuel for the coming of Saul (v. 15). There is an interesting expression here: "The Lord had told Samuel in his ear." We are not to understand this literally. Deane says, "It is an expression derived from the action of pushing aside the hair or headdress in order more conveniently to whisper something in a person's ear" (**Samuel and Saul: Their Lives and Times**). Thus it is a metaphor for a private and secret communication which was really spoken to Samuel's spirit. The communication told Samuel of the coming of Saul who was actually sent by God, unknown to himself, and he was the divinely chosen leader of Israel. The inner voice spoke again when Saul arrived (v. 17). This was the elected king of Israel!

It is clear from the divine choice of Saul, as also of David subsequently, that the Lord did not abdicate His sovereignty when He submitted to Israel's demand for a monarchy. He chose the king! There was no election, no discussion, no debate, no interviews. God personally and directly communicated His will to the prophet Samuel. The theocratic principle was still at work, certainly in the beginnings of the monarchy, though the very nature of hereditary monarchy would bring a change. In the future the theocratic government would be hidden and secret, more in the nature of overruling.

Samuel did not at once and entirely disclose the divine purpose to Saul. He gave several hints which stimulated Saul's interest and curiosity (vv. 20-24). Only on the following day did he tell the whole truth (vv. 25-27).

In the light of the New Testament (compare Acts 1:15-26; 6:1-8) is democracy compatible with the theocratic principle?

III. ANOINTING A LEADER (1 Samuel 10:1-27)

A. A Private Anointing (vv. 1-16)

Before dismissing Saul, Samuel led him to a place of privacy and there revealed to him the stunning news that God had chosen him to be "captain" over Israel (v. 1, see also 9:16). The Hebrew word rendered **captain (New English Bible, prince; New International Version, leader)** is not equivalent to **king.** Mauchline says, "The word means 'appointed one,' 'designated one,' somewhat like our term commissioner." Apparently, the whole truth was not yet to be disclosed to Saul. The private ceremony has four features:

1. **The Anointing** (v. 1). This consisted in pouring upon the head the special sacred oil compounded of a variety of spices (Exodus 29:7; 30:22-33). From Psalm 133:2 it seems that it was a very lavish anointing. It is symbolical of the enduing of the Holy Spirit for divine service.

2. **The Kiss** (v. 1). Some think this was a kiss of affection; others think it was the kiss of homage, as in Psalm 2:12, and as in the practice of kissing the sovereign's hand.

3. **The Proclamation** (v. 1). Why is this in the form of a question? Probably because Saul's face was reflecting surprise and wonder. What did all this mean? Samuel answers: Because the Lord has anointed you to be captain (or leader) of Israel!

4. **The Signs** (vv. 2-13). Samuel gives Saul three signs or proofs for his encouragement. (a) Two men will meet him to assure him that the lost asses which he had been seeking were found. (b) Three men will give to him of their sacrificial offerings, food which had been consecrated to God. (c) A company of prophets will meet him in a state of prophetic ecstasy, and he himself will be caught up into the same ecstasy. It should be noted that this "prophesying" was neither prediction nor preaching, but a kind of worshipful excitement. As Keil and Delitzsch say, "By the prophesying of these prophets we are to understand an ecstatic utterance of religious feelings to the praise of God, as in the case of the seventy elders in the time of Moses: Numbers 11:25" **(A Commentary on the Old Testament, The Books of Samuel,** p. 100).

These signs were all of an unusual and unexpected nature, and in an ascending order. The impact of them upon Saul would be to "turn him into another man" (v. 6). This is further described as, "God gave him another heart" (v. 9).

We must not read into these expressions the full theological and spiritual meaning of the New Testament. Neither regeneration, sanctification, nor the Pentecostal baptism with the Holy Spirit is meant. Nevertheless, it does describe a change in Saul from the temperament of a rustic farmer to that of a military and political leader, this change being effected by the Spirit of God. It is the equivalent of the charismatic endowment of the earlier judges (Gideon, Samson, and others). Keil and Delitzsch say, "This transformation is not to be regarded indeed as regeneration in the Christian sense, but as a change resembling regeneration, which affected the entire disposition of mind, and by which Saul was lifted out of his former modes of thought and feeling, which were confined within a narrow earthly sphere, into the far higher sphere of his new royal calling, was filled with kingly thoughts in relation to the service of God."

As a result of these signs, especially the last, Saul would know that God indeed had called and anointed him as leader of Israel.

If you were to suggest a Christian equivalent of Saul's experience, what would it be? Conversion, sanctification, or the Pentecostal Baptism? Why?

B. A Public Appointment (vv. 17-27)

17. And Samuel called the people together unto the Lord to Mizpeh;

18. And said unto the children of Israel, Thus saith the Lord God of Israel, I brought up Israel out of Egypt, and delivered you out of the hand of the Egyptians, and out of the hand of all kingdoms, and of them that oppressed you:

19. And ye have this day rejected your God, who himself saved you out of all your adversities and your tribulations; and ye have said unto him, Nay, but set a king over us. Now therefore present yourselves

before the Lord by your tribes, and by your thousands.

Samuel now calls a public assembly for the purpose of presenting Saul to the nation. The process of appointment is interesting as it describes election by the use of the sacred lot. It is also interesting that both Samuel and Saul knew beforehand what the result would be.

24. And Samuel said to all the people, See ye him whom the Lord hath chosen, that there is none like him among all the people? And all the people shouted, and said, God save the king.

25. Then Samuel told the people the manner of the kingdom, and wrote it in a book, and laid it up before the Lord. And Samuel sent all the people away, every man to his house.

26. And Saul also went home to Gibeah; and there went with him a band of men, whose hearts God had touched.

The process of ascertaining the divine choice led to Saul, and the people jubilently acclaimed him as "the king." (The crowning, however, did not take place until later. See 1 Samuel 11:12-15.) In fact there was a division of opinion (vv. 26, 27). This was overcome (as told in chapter 11) by a practical proof of Saul's charismatic anointing for military leadership.

Saul showed a strange reaction when the result of the sacred lot was announced (vv. 21, 22). How would you evaluate this: weakness or humility?

REVIEW QUESTIONS

1. How did the Lord consider the people's desire for a king?
2. How was Samuel used in the designation of Saul as the King?
3. How was Saul proclaimed king?
4. Who accompanied Saul to his home?
5. What practical applications for use in today's society do you draw from this lesson?

GOLDEN TEXT HOMILY

"GOD IS THE JUDGE: HE PUTTETH DOWN ONE, AND SETTETH UP ANOTHER" (Psalm 75:7).

A very serious thought is given that judgment belongs to God. He and He alone will bring it to pass. He will accomplish it according to His own timetable and not according to man's. God is the judge, and all depends on Him. Promotions and power do not come from human strength, skill, ingenuity, or from any other power on earth. Our success depends on God. He is over all; He can give success when it is least expected; and He can humble men when they have made the most ample preparation for their own success.

"He putteth down one, and setteth up another" is not only true for individuals, but for nations as well. The matter of "lifting up" or "promotion" depends on God. It was God who made Joseph a ruler throughout all of Egypt (Genesis 45:8).

The appropriate response for us is to trust and depend on Him in faith—faith that those who will forever declare their loyalty and trust in God can wait for God's workings. Esther's coronation is a true example of God's promotion. Those who are faithful in all things will be rewarded by divine providence, as God's plan unfolds in their lives.—**T. Paul Patton, pastor, Church of God, Chattanooga, Tennessee**

SENTENCE SERMONS

NO GROUP RISES higher than its leadership.
—**"NEA Journal"**

THE QUESTION, "Who ought to be the leader?" is like asking, "Who ought to be the tenor in the quartet?" Obviously, the man who can do the job!
—**Henry Ford**

IF YOU ARE NOT afraid to face the music, you may some day lead the band.
—**Spuck Tidings**

HE WHO LEADS without leading others to lead is no leader.
—**"Speaker's Sourcebook"**

EVANGELISTIC APPLICATION

PROPER LEADERSHIP HELPS TO MAKE THE CHURCH EFFECTIVE IN ITS EVANGELISTIC EFFORTS.

Many years ago an advert used to appear in a British magazine which used a cartoon drawing of a man brimming over with vigor and vitality, and holding the hand of a heart on legs, the heart being given human features which depicted buoyant happiness and strength. The caption read, "New Hearts for Old: Give your heart this new lease of life." It is in the most profound sense of all that God says, "A new heart also will I give you, and a new spirit will I put within you" (Ezekiel 36:26). To a degree, what God does through the gospel is portrayed in Saul. Before God gave him another heart, he appears to have had no personal awareness of the living God and no religious experience. His life was totally immersed in his father's farm. He sensed no higher destiny. His meeting with Samuel gave him "a new heart for the old one." His life gained a new dimension and a new direction. He began to see himself as an instrument for the service of Almighty God.

More profoundly, more grandly, this happens to those whose lives are touched and changed by Christ. "Old things are passed away; behold, all things are become new" (2 Corinthians 5:17).

ILLUMINATING THE LESSON

When a girl applies for admission to Vassar College, a questionnaire is sent to her parents. A father in a Boston suburb, filling out one of these blanks, came to the question, "Is she a leader?" He hesitated, then wrote, "I am not sure about this, but I know she is an excellent follower."

A few days later he received this letter from the president of the college: "As our freshman group next Fall is to contain several hundred leaders, we congratulate ourselves that your daughter will also be a member of the class. We shall thus be assured of one good follower."—**"The Journal of Education"**

A leader is best
When people barely know that he exists,
Not so good when people obey and acclaim him,
Worst when they despise him.
"Fail to honor people,
They fail to honor you."
But of a good leader, who talks little,
When his work is done, his aim fulfilled,
They will all say, "We did this ourselves."
—**Laotzu, "The Way of Life"**

DAILY DEVOTIONAL GUIDE

M. Leadership Traits. 1 Samuel 9:1-10
T. Divine Guidance. 1 Samuel 9:11-17
W. Spiritual Help. 1 Samuel 9:18-27
T. Anointed Leadership. 1 Samuel 11:4-15
F. Honorable Leadership. 1 Samuel 12:1-5
S. Godly Counsel. 1 Samuel 12:6-15

March 29, 1981

The Folly of Self-Will

Bible Background: 1 Samuel 13:1-14; 15:1-35

Time: Probably around 1018 B.C.

Place: Michmash, Bethel, Gibeah, Geba, Gilgal, Amalek, Carmel

Supplemental References: Psalm 75:1-10; Mark 14:32-39

Golden Text: "To obey is better than sacrifice" (1 Samuel 15:22).

Central Truth: Self-will can lead to heartache, disappointment, and broken fellowship with God.

Evangelistic Emphasis: "Thy will be done," must be the prayer of every soulwinner.

PRINTED TEXT

1 Samuel 15:10. Then came the word of the Lord unto Samuel, saying,

11. It repenteth me that I have set up Saul to be king: for he is turned back from following me, and hath not performed my commandments. And it grieved Samuel; and he cried unto the Lord all night.

13. And Samuel came to Saul: and Saul said unto him, Blessed be thou of the Lord: I have performed the commandment of the Lord.

14. And Samuel said, What meaneth then this bleating of the sheep in mine ears, and the lowing of the oxen which I hear?

15. And Saul said, They have brought them from the Amalekites: for the people spared the best of the sheep and of the oxen, to sacrifice unto the Lord thy God; and the rest we have utterly destroyed.

16. Then Samuel said unto Saul, Stay, and I will tell thee what the Lord hath said to me this night. And he said unto him, Say on.

17. And Samuel said, When thou wast little in thine own sight, wast thou not made the head of the tribes of Israel, and the Lord anointed thee king over Israel?

18. And the Lord sent thee on a journey, and said, Go and utterly destroy the sinners the Amalekites, and fight against them until they be consumed.

19. Wherefore then didst thou not obey the voice of the Lord, but didst fly upon the spoil, and didst evil in the sight of the Lord?

20. And Saul said unto Samuel, Yea, I have obeyed the voice of the Lord, and have gone the way which the Lord sent me, and have brought Agag the king of Amalek, and have utterly destroyed the Amalekites.

21. But the people took of the spoil, sheep and oxen, the chief of the things which should have been utterly destroyed, to sacrifice unto the Lord thy God in Gilgal.

22. And Samuel said, Hath the Lord as great delight in burnt-offerings and sacrifices, as in obeying the voice of the Lord? Behold, to obey is better than sacrifice, and to hearken than the fat of rams.

23. For rebellion is as the sin of witchcraft, and stubbornness is as iniquity and idolatry. Because thou hast rejected the word of the Lord, he hath also rejected thee from being king.

The Folly of Self-Will

DICTIONARY

Blessed be thou of the Lord—1 Samuel 15:13—A typical Hebrew form of greeting at the time of our lesson

Amalekites (AM-a-lek-kites)—1 Samuel 15:15—The plural form of "Amalek," the grandson of Esau. This term is used for the nomadic tribes which descended from Esau, and which occupies the Sinai peninsula between the Southern Judean hills and the borders of Egypt.

Agag (AA-gag)—1 Samuel 15:20—Probably a title like the Pharaoh of Egypt

LESSON OUTLINE

I. PERILS OF IMPATIENCE
 A. A National Emergency
 B. An Act of Folly
II. SERIOUSNESS OF DISOBEDIENCE
 A. The War With Amalek
 B. The Rebellion of Saul
III. PENALTY OF TRANSGRESSION
 A. The Sentence on Saul
 B. The Execution of Agag

LESSON EXPOSITION

INTRODUCTION

Though the Bible Background to our previous lesson included the twelfth chapter of the first Book of Samuel, it was not possible to comment upon it. However, it should be noticed at this point. It describes what has been called "Samuel's abdication" from his judgeship. It does not mean Samuel's retirement, for he continued to function as prophet throughout most of Saul's reign, as we shall see.

As we study our present lesson, we are bound to notice a striking contrast between the optimistic presentation of Saul in chapters 9 and 10, and of the Saul who is now king. The high hopes of the earlier chapters begin to be dimmed, and in later chapters of Samuel the picture gets even dimmer—to the point of total darkness.

This raises an important question: if the Lord knew beforehand (as He certainly did) the character of Saul and the total failure he would be, why did He choose such a person to be Israel's first king? The answer probably is that the Lord wanted the nation to learn a great spiritual lesson at the very beginning of the monarchy. He wished them to learn that what seemed an ideal form of government (a monarchy) was a vain illusion. If you put power into the hands of mortal man, whether he be judge, king, dictator, or president, his rule will be no better than his character. Saul was chosen because, in spite of his leadership potential, and even the charisma which was given him, he had a basic spiritual defect in his character which would bring about his own ruin and plunge the nation into near disaster.

In our present lesson this defect is exposed. God gave Israel the kind of leader they continually demanded, and they soon discovered what was in store for them. It sometimes happens like this in church life. God gives us up to what we clamor for—and we reap a bitter harvest.

I. PERILS OF IMPATIENCE (1 Samuel 13:1-14)

A. A National Emergency (vv. 1-7)

Two things are apparent from these verses:

(a) **Saul had provided for a standing army in Israel in the early days of his reign** (v. 2). The last clause of this verse, "and the rest of the people he sent every man to his tent," may look back to 11:15. After the war against the Ammonites (11:1-11), he disbanded the army, retaining only three thousand men. Of these, two thousand were under his own command at Michmash and Bethel. One thousand were under the command of his son Jonathan in Gibeah. These places were all within a few miles of Jerusalem. H. D. M. Spence says, "This was the first step towards the development of Israel into a great military power" **(Ellicott's Bible Commentary, Vol. 2).**

(b) **The Philistines had begun to reassert themselves** (v. 3). They had a garrison in Geba. The **New International Version** renders this, "the outpost at Geba" (see 1 Samuel 10:5). Verse 5 shows that the Philistines had gathered strength again and were bent on dominating the land. In this connection, the final verses of chapter 13 should be looked at (vv. 19-23), and should be read if possible in the **New International Version**. The Philistines had managed to gain a monopoly of iron and had made Israel wholly dependent upon them for military weapons and agricultural implements. Mauchline comments, "The Israelites were handicapped by their lack of military weapons (v. 22) and were agriculturally dependent on the Philistines. So they had a dependent prosperity in peace and an inadequacy amounting to impotence in war" **(New Century Bible, 1 and 2 Samuel).**

In these circumstances we are introduced to Jonathan, one of the most attractive men in the Bible, and surely one of the most unfortunate, in that he had Saul for a father. Both here and in chapter 14, we find Jonathan portrayed as a soldier of great courage and daring. He here launched an attack upon the Philistine garrison and thus opened a long war of attrition between Israel and the Philistines.

In consequence the Philistines mobilized for battle and Saul recalled his entire army to Gilgal (vv. 4, 5). However, the morale of Israel was so low that the army began to desert Saul in large numbers (vv. 6, 7). Thus, Saul had a dangerous situation on his hands.

Under the circumstances was Jonathan's action justified?

B. An Act of Folly (vv. 8-14)

This whole passage becomes meaningful once we have grasped the meaning of the statement, "And he tarried seven days, according to the set time that Samuel had appointed" (v. 8). As there is no reference to this appointment by Samuel in the immediate context, its meaning has been debated. Some have thought that it prescribes a general rule which Saul was always supposed to follow before going to battle—namely, to wait until the prophet Samuel had performed a sacrificial ceremony. Others think that it describes the instruction given to Saul on the occasion of his private anointing: "And thou shalt go down before me to Gilgal; and, behold, I will come down unto thee, to offer burnt-offerings, and to sacrifice sacrifices of peace-offerings: seven days shalt thou tarry, till I come to thee, and shew thee what thou shalt do" (1 Samuel 10:8). Keil and Delitzseh comment on this verse: "Placed as he was by Jehovah as king over His people, for the purpose of rescuing them out of the power of those who were at that time its most dangerous foes, Saul was not at liberty to enter upon the war against these foes simply by his own will, but was directed to wait till Samuel, the accredited prophet of Jehovah, had completed the consecration through the offering of a solemn sacrifice, and had communicated to him the requisite instructions from God, even though he should have to wait for seven days."

It is clear that Samuel had not surrendered his prophetic office and that Saul's exaltation to kingship did not give him license to act on his own without reference to the will of God whose anointed representative Samuel was.

As the story unfolds, we see that Saul was placed in a dilemma. He waited the seven days but Samuel did not arrive. The army of Israel was falling apart through panic. Each day intensified the danger should the superior Philistines attack. As soon as the time ran out, Saul took matters into his own hands and performed the appropriate ceremony. As soon as it was over, however, Samuel arrived and Saul hurried to meet him perhaps in order to receive his blessing before he went to battle. Instead of a blessing, however, he was given a scathing denunciation and was roundly told that through his attitude and action he had forfeited the Kingdom and would be replaced by a better man—"a man after his [God's] own heart" (vv. 13, 14).

Many feel great sympathy for Saul in his predicament, and some expositors have blamed Samuel for his delay. Some have even claimed that Samuel hated Saul. However, if we take the whole biography of Saul as it stands in the sacred record we cannot accept these opinions.

There was a radical defect in Saul's character. In spite of the ecstatic experience which had come to him, he had little real awareness of God and almost no spiritual perception. His will was not subordinated to the will of God. It has been suggested that the examples of his disobedience which are given in Scripture are only isolated instances of Saul's permanent disposition toward God. The seven-day delay at Gilgal seems to have been a divinely arranged test which exposed his carnal character.

David, as well as Saul, was guilty of failure, yet he was "a man after his [God's] own heart" (v. 14). What did David have which Saul had not?

II. SERIOUSNESS OF DISOBEDIENCE (1 Samuel 15:1-15)

The prophetic judgment upon Saul did not immediately fall. Rather the reverse, as chapter 14 shows. Though Israel was hopelessly outnumbered (see 1 Samuel 13:15, 16, 22), the Lord saved Israel in the battle of Michmash (14:23). The instrument in His hands was Jonathan, whose heroic action is narrated in chapter 14. The story, however, highlights again the rashness of Saul (14:24-46).

The Philistine threat being for the time overcome, Saul was able to give his attention to other aggressive neighbors (14:47-52), and he was able to build up a strong kingdom. This summary of his conquests reveals him to have been a great military commander, in spite of his fundamental defects of character and also in spite of the fact that he had incurred God's displeasure and was doomed to perish. This illustrates the saying, "The mills of God grind slowly." Samuel's prophecy did not immediately come to pass.

The fifteenth chapter, on which we now focus our attention, turns the spotlight on one of Saul's victorious battles summarized in the concluding verse of chapter 14.

What spiritual lesson may we learn from the fact that Saul continued to prosper for some years after Samuel declared his divine rejection, and in spite of his carnality?

A. The War With Amalek (vv. 1-7)

The war with Amalek is presented here as a war of divine retribution at the command of God through the prophet Samuel. It is not easy for the modern mind to understand, much less accept, such a concept. However, several considerations give relief to our minds.

First, we must realize that God is **righteous**, as well as loving. The fact of His love does not mean that He is weak and careless in judging wicked individuals and nations. Second, the ancient nations which were destroyed in biblical times, either by so-called "acts of God" in nature or by military extermination, are portrayed as so corrupt and cruel that they were a festering sore in the body of humanity which God in His wisdom and righteousness saw fit to remove, just as He had seen fit to destroy the whole world, except Noah's family, at the great Flood. Archaeological findings confirm the biblical verdict on these nations.

The people of Amalek were such a people. Blaiklock writes, "The Amalekites must be seen for what they were—a species of Bedouin tribe, ranging the eastern borderlands of Israel from Sinai and the Arabah northwards, harassing the frontier, raiding, looting, murdering. If peace was to reign in Palestine, their utter defeat was necessary. The war must be seen in the context of war such as this century has known, where beleaguered nations have had cruelty, aggression, and the determination of desperate guerrilla groups cursing their borderlands and damaging all peace" **(Bible Characters: Elkanah to David).**

B. The Rebellion of Saul (vv. 8-15)

Probably because of his strength and prosperity, Saul had been deceived into thinking that the judgment pronounced by Samuel was averted. Instead of a changed attitude toward the Lord and His Word we observe now a toughening of his rebellious spirit. He had become more bold and audacious. Consequently, though he was probably pleased to have the opportunity to destroy the Amalekite forces, he determined to enrich himself by the conquest, in complete contravention of God's command. He spared Agag (which is probably the official title of the Amalekite ruler), and also preserved and captured the best of the cattle (vv. 8, 9).

His motives for doing so are debated. Spence says, "Covetousness seems to have suggested the preservation of the choicest cattle, and pride probably induced the Hebrew king to save Agag alive, that he might show the people his royal capture." We may be sure that it was not for humanitarian reasons that Saul spared either Agag or his cattle. He did not live in the twentieth century A.D., and neither "human rights" nor "animal rights" was a factor. He planned to display his notorious prisoner before his people as the Philistines had done with Samson. And he was greedy for the cattle.

10. Then came the word of the Lord unto Samuel, saying,

11. It repenteth me that I have set up Saul to be king: for he is turned back from following me, and hath not performed my commandments. And it grieved Samuel; and he cried unto the Lord all night.

Saul's behavior shows how shallow his conception of God was and how little he understood Samuel's relationship with God. The shocking truth was disclosed to the old prophet in the nighttime, as had been the truth about Eli when Samuel was a mere boy. The word **repent** in reference to God, as used here and elsewhere, should be properly understood. Payne says, "**Repent** here signifies grief and a change of attitude, not a change of mind" **(New Bible Commentary Revised).**

Similarly Matthew Henry says, "Repentance in God is not, as in us, a change of mind, but a change of His method or dispensation. He does not alter His will, but wills an alteration. Saul had changed! He had 'turned back from following me.'" Says Keil and Delitzsch, "This was Saul's real sin. He would no longer be the follower and servant of the Lord, but would be absolute ruler in Israel."

13. And Samuel came to Saul: and Saul said unto him, Blessed be thou of the Lord: I have performed the commandment of the Lord.

14. And Samuel said, What meaneth then this bleating of the sheep in mine ears, and the lowing of the oxen which I hear?

15. And Saul said, They have brought them from the Amalekites: for the people spared the best of the sheep and of the oxen, to sacrifice unto the Lord thy God; and the rest we have utterly destroyed.

When Samuel approached Saul, the king put on an air of piety—a frequent trick of the "old man" (v. 13). This was a sugar-coating for an outright lie: "I have performed the commandment of the Lord." When asked to explain the bleating of the sheep and the lowing of the oxen, he laid the blame upon his soldiers and excused them on the grounds that they had done it for religious reasons (v. 15). Saul's conduct graphically illustrates the saying of Jeremiah, "The heart is deceitful above all things, and desperately wicked: who can know it?" (Jeremiah 17:9).

When God disclosed Saul's defection to Samuel, the prophet "cried unto the Lord all night." What do you think was the burden of his prayers?

III. PENALTY OF TRANSGRESSION (1 Samuel 15:16-33)

A. The Sentence on Saul (vv. 16-31)

16. Then Samuel said unto Saul, Stay, and I will tell thee what the Lord hath said to me this night. And he said unto him, Say on.

17. And Samuel said, When thou wast little in thine own sight, wast thou not made the head of the tribes of Israel, and the Lord anointed thee king over Israel?

18. And the Lord sent thee on a journey, and said, Go and utterly destroy the sinners the Amalekites, and fight against them until they be consumed.

19. Wherefore then didst thou not obey the voice of the Lord, but didst fly upon the spoil, and didst evil in the sight of the Lord?

Though Samuel was grief-stricken over Saul (compare verses 11 and 35), he knew he had to expose and judge him. His grief could not be allowed to deflect him from his duty to God and the nation. Samuel reminded Saul of the grace that had lifted him up from nothing and made him great, and charged him with presuming on that grace by his disobedience. Do we not often see this very thing among Christians?

20. And Saul said unto Samuel, Yea, I have obeyed the voice of the Lord, and have gone the way which the Lord sent me, and have brought Agag the king of Amalek, and have utterly destroyed the Amalekites.

21. But the people took of the spoil, sheep and oxen, the chief of the things which should have been utterly destroyed, to sacrifice unto the Lord thy God in Gilgal.

Saul, however, denied disobedience and repeated his excuses.

22. And Samuel said, Hath the Lord as great delight in burnt-offerings and sacrifices, as in obeying the voice of the Lord? Behold, to obey is better than sacrifice, and to hearken than the fat of rams.

23. For rebellion is as the sin of witchcraft, and stubbornness is as iniquity and idolatry. Because thou hast rejected the word of the Lord, he hath also rejected thee from being king.

Samuel's penetrating words in Hebrew are couched in the peculiar style of prophetic preaching (this is reflected in the **New International Version**). Blaiklock says, "Samuel in his stern rebuke shows himself the forerunner of the major prophets." Compare Isaiah 1:11-20. The message reaches over to our own times. It is popular and common for people to sugarcoat their disobedience by an outward show of religiousness. But God cannot be deceived, neither can He be satisfied with religiously covered immorality. Jesus even declared that a charismatic ministry is unacceptable to God if the life is not right (Matthew 7:21-23).

Thus exposed, Saul made a last-ditch stand, professing to repent (v. 24). However, his final plea, "Honor me, now, I pray thee, before the elders of my people, and before Israel," seems to show that he was more concerned with the appearance of things than with realities (v. 30). His sentence, therefore, was irrevocable.

Do you think Samuel was too hard on Saul?

B. The Execution of Agag (vv. 32, 33).

Let us not condemn Samuel's action. This was not a fierce murder, but a judicial execution upon a bloodthirsty, multiple murderer whose judgment was just. He had imagined that he had cheated the gallows, but he had reckoned without God and His prophet.

REVIEW QUESTIONS

1. What was Saul's first version to Samuel of what he had done?
2. What made Samuel know that Saul had disobeyed?
3. Why, according to Saul, had the various spoils been saved?
4. In the eyes of the Lord, what is more pleasing than merely the act of sacrificing?
5. What was the penalty for Saul's disobedience?

GOLDEN TEXT HOMILY

"TO OBEY IS BETTER THAN SACRIFICE" (1 Samuel 15:22).

Obedience is like a master key that unlocks a door that leads to a room full of a fabulously rich treasure! Obedience will bring peace, protection, and prosperity.

1. Peace. The blessing of happiness is a reality only when we are at peace with ourselves. Disobedience always produces conflict in the spiritual realm as well as in the natural realm. True contentment comes only to the obedient.
2. Protection. When we are disobedient to God we voluntarily step outside of His protective hand. Samuel told Saul that disobedience was as the sin of witchcraft (1 Samuel 15:23). When we disobey we are as susceptible to demon control as if we were involved in demon worship. God's great protection is for the obedient.
3. Prosperity. God always honors and blesses the obedient. It is His nature to do so. This is one principle that has not changed in any of the different dispensational dealings of God with man. God always rewards those who obey Him.

To rationalize that it is reasonable to do something other than what God has said is deadly. Adam and Eve, Lot, Saul, and Achan all rationalized that their actions were justifiable and yet they suffered severely for it. Many Christians today wrongly rationalize that it is more important to conform to society in their conduct, morals, and appearance than to what God has said. They will suffer for their actions, too.

Obedience is possible. It may seem as if it is beyond our potential, but Philippians 2:5 tells us, "Let this mind be in you, which was also in Christ Jesus." The mind of Christ was an obedient mind (Philippians 2:8). In the natural this is an impossible achievement, but the Lord has promised a renewed mind, by the transforming power of the Holy Spirit, to all believers who will allow it to happen.

Obedience really is best.—**Philip Siggelkow, President, International Bible College, Moose Jaw, Saskatchewan, Canada**

SENTENCE SERMONS

TO OBEY GOD in some things and not in others shows an unsound heart. Childlike obedience moves toward every command of God, as the needle points where the loadstone draws.

—**Thomas Watson**

THIRTY YEARS OF OUR Lord's life are hidden in these words of the Gospel: "He was subject unto them."

—**Jacques Bossuet**

TO BE MORE aware of God, we must be less aware of self.

—**"Notes and Quotes"**

HE WHO LIVES to benefit only himself, confers on the world a benefit when he dies.

—**Tertullian**

EVANGELISTIC APPLICATION

"THY WILL BE DONE," MUST BE THE PRAYER OF EVERY SOULWINNER.

The story of Saul pinpoints a fundamental truth which rings through the entire Bible: if a man is deliberately disobeying the Word of God nothing can make up for it.

Saul imagined that God could be induced to overlook his sin for the price of a few sheep and cattle. How shaken he was to learn the naked truth.

Later the Israelites had the same notion. They thought that they could practice the most flagrant wickedness under cover of many sacrifices to the accompaniment of much incense and excellent music. But God, declared the prophets, hated both the sight, the sound, and the smell of it all. Jesus denounced the Pharisees for similar practices.

Does mankind ever learn this lesson? We need to be absolutely clear that there is no substitute for simple obedience to the Word of God. If our religion lacks obedience, with all the sugarcoating in the world, it is unacceptable. We may build beautiful buildings, gather large crowds, provide appealing musical entertainment, lace it all with miracles, and give big donations to missions and benevolence, but without obedience it is nothing.

ILLUMINATING THE LESSON

Remember the little boy who had his hand fast in a vase? He ran to his father for help, and his father soon discovered that he had his fist tightly clinched inside the vase. "Open your hand, my son," said the father, "and it will come out easy enough." "But Papa," cried the child, "if I open my hand I'll drop my penny."

Two little girls were starting out to play. One insisted on going quite a distance away. "Why do you want to go so far?" the other asked. "So that if my mama calls me I won't hear her," was the candid reply.
—From **"Notes and Quotes"**

DAILY DEVOTIONAL GUIDE

M. Blessings of Obedience. Deuteronomy 7:12-16
T. Exhortation to Obedience. Proverbs 3:1-8
W. Valuable Counsel. Psalm 37:1-11
T. Divine Instruction. Matthew 7:21-27
F. Hearing and Doing. James 1:19-25
S. Godly Virtues. 2 Peter 1:3-11

April 5, 1981

God-Given Victory

Bible Background: 1 Samuel 17:1-58

Time: Probably around 1017 B.C.

Place: Philistine border

Supplemental References: 1 Kings 20:13-30; Revelation 3:21; 17:14

Golden Text: "The Lord saveth not with sword and spear: for the battle is the Lord's" (1 Samuel 17:47).

Central Truth: Spiritual victories are won, not by natural powers or abilities, but by complete reliance upon God.

Evangelistic Emphasis: Trust in God brings victory over Satan and sin.

PRINTED TEXT

1 Samuel 17:32. And David said to Saul, Let no man's heart fail because of him; thy servant will go and fight with this Philistine.

33. And Saul said to David, Thou art not able to go against this Philistine to fight with him: for thou art but a youth, and he a man of war from his youth.

34. And David said unto Saul, Thy servant kept his father's sheep, and there came a lion, and a bear, and took a lamb out of the flock:

35. And I went out after him, and smote him, and delivered it out of his mouth: and when he arose against me, I caught him by his beard, and smote him, and slew him.

36. Thy servant slew both the lion and the bear: and this uncircumcised Philistine shall be as one of them, seeing he hath defied the armies of the living God.

41. And the Philistine came on and drew near unto David; and the man that bare the shield went before him.

42. And when the Philistine looked about, and saw David, he disdained him: for he was but a youth, and ruddy, and of a fair countenance.

43. And the Philistine said unto David, Am I a dog, that thou comest to me with staves? And the Philistine cursed David by his gods.

44. And the Philistine said to David, Come to me, and I will give thy flesh unto the fowls of the air, and to the beasts of the field.

45. Then said David to the Philistine, Thou comest to me with a sword, and with a spear, and with a shield: but I come to thee in the name of the Lord of hosts, the God of the armies of Israel, whom thou hast defied.

46. This day will the Lord deliver thee into mind hand; and I will smite thee, and take thine head from thee; and I will give the carcases of the host of the Philistines this day unto the fowls of the air, and to the wild beasts of the earth; that all the earth may know that there is a God in Israel.

47. And all this assembly shall know that the Lord saveth not with sword and spear: for the battle is the Lord's, and he

will give you into our hands.

48. And it came to pass, when the Philistine arose, and came and drew nigh to meet David, that David hasted, and ran toward the army to meet the Philistine.

49. And David put his hand in his bag, and took thence a stone, and slang it, and smote the Philistine in his forehead, that the stone sunk into his forehead; and he fell upon his face to the earth.

DICTIONARY

Philistine (fill-LIST-teen)—1 Samuel 17:32—A wealthy seafaring people that occupied a border country beside Israel.

uncircumcised—1 Samuel 17:36—A word used in both Old and New Testament in several ways. Literally it refers to one who has not submitted to the Jewish rite of circumcision. Figuratively, it is used for the heathen.

LESSON OUTLINE

I. CHALLENGE OF THE ENEMY
  A. The Lines of Battle
  B. The Philistine Champion

II. RESPONSE OF FAITH
  A. The Providence of God
  B. The Confidence of David

III. VICTORY OVER THE ENEMY
  A. Preparation for the Fight
  B. Affirmation of Faith
  C. Destruction of the Foe

LESSON EXPOSITION

INTRODUCTION

We have previously seen that though the rejection of Saul was announced to him fairly early in his career (1 Samuel 13:8-14) he continued to prosper for some years. After the second pronouncement of his doom (1 Samuel 15:12-35), Saul's prosperity began to decline and even his personality began to disintegrate, as we shall see in subsequent lessons. But it was some years before his final collapse and tragic death (1 Samuel 31). Nevertheless God was already at work to fulfill the positive aspects of Samuel's prophecy, namely, the rise of a "neighbor" of Saul's who was better than he (1 Samuel 15:28).

Keil and Delitzsch summarize the situation as follows: "Saul's rejection was not followed by his outward deposition. The Lord merely took away His Spirit, had David anointed king by Samuel, and thenceforth so directed the steps of Saul and David, that as time advanced the hearts of the people were turned more and more from Saul to David; and on the death of Saul, the attempt of the ambitious Abner to raise his son to the throne could not possibly have any lasting success" **(A Commentary on the Old Testament, The Books of Samuel).**

The private anointing of the young David as successor to Saul, together with his charismatic enduement, is described in chapter 16. The rest of the first Book of Samuel describes the years of Saul's struggle to frustrate the purposes of God until his death. Our present lesson focuses on the way in which David was catapulted into public attention, God exalted him from obscurity to national fame in one hour.

I. CHALLENGE OF THE ENEMY (1 Samuel 17:1-11)

A. The Lines of Battle (vv. 1-3)

Several years had passed since the great battle of Michmash in which the smaller and greatly inferior forces of Israel crushed the powerful army of Philistia (14:1-23). Possibly other battles had followed (see 14:47, 52) but none have been described. Saul was now in a very strong position militarily, in spite of the fact that his personality had begun to disintegrate (see 16:14-23). At length, however, the Philistines massed their forces for a renewed attack, and Saul moved his army into position to face them.

We should carefully try to locate the battle lines. The Philistines dug in "between Shochoh and Azekah, in Ephes-dammim" (which means **the Boundary of Blood,** referring perhaps to the carnage of previous battles there). It was about fourteen miles southwest of Bethlehem on the border between Israel and Philistia. Saul placed his men "by the valley of Elah." This was a river valley running from the Judean hills toward the Mediterranean Sea.

Elah means "terebinth trees." Thus the armies faced each other across the valley, Israel in the north, the Philistines in the south. But between them was a ravine, according to Deane, "some twenty feet across, and having steep banks ten or twelve feet high" **(David: His Life and Times).** George Adam Smith says, "It is the very battlefield for those ancient foes; Israel in one of the gateways to her mountain land; the Philistines on the low hills they often overran, and between them the valley that divides Judah from the Shephelah or Lowland" **(Historical Geography of the Holy Land).** It has been suggested that this deep ravine which made direct engagement of troops difficult was one reason for the forty days stalemate (see v. 16).

B. The Philistine Champion (vv. 4-11)

Many years before, the Philistines had been harassed and humiliated by the Israelite, Samson. Now they had a champion of their own —Goliath by name. Some scholars suggest that Goliath was a descendant of the Anakim (Deuteronomy 2:20-23) who had found a home with the Philistines. The Bible tells us in Joshua 11:22 that remnants of the Anakim remained in the cities of Philistia. Goliath was of enormous stature, standing nearly ten feet tall. A number of such giants are mentioned by name in the Old Testament (Deuteronomy 3:11; 2 Samuel 21:16-22). The commentaries frequently mention the occasional appearance of a giant in several lands, and even in recent times. Some scientists claim that the occasional giant is produced by the abnormal working of the pituitary gland.

The Philistine had added to his terrifying size by wearing armor no less frightening (vv. 5-7). He wore a bronze helmet, and a coat of mail made of small plates of metal fastened on a surface of leather. This was a great weight, two hundred pounds, according to the **Living Bible.** His legs were equally well protected by bronze leggings. And he carried a fearful looking weapon, "a bronze javelin several inches thick, tipped with a twenty-five-pound iron spearhead" **(Living Bible).** He also carried a huge sword (see v. 51), and an attendant carried a large shield before him.

It seems he had a voice to match his size and his armor, for he could roar his challenge and his defiance at the Israelite armies across the valley. Night after night, and morning after morning he did this for forty days (v. 16). No wonder the Israelites were "dismayed, and greatly afraid" (v. 11). A decisive battle was difficult, and even if possible would have entailed many losses, in the valley of Elah. And the kind of champion-to-champion contest such as Goliath proposed left all the odds on the Philistine side.

We do not have to look far in the New Testament to find the spiritual counterpart of Goliath in Christian experience. Everywhere our attention is drawn to that diabolical giant to whom many names are given. He is called "the great dragon . . . that old serpent . . . the Devil, and Satan" (Revelation 12:9), "the prince of this world" (John 14:30), "the god of this world" (2 Corinthians 4:4). This diabolical champion defies "the armies of the living God," and seeks to terrorize every individual soldier in the army of the Lord. Each of us, at some time or other, comes to feel his malignant power and influence. In some lands and ages he has reduced the whole Church to silence and despair by his terrible threats and deeds.

Even Saul and Jonathan did not accept the giant's challenge. Can you suggest reasons for this?

II. RESPONSE OF FAITH (1 Samuel 17:12-37)

A. The Providence of God (vv. 12-23)

It is the design of the writer of 1 Samuel to remind his readers that the Lord had already provided the answer to Goliath's defiance. He here introduces David into the Goliath story and shows how it came about that he appeared on the battlefield. We should bear in mind, however, that David has already been introduced into the record as a whole in chapter 16. There, two things are narrated: (a) David's private anointing as successor to Saul by Samuel, and (b) David's employment as a musical entertainer to King Saul, as an antidote to his spasms of melancholia.

However, David was not permanently employed at Saul's court. He "went and returned from Saul to feed his father's sheep" (v. 15). The **New International Version** renders this, "David went back and forth from Saul to tend his father's sheep at Bethlehem." The **Living Bible** has, "David . . . was on Saul's staff on a part-time basis."

Three of David's brothers were in Saul's army which was dug in in the Valley of Elah fourteen miles southwest of Bethlehem.

David, who was apparently a youth too young for the military service, was sent by his father to the front with food for his brothers. By this simple circumstance Israel's anointed leader and deliverer was to be brought before the nation's attention. The writer plainly intends his readers to see the providence of God at work. This great truth is stamped upon the pages of the Bible from cover to cover, and it is a truth which we need to grasp for our own lives. "God moves in a mysterious way His wonders to perform," and very often this mysterious moving operates through the most ordinary circumstances and events of our everyday lives.

What other examples can you think of in Scripture which illustrate this great truth?

David arrived in the camp of Israel just as the armies were putting on their daily show of strength. We are not to imagine that verses 20 and 21 mean that a battle was imminent. It was probably no more than saber rattling. This climaxed, as it had done every day for forty days, with the appearance of Goliath, strutting and roaring his defiant challenge.

B. The Confidence of David (vv. 24-37)

Let us carefully note the reaction of the youthful David when he saw the mighty, roaring giant, and observed the terror of the Israelite soldiers. He said, "Who is this uncircumcised Philistine, that he should defy **the armies of the living God?**" (v. 26). That puts the thing into a true religious perspective. Payne says, "David injects the first theological note into the narrative" **(New Bible Commentary Revised).** Spence speaks of "the enthusiastic shepherd boy, glowing with religious fervor" **(Ellicott's Bible Commentary, Vol. 2).** Saul and his army could only survey the scene through natural eyes. David's language reveals him to be a deeply religious and spiritual youth who saw the scene through the eyes of **faith.** He thus belonged to the great company of men and women of faith whose praises are sung in the famous eleventh chapter of Hebrews.

In the final analysis, each of us belongs with David or with the Israelite army. We either evaluate things and face up to things from the perspective of faith in the living God, and thus "all things are possible." Or else we do so from the perspective of unbelief, and thus we are stymied and doomed. One David with faith in God can accomplish what a whole unbelieving army finds impossible or even unthinkable.

As David moved about among the soldiers, seeking information and expressing his belief that the giant could be conquered by faith in Jehovah, he came up against the hostility and resentment of his elder brother Eliab. Often in the Bible the elder brother appears in an unfavorable light (compare the brothers of Joseph, and of Jesus, and see Luke 15: 25-32). We may certainly take the lesson to heart that if we have a glowing heart of faith in God not all will appreciate it. Indeed one of the first obstacles for our faith to overcome is the spirit which was expressed in Eliab. Needless to say, this opposition does not always or necessarily come from our relatives, though it may and often does.

Eventually the eager, determined young man was reported to Saul, who sent for him (v. 31). "And David said to Saul, Let no man's heart fail because of him; thy servant will go and fight with this Philistine" (v. 32).

Here again David's living confidence in God shines out in the presence of the king. But he goes further than before. He himself offers to fight the Philistine. We must remember that David had already received a charismatic enduement (16:13). Therefore, it is highly probable (we could almost say, **certain)** that, just as Christ was driven or "led" by the Holy Spirit to combat Satan in the wilderness (Mark 1:12; Luke 4:1), so was David being stirred by the Holy Spirit to meet Goliath.

33. And Saul said to David, Thou art not able to go against this Philistine to fight with him: for thou art but a youth, and he a man of war from his youth.

It is not difficult to understand Saul's feelings. David's youth, inexperience, and lack of training disqualified him from the start. It was like a high-school amateur boxer offering to fight Muhammad Ali. Saul was not speaking harshly or caustically, but out of genuine fatherly feeling for the boy. This kind of tender concern can be as much a temptation of the devil to those who are seeking to follow the call of God as the bitter spirit of Eliab.

34. And David said unto Saul, Thy servant kept his father's sheep, and there came a lion, and a bear, and took a lamb out of the flock:

35. And I went out after him, and smote him, and delivered it out of his mouth: and

when he arose against me, I caught him by his beard, and smote him, and slew him.

36. Thy servant slew both the lion and the bear: and this uncircumcised Philistine shall be as one of them, seeing he hath defied the armies of the living God.

Here we have David's reply to Saul. First, he claimed that he was neither weak nor inexperienced. In his work as a shepherd he had actually killed both a lion and a bear which had attacked the flock (see **Living Bible**); therefore, he possessed both courage and stength. However, his confidence was **not self-confidence but God confidence.** "The Lord . . . delivered me out of the paw of the lion, and out of the paw of the bear, he will deliver me out of the hand of this Philistine." Thus David lifts the whole encounter out of a mere natural contest between two men, into the dimension of the spirit. Goliath was defying the armies of the living God. His sneers were directed against **the Lord.** And David would face him in the name of the Lord as the Lord's servant and representative. His past experiences had built up his faith for the present situation.

What steps can modern Christians take to build up the kind of faith which faces Goliaths with confidence?

III. VICTORY OVER THE ENEMY (1 Samuel 17:38-58)

A. Preparation for the Fight (vv. 38-40)

With well-meaning concern Saul clothed David with his own armor, but the young shepherd quickly removed it, knowing that it would hinder rather than help him in the fight. David had no intention of fighting the Philistine toe to toe—rather, he planned to fight him the only way he knew how, by the use of the sling and stone. This was a simple device used by shepherds to ward off wild animals from their flocks, and also to keep the sheep from straying. It was also used as a weapon of war in ancient nations (compare Judges 20:16; 1 Chronicles 12:2).

David had acquired great skill in this weapon during his work as a shepherd, as also with the harp (1 Samuel 16:18). J. D. Sanders makes the point that "David made good use of leisure hours while watching sheep. Out of this habit sprang the two great opportunities of his life. Long practice perfected his playing of the harp, and this first brought him to Saul's notice. Then he mastered the use of the sling which resulted in victory over Goliath. Many have missed God's best through a misuse of leisure" **(Men From God's School).**

B. Affirmation of Faith (vv. 41-47)

Equipped only with his sling and five smooth stones which he had picked up from the brook, David went forward to striking distance of Goliath.

41. And the Philistine came on and drew near unto David; and the man that bare the shield went before him.

42. And when the Philistine looked about, and saw David, he disdained him: for he was but a youth, and ruddy, and of a fair countenance.

43. And the Philistine said unto David, Am I a dog, that thou comest to me with staves? And the Philistine cursed David by his gods.

44. And the Philistine said to David, Come to me, and I will give thy flesh unto the fowls of the air, and to the beasts of the field.

Here we see two things: (a) David's very youthfulness and lack of military equipment had the effect of deceiving the Philistine into a false overconfidence. He was already off guard and psychologically defeated. (b) Goliath too, was religiously motivated, as is evident by the fact that he "cursed David by his gods." It was Dagon against Jehovah once again.

45. Then said David to the Philistine, Thou comest to me with a sword, and with a spear, and with a shield: but I come to thee in the name of the Lord of hosts, the God of the armies of Israel, whom thou hast defied.

46. This day will the Lord deliver thee into mine hand; and I will smite thee, and take thine head from thee; and I will give the carcases of the host of the Philistines this day unto the fowls of the air, and to the wild beasts of the earth; that all the earth may know that there is a God in Israel.

47. And all this assembly shall know that the Lord saveth not with sword and spear: for the battle is the Lord's and he will give you into our hands.

It is noteworthy that David, in his reply, does not even mention his weapon. It is true that he planned to use his sling and a stone, but his real confidence was in the Lord. He knew it was a religious and a spiritual battle—**Jehovah against Dagon**—and he had complete faith that Jehovah was the living God and Dagon but an idol. Therefore, his victory was certain.

Was not this the secret of the apostles of Christ when they went forth with their simple weapons to conquer the forces of imperial Rome? They knew that Jesus was the living Lord before whom no human or demonic power could stand.

The five stones out of the brook have sometimes been likened to five truths, or five promises, out of the Word of God, whereby we can go forth to meet the tempter. If you were to choose five such truths or promises, what would they be?

C. Destruction of the Foe (vv. 48-58)

48. And it came to pass, when the Philistine arose, and came and drew nigh to meet David, that David hasted, and ran toward the army to meet the Philistine.

49. And David put his hand in his bag, and took thence a stone, and slang it, and smote the Philistine in his forehead, that the stone sunk into his forehead; and he fell upon his face to the earth.

Spence makes this comment, "It has been well said that David was like one armed with a rifle, while his opponent had only a spear and a sword, and, if only he could take sure aim, the result was absolutely certain." But this is surely an overstatement. The "if" too, is important. And there was another factor. How could a stone penetrate such strong armor as Goliath wore? It may not have been bulletproof but it certainly was stone proof.

It seems, however, that there was one vulnerable spot in that armor, namely, in the shield which covered face and head. And David, equipped by long practice and guided by the Spirit of God which was upon him, aimed at that spot and unerringly found it.

Thus can the Lord guide all His Spirit-filled servants who have faithfully prepared themselves to accomplish their mission for God and to overcome all satanic opposition.

Can you name some modern Goliaths which threaten the Church of the living God today?

REVIEW QUESTIONS

1. What was the purpose of Goliath's daily trek to the valley to shout at Israel?

2. How did the weapons of the two champions compare?

3. Had the Philistine gods and Jehovah had encounters before? Explain.

4. How extensive a victory did David foresee? Did God do what David expected?

5. What application for life in today's world do you draw from this lesson?

GOLDEN TEXT HOMILY

"THE LORD SAVETH NOT WITH SWORD AND SPEAR: FOR THE BATTLE IS THE LORD'S" (1 Samuel 17:47).

Compare the characteristics of David to the giant Goliath. David, an average-size teenage boy; Goliath, a giant over nine feet tall. David, inexperienced in battle, a shepherd boy not old enough to be in the army of Israel; Goliath, an experienced Philistine warrior. David, with his staff and sling and five smooth stones; Goliath, with his armor, sword, spear, and shield. In the natural world, what a mismatch!

David looked at the circumstances he faced, made his own comparison and reached the conclusion that "the battle is the Lord's." He realized that in himself he was no match for Goliath. David recognized his power would have to come from the Lord, a fact which was later revealed unto Zerubbabel, "Not by might, nor by power, but by my spirit, saith the Lord of hosts" (Zechariah 4:6). It's not by any army, not by superior weapons, or the size of the enemy; victory comes through the Lord.

As we face the giants of our day—alcoholism, drug addiction, homosexuality, communism, cults, the occult, and so forth—we are as David in comparison to the giant. Let us be reminded that the battle is not ours, but the Lord's. Take courage, for, "Ye are of God, little children, and have overcome them: because greater is he that is in you, than he that is in the world" (1 John 4:4).—**Dennis Cox, Vice-President of Spiritual Affairs, Southwestern College, Oklahoma City, Oklahoma**

SENTENCE SERMONS

THEY CONQUER WHO believe they can. He has not learned the lesson of life who does not each day surmount a fear.
—**Ralph Waldo Emerson**

GREAT MINDS HAVE purpose; others have wishes. Little minds are tamed and subdued by misfortune, but great minds rise above them.
—**Washington Irving**

HE WHO HAS resolved to conquer or die is seldom conquered.
—**Anonymous**

NO MAN CAN choose what coming hours may bring
To him of need, of joy, of suffering,
But what his soul shall bring into each hour
To meet its challenge—that is in his power.
—**Anonymous**

EVANGELISTIC APPLICATION

TRUST IN GOD BRINGS VICTORY OVER SATAN AND SIN.

The Lord Jesus Christ is "great David's greater Son" who has conquered the satanic Goliath who has dominated and enslaved the human race.

When Jesus met this Goliath in the wilderness temptation He overcame him by the smooth stones of the Word of God. When He met him in the bloody battle on Calvary's hill He dealt him a blow from which he can never recover. Jesus himself said, "Now [**at the Cross**] shall the prince of this world be cast out" (John 12:31). He died that "he might destroy (or render powerless) him that had the power of death, that is, the devil" (Hebrews 2:14). Ultimately, Jesus will bind Satan in the abyss (Revelation 20:3), then cast him into the lake of fire (Revelation 20:10).

Part of the glorious gospel of God is that our David has conquered the satanic Goliath. The hosts of darkness have been vanquished and men and women can be loosed from the fear of him and domination by him. As "the men of Israel and of Judah arose, and shouted, and pursued the Philistines" (1 Samuel 17:52), so ought the Church to be shouting the victory and living in the victory which Christ has achieved for us. We ought not to be running from a victorious devil but resisting a defeated foe.

ILLUMINATING THE LESSON

After a bloody battle in World War I, won at terrific cost of life, a General walked over the field of carnage. The field was widely bestrewn with American dead. It was observed, however, that the heroic dead fell with their faces toward the enemy! What a lesson for God's children in this hour of cowardly compromise of the eternal verities of God's Word, whelming apostasy, and blatant denials of the only Lord God! May each soldier of the Cross face forward, marching triumphantly 'neath the all-conquering banner of the Captain, or "File-Leader" of our salvation! When we fall in death, should the Lord delay His coming, may our faces, with flint-like steadfastness, be toward the enemy!

—From **Knight's Masterbook of New Illustrations,** by Walter B. Knight. Used by permission.

We are told that just before the first battle of the Marne in the first World War, Marshal Foch, the great French General, reported: "My centre is giving; my left wing is retreating; the situation is excellent; I am attacking!" This was not mere military bombast, for the Marshal realized that apparent defeat could be turned into victory by acting with resolution and alacrity at the very moment when the enemy seemed to be triumphant.—**Harry A. Ironside**

DAILY DEVOTIONAL GUIDE

M. Defying God. 1 Samuel 17:1-11
T. Investigating the Crisis. 1 Samuel 17:19-30
W. Winning Victories. 1 Samuel 17:50-58
T. The Lord's Anointed. Psalm 2:1-12
F. The Christian's Warfare. Ephesians 6:10-18
S. The Final Victory. Revelation 19:11-21

April 12, 1981

Conquering Jealousy

Bible Background: 1 Samuel 18:1-30; 19:8-24

Time: Probably around 1016 B.C.

Place: Gibeah, about five miles north of Jerusalem

Supplemental References: Genesis 37:8-27; Judges 8:1-3; Matthew 20:1-15; Luke 15:25-32

Golden Text: "Charity suffereth long, and is kind; charity envieth not; charity vaunteth not itself, is not puffed up" (1 Corinthians 13:4).

Central Truth: If the attitude of jealousy is not conquered, it will lead to evil actions.

Evangelistic Emphasis: The new life which comes with salvation makes victory over jealousy possible.

PRINTED TEXT

1 Samuel 18:5. And David went out whithersoever Saul sent him, and behaved himself wisely: and Saul set him over the men of war, and he was accepted in the sight of all the people, and also in the sight of Saul's servants.

6. And it came to pass as they came, when David was returned from the slaughter of the Philistine, that the women came out of all cities of Israel, singing and dancing, to meet king Saul, with tabrets, with joy, and with instruments of musick.

7. And the women answered one another as they played, and said, Saul hath slain his thousands, and David his ten thousands.

8. And Saul was very wroth, and the saying displeased him; and he said, They have ascribed unto David ten thousands, and to me they have ascribed but thousands: and what can he have more but the kingdom?

9. And Saul eyed David from that day and forward.

10. And it came to pass on the morrow, that the evil spirit from God came upon Saul, and he prophesied in the midst of the house: and David played with his hand, as at other times: and there was a javelin in Saul's hand.

11. And Saul cast the javelin; for he said, I will smite David even to the wall with it. And David avoided out of his presence twice.

12. And Saul was afraid of David, because the Lord was with him, and was departed from Saul.

13. Therefore Saul removed him from him, and made him his captain over a thousand; and he went out and came in before the people.

14. And David behaved himself wisely in all his ways; and the Lord was with him.

28. And Saul saw and knew that the Lord was with David, and that Michal Saul's daughter loved him.

29. And Saul was yet the more afraid of David; and Saul became David's enemy continually.

30. Then the princes of the Philistines went forth: and it came to pass, after they went forth, that David behaved himself more wisely than all the servants of Saul; so that his name was much set by.

DICTIONARY

behaved . . . wisely—1 Samuel 18:5—The Hebrew verb here also indicates "had good success." David's general conduct contributed to his progress.

tabrets—1 Samuel 18:6—Tambourines. Small, shallow drums made from a wooden hoop, with animals skins stretched over one end. Jingling metal pieces are attached to the frame. The instrument is shaken or struck with the hand when played.

answered one another—1 Samuel 18:7—The women sang to one another antiphonally.

prophesied—1 Samuel 18:10—In this verse the term is used to describe Saul's deception. By pretending to prophesy he lured David close to him and tried to kill him, perhaps intending to blame the act on the Lord.

javelin—1 Samuel 18:10—A spear to be thrown by hand. One of the standard military weapons of that time. It appears that Saul's javelin served as a scepter and was a symbol of royalty (22:6).

LESSON OUTLINE

I. CAUSES OF JEALOUSY
   A. The Covenant With Jonathan
   B. The Praises of the People

II. EFFECTS OF JEALOUSY
   A. Homicidal Impulses
   B. Spiteful Actions
   C. Cunning Plots
   D. Persistence in Murder

III. ANTIDOTE FOR JEALOUSY
   A. Jonathan's Dilemma
   B. Jonathan's Solution

LESSON EXPOSITION

INTRODUCTION

Keil and Delitzsch say, "David's victory over Goliath was a turning point in his life which opened the way to the throne" **(A Commentary on the Old Testament, The Books of Samuel).** They also describe that event as "David's first step on the way to the throne to which Jehovah had resolved to raise him." No doubt this is the reason why the contest with Goliath is given so much space and is recounted with so much detail.

As a result of David's victory, Saul decided to bring the young man to his court and to give him a post in the army. The last few verses of chapter 17 have occasioned some perplexity, for they represent Saul as not being acquainted with David, whereas chapter 16 describes David as having been employed as a personal musician to Saul himself (1 Samuel 16:14-23). Various explanations have been offered. Perhaps the most satisfying is that Saul's mental sickness affected his memory. It is thought that David would only be called to the king during his spasms of derangement, and possibly in a darkened or heavily shaded room. Thus his memory of David was not likely to be clear. Others have suggested that his question to Abner related merely to David's lineage; he had simply forgotten who David's father was.

In contrast to the earlier period, when "David went back and forth from Saul" (1 Samuel 17:15, **New International Version),** he now began to reside at Saul's court (18:2). Here there came to him two greatly contrasted experiences: the great love of the crown prince Jonathan, and the murderous hatred of King Saul.

I. CAUSES OF JEALOUSY (1 Samuel 18:1-9)

A. The Covenant With Jonathan (vv. 1-4)

On David's return from his conquest, carrying the head of Goliath, Saul engaged him in conversation (1 Samuel 17:57, 58). Nothing is recorded of this conversation apart from a bare question and answer about David's parentage, but surely much more was said. Present at the conversation was Saul's son, Jonathan, whose heart was drawn out toward David in brotherly love. Spence comments on the word "knit" in 18:1: "The Hebrew is better rendered 'bound up.' This is a strong term and is used in Genesis 44:30 for Jacob's love for Benjamin, 'seeing that his life is bound up in the lad's life' " **(Ellicott's Bible Commentary, Vol. 2).** According to Keil and Delitzsch **knit** literally means "chained itself." Thus began a momentous friendship, one of the most beautiful and enduring narrated in the Bible.

The two men "made a covenant" (see also 1 Samuel 20:16; 23:18). This implies a pledge of loyalty to each other, and in all likelihood involved a religious ceremony. The Lord was brought into their covenant. As a seal of it Jonathan gave his clothes and his armor to David. Nothing is said of David's gifts to Jonathan. As Mauchline says, "David had no such possessions to give; he could but give himself in true friendship" **(New Century Bible, 1 and 2 Samuel).** Keil and Delitzsch, referring to Greek and Celtic traditions, say "this seems to have been a common custom in very ancient times."

When we compare the exploits of Jonathan recorded in chapters 13 and 14 with the exploits of David, it is not hard to see that these men were attracted to each other by the courage and heroism which was common to both. However, there was something more profound. Says Blaikie, "Besides all else about David that was attractive to Jonathan, as it was to everyone else, there was that strongest of all bonds, the bond of a common, all-prevailing faith, faith in the covenant God of Israel, that had now shown itself in David in overwhelming strength, as it had shown itself in Jonathan sometime before at Michmash" **(The Expositor's Bible, The First Book of Samuel).**

Sanders writes, "The love of Jonathan for David marks one of the ideal friendships of history, highlighted as it was against the dark background of Saul's jealousy and perfidy. Jonathan's loyalty and self-abnegation was an immense strength to David during his years of rejection" **(Men from God's School).** Yet this very fact was probably one of the causes of Saul's insane jealousy. He began to imagine that Jonathan was more loyal to David than to himself (see 1 Samuel 20:30, 31).

Jonathan was such an excellent character, with great faith in the Lord, that he would have made an excellent king. Why did God not permit this, instead of selecting David?

B. The Praises of the People (vv. 5-9)

5. And David went out whithersoever Saul sent him, and behaved himself wisely: and Saul set him over the men of war, and he was accepted in the sight of all the people, and also in the sight of Saul's servants.

It is evident that the battle which followed the conquest of Goliath did not end hostilities between the rival powers. "All the days of Saul there was bitter war with the Philistines" (1 Samuel 14:52, **New International Version).** David was now employed as an officer in the continuing war. The phrase, "behaved himself wisely," means that David was successful. "Whatever Saul sent him to do, David did it so successfully that Saul gave him a high rank in the army" **(New International Version).** Moreover, his fame and popularity grew rapidly.

6. And it came to pass as they came, when David was returned from the slaughter of the Philistine, that the women came out of all cities of Israel, singing and dancing, to meet king Saul, with tabrets, with joy, and with instruments of musick.

7. And the woman answered one another as they played, and said, Saul hath slain his thousands, and David his ten thousands.

8. And Saul was very wroth, and the saying displeased him; and he said, They have ascribed unto David ten thousands, and to me they have ascribed but thousands: and what can he have more but the kingdom?

Choral dancing was common in the ancient world, as it still is, at times of festivity or during triumphal occasions. The Hebrews were no exception. It was usual for them to greet Saul's return from his victories with dancing, singing, and music. Now, they included David in their praises, and in such a way as to arouse the king's jealousy. Some scholars say that there was no unfavorable contrast in the statement, "Saul hath slain his thousands, and David his ten thousands." It was merely a form of Hebrew poetry known as **parallelism,** and the expressions **thousands** and **tens of thousands** meant only "a large number." However, though they were only speaking poetically, Saul took it literally.

9. And Saul eyed David from that day and forward.

The New International Version renders this, "From that time on Saul kept a jealous eye on David." Though he could not have known of David's private anointing as king by Samuel, he must have remembered the prediction concerning "a neighbour of thine" (1 Samuel 15:28). His sick mind fed on the imagined slight of the dancing girls.

Can you think of other biblical examples of jealousy?

II. EFFECTS OF JEALOUSY (1 Samuel 18:10-30; 19:8-10)

A. Homicidal Impulses (18:10-12)

10. And it came to pass on the morrow, that the evil spirit from God came upon Saul, and he prophesied in the midst of the house: and David played with his hand, as at other times: and there was a javelin in Saul's hand.
11. And Saul cast the javelin; for he said, I will smite David even to the wall with it. And David avoided out of his presence twice.
12. And Saul was afraid of David, because the Lord was with him, and was departed from Saul.

We have previously noted that from the time of David's private anointing and charismatic enduement "the Spirit of the Lord departed from Saul, and an evil spirit from the Lord troubled him" (1 Samuel 16:14). This means, as Keil and Delitzsch say, that "Jehovah had sent the evil spirit upon Saul as a punishment." The marks of the evil spirit's influence were of two main kinds: (a) deep depression or melancholia, and (b) fits of homicidal frenzy.

Saul's condition is well known in the medical world. R. K. Harrison discusses it in his **Introduction to the Old Testament**. He describes it as a form of paranoid schizophrenia. It is marked by delusions of grandeur, feelings of persecution, extreme moodiness, and impulses to violence.

Though the Bible depicts Saul's condition as caused by an evil spirit, we must not jump to the illogical conclusion that all such sicknesses have a similar cause. **Demons** are only one of several causes of any kind of ill health, physical or mental, and it is irresponsible to name demons as the common cause. Furthermore, it is not said that Saul was **possessed** by the evil spirit, but "troubled" by it. There are different degrees of demon influence namely, **oppression, obsession,** and **possession.** Saul was probably obsessed rather than possessed, at this stage at any rate.

Previously, the effect of the evil spirit's influence was apparently deep depression which could be mitigated by appropriate music (see 1 Samuel 16:14-23).

First, "he prophesied" (v. 10). The rendering of the **New English Bible**—"he fell into a frenzy"—is to be preferred here. Also the **Living Bible** has "he began to rave like a madman." Keil and Delitzsch say, "The Hebrew word does not mean to prophesy in this instance, but **to rave."** It was not "prophecy" in the true divine sense. "There was something akin to the powerful emotions which agitated the true prophet: only it was not a true influence, but one springing from violent passions" **(Spence, Ellicott Bible Commentary, Vol. 2).**

Second, "Saul cast the javelin" at David, intending to kill him. He did this twice, but David was able to elude the throws. Blaiklock thinks that "the attempt was unsuccessful, for in David Saul was dealing with a superbly trained athlete" **(Bible Characters, Elkanah to David).** The Bible simply says "the Lord was with him" (v. 12).

The homicidal impulse clearly shows that the "prophesying" was evil. Let no one imagine that the prophesying was divine while the homicidal impulse was satanic. Both were evil. And let us, too, note that it was when Saul had yielded to the sin of jealousy that the evil spirit gained greater control of him. This underscores the close connection between character and the supernatural. A holy character fits one to be a channel of the Holy Spirit. An unholy character fits one to become a channel for evil spirits.

Some people have claimed that "carnal" people may possess and use the gifts of the Holy Spirit. In the light of Saul evaluate this.

B. Spiteful Actions (vv. 13-16)

13. Therefore Saul removed him from him, and made him his captain over a thousand; and he went out and came in before the people.
14. And David behaved himself wisely in all his ways; and the Lord was with him.

Some explain the words, "made him his captain over a thousand," as a promotion. Sometimes monarchs and others have removed rivals from their presence by this device. Such a trick tends to hide the real motivation from others. However, Mauchline claims that the biblical expression "can be interpreted as demotion in terms of his former military appointments as defined in 18:5." This is expressed by the **Living Bible:** "Saul banned him from his presence and demoted him to the rank of captain." In any case Saul was expressing his spite against David.

Nevertheless, like Joseph in the Genesis story, David prospered in the new position because "the Lord was with him." And his popularity with the nation grew.

C. Cunning Plots (vv. 17-30)

Frustrated in his direct attempts at murder, but provoked by David's increasing popularity, Saul sensed that his rival was under special divine protection. Instead of submitting to this, however, he became devilishly cunning in his methods.

First, he promised David the hand of his older daughter, Merab, if David would continue the campaigns against the Philistines. Note the touch of hypocrisy (v. 17). He called these "the Lord's battles." Yet the true motivation was very different. He hoped that David would get himself killed. When this failed he spitefully robbed David of the prize by marrying Merab to Adriel (v. 19).

Saul tried the trick a second time, promising Michal, who was said to have affection for David, to him if he brought evidence that he had killed a hundred Philistines. Again the motivation was murder (v. 25). Again David was preserved. This time the promise was honored. The outcome was that Saul's fear of David was deepened because he was signally preserved by the Lord.

Read Matthew 5:21, 22. In Saul we have seen two ways in which hatred may express itself. Can you think of others?

D. Persistence in Murder (19:8-10)

8. And there was war again: and David went out, and fought with the Philistines, and slew them with a great slaughter; and they fled from him.

9. And the evil spirit from the Lord was upon Saul, as he sat in his house with his javelin in his hand: and David played with his hand.

10. And Saul sought to smite David even to the wall with the javelin; but he slipped away out of Saul's presence, and he smote the javelin into the wall: and David fled, and escaped that night.

These three verses are but an introduction to a prolonged murder hunt by Saul. The continuing story now goes on for several chapters. However, our Bible Background for this lesson goes no further than the end of chapter 19. The special fact to notice is that Saul's jealous spirit which at first had shown itself in only spasmodic outbreaks of violence, and then in occasional plots of murder, eventually became a fixed and permanent obsession. The one great goal of Saul's life became the elimination of David. Saul began to consume all his energies and to organize his army in a determined, malignant crusade to kill David.

On one occasion, he sent assassins to David's home, and only the astuteness of Michal his wife saved him (vv. 11-18).

Incidentally, note that Michal lied twice over this matter. Is lying, then, justifiable?

On another occasion Saul sent his servants to "the company of the prophets" (probably a school or college at Ramah where Samuel trained the future prophetic leaders of the nation) where David had taken refuge in order that he might capture him. When they failed, Saul went himself (vv. 18-24).

This incident raises an intriguing question. Saul's servants (actually three successive teams) entered the school of the prophets during a religious service and as the prophets were prophesying, that is, worshiping God in ecstasy. We are astonished to find that one after another the three squads of armed men, and then the murderous king himself, began to "prophesy" with them. What does this mean, and how are we to account for it?

The commentators and expositors wrestle with this passage. Some simply conclude that Saul, if not his servants, was seized with the same mad frenzy as noted in 18:10. Pink writes it off as "a kind of trance" caused by God to allow David time to escape. Most, however, lean to the view that it was a genuine operation of the Holy Spirit sent to Saul as a final gracious effort to move him to repentance and renewal. Spence, for example, says, "Is it not better to explain the incident by understanding that once more the pitiful Spirit pleaded with the man whom the Lord had chosen to be His anointed? But alas! when the moment of strange excitement was over, the blessed pleading was forgotten. Is not this a matter of everyday experience?" One thing we must not do, and that is to use this incident in proof of the false idea that a person may be deliberately sinful or even demon possessed, and at the same time filled with the Holy Spirit.

Do you think that there is any relation between Saul's experience and such New Testament passages as Matthew 7:21-23 and 1 Corinthians 13:1-3?

III. ANTIDOTE FOR JEALOUSY (1 Samuel 19:1-7)

A. Jonathan's Dilemma (v. 1)

1. It should be noted that the portion of Scripture being discussed here chronologically precedes 1 Samuel 18:13-16, which was discussed earlier. 2. It begins by describing a further stage in Saul's murderous jealousy. Up to this point he had made two violent, personal, and probably unpremeditated assaults on David's life, followed by the vindictive demotion and two cunning plots to have him killed on the battlefront by enemy action. Now he comes out boldly with a plan to employ his own son Jonathan, as well as his servants, in the murder (v. 1).

B. Jonathan's Solution (vv. 2-7)

With this as the background, let us put the spotlight on verse 2, "But Jonathan Saul's son delighted much in David." This is one of the great **buts** of the Bible! Thus Jonathan found himself on the horns of a dilemma. His natural affection and filial loyalty to his father, coupled with his duty to the head of state, were in collision with his love for David and his solemn religious covenant with him.

It is wonderful and challenging to see how his love found a way to transcend the terrible difficulty. Putting his life in his hands, he determined to try to be a peacemaker. Did Jesus have Jonathan in mind when He said, "Blessed are the peacemakers" (Matthew 5:9)? Going to his father he sang David's praises and especially applauded David's loyalty both to Saul and the nation (vv. 4, 5).

What an example for us all to follow: Far too often when someone is maligned or denigrated before others, the others go along with it and thus feed the flames of hatred. By speaking well of David to his jealous father, Jonathan sought to assuage the hatred and provide an antidote to the poison in his soul.

For a time the remedy availed (vv. 6, 7). The crisis was averted. Unfortunately it was not to be a permanent cure. Deliverance from the deep soul-sickness of Saul needed a much more radical cure than even Jonathan's efforts could supply.

What is the real cure for such a sickness as Saul's?

REVIEW QUESTIONS

1. How did Saul reward David when he returned from the slaughter of the Philistine?
2. How did the women react to the return of the conquerors?
3. What first provoked Saul's jealousy toward David?
4. Did Saul have any real reason to be suspicious of David's conduct? Explain.
5. How did David conduct himself after the attempted assassination?

GOLDEN TEXT HOMILY

"CHARITY SUFFERETH LONG, AND IS KIND; CHARITY ENVIETH NOT; CHARITY VAUNTETH NOT ITSELF, IS NOT PUFFED UP" (1 Corinthians 13:4).

There is no possibility of mixing with human society without encountering many occasions of irritation. Indeed, human nature is such that conflicts of disposition and of habits will occur. It is so in the family, in civil life, and even in the Church. Hence impatience and irritability are among the most common of infirmities. And there is no more sure sign of a disciplined and morally cultured mind than a habit of forbearance, tolerance, and patience. But Christianity supplies a motive and power of long-suffering which can act in the case of persons of every variety of temperament and of every position of life. "Love suffereth long." "Love is kind."

Love is opposed to envy and jealousy. These are vices which arise from discontent with one's own condition as compared with that of others, and are justly deemed among the meanest and basest of which man is capable. But once again, Christianity proves its power of spiritual transformation by suppressing these evil passions from the heart, and by teaching and enabling men to rejoice in their neighbors' prosperity.

Love also destroys boastfulness. It "vaunteth not itself." With some personalities, there is a tendency toward display of abilities. These abilities may be real or a figment of the imagination; but a display of them is out of place in a Christian's life. Love delights not in the display of real power or the assumption of what does not exist. How can it? When love seeks the good of others, how can it seek their admiration?

Love is "not puffed up." The expression is sometimes rendered "does not swell and swagger," "is not inflated with vanity." The explanation of this is clear. The pretentious and arrogant man has a mind full of himself, of thoughts of himself, of thoughts of his own greatness and importance. Now love is the outflowing of the heart's affection in kindliness and benevolence towards others. He who is always thinking of the welfare of his fellow-man has no time and no inclination for thoughts of self-exaltation. Christianity introduces into human society a wholesome, purifying and sweetening influence. It can do no other, if it follows the footsteps of Jesus Christ.—**Adapted from "Pulpit Commentary" (Vol. 19, Corinthians)**

SENTENCE SERMONS

SUSPICION AND JEALOUSY never did help any man in any situation.
—**Abraham Lincoln**

JEALOUSY ALWAYS FINDS a target at which to shoot and a pretense upon which to fire.
—**"Notes and Quotes"**

JEALOUSY IS LIKE a spider which makes its home anywhere on seemingly nothing.
—**Selected**

THOSE WHO ARE green with envy often become red with anger.
—**"Notes and Quotes"**

EVANGELISTIC APPLICATION

THE NEW LIFE WHICH COMES WITH SALVATION MAKES VICTORY OVER JEALOUSY POSSIBLE.

One of the astounding aspects of the tragic story of Saul is the manner in which the Lord sought to reach the heart of the rebellious king in order to change his attitude—the sinful attitude which was the cause of his rejection and judgment.

The most striking was the powerful moving upon him, without any cooperation on his part, of the Holy Spirit in an uncontrollable ecstasy. Another was the strong appeal of Jonathan when he pleaded for the life of David. Yet another was the amazing grace shown to him by David on two occasions when David could so easily have killed him.

Saul seems to have been affected by these divine appeals, but not deeply and permanently. He hardened his heart in rebellion and jealousy and murder, until he was beyond hope and past redemption.

The Lord does not easily give the sinner or the backslider over to final judgment. Instead, God strives with him and appeals to him in many ways through providential happenings, through manifestations of grace, and, not least, through the direct working of the Holy Spirit on the mind, emotions, and conscience . . . often on special occasions such as a funeral, a wedding, an anniversary, or a revival. Sometimes, the Lord will make His presence known by the healing of the sinner's own body in a time of sickness.

Jesus takes every opportunity to stand outside the heart's door and knock. The road to hell is reached through many refusals and many hardenings of the heart.

ILLUMINATING THE LESSON

It is reported that a great wrestler was so envious of Theagenes, the prince of wrestlers, that he could not be consoled in any way; and after Theagenes died and a statue was lifted to him in a public place, his envious antagonist went out every night and wrestled with the statue, until one night he threw it, and it fell on him and crushed him to death. So jealousy is not only absurd, but it is killing to the body, and it is killing to the soul.—**Dewight Talmage**

DAILY DEVOTIONAL GUIDE

M. Jealousy Over Another's Blessing. Genesis 4:1-10

T. Jealousy in the Home. Genesis 37:1-11

W. Jealousy Among Believers. Matthew 20:20-28

T. Jealousy Over Another's Honor. Luke 15:25-32

F. Christian Relationships. Colossians 3:12-17

S. Love One Another. 1 John 3:11-24

April 19, 1981

Alive Forever

(Easter)

Bible Background: Matthew 28:1-15; Mark 16:1-20; Luke 24:1-53; John 20:1-23
Time: A.D. 30
Place: A garden near Calvary, possibly in the city of Jerusalem
Supplemental References: Psalms 16:1-11; 22:22-31
Golden Text: "I am he that liveth, and was dead; and, behold, I am alive for evermore" (Revelation 1:18).
Central Truth: The crucified Lord has risen and is alive forever.
Evangelistic Emphasis: Christians should take every opportunity to present the message that the risen Christ is the Savior.

PRINTED TEXT

Mark 16:1. And when the sabbath was past, Mary Magdalene, and Mary the mother of James, and Salome, had bought sweet spices, that they might come and anoint him.

2. And very early in the morning the first day of the week, they came unto the sepulchre at the rising of the sun.

3. And they said among themselves, Who shall roll us away the stone from the door of the sepulchre?

4. And when they looked, they saw that the stone was rolled away: for it was very great.

5. And entering into the sepulchre, they saw a young man sitting on the right side, clothed in a long white garment; and they were affrighted.

6. And he saith unto them, Be not affrighted: Ye seek Jesus of Nazareth, which was crucified: he is risen; he is not here: behold the place where they laid him.

7. But go your way, tell his disciples and Peter that he goeth before you into Galilee: there shall ye see him, as he said unto you.

8. And they went out quickly, and fled from the sepulchre; for they trembled and were amazed: neither said they any thing to any man; for they were afraid.

9. Now when Jesus was risen early the first day of the week, he appeared first to Mary Magdalene, out of whom he had cast seven devils.

10. And she went and told them that had been with him, as they mourned and wept.

11. And they, when they had heard that he was alive, and had been seen of her, believed not.

12. After that he appeared in another form unto two of them, as they walked, and went into the country.

13. And they went and told it unto the residue: neither believed they them.

14. Afterward he appeared unto the eleven as they sat at meat, and upbraided them with their unbelief and hardness of heart, because they believed not them which had seen him after he was risen.

15. And he said unto them, Go ye into all the world, and preach the gospel to every creature.

16. He that believeth and is baptized shall be saved; but he that believeth not shall be damned.

April 19, 1981

DICTIONARY

Mary Magdalene (MAG-duh-leen)—Mark 16:1—The Greek has "Mary **the** Magdalene," indicating that she was from the town of Magdala. Jesus healed her of demon possession.

Mary the mother of James—Mark 16:1—The mother of James the Less. Besides her appearance in today's lesson, she with Mary Magdalene and Salome witnessed the crucifixion (Mark 15:40) and the burial (Mark 15:47). Nothing more is known of her.

sat at meat—Mark 16:14—The Greek has "as they reclined," indicating that at this time people did not sit at a table as we do today, but rather "reclined" more horizontally, perhaps raising themselves on their elbows.

LESSON OUTLINE

I. THE LORD IS ALIVE!
  A. A Womanly Ministry
  B. An Angelic Announcement
II. PERSONAL FAITH NECESSARY
  A. The Witness of the Women
  B. The Witness of Mary Magdalene
  C. The Witness of the Emmaus Disciples
  D. The Witness of Jesus Himself
III. THE BELIEVERS COMMISSIONED
  A. Assignment
  B. Fulfillment

LESSON EXPOSITION

INTRODUCTION

"One thing is certain—if Jesus had not risen from the dead we would never have heard of Him. The attitude of the women [on Easter morning] was that they had come to pay the last tribute to a dead body. The attitude of the disciples was that everything had finished in tragedy. By far the best proof of the Resurrection is the existence of the Christian Church. Nothing else could have changed sad and despairing men and women into people radiant with joy and flaming with courage. The Resurrection is the central fact of the whole Christian faith" (W. Barclay, **Daily Study Bible, Mark**).

"Had there been no Resurrection, what then? There had been no Christian Church, no Christian propaganda, no Christian influence. Everything for which the lonely Nazarene stood lay murdered, dead, in the tomb when they rolled against it a great stone. His disciples had been scattered like chaff before the wind, and the whole movement stamped out. How did it live again? It lived again, and it lives, because He lived again, and lives!" (G. C. Morgan, **The Four Gospels, Mark**).

"Suppose that Jesus, having died on the Cross, had stayed dead. Suppose that, like Socrates or Confucius, He was now no more than a beautiful memory. Would it matter? We should still have His example and teaching; would not they be enough?

"Enough for what? Not for Christianity. Had Jesus not risen, but stayed dead, the bottom would drop out of Christianity" (J. I. Packer, **I Want to Be a Christian**).

"The first fact in the history of Christendom is a number of people who say they have seen the Resurrection. If they had died without making anyone else believe this 'gospel,' no Gospels would ever have been written" (C. S. Lewis, **Miracles**).

I. THE LORD IS ALIVE! (Mark 16:1-7)

A. A Womanly Ministry (vv. 1-3)

1. And when the sabbath was past, Mary Magdalene, and Mary the mother of James, and Salome, had bought sweet spices, that they might come and anoint him.

2. And very early in the morning the first day of the week, they came unto the sepulchre at the rising of the sun.

All four Gospels begin the account of the Resurrection with the coming of the women to the tomb, though they do not agree as to the number. Matthew names two; Mark, three; Luke merely says "the women"; and John gives only Mary Magdalene. However, these are not contradictions. The accounts complement each other. Calvin has a useful comment on this matter: "We know that it is customary with the sacred writers, when speaking of a great number, to name but a few of them. It may also be conjectured with great probability that Mary Magdalene whether she was sent before or ran forward of her own accord, arrived at the grave before the rest of the women" **(The Four Gospels).**

The very fact that the visit of these women is included and given such importance bears strong witness to the truth of the resurrection narrative, for in ancient Judaism a woman was commonly despised, and her testimony disregarded. It also portrays the new attitude toward womanhood introduced by Jesus.

These women had continuously ministered to Jesus for many months (see Luke 8:1-3; 23:55, 56). They had followed Joseph and Nicodemus to Christ's burial place and had bought spices and ointments for the body, late on Friday, with the intention of returning to the tomb. However, they could not do so until the Sabbath was over, namely after sunset on Saturday. Mary Magdalene seems to have been first at the tomb, "when it was yet dark" (John 20:1), and she was joined there by at least two other women as soon as the sun had risen. Their purpose was to place aromatic spices and oils on the body of Jesus. R. K. Harrison says, "While these did not significantly inhibit putrefaction, they served as deodorants and disinfectants" **(New Bible Dictionary,** "Spices"). W. L. Lane writes, "The preparations for returning to the tomb in performance of an act of piety show that the women had no expectation of immediate resurrection of Jesus. Since in the climate of Jerusalem deterioration would occur rapidly, the visit of the women with the intention of ministering to the corpse after two nights and a day must be viewed as an expression of intense devotion" **(New International Commentary, Mark).**

Though the women acted in ignorance of the scriptural prophecies of the Messiah's resurrection, as well as Christ's own predictions, they nevertheless acted in profound love for their Lord. Theirs was a love which enabled them to transcend their fear and weakness. How superior they were to the chosen apostles who, though taught by Christ himself, were weak in both faith and love at this dark hour.

3. And they said among themselves, Who shall roll us away the stone from the door of the sepulchre?

The women had witnessed the rolling of the great stone across the door of the tomb (Mark 15:46), but seem to have been ignorant of the sealing of the tomb and of the guard which had been set by Pilate's orders (Matthew 27:62-66). Their only concern was how they would be able to move the great stone so that they could have access to the body of Jesus.

In the women who visited the tomb of Jesus is portrayed a phenomenon which is quite common in the Church, both among women and men, namely, the combination of intense devotion and ignorance or imperfect understanding. Is this really acceptable to God?

B. An Angelic Announcement (vv. 4-7)

4. And when they looked, they saw that the stone was rolled away: for it was very great.

Even as the women were asking themselves the question, with downcast eyes, "Who shall roll away the stone for us?", **they looked up** (literal rendering) and discovered that their problem was already solved—"the stone was rolled away." How often it is like this in Christian experience. We may be preoccupied and overwhelmed by problems which do not exist except in our own minds. When we look up we may find that the problem has already been solved by the hand of God.

5. And entering into the sepulchre, they saw a young man sitting on the right side, clothed in a long white garment; and they were affrighted.

Lane writes, "Inside the large opening in the facade of the tomb was an antechamber at the back of which a rectangular doorway about two feet high led inside. Small low doorways between the antechamber and the burial chamber were standard features of Jewish tombs in this period. The inner chamber where the body had been laid was perhaps six or seven feet square, and about the same height." Inside the burial chamber the women saw "a young man sitting on the right side." What Mark calls "a young man," Matthew calls an "angel" (Matthew 28:2). There is no contradiction. As Alford says, "In Mark he is described **as he appeared** (that is, as he appeared to the women), and we are left to infer what he was" **(Greek Testament, Vol. 1).** The women's reaction was perfectly natural. The word rendered "affrighted" in the **King James Version** is given various renderings in the modern versions: "dumbfounded" **(New English Bible),** "astonished" **(Phillips),** "startled" **(Living Bible),** "alarmed" **(New International Version).**

6. And he saith unto them, Be not affrighted: Ye seek Jesus of Nazareth, which

was crucified: he is risen; he is not here: behold the place where they laid him.

The resurrection of Christ was not witnessed by any human being. Neither was the risen Lord himself the first to communicate the news. It was announced by the angel who had rolled the stone away (Matthew 28: 2-7).

There are two features of this announcement: (a) "He is risen." (b) "He is not here: behold the place where they laid him." These aspects are integrally linked. The one fact that "He is risen" is proved by the other fact that the tomb was empty; the body of Jesus had gone. Again, the fact that the tomb was empty is explained by the fact that Jesus was risen. In John's account, a further fact is given: the voluminous graveclothes of Jesus were still lying in the tomb **undisturbed** (John 20:6, 7). Liberal thinkers endeavor to explain away the empty tomb and the missing body, and claim that these matters are of no importance to the truth of the Resurrection. However, we may be sure that the Roman and Jewish authorities would leave no stone unturned to trace the body and find the explanation of the empty tomb. If the tomb had not been empty and the body not there, would anyone have believed that Christ was risen?

7. But go your way, tell his disciples and Peter that he goeth before you into Galilee: there shall ye see him, as he said unto you.

Is it not wonderful that the chosen apostles were to receive the gospel of the Resurrection first of all from these women? But would the apostles listen? In order to convince them and excite their interest the angel added two details: (a) "And Peter." This seems to allude to the tragedy of Peter's betrayal (Mark 14:66-72). A special word for him would surely reach his heart. (b) "He goeth before you into Galilee: there shall ye see him, as he said unto you." This looks back to Mark 14:28. Such a statement would be a sure mark of authenticity to the apostles.

Can you think of any reasons why the news of Christ's resurrection was communicated, in the first place, by an angel and not by Christ himself?

II. PERSONAL FAITH NECESSARY (Mark 16: 8-14)

A. The Witness of the Women (v. 8)

8. And they went out quickly, and fled from the sepulchre; for they trembled and were amazed: neither said they any thing to any man; for they were afraid.

In order to get the full story of the reaction of the women to the angel's announcement, this one verse in Mark needs to be supplemented by the accounts in the other Gospels (see Matthew 28:8, 9; Luke 24:8-12; John 20: 1-10). At first sight these appear to contradict Mark. It is better, however, to view them as complementary. Moreover, there were no doubt many happenings on that morning which the Holy Spirit has not seen fit to preserve for us. If we had all the details we should have a perfect picture. What does seem clear is that the women got over their fear and shock, and "did run to bring his disciples word" (Matthew 28:8). John especially mentions Mary Magdalene **running** to Peter and to John (John 20:2), who **ran** to the tomb to see for themselves, followed by Mary Magdalene (John 20:3-11). Up to this point no one had seen the risen Lord. But plainly Peter and John believed the news about the empty tomb and John believed what the empty tomb implied.

B. The Witness of Mary Magdalene (vv. 9-11)

9. Now when Jesus was risen early the first day of the week, he appeared first to Mary Magdalene, out of whom he had cast seven devils.

10. And she went and told them that had been with him, as they mourned and wept.

11. And they, when they had heard that he was alive, and had been seen of her, believed not.

Mark's account merely summarizes the lengthy account of John (John 20:11-18). As women had been the first people to enter the empty tomb and to hear the news of the Resurrection, so a woman was the first to see the risen Lord. James S. Stewart beautifully describes it: "The greatest news that ever broke upon the world, the news which was to change the whole life of humanity and shake down thrones and revolutionize kingdoms, the news which still today girdles the earth with everlasting hope and sends a thrill through every Christian soul on Easter morning, was given first to one humble, obscure woman out of whom seven devils had gone, who had nothing to distinguish her but her forgiven heart, and no claim at all but her love" **(The Life and Teaching of Jesus Christ).**

John does not tell us how the disciples reacted to the story, but Mark does. She found them mourning and weeping. What a contrast to the women, especially to Mary Magdalene! But perhaps Peter and John were not with these mourners and weepers. Note that John says they "went away again unto their own home" (John 20:10). Mary's news should have been enough to stop their weeping at least, but they didn't believe her. Luke says that the news seemed as "idle tales" (Luke 24: 11), "a fairy tale" **(Living Bible).**

It is commonplace to represent the apostles as credulous easy-believers who were eager to swallow the story of the Resurrection. But, as H. B. Swete says, "So far was Mary of Magdala from creating the belief in the Lord's resurrection, that for hours, as it appeared, she alone believed; or if there were others who shared her conviction, they were not to be found among the apostles or the men of their company" **(The Appearances of Our Lord After His Passion).**

Why did Jesus appear first to a woman rather than to an apostle?

C. The Witness of the Emmaus Disciples (vv. 12, 13)

12. After that he appeared in another form unto two of them, as they walked, and went into the country.

13. And they went and told it unto the residue: neither believed they them.

This brief account is greatly expanded in Luke's Gospel (Luke 24:13-35). There is a problem, however, over the two accounts. Mark says that when the favored two reported their experience to "the residue" (or "the rest,") "neither believed they them," whereas Luke reports that "the eleven" were already claiming, "The Lord is risen indeed, and hath appeared to Simon" (Luke 24:34). There are various explanations. Perhaps "the residue" was a different company of disciples from "the eleven."

D. The Witness of Jesus Himself (v. 14)

14. Afterward he appeared unto the eleven as they sat at meat, and upbraided them with their unbelief and hardness of heart, because they believed not them which had seen him after he was risen.

According to the other three Gospels, the risen Lord made several appearances to "the eleven" (which is a technical term for the apostolic team), and it is not clear to which of these appearances Mark refers, or if he speaks of a different one. Alford thinks he merely summarizes the others in a single statement. He especially makes mention of the charge of unbelief which Christ brought. Barnes comments, "This is a most important circumstance in the history of our Lord's resurrection. Never were men more difficult to convince of anything than **they** were of that fact. And this shows, conclusively, that they had not conspired to impose on the world; that they had given up all for lost when He had died; that they did not expect His resurrection, and all this is the strongest proof that He truly rose" **(Notes on the Four Gospels).**

Liberal critics say that the Resurrection was a "myth" created by the faith of the early Christians. What evidence to challenge this opinion emerges from our study?

III. THE BELIEVERS COMMISSIONED (Mark 16:15-20)

A. Assignment (vv. 15-18).

15. And he said unto them, Go ye into all the world, and preach the gospel to every creature.

There is a gap of possibly many days between verses 14 and 15. All of the events of the first fourteen verses took place on Easter day in or near Jerusalem, whereas the Great Commission was given on a mountain in Galilee (Matthew 28:16).

Alford makes the comment, "By these words the missionary office is bound upon the Church through all ages, till every part of the earth shall have been evangelized" **(Greek Testament, Vol. 1).** Thus this command is as binding on the Church of today, and upon every believer of today, as upon those who heard it from the lips of Christ. **Are we obeying it?** Are we actively involved in some way in the Great Commission?

16. He that believeth and is baptized shall be saved; but he that believeth not shall be damned.

The language of this verse should be carefully noted. Baptism is included in the first clause but not in the second. This implies that faith in Christ should always (except in very exceptional circumstances, example: the dying thief) be followed by Baptism, but that final condemnation is for unbelief, not for lack of Baptism. As Wesley says, "Every one that believed was baptized. But whether baptized or unbaptized, he that believeth not shall perish everlastingly" **(Explanatory Notes Upon the New Testament).**

This preaching of the gospel, said Jesus, would be followed by miraculous signs, which are enumerated (vv. 17, 18). Most of these are illustrated in the Acts of the Apostles. But what is meant by "them that believe," literally "the believing ones"? The context surely means those who have believed the gospel and are saved (as v. 16), the whole company of those who believe, namely the Church, not necessarily each individual believer. It has never been true and is not true today that miracles have followed every believer. But it has always been true and is still true today that miracles have followed the collective company of believers. And in that we should rejoice. I may not work miracles, but the **Church** of which I am a part does!

Barnes comments, "Miracles were necessary for the establishment of religion in the world; they are not necessary now." How would you evaluate this opinion?

B. Fulfillment (vv. 19, 20)

Again (in the light of Luke's Gospel) there is a gap in Mark's record. From Luke 24:44-53 and Acts 1:4-9 we know that the Ascension took place from the Mount of Olives, and from Acts 1:15—2:4 we know that the disciples waited for, and received, the power of the Holy Spirit before they began to obey the Great Commission. Thenceforward "they went forth, and preached every where" (v. 20). This statement describes the entire period of the Acts of the Apostles. But, of course, it describes the continuous ministry of "the believing ones" throughout the centuries and at the present time. The believing ones are still going forth and preaching everywhere.

The believing ones did the going and the preaching, but **the Lord** did the working and the confirming. And He still does! If the Church is faithful in its going and its preaching, the Lord will be faithful in His working and His confirming.

Which is more important: to preach the gospel without miracles, or to work miracles without preaching the gospel?

REVIEW QUESTIONS

1. What accounted for the presence of Mary Magdalene, Mary the mother of James, and Salome, at the tomb?

2. What do you feel would have happened to the disciples if Jesus had not risen from the dead?

3. To whom did Jesus appear first after His resurrection?

4. What reactions did Mary Magdalene receive when she informed those who had been with her, of the resurrection of Jesus?

5. What was the final admonition Jesus gave the disciples before He was taken up into heaven?

GOLDEN TEXT HOMILY

"I AM HE THAT LIVETH, AND WAS DEAD; AND, BEHOLD, I AM ALIVE FOR EVERMORE" (Revelation 1:18).

Christ makes the startling statement in this text that He died. Many have followed the theory that Christ only fainted, swooned, or was unconscious for a time. Satan's work is to plant doubts in our mind concerning the authenticity of Christ's sonship, His Word, His death, His resurrection, and His ascension. Religionists were first to propose the Resurrection denial. Christ's credibility is at stake. His statement of dying should suffice. If He is not "the truth" then He is not "the way" or "the life."

Paul the Apostle masterfully dealt with the negative supposition of some in the Corinthian church that Christ was not risen. His conclusion—if so, we are yet in our sins (see 1 Corinthians 15:12-19).

The resultant evidences of Christ's resurrection and ascension are manifold: (1) Both events were verified by many witnesses. (2) Both Christ and Paul made positive statements attesting to the truth of the two events—"I am alive" and "Now is Christ risen" (1 Corinthians 15:20). (3) The Holy Ghost came on the Day of Pentecost as He promised. (4) With the keys

He possessed in His death He released the prisoners; in His raising He took the sting from death—dead saints were seen walking the streets of Jerusalem. (5) Changed lives wrought by His Spirit continue to attest to the fact of His resurrection and ascension (Romans 8:11).

Because He lives I can live also—now and forever. Whom the Son makes free is free indeed.

The evidence is in—He is risen!—**Fred H. Whisman, Cost Analyst, Church of God Publishing House, Cleveland, Tennessee**

SENTENCE SERMONS

FAITH CANNOT LONG keep death in view. Resurrection is that which fills the vision of faith; and in the power thereof, it can rise from the dead.
—**Charles Mackintosh**

THE RESURRECTION IS a true sunrising, the inbursting of a cloudless sky on all the righteous dead.
—**Horace Bushnell**

YOU CAN'T WRECK the Resurrection by open attack, deliberate denial, or intentional ignorance.
—**"Notes and Quotes"**

I DO BELIEVE, that die I must,
And be returned from out my dust:
I do believe, that when I rise,
Christ I shall see, with these same eyes.
—**Robert Herrick in "Noble Numbers"**

EVANGELISTIC APPLICATION

CHRISTIANS SHOULD TAKE EVERY OPPORTUNITY TO PRESENT THE MESSAGE THAT THE RISEN CHRIST IS THE SAVIOR.

The last chapter in Mark contains some things omitted in Matthew, and some things of fearful import. We learn from it that the gospel is to be preached to all mankind. Every man is to be offered eternal life; and he rejects it at his peril. The condition of the man who will not believe is fearfully awful. The Son of God has solemnly declared that he shall be damned. **He** will judge the world; and there is none that can deliver out of His hand. No excuse will be allowed for **not** believing. Unless a man has faith, he **must** be lost forever. This is the solemn assurance of the whole Bible; and in view of this awful declaration of the **merciful** Redeemer, how sad is the condition of him who has no confidence in Jesus, and who has never looked to Him for eternal life! And how important that without delay he should make his peace with God, and possess that faith which is connected with eternal life (Barnes, **Notes on the Four Gospels).**

ILLUMINATING THE LESSON

William Jennings Bryan describes securing a few grains of wheat when in Cairo that had slumbered thirty centuries in an Egyptian tomb. Upon thinking of the unbroken chain of life of the grain we sow and harvest today, he wrote, "If this invisible germ of life in the grain of wheat can pass unimpaired through three thousand resurrections, I shall not doubt that my soul has power to clothe itself with a new body suited to its new existence when this earthly frame has crumbled to dust."
—**"Notes and Quotes"**

"It seems but the other day, though a full seventy years have passed since then, that I heard two boys talking under my little east window that looked out upon the sea. It was springtime, and good old black Enoch was planting flowers." "I don't like to see seeds bein' planted," said the older boy; "makes me think o' diggin' graves an' buryin' folks." "It don't make me feel that way a bit," said the younger. "I just look ahead and see 'em wake right up into posies."

"Who verily was foreordained before the foundation of the world, but was manifest in these last times for you. Who by him do believe in God, that raised him up from the dead, and gave him glory; that your faith and hope might be in God" (1 Peter 1:20, 21).—**"Sunday School Times"**

DAILY DEVOTIONAL GUIDE

M. Prophecy of Resurrection. Psalm 16:1-11
T. Messengers of the Resurrection. Matthew 28:1-10
W. Unbelieving Disciples. Luke 24:4-12
T. The Master's Commission. Matthew 28:16-20
F. Joyful Worship. Luke 24:49-53
S. Believers' Resurrection Hope. 1 Corinthians 15:1-11

April 26, 1981

Responsibilities of Friendship

Bible Background: 1 Samuel 19:1-7; 20:1-42

Time: Probably 1015 B.C.

Place: Near Gibeah, about five miles north of Jerusalem

Supplemental References: 2 Samuel 9:1-13; Mark 5:19; Philippians 4:10-18; 2 Timothy 1:16-18

Golden Text: "A man that hath friends must shew himself friendly: and there is a friend that sticketh closer than a brother" (Proverbs 18:24).

Central Truth: Jonathan is a picture of that greater Friend who loved us and gave Himself for us.

Evangelistic Emphasis: Christ is the great Friend of sinners.

PRINTED TEXT

1 Samuel 20:4. Then said Jonathan unto David, Whatsoever thy soul desireth, I will even do it for thee.

5. And David said unto Jonathan, Behold, to morrow is the new moon, and I should not fail to sit with the king at meat: but let me go, that I may hide myself in the field unto the third day at even.

6. If thy father at all miss me, then say, David earnestly asked leave of me that he might run to Beth-lehem his city: for there is a yearly sacrifice there for all the family.

7. If he say thus, It is well; thy servant shall have peace: but if he be very wroth, then be sure that evil is determined by him.

8. Therefore thou shalt deal kindly with thy servant; for thou hast brought thy servant into a covenant of the Lord with thee: notwithstanding, if there be in me iniquity, slay me thyself; for why shouldest thou bring me to thy father?

9. And Jonathan said, Far be it from thee: for if I knew certainly that evil were determined by my father to come upon thee, then would not I tell it thee?

10. Then said David to Jonathan, Who shall tell me? or what if thy father answer thee roughly?

11. And Jonathan said unto David, Come, and let us go out into the field. And they went out both of them into the field.

12. And Jonathan said unto David, O Lord God of Israel, when I have sounded my father about to morrow any time, or the third day, and, behold, if there be good toward David, and I then send not unto thee, and shew it thee;

13. The Lord do so and much more to Jonathan: but if it please my father to do thee evil, then I will shew it thee, and send thee away, that thou mayest go in peace: and the Lord be with thee, as he hath been with my father.

14. And thou shalt not only while yet I live shew me the kindness of the Lord, that I die not:

15. But also thou shalt not cut off thy kindness from my house for ever: no, not when the Lord hath cut off the enemies of David every one from the face of the earth.

Responsibilities of Friendship

DICTIONARY

the new moon—1 Samuel 20:5—The first day of the lunar month was generally celebrated with some type of religious festivity. It was observed as a day of rest, worship, and religious instruction (Amos 8:5; 2 Kings 4:23; Isaiah 66:23).

a covenant of the Lord—1 Samuel 20:8—The covenant made in 18:3 was considered witnessed by God; it was binding too, for God was the guardian of it.

into the field—1 Samuel 20:11—The only place where Jonathan felt sure they would have adequate privacy.

LESSON OUTLINE

I. FRIENDSHIP—HELPING EACH OTHER
II. FRIENDSHIP—A LASTING BOND
   A. David's Confidence in Jonathan
   B. Jonathan's Confidence in the Lord
III. FRIENDSHIP—RESPONSIBILITIES ACCEPTED
   A. The Plan
   B. The Outcome
   C. The Climax

LESSON EXPOSITION

INTRODUCTION

From this point onward our studies of Saul, David, and Jonathan become less continuous and detailed. Emphasis will be made on just a few specific events, all of which turn the spotlight on David. Apart from the present lesson, Saul and Jonathan drop almost entirely out of the picture. They do not do so in the biblical record, however. Indeed, in the twelve remaining chapters of the first Book of Samuel and the first four chapters of the second Book of Samuel there is recurring interaction between David and the house of Saul.

An important point to note is the length of time which elapsed between David's private anointing and charismatic enduement when he was still a youth, almost certainly in his teens, and his coming to the throne. He was thirty years old before he became king of Judah upon the death of Saul, and it was a further seven and a half years before he reigned over the whole nation of Israel (2 Samuel 5:4, 5).

Thus, a period of twenty years or so elapsed between David's anointing and enduement and the beginning of his full reign. These years were filled with trouble and strife, with testing and trials of many kinds. The question forces itself upon us—**why?** Why did not the Lord remove Saul at once and place David on the throne?

The answer would seem to be that something more was required than even charismatic enduement. He needed disciplined character. Both Samson and Saul had charismatic enduement but they failed for lack of disciplined character. David was put under divine discipline for almost twenty years before he was placed on the throne. Surely this tells us something of importance for our own times!

A part of David's training was his rich friendship with Jonathan which we now consider. Jonathan imparted something precious to David's life. How rewarding good friendship can be!

I. FRIENDSHIP—HELPING EACH OTHER (1 Samuel 19:1-7)

We have already had occasion to comment upon this passage when thinking of the antidote for jealousy (lesson 7). We saw that by his intervention Jonathan performed an inestimable service for both Saul and David. By his one action he held back his father from murder and saved the life of David.

Our second look at this passage draws attention to the mutual love of Jonathan and David. In lesson 7 we also commented upon the opening verses of chapter 18 which describe the covenant of friendship formed by Jonathan and David after the slaying of Goliath and the slaughter of the Philistines. That covenant bound them to support each other and stand by each other whatever the cost. Neither could have imagined at that stage how dangerous and how costly to both of them the covenant would prove, but more especially to Jonathan.

How Jonathan reacted in the early stages of his father's hatred toward David we are not told. But when Saul called upon Jonathan to kill David he had to make a decision. We are left to imagine the agony of his conflict. Ties of blood and responsibilities of state bound him to his father. But he was bound to David by a covenant of friendship.

Moreover Jonathan was a God-fearing man to whom the sixth commandment ("Thou shalt not kill") was a powerful moral imperative. Furthermore, he surely must have been tempted to consider the fact that David was a serious threat to his own future position. His mind must have been in great turmoil as he battled the issues.

But Jonathan did not draw back. He intervened with Saul in an endeavor to dissuade him from his mad enterprise. He crucified his self-interest. It is probable he risked his own life, for Saul, thwarted in his schemes, might easily react against even his own son.

It has been suggested that the passage in Proverbs 18:24 ("There is a friend that sticketh closer than a brother") was written or preserved by Solomon with David and Jonathan in mind. It is a lesson which Christians should seek to apply in the precious fellowship of the church. Our covenant with Christ joins us also to each other, and when our brother or sister is in peril or want we should stick close to him or her, as Jonathan did to David. C. H. Spurgeon, in his typical style, writes: "If you belong to the army of Immanuel, and our persecuted brother has done no wrong, let us stand or fall by him. Let us never desert a comrade. If the world says, 'Down with him! down with him! down with him!' we will rush like the old Greek hero to the rescue, and hold our shield over the fallen one, fighting for him till he can get up again, for one of these days we will be down too, and we may want a brother soldier to cover us from the enemy. Let us pray our brethren out of their troubles and not desert them."

In the above quotation Spurgeon inserts a qualification, "and [if] our persecuted brother has done no wrong." What does this imply? Are there some circumstances when we are free from a covenant of friendship such as that between David and Jonathan?

II. FRIENDSHIP—A LASTING BOND (1 Samuel 20:1-17)

A. David's Confidence in Jonathan (vv. 1-10)

This whole chapter, so full of detail, is especially important in that it narrates the last days (strictly, **hours**) that David and Jonathan were able to spend before the tragic circumstances separated them, physically though not in heart. It is plain, as most commentators point out, that these details must have been communicated by one of the two friends.

We must not forget that between our first and second divisions Saul had failed to honor his solemn pledge to Jonathan, **made on oath,** that David would not be slain. After a further Davidic victory over the Philistines, Saul's insane jealousy had revived, opening him once again to the evil spirit and resulting in the hunt for David's life which we examined in lesson 7 (2 Samuel 19:8-24).

We should note, too, that David had no confidence in the long-term effects of the religious experience which came to Saul at Ramah. Maybe he felt that a man who could perjure himself as Saul had done (compare 2 Samuel 19:6) was not to be trusted regardless of his charismatic experience. Let it be insisted that charismatic experience is not above or outside ethical criteria. Charisma must be evaluated by character.

David had fled from Saul to his wife. Then he had fled from his wife to Samuel. Where now could he flee? To his covenant friend Jonathan. Nothing more strikingly reflects the solidarity of this friendship than the fact that David fled to Jonathan at this time. He felt there was a bond between them which would be honored even though Saul was Jonathan's father and David would receive the crown which by heredity belonged to Jonathan.

When, however, David insisted that Saul was hunting his life Jonathan refused to believe it (v. 2). Pink, who seems to see Jonathan through jaundiced eyes, claims that Jonathan was "not a saved man," and that "he had not the moral courage to acknowledge the truth." Blaikie, on the other hand, sees him as "noble in character. Guileless himself, he suspected no guile in his father" **(Expositor's Bible, 1 Samuel).** Possibly the simple truth is that Jonathan so loved his father that he found it difficult to believe that he was capable of the deliberate murder of David. And his whole attitude was tempered by the fact that his father was mentally ill. Nevertheless, as Spence says, "David, with his clear, bright intellect, looked deeper into Saul's heart than did the heroic, guileless son" **(Elliott's Bible Commentary, Vol. 2).** He was so sure of Saul's deadly designs that he "sware," that is, declared on oath, that it was so (v. 3).

4. Then said Jonathan unto David, Whatsoever thy soul desireth, I will even do it for thee.

5. And David said unto Jonathan, Behold, to morrow is the new moon, and I should not fail to sit with the king at meat: but let me go, that I may hide myself in the field unto the third day at even.

Convinced, Jonathan agreed to help his friend, and David put a plan to Jonathan whereby they both might know beyond all doubt how to act. In reference to the **new moon,** which was a religious festival (see Numbers 10:10; 28:11-15), Keil and Delitzsch say, "This request implies that Saul gave a feast at the new moon, and therefore that the new moon was not merely a religious festival, but that it was kept as a civil festival also, and in the latter character for two days" **(A Commentary on the Old Testament, The Books of Samuel).** Spence writes, "The sacrificial and ceremonial rites were accompanied by a state and family banquet, at which David, as the king's son-in-law, and also as holding a high post in the royal army, was expected to be present" (p.377). David's plan was to absent himself from this banquet. Instead he would go and hide "in the field," that is, the open country away from the city.

6. If thy father at all miss me, then say, David earnestly asked leave of me that he might run to Beth-lehem his city: for there is a yearly sacrifice there for all the family.

7. If he say thus, It is well; thy servant shall have peace: but if he be very wroth, then be sure that evil is determined by him.

David's request to Jonathan apparently involved a deliberate lie—"that he might run to Beth-lehem." Nevertheless, as Bethlehem was only a few miles from Gibeah, where Saul resided, the double journey was no problem, well within the space of the three days. However, some scholars frankly acknowledge the prevarication, claiming that in those ancient times few would raise their eyebrows at such lying. Others, rightly, point out that the biblical historian merely records the lie but does not thereby sanction it.

Discuss: What should be the Christian attitude both to lying and to oaths to enforce statements?

David's plan was that Saul's reaction to his absence from the banquet would be a sign of the king's intentions. If he accepted the news amicably, all was well. But if Saul became angry, the situation was indeed dangerous.

8. Therefore thou shalt deal kindly with thy servant; for thou hast brought thy servant into a covenant of the Lord with thee: notwithstanding, if there be in me iniquity, slay me thyself; for why shouldest thou bring me to thy father?

The Hebrew word rendered "deal kindly" here is considered to be one of the most significant terms in the Old Testament **(chesed),** involving more than what we usually mean by kindness or even love. The **New English Bible** renders it here "keep faith"; the word is also sometimes rendered "steadfast love." It means "covenant love." David requests Jonathan to be loyal to the covenant which they had made. This is further enforced by the statement, "you and I have entered into a solemn compact before the Lord" **(New English Bible).** However, this verse is interesting in that it shows that "covenant love" was not without qualifications. If David were a criminal Jonathan would not be bound to protect him from the law. Indeed he could exact it.

9. And Jonathan said, Far be it from thee: for if I knew certainly that evil were determined by my father to come upon thee, then would not I tell it thee?

10. Then said David to Jonathan, Who shall tell me? or what if thy father answer thee roughly?

The archaic phrase "Far be it from thee" is a protestation on Jonathan's part, almost an oath. The **New English Bible** renders it "God forbid!" and the **New International Version** says "Never!"

B. Jonathan's Confidence in the Lord (vv. 11-17)

11. And Jonathan said unto David, Come, and let us go out into the field. And they went out both of them into the field.

One problem remained in the minds of the two men: how to convey information to David concerning Saul's reaction. They decided to go into "the field" for further discussion.

12. And Jonathan said unto David, O Lord God of Israel, when I have sounded my father about to morrow any time, or the third day, and, behold, if there be good toward David, and I then send not unto thee, and shew it thee;

13. The Lord do so and much more to Jonathan: but if it please my father to do

thee evil, then I will shew it thee, and send thee away, that thou mayest go in peace: and the Lord be with thee, as he hath been with my father.

The phrase "O Lord God of Israel" is not the beginning of a prayer, as the rest of the verse shows. Jonathan was speaking to David, not to God, but he introduced his statement by either an invocation or an oath: "By the Lord, the God of Israel" **(New International Version);** "I promise you, David, in the sight of the Lord the God of Israel" **(New English Bible).** Jonathan solemnly pledged himself to let David know the whole truth about Saul's intentions. He ended his promise with a very revealing wish: "And the Lord be with thee, as he hath been with my father." As Keil and Delitzsch say, "In this wish there is expressed the presentiment that David would one day occupy that place in Israel which Saul occupied then, i.e. the throne."

14. And thou shalt not only while yet I live shew me the kindness of the Lord, that I die not:

15. But also thou shalt not cut off thy kindness from my house for ever: no, not when the Lord hath cut off the enemies of David every one from the face of the earth.

Again the important Hebrew word for covenant love **(chesed)** occurs in these two verses, rendered "kindness." Jonathan plainly expresses his confidence in David's future. Indeed he almost makes a prophecy, "when the Lord hath cut off the enemies of David every one from the face of the earth." He was sure that Jehovah would both protect David from Saul and all other enemies, and bring him to the throne. Therefore, as Jonathan pledges his steadfast love to David in his hour of need, so he pleads for David's steadfast love not only to himself but to his "house," that is, his descendants, "for ever."

The remaining two verses of our second division (vv. 16, 17) summarize in the historian's own words the covenant which the two men made with each other.

Does your church have a **covenant?** How do you evaluate it? Do you consider it binding?

III. FRIENDSHIP—RESPONSIBILITIES ACCEPTED (1 Samuel 20:18-42)

A. The Plan (vv. 17-23)

David had previously laid out his plan to Jonathan (see vv. 5-8). One thing was undecided: the method of passing on the information concerning Saul's intentions. Jonathan then decided what he would do. At the end of the three days David would place himself in the agreed place. Jonathan would shoot three arrows in his direction. If they fell short of him he would know that all was well. However, if the arrows went further he would send a lad to collect them, calling after him, "The arrows are beyond thee." This would indicate bad news, and David must be ready for flight.

B. The Outcome (vv. 24-34)

These verses describe what happened at the family banquet. On the first day Saul passed no comment on David's absence, assuming that he must be ceremonially unclean for some reason (see Leviticus 15 for examples). However, when he was missing on the second day Saul became inquisitive. When Jonathan gave the reply which he and David had agreed upon, the king flew into a violent rage in which he insulted both Jonathan and his mother and threw a javelin at his son. However, his insulting remarks revealed to all the basic cause of his insane jealousy. It was not merely David's superior prowess and greater popularity, but that he was aware that David was the "neighbour" of his, the man after God's "own heart," of whom Samuel had prophesied (see 1 Samuel 13:14; 15:28). So long as David lived, Saul bellowed, "thou shalt not be established, nor thy kingdom" (v. 31). Saul had deliberately set himself to fight against God.

Outraged, Jonathan left the banquet. Not until the next morning, however, did he go out to the place of meeting with David.

C. The Climax (vv. 35-42)

These remaining verses tell their own story simply and dramatically. Jonathan conveyed his bad news to David as they had planned. He added the words, "Make speed, haste, stay not" (v. 38)—intended of course for David, not merely the lad who collected the arrows. However, David was not about to run before meeting with Jonathan for a farewell. Both men seemed to realize that this might be their last meeting. Only this presentiment can explain the pathos and passion of their affection. The phrase "until David exceeded" (v. 41) is rendered by the **New International Version,** "but David wept the most." The **Living Bible** translates, "until David could weep no more."

The crown prince had to choose the hard pathway of duty, and return to his insane father, his own wife and family, his responsibilities at court, and eventually to die in one of the most tragic battles in Israel's history, by the side of his father and two brothers (1 Samuel chapter 31). Both David and Saul were destined to undergo several long, hard years.

Can you imagine the consequences if Jonathan had gone with David?

REVIEW QUESTIONS

1. What occasion was King Saul about to celebrate?
2. Where was David planning to be during this occasion?
3. Where were David and Jonathan when they made their covenant?
4. Who witnessed the covenant between David and Jonathan?
5. What was Jonathan's condition that he required of David?

GOLDEN TEXT HOMILY

"A MAN THAT HATH FRIENDS MUST SHEW HIMSELF FRIENDLY: AND THERE IS A FRIEND THAT STICKETH CLOSER THAN A BROTHER" (Proverbs 18:24).

Most of us have very few close friends; however, as a Christian the act of being friendly is a personal, positive approach to everyone with whom we have contact.

The act of being friendly should be consistent both in good times and in times of stress.

Often, the people that we associate with will want to know more about us if we are basically friendly and warm. As time goes by, they will discover that this attitude of friendliness is the result of our Christian experience.

When I was a child we sang the song, "The Old Time Religion," and after someone was converted we sang the line, "Makes me love everybody." With this attitude, we have another form of Christian witness.

Jesus was accused of being a friend of publicans and sinners (Matthew 11:19). By being friendly with those with whom we come in contact, we can let our close friend, Jesus Christ, shine forth through the sincere friendship that we emit.—**Scott T. Muse, Jr., Ph.D., President, Southwestern College, Oklahoma City, Oklahoma**

SENTENCE SERMONS

A FAITHFUL FRIEND is a strong defense.
—**Anonymous**

FRIENDSHIP IS A STRONG and habitual inclination in two persons to promote the good and happiness of each other.
—**Addison**

REAL FRIENDSHIP IS a slow growth and never thrives unless engrafted upon a stock of known and reciprocal merit.
—**Lord Chesterfield**

FRIENDSHIP DOES NOT mean knowing all about a person. It is knowing him.
—**Henrietta Mears**

EVANGELISTIC APPLICATION

CHRIST IS THE GREAT FRIEND OF SINNERS.

David the conqueror of Goliath was rejected, opposed, and persecuted by King Saul for many years. Jesus too, "great David's greater Son," the conqueror of Satan in the wilderness and on the Cross, was rejected and opposed by large numbers of His own people. "He came unto his own, and his own received him not" (John 1:11). He is still being rejected and opposed by vast numbers of people. As a well-known hymn has it, "Our Lord is now rejected, And by the world disowned."

However, David from the first found one wonderful friend in his rejection—Jonathan, whose heart was chained to his heart in a covenant of loyal love. Later, hundreds were to turn to him during his time of rejection.

Jesus too found friends. There were those who "received him" (John 1:12). Throughout Christian history this company has been swelled by the millions. Each one has a kind of Jonathan relationship to Christ. The heart of the true Christian is knit, bound, chained to the heart of the Lord in covenant love.

ILLUMINATING THE LESSON

If you would win a man to your cause, first convince him that you are his true friend. Therein is a drop of honey that catches his heart, which, say what he will, is the greatest highroad to his reason, and which when once gained, you will find but little trouble in convincing his judgment of the justice of your cause, if, indeed, that cause be really a just one. On the contrary, assume to dictate to his judgment, or to command his action, or to make him as one to be shunned or despised, and he will retreat within himself, close all the avenues to his head and heart; and though your cause be naked truth itself, transformed to the heaviest lance, harder than steel and sharper than steel can be made, and though you throw it with more than Herculean force and precision, you shall be no more able to pierce him than to penetrate the hard shell of a tortoise with a rye straw.—**Abraham Lincoln**

DAILY DEVOTIONAL GUIDE

M. Love Is Friendship's Bond. 1 Samuel 18: 1-4
T. The Covenant of Lasting Friendship. 1 Samuel 20:16-34
W. Friendship's Covenant Includes the Family. 1 Samuel 20:35-42
T. Friends—A Source of Encouragement. 1 Samuel 23:16-18
F. Honoring the Covenant of Friendship. 2 Samuel 9:1-13
S. Love—A Mark of Discipleship. John 13:34, 35

May 3, 1981

Demonstrating True Greatness

Bible Background: 1 Samuel 24:1-12; 26:1-21; 28:1-25; 31:1-13; 2 Samuel 1:1-27; 2:1-4
Time: Around 1010 B.C.
Place: Ziklag, a city in the south of Palestine
Supplemental References: Proverbs 3:3, 17; Micah 6:8; Mark 11:25; Luke 17:3, 4; Colossians 3:12-14; James 3:17; 1 Peter 4:8
Golden Text: "Let nothing be done through strife or vainglory; but in lowliness of mind let each esteem other better than themselves" (Philippians 2:3).
Central Truth: One's attitude toward the blessings and problems of others indicates the quality of his character.
Evangelistic Emphasis: The Christian, by his attitudes and actions, is an example to the ungodly.

PRINTED TEXT

2 Samuel 1:17. And David lamented with this lamentation over Saul and over Jonathan his son:

19. The beauty of Israel is slain upon thy high places: how are the mighty fallen!

20. Tell it not in Gath, publish it not in the streets of Askelon; lest the daughters of the Philistines rejoice, lest the daughters of the uncircumcised triumph.

21. Ye mountains of Gilboa, let there be no dew, neither let there be rain, upon you, nor fields of offerings: for there the shield of the mighty is vilely cast away, the shield of Saul, as though he had not been anointed with oil.

22. From the blood of the slain, from the fat of the mighty, the bow of Jonathan turned not back, and the sword of Saul returned not empty.

23. Saul and Jonathan were lovely and pleasant in their lives, and in their death they were not divided: they were swifter than eagles, they were stronger than lions.

24. Ye daughters of Israel, weep over Saul, who clothed you in scarlet, with other delights, who put on ornaments of gold upon your apparel.

25. How are the mighty fallen in the midst of the battle! O Jonathan, thou wast slain in thine high places.

26. I am distressed for thee, my brother Jonathan: very pleasant hast thou been unto me: thy love to me was wonderful, passing the love of women.

27. How are the mighty fallen, and the weapons of war perished!

DICTIONARY

Gath—2 Samuel 1:20—One of five great Philistine cities. Its people were the Gittites of whom were Goliath and other giants.

Gilboa (gil-BOW-ah)—2 Samuel 1:21—A range of barren hills on the eastern side of the Plain of Esdraelon, named from a noted spring. The mean elevation is about 1,600 feet.

LESSON OUTLINE

I. EXPRESSING SORROW
   A. The Background
   B. The Incident
   C. The Lamentation

II. RECOGNIZING THE WORTH OF OTHERS
   A. A General Lament for Saul and Jonathan
   B. A Special Lament for Jonathan

III. ACCEPTING RESPONSIBILITY
   A. Directed by the Lord
   B. Crowned by Judah

LESSON EXPOSITION

INTRODUCTION

A glance at our Bible Background in comparison with our lesson outline will show that our study is limited to only a part of it, the two concluding portions. However, we are expected to be aware of the background material, for only thus can we grasp the significance of the early chapters of the second Book of Samuel.

With David's flight from Saul's court and his emotional parting from Jonathan, he entered a new and painful period of his life, covering possibly seven or eight years (1 Samuel 21—31). He was forced to live the life of a fugitive and an outlaw.

We may divide this period into three phases: 1. He made an attempt to settle in Philistia, but was forced to withdraw in an ignominious manner (1 Samuel 21). It is a rather bizarre story. 2. Returning to Judea he lived as an exile continually hunted by the implacable Saul (1 Samuel 22—26). 3. In utter desperation he led his band of outlaws to Philistia where he was given asylum in Ziklag. However, this was a retrograde step through which his entire cause was nearly ruined (1 Samuel 27—31).

In this period David appeared to be a very mixed-up person, almost like the carnal Christian of Galatians 5:17, "The flesh lusteth against the Spirit, and the Spirit against the flesh." Some of his doings were extremely carnal, yet he could rise to great heights of spirituality. This is especially evident in his treatment of the mad King Saul. On two occasions the hunter found himself at the mercy of the hunted, and David showed Saul incredible kindness and grace, especially considering the cruelty of the times, and his own situation. On these occasions David demonstrated true greatness. For this reason the passages which describe them are included in our background readings. This magnanimous spirit of David comes to special focus in our outline. David might well have seen the death of Saul as a cause for jubilation. This was far from being the case, as we shall see.

I. EXPRESSING SORROW (2 Samuel 1:1-12)

A. The Background (v. 1)

This opening verse of the chapter crisply summarizes the last two chapters of the first Book of Samuel and leads into the story which is recounted.

The death of Saul is described in 1 Samuel 31. After years of rebellion against the Lord, years especially of a violent and malicious campaign against David whom, by killing, he hoped to keep the kingship in his own family, Saul died on the battlefield of Mount Gilboa in the valley of Jezreel. In the same battle, Saul's three sons, Jonathan, Abinadab and Malchishua, also died, and the forces of Israel suffered a shocking defeat at the hands of the Philistines. The Philistine success, so far north in Canaan, put them in a commanding position and threatened the whole future of the Israel nation (see 31:7). The tragedy of Saul was heightened by the fact that he was not slain outright in the battle, but left wounded, and in order to save himself from humiliation and disfigurement as a Philistine prisoner, he committed suicide (31:4, 5).

The slaughter of the Amalekites by David is described in 1 Samuel 30. It is one of the most dramatic stories in the whole Bible, full of important spiritual lessons. David had chosen exile in Philistia together with his six hundred followers and their families (1 Samuel 27) in order to escape from Saul. He had been received as a defector from Israel and was treated as a potent ally, being given the city of Ziklag in the southern border region between Judah and Philistia. During this period David virtually lived as a guerilla, fighting and pillaging various groups, including the Amalekites. The latter, however, inflicted a terrible revenge on David. While he and his troops were marching northward with the Philistine forces to do battle with Saul (from which he was dismissed because his motives were suspected by the Philistine leaders), the Amalekites attacked and destroyed Ziklag, capturing all the women and children and goods. When David's forces returned, they were so distraught that they were ready to mutiny and kill their leader. However, through prayer and the leading of the Lord, David survived, turned the tables on the Amalekites, and "reversed his reverses."

It was during this very time of disaster and recovery that Saul met his tragic doom, about one hundred miles to the north of Ziklag.

Expositors usually express the opinion that David was in a "backslidden" state during his exile in Ziklag, and that his disaster led to his spiritual restoration. Can you suggest reasons for this belief?

B. The Incident (vv. 2-10)

On the third day after David had returned from the slaughter of the Amalekites, a man came to Ziklag bearing signs of deep mourning. He brought the terrible news of the defeat of Israel on Mount Gilboa. He carried with him Saul's crown and a bracelet. He announced that he had found Saul wounded on the battlefield and in danger of capture by the Philistines. Saul had entreated him to put his life to an end. He had done so and now had come to David with the news and the crown.

There is an obvious discrepancy between this story and the account given in 1 Samuel 31. What is the explanation? Did Saul commit suicide, or was he, at his own request, slain by the Amalekite? Josephus harmonizes the two accounts by stating that when Saul found difficulty in taking his own life, he enlisted the help of the Amalekite **(Antiquities of the Jews, Book 6,** Chapter 14). Liberal scholars treat both accounts as "variant traditions," a solution which is abhorrent to reverent conservative expositors. The common conservative explanation is that the Amalekite was lying. The truth was that he had found Saul dead on the battlefield and had robbed the body of the kingly jewels. However, conservatives are then divided. Some think that the Amalekite had gone to David thinking to ingratiate himself with one whom he obviously believed would be Israel's next king. Others believe that he encountered David unexpectedly on his way south and fabricated the explanation in an effort to save his skin.

C. The Lamentation (vv. 11, 12)

The Amalekite's story, whether truth, lies, or a mixture, plunged David and his people into profound anguish and deep mourning. Only a few days before, they had wept and cried over their personal losses (31:3-6). Now,

they mourned "for Saul, and for Jonathan his son, and for the people of the Lord, and for the house of Israel" (2 Samuel 1:12). Dr. F. Gardiner comments, "The whole narrative shows that David not only, as a patriotic Israelite, lamented the death of the king, but also felt a personal attachment to Saul, notwithstanding his long and unreasonable hostility" **(Ellicott's, Bible Commentary, Vol. 2).** Keil and Delitzsch quote an older commentator: "The only deep mourning for Saul, with the exception of that of the Jabeshites (1 Samuel 31:11) proceeded from the man whom he had hated and persecuted for so many years even to the time of his death; just as David's successor (Christ) wept over the fall of Jerusalem, even when it was about to destroy Himself" **(A Commentary on the Old Testament, The Books of Samuel,** p. 287).

Not without reason is our lesson entitled "Demonstrating True Greatness." Both in life and in death David treated his relentless persecutor with amazing magnanimity. Often Christians who have so much more light from heaven and enjoy so much more of the Holy Spirit's grace, fall immeasurably below David in this kind of greatness.

What steps can we take in order to have this kind of greatness exhibited by David toward Saul?

II. RECOGNIZING THE WORTH OF OTHERS (2 Samuel 1:17-27)

Before proceeding to examine David's "lament" or "elegy," we should take a look at verses 13-16 which describe David's treatment of the lying Amalekite.

This was not a personal, vindictive, and savage murder, but the righteous execution of one who claimed to have committed a capital crime, the crime of regicide or murder of the king. We must realize that David had no knowledge of the truth. He condemned and sentenced the man on his own confession and evidence. Gardiner comments, "Regicide was not in David's eyes merely a political crime; he had showed on more than one occasion of great temptation (1 Samuel 24:6; 26:9, 11, 16) that he considered the taking the life of 'the Lord's anointed' as a religious offence of the greatest magnitude. It was an especially grievous thing for a foreigner and an Amalekite thus to smite him whom God had appointed as the monarch of Israel.''

David lived before the revelation of God in Christ. How would he have acted toward the Amalekite in modern times? Are kings and other heads of state to be treated as specially sacred today?

A. A General Lament for Saul and Jonathan (vv. 17-24)

17. And David lamented with this lamentation over Saul and over Jonathan his son.

This "lament" is a striking example of David's poetry. It is not a "psalm" but more like a ballad poem, or a poem narrating a popular story, to be set to music.

It will be noticed that in verse 18 the words "the use of" are in italics, and thus not in the original. It seems that the translators of the **King James Version** misunderstood the meaning of this verse. "The bow" does not refer to the weapon called a bow, but is the name of this poem. David ordered that the poem which he had composed on the death of Saul and Jonathan, which he called "The Bow," should become one of the national songs. The **New International Version** translates, "And ordered that the men of Judah be taught this lament of the bow" (2 Samuel 1:18).

The Book of Jashar here mentioned means "the book of the upright." This book is also mentioned in Joshua 10:13. Gardiner says, "It is supposed to have been a collection of songs relating to memorable events and men in the early history of Israel, and it appears that this elegy was included among them."

19. The beauty of Israel is slain upon thy high places: how are the mighty fallen!

The word rendered "beauty" in the **King James Version** is rendered "glory" in the **New International Version,** whereas the **New English Bible** renders it "prince." Mauchline comments, "The term should be rendered as 'glory' with reference to Saul and Jonathan or to the 'glory,' the national prestige and dignity of Israel as a whole" (**New Century Bible, 1 and 2 Samuel**). "Thy high places" means the mountains of Gilboa where the fateful battle had been fought (see verse 21).

20. Tell it not in Gath, publish it not in the streets of Askelon; lest the daughters of the Philistines rejoice, lest the daughters of the uncircumcised triumph.

Gath and Askelon were two of the Philistine cities. David's language is a poetic way of saying that the whole of Philistia will be jubilant at the defeat of Israel and the death of Saul and his sons.

21. Ye mountains of Gilboa, let there be no dew, neither let there be rain, upon you, nor fields of offerings: for there the shield of the mighty is vilely cast away, the shield of Saul, as though he had not been anointed with oil.

This is poetic language. David is not expressing a hope that the Gilboa region would become desert, but simply saying that henceforth it would be remembered with mourning, such mourning as even nature ought to share.

22. From the blood of the slain, from the fat of the mighty, the bow of Jonathan turned not back and the sword of Saul returned not empty.

A poetic description of Saul and Jonathan as mighty warriors. David is thinking not of the battle of Gilboa but of their previous record of military successes. The reference to Jonathan's bow is probably one reason for calling the whole poem "The Bow."

23. Saul and Jonathan were lovely and pleasant in their lives, and in their death they were not divided: they were swifter than eagles, they were stronger than lions.

This is one of the most lovely and generous-hearted parts of the whole poem. David had suffered unjustly and harshly at the hands of Saul, but he did not allow bitter memories to poison his soul and cloud his judgment concerning the greatness of Saul. Father and son together had done great and mighty things for Israel (see chapter 14), and David did not forget it. Moreover, there was a close personal attachment of Saul and Jonathan both in life and in death. "They were not divided." Even the covenant of friendship which existed between David and Jonathan had not been allowed to destroy that unity, though it had come under severe strain.

24. Ye daughters of Israel, weep over Saul, who clothed you in scarlet, with other delights, who put on ornaments of gold upon your apparel.

Gardiner comments, "This refers to Saul's division among the people of the spoil of his conquered foes, and to the prosperity resulting from his many successful campaigns."

This lament over Saul, especially, highlights the greatness of David's spirit. The saying is attributed to Winston Churchill, "A people should be defiant in defeat but magnanimous in victory." He might have been describing the character of David. David certainly did not glory and jubilate at Saul's death though he was to profit by it, but rather celebrated his successes and remembered his virtues.

B. A Special Lament for Jonathan (vv. 25-27)

25. How are the mighty fallen in the midst of the battle! O Jonathan, thou wast slain in thine high places.

26. I am distressed for thee, my brother Jonathan: very pleasant hast thou been unto me: thy love to me was wonderful, passing the love of women.

27. How are the mighty fallen, and the weapons of war perished!

David had not seen Jonathan for several years but he cannot forget their covenant and deep friendship. Unscrupulous homosexual propaganda has perverted and sullied the language of David, but there is no suggestion of anything but noble and manly regard and loyalty. As Gardiner says, "It was such an affection as could only exist between noble natures and those united in the fear of God."

Professor E. M. Blaiklock thinks that David's poem, in addition to its expressions of personal grief, also expresses David's patriotism, and says "There is no reproach in patriotism." What do you think?

III. ACCEPTING RESPONSIBILITY (2 Samuel 2:1-4)

A. Directed by the Lord (vv. 1-3)

During David's days of rejection he was joined by a surviving descendant of Eli who had inherited the priesthood (see 1 Samuel 14:3; 22:18-23). This priest carried the ephod, a special high-priestly garment. Situated on the breastplate of the ephod in a pouch were the Urim and Thummim which were used in obtaining divine guidance on particular matters (see Exodus 28:30; Leviticus 8:7, 8). These are thought to have been two stones, but how they functioned is a matter of debate (see the brief but excellent article in **The New Bible Dictionary).** What does seem clear is that by means of the stones a negative, positive, or neutral reply could be given to a person's quest for guidance.

David used this means of ascertaining God's will for him in the earlier period of his time of rejection by Saul (1 Samuel 23:1-12). Matthew Henry points out, however, that he seems to have made his decision to seek asylum in Philistia without consulting the will of God (1 Samuel 27:1). His stay there proved to be disastrous, but a turning point in his fortunes came: "David enquired at the Lord" (1 Samuel 30:8).

Now that Saul and Jonathan were dead and the nation was without a leader, the question was forced upon David: Is it time for me to return to my people? The fact that the Philistines were in a commanding position made the matter urgent. But David had learned his lesson. Expediency was a poor guide. He must get the will of God! Though the record does not say so; we may feel sure (by comparing the incident with 1 Samuel 23:1-12) that his guidance came through Abiathar and his use of the Urim and Thummim.

His guidance was to leave Ziklag and make his headquarters in Hebron, a town in the Judean hills about twenty miles from Jerusalem. This was an ancient city having historic and sacred associations from the days of Abraham (see Genesis 13:18; 23:1-20; 25:7-10). It was also strategically situated.

In Old Testament days, divine guidance for particular occasions was given in various ways: by dreams, the sacred lot, the prophetic voice, the Urim and Thummim. Can we expect clear guidance today? How can we know the will of the Lord?

B. Crowned by Judah (v. 4)

David had known for about twelve years that he was the anointed king of Israel. His anointing, however, had been private and secret (1 Samuel 16:1-13). Nevertheless, his family knew of it, and the knowledge must have spread to some extent through the years. Moreover, for some years he had captained his own private army. These men and their families would certainly believe in David's kingship. Also, during his years as an exile he had built up a large amount of goodwill in Judea (1 Samuel 30:26-31). It is not surprising, therefore, that when David and his private army established themselves in Hebron, "the men of Judah came, and there they anointed David king over the house of Judah."

However, his struggles were not over. Saul's

commander in chief, Abner, was not about to surrender his personal authority and power so easily. Possibly motivated in part by self-interest, though loyalty to Saul must not be excluded, he put forward a remaining son of Saul as king. This precipitated civil war in the nation, the northern tribes rallying to Ish-bosheth, the tribe of Judah to David.

David had to wait for a further seven and a half years before God's complete plan for his life could be realized.

W. J. Deane writes, "From the sheepfold to the throne David has passed by a series of stages which were his education, each of which contributed some trait, left some impression to stamp upon him the character which has won not only the admiration, but also the warm love of all who hear his story" **(David: His Life and Times).** His sufferings helped to create the character which could carry responsibility.

Is it true that suffering and trial are essential for leadership ability?

REVIEW QUESTIONS

1. What caused David to always hold Saul in highest respect?
2. What phrase is used to describe the respect with which David held Saul?
3. What did David do to remember Saul and Jonathan?
4. At this occasion, why would "the daughters of the Philistines," have cause to rejoice?
5. What comparison does David use to describe Saul's and Jonathan's swiftness and strength?

GOLDEN TEXT HOMILY

"LET NOTHING BE DONE THROUGH STRIFE OR VAINGLORY; BUT IN LOWLINESS OF MIND LET EACH ESTEEM OTHER BETTER THAN THEMSELVES" (Philippians 2:3).

Nothing so separates souls and breaks the unity of spirit as vainglorious strife. Competition, be it ever so generous, cannot be tolerated in the body of Christ except it be competition for the lowest place and the severest service. Competition for the seats in society, in the world's market, and in the sphere of power is always prejudicial to the Christian spirit and the unity which comes from heaven.

In humbleness of mind let each esteem others better than themselves. This implies that we have a modest view of ourselves. Paul said for "every man that is among you, not to think of himself more highly than he ought to think; but to think soberly" (Romans 12:3). We also must have a just idea of others' abilities, and accept them without sarcasm. And, in honor we are to prefer one another (Romans 12:10).

Again Paul says, "Let the elders that rule well be counted worthy of double honour, especially they who labor in the word and doctrine" (1 Timothy 5:17). If we practice the law of respect for others, no longer will we complain of any lot God gives us. We accept it as better than we deserve, and in panoply of humility we are safe from all assault.—**Wayne DeHart, Pastor, Clarksburg, West Virginia**

SENTENCE SERMONS

ONE'S ATTITUDE TOWARD the blessings and problems of others indicates the quality of his character.
—**Selected**

THE TROUBLE IS—before you can be a "former great" you have to be a "great."
—**Charlie Brown (Schultz)**

ONE OF THE MARKS of true greatness is the ability to develop greatness in others.
—**J. C. MacAulay**

A TRUE FRIEND doesn't sympathize with your weakness—he helps summon your strength.
—**Selected**

EVANGELISTIC APPLICATION

THE CHRISTIAN, BY HIS ATTITUDES AND ACTIONS, IS AN EXAMPLE TO THE UNGODLY.

"By this shall all men know that ye are my disciples," said Jesus, "if ye have love one to another" (John 13:35). Also Jesus prayed for his followers, "That they all may be one . . . that the world may believe that thou hast sent me" (John 17:21). This is not referring to the oneness of organization, but the oneness of love—that quality of love which was exhibited so beautifully in the brotherhood of David and Jonathan.

This quality of love is more influential than all speech and all miracles and all knowledge, as Paul so profoundly affirms in the thirteenth chapter of 2 Corinthians.

It is said that the pagans of the Roman Empire in the early centuries cried, "See how these Christians love one another!" No wonder the Greek and Roman dagons were toppled before such a demonstration of Jesus Christ.

ILLUMINATING THE LESSON

A Union soldier, bitter in his hatred of the Confederacy, lay wounded at Gettysburg. At the close of the battle General Lee rode by, and the soldier, though faint from exposure and loss of blood, raised his hands, looked Lee in the face, and shouted as loudly as he could, "Hurrah for the Union!" The General heard him, dismounted, and went toward him, and the soldier confesses: "I thought he meant to kill me. But as he came up, he looked at me with such a sad expression upon his face that all fear left me, and looking right into my eyes, he said, 'My son, I hope you will soon be well.' If I live a thousand years, I shall never forget the expression on General Lee's face. There he was, defeated, retiring from a field that had cost him and his cause almost their last hope, and yet he stopped to say words like those to a wounded soldier of the opposition who had taunted him as he passed by. As soon as the General left me I cried myself to sleep there upon the bloody battleground."—**"New Century Leader"**

DAILY DEVOTIONAL GUIDE

M. Honor for God's Anointed. 1 Samuel 24:1-7

T. Humility. Romans 12:10, 16

W. Forgiving Spirit. Romans 12:17-21

T. Charitableness. 1 Corinthians 13:6

F. Kindness. Ephesians 4:31, 32

S. Respect for Others. James 2:8

May 10, 1981

Following God's Plan

Bible Background: 2 Samuel 5:1-25
Time: Probably 1004 B.C.
Place: Hebron, Jerusalem, Zion, Millo
Supplemental References: 2 Samuel 2:1-15; 4:1-12; Psalm 101:1-5; Romans 13:1-5
Golden Text: "David went on, and grew great, and the Lord God of hosts was with him" (2 Samuel 5:10).
Central Truth: Cooperation with God in His plan for our life brings us to a place of maximum usefulness.
Evangelistic Emphasis: Man can win the victory over sin through the power of Christ.

PRINTED TEXT

2 Samuel 5:4. David was thirty years old when he began to reign, and he reigned forty years.

5. In Hebron he reigned over Judah seven years and six months: and in Jerusalem he reigned thirty and three years over all Israel and Judah.

6. And the king and his men went to Jerusalem unto the Jebusites, the inhabitants of the land: which spake unto David, saying, Except thou take away the blind and the lame, thou shalt not come in hither: thinking, David cannot come in hither.

7. Nevertheless David took the strong hold of Zion: the same is the city of David.

8. And David said on that day, Whosoever getteth up to the gutter, and smiteth the Jebusites, and the lame and the blind, that are hated of David's soul, he shall be chief and captain. Wherefore they said, The blind and the lame shall not come into the house.

9. So David dwelt in the fort, and called it the city of David. And David built round about from Millo and inward.

10. And David went on, and grew great, and the Lord God of hosts was with him.

11. And Hiram king of Tyre sent messengers to David, and cedar trees, and carpenters, and masons: and they built David an house.

12. And David perceived that the Lord had established him king over Israel, and that he had exalted his kingdom for his people Israel's sake.

23. And when David enquired of the Lord, he said, Thou shalt not go up; but fetch a compass behind them, and come upon them over against the mulberry trees.

24. And let it be, when thou hearest the sound of a going in the tops of the mulberry trees, that then thou shalt bestir thyself: for then shall the Lord go out before thee, to smite the host of the Philistines.

25. And David did so, as the Lord had commanded him; and smote the Philistines from Geba until thou come to Gazer.

DICTIONARY

Hebron (HE-bron)—2 Samuel 5:15—One of the most ancient towns, built seven years before Zoan. Abraham, Isaac and Jacob spent many years in Hebron. It became David's royal residence for seven and one-half years (2 Samuel 2), and then David moved the royal palace to Jerusalem.

Jebusites (JEB-you-sites)—2 Samuel 5:5—Occupants of Jebus, a part of Jerusalem, who held out for three hundred years until David captured the citadel. The remnant of the tribe later was made tributary to Solomon (1 Kings 9:20).

the blind and lame—2 Samuel 5:6—So confident were the defenders of the citadel of Jebus that they boasted that even if it were manned by only the blind and lame, it could not be captured.

Zion—(ZI-on)—2 Samuel 5:9—"The city of David, which is Zion" (1 Kings 8:1).

Millo (MILL-lo)—2 Samuel 5:9—An ancient Jebusite stronghold. The name of part of the citadel of Jerusalem.

Hiram (HIGH-ram)—2 Samuel 5:11—This cannot be the Hiram who helped Solomon with the building of the Temple. He was probably the father of Soloman's close ally. This one was a great admirer of David (1 Kings 5:1).

Tyre (TIRE)—2 Samuel 5:11—With Sidon, this city of the Phoenicians was famous for its commerce, craftsmen, and wealth. It was probably the similarity of language, the closeness geographically, the trade, and perhaps the common Philistine enemy that brought the Phoenicians and the Hebrews close together.

LESSON OUTLINE

I. GOD PROVIDES LEADERS
   A. Recognition
   B. Coronation

II. GOD PROVIDES FACILITIES
   A. The Conquest of Jerusalem
   B. The Enlargement of Jerusalem

III. GOD HELPS BRING VICTORY
   A. First Victory Over the Philistines
   B. Second Victory Over the Philistines

LESSON EXPOSITION

INTRODUCTION

Between our lessons 10 and 11 there is a gap of seven and a half years, covered by 2 Samuel 2:5—4:12. It would be helpful to review these chapters as a prelude to our study of chapter 5. The following analysis will serve as a guide.

1. **David's commendation of the men of Jabesh-gilead** (2 Samuel 2:5-7). This passage looks back to 1 Samuel 31:11-13 which describes a deed of heroism and kindness performed by the men of Jabesh-gilead, a town in Transjordan, to the mortal remains of Saul and his sons. David's first act after becoming king of Judah was to honor them for this.

2. **The coronation of Ish-bosheth, the remaining son of Saul, as king over the northern tribes** (2 Samuel 2:8-11). Abner, Saul's commander in chief, was closely related to Saul. For both family and political reasons he was motivated to oppose David in this way. The fact that Ish-bosheth reigned only two years may imply that this coronation did not take place until five and a half years after the death of Saul. The presence of Philistine forces in northern Canaan may have prevented it before.

3. **Civil war** (2 Samuel 2:12—3:1). The beginnings of open war between the rival monarchies is here vividly narrated, together with a one-verse summary of its progress.

4. **David's polygamous household** (2 Samuel 3:2-5). This passage should be noted, as it provides a key to much of the tragedy of David's later life. Blaiklock writes, "There was an unsanctified corner in his personality. Such a bridgehead of evil can be the source of inroads of catastrophe. Observe the process in the rest of David's story **(Bible Characters: Elkanah to David).**

5. **The collapse of Ish-bosheth** (2 Samuel 3:6—4:12). Seeing disaster approaching, Abner found an occasion to transfer his allegiance to David, and to conspire to join the kingdom of Ish-bosheth to that of David. Before he could complete the negotiations he was murdered by Joab, David's commander in chief, as a revenge for Abner's killing of his brother Asahel in the war. David, however, publicly condemned Joab for the deed, and thus conciliated the northern tribes. Subsequently Ish-bosheth, too, was murdered by two of his army captains who imagined that

by the assassination they would ingratiate themselves with David. However, David executed them for the foul deed and gave honorable burial to the head of Ish-bosheth which the assassins had brought to him.

Two things became increasingly clear to the northern dissenters as a result of these events: (a) **The Lord was with David,** and (b) **David bore no ill will** either to the family of Saul or to the northern tribes, but desired the good of all. Thus all opposition to his rule melted away and the time arrived for him to reign over the whole kingdom of Israel. Thus commenced **the united monarchy** which was to last, however, only about seventy-five years, until the death of Solomon.

I. GOD PROVIDES LEADERS (2 Samuel 5:1-5)

A. Recognition (vv. 1, 2)

Events had forced the northern tribes to recognize the fact that the only person who could effectually unite the nation and meet the Philistine threat was David. Mauchline sums up the situation thus: "No claimant of the house of Saul was available to succeed Ish-bosheth apart from the young child Mephibosheth, Jonathan's son (2 Samuel 4: 4). On the other hand, David had strong claims and much popular support. Already a leader of repute in Israel in Saul's time (2 Samuel 5:2), allied by marriage with Saul's house (1 Samuel 18:27-29; 25:44; 2 Samuel 3:14-16), and acknowledged as king of Judah (2 Samuel 2:4), he had no rival; more important still, the belief was held that David was to be king of Israel (2 Samuel 3:9, 10). The basis for this belief may have been, for some, the knowledge of his anointing by Samuel (1 Samuel 16:13), but for many others, it was the signs he had given of being possessed by God's Spirit" **(New Century Bible, 1 and 2 Samuel).**

We are not to think that the expression, "then came all the tribes of Israel . . . unto Hebron," means the total population. Rather, all the tribes sent delegates to put their request to David. The delegates gave three reasons for their change of heart.

1. **"Behold, we are thy bone and thy flesh."** This is equivalent to our modern expression "your own flesh and blood," and it is so rendered by the **New English Bible** and the **New International Version.** The delegates were acknowledging the unity of the twelve tribes as common descendants of Abraham, Isaac, and Jacob. This gave the foundation for one monarchy and kingdom.

2. **"Thou wast he that leddest out and broughtest in Israel."** This refers to the fact that even during Saul's reign (before David's demotion and exile), David was an experienced military leader. The **New International Version** renders it, "you were the one who led Israel on their military campaigns." A further ground for kingship: David was a tried and proved leader.

3. **"The Lord said to thee, Thou shalt feed my people Israel, and thou shalt be a captain over Israel."** The former part of this statement is rendered "you shall be shepherd" in the **New English Bible** and "you will shepherd my people" in the **New International Version.** This is the first instance of this term in the Bible as a metaphor for kingship. It clearly implies that the king of Israel was not to be a despot but a man with a pastoral care. It is also used of the coming Messiah (Isaiah 40:11; Ezekiel 34:23; 37:24). The same Hebrew word is used of the religious leaders of Israel (Jeremiah 3:15; 23:4; Ezekiel 34:2). Also the Greek equivalent is used in the New Testament both of Christ (John 10:2, 11, 14; Hebrews 13:20; Revelation 7:17; 19: 15), and of Christian ministers (John 21:16; Acts 20:28; Ephesians 4:11; 1 Peter 5:2). The term beautifully unites the characteristics of strength and compassion, both of which are required in church leaders, and, as reflected in the Bible, in the political leader.

The delegates from the northern tribes seemed to be aware of the divine prophecies which attributed these qualities to David, and had clearly perceived that he possessed them.

Read Revelation 2:27—"He shall rule (literally, **shepherd**) them with a rod of iron." Do you think that the concepts of "shepherding" and "a rod of iron" are compatible?

B. Coronation (vv. 3-5)

This does not refer to a different event from that described in verses 1 and 2, but more explicitly shows that it was delegates ("the elders of Israel") who assembled at Hebron to recognize and to crown David as king over the whole nation. The word **league** is rendered "covenant" in the **New English Bible. Before the Lord** shows that it was a solemn religious covenant. This was consummated with David's **anointing** as king.

We should note that this was David's third kingly anointing. The first anointing was privately conducted by Samuel when David was still a teenage shepherd (1 Samuel 16:1-13). The second, when he was thirty, was a public ceremony which made him king over Judah (2 Samuel 2:1-4). Now, at thirty-seven years of age, he was at last anointed to be king over the whole united nation.

If David was a type of Christ, can you suggest a parallel in the experience of Jesus? Is there a threefold anointing of Jesus for His messianic work?

---

4. David was thirty years old when he began to reign, and he reigned forty years.

5. In Hebron he reigned over Judah seven years and six months: and in Jerusalem he reigned thirty and three years over all Israel and Judah.

We need not comment on these verses except to say that they provide a useful chronological outline for the study of David's life.

II. GOD PROVIDES FACILITIES (2 Samuel 5:6-12)

A. The Conquest of Jerusalem (vv. 6-8)

6. And the king and his men went to Jerusalem unto the Jebusites, the inhabitants of the land: which spake unto David, saying, Except thou take away the blind and the lame, thou shalt not come in hither: thinking, David cannot come in hither.

7. Nevertheless David took the strong hold of Zion: the same is the city of David.

8. And David said on that day, Whosoever getteth up to the gutter, and smiteth the Jebusites, and the lame and the blind, that are hated of David's soul, he shall be chief and captain. Wherefore they said, The blind and the lame shall not come into the house.

The Israelites had been in Canaan for about three hundred years, but they had not yet conquered the ancient city of Jerusalem. This city existed in Abraham's time, known then as Salem (Genesis 14:18). The conquest of this city mentioned in Judges 1:8 is implied in Scripture itself to be only a partial victory (compare Judges 1:21 and Joshua 15:63). Keil and Delitzsch say that the part of the city which was occupied by Israel was the lower section in the north, but the fortress or citadel in the south remained the possession of the Jebusites **(A Commentary on the Old Testament, The Books of Samuel).** Unger writes, "Situated on a plateau of commanding height twenty-five hundred feet above the Mediterranean and thirty-eight hundred feet above the Dead Sea, the Jebusite fortress, scarped by natural rock for defense, with stout walls, gates, and towers, was considered impregnable" **(Archaeology and the Old Testament).**

David was attracted to Jerusalem for several reasons: (a) He needed territory which was neutral ground between the rival groups of Israeli tribes. (b) So long as it was controlled by a foreign power it could effectively separate the northern and southern divisions of his kingdom. (c) Its impregnable situation was ideal as a capital. Subsequent history for a thousand years was to confirm this.

The statement of verse 6 becomes clearer when read in the **New International Version.** "The Jebusites said to David, 'You will not get in here; even the blind and the lame can ward you off.' They thought, 'David cannot get in here.'" Josephus interpreted this literally. He thought that the Jebusites, in their self-confidence, actually placed blind and lame people as sentinels **(Antiquities,** 7:3:1). More likely it was a taunt: "We are so secure that cripples and blind people can protect us!"

"Nevertheless," says the Bible historian, "David took the strong hold of Zion" (v. 7). "Zion" was another name given to the Jebusite citadel which was situated in the southeastern section of the city (a map of ancient Jerusalem should be consulted).

Thank God for this **nevertheless**. The task confronting David was considered impossible. "Nevertheless," David did it! Just as he had conquered Goliath earlier. And just as he did on many occasions (compare Psalm 60:9-12). He had learned how to change impossible situations through faith in the Lord.

The eighth verse tells us how the fortress was conquered, but the exact meaning of the verse is debated. The use of italics here bears witness to the problem of translation from Hebrew into English. The word **gutter** seems obscure. Modern versions lean either to **water tunnel (Living Bible)** or **grappling-iron (New English Bible).** The **New International Version** has **water shaft** in the text but gives **scaling hooks** in the margin as an alternative. Either alternative vividly shows how David succeeded. If the former, he sent commandos up a water tunnel. Such a tunnel for the conducting of water into the city was discovered by Sir Charles Warren, dating back to Jebusite times. If the latter, an even more intrepid commando maneuver took place.

The statement, "smiteth . . . the lame and the blind, that are hated of David's soul," does not mean that David actually commanded his men to kill the lame and the blind. He was referring to the taunt of the Jebusites of verse 6. He is using their metaphorical, taunting language. Similarly, the proverb mentioned by the historian at the end of verse 8. The lame and the blind were not actually forbidden to enter houses (or probably, the Temple). The phraseology became a proverb to describe repulsive or unwanted people.

What important spiritual truth may be learned from David's conquest of Jerusalem?

B. The Enlargement of Jerusalem (vv. 9-12)

9. So David dwelt in the fort, and called it the city of David. And David built round about from Millo and inward.

It must be understood that the fortress hill of Zion was only a small part of the Jerusalem of later. The excellent article in the **Zondervan Pictorial Bible Dictionary** describes the Zion portion of Jerusalem as only "about eight to ten acres, shaped somewhat like a gigantic human footprint about 1,250 feet long and 400 feet wide," and having a population of approximately 1,230 people.

David made his residence there at once and gave his name to the city. He also instituted a building program. The word **Millo** in this verse is debated. Mauchline says, "The Millo must have been something filled in, like a ramp or a leveled platform and so has sometimes been thought of as a raised processional way from the city of David to that area north of it in which the Temple was built in the reign of Solomon" **(New Century Bible, 1 and 2 Samuel).**

10. And David went on, and grew great, and the Lord God of hosts was with him.

Here the sacred historian draws attention to David's ongoing prosperity from his coronation and the conquest of Jerusalem. He attributes this prosperity to the fact that "the Lord God of hosts **(Jehovah-tsabaoth)** was with him."

11. And Hiram king of Tyre sent messengers to David, and cedar trees, and carpenters, and masons: and they built David an house.

The verse is a significant witness to David's rise to power. As Mauchline says, "We must assume that, by his capture of Jerusalem and in view of the prospect of his uniting Israel and Judah into one kingdom, David had now taken a prominent place in the eyes of the surrounding peoples, so that a courtesy gift to him from the Phoenicians is easily understood at this stage." Though this friendship as it developed in the days of Solomon brought some good, it proved to be also the cause of much evil for the nation.

The Phoenicians were experienced in construction and built "an house," presumably a palace for David.

12. And David perceived that the Lord had established him king over Israel, and that he had exalted his kingdom for his people Israel's sake.

As Gardiner writes, "David's prosperity had not blinded him to the fact that his blessings came to him as the head of the theocracy, and for the sake of God's chosen people" **(Ellicott's Bible Commentary, Vol. 2).**

Though the next four verses are excluded from our study, we should take a passing glance at them. They illustrate once again that "unsanctified corner of David's personality" to which allusion was previously made. He was to reap a bitter harvest from this "sowing to the flesh."

What are the special dangers of polygamy? Illustrate from David's own life.

III. GOD HELPS BRING VICTORY (2 Samuel 5:17-25)

A. First Victory Over the Philistines (vv. 17-21)

Most scholars think that this incident, which describes the beginning of David's renewed conflict with the Philistines (after his period of conciliation narrated in 1 Samuel, chapters 27-31), took place while he was at Hebron before his capture of Jerusalem. The reason for this opinion is the fact that David "went down to the hold." As Keil and Delitzsch say, "The 'hold' cannot be the citadel of Zion (as in vv. 7, 9), because this was so high that they had to go **up** to it on every side."

And he was not likely to leave the citadel of Zion for any other "hold." The "hold" was probably the cave of Adullam (see 1 Samuel 22:1-5) or some other equally strategic place from which to operate. But he was only likely to go there from Hebron, not from Jerusalem.

The Philistines must have been deeply disturbed when the monarchy was united under David, and they decided to crush him right away. They stationed their armies in "the valley of Rephaim," which lay to the south of Jerusalem towards Bethlehem. Thus the Philistines sought to separate David from the northern tribes.

Once again we find David seeking divine direction—a most important guideline for spiritual victory in the Christian life! God is not committed to give victory to those who plan and promote without reference to His holy will.

Under the Lord's leadership David did not wait to be attacked but took the initiative and gained a great victory. As Mauchline puts it, "He swept clean through the Philistines like a river in spate bursting its banks." For this reason he called the place **Baal-perazim,** which means "the lord who breaks out" **(New International Version).** Let Christians never forget, "this God is our God," the Lord of breaking through!

B. Second Victory Over the Philistines (vv. 22-25)

It is not clear whether, when the Philistines renewed the fight, David was still in Hebron or had settled in Jerusalem. Mauchline favors the latter supposition. More important is the fact that David again sought the Lord's guidance. He did not assume that because God had guided and blessed his previous methodology that he must always proceed in this way. How many of us make mistakes along these lines!

On the second occasion the Lord revealed a different strategy, although the Philistines were massed in the same area as before.

23. And when David enquired of the Lord, he said, Thou shalt not go up; but fetch a compass behind them, and come upon them over against the mulberry trees.

24. And let it be, when thou hearest the sound of a going in the tops of the mulberry trees, that then thou shalt bestir thyself: for then shall the Lord go out before thee, to smite the host of the Philistines.

25. And David did so, as the Lord had commanded him; and smote the Philistines from Geba until thou come to Gazer.

Instead of confronting the enemy in a head-on attack as before, David was commanded to "fetch a compass behind them." This is an archaic phrase meaning "wheel round and take them in the rear" **(New English Bible);** "circle around behind them" **(New International Version).** In modern military jargon he was to make a flank attack. There is something to learn from this. Some ardent Christians imagine that to effectively "resist the devil" we must always run into a head-on collision. But there are other strategies of spiritual warfare. We may have to match his craft with craft, such as a flank attack.

The word rendered **mulberry trees** is rendered "balsam trees" by the **New International Version.** The original is **baca trees or shrubs,** meaning "weeping trees." God gave David a sign to reveal the moment of attack: "the sound of marching in the tops of the balsam trees" **(New International Version).** At that moment he was to "move quickly" **(New International Version).** The sound indicated to David that the army of Jehovah-tsabaoth ("the Lord of hosts") had moved to attack the Philistines. In other words: **Until God moved, David must wait. When God moved David must move with Him.**

Matthew Henry used the Lord's command in verse 24 as a portrait of the Day of Pentecost. What does this mean?

REVIEW QUESTIONS

1. How old was David when he began to reign?
2. What were the three reasons for David's being selected?
3. What were the qualifications David required of the man who was to become his captain?
4. Why did the Jebusites boast that even the blind and lame could hold their fortress?
5. Who was responsible for building David's house?

GOLDEN TEXT HOMILY

"DAVID WENT ON, AND GREW GREAT, AND THE LORD GOD OF HOSTS WAS WITH HIM" (2 Samuel 5:10).

Some men are apparently destined for greatness, and it appears obvious early in their lives. Their gifts seem so striking that their rise to greatness appears inevitable to all who watch their development.

David was such a man. As a youngster he was marked by qualities that were too rare for anyone to ignore. He seemed to be inevitably bound for greatness, with only time needed for that greatness to emerge.

This verse refers to that emerging greatness, but it contains a subtle reminder as well. Having reported that David "went on, and grew great," this verse adds that the "Lord God of hosts was with him." It was the presence of the hand of God in his life that was the source of David's greatness. Without God's help, David proved to be weak and full of flaws, as his affair with Bathsheba later demonstrated.

More great men of God fail because they forget that God is the source of their greatness than for any other reason. Because greatness comes so easily to them and because their growth in stature seems so steady and inevitable, it is easy for them to begin to regard their success as being independent of God's presence. David learned, amid tragedy and pain, that when he deserted the Lord God of hosts, he left behind his greatness as well.—**Selected**

SENTENCE SERMONS

COOPERATION WITH GOD in His plan for our life brings us to a place of maximum usefulness.
—**Selected**

GOD IS NOT GREATER if you reverence Him, but you are greater if you serve Him.
—**Augustine**

WHEN GOD MEASURES men He puts the tape around the heart, not the head.
—**"Speaker's Sourcebook"**

EVEN AS YOU CAN'T outrun God when you dodge His will, it is equally impossible to outrun His care when you are in His will.
—**Cal Guy**

EVANGELISTIC APPLICATION

MAN CAN WIN THE VICTORY OVER SIN THROUGH THE POWER OF CHRIST.

Arthur Pink likens the surrender of the northern tribes to David to Christian conversion. Hitherto they had followed the house of Saul with its implacable hatred of David, just as unregenerate people are under the authority and influence of the devil. But they abandoned the old master for a new one and crowned David as their king.

Says Pink, "Conversion consists not **(merely)** in believing certain facts or truths made known in Holy Writ, but lies in the complete surrender of the heart and life to a divine person. It consists in the throwing down of the weapons of our rebellion against Him. It is the total disowning of allegiance to the old master—Satan, sin, self—and a declaring, 'We **will** have this Man to reign over us' (Luke 19: 14). It is owning the claims of Christ and bowing to His rights of absolute dominion over us. It is taking His yoke, submitting unto His scepter, yielding to His blessed will. In a word it is 'receiving Christ Jesus as the **Lord**' (see Colossians 2:6), giving Him the throne of our heart, turning over to Him the control and regulation of our life. Nothing short of this is a scriptural **conversion:** anything else is a make-believe, a lying substitute, a fatal deception."

ILLUMINATING THE LESSON

The passengers on the train were uneasy as they sped along through the dark, stormy night. The lightning was flashing, black clouds were rolling and the train was traveling fast. The fear and tension among the passengers was evident.

One little fellow, however, sitting all by himself, seemed utterly unaware of the storm or the speed of the train. He was amusing himself with a few toys.

One of the passengers spoke to him. "Sonny, I see you are alone on the train. Aren't you afraid to travel alone on such a stormy night?"

The lad looked up with a smile and answered, "No ma'am, I ain't afraid. My daddy's the engineer."

When God is in charge of the plans, we have no need to be afraid.—**"Brethren Quarterly"**

DAILY DEVOTIONAL GUIDE

M. Respecting God's Anointed Leaders. 2 Samuel 1:1-16

T. Lamenting the Death of a Leader. 2 Samuel 1:17-27

W. Anointed for Service. 2 Samuel 2:1-11

T. Facing Difficulties Courageously. 2 Samuel 3:22-39

F. Making Commitments to God. Psalm 101: 1-8

S. Trusting God's Guidance. Acts 16:6-11

May 17, 1981

Doing Things God's Way

Bible Background: 2 Samuel 6:1-23; Psalm 132:1-18
Time: Probably 1003 B.C.
Place: Perez-uzzah, City of David
Supplemental References: Numbers 4:1-15; 1 Chronicles 16:1-11; Psalm 24:1-10; Acts 5:1-16
Golden Text: "And whatsoever ye do in word or deed, do all in the name of the Lord Jesus, giving thanks to God and the Father by him" (Colossians 3:17).
Central Truth: Doing God's work in God's way brings success and happiness.
Evangelistic Emphasis: Man is not saved by good intentions but by obedience to God's Word.

PRINTED TEXT

2 Samuel 6:6. And when they came to Nachon's threshingfloor, Uzzah put forth his hand to the ark of God, and took hold of it; for the oxen shook it.

7. And the anger of the Lord was kindled against Uzzah; and God smote him there for his error; and there he died by the ark of God.

8. And David was displeased, because the Lord had made a breach upon Uzzah: and he called the name of the place Perez-uzzah to this day.

9. And David was afraid of the Lord that day, and said, How shall the ark of the Lord come to me?

10. So David would not remove the ark of the Lord unto him into the city of David: but David carried it aside into the house of Obed-edom the Gittite.

11. And the ark of the Lord continued in the house of Obed-edom the Gittite three months: and the Lord blessed Obed-edom, and all his household.

12. And it was told king David, saying, The Lord hath blessed the house of Obed-edom, and all that pertaineth unto him, because of the ark of God. So David went and brought up the ark of God from the house of Obed-edom into the city of David with gladness.

13. And it was so, that when they that bare the ark of the Lord had gone six paces, he sacrificed oxen and fatlings.

14. And David danced before the Lord with all his might: and David was girded with a linen ephod.

15. So David and all the house of Israel brought up the ark of the Lord with shouting, and with the sound of the trumpet.

16. And as the ark of the Lord came into the city of David, Michal Saul's daughter looked through a window, and saw king David leaping and dancing before the Lord; and she despised him in her heart.

17. And they brought in the ark of the Lord, and set it in his place, in the midst of the tabernacle that David had pitched for it: and David offered burnt-offerings and peace-offerings before the Lord.

18. And as soon as David had made an end of offering burnt-offerings and peace-offerings, he blessed the people in the name of the Lord of hosts.

19. And he dealt among all the people, even among the whole multitude of Israel, as well to the women as men, to every one a cake of bread, and a good piece of flesh, and a flagon of wine. So all the people departed every one to his house.

DICTIONARY

Uzzah (UZ-zah)—2 Samuel 6:6—One of three sons of Abinadab at whose house the Ark remained for twenty years. Ahio, probably a younger brother went before the new cart (1 Chronicles 13:7), and Uzzah walked by the side.

Nachon (NAY-chon)—2 Samuel 6:6—Exact site is unknown. It is the place where Uzzah was struck dead for irreverence.

Perez-uzzah (PE-rez-UZ-zah)—2 Samuel 6:8—Name given by David to the place where Uzzah was struck dead. The name means "breach of Uzzah." The location is unknown.

Obededom (OH-bed-EE-dom)—2 Samuel 6:10—A Gittite, very probably a native of Philistine Gath.

ephod (EF-fod)—2 Samuel 6:14—A sacred vestment used by the priests, but worn by both Samuel (1 Samuel 2:18) and David when the Ark was taken to Jerusalem.

LESSON OUTLINE

I. THOUGHTLESS IRREVERENCE
   A. A Worthy Purpose
   B. A Faulty Method

II. BLESSINGS THROUGH GODLY FEAR
   A. Obed-edom Blessed
   B. David Blessed

III. JOYOUS OBEDIENCE
   A. David's Happiness
   B. David's Generosity
   C. David's Cross

LESSON EXPOSITION

INTRODUCTION

As we saw in our previous lesson, David now had a capital city which was admirable in many ways. F. F. Bruce writes, "Politically it was admirably adapted to be his royal city, for it was neither Israelite nor Judaean, and neither Israel nor Judah could complain that the other was favored in this respect. It remained a city-state in its own right, governed by the king of Israel and Judah, who now succeeded to its ancient dynasty of priest-kings. A sacred city of such ancient prestige was a worthy capital for the founder of a new dynasty under which all elements in the population of Canaan were to be united; it had venerable associations in Israelite as well as in Canaanite eyes, for did not Melchizedek, priest of El-Elyon come forth from there to greet Abraham when the patriarch returned from the rout of the invading kings from the east? Did he not bestow his priestly blessing on Abraham and receive tithes of the spoil from him? And did not David now sit on the throne of Melchizedek as king of Jerusalem as well as on the joint throne of Israel and Judah?" **(Israel and the Nations).**

There remained one thing more, however, for David to do. He needed to make Jerusalem the spiritual and religious center of the nation. This would be the final bond to unify the nation. At the time of his coronation the worship of Jehovah was divided into several sections, none of which, of course, was located in Jerusalem. The "school of the prophets" was located in Ramah, about fifteen miles north of Jerusalem (1 Samuel 19:18-26). The sacred Ark of the Covenant was at Kirjath-jearim, about fifteen miles west of Jerusalem (1 Samuel 7:1). Very probably the altar of sacrifice was at Gibeon a few miles north of Jerusalem (1 Chronicles 16:39). Even Solomon sacrificed there (1 Kings 3:4). And the high priest Abiathar resided with David, both at Hebron and Jerusalem, with the Urim and Thummim (2 Samuel 5:19, 23).

Therefore, David planned to bring all these elements together. In fact, he was only able to bring to Jerusalem Abiathar and his Urim and Thummim, and the sacred Ark. The completion of the task was left to Solomon. Nevertheless, David's achievement, as John Bright says, "was a masterstroke. It must have done more to bind the feelings of the tribes to Jerusalem than we can possibly imagine" **(A History of Israel).**

How David performed his masterstroke is the subject of our present lesson.

I. THOUGHTLESS IRREVERENCE (2 Samuel 6:1-7)

A. A Worthy Purpose (vv. 1, 2)

The Ark of the Lord was Israel's number one national treasure. By the time of David it was several hundred years old. It had been constructed by Moses after a pattern divinely given during his forty days and nights in the presence of God on Mount Sinai. Normally no one but the high priest could see it, for it was kept behind curtains in the most holy place of the Tabernacle. Above it on the mercy seat, between the cherubim, dwelt the Shekinah Glory—the manifested presence of Jehovah. It might be described as Jehovah's private residence on earth. And it was His special symbol. Moreover, it had been associated with some of the most important events of Israel's history—the wanderings in the wilderness, the crossing of the Jordan, the fall of Jericho. No wonder, then, when the sacred Ark was captured by the Philistines in the decadent days of Eli and his sons, the cry went up, **Ichabod—there is no glory!** (1 Samuel 4:21, 22).

After its dramatic capture and the mysterious consequences for the Philistine people, the Ark was returned to Israel, first to Bethshemesh and then to Kirjath-jearim (1 Samuel 5:1—7:2). It had remained in the latter place, preserved and attended by the descendants of Abinadab, throughout the lives of Samuel and Saul.

This raises an important question: Why is there no mention of the Ark during these long years? If the Ark was so important and so precious, why the neglect of it? Some have blamed the rebellious spirit and indifference of Saul. But what about Samuel? Surely, if the Ark was accessible, he, of all people, would have been the first to approach it. On these grounds A. R. S. Kennedy writes, "That this precious shrine, whose presence was as the presence of Yahweh, and whose loss was the passing of the glory from Israel, should have played no part in the revival of national and religious life which culminated in the institution of the monarchy is surely to be explained only by the hypothesis that the Ark was inaccessible to the leaders and to all who rallied round them" **(Century Bible, 1 and 2 Samuel).** Mauchline adds, "Kirjath-jearim was a border town very much under Philistine rule and the Israelites, until now [the reign of David], had neither the confidence nor the military resources to make an assault upon the town" **(New Century Bible, 1 and 2 Samuel).** Kennedy also favors this view, and says, "Only when the Philistine power had been completely broken was it possible for Israel to regain possession of the Ark" (p. 218).

But now, the Philistine power was completely broken (see last lesson on 2 Samuel 5:17-25). The way was open and the time was ripe for the recovery of the sacred Ark.

In our introduction we have shown that the recovery of the Ark and its installation in the capital city of Jerusalem was a matter of political strategy and expediency for David. However it was more. The narrative reveals that it was a matter of personal religious devotion for David. He threw himself into the proceedings with holy joy and enthusiasm. This devout spirit also shows itself in some of the psalms which are related to the event (see Psalms 24 and 132). It was, therefore, a worthy and honorable purpose which motivated David when he planned to recover the Ark of the Lord. He coveted for himself and for the united nation not merely a national treasure and religious symbol, but the spiritual reality which it manifested, the Shekinah Glory of the Lord.

What is its meaning for us? Surely nothing less than the Holy Spirit in all His fullness! To have forfeited the glorious Pentecostal fullness, whether in the church as a whole or in our individual lives, is a momentous calamity. Nothing can make up for the loss. We may have everything else, as David and Israel had everything else when Jerusalem was conquered. But without the glorious presence and power of the Holy Spirit, we are deficient. We need to sense our deficiency, as David did, and begin to yearn and long and pray and plan to "bring up the Ark of the Lord."

If the recovering of the Ark has some such spiritual significance for the Christian as we have suggested, what would be the meaning of the conquest of the Philistines as a prelude to that recovery?

B. A Faulty Method (vv. 3-7)

The Ark had been in the house of Abinadab for seventy years (Samuel = 20 years; Saul = 40 years; David = 10 years). Therefore, the reference to "the sons of Abinadab" probably means **grandsons.** This mode of description is fairly common in Scripture.

David planned a great religious procession, almost a carnival, to celebrate the recovery of the Ark: a new cart pulled by oxen, accompanied by thirty thousand men, and a large orchestra. There was to be singing and dancing along the way. It was to be almost a riot of joy (vv. 3-5). (See also 1 Chronicles 13:1-8.)

6. And when they came to Nachon's threshingfloor, Uzzah put forth his hand to

the ark of God, and took hold of it; for the oxen shook it.

7. And the anger of the Lord was kindled against Uzzah; and God smote him there for his error; and there he died by the ark of God.

What is here called "Nachon's threshingfloor" is referred to as the "threshingfloor of Chidon" in 1 Chronicles 13:9. Keil and Delitzsch say, **"Nachon** means 'the stroke,'" and **"Chidon** means 'destruction or disaster.'" Its location is unknown. The names were probably given as a result of the calamity which befell David's procession. In view of David's worthy motives and of the success and blessing which had accompanied his endeavors thus far, the statements in verses 6 and 7 come as a terrible shock. Even a mere accident or temporary setback would be a puzzle. But the record attributes the disaster to an act of divine judgment. We are bound to ask, Why? This is especially so in respect of the present generation of Evangelicals. The concept of "a good God" has weakened our understanding of God's "righteousness" and "wrath." These are uncomfortable words and doctrines in our ears.

Two reasons may be given for the divine displeasure.

1. **David neglected to seek divine counsel before he went ahead with his plans.** Arthur Pink draws attention to this: "Each time the Philistines came up against him, David 'enquired of the Lord, but nothing is said of **that** now that he proposed to conduct the Ark into a suitable habitation for it." He consulted with his generals (1 Chronicles 13:1) but took it for granted that the Lord would rubber-stamp this plan. How often in our church and interchurch schemes for revival we make the same mistake!

2. **David set aside the divine pattern and followed a Philistine methodology.** The Mosaic law clearly laid down the divine arrangement for moving the sacred Ark (see Numbers 3:29-39; 4:15; 7:9). It must be borne upon the shoulders of the Levites. The Philistines had used a new cart (1 Samuel 6:7) in which to get rid of the Ark. Now David used a new cart to recover it. Blaikie draws the lesson: "It was substituting a heathen example for a divine rule in the worship of God" **(Expositor's Bible, The Second Book of Samuel).** Has not this been a frequent mistake throughout the history of the Church? And not least in respect of revival. Man seems prone to ignore the principles of the Bible. He loves to make a new cart.

Can you suggest examples of the "new cart" in modern times?

II. BLESSINGS THROUGH GODLY FEAR (2 Samuel 6:8-13)

A. Obed-edom Blessed (vv. 8-11)

8. And David was displeased, because the Lord had made a breach upon Uzzah: and he called the name of the place Perez-uzzah to this day.

9. And David was afraid of the Lord that day, and said, How shall the ark of the Lord come to me?

Blaikie says that the sudden calamity which stopped the procession "was like the bursting of a thunderstorm on an excursion party that rapidly sends everyone to flight." David himself reacted in "displeasure" ("anger" in modern versions) and fear of the Lord. His anger was not directed against God, but most probably against the unfortunate Uzzah whose irreverent and religiously unlawful action had brought about God's judgment. He was angry because his plans had been thwarted and that the great occasion had been marred. "Fear of God" may be either godly fear (reverence) or terror. Here it was the latter. As Pink says, "That holy vessel of the tabernacle which had been the object of his veneration, now became an occasion of dread."

David's cry might well express the feelings of God's own people today who long for true biblical revival and the outpouring of the Holy Spirit: "How shall . . . the Lord come to me?"

10. So David would not remove the ark of the Lord unto him into the city of David: but David carried it aside into the house of Obed-edom the Gittite.

11. And the ark of the Lord continued in the house of Obed-edom the Gittite three months: and the Lord blessed Obed-edom, and all his household.

David had the good sense to realize that God had stopped his religious procession. He would go no further, but placed the sacred Ark in a nearby residence, "the house of Obed-edom [meaning 'servant of Edom'] the Gittite." Some think this man was a Philistine, as **Gittite** means "of Gath," a Philistine city. If so this man was an alien who had settled in Israel near Jerusalem and had become a part of Israel. Six hundred of these had followed David in his army (2 Samuel 15:18-22; 18:2). Others think the word **Gittite** here refers to **Gath-rimmon** in the tribe of Dan (Joshua 19:45; 21:24), and that Obed-edom was a Levite whose birthplace was this place.

David did nothing more about the Ark for three months, when the astonishing news came to him that the Lord blessed Obed-edom and all that he had. Probably this was an act of grace not only to Obed-edom himself but to David also. By this happening, the interest of David was attracted. He perceived that the Ark itself was not to be feared. It could be a source of blessing as well as of judgment.

"How shall the ark of the Lord come to me?" If a person seeking the fullness of the Holy Spirit asked such a question, what would be the answer?

B. David Blessed (vv. 12, 13)

12. And it was told king David, saying, The Lord hath blessed the house of Obed-edom, and all that pertaineth unto him, because of the ark of God. So David went and brought up the ark of God from the house of Obed-edom into the city of David with gladness.

13. And it was so, that when they that bare the ark of the Lord had gone six paces, he sacrificed oxen and fatlings.

These verses should be supplemented by 1 Chronicles 15:2-26 which gives a much fuller picture of David's second attempt to recover the Ark. This time he consulted with the religious leaders of the nation. He realized that his mistake lay in not using the Levites to transport the Ark upon their shoulders (1 Chronicles 15:12, 13). We may observe that in changing his methodology David felt no obligation to change the celebrations into a lower key. The crowds once again were present; the orchestration was, if anything, greater (1 Chronicles 15:14-28). But he abandoned the worldly way of the new cart and followed the Bible way of the Levitical shoulders. Thus, his panicky fear of the Lord, his terror, was transformed into godly fear or true reverence for the Word of God.

In 1 Chronicles 15:12 David commanded the Levites to "sanctify yourselves ... that ye may bring up the ark." What is the special significance of this for Christian's seeking revival or the Holy Spirit's fullness?

III. JOYOUS OBEDIENCE (2 Samuel 6:14-23)

A. David's Happiness (vv. 14-16)

14. And David danced before the Lord with all his might; and David was girded with a linen ephod.

15. So David and all the house of Israel brought up the ark of the Lord with shouting, and with the sound of the trumpet.

If we compare this record with 1 Chronicles 15:16-24 we get the impression that the religious ceremonial which accompanied the bringing of the Ark to Jerusalem was a happy mixture of planned liturgy and spontaneity. There were well-prepared choirs and orchestras, and many commentators agree that Psalm 24 was composed for this occasion. Sung antiphonally by two choirs, this psalm vividly portrays the thrilling occasion. However, there was much spontaneity, the most surprising example being David, who let himself go into the festivities with relish, even to the point of putting off his royal robe and dancing in a linen ephod, which was a short garment hanging from the shoulders. The word "dance" might be rendered "whirled." It is the only time this Hebrew word is used in the Old Testament, and means "to whirl about." It implies a very intensive and vigorous form of movement. The **New English Bible** translates, he "danced without restraint." The king was absolutely exuberant in his gladness.

B. David's Generosity (vv. 17-19)

17. And they brought in the ark of the Lord, and set it in his place, in the midst of the tabernacle that David had pitched for it: and David offered burnt-offerings and peace-offerings before the Lord.

The "tabernacle" here referred to was not the tabernacle of Moses, but a new "tent" (modern versions) which David had prepared to house it (1 Chronicles 15:1). It is assumed by expositors that this would be modeled on the Mosaic tabernacle. In this tent, no doubt its "outer court," David offered sacrifices unto the Lord, probably for the consecration of the new tabernacle.

18. And as soon as David had made an end of offering burnt-offerings and peace-offerings, he blessed the people in the name of the Lord of hosts.

19. And he dealt among all the people, even among the whole multitude of Israel, as well to the women as men, to every one a cake of bread, and a good piece of flesh, and a flagon of wine. So all the people departed every one to his house.

Two things are mentioned here: (a) **He blessed the people** (v. 18). For examples of such a procedure see Numbers 6:22-26 and 1 Kings 8:14-55. (b) **He distributed (Amplified)** gifts of food to the people (v. 19).

There is a close association of joy with generosity. This is seen in conspicuous fashion in the days immediately following Pentecost (Acts 2:45; 4:34-37). The joy of the Lord touches the springs of generosity. God's blessings cannot be contained, they must be communicated.

C. David's Cross (vv. 20-23)

These verses look back to verse 16—Michal, David's wife, "despised him in her heart," as she witnessed his exuberant participation in the whirling dance. Apparently she bottled up her embarrassment and anger at the time. It was different at home. "David returned to bless his household." But what a reception! His wife really tore him apart. Expositors discuss the reason for Michal's attitude. Most likely her motivation was deeper and more prolonged than her embarrassment at his dancing. This was merely an occasion which triggered deep resentment at her husband's spirituality. She had originally fallen in love with a hero and soldier, not a religious enthusiast. She may have come to share her father's feelings about David, as she had been forcibly taken from her second husband (see 2 Samuel 3:13-16). Pfeiffer suggests that "she may have been angered to discover that she was but one of David's many wives" **(Old Testament History).**

In any case, David discovered that not everyone, even in his family, appreciated or even understood his enthusiastic devotion to the Lord. There was a cross to be borne. His reply has become immortal: "I will yet be more vile than thus." We should note that the old English word **vile** does not mean immoral, but "undignified" **(New International Version).** Wesley referred to this to justify his adoption of field preaching, which in his day was a contemptible and undignified thing.

REVIEW QUESTIONS

1. Describe the arrangements by which the Ark was to be transported.

2. What unfortunate incident developed when the Ark was being moved onto the threshing floor at Nachon?

3. After the unfortunate incident, where did David take the Ark?

4. How long did the Ark remain at Obed-edom's house?

5. How did David react to the Lord's allowing him to take the Ark to Jerusalem?

GOLDEN TEXT HOMILY

"AND WHATSOEVER YE DO IN WORD OR DEED, DO ALL IN THE NAME OF THE LORD JESUS, GIVING THANKS TO GOD AND THE FATHER BY HIM" (Colossians 3:17).

Doing all in the name of the Lord Jesus suggests that everything is hallowed to the Christian. Not just churchgoing or praying or singing, but even our eating and drinking. Nothing is too small to be done in his name. A cup of cold water takes on a far greater significance when it is offered because of Him. God delights to use common things for His glory. He does not ask for our body to be burned, but that our living offering shall be our actions, our speech, and our attitudes, reflecting His presence. And this, too, is for our benefit. Even the most common iron becomes magnetic if associated closely with a powerful magnet.

This verse calls to its proper place the motive of our life. If anything that we do brings Him no glory we must certainly evaluate our reason for doing it. We need not always say we do it for His glory or even consciously think about doing it for His glory, for since we are His and He is ours there is no other acceptable way because "in him we live, and move, and have our being" (Acts 17:28). It is in His name that Christians fellowship with Christians and in His name that we share the gospel with those who are lost.

To do everything in His name is to do nothing unworthy of His name. Here is the great challenge for the child of God. Little debate is needed as to whether a thing is right or wrong. The simple test is whether it can be done so as to bring glory to Him. This rule is good in all places, under all circumstances, at all times, and for any age. It is the rule by which God tests the length and the breadth of our Christian commitment.

The unconverted cannot relate to this text because it requires Christ to be first, last, and in all.

To do everything in His name is to do nothing in our own name. Although men may conceive of us as performing it, in our own heart we do it unto Him. We accept responsibility for our actions but point always to Him whose ambassadors we are. One of our former presidents said that there were two people in the White House: Truman the President and Truman the man. The implication was that Truman the man could do what he pleased and the people had no reason to question it, while Truman the President must be responsible to the people for his actions and deeds. This is not true in the Christian religion. All that we do represents Him whose ambassadors we are. Our private life and our public life speaks one message.

This statement implies also that the Christian does all in His strength. By what power do we preach? By whose strength do we endure? What secret supply is available to the Christian? "I can do all things through Christ which strengtheneth me" (Philippians 4:13) is the declaration of God's children everywhere. We have no power but His; but having His power we need none other. We have no authority but His; but having received His authority we desire none of our own. We give thanks by Him because He is the channel through which God's blessings flow to us and to a needy world.—**Laud O. Vaught, Ph.D., President, Northwest Bible College, Minot, North Dakota**

SENTENCE SERMONS

OBEDIENCE TO GOD is the most infallible evidence of sincere and supreme love to Him.
—**Nathanael Emmons**

JOY IS MORE divine than sorrow, for joy is bread and sorrow is medicine.
—**Henry Ward Beecher**

DOING GOD'S WORK in God's way brings success and happiness.
—**Selected**

ONE MIGHT SACRIFICE without obeying, but he cannot obey without sacrificing.
—**"Notes and Quotes"**

EVANGELISTIC APPLICATION

MAN IS NOT SAVED BY GOOD INTENTIONS BUT BY OBEDIENCE TO GOD'S WORD.

The sacred Ark of the Lord which David coveted for his capital city, Jerusalem, is a wonderful type of the Lord Jesus Christ. It is even more important that men and women should welcome Christ into their heart than that David should welcome the Ark to Jerusalem.

Without the Ark the city of Jerusalem was minus the greatest treasure of the nation. Without Christ the heart of man is minus the pearl of greatest price. Man, like Jerusalem, may possess so much that is important and beautiful, but without Christ he lacks eternal value and is doomed to perish.

Recognizing his need, David cried, "How shall the ark of the Lord come to me?" It is a great day for a sinner when, recognizing his need, he cries, "What must I do to be saved?" or "How can I receive Jesus Christ into my heart and life?"

David found the answer to his cry in the Bible. When he followed the Bible way, he was enabled to bring the Ark to Jerusalem with great rejoicing. It is so in regard to the way of salvation. There is only one way and that is the Bible way. There are two clear-as-crystal steps in this way. Repent! that is, change your attitude, forsake your sins. And, believe on the Lord Jesus Christ and thou shalt be saved! that is, put your entire trust and confidence in Him!

All who follow this way welcome Christ with great rejoicing.

ILLUMINATING THE LESSON

One Sunday morning a Christian layman from Louisville, Kentucky walked down the streets in St. Louis, Missouri, trying to find a place to worship. The streets were rather deserted, but he saw a police officer; so he went up to him and said, "Officer, I'm a Protestant, and I want to go to church to worship. Could you suggest a place?"

The officer said, "I will," and he named a church and gave him directions as to how to get there. The man thanked him and started to go; then suddenly he stopped, turned around, and said, "By the way, officer, there must be several churches on your beat. Why have you named this particular one for me to go to?"

And the officer said, "I'll tell you why! I'm not a very religious man; I'm not a church man. There are several churches on my beat. I'm sending you to this one because I've observed for years that the people who come out of that church are the happiest-looking church people in St. Louis!" How little these people realized that an ungodly police officer had taken notice of the fact that there was the evidence of the joy of the Lord upon their countenances, as they came out of His sanctuary.—**Paul Reese**

DAILY DEVOTIONAL GUIDE
M. Achieving Victory. Exodus 15:1-8
T. Enduring God's Testings. Psalm 30:1-12
W. Following God's Precepts. Psalm 119:161-168
T. Knowing God's Righteousness. Psalm 132:1-10
F. Sorrowing Turned to Joy. John 16:16-24
S. Proclaiming God's Redemption. Acts 5:33-42

May 24, 1981

The Consequences of Rebellion

Bible Background: 2 Samuel 13:37—15:37; 18:1-33

Time: Around 980 B.C.

Place: Hebron, Geshur, Syria, Giloh, Jerusalem

Supplemental References: 2 Samuel 13:23-39; Psalms 3:1-8; 5:6-9; Proverbs 23:6, 7

Golden Text: "Woe to the rebellious children, saith the Lord, that take counsel, but not of me" (Isaiah 30:1).

Central Truth: All sin is rebellion against God, the Sovereign of the Universe.

Evangelistic Emphasis: Reconciliation with God is freely offered to man through Christ, the atoning sacrifice.

PRINTED TEXT

2 Samuel 15:1. And it came to pass after this, that Absalom prepared him chariots and horses, and fifty men to run before him.

2. And Absalom rose up early, and stood beside the way of the gate: and it was so, that when any man that had a controversy came to the king for judgment, then Absalom called unto him, and said, Of what city art thou? And he said, Thy servant is of one of the tribes of Israel.

3. And Absalom said unto him, See, thy matters are good and right; but there is no man deputed of the king to hear thee.

4. Absalom said moreover, Oh, that I were made judge in the land, that every man which hath any suit or cause might come unto me, and I would do him justice!

5. And it was so, that when any man came nigh to him to do him obeisance, he put forth his hand, and took him, and kissed him.

6. And on this manner did Absalom to all Israel that came to the king for judgment: so Absalom stole the hearts of the men of Israel.

7. And it came to pass after forty years, that Absalom said unto the king, I pray thee, let me go and pay my vow, which I have vowed unto the Lord, in Hebron.

8. For thy servant vowed a vow while I abode at Geshur in Syria, saying, If the Lord shall bring me again indeed to Jerusalem, then I will serve the Lord.

9. And the king said unto him, Go in peace. So he arose, and went to Hebron.

10. But Absalom sent spies throughout all the tribes of Israel, saying, As soon as ye hear the sound of the trumpet, then ye shall say, Absalom reigneth in Hebron.

11. And with Absalom went two hundred men out of Jerusalem, that were called; and they went in their simplicity, and they knew not any thing.

12. And Absalom sent for Ahithophel the Gilonite, David's counsellor, from his city, even from Giloh, while he offered sacrifices. And the conspiracy was strong; for the people increased continually with Absalom.

DICTIONARY

Hebron (HE-bron)—2 Samuel 15:7—An ancient city, midway between the Mediterranean

Sea and the Dead Sea in Judah. Hallowed by the patriarchs. For a time it was the royal residence of David.

Geshur (GESH-ur or GE-shur)—2 Samuel 15:8—A place in northeast Bashan (Deuteronomy 3:14). David married Maachah, the daughter of Talmai, King of Geshur (2 Samuel 3:3). She was also the mother of Absalom. Geshur is a district now called El Lejah.

Syria (SIHR-ee-uh)—2 Samuel 15:8—A heathen country northeast of Palestine.

Giloh (GI-loh)—2 Samuel 15:12—A village in Judah (Joshua 15:5) named with the towns to the south of Hebron.

simplicity—2 Samuel 15:11—A state of being innocent regarding a matter.

LESSON OUTLINE

I. DECEITFULNESS OF REBELLION
II. ANGUISH OF REBELLION
III. RESULTS OF REBELLION
IV. CONCERN FOR THE REBELLION

LESSON EXPOSITION

INTRODUCTION

In presenting our thirteenth lesson we are taking a great leap forward across seven chapters of the Bible, several of which are nevertheless of crucial importance for evaluating the life and work of David. In these chapters are narrated the making of the Davidic Covenant (chapter 7); the growth of the Davidic empire (chapters 8 and 10); the lovely story of David's kindness to Mephibosheth, the son of Jonathan, in remembrance of the covenant of David and Jonathan (chapter 9); David's fall into the sins of adultery and murder, and his repentance and forgiveness (chapters 11 and 12); and the firstfruits of the harvest of sorrow which David reaped as a consequence of his polygamous household (chapter 13).

It is within the context of chapter 13, which narrates a sordid story of rape and murder in the royal household, that David's son Absalom, the subject of our present lesson, appears on the scene. His very first appearance is as the murderer of his half brother Amnon, in revenge for his rape of Absalom's sister.

The seven chapters which are devoted to the history of Absalom reveal how near David came to total collapse through the deceitfulness and rebellion of his son.

Probably a period of twenty years is spanned between the recovery of the Ark and the tragic story here recorded.

I. DECEITFULNESS OF REBELLION (2 Samuel 15:1-12)

When Nathan the prophet had faithfully uncovered David's sin of adultery and murder, he proclaimed a stern prophecy: "Now therefore the sword shall never depart from thine house; because thou hast despised me, and hast taken the wife of Uriah the Hittite to be thy wife" (2 Samuel 12:10). Though David was forgiven when he repented, the consequences of his actions were not canceled. With the immoral and brutal behavior of his sons, Amnon and Absalom, which is described in chapter 13, harvesttime began. It is a fallacy out of harmony with Scripture and experience to think that divine forgiveness will automatically let us off the temporal results of our actions.

When Absalom murdered his brother Amnon he fled for protection to his father-in-law in Geshur, a region between Syria and Transjordan, where he remained for three years (2 Samuel 13:37-39). However, through the negotiating skill of Joab, David's commander in chief and nephew, Absalom was allowed back in Jerusalem, and eventually was restored to the king's favor (chapter 14).

It is at this point of the Absalom story that we turn to our lesson outline. Blaikie makes the comment, "David lets Absalom loose, as it were, on the people of Jerusalem" **(Expositor's Bible, 2 Samuel).** The consequences were dramatic and fearful. As the story unfolds, it becomes evident that Absalom had not been changed by his five years of discipline. Indeed the criminal had only become more ambitious, clever, and cunning.

1. And it came to pass after this, that Absalom prepared him chariots and horses, and fifty men to run before him.

Kennedy says, "A chariot, horses, and runners were marks of royalty (1 Samuel 8:11).

Compare Adonijah's similar pretensions, 1 Kings 1:5" **(Century Bible, 1 and 2 Samuel).** Mauchline says, "It may even have had the appearance of a private army" **(New Century Bible, 1 and 2 Samuel).**

2. **And Absalom rose up early, and stood beside the way of the gate: and it was so, that when any man that had a controversy came to the king for judgment, then Absalom called unto him, and said, Of what city art thou? And he said, Thy servant is of one of the tribes of Israel.**

3. **And Absalom said unto him, See, thy matters are good and right; but there is no man deputed of the king to hear thee.**

4. **Absalom said moreover, Oh that I were made judge in the land, that every man which hath any suit or cause might come unto me, and I would do him justice!**

Absalom's clever strategy now begins to appear. "The way of the gate," was a strategic place for Absalom to promote his cause, being the place where people came in and out and congregated, and in which in ancient times the city magistrates often conducted their business. Here the crafty Absalom pretended to be compassionately concerned about cases of injustice and need. A modern analogy is the political vote-seeker—"If you would only make me president, or governor, or senator!"

5. **And it was so, that when any man came nigh to him to do him obeisance, he put forth his hand, and took him, and kissed him.**

6. **And on this manner did Absalom to all Israel that came to the king for judgment: so Absalom stole the hearts of the men of Israel.**

These verses show the extent to which the conspirator was ready to go in order to ingratiate himself with the people. By this show of affection he "stole the hearts of the men of Israel." Keil and Delitzsch say of the word **stole**: "This does not mean to deceive or cheat, but to steal the heart, i.e. to bring a person over to his side secretly and by stratagem" **(A Commentary on the Old Testament, The Books of Samuel).** We must realize that Absalom had great natural gifts. He not only was a great promoter but he also was a person of magnificent personality (see 2 Samuel 14:25, 26). To use the modern jargon, he had great **charisma**, not in the true spiritual sense of the Holy Spirit's anointing, but in the natural, worldly sense of impressive and powerful personality.

The question is sometimes asked: What was David doing while Absalom promoted his cause? Some answer: He was very ill from a disease (compare Psalms 41 and 55). What is your opinion?

---

7. **And it came to pass after forty years, that Absalom said unto the king, I pray thee, let me go and pay my vow, which I have vowed unto the Lord, in Hebron.**

8. **For thy servant vowed a vow while I abode at Geshur in Syria, saying, If the Lord shall bring me again indeed to Jerusalem, then I will serve the Lord.**

9. **And the king said unto him, Go in peace. So he arose, and went to Hebron.**

It should be noted that modern versions and many commentators change "forty years" into "four years" (v. 7), as also does Josephus. These verses uncover still another aspect of Absalom's bad character. Under the pretense of fulfilling a religious vow made during his exile, he asked the king's permission to go to Hebron. His real purpose was to bring his plotting and planning to a climax, as the subsequent verses show.

10. **But Absalom sent spies throughout all the tribes of Israel, saying, As soon as ye hear the sound of the trumpet, then ye shall say, Absalom reigneth in Hebron.**

11. **And with Absalom went two hundred men out of Jerusalem, that were called; and they went in their simplicity, and they knew not any thing.**

12. **And Absalom sent for Ahithophel the Gilonite, David's counsellor, from his city, even from Giloh, while he offered sacrifices. And the conspiracy was strong; for the people increased continually with Absalom.**

The word "spies" (v. 10) is rendered "secret messengers" **New International Version** and "runners" by the **New English Bible.** The implication is that Absalom had already prepared groups of conspirators throughout the land, and the runners were sent to alert them that the moment for rebellion had arrived. But why did he invite the two hundred men from Jerusalem who had no knowledge of what was happening? Gardiner thinks they were "prominent and influential citizens of Jerusalem" **(Ellicott's**

Bible Commentary, Vol. 2). We are familiar with hostages in our own times, and it may be that these men provided Absalom with a similar kind of insurance if things went wrong.

Ahithophel was a king's counselor who appears to have been completely committed to the rebellion. Various guesses have been made concerning his change of allegiance. One suggestion is that as Bath-sheba's grandfather (2 Samuel 11:3; 23:34) he had not forgiven David for seducing her. Another is that the growth of the kingdom and the coming into influence of other leaders had weakened his power, and he felt rejected. The passages in Psalms 41:9 and 55:13 (David's "familiar friend" or "acquaintance") are thought to refer to Ahithophel.

Large numbers of the tribes of Israel appeared ready to join the rebellion. Can you think of any defects in David's administration which influenced them?

II. ANGUISH OF REBELLION (2 Samuel 15: 13-37)

As soon as David learned that Absalom had raised a rebellion, he decided to flee from Jerusalem. At first sight we might think that David acted in weakness and panic. Why did he so easily run? However, as we look more deeply into this chapter (and the next two chapters) it becomes clear that David's decision to flee the city was an act of military strategy, even though he was stricken with grief.

David had a choice: either to defend the city or to move out, rally his forces, and meet the rebel forces in open ground. If he had done the former, he would have been cut off from his friends and soldiers outside Jerusalem and he would have exposed the holy city and its entire population to a seige which might have lasted a long time. Moreover, he did not know how many allies Absalom had in Jerusalem. By leaving the city, he avoided these dangers and placed himself in a position where he himself could take the initiative against the rebels.

The title of our second division—**Anguish of Rebellion**—focuses on the suffering which Absalom's ambitions brought upon the nation. Note verses 23 and 30 which vividly portray the anguish, not only of David himself, but also of his close associates and of all his supporters in Jerusalem. The place of this drama was the Mount of Olives, and we might even think of this experience as a Gethsemane agony for David and his government. How often in the long history of state and church has the selfish ambition of some individual, though frequently camouflaged as altruism or justice, or even the will of God, brought whole nations and communities into anguish!

We should not fail to take note of David's remarkable meekness and humility in the face of his adversity (see 2 Samuel 15:24-26; 16: 5-14). He must have recalled the prophecy of Nathan and realized that his cup of suffering came to him within the will of God and, therefore, for his good. The devil inspired it but the Lord graciously would use it! To face suffering of any kind with this understanding and attitude will cast a tree of sweetening into the bitterest Marah.

In evaluating suffering can you think of any guidelines by which we may determine whether we are "suffering according to the will of God"? (See 1 Peter 4:19.)

There are, however, some other noble aspects of David's spirit which shine out in his suffering.

One is his attitude of prayer and worship (vv. 31, 32). David may have been deeply disturbed when he learned that Ahithophel had defected to Absalom. But he "took it to the Lord in prayer." Is not this the greatest thing we can do in such a situation? God can even use the counsel of a defector for our good—as indeed He did in David's case (see 2 Samuel 17:1-14). Reference should also be made to Psalm 3, which was born out of the Absalom rebellion, and shows how David prayed through to victory at this time.

Another is his faith in the Word of God. Stored up in David's memory were a number of divine disclosures to him concerning his successors. He could think back over forty years to his anointing by Samuel. He could recall the Lord's providences and deliverances on many occasions. Even the farseeing words of Nabal's wife Abigail, whom David married, would come to mind (1 Samuel 25:28-30). Outstanding in his thoughts would be the great promises of Jehovah's covenant with him (2 Samuel 7:4-29; Psalm 89). Moreover, God had given David a special revelation which assured him that his heir would be

Solomon, who at the time of the rebellion was about ten years old (1 Chronicles 22:6-10). Thus, in this time of great shaking David had a firm foundation for his faith. Reasoning from these prophecies and promises, he knew that Absalom's conspiracy was doomed to failure. He expressed his faith by sending the Ark of the Lord back to Jerusalem when Zadok would have carried it out after David (vv. 24-26).

Here is portrayed real biblical faith, which is not merely positive thinking, but a confidence and a hope which reasons and rests on the Word of the living God.

Yet another aspect of David's wonderful spirit is the practical wisdom which he displayed. He may, as some think, have been seriously sick for some time, but the crisis which forced him out of the hospital showed that he had lost none of his shrewd and courageous generalship. Grief-stricken, though he was, he nevertheless had the situation under control. His vacating of Jerusalem was tactical wisdom. The sending back of the priests and Hushai into the very camp of Absalom was a shrewd and calculated stroke of diplomacy. In Cromwell's language, "he trusted in God but kept his powder dry." As Mauchline says, "David shows that he did not think of his trust in Yahweh as absolving him from the responsibility of taking all possible measures on his own account for the success of his cause."

What can we learn from David's attitude about believing prayer and the use of means?

III. RESULTS OF REBELLION (2 Samuel 18: 1-23)

Two chapters of the biblical record (2 Samuel 16 and 17) are omitted, both from our lesson outline and our Bible Background. We advise, however, that they be carefully read both for their interest and because they vividly describe the developments of the drama which began to be unfolded in chapter 15 and which comes to a climax in chapter 18. We shall more clearly follow chapter 18 if we have followed the progress of the rebellion, both in Jerusalem where Absalom had assumed the kingship (2 Samuel 16:15—17:23) and in Transjordan (Mahanaim,) where David had placed himself (2 Samuel 17:24-29).

At the point where our first division begins, both David and Absalom, with their armies, were situated in "Gilead," that is, central Transjordan. Absalom had gone there following the shrewd counsel of Hushai, who was really working for David. David had gone there, specifically to Mahanaim on the Jabbok (the place of Jacob's Peniel experience—see Genesis 32:1-32), when advised by Hushai through the two high priests' sons of Absalom's intentions (2 Samuel 17:15-22).

From Psalm 3:5-8 we see that David had complete assurance that Absalom would be defeated in the coming battle. This is reflected in the Samuel record in two ways: (a) His confident planning of the battle (vv. 1-4). (b) His concern for Absalom's welfare (v. 5). This concern assumes that Absalom would be defeated. Some have criticized David for this concern. However, surely it reveals David's agony of soul, torn as he was between his public duty and fatherly love.

The battle is only briefly described (vv. 6-8). The hastily gathered rebel army was no match for the royalist troops under skillful and experienced generalship. David had strategically chosen to fight Absalom in what the **King James Version** calls "the wood," a term which scarcely pictures the scene. Modern versions describe it as a "forest," and the **Oxford Annotated Bible** describes it as "a trackless jungle from which there was no escape."

In the battle, Absalom himself met a bizarre and humiliating death (vv. 9-18). Either his head or his hair was caught in the fork of a tree. His mule fled and the rider was left suspended and helpless in the tree. His plight was reported to Joab who, with ten armor-bearers, killed Absalom and threw the body into a large hole and covered it with stones. Then, calling off further bloodshed, Joab sent the news to David.

How, do you think, could Joab justify his killing of Absalom in defiance of the king's orders?

IV. CONCERN FOR THE REBELLION (2 Samuel 18:24-33)

With the death of Absalom, and that done brutally by Joab's own hand, the general was left with the extremely difficult task of communicating to David the double news of victory and of the slaying of Absalom. News was carried in those times by fast runners.

Ahimaaz, the son of Zadok one of the two high priests, offered to run with the news to David, but was rejected by Joab in favor of a Cushite, probably an Ethiopian slave. The most probable reason for this would be that Joab wished to spare Ahimaaz from becoming the victim of a violent, emotional reaction when David got the news of Absalom's death. He had no such scruples about the Cushite. Nevertheless, after the Cushite had started, Ahimaaz again requested permission to run, and now permission was given. Joab no doubt thought that the Cushite's news would have reached David before Ahimaaz arrived. However, the reverse happened, because the Cushite took the stiffer though shorter route, while Ahimaaz took the easier though longer route.

It seems that when Ahimaaz reached David he lacked the courage to tell the whole story. He reported the victory but lied about the death of Absalom. However, the Cushite filled in the picture. As things worked out the news was broken gradually and gently to the king. Even so he was overcome by violent emotion (v. 33).

In order to get the complete story we should read on into chapter 19 which describes the effects of the king's grief upon the army. The impression is given that the emotion of the king was hard for the soldiers to comprehend. As Mauchline sums it up, "The impression given by verse 33 is of a king enveloped in personal grief to the exclusion of everything else. But it was not a private danger from which he had been saved at Mahanaim; it was a national disaster. Others had died there, fighting for the king; many more had been wounded. That is the point of 19:1-4. An occasion of national rejoicing for victory had been overshadowed and had been effectually ruled out by the king's mourning." Other commentators make similar comments. It was not that David's grief was wrong. It was natural and normal. But David not only was a parent but also a public figure. And a public figure may be called upon to subordinate his own interests, and even his own deepest feelings, to the public good. This is so both in church and in state. Arthur Pink asserts that David's mourning for Absalom was "inordinate." In this he follows Matthew Henry.

In this evaluation there is a message for us all. Affections and emotions may be, in themselves, perfectly proper. But if we are carried away and overwhelmed by them to the point where our usefulness, our influence, and our example, are spoiled, they have become "inordinate," and therefore blameworthy.

Consider Joab's rebuke to King David (2 Samuel 19:5-7). Was this justified?

REVIEW QUESTIONS

1. How did Absalom gain most of his followers?
2. How did Absalom deceive David?
3. What method did Absalom plan to use to make himself king?
4. How many men accompanied Absalom out of Jerusalem?
5. Did Absalom appear to be succeeding in his revolt?

GOLDEN TEXT HOMILY

"WOE TO THE REBELLIOUS CHILDREN, SAITH THE LORD, THAT TAKE COUNSEL, BUT NOT OF ME" (Isaiah 30:1).

There are two types of rebellion to consider: active and passive. Active rebellion consists of getting our information from outside sources and acting on that same information, putting into operation the full knowledge of the consequences of acts that are against God. This is active rebellion. What about that person on the sidelines who passively rebels by doing nothing? He sits in the counsel of the confused, the counsel of fear—neurotic fear. He is afraid to step left or to step right, so he steps neither way and passively lets the situation go by. These are two types of rebellion. They take their counsel not from the Lord; they take their counsel from the outside and from the confused.

Why can't we hear what the Lord says? We hear, but we're not listening. We can't hear God's counsel because we hear what we want to hear. We hear what we are and what our fantasies are. And our fantasies get in our way. Some of us are like small children. We grasp for what is here and now—what we can see or get into our hands. Our immaturity drives us toward short-term goals. It is the Lord's people who are willing to wait over long periods of time to achieve certain goals that God has planned for them.

Short-term goals cause us to become victims of self-deception. Our logic becomes clouded by the idea of material gains or personal status. It drives some of us to do things ourselves, to massage our ego in one form or another. And we are willing to manipulate anyone or anything to achieve our particular goals for that moment.

Now, we know that communication is a learned thing. So is the ability to listen. It is something that has to be cultivated. William Penn put it this way: "Men may tire themselves out in the church and talk of God. But if we would know Him, it must be from the impressions we receive of Him. And the softer our hearts are, the deeper and livelier those impressions will be upon us."

In a recent book entitled **Jonathan Livingston Seagull,** there is a statement that goes like this: "Look with your understanding, find out what you already know, and you will see the way to fly."

Now, we know God calls us rebellious if we get our counsel from any source other than Him. And He has given us the Spirit which He says will lead us into all truth.
—Selected

SENTENCE SERMONS

FOOLS MEASURE ACTIONS after they are done, by the event; wise men beforehand, by the rules of reason and right.
—Richard Hill

SIN IS REBELLION against God, the Sovereign of the universe.
—Selected

WE SHALL BE JUDGED, not by what we might have been, but what we have been.
—William Sewell

REASON NEVER SHOWS itself so unreasonable as when it ceases to reason about things which are above reason.
—"Speaker's Sourcebook"

EVANGELISTIC APPLICATION

RECONCILIATION WITH GOD IS FREELY OFFERED TO MAN THROUGH CHRIST, THE ATONING SACRIFICE.

As Absalom treated David, so has humanity treated God. In Isaiah 1:2 the Lord himself calls upon the heavens and the earth to take note of the astonishing truth: "I have nourished and brought up children, and they have rebelled against me." Though this strictly has Israel in mind, it is nevertheless true of all mankind. "All have sinned." That is, all have **rebelled** against God.

The Lord can no more accept or overlook this rebellion than could David overlook the rebellion of Absalom. He must resist it. He will put it down. And the end of every rebel will be worse than that of Absalom. "For the wages of sin is death" (Romans 6:23).

Yet God no more wills the death of the sinner than did David the death of Absalom. Even while His justice pursues him, His love yearns to save him from the tragic consequences of his evildoing.

David could only cry, "Would God I had died for thee, O Absalom, my son!" The eternal God actually **did die** for a rebel race.

How truly Wesley's hymn expresses the wonder and mystery of it:

And can it be, that I should gain
An interest in the Savior's blood?
Died He for me, who caused His pain?
For me, who Him to death pursued?
Amazing love! how can it be
That Thou my God, shouldst die for me?

ILLUMINATING THE LESSON

A petted soldier of the Macedonian army was shipwrecked and cast upon the shore apparently lifeless. A hospitable Macedonian discovered him, revived him, took him to his home and treated him in a princely manner and, when he departed, gave him money for his journey.

The rescued soldier expressed warm thanks and promised royal bounty to his benefactor. Instead, when he came before Philip, he related his own misfortunes and asked to be rewarded by the gift of the house and lands of his rescuer. His request was granted and he returned and drove out his former host.

The latter hastened to lay the true state of the case before the king; he restored the land and caused the soldier to be branded in the forehead, "The Ungrateful Guest," as the reward of his baseness.—Selected

DAILY DEVOTIONAL GUIDE

M. Seeds of Selfish Ambition. 2 Samuel 13:37—14:3
T. Results of Selfish Ambition. 2 Samuel 18:9-33
W. Deceitfulness of Rebellion. Psalm 5:1-12
T. Preventing Rebellion. Deuteronomy 6:4-7
F. Judgment of Rebellion. Romans 1:16-20
S. Victory Over Selfish Ambition. Philippians 3:4-14

May 31, 1981

The Importance of Choice

Bible Background: 2 Samuel 24:1-25

Time: Around 974 B.C.

Place: In all Israel and in Jerusalem

Supplemental References: Jeremiah 21:8-14; John 6:66-69; 2 Timothy 4:10

Golden Text: "Trust in the Lord with all thine heart; and lean not unto thine own understanding" (Proverbs 3:5).

Central Truth: A person's decisions and actions affect not only his life but also the lives of others.

Evangelistic Emphasis: A man makes his most important choice when he decides to serve God.

PRINTED TEXT

2 Samuel 24:10. And David's heart smote him after that he had numbered the people. And David said unto the Lord, I have sinned greatly in that I have done: and now, I beseech thee, O Lord, take away the iniquity of thy servant; for I have done very foolishly.

11. For when David was up in the morning, the word of the Lord came unto the prophet Gad, David's seer, saying,

12. Go and say unto David, Thus saith the Lord, I offer thee three things; choose thee one of them, that I may do it unto thee.

13. So Gad came to David, and told him, and said unto him, Shall seven years of famine come unto thee in thy land? or wilt thou flee three months before thine enemies, while they pursue thee? or that there be three days' pestilence in thy land? now advise, and see what answer I shall return to him that sent me.

14. And David said unto Gad, I am in a great strait: let us fall now into the hand of the Lord; for his mercies are great: and let me not fall into the hand of man.

15. So the Lord sent a pestilence upon Israel from the morning even to the time appointed: and there died of the people from Dan even to Beer-sheba seventy thousand men.

16. And when the angel stretched out his hand upon Jerusalem to destroy it, the Lord repented him of the evil, and said to the angel that destroyed the people, It is enough: stay now thine hand. And the angel of the Lord was by the threshingplace of Araunah the Jebusite.

17. And David spake unto the Lord when he saw the angel that smote the people, and said, Lo, I have sinned, and I have done wickedly: but these sheep, what have they done? let thine hand, I pray thee, be against me, and against my father's house.

18. And Gad came that day to David, and said unto him, Go up, rear an altar unto the Lord in the threshingfloor of Araunah the Jebusite.

19. And David, according to the saying of Gad, went up as the Lord commanded.

DICTIONARY

heart smote him—2 Samuel 24:10—His conscience convicted him.

Gad, David's seer—2 Samuel 24:11—A prophet who seems to have joined David when he was fleeing Saul (1 Samuel 22:5). We are told that he wrote a book of the acts of David (1 Chronicles 29:9), and is also said to have helped in the arrangements for the musical service of the "house of the Lord" (2 Chronicles 29:25).

I offer thee—2 Samuel 24:12—More literally and graphically translated, "I hold over thee."

from Dan to Beer-sheba—2 Samuel 24:15—A customary way of speaking of the extent of Palestine from north to south.

Araunah (ah-RAU-nah)—2 Samuel 24:16—One of the original Jebusites inhabitants of Jerusalem. His threshingfloor, which he sold to David, was later the site of the Temple built by Solomon.

LESSON OUTLINE

I. A FOOLISH DECISION
  A. David's Plan
  B. David's Persistence
II. A BITTER RESULT
  A. A Smitten Conscience
  B. A Smitten Nation
III. CORRECTING A MISTAKE
  A. David's Appeal
  B. David's Actions

LESSON EXPOSITION

INTRODUCTION

Our previous lesson ended on a note of incompleteness. David was overcome with emotion at the untimely death of his son, and the army was embarrassed and bewildered to witness such an anticlimax to their loyalty. However, the full story does not end on that jarring note but goes on to describe Joab's intervention and the recall of the king and his legal government to the capital (chapter 19).

The rebellion of Absalom, however, was not the last of David's troubles. The civil war left a legacy of discontent among the northern tribes (2 Samuel 19:41-43). Then, a further revolt broke out, though of smaller dimensions, which had to be put down (chapter 20).

It is generally considered that the concluding four chapters of the second Book of Samuel are an appendix, the historical sequence beginning again with the first Book of Kings. There is a gap of about ten years between the revolt of Sheba and the situation described in the opening chapters of the first Book of Kings. However, the picture is filled in by the final chapters of the first Book of Chronicles (1 Chronicles chapters 21—29).

It is seen from these chapters that the last ten years of David's reign were chiefly occupied with preparing the plans for the Temple, accumulating the materials, and planning the Temple liturgy. The first of these chapters (1 Chronicles 21), however, deals with the same subject of our present lesson based on 1 Samuel 24. As we study this lesson, though we focus chiefly on a further sin of David and the divine judgment which it brought, we must not fail to note that it climaxed in an event which was a fundamental part of the Temple preparation, namely, David's purchase of the threshing floor of Ornan which became the site for the future Temple. Indeed, one great reason for including this incident in the biblical narrative seems to have been to place on permanent record the circumstances which led to the provision of the Temple site.

I. A FOOLISH DECISION (2 Samuel 24:1-9)

A. David's Plan (vv. 1, 2)

Before discussing the nature of David's plan it is necessary to compare this account in 2 Samuel with that of 1 Chronicles. The account in 2 Samuel says that "the Lord" moved David to number Israel, whereas 1 Chronicles 21:1 says that "Satan . . . **provoked** David to number Israel." The same Hebrew word is used in both texts, meaning "to incite, allure, instigate." The same incitement is attributed both to the Lord and to Satan. This is one of those cases where contradiction is supposed to exist. However the contradiction is merely supposition. Arthur Pink says, "These two statements are not, as some have foolishly supposed, contradictory, but are complementary. Though God is not the author of sin, and can never be charged with evil, yet as the governor of the universe He is the controller and director of it, so that when it serves His righteous purpose even Satan and his hosts are requisitioned by Him." Dr. D. F. Payne comments, "This writer (Samuel) recognizes the overruling hand of God, whereas the later historian (Chronicles) was more interested in the mode of incitement, namely satanic tempting" **(New Bible Commentary Revised).** In other words, Satan was God's agent or instrument in this matter.

There is, however, a more difficult problem. Does God really "incite" people, more especially His own people, to commit sin? The New Testament definitely says **No** (see James 1: 13). How then, must we understand those Old Testament statements, if we are to reject the liberal opinions which view them as imperfect representations of God?

There are two explanations. One is stated by Dr. Kirkpatrick (in the **Cambridge Bible, 2 Samuel):** "It cannot mean that the Lord **compelled** David to sin, but in order to test and prove his character He allowed the temptation to assault him." This puts the incident in the same category as Abraham's offering up of Isaac (Genesis 22) and the sufferings of Job (Job 1 and 2). The other explanation is promoted by Keil and Delitzsch. Writing of this and other incidents where God is said to instigate men to evil, they write: "These passages show that God only instigates those who have sinned against Him to evil deeds. . . . The instigation of a sinner to evil is simply one peculiar way in which God, as a general rule, punishes sins through sinners; for God only instigates to evil actions such as have drawn down the wrath of God upon themselves in consequence of their sins" **(A Commentary on the Old Testament, The Books of Samuel).**

Which of the above explanations appeals to you? Why?

In view of the opening clause of 2 Samuel 24:1—"the anger of the Lord was kindled against Israel"—it seems that the second of the above opinions is nearer the truth. God's incitement of David through Satan was a judgment upon king and nation for some sin. What was this sin?

Many scholars believe that the nature of David's sin is revealed by the nature of the temptation which came to him at this time. The temptation appealed to his pride and arrogance and lust for worldly greatness. These passions were already controlling his heart. The temptation stimulated what was already there. It brought his lust for worldly power and greatness into open manifestation. As Keil and Delitzsch say, "The true kernel of David's sin was to be found, no doubt, in self-exaltation." F. B. Meyer says, "David was animated by a spirit of pride and vainglory. He was eager to make a fine show among the surrounding nations" **(David: Shepherd, Psalmist, King).** Gardiner comments, "It would appear that prosperity and power, the natural generators of pride, had momentarily affected even David's humble dependence upon God, and led him to wish to organize his kingdom more perfectly as a worldly power among the nations of the earth" **(Ellicott's Bible Commentary, Vol. 2).**

As far as the nation was concerned, some commentators are of the opinion that the judgment was also a punishment for its previous rebellions in following Absalom and Sheba.

There are two clear warnings for the Church, whether we think of it as universal, denominational, or local. Of the many sins which may bring down God's judgment upon us, two are here portrayed: (a) the sin of internal strife and division, and (b) the lust for worldly greatness. How does God judge these sins? In the same way as He judged the Davidic kingdom: by taking His hand off, by removing restraining influences and giving opportunity for these evils to break out. As He "gave up" the ancient nations to their own lusts (Romans 1:24, 26, 28), so He may give up the Church to its lusts. Is not this seen repeatedly in Church history?

The medieval Roman Catholic Church is one clear example of the principle described above. Can you suggest others?

B. David's Persistence (vv. 3-9)

The ambitions of David's heart were stimulated to action by a plan to "number Israel and Judah." The fact that Joab was ordered to carry out this scheme suggests, as Payne says, that "the purpose of the census will have been the reorganization of the tax, military service, and forced labor systems."

But now comes a surprising intervention. Joab is the last man one would expect to oppose a grandiose scheme of kingdom and empire. He was a strong and unscrupulous man with great love of power. Yet he felt that David's plan was wrong. Some expositors see his misgivings as political shrewdness. He felt that the nation would resent the census. However, we may not see it as a gracious warning from God? Pink thinks so: "God did not utterly forsake David and give him up to his heart's lusts. Instead, He placed an obstacle in his path, in the form of Joab's opposition, which rebuked his folly, and rendered his sin more excuseless."

We see this so often in Bible characters, and in our own lives. His judgments are tempered by mercy. He does everything possible to protect us, even when in wisdom and righteousness He permits Satan to tempt us. He puts up fences and warning notices along the pathway—the warnings of parents (as in Samson's case), and of friends and colleagues (as in David's case), even the mouth of an ass (as in Balaam's case).

But David went on heedless in his ambition and arrogance, and Joab organized and carried through the census which took almost ten months to complete. The numbers given in verse 9 support the view that David's motive was military greatness.

II. A BITTER RESULT (2 Samuel 24:10-16)

A. A Smitten Conscience (v. 10)

10. And David's heart smote him after that he had numbered the people. And David said unto the Lord, I have sinned greatly in that I have done: and now, I beseech thee, O Lord, take away the iniquity of thy servant; for I have done very foolishly.

We do not know if David had suffered any pangs of conscience during the ten months of the census, or whether others besides Joab among his friends and counselors had reasoned with him. The record only draws our attention to the fact that "David's heart smote him (meaning his **conscience,** for the heart in Scripture is not merely the emotions but the source of reason, conscience, and will also) after that he had numbered the people." It is a healthy sign when one has a conscience that really works. Individuals and communities are dangerously sick when conscience has ceased to work, or as the New Testament puts it, is "seared" (1 Timothy 4:2).

What stirred David's conscience we are not told. In the matter of Bath-sheba it had been Nathan the prophet (2 Samuel 12:1), but on the present occasion God sent his prophet, this time Gad (v. 11), after conscience had done its painful but fruitful work. Deane thinks that David's conscience was stirred as a result of his own reflections: "When the results of the census, so far as it had gone, were brought before him, he reflected with himself on the motives which led him to the undertaking and the use which he had thought to make of it; he compared his worldly ambition with the theocratic idea which had hitherto controlled his conduct; he weighed his actions in the balance of religion, and his heart smote him" **(David: His Life and Times).**

The New Testament brings two factors together in a conscience-stirring ministry. One is the Holy Spirit: "And when he is come, he will reprove [**convict, New International Version**] the world of sin" (Johh 16:8). Though this speaks of the Holy Spirit's work in the world it does not **confine** His convicting work to the world. Believers need that ministry too!

The other factor is the Word of God: "For the word of God is quick, and powerful, and sharper than any twoedged sword, piercing even to the dividing asunder of soul and spirit, and of joints and marrow, and is a discerner of the thoughts and intents of the heart" (Hebrews 4:12). These two factors are closely connected. The Word of God is the Spirit's sword (Ephesians 6:17), that is, the sword both forged and used by the Holy Spirit.

We may be sure that when a believer is exposed to the light of the Word of God, read or proclaimed in the power of the Holy Spirit, his worldliness and carnality will be brought to the surface. He will feel far from good. Indeed, he is likely to feel very bad. Many of the grandiose schemes which the Church often pursues, in imitation of worldly pomp and power, may be seen as carnal and egotistical ambitions when the Holy Spirit applies His twoedged sword.

Of course, conviction does not always lead to repentance. In David's case it did. What a great example to backsliding Christians he is in this!

Compare David with Saul in respect of conviction of sin (see 1 Samuel 13:8-23). Can you describe the fundamental difference between the two men?

B. A Smitten Nation (vv. 11-16)

11. For when David was up in the morning, the word of the Lord came unto the

prophet Gad, David's seer, saying,

12. Go and say unto David, Thus saith the Lord, I offer thee three things; choose thee one of them, that I may do it unto thee.

13. So Gad came to David, and told him, and said unto him, Shall seven years of famine come unto thee in thy land? or wilt thou flee three months before thine enemies, while they pursue thee? or that there be three days' pestilence in thy land? now advise, and see what answer I shall return to him that sent me.

We noted in our previous lesson that although David acknowledged his sins of adultery and murder in the case of Bath-sheba, and although he received divine forgiveness, he was not let off the consequences of his folly. It is also true in regard to his present sin of pride and arrogance, as also in regard to the nation's participation in rebellion and conflict. David and the nation were divinely forgiven, but they were also divinely punished.

We may regard the choice of three forms of chastisement offered to David as a further form of testing. The decisions men and women make when presented with alternatives reveal their inner character. Every day of our lives we are placed in situations, sometimes insignificant in themselves, sometimes hugely important, in which we have to make a choice, and the choice exposes us for what we really are. Some people are notorious for always snatching the creamiest cake, or the tastiest piece of chicken, or the coziest seat, or the easy way out. Others follow the Jesus way in both things big and things little.

14. And David said unto Gad, I am in a great strait: let us fall now into the hand of the Lord; for his mercies are great: and let me not fall into the hand of man.

When confronted with a choice David said, "Let us fall now into the hand of the Lord." What did he mean? Keil and Delitzsch think "he chose the third judgment since pestilence comes from God." But the same could be said of famine. Adam Clarke thinks that in choosing pestilence David was chosing a form of suffering which could affect himself and his household in a more certain way than famine or sword. He says, too, that by this choice David revealed his moral greatness. Certainly that would be the Jesus way. However, it may be that by this statement David was really declining to choose for himself, and was submitting himself and his nation utterly to God. He chose not to choose.

This is often the way of the true saint. In the words of a delightful hymn—"Yea, choose the path for me, although I may not see/The reason Thou dost will to lead me so./ I know the toilsome way will lead to realms of day/Where shall dwell with thee, O mighty Savior."

The modern Christian of the Western world is heavily influenced by the pragmatic world around him. He is strong on claiming and demanding and appropriating from God, but inclined to be weak on qualities of humility, meekness, and submission. But these, too, are equally a part of Christian character.

15. So the Lord sent a pestilence upon Israel from the morning even to the time appointed: and there died of the people from Dan even to Beer-sheba seventy thousand men.

16. And when the angel stretched out his hand upon Jerusalem to destroy it, the Lord repented him of the evil, and said to the angel that destroyed the people, It is enough: stay now thine hand. And the angel of the Lord was by the threshingplace of Araunah the Jebusite.

The fifteenth verse describes the duration of the divine judgment and the number of those who died. The expression, "even to the time appointed," is debated. Some think it means the third of the three days of verse 13. Others think it is a technical expression for the hour of the evening sacrifice on the same day that the pestilence began. This would mean that the plague lasted only a part of one day. The sixteenth verse leads to the climax of the story. It describes the approach of the messenger of judgment toward Jerusalem, but before he could begin his work he was arrested by the Lord at a spot just north of the city, "the threshingplace of Araunah the Jebusite."

Some say: "A God of love cannot act like this!" How would you answer such a charge?

III. CORRECTING A MISTAKE (2 Samuel 24: 17-25)

A. David's Appeal (vv. 17-19)

17. And David spake unto the Lord when he saw the angel that smote the people, and said, Lo, I have sinned, and I have

done wickedly: but these sheep, what have they done? let thine hand, I pray thee, be against me, and against my father's house.

18. And Gad came that day to David, and said unto him, Go up, rear an altar unto the Lord in the threshingfloor of Araunah the Jebusite.

19. And David, according to the saying of Gad, went up as the Lord commanded.

Keil and Delitzsch say, "The threshing floor of Araunah was situated, like all other threshing floors, outside the city, and upon an eminence, or, according to the more precise statement which follows, to the northeast of Zion, upon Mount Moriah." We must realize that the city of David was very small at that time (see a map of ancient Jerusalem). It did not include the Temple site. From his house in the city David saw the angel standing in Araunah's threshing floor to the north. At once David turned to **the Lord** (not the angel) in prayer for mercy. Not mercy for himself, but for the inhabitants of Jerusalem. He confessed that he personally was responsible and pleaded that others might be spared.

In this David showed himself a true shepherd of his people which, as we pointed out in a previous lesson, was the Hebrew ideal of monarchy, and of all leadership.

What can leaders in the church learn from David's appeal for his people?

B. David's Actions (vv. 20-25)

God revealed to David that an atoning sacrifice was required in order that his sin might be covered and the pestilence stayed. The place where the angel had stopped at God's command was to become the site for a new altar. At this very place, hundreds of years before, the Lord had provided Abraham with a substitute for Isaac (Genesis 22:1-14).

The account in 2 Samuel needs to be augmented by the account in 1 Chronicles 21:18—22:1. As a result of his experience David came to see that this place must become the site for the future Temple. Thus the terrible and tragic event was wonderfully overruled and was woven into the messianic and redemptive fabric of the Bible.

Consider verse 24. What message does this have for Christians?

REVIEW QUESTIONS

1. Who delivered God's Word to David?
2. What three choices did God give David for his punishment?
3. Which punishment was sent upon the land?
4. Where was the angel of destruction when the Lord told him to stay his hand?
5. What was required of David to atone for his sin?

GOLDEN TEXT HOMILY

"TRUST IN THE LORD WITH ALL THINE HEART; AND LEAN NOT UNTO THINE OWN UNDERSTANDING" (Proverbs 3:5).

I had a business associate who refused to attend church or have anything to do with religion. He said he was an agnostic. He prided himself in his ability to make his way in life without the help of anyone "including God."

There is no question about it, he was a brilliant man and very successful in his chosen profession. After a few years of operating his own business, he became extremely wealthy and began to travel around the world.

He told me in confidence one day that he was seeking the most beautiful place in the world to settle down; the most secure place where he could live in regal splendor without being disturbed by the many accouterments of modern civilization. Finally one day, he reported to me that he had found it. He said he was investing $150,000 in a ranch house on a distant seashore with a beach of coal black sand. It was a semitropical climate he said, and lush with all the fruitage you could want. He spoke enthusiastically of the natives. "They are a warm-hearted, friendly, generous people," he said, "who would work hours on end with little or no pay except their sustenance. They really appreciate what I am doing for them down there in the construction of this house and the improvement of the surrounding land."

This gentleman disappeared from town for long periods of time, returning with increasingly glowing accounts of his new paradise.

One day in a final burst of enthusiasm he said, "This is heaven on earth. I have found it. I have found absolute security and contentment. This is real religion to me, boy. This is my religion. This is what you ought to go for too."

The place was the Isle of Pines just off the coast of Cuba. It is today Castro's maximum security prison camp, and my friend's house is occupied by the commandment of that prison camp.

It is a classic example of what happens to those who lean on their own understanding and trust not in the Lord.—**Lambert Huffman, Winona Lake, Indiana**

SENTENCE SERMONS

WHO SINS AND MENDS commends himself to God.
—**Miguel de Cervantes**

SIN IS NOT HURTFUL because it is forbidden, but it is forbidden because it is hurtful.
—**Benjamin Franklin**

REPENTANCE WITHOUT AMENDMENT is like continually pumping without mending the leak.
—**Lewis W. Dillwyn**

THE SERENE, SILENT beauty of a holy life is the most powerful influence in the world, next to the might of God.
—**Pascal**

IN THE FOOTPRINTS on the sands of time some people leave only the marks of a heel.
—**"Speaker's Sourcebook"**

EVANGELISTIC APPLICATION

A MAN MAKES HIS MOST IMPORTANT CHOICE WHEN HE DECIDES TO SERVE GOD.

On Mount Moriah Abraham took the ram which the Lord himself had provided and "offered him up for a burnt-offering in the stead of his son" (Genesis 22:13). Hundreds of years later, at the very same spot, "David built there an altar unto the Lord, and offered burnt-offerings and peace-offerings. So the Lord was intreated for the land, and the plague was stayed from Israel" (2 Samuel 24:25). Almost a thousand years later, not far from this same site, Jesus the Lamb of God, "that he might sanctify the people with his own blood, suffered without the gate" (Hebrews 13:12). What Abraham did and what David did were signposts to what Jesus did upon the altar of His cross. As death was averted from Isaac and as the pestilence was averted from Israel, so has eternal judgment been averted for all who truly trust in Christ.

The heart of the gospel is the message that atonement is accomplished, the plague is stayed, and all who will believe may be saved.

ILLUMINATING THE LESSON

A revival meeting was being held in a village church. Many had been saved during the meetings. At the end of the sermon one night, the preacher said, "Is the person here who most influenced you in becoming a Christian? Maybe it is your mother, your pastor, your Sunday school teacher, your neighbor. I wish you would now rise and go and shake hands with the one who most influenced you to accept Christ as your Saviour."

A glorious scene followed! Pupils went to their Sunday school teachers. Some went to the Sunday school superintendent. Some went to the pastor. To the left of the preacher sat an aged woman, wearing a sun bonnet. She had never spoken in public. She was not a Sunday school teacher. She was not an officer in the church. She was only a faithful, consecrated Christian mother and wife. She was more than seventy-five years old. A long line went to where she sat. Some took her by the hand. Some placed their arms about her. They said, "Your quiet, faithful, consecrated life; your personal work and testimony for Christ, when we were in your home, led us to Christ, the Saviour!" It was the beautiful, holy life which the Christian woman had led throughout the years that had won so many to the Saviour.—**"Gospel Herald"**

DAILY DEVOTIONAL GUIDE

M. Choice Offers Two Ways. Deuteronomy 30: 11-20
T. Choice Includes Commitment. Joshua 24: 14-26
W. Choice Affects Others. 2 Samuel 24:10-17
T. Choice Is Inescapable. Psalm 139:1-12
F. Choice Implies Responsibility. Matthew 7: 13-27
S. Choice Involves Eternity. Hebrews 11:24-27

INTRODUCTION TO SUMMER QUARTER

The lessons for the summer quarter (June, July, August) are presented under the theme "A Nation in Transition." This three-month series of studies is taken from the Books of 1 and 2 Kings, 2 Chronicles, and Isaiah. One lesson, however, comes from the Book of 2 Samuel as we focus attention on Pentecost Sunday. Perhaps this lesson on the work of the Holy Spirit will provide a proper starting point and serve as a vital source of strength and understanding as the remaining twelve lessons of the quarter are considered.

In this series of lessons we will consider a part of the reign of King Solomon, but more particularly the lessons will focus on the kings of Judah after the transition to the divided kingdom around 931 B.C. The quarter of studies concludes with a lesson relating to the seige of Jerusalem by the Babylonians in 586 B.C.

Although the lessons are historical in nature, they provide a look at leaders, some of which were godly kings, but all of which were subject to human failures. At times, God through His prophets, brought messages of judgment to the leaders. At other times, God gave miraculous victory to the nation when they were threatened by heathen neighbors. Taken as a whole, the quarter of studies is certain to leave the diligent student with a greater appreciation for the providential care of a loving Heavenly Father.

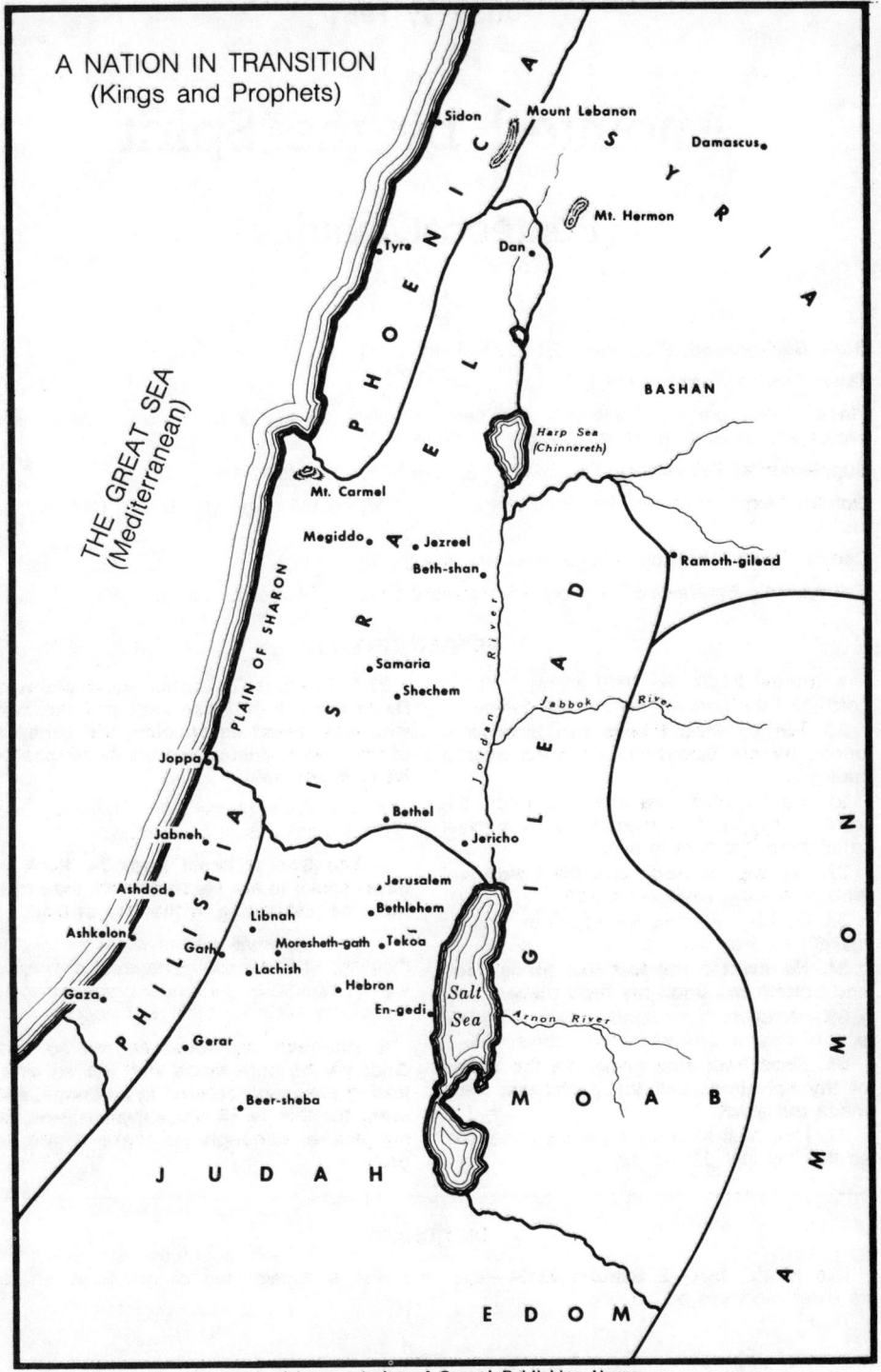

June 7, 1981

Anointed by the Spirit

(Pentecost Sunday)

Bible Background: 2 Samuel 22:1—23:5; Luke 4:16-21
Time: Probably around 974 B.C.
Place: Exact place is unknown, but some scholars suggest that the place of David's prayer was at Gath in the land of the Philistines.
Supplemental References: Psalm 133:1-3; Isaiah 61:1-3; Acts 19:1-6
Golden Text: "When he, the Spirit of truth, is come, he will guide you into all truth" (John 16:13).
Central Truth: The Holy Spirit anoints and guides believers.
Evangelistic Emphasis: The Holy Spirit gives the believer power to witness.

PRINTED TEXT

2 Samuel 22:29. For thou art my lamp, O Lord: and the Lord will lighten my darkness.
30. For by thee I have run through a troop: by my God have I leaped over a wall.
31. As for God, his way is perfect; the word of the Lord is tried: he is a buckler to all them that trust in him.
32. For who is God, save the Lord? and who is a rock, save our God?
33. God is my strength and power: and he maketh my way perfect.
34. He maketh my feet like hinds' feet: and setteth me upon my high places.
35. He teacheth my hands to war; so that a bow of steel is broken by mine arms.
36. Thou hast also given me the shield of thy salvation: and thy gentleness hath made me great.
37. Thou hast enlarged my steps under me; so that my feet did not slip.

23:1. Now these be the last words of David. David the son of Jesse said, and the man who was raised up on high, the anointed of the God of Jacob, and the sweet psalmist of Israel, said,
2. The Spirit of the Lord spake by me, and his word was in my tongue.
3. The God of Israel said, the Rock of Israel spake to me, He that ruleth over men must be just, ruling in the fear of God.
4. And he shall be as the light of the morning, when the sun riseth, even a morning without clouds; as the tender grass springing out of the earth by clear shining after rain.
5. Although my house be not so with God; yet he hath made with me an everlasting covenant, ordered in all things, and sure: for this is all my salvation, and all my desire, although he make it not to grow.

DICTIONARY

like hinds' feet—2 Samuel 22:34—The hind was a female stag or gazelle noted for its surefootedness and agility.

June 7, 1981

Jesse—2 Samuel 23:1—Son of Obed, father of David, and grandson of Boaz.

LESSON OUTLINE

I. STRENGTHENED BY THE LORD
  A. Divine Deliverance
  B. Divine Reward
  C. Divine Victory

II. ANOINTED BY THE SPIRIT
  A. The Royal Singer
  B. The Righteous Ruler
  C. The Everlasting Covenant
  D. The Destruction of Evil Men

III. MINISTERING IN THE SPIRIT
  A. A Customary Sabbath Observance
  B. A Significant Scripture Lesson
  C. An Astounding Exposition
  D. A Hostile Response

LESSON EXPOSITION

INTRODUCTION

The Christian Church has for many centuries set aside one day in its calendar for the celebration of the outpouring of the Holy Spirit upon the infant New Testament Church. It is obviously appropriate that we study the nature and activity of the third person of the Trinity on this day—the Day of Pentecost.

The New Testament is replete with references to the Holy Spirit—as Baptizer, Revealer, Comforter, Agent of divine grace. But the careful student of God's Word soon discovers that the operations of the Spirit are also clearly evident in the Old Testament. Although the Old Testament does not on every occasion distinguish the personality and functions of each of the three members of the Godhead, both distinctions of person and individual functions of members of the Trinity are always present implicitly and on occasion explicitly.

The Holy Spirit, for example, was quite evidently active in creation itself: "The Spirit of God moved upon the face of the waters" (Genesis 1:2). His function as agent of conviction of sin or as means of moving the human heart toward recognition of God's claims upon human life also appears early in the Old Testament: "The Lord said, My spirit shall not always strive with man, for that he also is flesh: yet his days shall be an hundred and twenty years" (Genesis 6:3). The Holy Spirit, moreover, centuries later, heightened the natural artistic abilities of Bezaleel so that he might exhibit ingenious craftsmanship in the construction of the Tabernacle: "See, I have called by name Bezaleel the son of Uri, the son of Hur, of the tribe of Judah: And I have filled him with the spirit of God, in wisdom, and in understanding, and in knowledge, and in all manner of workmanship" (Exodus 31:2, 3). This occurrence exemplifies the anointing of the Holy Spirit for a specific task.

Quite clearly, while there was no general outpouring of the Holy Spirit "upon all flesh" during the Old Testament era, there were special anointings for particular purposes, ministries, or functions. Moses, for instance, operated with unusual spiritual force because of such an anointing, and Miriam, his sister, rejoiced before the Lord with hilarious abandon under the power of the Holy Spirit. Priests, prophets, and kings seemed to receive a special anointing upon the occasion of their consecration to office. King Saul, for example, prophesied among a company of the prophets immediately following Samuel's designation of him as king and anointing of him with oil (1 Samuel 10:1, 6, 9, 11). Elisha performed many miracles after receiving the mantle of Elijah (2 Kings 2:14).

The greatest of Old Testament kings, David, exhibited unusual evidences of the activity of the Holy Spirit in his life. After God's rejection of Saul, Samuel the prophet—directed by God—went to the house of Jesse, where he anointed the young David with oil, symbolic of his designation for the royal office (1 Samuel 16:1-13). David began to exhibit physical prowess (1 Samuel 17:34-36), military skill (1 Samuel 17:51-53; 18:6-8), and unusual wisdom (1 Samuel 20:5-7; 21:13-15).

Although he evidently was not without flaws, King David, under the leadership of the Spirit, acceded to power, consolidated his kingdom, defeated foreign enemies, and established effective administrative practices. When he became willful and disobedient, he was chastised by the Lord and, as a result of failure to follow divinely ordained principles for the family, found himself fleeing before military forces loyal to Absalom, his rebellious son. Clearly then, in the Old Testament as well as in the New, leadership by the Spirit depends upon consistency in consecration and constancy in holy behavior. In any case,

David's life, despite his serious lapses in behavior, stands as a witness to the possibility of extraordinary results when dedicated genius receives spiritual anointing for a divinely ordained task

I. STRENGTHENED BY THE LORD (2 Samuel 22:1-51)

In the Book of 2 Samuel appear four great psalms of David: (1) 2 Samuel 1:17-27, a lament; (2) 2 Samuel 7:18-29, a prayer; (3) 2 Samuel 22:1-51, a thanksgiving; (4) 2 Samuel 23:1-7, a valediction. In the third and fourth of these poetic utterances—hymns of praise and valediction—one views clear evidences of the activity of the Holy Spirit in the life of the great king.

David might well have composed the psalm of thanksgiving of 2 Samuel 22 just after he consolidated his kingdom and conquered his military enemies. The eighth chapter of 2 Samuel catalogs the remarkable victories achieved over the Moabites, Syrians, Ammonites, Philistines, Amalekites, and Edomites; 2 Samuel 22:1 says, "David spake unto the Lord the words of this song in the day that the Lord had delivered him out of the hand of all his enemies, and out of the hand of Saul." Conceivably, then, the psalm of chapter 22 might fit quite smoothly after chapter 8. It is also appropriate, however, that this psalm appear at the end of David's life—in celebration of divine guidance throughout forty years of rule and despite the frailties of the flesh which this "man after God's own heart" fell prey to.

A. Divine Deliverance (vv. 1-20)

The presence and activity of the Holy Spirit are implicit rather than explicit in this hymn of thanksgiving. The designations of deity are invariably "the Lord" and "God." But the activity of the Spirit is nonetheless discernible.

In the first major division of the psalm (vv. 1-20), David exalts the Lord as **rock, fortress, deliverer, shield, horn, high tower,** and **refuge** (vv. 2, 3). The idea conveyed is that of a massive, towering rock in a mountain fastness, difficult of access and therefore a safe retreat—a natural fortress securing one against enemies. In other words David has found his God a strong, never-failing refuge in times of trouble (v. 4).

The psalmist proceeds to describe a period of intense distress (vv. 5, 6), perhaps when he was fleeing from Saul. During this time of anguish he cries out to God (v. 7) and receives a mighty vision of the divine presence, conveyed through nature images of enormous force (vv. 8-20). The result of this experience is conveyed in verse 20: "He brought me forth also into a large place: he delivered me, because he delighted in me." What committed Christian has not known constrictions analogous to those experienced by King David during those early years when he was in constant flight from King Saul—physical, psychological, intellectual, spiritual—a sense of being hemmed in. Then God, in His own time and in His own way, sends deliverance, and the soul experiences a sense of enlargement—increased resources, widened space—for breathing, living, ministering.

Could you testify to such a sense of release and enlargement through the Holy Spirit as David attests to in 2 Samuel 22:20?

B. Divine Reward (vv. 21-32)

The second major division of David's great psalm of thanksgiving speaks of **divine reward** based upon **personal commitment.** He declares, "According to the cleanness of my hands hath he recompensed me" (2 Samuel 22:21). The psalmist proceeds in verses 22-24 to avow his avoidance of evil and his blamelessness before the Law. Then in verse 25 he exults, "The Lord has rewarded me according to my righteousness, according to my cleanness in his sight" **(New International Version).** The Lord **matches** and far surpasses **in kind** the faithfulness (v. 26), the blamelessness (v. 26), and the purity (v. 27) of the upright man, but he responds shrewdly (v. 27, **New International Version)** toward crookedness, and He humiliates haughtiness (v. 28). One notes that the Holy Spirit is the agent of sanctification, burning away impurity and making possible that fidelity and holiness of character which God rewards through His own faithfulness and holiness.

29. For thou art my lamp, O Lord: and the Lord will lighten my darkness.

That life without the divine presence often experiences the blackest night of confusion, aimlessness, and moral obliquity. But when "the light of the world" floods that corner in which such a life lies huddled, values are clarified, directions are set, and behavior patterns are changed. Even the Christian on occasion may become self-willed and wander into the shadows of disbelief or halfhearted commitment, but, upon a sincere cry to God, his darkness is lightened. As a Christian matures, however, he learns that spiritual rewards become available as he consistently walks in the light. He learns that he must allow the Lord to be a **lamp** which sheds its beams in a wide radius surrounding him and makes it possible for him to see potential pitfalls, while also providing a source of illumination for darkened souls wandering close by.

30. For by thee I have run through a troop: by my God have I leaped over a wall.

David here employs military terminology to express the Lord's reward to him because of his faithfulness. This king and commander has been able to overrun single-handedly a band of marauders, and he has possessed the physical agility to leap over a fortification, to "scale a wall" (v. 30, **New International Version**). One witnesses here that activity of the Spirit which heightens natural abilities, leading to the performance of unusual exploits, but which is always rooted in single-minded dedication to the divine will.

31. As for God, his way is perfect; the word of the Lord is tried: he is a buckler to all them that trust in him.

That pattern of righteous behavior revealed in the written Word of God **works**—because it is consistent with the very laws of the universe. When one, moreover, bases his life upon this revealed will of God, he places himself under the divine protection: God becomes his **buckler,** or **shield.** Here, one sees once more the operation of an already-declared principle—man's faithfulness divinely rewarded.

32. For who is God, save the Lord? and who is a rock, save our God?

David's words were spoken during an age of competing deities, when every tribe and nation had its god or gods, thought to be powerful within their limited sphere. The psalmist, however, enunciates a unique principle: There is only one God—the Lord God of Israel; and He is the refuge of those who place their trust in Him.

David's question, however, has much more relevance to **modern** culture than at first might be imagined. Modern man also has his competing deities—mistaken concepts of religion with attendant false ideas of the nature and function of God—or substitutes for religion in the material (things) or intellectual (systems)realm. In any case, they are idols—false gods without power, without meaning, and even without existence. David opts for the God of Israel—the God of power, the only true God. And he proclaims the faithfulness of God to His Word and His rewards to men who consistently trust in Him.

C. Divine Victory (vv. 33-51)

The third major division of David's hymn of praise celebrates victory—military, personal, spiritual. He sees no dichotomy between his military prowess and his spiritual stature. As king and military commander, he unites all personality resources in an offering of himself to God. The Lord in turn honors him with personal renown, national victory, and a strong sphere of royal influence and control which stretches far beyond the boundaries of Israel itself.

34. He maketh my feet like hinds' feet: and setteth me upon my high places.

David can run like a deer—according to this vivid image of physical prowess and exultant joy. And he attributes this **physical effect** to **divine agency,** implicitly ascribing his strength and agility to the agency of the Holy Spirit. David, moreover, stands on the tops of the mountains—emblematic of divine protection, personal and national victory, and, again, of gladness and lightness of heart.

35. He teacheth my hands to war; so that a bow of steel is broken by mine arms.

The psalmist sees no inconsistency in the idea of Deity revealing military tactics. Certainly, God did not ordain or originate military conflict, yet occasions arise when forces of justice and right must be arrayed against opponents of good. In our own century the very survival of sane civilization has more than once depended upon the willingness of free men to engage in military combat. But such is not to condone resorting to battle to settle any territorial or other dispute which might happen to arise, particularly when means of peaceful settlement of such issues are available, given patience and goodwill on both sides. King David has no doubt that he has fought just and necessary battles and therefore can attest indubitably to divine presence and divine enablement.

36. Thou hast also given me the shield of thy salvation: and thy gentleness hath made me great.

A shield protects the upper torso and is hence maneuverable by the bearer. According to verse 36, God has become David's shield, the protector of his **vital parts** from all danger, since He is totally capable of resisting successfully all foes, regardless of their stance or their weapon.

But note the surpassing beauty of the second half of the verse: "You stoop down to make me great" **(New International Version).** Christ himself said, "Come unto me, all ye that labour and are heavy laden, and I will give you rest. Take my yoke upon you, and learn of me; for I am meek and lowly in heart: and ye shall find rest unto your souls. For my yoke is easy, and my burden is light" (Matthew 11:28-30). David had achieved renown—genuine acclaim—among men as a result of God's patient, tender care throughout years of painful development. And since he had yielded, however wincingly at times, to the ministrations of Deity, he had now achieved greatness—not only in the eyes of men but also in the sight of God. The ultimate example of this profound truth, however, lies in Calvary, even as Scripture so eloquently declares: "He humbled himself, and became obedient unto death, even the death of the cross. Wherefore God also hath highly exalted him" (Philippians 2:8, 9). And in His humiliation lies our redemption, while in His exaltation rests our daily victory, as we rely upon His present intercessory position at the right hand of His Father.

37. Thou hast enlarged my steps under me; so that my feet did not slip.

Who among us could not testify to an occasional vivid sense of the divine presence which prevented our stumbling over some spiritual pitfall? The image of verse 37 is that of climbing a steep, narrow mountain path and almost stumbling when a rock loosened or a bit of earth crumbled—but then of miraculously seeing the path suddenly expand, thereby preventing sure disaster. Divine providence constantly attends us and prevents evil from befalling us—through both natural and supernatural means.

38. I have pursued mine enemies, and destroyed them; and turned not again until I had consumed them.

One's sensibilities might be wounded by the violence of this verse—by David's ruthless pursuit of fleeing enemy troops until not one soldier remained alive. But if God had commanded the total destruction of alien cultures whose way of life threatened the righteousness and total spiritual stability of Israel, then this supposedly heartless action is not improper; rather, it is in fact enabled by God and is an appropriate subject of praise and celebration.

39. And I have consumed them, and wounded them, that they could not arise: yea, they are fallen under my feet.

Through divine enablement David's victory over his military foes is complete, and he exults over their abject defeat. The spiritual lesson obviously lies in our appropriation of resources of the Holy Spirit for the defeat of the world, the flesh, and the devil. Paul's letter to the Ephesians describes that spiritual warfare which every Christian must inevitably wage, but it also offers **attire, weaponry,** and **strategy** for the soldier (see Ephesians 6:10-18). Indeed, if one avails himself of the resources available through the Holy Spirit, the Word of God, prayer, and the fellowship of believers, he cannot be defeated by our spiritual foe.

In 1 Samuel 22:40-43 David continues to describe his defeat of his enemies. Then in verses 44-46 he mentions his deliverance from civil conflict and celebrates his extension of rule over foreign subjects. Finally, in verses 47-51 he rises to a mighty climax of praise in which he attributes all his successes to the Lord. In the words of verse 51: "He is the tower of salvation for his king: and sheweth mercy to his anointed, unto David, and to his seed for evermore."

Can the twentieth-century Christian find in this psalm principles which will guide him to divine reward, divine deliverance, and divine victory?

II. ANOINTED BY THE SPIRIT (2 Samuel 23:1-7)

A. The Royal Singer (vv. 1, 2)

1. Now these be the last words of David. David the son of Jesse said, and the man who was raised up on high, the anointed of the God of Jacob, and the sweet psalmist of Israel, said,

2. The Spirit of the Lord spake by me, and his word was in my tongue.

Here occurs David's valediction, his parting words, and one notes that they are not personal in character but, under the inspiration of the Holy Ghost, ultimately of universal significance. They state divinely ordained principles of national leadership and describe the magnificent result of the operation of such principles and the devastating result of their violation. David himself is characterized as: (1) "son of Jesse"—an indication of the genealogical record; (2) "the man who was raised up on high" an indication of the divine prerogative; (3) "the anointed of the God of Jacob"—an indication of supernatural enablement by unalterable divine authority; (4) "the sweet psalmist of Israel"—an indication of the spiritual submission, the inner wholeness, and the aesthetic release of this divinely appointed leader. Because of the above-named qualities, the Spirit of God could entrust divine truth to David. Hence, he speaks as the oracle of God, even as 2 Peter 1:21 acknowledges centuries later: "Holy men of God spake as they were moved by the Holy Ghost."

B. The Righteous Ruler (vv. 3, 4)

3. The God of Israel said, the Rock of Israel spake to me, He that ruleth over men must be just, ruling in the fear of God.

4. And he shall be as the light of the morning, when the sun riseth, even a morning without clouds; as the tender grass springing out of the earth by clear shining after rain.

Stated here are two biblical principles of leadership which are grounded in the character of God himself. It is not incidental that the "God of Israel" is here designated as the "Rock of Israel." It is that God who has sustained the nation of Israel since its existence in the loins of Abraham who is now described as an impregnable natural fortress—a bastion of strength. And it is intended that those qualities of Deity be in mind when the psalmist expresses the two characteristics of proper leadership inspired by God. Obviously, any great leader must have intelligence, administrative skill, and the capacity to inspire and to command men. The qualities denominated by the psalmist, however, are additional ingredients essential to true greatness. First, a ruler must be righteous—possessed of integrity and moral uprightness, an exemplar of the moral and ethical imperatives of society, assumed here to be those ideals proclaimed in the Mosaic Code. Second, he must rule in the fear of God; that is, he must live in proper spiritual relationship to God and behave in every personal and leadership role he assumes in a manner consonant with that relationship to God. Of course, every duty of government, of statecraft, which he performs will reflect his moral and spiritual character, and that he stands in awe of Deity will eventually become obvious to all men.

Such a ruler will provide a glorious spectacle to all mankind and will serve as a model for all mankind. The image of verse 4—that of the early morning sun on a cloudless morning and its positive effects—has marvelous appropriateness. For such a national leader **provides clear guidance** (light) and **sustains his people** (energy), functioning as a **moral force** as well as a politician and administrator.

C. The Everlasting Covenant (v. 5)

5. Although my house be not so with God; yet he hath made with me an everlasting covenant, ordered in all things, and sure: for this is all my salvation, and all my desire, although he make it not to grow.

The King James Version rendering of this verse suggests that David is well aware that during his own forty years of rule he has often fallen short of the ideal he has just enunciated. Yet he asserts that God has made "an everlasting covenant" with him, and the Old Testament prophets assert the truth of David's declaration again and again. Isaiah for example, asserts that the Messiah shall govern forever "upon the throne of David" (Isaiah 9:7). In other words, it was divinely ordained that this "man after God's own heart" initiate a royal house which should culminate in the reign of Jesus Christ himself—at that time when He should conquer the forces of the Antichrist and establish His millenial kingdom, to rule in righteousness for a thousand years. The **New International Version** phrases verse 5 as a series of questions, the last of which is: "Will he not bring to fruition my salvation and grant me my every desire?" Expressed thus, these words proclaim the assurance rather than the doubt of the psalmist, David's confidence that God will accomplish that which He has ordained.

D. The Destruction of Evil Men (vv. 6, 7)

The psalmist concludes his valedictory address with an appropriate warning that "sons of Belial"—evil rulers, one might assume, since they stand in contrast to the righteous ruler—will be treated as sons of worthlessness deserve to be treated. Imagery of the burning of thorns expresses the basic lack of worth of such men, their danger to those who come into contact with them, and their ultimate destruction.

Do the principles of national leadership here enunciated apply to the United States in 1981?

III. MINISTERING IN THE SPIRIT (Luke 4:16-30)

In this New Testament passage we observe the Spirit-anointed and Spirit-directed Christ as He visits his hometown synagogue, reads publicly a scripture with pointed reference to His own ministry, explains the significance of that passage from the prophet Isaiah, and suffers a hostile reaction from his neighbors.

A. A Customary Sabbath Observance (v. 16)

That Jesus did not flaunt established custom becomes apparent in this verse which shows Him engaging in worship in the synagogue on the Sabbath day, "as his custom was." When tradition conflicted with truth, He abandoned tradition. But, given the absence of such conflict, He unhesitatingly promoted the observance of traditional pieties. Indeed, He gave them new life. Attendance at the synagogue by the Jewish male was allowable from age five and mandatory from age thirteen. Our Lord was now conforming to this traditional requirement as He also engaged in sincere worship of His Father.

Any Jewish male might be asked by the ruler of the synagogue to read the assigned Scripture lesson, and if he was well reputed as a teacher, he might be invited to give comment. Apparently, Jesus' growing reputation as a teacher had now reached his hometown, so he read and taught according to the accepted custom.

B. A Significant Scripture Lesson (vv. 17-20)

Jesus read the Septuagint rendering of Isaiah 61:1, 2, a scripture universally acknowledged to be messianic in its import. Jesus, just recently come from His baptism at the hands of John the Baptist and that most remarkable visible descent of the Holy Spirit upon Him, and highly conscious of Holy Spirit leadership, was now reading the most appropriate text possible. The anointing of the Spirit is said to be upon the Messiah for several specific functions: **to preach** the gospel, **to heal** the brokenhearted, **to proclaim** freedom to prisoners and recovery of sight to the blind, **to release** the oppressed, and **to proclaim** the acceptable year of the Lord. In other words, through the power of the Holy Spirit, He would minister to the **entire person**—spiritually, intellectually, physically, emotionally, and socially—as He proclaimed the advent of the kingdom of God His Father. Having read this powerful text, Jesus rolled up the scroll and **sat down** to teach, as was expected.

C. An Astounding Exposition (vv. 21-27)

Jesus immediately and forthrightly applied the text to Himself, asserting, "This day is this scripture fulfilled in your ears" (v. 21). He continued with a rich, pleasing exposition of this passage from the prophet Isaiah which induced wonder (v. 22) in His hearers. They soon, however, began to question how a carpenter's son from their own hometown could speak so graciously (v. 22). Christ discerned this changed response and met it with the contention that a prophet is always rejected in his own country, giving as examples Elijah's miraculous sustenance of a foreign widow and Elisha's cleansing of Naaman, the leprous Syrian general.

D. A Hostile Response (vv. 28-30)

The attendants at the synagogue hereupon became incensed at Jesus and attempted to throw Him over a cliff. He, however, "passing through the midst of them went his way," saved through either miracle or ingenuity. This passage shows our Lord teaching **about** His anointing by the Spirit while **under** the anointing of that same Holy Spirit. It also reveals that response to one's witness is in itself no sure indication of spiritual direction. Some see persecution as a sure sign of divine favor, and others see success as an undeniable proof of spiritual leadership. Neither view is automatically correct, although the Spirit-led believer may discover himself in either circumstance.

Will the Spirit-controlled Christian resemble his Lord in the production of activity similar to that in Luke 4:18, 19?

Our lesson for Pentecost Sunday has shown us the Spirit of God at work in the life of King David in the Old Testament and in the life of our Lord himself in the New Testament. We have seen implicit evidences of the activity of the Holy Spirit in 2 Samuel 22, the inspired result of His anointing in 2 Samuel 23:1-7, and the fulfilled prediction of His anointing of the Christ himself in Isaiah 61:1, 2 and Luke 4:16-30. How enriching and inspiring it is to delve with whatever acuity into the mysteries of Divinity—as revealed by the inspired Word of God.

REVIEW QUESTIONS

1. What central image does the psalmist employ repeatedly when speaking of God in 2 Samuel 22?
2. What is the predominant tone of this inspired poetic utterance (2 Samuel 22)?
3. What is the central idea of David's valedictory address?
4. What is the mission of the Messiah, according to Isaiah 61:1, 2 and Luke 4:18, 19?
5. What response did Jesus' words concerning His mission elicit?

GOLDEN TEXT HOMILY

"WHEN HE, THE SPIRIT OF TRUTH, IS COME, HE WILL GUIDE YOU INTO ALL TRUTH" (John 16:13).

The Holy Spirit is a Person. He is the Third Person of the Trinity, and is now the administrator of the work of God in and through the Church. Among His many duties is that of leading us into all truth so that we may know what the will of God is for our lives. Jesus said, "Ye shall know the truth and the truth shall make you free." It is only as the Holy Spirit teaches and leads us that we can really know the truth. Paul clearly indicates that there are some things that cannot be known by natural wisdom and learning but that must be taught to us by the Holy Spirit.

Jesus indicated to His disciples, before He went back to heaven, that there were some things that He himself could not teach them. He told them that when the Holy Spirit was come, He would lead them into all truth and teach them the things that they needed to know.

One cannot really know the truth about Christ except as it is revealed to him by the Holy Spirit. The Bible was written under the inspiration of the Holy Spirit, and it is only as we are taught by the Holy Spirit that we can understand the truth as it is given to us in the Word of God. The Holy Spirit is the supreme Teacher. Let Him be your guide, and ye shall know the truth as it is given to us in Christ, and through the Bible.—**Selected**

SENTENCE SERMONS

I SHOULD AS soon attempt to raise flowers if there were no atmosphere, or produce fruit if there were neither light nor heat as to try to regenerate men if I did not believe there is a Holy Ghost power.

—**Henry Ward Beecher**

ALL THAT HAS been done by God the Father and by God the Son must be ineffectual to us, unless the Spirit shall reveal those things to our souls.

—**Charles H. Spurgeon**

HE WHO HAS the Holy Spirit in his heart and the Scripture in his hands has all he needs.

—**Alexander MaClaren**

THE HOLY GHOST power is given to enable us to do spiritual things in a spiritual way in an unspiritual world.

—**Malcom Cronk**

EVANGELISTIC APPLICATION

THE HOLY SPIRIT GIVES THE BELIEVER POWER TO WITNESS.

Even the Old Testament gives abundant evidence of the powerful effect of the anointing of the Holy Spirit upon the human tongue—whether observed in Saul (prophesying with the school of prophets), or David (singing inspired psalms), or one of the prophets such as Daniel (uttering remarkable truths in witness to his faith while under immense pressure).

In the light of such possibilities for Spirit-inspired utterance, is it not shameful for men indwelt by the Spirit to use their tongues for less than noble purposes? For gossip? For off-color humor? For negative comment? **Latent** within many of us (rather than **already tapped**) is a tremendous source of power for positive, spiritual use of the tongue. The Holy Spirit can and will enable us, as we become His yielded vessels, to proclaim gospel truth to those persons whom we can best influence to receive the truth.

He will grant us wisdom so that our words do not offend. Rather, they will become responses to the specific need of the person to whom we speak, showing that individual how the good news about Jesus Christ constitutes the answer for his deepest problems—whether physical, mental, emotional, social, financial, marital, or basically spiritual. Indeed, Acts 1:8 declares bedrock truth: "But you will receive power when the Holy Spirit comes on you; and you will be my witnesses in Jerusalem, and in all Judea and Samaria, and to the ends of the earth" **(New International**

Version). Does the Holy Spirit have control of your tongue? Are you witnessing daily through the Holy Spirit to the saving power of Jesus Christ?

ILLUMINATING THE LESSON

Dr. Walter L. Wilson in his book **Miracles in a Doctor's Life,** tells of an interesting answer which Mr. Samuel Levermore of London made. He had told his sister about the call of God to serve as a missionary in France, whereupon she replied, "Sammy, you will be wasting your time: to find a troubled soul in France would be like looking for a needle in a haystack." "Yes," answered Mr. Levermore, "that is quite true, but you must remember, sister, that the Holy Spirit knows where the needle is, and He will direct me to it."

—From **3,000 Illustrations for Christian Service,** by Walter B. Knight. Used by permission.

DAILY DEVOTIONAL GUIDE

M. Anointing for Holy Service. Isaiah 61:1-11
T. Teaching the Things of God. John 14:16-26
W. Guiding the Followers of Christ. John 16:4-15
T. Empowering for Christian Witnessing. Acts 1:1-8
F. Baptism in the Holy Spirit. Acts 19:1-6
S. Indwelling for Holy Living. Romans 8:1-11

June 14, 1981

The Results of Choice

Bible Background: 1 Kings 3:1-15; 11:1-13; 2 Chronicles 11:1-13
Time: Soon after Solomon became king, probably 970 B.C.
Places: Gibeon and Jerusalem
Supplemental References: Proverbs 8:1-21; Ecclesiastes 2:4-8, 11; James 3:13-18
Golden Text: "But seek ye first the kingdom of God, and his righteousness; and all these things shall be added unto you" (Matthew 6:33).
Central Truth: Choosing God's best prepares the way for His blessing, but choosing materialism and sensualism leads ultimately to judgment.
Evangelistic Emphasis: Choosing to take Christ as Savior is life's greatest and wisest decision.

PRINTED TEXT

1 Kings 3:5. In Gibeon the Lord appeared to Solomon in a dream by night: and God said, Ask what I shall give thee.

6. And Solomon said, Thou hast shewed unto thy servant David my father great mercy, according as he walked before thee in truth, and in righteousness, and in uprightness of heart with thee; and thou hast kept for him this great kindness, that thou hast given him a son to sit on his throne, as it is this day.

7. And now, O Lord my God, thou hast made thy servant king instead of David my father: and I am but a little child: I know not how to go out or come in.

8. And thy servant is in the midst of thy people which thou hast chosen, a great people, that cannot be numbered nor counted for multitude.

9. Give therefore thy servant an understanding heart to judge thy people, that I may discern between good and bad: for who is able to judge this thy so great a people?

11:9. And the Lord was angry with Solomon, because his heart was turned from the Lord God of Israel, which had appeared unto him twice,

10. And had commanded him concerning this thing, that he should not go after other gods: but he kept not that which the Lord commanded.

11. Wherefore the Lord said unto Solomon, Forasmuch as this is done of thee, and thou hast not kept my covenant and my statutes, which I have commanded thee, I will surely rend the kingdom from thee, and will give it to thy servant.

12. Notwithstanding in thy days I will not do it for David thy father's sake: but I will rend it out of the hand of thy son.

13. Howbeit I will not rend away all the kingdom; but will give one tribe to thy son for David my servant's sake, and for Jerusalem's sake which I have chosen.

DICTIONARY

Gibeon (GIB-ee-on)—1 Kings 3:5—An ancient town six miles northwest of Jerusalem and the location of one of the principal "high places."

rend the kingdom from thee—1 Kings 11:11—To take away regardless of the magnificence or self-exalting strength.

LESSON OUTLINE

I. OPPORTUNITY TO CHOOSE
   A. Irregular Worship
   B. Sincere Worship
   C. Extravagant Worship
   D. Divine Response to Worship

II. A WISE CHOICE
   A. Humility Demonstrated
   B. Wisdom Requested
   C. Blessings Granted
   D. Wisdom Demonstrated

III. THE FOLLY OF WRONG CHOICES
   A. Forbidden Marriages
   B. Resultant Idolatry
   C. Divine Retribution

LESSON EXPOSITION

INTRODUCTION

Seldom in our sacred writings have such opposite qualities manifested themselves in a single individual as appeared in King Solomon. Early in his reign, his sound choices led to divinely granted wisdom, wealth, and renown. Later in his reign, politically prudent but spiritually devastating marriages with foreign princesses led him into idolatry, and, ultimately, both spiritual and temporal loss resulted—for both the royal office and the nation.

David must have loved Solomon intensely; after all, he was the first surviving child of Bathsheba, with whom David had experienced that most passionate and most costly love affair. It stands to reason, moreover, that David certainly would have wished this beloved son to have benefited from highly positive influences during his childhood and adolescence. Solomon, however, grew up during David's declining years and must inevitably have absorbed negative influences from palace intrigue, family bickering, the moral heinousness of Amnon's behavior toward his half sister, Tamar, and the outright rebellion of Solomon's older half brother Absalom. One would speculate that the guidance of Nathan the prophet, traditionally supposed to have served as the young Solomon's mentor, might have done much to offset such pervasive counter-influences. But it is nonetheless very likely that the decadent state of affairs in the royal family left its indelible mark on the young prince.

By royal promise to his mother—through the intervention of both Bathsheba and the prophet Nathan, and with divine sanction (see 1 Kings 1)—Solomon, at approximately twenty years of age, assumed the kingship and ruled from about 1015 B.C. to 975 B.C. The early years of his reign would have fulfilled the fondest dreams of a pious and aspiring Israelite, for the young king proved to be a model of piety, prudence, sound judgment, administrative acumen, and diplomatic skill; in fact, at this point in his reign he almost invariably made both worldly wise and spiritually sound decisions. King Solomon, however, gradually immersed himself so fully in royal luxury, adapting himself so totally to customs common among Oriental monarchs but contrary to divine commands, that he departed widely from that covenant made with the Lord early in his reign and renewed at the dedication of the Temple. As a direct result of this departure, he brought divine judgment upon both his royal house and his nation. This week's Sunday school lesson emphasizes Solomon's early exemplary leadership but also points out the diametrical contrast between early and later years as it details the reprehensible result of Solomon's later practice of forbidden activity and mentions briefly the supernaturally imposed penalty.

I. OPPORTUNITY TO CHOOSE (1 Kings 3: 1-5)

A. Irregular Worship (vv. 1, 2)

Before Solomon built the Temple in Jerusalem, Israel worshiped—with apparent sincerity—at local sacred places on the hilltops, offering their own animal sacrifices. Although such irregular worship did not conform completely to the divine will, the Lord appears to have tolerated it during a period of relative ignorance of the Law and disorganization of the religious institutions. (The Ark of the Covenant, for instance, rested in Jerusalem—not in the Tabernacle at Gibeon where God had ordained its placement and its sacred function within the holy of holies.) God obviously discerned within the majority of Israelites a sincerity of intention which caused Him to tolerate a pattern of worship which, while not idolatrous, did not conform perfectly to His present will for the national community.

B. Sincere Worship (v. 3)

King Solomon participated in these irregular worship practices of his people, the one imperfect element in an otherwise highly upright early life. Verse 3 assures us that the king "loved the Lord, walking in the statutes of David his father." This love for God should not be viewed, however, as sentimental attachment but as a continuous response of intellect and will which assuredly induced positive emotions but which, more importantly, impelled the king toward the formation of a godly pattern of behavior. The devoted heart spontaneously seeks to worship the Creator and Sustainer of life. Hence, Solomon engaged in acts of worship which, although not totally according to the divine intention for his era, were beyond doubt the sincere expressions of a godly heart. One recalls that such individually performed acts of animal sacrifice as King Solomon performed on this occasion had been the norm during the patriarchal period, so that Solomon and his people were engaging in practices once divinely sanctioned but now rendered obsolete with the institutionalization of religion.

C. Extravagant Worship (v. 4)

Solomon's intensity of devotion induced him to extravagant expression in worship. Gibeon was the location of the Tabernacle, where priests officiated regularly. But now the king himself offered—because of impulses from a grateful heart—a thousand burnt offerings. Mary performed an analogous act of extravagant worship of our Lord in John 12:2-6 when she poured the precious ointment upon His feet. In each case God responded to the extravagant expression of intense devotion.

What is the New Testament pattern of worship? How planned or how spontaneous should worship be, according to this pattern?

D. Divine Response to Worship (v. 5)

5. In Gibeon the Lord appeared to Solomon in a dream by night: and God said, Ask what I shall give thee.

On occasion in both the Old and New Testaments, God spoke to men through dreams. Joseph, of course, comes immediately to mind (Genesis 37:5-11), but the Apostle Paul also received a divine communication by means of a dream vision during the night which changed the very course of his life (Acts 16:9, 10). God responded to King Solomon's sincere expression of love and devotion in the above-mentioned rites of worship by communicating with the king in a dream vision which beyond doubt determined the nature of his life and his kingship. The person truly dedicated to God always worships out of a grateful heart, not with some ulterior motive. Hence, Solomon surely was not engaging in worship (as some scholars suggest) in order to **induce deliberately** a communication from God through a dream. Such a motive smacks of a magical conception of religious life. But God does respond—often indeed with apparent extravagance—to the honest expressions of His people, even as He did during King Solomon's dream: "Ask what I shall give thee." Jesus, moreover, urged upon His disciples the following almost startling principle: "I tell you the truth, my Father will give you whatever you ask in my name. Until now you have not asked for anything in my name. Ask and you will receive, and your joy will be complete" (John 16:23, 24; **New International Version).** Prayer, in whatever form, is not a magic talisman to be evoked upon demand by a carnal mind. It is, however, the prerogative and the joy of the dedicated believer who asks and receives in accordance with the divine will.

II. A WISE CHOICE (1 Kings 3:6-28)

A. Humility Demonstrated (vv. 6-8)

6. And Solomon said, Thou hast shewed unto thy servant David my father great mercy, according as he walked before thee in truth, and in righteousness, and in uprightness of heart with thee; and thou hast kept for him this great kindness, that thou hast given him a son to sit on his throne, as it is this day.

Solomon's reply indicates his recognition of his father's covenant relationship with the Lord. God's response to David's righteousness, however, was beyond that which was deserved—"great mercy." David, moreover, related to God **as slave to master**, according to these words of his son, and thereby must offer implicit obedience, rendering himself a ready instrument of the divine will on any occasion. We know that David did not always live out this ideal expression of his relationship to Deity, but he did, through contrition after any act of disobedience, maintain his covenant with God. God therefore honored him by continuing his royal lineage in Solomon. This statement by Solomon in verse 6 reveals the son's basic recognition of God's claims upon the sovereign of Israel.

7. And now, O Lord my God, thou hast made thy servant king instead of David my father: and I am but a little child: I know not how to go out or come in.

Solomon must now enter into a relationship with God like that which his father had maintained before him. As king of God's chosen people, he must behave as **servant of Deity**. At the moment of recognition of the awesome role he had assumed, Solomon seemed overwhelmed by a sense of inadequacy. The symbolic expression "I am but a little child" reveals the young king's humility before God, his sense of a lack of fitness for the responsibility he must fulfill. One should not, however, view such an expression of humility as perfunctory or false, and neither should one see it as indicative of actual inadequacy. With huge responsibilities looming before him and cognizant of the presence of Divinity, any honest man must sense whatever ability he has as insufficient. That ruler, moreover, who cockily expressed complete confidence in his personal acumen under such circumstances would reveal supreme arrogance as well as obvious foolishness. No man could be sure of sufficient personal resources to meet yet unforeseen contingencies of national leadership.

8. And thy servant is in the midst of thy people which thou hast chosen, a great people, that cannot be numbered nor counted for multitude.

Solomon continued to express his sense of awe at the position in which he found himself. He also indicated his recognition of the special nature of the kingdom which he was to rule—"people which thou hast chosen." From the time of Abraham that special destiny of Israel had been charted by Deity, a destiny which Solomon could not foresee in its fulness. But the king was well aware of God's special dealings with Israel during the past centuries and even during his father's own recent reign. He most likely spoke figuratively of Israel's numbers—a symbolic expression of royal pride in his people, who in actuality constituted a relatively small kingdom in comparison with Egypt or Assyria, but whose numbers were nonetheless imposing and which was a "great" nation—in national character and divinely ordained destiny as well as size.

Solomon's genuine humility might serve as a model for any man in any role in any age. Is not humility the inevitable accompaniment of honest, in-depth self-assessment? And does not the proud man always deceive himself? For, in fact, no man can boast of uniformly high accomplishment in every single area of his life. If he is honest, moreover, he must acknowledge that his talents and capabilities ultimately stem from God. Such recognition of personal reality will produce humility before one's Maker—both the acknowledgment of personal limitations and thanksgiving for divine enablement.

B. Wisdom Requested (v. 9)

9. Give therefore thy servant an understanding heart to judge thy people, that I may discern between good and bad: for who is able to judge this thy so great a people?

Solomon's request reveals that he already possessed valuable qualities of character and spirit—piety, self-discernment, and a properly ordered sense of values, for example. Now he was asking God for "a heart with skill to listen" **(New English Bible)**, and the word **heart** in this context denotes "mind" or "intellect." An important function of the king of Israel was the task of **judgment**, that role assumed by the judiciary in more complex later cultures. While the king certainly would not decide every such case, to make decisions in specific cases was nonetheless an expectation of his office. The request encompasses a much broader scope, however, for the ruling monarch would need "an understanding heart" in a multiplicity of roles, such as planning with administrative subordinates and consulting with diplomatic advisors. That the **seeds** of some of his later acquired wisdom already rested within his heart appears in the very fact that he made this most discerning petition. But Solomon, whether consciously or not, was now asking for a supernatural endowment through the agency of the Holy Spirit, who, as we know, granted such specific anointings for specialized purposes during Old Testament times.

The king here exercised **judicious choice**. Viewed from one perspective, life consists of such freely made choices. Each choice, moreover, propels the chooser in a particular direction and thereby helps to form his very being, to shape his basic character. Having chosen, one usually cannot retrace his steps. Often, having chosen foolishly, one must wander through a thicket of confusion and despair before regaining the path forsaken as a matter of free personal choice. Hence, to weigh carefully each of those successive decisions which constitute the ongoing life process is vital to one's spiritual health. In verse 9, one sees that Solomon—at this point—was choosing most wisely.

Is it possible, however, that Solomon—even in childhood, perhaps—had already made choices which would make easier his later very foolish choices?

C. Blessings Granted (vv. 10-15)

God was pleased with Solomon's request. The king had avoided the mean, the selfish, and the sensual in his petition and had thereby revealed a godly heart. First, he did not request "long life," always **conditional** and possibly contrary to God's will in a particular given case. Second, he did not request **riches**—considered in Old Testament times as an indication of divine favor, hence, not an unreasonable request, but certainly one **relatively low** in priority. Finally, he did not pray for divine vengeance upon his enemies, although various psalms indicate that to request divine judgment upon men who had behaved wickedly would not be indicative of an unspiritual mind during the Old Testament era.

Hence, God granted Solomon's request, giving him "a wise and discerning heart" (v. 12, **(New American Standard Bible)** so that he would surpass in wisdom all before or after him. Abundant evidence exists that God endowed Solomon with wisdom of supernatural scope and depth. For instance, 1 Kings 4:29-34 states regarding this divine gift that Solomon (a) excelled the sages of other lands and cultures in wisdom, (b) devised 3,000 proverbs and 1,005 songs, (c) exhibited knowledge of **natural history,** and (d) attracted visitors who had heard of his wisdom from among "all people." Conservative Bible scholars, moreover, attribute to King Solomon at least two of the Psalms, much of the Book of Proverbs, Ecclesiastes, and the Song of Solomon, sections of Scripture which illustrate well both the breadth and the intensity of his wisdom.

D. Wisdom Demonstrated

Two specific incidents illustrate quite well the depth and the scope of that wisdom. In 1 Kings 3:16-28, the Bible tells of two prostitutes who came before the king with claims and counterclaims as to which of them had accidentally caused her child's death and which of the two was mother of a surviving child. The well-known answer of the king revealed depth of wisdom in that it elicited the basic maternal response, unmistakable in a woman who was influenced little if at all by proprieties. Since these prostitutes lived outside the pale of respectable society, there would be little if any impulse to say the expected thing—even to the king. Hence, the "nonmother" cared little for the child's life and said so, whereas the real mother demonstrated her concern for the survival of the child, even if she must forfeit both her custody of the child and her emotional satisfaction to assure that survival. Solomon's depth of wisdom lay in his instinctive perception that such would be the case.

The other incident (1 Kings 10:1-13) illustrates well both the depth and the scope of the wisdom of Solomon. The Queen of Sheba (a land usually identified with modern Yemen) came to Jerusalem, with her imposing Oriental retinue, expressly "to test him with difficult questions" (v. 1, **New American Standard Bible**). She was amazed to discover that he had a satisfactory answer for every question. She, moreover, marvelled at the luxury of his court, exchanged rich gifts with him, and, most importantly, praised the God of Israel for Solomon's glorious reign (v. 9).

III. THE FOLLY OF WRONG CHOICES (1 Kings 11:1-13)

A. Forbidden Marriages (vv. 1-3)

At what point in his reign Solomon began to veer away from that strong dedication evident in earlier chapters of 1 Kings, one cannot discern. At some point, however, he began to make choices devastating to his own ethical purity, to the separation demanded by the God of Israel as a nation, and to the well-being of future generations of Israelites. These choices lay in the realms of both statecraft and personal affairs, which in this case were very closely intertwined anyway. The glittering luxury of his court may be viewed as the fulfillment of a divine promise, but in its later excess it may also well be seen as a departure from the divine will.

Central to Solomon's moral and spiritual decline, however, were those multiple marriages with foreign princesses. If the daughter of Pharaoh was Solomon's first wife and if she became a proselyte to the Jewish religion, then this marriage was neither forbidden nor harmful. Our information is incomplete regarding these factors. The presence of the many other occupants of Solomon's harem, however, was in express violation of God's commands against foreign entanglements, and Solomon's inevitable emotional involvements with this vast plurality of wives could only lead to further violations of God's clear-cut instructions to His people. The divine expectation of Israel's separation is declared in Exodus 33:16, and Exodus 23:31-33 and 34: 12-16 expressly forbid any sort of relationship with the seven nations of Canaan, some of which were sources for Solomon's harem. Polygamy itself violated God's basic will for man (Genesis 2:18-25), although it had existed since "Lamech took unto him two wives" (Genesis 4:19); moreover, Solomon's father David's domestic problems illustrate some of the inevitable difficulties of a polygamous home. Hence, the plurality of marriages must in itself have produced its ever attendant evils. It apparently would not in itself have brought the direct divine judgment inevitable in the present case, however.

Solomon's marriages to foreign princesses must have created some purely cultural problems since customs would without doubt have been greatly different in the domestic, social, and religious realms. It takes intelligence, persistence, cultural insight, and a high degree of personal maturity in both partners for an intercultural marriage to succeed. But the religion of Israel pervaded every aspect of life (as true religion must always); therefore, how an Israelite behaved in every sphere of life mattered—immensely. For this reason God had prohibited all entanglements which might affect any phase of the life of His people. And marriage obviously constituted the most crucial relationship of all in this regard. In King Solomon's case, 1 Kings 11:3 graphically declares the sad truth: "He had seven hundred wives, princesses, and three hundred concubines: and his wives turned away his heart."

B. Resultant Idolatry (vv. 4-8)

It should not surprise anyone that Solomon's foreign wives would wish to worship their gods. After all, they had had such worship practices inculcated from infancy, their consciences had been formed in cultural **milieus** with those religions at the center of each given culture. They had, as members of royal households in their respective kingdoms, likely practiced their religions devotedly before coming to Jerusalem.

It would have been Solomon's hard duty to have taught these wives the religion of Israel, having brought them to his kingdom, but the same impulse which led him to such typical behavior of the Oriental monarch as the creation of a harem also inclined him, first, toward the toleration of their false gods and, ultimately, toward the embracing of such worship of idols himself (1 Kings 11:4). **Ashtoreth** (v. 5), of the Zidonians, was apparently a moon goddess associated with fertility rites among the Canaanites, and morally impure ceremonies were involved in her worship. **Milcom,** the national god of the Ammonites, had his shrine, constructed by King Solomon, within sight of the Temple itself. **Chemosh,** national deity of the Moabites, is to be identified with **Milcom** in this context (see 1 Kings 11:5, 7). According to verse 8, Solomon also built shrines for other false deities. The great seventeenth-century poet John Milton in memorable language deplores such wicked activity:

By that uxorious King, whose heart though large,
Beguil'd by fair Idolatresses, fell
To Idols foul. **(Paradise Lost, I)**

By what forms of idolatry are twentieth-century Christians tempted?

C. Divine Retribution (vv. 9-13)

9. And the Lord was angry with Solomon, because his heart was turned from the Lord God of Israel, which had appeared unto him twice.

It may startle some modern Christians to read of the **anger** of the Lord, for our natural and appropriate preference for the positive, beneficent qualities of Deity may at times produce an embalance of emphasis which, in turn, produces an ignoring of God's stern justice and outright wrath against evil. Solomon's wicked behavior provoked God's wrath, particularly in view of the fact that God had granted the king remarkable and gracious evidences of His presence and power. Solomon's failure, moreover, could not in any sense be construed as the result of ignorance or of unconscious straying from the appointed path. He knew well God's requirements, he had experienced the divine presence, and he had **covenanted** with God to walk uprightly and to lead his nation wisely.

10. And had commanded him concerning

this thing, that he should not go after other gods: but he kept not that which the Lord commanded.

It is clear that Solomon not only provided for idolatrous worship for his many wives but also himself joined in these forbidden religious practices—a remarkable lapse from piety in one who had earlier walked before the true God in intimate fellowship. If one's religious faith is merely traditional and not rooted in personal experience, a lapse into false religion or the total absence of religious faith is quite understandable. But for a man who has experienced the true God to turn to idolatrous practices constitutes the most heinous of offenses.

11. Wherefore the Lord said unto Solomon, Forasmuch as this is done of thee, and thou hast not kept my covenant and my statutes, which I have commanded thee, I will surely rend the kingdom from thee, and will give it to thy servant.

Did the Lord on this occasion appear directly to Solomon, or did He send a prophet? Since the king had broken his covenant with God and had through his wicked behavior forfeited his right to intimate fellowship with God, the mode was likely that of the prophet. The message was not conditional; the divine retribution was inevitable. It was, moreover, particularly humiliating: not only would Solomon indirectly lose the kingdom, he would also lose it to one of his own subordinates.

12. Notwithstanding in thy days I will not do it for David thy father's sake: but I will rend it out of the hand of thy son.

Solomon received a personal respite—not for his own sake but for David's sake. This fact, however, must have made his humiliation more complete. He must, moreover, live with the knowledge that both his son and his entire kingdom would suffer after his decease. The verb **rend** or **tear (New International Version),** which, to emphasize its force, occurs three times—in verses 11, 12, and 13—connotes "violence." Hence, one learns that King Solomon's rebellion would bring devastating turmoil upon his entire kingdom. How selfish is the sinner—always! Inevitably, he brings a harvest of evil circumstance not upon himself only but also upon those whom he may love most.

Does sin always bring retribution? (See Galatians 6:7, 8)

---

13. Howbeit I will not rend away all the kingdom; but will give one tribe to thy son for David my servant's sake, and for Jerusalem's sake which I have chosen.

Solomon was a part of something far larger than himself. God had a destiny for Israel and for Jerusalem which was closely intertwined with the house of David, and one man's disobedience would not foil the divine plan. In 2 Samuel 7:12-15, God had promised David, concerning Solomon, that He would "establish the throne of his kingdom for ever" (v. 13). He also had pledged to punish Solomon if he committed iniquity (v. 14); but, crucially, He had assured David that divine "mercy shall not depart away from him" (v. 15). God was now keeping His word to David and to Solomon, even in this act of judgment.

The life of King Solomon teaches twin lessons—the rewards of wise choice and the perils of evil choice. We know, moreover, that God does not change, that His moral law is ageless, and that men who flout the divine will and ignore the divine Word pay—always.

REVIEW QUESTIONS

1. What were the circumstances of Solomon's dream vision?

2. What wise choice did Solomon make, and what resulted from that choice?

3. What are some specific evidences of Solomon's supernaturally granted wisdom?

4. What factors induced King Solomon to stray from his covenant with God?

5. How was Solomon punished for his sin?

GOLDEN TEXT HOMILY

"BUT SEEK YE FIRST THE KINGDOM OF GOD, AND HIS RIGHTEOUSNESS; AND ALL THESE THINGS SHALL BE ADDED UNTO YOU" (Matthew 6:33).

It is very easy for us, even in the work of the Lord, to ignore this simple verse.

The verse is both a command and a promise. The clause which tells us to seek first the kingdom of God is a no-nonsense order. It speaks to the ordering of our priorities.

The second clause is a promise. It says that if we put God first, the more tangible aspects of life will be taken care of. The implication is that the very things which we are tempted to put ahead of God will turn out all right if we keep them in their proper place.

Some seem to believe that this verse is purely an evangelistic one, warning those who have ignored God altogether to make provision for Him in their lives. But the scope of the verse is much broader than that. Even in the work of God it is easy to get "the cart before the horse." It is easy to value our reputations as good Sunday school teachers over the lives of our students. It is easy to place a higher value on building a new church building than on finding the perfect will of God.

Even for churches and church people, the message from Jesus is clear: "Seek ye first the kingdom of God."—**Selected**

SENTENCE SERMONS

CHOOSING GOD'S BEST prepares the way for His blessings, but choosing materialism and sensualism leads ultimately to judgment.
—**Selected**

LITTLE CHOICES DETERMINE habit;
Habit carves and molds character
Which makes the big decisions.
—**Selected**

GOD ALWAYS GIVES His best to those who leave the choice with Him.
—**"Speaker's Sourcebook"**

CHOICE, NOT CHANCE, determines human destiny.
—**"Speaker's Sourcebook"**

EVANGELISTIC APPLICATION

CHOOSING TO TAKE CHRIST AS SAVIOR IS LIFE'S GREATEST AND WISEST CHOICE.

"Decisions! Decisions!" we sometimes say in mock despair, giving vent to our mild displeasure during some moment of slight consternation. But we thereby focus attention on a crucial element of living. Constantly, we must **decide**—often when we feel least ready to do so. In late adolescence the decision may be **whom to marry** or **how to earn a living**. In middle age we are forced to decide **how to rear children** or **whether or not to change jobs**. In the later years the choice may be **when to retire** or **whether to retain the family dwelling**. Life is without doubt a succession of often agonizing choices.

The greatest tragedy of many lives, however, lies in the fact that those inevitable decisions of the life process are made without recourse to the very Fount of wisdom, to the One who said, "I am the way, the truth, and the life" (John 14:6). The reason, of course, is the failure to make that most crucial decision—a commitment to Jesus Christ as Savior and Lord.

Making this choice does not remove one from the sphere of exciting action or relegate him to the sidelines. It does provide him, however, with a frame of reference for making those other necessary decisions, and it endows him with power for vibrant living. After all, having decided for Christ, he has placed himself in harmony with the forces of the universe. How could one lose?

ILLUMINATING THE LESSON

The Swedish Nightingale, Jenny Lind, won great success as an opera singer, and money poured into her purse. Yet, she left the stage while she was singing her best, and never returned to it. She must have missed the money, the fame, and the applause of thousands, but she was content to live in privacy.

Once an English friend found her sitting on the sea sands with a Bible on her knee, looking out into the glory of the sunset. They talked, and the conversation finally led to the inevitable question: "Oh, Madame Goldschmidt, how is it that you came to abandon the stage at the very height of your success?"

"When every day," was the quiet answer, "it made me think less of this (laying a finger on the Bible) and nothing at all of that (pointing to the sunset), what else could I do?"

—From **Springs in the Valley,** by Mrs. Charles E. Cowman

DAILY DEVOTIONAL GUIDE

M. Importance of a Wise Choice. Deuteronomy 30:11-20

T. Necessity of Choice. Joshua 24:1-15

W. Choice Affects Others. 2 Samuel 24:10-17

T. Response to a Wise Request. 1 Kings 3:10-15

F. Dangers of Wrong Choice. Proverbs 1:24-33

S. Promise of Wisdom. James 1:5-11

June 21, 1981

The Value of Wise Counsel

Bible Background: 1 Kings 11:11—12:33; 2 Chronicles 10:1-19
Time: Probably 931 B.C.
Place: Shechem
Supplemental References: Psalms 10:4; 133:1-3; Proverbs 13:10; 16:18; 26:12; Jeremiah 43:2; 49:16; Hosea 7:9, 10
Golden Text: "The way of a fool is right in his own eyes: but he that hearkeneth unto counsel is wise" (Proverbs 12:15).
Central Truth: Decisions made in total disregard of wise counsel lead to disaster.
Evangelistic Emphasis: Hearing and obeying the counsel of God's Word leads to eternal life.

PRINTED TEXT

1 Kings 12:12. So Jeroboam and all the people came to Rehoboam the third day, as the king had appointed, saying, Come to me again the third day.

13. And the king answered the people roughly, and forsook the old men's counsel that they gave him;

14. And spake to them after the counsel of the young men, saying, My father made your yoke heavy, and I will add to your yoke: my father also chastised you with whips, but I will chastise you with scorpions.

15. Wherefore the king hearkened not unto the people; for the cause was from the Lord, that he might perform his saying, which the Lord spake by Ahijah the Shilonite unto Jeroboam the son of Nebat.

16. So when all Israel saw that the king hearkened not unto them, the people answered the king, saying, What portion have we in David? neither have we inheritance in the son of Jesse: to your tents, O Israel: now see to thine own house, David. So Israel departed unto their tents.

17. But as for the children of Israel which dwelt in the cities of Judah, Rehoboam reigned over them.

18. Then king Rehoboam sent Adoram, who was over the tribute; and all Israel stoned him with stones, that he died. Therefore king Rehoboam made speed to get him up to his chariot, to flee to Jerusalem.

19. So Israel rebelled against the house of David unto this day.

20. And it came to pass, when all Israel heard that Jeroboam was come again, that they sent and called him unto the congregation, and made him king over all Israel: there was none that followed the house of David, but the tribe of Judah only.

DICTIONARY

Jeroboam (jer-oh-BOH-um)—1 Kings 12:12—The son of Nebat and first king of the Northern tribes after the disruption of the kingdom at the death of Solomon.

Rehoboam (re-oh-BOH-um)—1 Kings 12:12—Son of Solomon and the first king of the Southern kingdom after his father's death.

scorpions—1 Kings 12:14—An ordinary whip with barbs of metal fastened near the end.

Ahijah the Shilonite (ah-HIGH-jah, SHY-lo-nite)—1 Kings 12:15—A prophet from the city of Shiloh, otherwise unknown except for the incident referred to in our text.

Adoram (ah-DOOR-am)—1 Kings 12:18—The son of Abda. He was a high official in the courts of David, Solomon, and Rehoboam, with a long record of service in charge of the forced labor groups. He was the overseer of a force of thirty thousand under Solomon (1 Kings 5:13, 14).

LESSON OUTLINE

I. OFFERING WISE COUNSEL
   A. The Assembly at Shechem
   B. The Request of the People
   C. The Counsel of the Elders

II. HEEDING UNWISE COUNSEL
   A. Consulting the Young Men
   B. Obtaining Foolish Counsel
   C. Following the Bad Advice

III. SUFFERING THE CONSEQUENCES
   A. The Rebellion of Israel
   B. A Shocking Aftermath
   C. The Selection of Israel's King

IV. ACCEPTING GOD'S COUNSEL
   A. Rehoboam's Intention
   B. Shemaiah's Warning

LESSON EXPOSITION

INTRODUCTION

One must view the sad events of this week's lesson from a double perspective. King Solomon, through wicked behavior, had caused ten tribes of Israel to be removed from rulership by the Davidic royal line. Solomon's son Rehoboam, however, must undergo this divinely imposed penalty—and that regardless of his personal behavior. The divine retribution, affecting direly the fortunes of Rehoboam, was an inevitable fact since a true prophet had proclaimed God's sovereign will regarding the matter long before Rehoboam's accession to the throne. Rehoboam, nonetheless, without doubt functioned as the immediate instrument of his own downfall. His unfortunate destiny was rooted not only in his father's sin, but also in his own rash nature and immature behavior. It is reasonable yet again, however, to suppose that influence from the father had helped to shape the character of the son. In fact, that very marriage alliance with the Ammonitish princess which produced Rehoboam demonstrates the negative nature, on the whole, of the influence exerted by Solomon during his later years.

King Solomon, then, imposed a double penalty upon Rehoboam. By his overt wickedness he brought about a divine judgment, the effects of which devolved upon his son; however, Solomon had already, through the total effect of his parental example, been instrumental in the creation of Rehoboam's faulty character, and that, beyond doubt, was the worse of the two effects.

I. OFFERING WISE COUNSEL (1 Kings 12: 1-7)

A. The Assembly at Shechem (vv. 1, 2)

Shechem was an important city of Ephraim, a powerful, influential tribe; hence, it is likely that Rehoboam's going to this city to be crowned (outside the boundaries of Judah, his own tribe) in itself indicates the precariousness of his position. He must have recognized the existence of this rival power center and its potential threat to his own position and must have been seeking to placate the northern tribes. Apparently the rumblings of dissent had already reached Jerusalem before they surfaced so audibly at the assembly at Shechem. Rehoboam's later naively rash actions, however, cast some doubt upon these assumptions of highly reasonable behavior on his part.

Jeroboam, already deemed a threat during Solomon's lifetime, had returned from exile in Egypt upon Solomon's death and now functioned as spokesman for the smoldering tribes.

B. The Request of the People (vv. 3-5)

The message conveyed to the young king by the representatives of the northern tribes was clear: their dissatisfaction with the harshness of Solomon's rule was severe, and their willing acceptance of Rehoboam's rule depended upon redress of their grievances. It is important, however, to note that the tone of 1 Kings 12:4 is not one of unalterable rebellion: ' "Your father put a heavy yoke on us, but now lighten the harsh labor and the heavy yoke he put on us, and we will serve you' " **(New International Version).** They had loved King David and had gloried in King Solomon's successes, and they would not forsake Rehoboam and the royal house of David which he represented lightly and easily.

Their grievances seem to have been entirely legitimate and indeed quite heavy. King David had employed forced labor during his reign but had used only foreigners for such tasks. King Solomon, however, had begun to employ Israelites for hard forced labor—a kind of serfdom contrary to the spirit, if not the letter, of the Mosaic Code (see Leviticus 25:39-46). Solomon, moreover, had imposed tax levies upon the people in support of his lavish court, and this practice may well have contributed to the feeling of the people that they had been treated unjustly. The northern tribes, furthermore, had accepted David as king only after seven years of resistance and after various intrigue. They had exhibited signs of rebelliousness on more than one occasion. After all, Judah was not at the center of the kingdom, and there might well have existed feelings of resentment that this "outlying district" should contain the seat of government.

On the present occasion, these long accumulated and deeply divisive tribal feelings probably smoldered beneath the surface while remaining unarticulated, but they nonetheless contributed intense emotional tension and potential explosiveness to the situation. It was imperative, then, that calm reason prevail and that complaints which proved justifiable be redressed immediately. King Rehoboam at this point dismissed the assembly for three days, apparently so that careful deliberation regarding these requests of the people might ensue.

C. The Counsel of the Elders (vv. 6, 7)

Rehoboam first consulted the advisers of his father—men who were elderly, experienced, and wise. **Elders** need not by definition be **elderly,** despite the root meaning of the word (which has undergone development in meaning), but in this case the counselors surely **were** in many cases elderly, since they had been advisers to King Solomon, now dead after a forty-year reign. Rehoboam, if he made it in sincerity, was well advised in his decision to consult these seasoned men. These advisers were loyal to King Solomon and now to his son, but they were also quite cognizant of Solomon's excesses and, through extensive experience, well able to read the political climate and to sense undercurrents of which Rehoboam might have had no notion.

Their advice, carefully couched, is the very essence of political wisdom. They recognized that in yielding to the desires of the assembly Rehoboam would seem to stoop, a hard posture for the proud young king. So they acknowledged: ' "If today you will be a servant to these people and serve them and give them a favorable answer, they will always be your servants' " (1 Kings 12:7, **New International Version).**

In so doing, moreover, the elders enunciated a basic principle of statecraft as well as of personal living—that of mutual service. While often remaining unstated and indeed sometimes unacknowledged, this principle nonetheless operates relentlessly and unexceptionally. Even in totalitarian societies this mutual service bond between ruler and ruled ultimately obtains. There may exist in such societies cruelty and the denial of personal liberties, but at some point a level of intolerability is reached, and the government then either backs off and satisfies basic demands, or else the people revolt. Enlightened societies operate consciously and purposefully on the basis of such a principle of mutual service between government and people. There is in such societies a clear perception of the purposes of government: (1) the preservation of order, (2) the protection of the life and property of the citizenry, and (3) the conveyance to the people of whatever other rights and benefits the particular society has agreed to be just and fitting. Hence, the elders stated quite sagely, "Serve, and you will be served."

Does this principle of mutual service between leader and follower operate in leadership positions in every sphere of society? What about within the church?

II. HEEDING UNWISE COUNSEL (1 Kings 12:8-15)

A. Consulting the Young Men (vv. 8, 9)

Some commentators believe that Rehoboam had dismissed the assembly for three days for the express purpose of giving his young friends opportunity to travel from Jerusalem to Shechem. In this case, the consultation with the elders would have been little more than a ruse or a delaying tactic, while advice more to his taste was made available. These younger advisers likely had grown up with Rehoboam in the harem and would share his unversed viewpoints and sympathize more fully with that despotic view of rulership common in the Orient and apparently held, most foolishly, by Rehoboam. Hence, the inexperienced king rejected the sage advice of seasoned counselors and turned to untried and unwise advisers. Perhaps Rehoboam knew already what he wished to hear and was merely seeking to have it articulated—a very human but also often an extremely shortsighted tendency.

If the translators have captured the precise tone of the original text, one can discern in 1 Kings 12:9 **(New International Version)** just a hint of sarcasm in the king's request to the young men: ' "What is your advice? How should we answer these people who say to me, "Lighten the yoke your father put on us"?' " If the tone is slightly sarcastic, then Rehoboam is suggesting the answer he desires through the phrasing of the question.

B. Obtaining Foolish Counsel (vv. 10, 11)

The advice of the king's young counselors was enormously foolish and entirely wrongheaded. One wonders if they had read the mood of the assembly at all; certainly they either had not accurately discerned the threatening national climate or else presumed that despotic threats would cow a deeply disturbed people. Often, naively authoritarian leadership assumes that tightening the screws upon a restive group will quell any disturbance, and indeed at times such a tactic might seem to succeed. In such a case, however, the underlying causes lie unaddressed, remaining to fester, to create fresh problems, and eventually to explode into angry rebellion.

The young men suggested first that Rehoboam acknowledge the harshness of his father's rule. But the mitigation of harshness naturally expected to follow such an acknowledgement would not ensue, for the young advisers next counseled Rehoboam to threaten to rule even more harshly. The foolishness of such counsel is rendered even more evident to us because we can view the total context of the situation. Any close observer, however, should have sensed the ominous implications. Jeroboam, threatened with execution during Solomon's reign, had now returned from exile in Egypt and stood waiting in the wings to "usurp" leadership over the northern tribes. Jeroboam's presence, moreover, was evidently visible, inasmuch as he was serving as spokesman. In sum, if Rehoboam heeded the advice of his young counselors, he would be courting sure disaster for himself and for the kingdom.

C. Following the Bad Advice (vv. 12-15)

12. So Jeroboam and all the people came to Rehoboam the third day, as the king had appointed, saying, Come to me again the third day.

13. And the king answered the people roughly, and forsook the old men's counsel that they gave him;

14. And spake to them after the counsel of the young men, saying, My father made your yoke heavy, and I will add to your yoke: my father also chastised you with whips, but I will chastise you with scorpions.

Mentioned most prominently (and most ominously for Rehoboam) is the leadership of Jeroboam. In this light, how amazing it was that Rehoboam could not discern the inevitable result of the harshly despotic answer which he now gave the people! Had he (and his young counselors) been reared in such total isolation as to have absolutely no insight into or sensitivity regarding national moods and currents of feeling? Could he not even sense so obviously threatening a situation as this? Evidently not. For his answer was not only unfavorable but also highly insulting: **If things have been bad, you can now expect them to get worse.** Rehoboam must have reminded those Israelites who knew their national history of the Egyptian Pharaoh and his reaction to Moses—here was a ruler of Israel behaving like an Eastern despot.

Were they also reminded of Samuel's reply to Israel in 1 Samuel 8:10-18 upon their first request for a king? They had wanted to be like other nations. (And indeed they would be!) Samuel at that time informed Israel that a king would force their sons and daughters into employment as his personal servants, soldiers, farmers, artisans, cooks, and bakers; that he would appropriate their properties and seize their slaves for his own use; and that he would forcibly take their flocks. Samuel, moreover, solemnly warned: "Ye shall cry out in that day because of your king which ye shall have chosen you; and the Lord will not hear you in that day" (1 Samuel 8:18). And, in fact, the ten northern tribes were actually merely trading one despot for another.

Rehoboam used the most lacerating words possible: ' "My father scourged you with whips; I will scourge you with scorpions' " (1 Kings

12:14, **New International Version). Scorpions** likely refers to "whips" which sting like scorpions, since it would seem virtually impossible to whip with literal scorpions (as if with snakes). Yet his cruel intention of subjecting his people to the severest inhumanity is clearly evident.

Throughout the Old Testament a recurring, emphatic prophetic theme is that of the heinousness of social and political injustice and God's sure vindication of those upon whom such injustice fell. As early as Deuteronomy 24:14-22, this scriptural motif can be found, and in prophetical book after prophetical book it recurs. For instance, this scripture thunders forth: "Is not this the fast that I have chosen? to loose the bands of wickedness, to undo the heavy burdens, and to let the oppressed go free, and that ye break every yoke? Is it not to deal thy bread to the hungry, and that thou bring the poor that are cast out to thy house? when thou seest the naked, that thou cover him; and that thou hide not thyself from thine own flesh?" (Isaiah 58:6, 7). In stating his intention to violate the basic principles of humane treatment of his subjects, violations like those detailed above, King Rehoboam was contradicting the very reasons for the existence of government. Unwittingly, he was lending his support to those forces of anarchy, disorganization, and social immorality which ultimately must lead to the demise of leadership and the disintegration of kingdoms.

Does the Christian gospel speak to the social concerns of man, even as it addresses the needs of his immortal soul?

15. Wherefore the king hearkened not unto the people; for the cause was from the Lord, that he might perform his saying, which the Lord spake by Ahijah the Shilonite unto Jeroboam the son of Nebat.

From a totally human perspective, Rehoboam must be seen as either almost stupidly unperceptive or else as almost insanely arrogant, even to the point of believing that he could quell any possible rebellion. Why else would he have been so totally unresponsive to representatives of his kingdom gathered in solemn assembly and with legitimate complaints, even by his own admission?

Another dimension, however, remains to be considered: "The cause was from the Lord."

While Rehoboam's response was without doubt rooted in defective character, on another occasion—with different antecedent events—he nonetheless might have been able to behave differently despite his rashness of character. But an issue far larger than that of Rehoboam's destiny was being worked out here, and his role was at least partially predetermined. God, some time before, had through His prophet informed Solomon that he would lose the ten northern tribes (1 Kings 11:11, 12). Later, an admirable servant of King Solomon, Jeroboam, had been accosted by Ahijah the prophet and informed in a dramatic encounter that he would be granted rule over the ten northern tribes (1 Kings 11:26-40). Now the scenario which would bring about the fulfillment of those prophecies was playing itself out. Rehoboam, through his naivete and gross misjudgment, was performing his crucial role in that real-life drama.

III. SUFFERING THE CONSEQUENCES (1 Kings 12:16-20)

A. The Rebellion of Israel (vv. 16, 17)

16. So when all Israel saw that the king hearkened not unto them, the people answered the king, saying, What portion have we in David? neither have we inheritance in the son of Jesse: to your tents, O Israel: now see to thine own house, David. So Israel departed unto their tents.

The conclusion drawn by the leadership of the northern tribes was that their interests were not to be served by this royal representative of the house of David. They, in all likelihood, knew nothing of the prophecies mentioned earlier in this lesson. Instead, they reacted purely on the basis of the king's intention to continue what they rightly perceived to be political and social injustice. Hence, one gets a double perspective: men, on the one hand, acting so as to fulfill what they considered their best interests; God, on the other hand, both bringing about retribution for the sins of an individual (King Solomon) and at the same time working out the long-term destinies of two kingdoms, a chosen people, and a divinely designated royal house.

The passage which presents the rejection of the house of David by the northern tribes is couched in beautifully poignant phrasing. It is a statement packed with emotion—emotion producible only by the intensity generated by a crisis moment when all the mental energies of whoever spoke for the people (was it Jeroboam himself?) were focused upon vehement expression of bitter rejection.

The sense of the expression is that the northern tribes could hope for no justice from this king from Judah and that therefore they would offer him no allegiance. Their repudiation, however, was not merely personal. They at the same time were rejecting the royal house represented by Rehoboam—a divinely appointed lineage of rulers which would one day produce the Messiah himself. There lies the tragedy of this real-life drama. In rejecting the rash, foolish young king, they must also reject that entire line of kings descending from Israel's most glorious king—David. They must dissociate themselves from that "royal vine" which would one day, despite all sins, weaknesses, and excesses, produce "the Branch," the Messiah himself.

17. But as for the children of Israel which dwelt in the cities of Judah, Rehoboam reigned over them.

Those ancestral members of the ten northern tribes who resided in Judah continued in loyalty to Rehoboam. Their ancestral loyalties had likely weakened as they interacted with members of the tribe of Judah. There were clear advantages, moreover, to continued allegiance to Rehoboam: (1) if they declared their loyalty to Jeroboam, they would find it necessary to relocate within their former tribal areas, and (2) such a disruption of life would affect them materially and perhaps even spiritually, for (3) they must in such a case give up their home and start over in a new location; moreover, (4) they were presently within easy access of the Temple in Jerusalem, whereas in their ancestral homes, particularly given the divided kingdom, they would find continued participation in woship in the Temple in Jerusalem most difficult.

B. A Shocking Aftermath (vv. 18, 19)

18. Then king Rehoboam sent Adoram, who was over the tribute; and all Israel stoned him with stones, that he died. Therefore king Rehoboam made speed to get him up to his chariot, to flee to Jerusalem.

19. So Israel rebelled against the house of David unto this day.

Adoram, in certain manuscripts of the Old Testament called **Adoniram**, usually is identified with that public official who had performed the same duties under David and Solomon (see 2 Samuel 20:24 and 1 Kings 4:6; 5:14). If this identification, as is likely, is accurate, by this time he would be quite aged.

To stone a person in Israel was to end that person's life through an act (often, but not here, an official execution) which expressed the utmost outrage and contempt. That a long-standing public servant, who must be seen as having enjoyed high respect since he had served in his position so long and under three kings, should be subjected to such treatment indicates the extremely hostile attitudes toward the authority of Rehoboam prevailing in Israel. The act, while totally unjustifiable on moral grounds, is easily comprehensible, as is that similar expression of hostility which caused Rehoboam to flee unceremoniously to Jerusalem. Rehoboam had proved himself intolerable to the ten northern tribes, and now they expressed their total rejection of his royal authority in the most clearcut manner possible. One is also reminded, however, that the loss of the ten northern tribes to Rehoboam had been mandated by the divine will and therefore would not be circumvented or countermanded.

C. The Selection of Israel's King (v. 20)

20. And it came to pass, when all Israel heard that Jeroboam was come again, that they sent and called him unto the congregation, and made him king over all Israel: there was none that followed the house of David, but the tribe of Judah only.

There is no real discrepancy between verse 20 and verse 1. "All Israel" in verse 1 clearly refers to a representative group from all the tribes, whereas "all Israel" in verse 20 undoubtedly refers to the general population. "Congregation," in verse 20, like "all Israel" in verse 1, most likely refers to a representative group from the ten northern tribes. In any case, the "congregation" crowned Jeroboam, a gifted leader with a divine mandate to rule given through a reliable prophecy (1 Kings 11:29-39), as their king.

Apparently the tiny tribe of Benjamin was commonly subsumed under Judah during this age since verse 20 does not mention the fact that it remained under Rehoboam's rule. Also, 2 Chronicles 11:13, 14 states that all the Levites left their appointed districts within the ten northern tribes and came to Judah and Jerusalem. Hence, in reality, the house of David continued to rule over **three** tribes, which still left **ten** northern tribes under Jeroboam's rule since the descendants of Ephraim and Manasseh, sons of Joseph, had long before been formed into **two** tribes. The geographical area controlled by Rehoboam and his successors, however, was **primarily** that of the **one** tribe of Judah since Benjamin constituted a very small area and since "the priesthood of the Lord" was the Levites' only "inheritance" (see Joshua 18:7).

IV. ACCEPTING GOD'S COUNSEL (1 Kings 12:21-24)

A. Rehoboam's Intention (v. 21)

Rehoboam yet had no intention of allowing the ten northern tribes to remain free of his rule, although one would think that the extreme hostility experienced by himself and his servant at their hands should have convinced him that the division of the kingdom was, at least for the present, not to be healed—and certainly not through his relatively weak military force. Was not Rehoboam, moreover, aware of the prophecies which mandated this division of the kingdom? Whatever his knowledge and with whatever rationale, he assembled a fighting force of 180,000 men (which Israel would have easily far surpassed in numerical strength) and prepared to wage war against the ten northern tribes.

Does modern man, like Rehoboam, often cause himself grief and trouble through rashness and willfulness? Discuss submission and rebellion as spiritual alternatives.

B. Shemaiah's Warning (vv. 22-24)

God sent a prophet to Rehoboam to warn him against fighting his "brothers." In fact, the Lord constantly extends His mercies to man (as in the present context to Rehoboam)— undeserving though he be. Rehoboam surely would have been defeated had he persisted in his military plans, not merely because of the highly superior numerical strength of Israel but, rather, because God had mandated the national division. The word from God was, "This is my doing" (1 Kings 12:24, **New International Version**); therefore, it was to be done. If Rehoboam had continued to work counter to the divine will, he would have been completely crushed and humiliated. At this point, however, he was ready to accept what prophecy had decreed and his own rashness of character had directly brought about: "So they obeyed the word of the Lord and went home again, as the Lord had ordered" (v. 24, **New International Version**).

REVIEW QUESTIONS

1. Why did Rehoboam go to Shechem to be crowned?
2. What major grievance did the national assembly present to Rehoboam?
3. What answer did King Rehoboam return after three days?
4. How did Israel react to the king's harshness?
5. What was the final outcome of this grave national crisis?

GOLDEN TEXT HOMILY

"THE WAY OF A FOOL IS RIGHT IN HIS OWN EYES: BUT HE THAT HEARKENETH UNTO COUNSEL IS WISE."

In making a decision it is wise to get the best counseling possible, consider the options and select the best one before adopting a course of action. Even if this process is followed, we may still make mistakes. We need to realize that we are responsible for our own decisions. We should not blame others for giving us bad advice. However, we are less likely to get into difficulty if we follow this procedure than if we make self-willed choices without seeking counsel.

Our Heavenly Father has not left us to grope through life in darkness, but has provided His word to lighten our way. (Psalm 119:105) Before making a decision we should make sure that it is not in conflict with God's word.

Spirit-filled Christians have a paraclete—a counselor, advocate, comforter to guide and assist them. Decisions should be made through prayer, seeking the guidance of the Holy Spirit as our ultimate counselor.—**Richard Y. Bershon, Chief, Chaplain Service, V. A. Medical Center, Tomah, Wisconsin.**

SENTENCE SERMONS

IT IS CERTAIN that either wise hearing or ignorant speech is caught; therefore, let men take heed of their company.
—**William Shakespeare**

ADVICE IS SELDOM welcome; and those who want it most always like it the least.
—**Lord Chesterfield**

TO PROFIT FROM good counsel requires more wisdom than to give it.
—**Churton Collins**

DECISIONS MADE IN total disregard of wise counsel leads to disaster.
—**Selected**

EVANGELISTIC APPLICATION

HEARING AND OBEYING THE COUNSEL OF GOD'S WORD LEADS TO ETERNAL LIFE.

Man today is bombarded with both verbal and nonverbal messages—through mass communication media and through direct contacts with representatives of the multiplicity of both secular and religious life views promulgated constantly. If one responds indiscriminately, he is bound to dwell perpetually in a state of confusion and bewilderment. Somehow, he must filter out the trash, the nonsense, and the poison and accept only the worthwhile.

How can he do it? Only through an overarching set of principles so deeply rooted that they guide him implicitly, even automatically, as he threads his way through the welter of conflicting ideas and opinions pressing upon him from every side.

The only totally adequate set of such guiding principles is to be derived from the Bible, man's only safe and reliable spiritual and moral guide. The Book of books has long since proved itself entirely adequate. It tells of encounters with God, directives from God, and supernatural interventions by God. Those who have mastered its principles and followed its precepts have discovered their total truth and utter reliability.

In fact, to obey the Word of God is to discover **soul peace, spiritual joy,** and **everlasting life;** to deny God's Word or to disobey it is tantamount to disaster—ultimately if not immediately. Man was not created to be wholly self-reliant; therefore, he cannot fulfill his basic reason for existence alone. St. Augustine said it best centuries ago: "Thou hast made us for Thyself, O Lord; and our heart is restless until it rests in Thee." Having acquiesced in and appropriated this truth, man has entered upon the path to ultimate fulfillment. The instructions for forming such a healthful relationship with God, however, are found only in the Bible—God's written Word. Taste it, chew it, devour it, assimilate it, obey it, act it out—and live eternally!

ILLUMINATING THE LESSON

Don't Let This Happen to You.

There was a man who lived by the side of the road and sold hot dogs.

He was hard of hearing so he had no radio.

He had trouble with his eyes so he read no newspapers.

But he sold good hot dogs.

He put up signs on the highway telling how good they were.

He stood on the side of the road and cried, "Buy a hot dog, Mister?"

And people bought his hot dogs.

He increased his meat and bun orders.

He bought a bigger stove to take care of his trade.

He finally got his son home from college to help out.

But then something happened.

His son said, "Father, haven't you been listening to the radio?

"Haven't you been reading the newspaper?

"There's a big recession on.

"The European situation is terrible.

"The Domestic situation is worse."

Whereupon the father thought, "Well, my son's been to college, he reads the papers and he listens to the radio, and he ought to know."

So the father cut down his meat and bun orders, took down his signs, and no longer bothered to stand out on the highway to sell his hot dogs.

His sales fell overnight.

"You're right, son," the father said to the boy.

"We certainly are in the middle of a big recession."

—From **Speaker's Sourcebook**

DAILY DEVOTIONAL GUIDE

M. Disobedience Brings Disfavor. 1 Kings 11: 9-13

T. God's Sovereignty in Men's Affairs. 1 Kings 11:26-37

W. Folly of Bad Advice. 1 Kings 12:1-11

T. Folly of Pride. Psalm 36:1-12

F. Wisdom of Unity. Psalm 133:1-3

S. Wise Counsel. 2 Timothy 3:14-17

June 28, 1981

No Other Gods

Bible Background: 1 Kings 12:21—13:34; 2 Chronicles 11:14-17; Matthew 4:8-11
Time: Around 931 B.C.
Places: Shechem, Bethel
Supplemental References: Exodus 20:1-6; Deuteronomy 4:15-19; 5:7-9; Romans 1:18-23
Golden Text: "Thou shalt worship the Lord thy God, and him only shalt thou serve" (Matthew 4:10).
Central Truth: To worship at the shrine of convenience, materialism, or the occult is to indulge in idolatry, and to set the course for failure.
Evangelistic Emphasis: Salvation comes through obedient faith, not by the works of men.

PRINTED TEXT

1 Kings 12:25. Then Jeroboam built Shechem in mount Ephraim, and dwelt therein; and went out from thence, and built Penuel.

26. And Jeroboam said in his heart, Now shall the kingdom return to the house of David:

27. If this people go up to do sacrifice in the house of the Lord at Jerusalem, then shall the heart of this people turn again unto their lord, even unto Rehoboam king of Judah, and they shall kill me, and go again to Rehoboam king of Judah.

28. Whereupon the king took counsel, and made two calves of gold, and said unto them, It is too much for you to go up to Jerusalem: behold thy gods, O Israel, which brought thee up out of the land of Egypt.

29. And he set the one in Beth-el, and the other put he in Dan.

30. And this thing became a sin: for the people went to worship before the one, even unto Dan.

13:1. And, behold, there came a man of God out of Judah by the word of the Lord unto Beth-el: and Jeroboam stood by the altar to burn incense.

2. And he cried against the altar in the word of the Lord, and said, O altar, altar, thus saith the Lord; Behold, a child shall be born unto the house of David, Josiah by name; and upon thee shall he offer the priests of the high places that burn incense upon thee, and men's bones shall be burnt upon thee.

3. And he gave a sign the same day, saying, This is the sign which the Lord hath spoken; Behold, the altar shall be rent, and the ashes that are upon it shall be poured out.

4. And it came to pass, when king Jeroboam heard the saying of the man of God, which had cried against the altar in Beth-el, that he put forth his hand from the altar, saying, Lay hold on him. And his hand, which he put forth against him, dried up, so that he could not pull it in again to him.

5. The altar also was rent, and the ashes poured out from the altar, according to the sign which the man of God had given by the word of the Lord.

6. And the king answered and said unto the man of God, Intreat now the face of the Lord thy God, and pray for me, that my hand may be restored me again. And the man of God besought the Lord, and the king's hand was restored him again, and became as it was before.

DICTIONARY

Jeroboam (jer-oh-BOH-um)—1 Kings 12:25—See Lesson Three.

Shechem (SHECK-em)—1 Kings 12:25—A city located in the hill country of Ephraim.

Penuel (pa-NEW-el)—1 Kings 12:25—A city east of the Jordan River situated on the River Jabbok. The name is a variation of the name Jacob gave the place when he wrestled with an angel, Peniel. Nothing is mentioned about the city for nearly 200 years before this event. Probably the city lay in ruins until the time of Jeroboam.

Rehoboam (re-oh-BOH-um)—1 Kings 12:27—See Lesson Three.

Bethel—1 Kings 12:29—A city located just north of the boundary line running between the kingdoms of Israel and Judah. Of all the cities of Palestine, only Jerusalem was mentioned more often than Bethel.

Dan—1 Kings 12:29—The northernmost city in Palestine to which the Danites migrated (Judges 18), giving it its name.

Josiah—1 Kings 13:2—King of Judah who reigned from 640 B.C., which was approximately three hundred years after the prophecy here given.

LESSON OUTLINE

I. MAKING FALSE GODS
 A. Political Consolidation
 B. Religious Consolidation
II. WORSHIPING FALSE GODS
 A. Establishing Shrines
 B. Instituting a Festival
III. GOD JUDGES IDOLATRY
 A. Prophecy
 B. Reaction
 C. Disobedience
 D. Retribution
IV. WORSHIPING THE TRUE GOD

LESSON EXPOSITION

INTRODUCTION

During the reign of Solomon, Jeroboam, son of Nebat, served as supervisor of forced labor and as collector of taxes for the tribe of Ephraim (some think for all the northern tribes). According to 1 Kings 11:27, however, Jeroboam "lifted up his hand against the king." The circumstances of that rebellion remain uncertain. Nonetheless, in 1 Kings 11: 29-39 the Bible does inform the reader that the prophet Ahijah met Jeroboam "out in the country" (v. 29, **New International Version**). In a dramatic gesture, the prophet tore his new robe into twelve pieces, giving Jeroboam ten pieces and informing him that he would receive ten tribes of Israel over which to rule and that only Judah and Benjamin would remain under the rule of the house of David. Did Jeroboam rebel against Solomon as a direct result of that meeting with Ahijah? That, Scripture does not reveal. It states, however, that Solomon sought to have Jeroboam executed and that, as a result, this divinely designated "usurper" fled to Egypt, where he remained until Solomon's death.

When the smoldering northern tribes confronted Rehoboam at Shechem with demands for redress of their quite legitimate grievances, Jeroboam emerged as leader. As we know from last Sunday's lesson, when Rehoboam responded in despotic fashion, the ten northern tribes (thereafter known as **Israel**, although also called **Ephraim**, after the most influential tribe, or **Samaria** at times) rebelled and chose Jeroboam (known as **Jeroboam I** in the chronologies of the kings of Israel and Judah) as king. So, even man's disobedience ultimately serves the divine purpose, in this case God's purpose being the already-prophesied accession of Jeroboam to the throne of northern Israel.

The divine mandate, however, was not unconditional. It served as no license for Jeroboam to behave, with assurance of impunity, exactly as suited his whim or convenience. Not long after his accession to the throne, this obviously accomplished leader—who had begun his reign with the opportunity to prove himself godly and his dynasty long lived—forfeited divine approval and insured the early end of the occupancy of Israel's throne by his lineage.

I. MAKING FALSE GODS (1 Kings 12:25-28)

A. Political Consolidation (v. 25)

25. Then Jeroboam built Shechem in mount Ephraim, and dwelt therein; and went out from thence, and built Penuel.

The assembled members of the ten northern tribes chose Jeroboam, already under divine appointment to the office, as their king. At the outset of his reign, he had the opportunity to chart a course for himself and his people which would reverse that growing trend in Israel away from adherence to the Mosaic law and toward absorption of elements of Canaanitish culture.

A forceful, popular leader with the people virtually in the palm of his hand, Jeroboam could have insured the fulfillment of that word from God given to him through Ahijah the prophet and recorded in 1 Kings 11:38: "And it shall be, if thou wilt hearken unto all that I command thee, and wilt walk in my ways, and do that is right in my sight, to keep my statutes and my commandments, as David my servant did; that I will be with thee, and build thee a sure house, as I built for David, and will give Israel unto thee." Jeroboam, however, during that shrewdly conceived process of consolidation of his kingdom which ensued immediately upon his elevation to the throne, laid the foundations of ultimate national ruin and personal loss.

Jeroboam's first steps were to rebuild the city which would serve as his capital and to provide for protection of that capital city from any potential military invasion. Perhaps Shechem had been previously subjected to attack and partially destroyed. Of that we cannot be certain. Perhaps Jeroboam simply wished to make less vulnerable a city whose very geographical location rendered it difficult to defend since it lay in a narrow valley between Mount Ebal and Mount Gerizim, a rather precarious position in case of military assault.

Penuel lay across the Jordan River, a few miles east of Shechem. The **New International Version** notes that Jeroboam "went out and built up Peniel" (a variant of **Penuel**). Apparently, the king fortified the city militarily in order to create an outpost of defense for his capital city. Jeroboam nonetheless later moved his capital to Tirzah, a few miles north of Shechem, perhaps because it was more easily defensible. (There is archaeological, although not scriptural, evidence that Shishak, Pharaoh of Egypt, invaded Israel as well as Judah, and this invasion could have precipitated Jeroboam's relocation of his capital.)

B. Religious Consolidation (vv. 26-28)

26. And Jeroboam said in his heart, Now shall the kingdom return to the house of David:

27. If this people go up to do sacrifice in the house of the Lord at Jerusalem, then shall the heart of this people turn again unto their lord, even unto Rehoboam king of Judah, and they shall kill me, and go again to Rehoboam king of Judah.

Jeroboam's first steps of consolidation—military measures—were the prudent acts of a politically sagacious ruler. To make himself secure militarily was sensible, and to engage in such shoring-up activity could only increase the confidence of his people in his leadership ability. But his next step, however shrewd politically, would have enormously far-reaching spiritual effects upon Jeroboam and upon Israel. It was a step which would pull his people away from the divinely constituted pattern of worship and thereby alienate them from their God.

All Israel, since the construction of the Temple in Jerusalem, had assembled in the city of David three times yearly for the great festivals of worship—Passover, Weeks, and Tabernacles. These sacred occasions of national celebration had indeed served to increase national unity and to cement the kingdom into a more close-knit entity. (Obviously, though, the celebrations had not been entirely successful. The northern tribes had been ready to rebel and to sever themselves from Judah and Benjamin when subjected to the hard duress of Solomon's later years.)

Jeroboam now feared that if he permitted his subjects to continue these frequent pilgrimages for worship to what was now their capital city of a rival political power they would be lured back into allegiance to Rehoboam. (Indeed, Rehoboam might well, in the case of such continued worship at Jerusalem by the northern tribes, have been tempted to exact allegiance to himself as a condition of his permission for their entrance into his kingdom.)

Jeroboam's uneasiness and his alternate plan for national worship showed natural intelligence but a great deficiency in spiritual wisdom, for God had given His sure word that if Jeroboam met His conditions He would insure his continuance on the throne. Furthermore, the accomplishment of God's will was by no means contingent upon the carrying out of human plans which in themselves were contrary to the divine will. But Jeroboam, not unlike the vast majority of men, was intent upon insuring his success through the carrying out of a carnal, indeed wicked, scheme which ignored the divine will while enhancing his own power. Had this king relied upon divine resources, could not God have enabled him to accomplish his political purpose without that great spiritual loss which ensued as a result of Jeroboam's creation of a system of idolatry?

How important is it to seek divine guidance in all spheres of living—the so-called secular as well as the obviously religious?

28. Whereupon the king took counsel, and made two calves of gold, and said unto them, It is too much for you to go up to Jerusalem: behold thy gods, O Israel, which brought thee up out of the land of Egypt.

With whom the king counseled one cannot be certain. Perhaps he counseled with the elders of Israel in order to obtain advice as to a **precise form** for this deliberately created national system of worship which he was inaugurating. Perhaps he counseled as well with the artisans who would construct these new objects of worship. Obviously, he did not seek instruction from Ahijah the prophet, who surely would have warned him away from this religious scheme, concocted to insure the political loyalty of his subjects.

Jeroboam's immediate appeal was to the **convenience** of his people. He suggested that it was simply too much trouble for them to continue their worship in the Temple at Jerusalem. The question is, of course, whether Jeroboam would have resorted to more tyrannical measures in order to insure his continued control, had this appeal not been sufficient.

This argument to the convenience of his people by the king in any case appealed to base instincts. In the face of a divine imperative, mere convenience must never be a factor in determining one's obedience. In fact, the surest test of sterling character lies in one's willingness to go to any lengths to conform to the revealed will of God—whether the specific occasion calls for compliance with the moral law under difficult circumstances or for implicit obedience to a divine command when personal desires pull in contrary directions.

Jeroboam next unveiled before the assembled people the images which he had ordered created. He clearly (according to all translations of the verse) called the images "your gods." Scholars have identified these images variously:

1. Some insist that the calves were not idols, but simply **aids to worship,** like those in Solomon's temple. They further contend that bulls had long been associated with the worship of Jehovah in the northern kingdom, so that Jeroboam, by providing them, was merely reverting to ancient custom. Even these commentators, however, admit that the golden calves, although in their view not false gods, were **forbidden images,** in light of Exodus 20:4 and Deuteronomy 5:8.

2. Other interpreters believe that the calves were representations of Mnevis, the sacred calf worshiped in Egypt. These scholars think that Jeroboam, who had resided in Egypt for some years, was now importing an idolatrous system of calf worship from Egypt.

3. Still other commentators on the passage believe that the golden calves represented a Canaanitish fertility deity. This is perhaps the most sensible position in view of the scriptural identification of the objects as "gods" (which rules out the first view mentioned above) and in view of the ease with which Jeroboam secured the compliance of the northern tribes with this new religious system (which makes the second view mentioned above unlikely). It is probable that many Israelites had already been influenced by Canaanitish practices and found it easy to comply with a religious system which resembled those idolatrous rituals. The argument, often broached, that Jeroboam could not have secured compliance with an idolatrous system which resembled so closely Aaron's golden calves and that therefore the images were **irregular but not idolatrous aids to worship of Jehovah** is not very convincing when one considers the frequent disobedience of the nation of Israel both before and after this occasion—disobedience through gross immorality and through flagrant idolatry.

What are some modern substitutes for true religion, less demanding and more alluring to fallen human nature?

II. WORSHIPING FALSE GODS (1 Kings 12: 29-33)

A. Establishing Shrines (vv. 29-31)

29. And he set the one in Beth-el, and the other put he in Dan.

Bethel lay on the border of Benjamin and technically within the boundary of that tribal area. Apparently, this city had for some unknown reason passed under the control of the northern kingdom. Bethel was an ancient shrine; the very name, in its root meaning, denotes **house of God.** Here, Jacob had had a marvelous vision of a lader upon which angels were ascending and descending and with the throne of God at the top. In his awe at God's presence he had renamed the place (formerly called **Luz**) Bethel because he thought that it could be none other than the **house of God** (see Genesis 28: 10-22). A school of the prophets also had resided here (and perhaps yet did). Clearly, Jeroboam had with his usual shrewdness chosen a location with associations of sacredness and thus with possibilities for easy acceptance as a center for his new system of worship.

Dan, also the location of an ancient shrine, lay far north on Israel's border with Syria. This locale seems as unlikely as Bethel seems inevitable since Dan was so far removed from the political center of the kingdom.

30. And this thing became a sin: for the people went to worship before the one, even unto Dan.

The thrust of this passage is that the people of the northern tribes committed the sin of idolatry by worshiping at the shrines which Jeroboam had established. Each family who participated apparently chose that shrine which was most convenient or otherwise most attractive; whether Dan, on Israel's northern border, or Bethel, on Israel's southern border. There seems to be the implication that some persons traveled considerable distances to Dan, perhaps even when Bethel was closer.

Moreover, "this thing became a sin" at the precise point when rituals of worship were instituted, since the worship of concrete images was thereby substituted for the worship of the invisible true God, Jehovah. In the words of John 4:24, "God is a Spirit: and they that worship him must worship him in spirit and in truth." The first commandment, furthermore, declares: "Thou shalt have no other gods before me" (Exodus 20:3)—a clearcut divine imperative handed to Moses directly by God on Mount Sinai. The sin, then, was a most heinous infraction of the divine law—unmistakable, flagrant, and rendering the violator subject to divine judgment.

Verse 31 informs the reader of two most revealing aspects of Jeroboam's activity: (1) He created shrines or temples, apparently at each location ("an house of high places"); hence, each locale would contain an imposing structure to house its golden calf. (2) He instituted a priesthood—not composed of members of the tribe of Levi, since all the Levites had migrated to Judah, but apparently of whoever was willing to serve. Obviously, Jeroboam was not very discriminating in his choices, for he "made priests of the lowest of the people." This first king of northern Israel comes across as a highly pragmatic individual whose motives and acts in the political and religious spheres were primarily self-serving. His object was self-perpetuation, and a new religion seemed to be one effective means to this end. Hence, whatever would make this religious system functional, he would do.

B. Instituting a Festival (vv. 32, 33)

The Feast of Tabernacles occurred during the seventh month of the Hebrew calendar. Jeroboam planned for his rival festival to be held during the eighth month, a date well suited to the later growing season of northern Palestine, but also "in the month which he had devised of his own heart." Hence, **convenience** rather than obedience to a divine principle motivated the king, in itself indicative of his sinful rather than spiritual purposes. During this festival the king himself offered animal sacrifices and incense upon the altar at the shrine he had established in Bethel. Since God had accepted Solomon's offering of sacrifices at Gibeon and had sanctioned Jeroboam's accession to the throne of northern Israel, one can assume that the king's wrongdoing lay in the idolatrous system of worship itself rather than in the fact of his offering sacrifices.

III. GOD JUDGES IDOLATRY (1 Kings 13: 1-32)

A. Prophecy (vv. 1-3)

1. And, behold, there came a man of God out of Judah by the word of the Lord unto Beth-el: and Jeroboam stood by the altar to burn incense.

The word **prophet** is neutral; there are **false** prophets as well as **true** prophets. But **man of God** is unmistakable in its reference. This unnamed figure, then, was **God's man**, subject to His will and ready to do His bidding. Hence, at great risk to his life he— "by the word of the Lord"—went across the national border into Jeroboam's kingdom for the express purpose of conveying a divine message of condemnation directly to King Jeroboam.

Can twentieth-century Christians—whether lay or clergy—have such an assurance of divine commission that they speak boldly and fearlessly when occasion demands?

2. And he cried against the altar in the word of the Lord, and said, O altar, altar, thus saith the Lord; Behold, a child shall be born unto the house of David, Josiah by name; and upon thee shall he offer the priests of the high places that burn incense upon thee, and men's bones shall be burnt upon thee.
According to verse 1, Jeroboam was officiating at the altar at the moment of the unnamed prophet's arrival. This messenger of God, however, seemed to ignore the royal officiant completely and, instead, to address the altar itself in a remarkable example of that figure of speech known as **apostrophe** (addressing an object, animal, or dead or absent person as if present and able to respond).

The message was direct and explicit, although three hundred years would elapse before its fulfillment. Josiah, a late reformer among the kings of Judah about a century after the destruction of the kingdom of northern Israel by Assyria, would personally desecrate this unauthorized and idolatrous altar. Scripture records the precise fulfillment of this prophecy: "Even the altar at Bethel, the high place made by Jeroboam son of Nebat, who had caused Israel to sin—even that altar and high place he demolished. He burned the high place and ground it to powder, and burned the Asherah pole also. Then Josiah looked around, and when he saw the tombs that were there on the hillside, he had the bones removed from them and burned on the altar to defile it, in accordance with the word of the Lord proclaimed by the man of God who foretold these things" (2 Kings 23:15, 16, **New International Version).**

3. And he gave a sign the same day, saying, This is the sign which the Lord hath spoken; Behold, the altar shall be rent, and the ashes that are upon it shall be poured out.
This **unknown** prophet (most probably) had boldly made a remarkable prediction—in the very presence of that king whom it was bound to incense. It was imperative that this man of God be **authenticated** so that the divine mission would not be discredited and the messenger of God immediately destroyed. Even had such happened, truth would have ultimately prevailed, but the impact upon that man whom God intended to hear the message would have been greatly blunted. Hence, a supernatural sign would occur which would make obvious to everyone God's authentication of the messenger and the message.

B. Reaction (vv. 4-10)

4. And it came to pass, when king Jeroboam heard the saying of the man of God, which had cried against the altar in Beth-el, that he put forth his hand from the altar, saying, Lay hold on him. And his hand, which he put forth against him, dried up, so that he could not pull it in again to him.
The words which Jeroboam had heard should at least have given him pause. But the king instead acted rashly and arrogantly by instructing his servants to seize the prophet. Jeroboam apparently had relinquished, during that process of inaugurating his idolatrous religious system, all sensitivity to the Spirit of the true God, so that he now could boldly defy a prophet sent by God. One thinks that he might at least have waited to see whether divinely induced action would follow the words of the prophet. Momentarily at least, Jeroboam was jolted back into spiritual reality, for God authenticated the words of His messenger and protected his person by striking that very hand which had been stretched forth in signal against God's man.

5. The altar also was rent, and the ashes poured out from the altar, according to the sign which the man of God had given by the word of the Lord.
The authenticating sign occurred as predicted. Throughout the Bible God repeatedly authenticated both His Word and His mouthpiece through supernatural signs. Miracles do not invariably occur within or outside Scripture solely for authentication. They may also be acts of compassion or, in a few cases, of judgment. Indeed, Christ's authenticating miracles normally also had an important second reason—the desire of a compassionate Savior to relieve human suffering, to minister to the whole human person. But in the present case God interposed upon **the natural order supernatural interventions** which in a spec-

tacular manner unmistakably announced His presence, authenticated a predicted action of one of His servants, and brought judgment upon a rash opponent of His sovereign will.

6. And the king answered and said unto the man of God, Intreat now the face of the Lord thy God, and pray for me, that my hand may be restored me again. And the man of God besought the Lord, and the king's hand was restored him again, and became as it was before.

Jeroboam, at least for the moment, was humbled. However rash and arrogant he might be and however deliberately ignorant of spiritual reality, he recognized now the obvious presence of the supernatural and submitted. The mercy of God is boundless and inexplicable by human reason. He could have left Jeroboam maimed as a permanent reminder of his sin and of the divine power to judge that sin. He, however, did not. Instead, He gave the wicked king a further sign of the supernatural—a benevolent sign of His grace—through the restoration of his withered hand.

Jeroboam's response to the unnamed messenger of God now was positive. He invited him to dine. The man of God, however, revealed that he must accept no such invitation but instead return home immediately by a different road from that taken to Bethel. Why the divine instructions were so severe one cannot be certain. But one can be certain that, having received an explicit command from God, His servant must obey unquestioningly. Perhaps God knew that social intercourse would compromise the impact of the message. Perhaps God merely was testing his **trustworthiness**. For, to be used of God, one must always be unfailing in his obedience; else the force of God's word is muted. A disobedient vessel, is unworthy of use by the Master, thereby rendering itself fit only to be cast aside.

C. Disobedience (vv. 11-19)

Why the also unnamed old prophet of Bethel induced this true man of God to be disobedient, Scripture does not make certain. Perhaps God allowed this further test of obedience in order to make certain that His man would be unvarying in his conformity to all divine instructions. After all, God had spoken directly to the prophet from Judah. To have further usefulness he must prove himself trustworthy in every situation. Perhaps the old prophet, out of harmony with God's will, deliberately deceived the younger prophet because he had himself become the instrument of evil and wished to destroy that which reminded him of what he once had been. In any case, the man of God from Judah was induced, directly in opposition to God's expressed will, to return to Bethel for a meal.

D. Retribution (vv. 20-32)

God's retribution was severe. The man of God from Judah had taken **a secondhand message, purported** to have come from an angel of God, over God's direct instructions to him. He thereby brought upon himself the divine judgment, necessary to demonstrate that God had sent him in the first place with precise instructions as to what to say and how to behave. Otherwise, the entire mission might have been discounted by superstitious people who might ascribe even supernatural acts to a force other than the power of Jehovah God. So the man of God from Judah, sent to Bethel to proclaim God's judgment, was himself finally a victim of God's just punishment—slain by a lion and buried by the old prophet from Bethel who had been the agent of his ruin.

IV. WORSHIPING THE TRUE GOD (Matthew 4:8-11)

During His forty days of temptation in the wilderness, Jesus was repeatedly tempted by Satan and, either then or later, in every area of His life—"in every way, just as we are" (Hebrews 4:15, **New International Version).** In fact, He was tempted to commit the ultimate act of idolatry—to bow down and worship Satan himself—as a shortcut to power and glory. It was a **real** temptation, real in the sense that Jesus **felt most strongly** that pull away from the ultimate glory of the Cross and toward temporary glory without the Cross.

But He conquered His temptation through His knowledge of God's Word: "It is written, Thou shalt worship the Lord thy God, and him only shalt thou serve" (v. 10). Thereby He provided us with the answer when Satan approaches us with those subtle forms of idolatry with which he seeks to deflect us from our proper course—worship of God through our every act and as a result of our ultimate commitment to His will. The aftermath of Jesus' temptation gives us the assurance of **supernatural ministry**—in this case through angels (see Hebrews 1:14)—as we stand firm against every inducement to evil, even against that particular inducement tailor-made by Satan to fit our particular disposition and circumstance.

REVIEW QUESTIONS

1. How did Jeroboam attain the throne of northern Israel?
2. By what action did Jeroboam forfeit the divine approval?
3. How did Jeroboam respond to the prophetic message which denounced his actions?
4. How can we account for the sad demise of the man of God from Judah who had proclaimed God's judgment?
5. What action of Jesus serves to instruct the Christian met with a modern inducement to idolatry?

GOLDEN TEXT HOMILY

"THOU SHALT WORSHIP THE LORD THY GOD, AND HIM ONLY SHALT THOU SERVE" (Matthew 4:10).

Christ achieved an amazing triumph over Satan by quoting the imperial decrees of heaven as recorded in Deuteronomy 6:13. This was the crowning victory in His progressive testing through a forty-day period. Satan's most vigorous assault was repulsed, and being utterly defeated, Satan fled (Matthew 4:11).

With three great principles, Christ confronted Satan:

First, there is **only one object of worship,** the Lord God. As God, He is the powerful Creator and Sustainer of the universe. As Lord, He is the Sovereign over all created intelligences.

Second, this fact calls for worship **as the supreme object of wonder.** This means a recognition of the greatness and preeminence of God and demands a response consisting of humiliation and submission.

Third, this **must ultimately result in performance** of service to the high and lofty One. The word used for "serve" has a twofold significance: this is sacred service of religious devotion, and servile bondage in the entire round of life.—**Selected**

SENTENCE SERMONS

WHEN GOD COMES in, the idols tumble down.
—**"Speaker's Sourcebook"**

TO WORSHIP AT the shrine of convenience, materialism, or the occult is to indulge in idolatry, and to set the course for failure.
—**Selected**

"YOU SHALL WORSHIP the Lord your God and Him alone shall you serve."
—**Jesus** (Matthew 4:10, Amplified Bible)

GOD IS NOT greater if you reverence Him, but you are greater if you serve Him.
—**Augustine**

EVANGELISTIC APPLICATION

SALVATION COMES THROUGH OBEDIENT FAITH, NOT BY THE WORKS OF MEN.

Any object, tangible or intangible, which replaces God in one's life thereby becomes an idol. **He** deserves to be enthroned as sole ruler in our life by right of creation. When we give His place to anything else, ascribing ultimate value to that which is merely temporary, we turn our life topsy-turvy and bring upon ourselves needless confusion and misery.

Sometimes our **supposed** acts of worship are themselves less than God demands, for we either merely go through the motions while our hearts are elsewhere or we use the very means of corporate worship activity to serve carnal interests and to meet nonspiritual needs.

God, however, has provided a means whereby man can transcend self and sin and come into fellowship with Him. Through faith in the merits of Christ, purchased through His obedience to the Cross, man can attain harmony with God and come to know through daily fellowship with the Divine the joy of full surrender. Man tries constantly to lift himself by his own bootstraps, to attain spiritual life through his own merits, only to find himself a failure—miserable and unfulfilled. By renouncing his own efforts, however, and abjectly casting himself upon the mercies of Christ, that Lamb of God who took upon Himself the sin of the world and thereby appeased God's wrath against the repentant sinner, man can find peace. Man can enter upon a lifestyle which makes for peace as he crowns Jesus Christ as truly Lord and King and brings **his** will into full conformity with **His** will.

ILLUMINATING THE LESSON

Two missionaries were walking around the Temple of Siva, or Great Pagoda of Tanjore, India, when they noticed the people carrying out one of the brass idols in procession. It being a warm sunny day, it became heated. Some one happened to touch it, and perceiving that it was very warm, concluded **it must have a fever!** The rajah, being present, sent for a physician. He came, and told them they need not be troubled, for the god was well enough. But the rajah called him a fool and sent him home, and ordered that another physician should be called. When he came he told them that the god was very sick, had a high fever, and remedies must be applied immediately or he would die. So he directed them to put him in a shady place, and washed him with some cool liquid, and when he was well cooled off the doctor pronounced him **cured!** And the rajah gave him three thousand rupees for saving the life of his god.

—Selected

DAILY DEVOTIONAL GUIDE

M. God's Eternal Principles. Exodus 20:1-6

T. God's Warnings Against Idolatry. Exodus 34:13-16

W. Jesus Summarizes God's Law. Matthew 22:35-40

T. The Degrading Nature of Idolatry. Romans 1:18-23

F. Blessings of Separation From Idols. 2 Corinthians 6:15-18

S. Freedom From Idolatry's Enslavement. Galatians 4:1-9

July 5, 1981

Seeking God's Help

Bible Background: 1 Kings 15:1-24; 2 Chronicles 14:1—15:19
Time: Around 910 to 896 B.C. (Reign of Asa 910-870 B.C.
Place: Jerusalem, from the valley of Zephathah to Gerar
Supplemental Reference: Acts 3:19-26
Golden Text: "Help us, O Lord our God; for we rest on thee" (2 Chronicles 14:11).
Central Truth: God's power is always available to the one who seeks to do God's will.
Evangelistic Emphasis: When men seek God, they will find Him.

PRINTED TEXT

2 Chronicles 14:1. So Abijah slept with his fathers, and they buried him in the city of David: and Asa his son reigned in his stead. In his days the land was quiet ten years.

2. And Asa did that which was good and right in the eyes of the Lord his God:

3. For he took away the altars of the strange gods, and the high places, and brake down the images, and cut down the groves:

4. And commanded Judah to seek the Lord God of their fathers, and to do the law and the commandment.

5. Also he took away out of all the cities of Judah the high places and the images: and the kingdom was quiet before him.

6. And he built fenced cities in Judah: for the land had rest, and he had no war in those years; because the Lord had given him rest.

7. Therefore he said unto Judah, Let us build these cities, and make about them walls, and towers, gates, and bars, while the land is yet before us; because we have sought the Lord our God, we have sought him, and he hath given us rest on every side. So they built and prospered.

8. And Asa had an army of men that bare targets and spears, out of Judah three hundred thousand; and out of Benjamin, that bare shields and drew bows, two hundred and fourscore thousand: all these were mighty men of valour.

9. And there came out against them Zerah the Ethiopian with an host of a thousand thousand, and three hundred chariots; and came unto Mareshah.

10. Then Asa went out against him, and they set the battle in array in the valley of Zephathah at Mareshah.

11. And Asa cried unto the Lord his God, and said, Lord, it is nothing with thee to help, whether with many, or with them that have no power: help us, O Lord our God; for we rest on thee, and in thy name we go against this multitude. O Lord, thou art our God; let not man prevail against thee.

12. So the Lord smote the Ethiopians before Asa, and before Judah; and the Ethiopians fled.

13. And Asa and the people that were with him pursued them unto Gerar: and the Ethiopians were overthrown, that they could not recover themselves; for they were destroyed before the Lord, and before his host; and they carried away very much spoil.

DICTIONARY

Abijah (uh-BYE-jah)—2 Chronicles 14:1—Son of Rehoboam and father of Asa. He reigned over Judah for about three years.

high places—2 Chronicles 14:3—Worship centers built on small hills generally, but sometimes in valleys (Jeremiah 7:31).

images—2 Chronicles 14:3—The Hebrew says "pillars." These were stones standing upright by the side of an altar as a symbol of the god worshiped and were regarded as sacred.

groves—2 Chronicles 14:3—The Hebrew has "asherim," the plural form for asherah, an upright wooden pole placed by the side of an altar; also a symbol of a god or goddess.

images—2 Chronicles 14:5—This is a different word in the Hebrew from that of verse 3; it means "sun-images." They were stones used in connection with the high place and were probably dedicated to the sun god.

Zerah (ZEE-rah) the Ethiopian—2 Chronicles 14:9—The Hebrew calls him Zerah the Cushite. He was probably a Nubian prince who ruled over the region around Gerar, probably with Egyptian protection. From this base he tried to conquer areas of Judah.

Mareshah (mah-RAY-shah)—2 Chronicles 14:9—One of the cities that Rehoboam fortified to protect his southern boundary against Egypt.

Zephathah (ZEF-ah-thah)—2 Chronicles 14:10—The place is not known since it is mentioned only here in the Bible.

Gerar (GE-rar)—2 Chronicles 14:13—The ancient trade route city located between Gaza and Beersheba on the border between Canaan and Egypt.

LESSON OUTLINE

I. FORSAKING IDOLATRY
   A. Quiet Rule
   B. Thorough Reform

II. ENJOYING PEACE
   A. Fortification in Time of Peace
   B. Mobilization in Time of Peace

III. GAINING VICTORY
   A. Military Engagement
   B. Humble Petition
   C. Remarkable Victory

IV. SEEKING GOD
   A. Prophetic Advice
   B. Courageous Response
   C. Entire Cooperation
   D. Radical Removal
   E. Generous Gifts
   F. Extended Peace

LESSON EXPOSITION

INTRODUCTION

Once the kingdom of Israel had been divided, the resulting two kingdoms took far different directions. The northern kingdom moved ever downward—ever further below those moral and spiritual values embodied in the Mosaic Code. Judah did not form a total contrast to the northern kingdom, but neither did that kingdom take an equally disastrous national course. Interspersed among the kings of Judah were five great reformers—Asa (910-869 B.C.), Jehoshaphat (872-848 B.C.), Joash (835-796 B.C.), Hezekiah (715-686 B.C.), and Josiah (640-609 B.C.). These godly kings called Judah repeatedly back to the worship of Jehovah and to the keeping of His law and thereby stemmed somewhat that tide of immorality and idolatry which always threatened to engulf the kingdom.

Ultimately Judah suffered a fate similar to that of Israel, but there were several crucial differences. Judah: (1) survived as a nation more than a century longer than did Israel; (2) maintained a single dynasty—and that the house of David—on its throne; and (3) after seventy years of captivity, returned from Babylon with a strong leadership structure intact to rebuild Jerusalem and the Temple and to resume national life.

The first of the reforming kings of Judah was Asa. His grandfather Rehoboam had helped to lead Judah away from God and into idolatrous practices similar to those fostered by King Jeroboam I and his successors in northern Israel. Abijah, however praiseworthy his military victory over Jeroboam I, appears not to have reversed that course pursued by his father Rehoboam. Abijah's son Asa, however, ascending the throne at approximately ten years of age, took a remarkable course of action which turned Judah completely around. The religious reforms which he instituted reached the royal palace itself and radically affected the lives of his subjects.

I. FORSAKING IDOLATRY (2 Chronicles 14: 1-5)

A. Quiet Rule (v. 1)

1. So Abijah slept with his fathers, and they buried him in the city of David: and Asa his son reigned in his stead. In his days the land was quiet ten years.

Abijah, Asa's father, had become a powerful ruler following his victory over Jeroboam, a fact attested to by his royal harem (2 Chronicles 13:21), normally a sign of eminence among Near Eastern monarchs of that age. There is no evidence, however, of **spiritual might**. In fact, the reforms of Asa's reign themselves constitute strong evidence of the moral and spiritual decay which was allowed to proceed unchecked under the rule of Abijah, Asa's father.

Chronological evidence in the Bible leads one to conclude that Asa was a mere lad at the time of his father's death—ten years old approximately. Michaiah (or Maachah), Asa's **grandmother** (not his mother, according to virtually all recent Old Testament scholars), was queen mother upon Asa's accession to the throne—a position of considerable respect and power. Asa's own mother likely either was dead or else lacked sufficient power to unseat this forceful lady. Remarkably, Asa, even as a boy-king and despite the strong counterinfluence of Michaiah, provided powerful, positive leadership. At least partially as a result, his kingdom enjoyed a decade of peace and calm before that unceasing conflict with Israel began and that remarkable battle with the Ethiopians occurred.

It has been suggested that Asa's youthfulness induced potential adversaries to desist or to wait, an explanation often broached to account for the decade of peace but certainly not an inevitable outcome (indeed, the very opposite outcome might be expected). An explanation more in keeping with the spirit of the entire record of Asa's life and accomplishments is that of **divine providence**. God granting a youthful monarch, whose heart He knew to be pure, the time to gain administrative experience and to sharpen his political acumen before allowing him to face potentially overwhelming adversaries.

Does God intervene supernaturally in the mundane affairs of men and nations today?

B. Thorough Reform (vv. 2-5)

2. And Asa did that which was good and right in the eyes of the Lord his God.

During the period of the divided kingdom, conditions were such in both Israel and Judah that one can be certain of the moral and spiritual integrity of a ruling monarch only if the Bible states outrightly that such was the case, although one might prefer the opposite to be true. Of the youthful Asa the record so declares. He did not swerve toward idolatry; he did not embrace immorality. Instead, he clung firmly to the commands of the Torah —the law of Moses; and that document offered him guidance in every sphere of personal and national life.

Good is a word used so often and so carelessly as to be meaningless to many persons. The meaning of **right** in our own relativistic age would be seen by many to depend solely upon the perspective of the user. In 2 Chronicles 14:2, however, we find a context for both of these words which establishes their meaning for time and eternity— "in the eyes of the Lord his God." God's direct communication with Moses on Mount Sinai had established for all time the basic spiritual and ethical meanings of these terms, and only outflowing regulations for living and worship would change with time, not the basic truth behind those regulations.

3. For he took away the altars of the strange gods, and the high places, and brake down the images, and cut down the groves.

Judah had already advanced deeply into idolatrous forms of worship. The idolatrous customs of the Canaanites appealed strongly to persons holding weak faith in the true spiritual realm and to man's ever-present tendencies toward sensuality. Spurred on by that dual appeal, idolatry had by now swept completely the northern kingdom and was making strong inroads into the kingdom of Judah.

Verse 3, however, specifies four distinct corrective actions taken by the young king: (1) He removed the altars dedicated to false gods—his first order of business since these objects would be central to the idolatrous worship rituals. (2) He removed the high places—although he must not have obliterated **all** such places, since 1 Kings 15:14 informs us that Asa left certain shrines intact. (Perhaps he removed those dedicated to the worship of false gods and left those used— irregularly—in the worship of Jehovah.) (3) He destroyed the images—of Asherah, the moon-goddess, and of Baal, the sun-god, as well as those of other deities common in Canaanitish culture. (4) He hacked down the "groves" or "Asherah poles." These were not **sacred trees** but, rather, **vertical images,** symbolic representations of the fertility goddess, which likely bore obscene figures.

4. And commanded Judah to seek the Lord God of their fathers, and to do the law and the commandment.

The king employed his authority as the properly designated ruler to insure compliance with his religious reforms: **He commanded.** Judah was not a democracy with attendant total freedom of worship; it was a monarchy under the ultimate governance of Jehovah and with the king as the subaltern of Jehovah. The king therefore had the **authority** and even the **obligation** to insure that his subjects engaged in that public worship authorized by Jehovah. He could not command their conscience, but he could forbid unlawful practices and prescribe the proper ones.

Seeking "the Lord God of their fathers" as mentioned in verse 4 is in direct contrast with the worshiping of idols which verse 3 declares was forbidden by the young king. Rather than employing incantations to false gods, offering sacrifices to such nondeities, and participating in rites and festivals dedicated to them, the inhabitants of Judah now would serve God alone. They would worship solely at the Temple in Jerusalem, attend the three great festivals celebrated annually there, offer proper sacrifices to the true God, pray sincerely to Him, and adhere unremittingly to the commands and regulations given by God to Moses.

To seek God, moreover, is to find the proper answer to many maladies afflicting both individuals and societies today. The pervasive insecurity and instability which threaten at both the personal and national levels are rooted essentially in estrangement from God. When man attempts to chart his own destiny, he inevitably cuts himself off from the Author of destiny and thereby makes himself subject to the ever-shifting currents of chance and fortune. When man seeks primarily for temporal benefits—power, wealth, ego-enhancement, pleasure—he may or may not attain those goals, but he will certainly fail to satisfy those deep longings of his inner nature for communion with his Creator. The spiritual alternative appears in Matthew 6:33: "But seek ye first the kingdom of God, and his righteousness; and all these things shall be added unto you."

Asa commanded his subjects, first, to worship properly and, second, to practice moral and ethical uprightness. The two always go hand in hand. If one is to walk with God—to be a citizen of His kingdom—he must allow God to rule in his everyday life. For only so will the channel of communication between himself and God remain unobstructed, and only so will he enjoy the benefits from God which flow to the completely surrendered life.

5. Also he took away out of all the cities of Judah the high places and the images: and the kingdom was quiet before him.

The emphasis of verse 5 is upon "the cities of Judah." The king's reform edict had force not only in the countryside but also in the population centers. It is in the cities that evil frequently exists in more heinous forms. Godless influences crowd in upon even the resistant heart with greater force than in rural areas with their simpler lifestyles and lack of such ready accessibility to wicked tendencies. The removal of both shrines (high places) and images **from the cities** receives strong emphasis here. This is perhaps an indirect explanation of 1 Kings 15:14, which declares that not **all** high places (or **shrines**) were destroyed by King Asa.

Do modern churches sometimes need radical reform akin to that accomplished by King Asa?

Having acted in strict obedience to the law of God, Asa could now enjoy a period of respite from trouble—whether produced by internal dissension or by invasion by enemy forces. At times the conquering saint of God experiences a similar blessing in the spiritual realm. An onslaught of temptation or persecution might previously have left such an adherent to godliness prostrate with exhaustion. But he has stood in the face of every spiritual adversary (Ephesians 6:13, 14), and God now brings him into a period of recuperation, **recreation,** and relaxation. This respite is never permanent but is nonetheless welcome, invigorating, and **preparatory** to whatever battles next ensue.

II. ENJOYING PEACE (2 Chronicles 14:6-8)
A. Fortification in Time of Peace (vv. 6, 7)

6. And he built fenced cities in Judah: for the land had rest, and he had no war in those years; because the Lord had given him rest.

The young king here demonstrated rare leadership acumen. An almost universal tendency exists among nations to settle into apathy during peacetime and to allow their military defenses to deteriorate. Also, ethical discipline and moral purity often decline during such periods of peace, progress, and prosperity. King Asa nonetheless achieved the opposite result; however, it **was** an achievement and not the mere result of chance. To strengthen the national moral fiber during such a period of national calm would require intense, unremitting fervor and stamina—qualities not possessed by every national leader. From some source, perhaps from his unnamed mother (certainly not Michaiah, his wicked grandmother), Asa had absorbed godly influences which resulted in deep piety, impeccable character, and great strength of will—a reservoir of strength which he could now share with the nation he was destined to rule.

During this time of national calm Asa "built fenced cities" able to withstand siege for extended periods. One would presume that this was a farsighted move for a nation which lay (like the northern kingdom next door) directly in the path of any advancing army from north or south.

7. Therefore he said unto Judah, Let us build these cities, and make about them walls, and towers, gates, and bars, while the land is yet before us; because we have sought the Lord our God, we have sought him, and he hath given us rest on every side. So they built and prospered.

The king apparently addressed an assembly of his subjects, at the outset of his program to insure military preparedness, in a highly successful attempt to rally them behind this peacetime military effort. He specified the kinds of fortifications contained in his plans. The cities probably existed already, and he now sought to add to them means which would insure tight security during times of siege or assault—walls for basic protection, towers to serve as lookouts, and gates and bars to allow ingress and egress without in the least compromising safety.

To paraphrase the continuation of Asa's address, "**As a nation** we have returned to Jehovah, praying, worshiping, and behaving properly, and as a direct result He has now granted us peace. It therefore is imperative that we take advantage of this period of respite from external invasion in order to prepare for that inevitable time when it shall appear." The outcome is stated cryptically: "So they built and prospered." Fortunately, Asa knew that while good times come and it is both safe and proper to enjoy them, such favorable periods may give way eventually to the worst of times. It is therefore only good sense to prepare for the inevitable periods of duress.

B. Mobilization in Time of Peace (v. 8)

8. And Asa had an army of men that bare targets and spears, out of Judah three hundred thousand; and out of Benjamin, that bare shields and drew bows, two hundred and fourscore thousand: all these were mighty men of valour.

There were 480,000 men from the small kingdom of Judah—this was **all-out** mobilization. Particularly surprising is the strong force from tiny Benjamin, while also notable is the diversification in weaponry—Judah providing heavy weaponry and Benjamin lighter weaponry.

One should not view the comment in verse 8 on the courage of these men as merely perfunctory. In an era when strong leadership exists in the highest office of a nation and the entire culture projects a highly positive outlook, great courage and high valor might well prove to be an ordinary occurrence among that nation's fighting men rather than extraordinary. The kingdom of Judah was perpetually subjected to military threats from Isreal, Syria, Egypt, or other states; hence, the emphasis upon **heroic** virtues—such as amazing physical prowess and strong courage—should not be unexpected. Neither should one consider such an emphasis to conflict with spiritual values. In fact, during his reign over the kingdom of Judah, Asa struck quite an appropriate balance between the spiritual and the heroic, as indeed the divinely granted victory over Ethiopia proved.

Can one draw an analogy to aspects of Christian living from King Asa's preparedness in peacetime?

III. GAINING VICTORY (2 Chronicles 14:9-15)
A. Military Engagement (vv. 9, 10)

9. And there came out against them Zerah the Ethiopian with an host of a thousand thousand, and three hundred chariots; and came unto Mareshah.

Scholars have not identified the precise location of Zerah's kingdom. There exists no certainty that **modern** Ethiopia is that location since groups ethnically identifiable as Cushites inhabited a much larger area than what is presently called Ethiopia. In any case, Zerah had assembled a massive army—one million strong—and was advancing north toward Judah, having already reached Mareshah. The sheer psychological effect of such massive numbers upon a small kingdom must have been devastating, for Asa and his subjects knew that they could never match these numbers.

10. Then Asa went out against him, and they set the battle in array in the valley of Zephathah at Mareshah.

Despite the natural odds against victory, Asa must muster his hopelessly outnumbered forces and prepare for battle. One can imagine that this sagacious king never for once behaved as if anything other than victory were a possibility. He marched proudly before his troops, conscious of Judah's admirable past and unashamed because of his sure knowledge of the high quality of his troops. The two armies ranged themselves at locations opposite each other in the valley of Zephathah, which provided more level ground for fighting than the surrounding hillsides.

B. Humble Petition (v. 11)

11. And Asa cried unto the Lord his God, and said, Lord, it is nothing with thee to help, whether with many, or with them that have no power: help us, O Lord our God; for we rest on thee, and in thy name we go against this multitude. O Lord, thou art our God; let not man prevail against thee.

Asa's prayer might have been public—before his troops. However, I prefer to think that the king prayed this honest prayer (which might have demoralized his troops had they heard it) privately and reported it later—after his (or **God's**) glorious victory. It was, however, a prayer of faith. The king acknowledged his severe weakness but also recognized God's limitless power. He understood that divine power depends not in the least upon human resources.

God can employ, as in the case of Nebuchadnezzar centuries after this event, a heathen horde to scourge his disobedient people; or he can, as in the case of Gideon centuries before this event, rout markedly superior forces with a few dedicated men. As the angel informed Zechariah in Zechariah 4:6: "This is God's message to Zerubbabel: 'Not by might, nor by power, but by my Spirit, says the Lord of Hosts—you will succeed because of my Spirit, though you are few and weak' " **(Living Bible)**.

The king here acknowledged God's supremacy and His lordship over Judah, but one notes that this prayer was really an affirmation of an act of dedication which the king and his subjects had made to God some time earlier. They were not merely calling upon God to get them through an emergency; this royal petition was the natural outcry of an anguished but also fully committed heart.

Only one who has served in a leadership capacity could fully identify with the conflicting emotions which must have surged through the breast of the king. If God did not undertake, a massive heathen force would overwhelm this smaller army dedicated to Jehovah—the true God. If, as would not be very likely, the nation survived at all, they would be slashed numerically, totally demoralized, and filled with spiritual doubt and bitterness. Hence, Asa concluded, "O Lord, thou art our God; let not man prevail against thee."

C. Remarkable Victory (vv. 12-15)

12. So the Lord smote the Ethiopians before Asa, and before Judah; and the Ethiopians fled.

We are not given notice here of a miraculous intervention which **prevented** battle, that would not have convinced future invaders of Judah's mettle. Rather, we are informed that God enabled vastly outnumbered troops to achieve a marvelous military victory. The miracle was wrought upon the **men** of Judah, a miracle of strategy, of strength and prowess, and of stamina. This was precisely the sort of intervention needed to raise Judah's confidence in God to a high level and to serve notice upon her neighbors that she was not easily to be tampered with. Therefore, one reads in the account that "the Lord smote" and that "the Ethiopians fled."

13. And Asa and the people that were with him pursued them unto Gerar: and the Ethiopians were overthrown, that they

could not recover themselves; for they were destroyed before the Lord, and before his host; and they carried away very much spoil.

Judah's rout of the vast Ethiopian army was total; moreover, the equipment and personal properties of these soldiers appear also to have been confiscated. The invading army was unable to recoup its losses and to reorganize as a military force, an unusual occurrence, given the vast numbers of the Ethiopian force. The victory is attributed entirely to the Lord; in fact, Judah's army is called "his host." Whatever the sphere of conflict may be, when one is God's servant doing His bidding, he can be assured of whatever divine resources are necessary to achieve a favorable outcome. Indeed, in such a case the battle is the Lord's, and one can rest confidently in the expectation that He will wage effective warfare. Asa's forces even subdued those cities surrounding the area of battle with the Ethiopians, taking much spoil, before returning jubilantly to Jerusalem.

Have you recently enjoyed a spiritual victory of great magnitude which could be attributed only to supernatural forces operating on your behalf?

IV. SEEKING GOD (2 Chronicles 15:1-19)

A. Prophetic Advice (vv. 1-7)

Immediately upon Asa's return from battle, he was met by the prophet Azariah—at a moment most propitious for the king's hearing and heeding of sound advice. King Asa was surely both subdued and joyous—if such conflicting emotions can coexist in a single heart. He recognized what a perilous spot he had been in and who had extricated him from that predicament. At this exactly proper moment Azariah had for the king a message from God which contained both a promise and a warning.

God presently was with Judah and would continue to be so long as that nation remained in harmony with Him. But should they forsake God, they would assuredly be forsaken by Him. The prophet reviewed a portion of Israel's history—most likely that to-a-great-extent anarchic period of the judges when the nation lapsed into, first, spiritual ignorance, then spiritual anarchy, and ultimately idolatry. Azariah described graphically the insecure condition of Israel during that period and attributed that state to God's judgment. He concluded with a powerful directive which contained an encouraging promise: "But as for you, be strong and do not give up, for your work will be rewarded" (2 Chronicles 15:7 **New International Version**).

B. Courageous Response (vv. 8, 9)

Asa was heartened by this message from the Lord, with its assurance of His faithfulness and integrity. There was, however, yet reforming work to be accomplished. It appears that after the king's initial effort, described in 2 Chronicles 14:2-5, sections of his realm had lapsed once more into the forbidden idolatrous practices. Once again, Asa thoroughly removed the offensive religious objects—all "abominable idols." Then he repaired the altar in the Temple, which was apparently suffering either from fifty years of wear or else from that neglect of God's house which commonly accompanies backsliding. The king also summoned the entire nation to a festival of celebration and dedication, a summons responded to even by some inhabitants of the kingdom of Israel, impressed by evidences of divine favor upon King Asa and the kingdom of Judah.

C. Entire Cooperation (vv. 10-15)

The multitude of his subjects who responded to Asa's summons came to a special called assembly, not to one of the regular annual feasts, a fact which attests to the confidence of the people in their king. Once the festival had begun, several distinct activities occurred: (1) worship—through the offering of sacrifices, (2) the making of a covenant to seek God and to put to death whoever refused to do so, (3) the enunciation of a resounding oath that they would keep the covenant just made, and (4) joyous celebration—the logical outcome of such solemn, deeply sincere dedication to God. The result of this entire dedication was visible to all who would see: Judah sought God, discovered Him (as He had assured them would be the case), and, as a direct outcome, enjoyed an extended period of genuine peace.

D. Radical Removal (vv 16, 17)

From the beginning of Asa's reign it would have been clearly apparent that he thoroughly disapproved of his grandmother Michaiah's ungodly behavior. Now the king was sufficiently powerful to remove her from her position as queen mother and to destroy her detested objects of idolatrous worship. The king's intention toward radical obedience of Jehovah at this point passed its most crucial test, for as long as a prominent role model in the kingdom defied his commands of religious reformation, the entire nation would likely be influenced back into idolatrous practices. Even yet, however, certain hill-shrines remained, perhaps irregular centers of worship of the true God rather than idolatrous shrines. One nonetheless learns that Asa's consecration was entire: "The heart of Asa was perfect all his days" (v. 17).

E. Generous Gifts (v. 18)

Spiritual renewal normally is accompanied by generosity. Love for God receives spontaneous concrete expression through the giving of both currency and property to His cause. Even so, Asa presented lavish gifts to the Temple—silver, gold, and precious containers.

F. Extended Peace (v. 19)

For twenty years following Asa's remarkable act of dedication to Jehovah, the land remained free from war, a great temporal and spiritual blessing. Now the arts of peace could flourish—manufactures, music, poetry, and the cultivation of religious faith. An entire generation of children grew up without experiencing the trauma of ancient warfare with its cruel hand-to-hand combat and atrocities visited upon the innocent.

Later, of course, Asa was threatened by the northern kingdom (Israel) and, in a moment of doubt or else in a time of spiritual laxity, made an alliance with Syria which caused him to be reprimanded and warned by the prophet Hanani. Asa's reaction on this occasion is a blot upon a good record, for he imprisoned the prophet and at the same time took oppressive measures against others among his subjects (2 Chronicles 16:10, 11). After forty-one years of rule King Asa died, likely of heart dropsy, after failure to seek God for healing. Regrettably, then, one must end the discussion of a notable reign in Judah on a sad note since a leader who had faithfully obeyed God for many years became at least to some extent rebellious late in his life. Perhaps his successes had produced pride—always "the beginning of a fall."

REVIEW QUESTIONS

1. What action taken during Asa's youthful years of reign brought peace to Judah?

2. How did Asa behave during the ensuing period of peace?

3. What divine intervention kept the kingdom of Judah from great disaster?

4. How did Asa respond to the message of the prophet Azariah?

5. What radical act demonstrated most clearly the depth of King Asa's spiritual commitment?

GOLDEN TEXT HOMILY

"HELP US, O LORD OUR GOD; FOR WE REST ON THEE" (2 Chronicles 14:11).

Asa is described as a zealous reformer who broke down many of the altars of the strange gods and commanded Judah to seek God. The kingdom was then quiet before him, and he began to build cities, walls, and tower gates.

As always when we take a position to serve God, we are faced with opposition from the enemy. Asa was no exception. Asa found himself and the army of Judah pitted against Zerah and his host of thousands. We can all be taught by Asa's example when he said: "Lord, it is nothing with thee to help, whether with many, or with them that have no power: help us, O Lord our God; for we rest on thee, and in thy name we go against this multitude." Let us never rest in our own strength.

Consider verse 12: "So the Lord smote the Ethiopians"; the battle is the Lord's as well as the victory. There will be battles in every Christian's life. The length or severity of the battles are not what is important. The most important thing for any Christian to remember is that God has never lost and will never lose a battle.—**Henry H. Kinsey, Servicemen's Representative, Stateside, Cleveland, Tennessee**

SENTENCE SERMONS

GOD'S POWER IS always available to those who seek to do His will.
—Selected

WHAT CANNOT BE told to human ears can be poured into God's sympathetic ear.
—"Speaker's Sourcebook"

THE CHRISTIAN ON his knees sees more than an unregenerate philosopher on tiptoes.
—Selected

WHERE GOD'S FINGER points, there God's hands will make a way.
—"Speaker's Sourcebook"

EVANGELISTIC APPLICATION

WHEN MEN SEEK GOD, THEY WILL FIND HIM.

Dwight L. Moody once expressed his belief that the world has yet to witness the result of entire dedication to God. Moody's statement was not skeptical but confident; he was convinced that the man who seeks God earnestly, who yields himself fully, will tap the resources of the supernatural realm and release spiritual power to an ever-widening circle of human contacts.

What is it, then, truly to seek Him? Obviously, it is to send up impassioned prayer from a sincere heart. But it is more. It is to search the heart for any symptom of spiritual illness and to ascertain that every vestige of known sin is removed. It is to make all necessary changes in lifestyle, as one is impressed by the Holy Spirit, so as to free oneself from those weights which deflect him from his carefully determined spiritual course. It is, furthermore, to present oneself daily as a yielded vessel, ready to receive, ready to obey—ready for radical submission, ready for any commission to service from the King who is resident within every yielded human heart.

The Lord has assured us that "everyone who asks receives; he who seeks finds; and to him who knocks, the door will be opened" (Matthew 7:8, **New International Version**). We are the children of an infinitely benevolent Heavenly Father who desires communion with us and who is eager to spread His blessings upon those who open themselves up to Him. Why should we deprive ourselves of benefits available to all who seek Him?

ILLUMINATING THE LESSON

Dr. Harry A. Ironside was asked: "If you had prayed all your life for the salvation of a loved one, and then you got word that that person had died without giving any evidence of being saved, would your belief in prayer or faith in God be shattered?"

Dr. Ironside answered by telling the story of an unsaved man who had gone to sea. One night his mother awakened with a deep sense of need. A burden for her unsaved boy rested heavily upon her heart. She earnestly prayed for his salvation.

Weeks passed. Then, one day, there was a knock at her door and there stood her son! "Mother, I'm saved," he exclaimed joyfully. Then he told her: "A few weeks ago, our ship was caught in a fearful storm. The waves seemed mountain high. Hope of our outriding the storm vanished. Suddenly the ship gave a lurch and I was swept overboard. As I began to sink, the awful thought came to me: 'I'm lost forever! Where will I spend eternity?' In agony of heart I cried out, 'O God, I look, I look to Jesus!' Then I lost consciousness. After the storm had abated, the Sailors came out to clear the deck. They found me lying, unconscious, against a bulwark!"— **Walter Brown Knight**

DAILY DEVOTIONAL GUIDE

M. Godliness Produces Obedience. Judges 7:9-22

T. Godliness Produces Godly Acts. 1 Kings 15:11-15

W. Encouragement to Those Who Obey. 2 Chronicles 15:1-7

T. Reforms Under Godly Leadership. 2 Chronicles 15:8-19

F. Blessings of Serving God. Psalm 1:1-6

S. Blessings on the Repentant. Acts 3:19-26

July 12, 1981

Courage to Champion God's Cause

Bible Background: 1 Kings 18:1-46
Time: Around 867 B.C.
Places: Jezreel, Mount Carmel
Supplemental References: Numbers 16:1-50; 23:1-30; 1 Chronicles 21:25-30; Romans 12:21
Golden Text: "Greater is he that is in you, than he that is in the world" (1 John 4:4).
Central Truth: Faith in God can make us more than conquerors over the forces of wickedness.
Evangelistic Emphasis: Freedom to accept or reject Christ means that each man determines his own destiny.

PRINTED TEXT

1 Kings 18:17. And it came to pass, when Ahab saw Elijah, that Ahab said unto him, Art thou he that troubleth Israel?

18. And he answered, I have not troubled Israel; but thou, and thy father's house, in that ye have forsaken the commandments of the Lord, and thou hast followed Baalim.

19. Now therefore send, and gather to me all Israel unto mount Carmel, and the prophets of Baal four hundred and fifty, and the prophets of the groves four hundred, which eat at Jezebel's table.

20. So Ahab sent unto all the children of Israel, and gathered the prophets together unto mount Carmel.

21. And Elijah came unto all the people, and said, How long halt ye between two opinions? if the Lord be God, follow him: but if Baal, then follow him. And the people answered him not a word.

22. Then said Elijah unto the people, I, even I only, remain a prophet of the Lord; but Baal's prophets are four hundred and fifty men.

23. Let them therefore give us two bullocks; and let them choose one bullock for themselves, and cut it in pieces, and lay it on wood, and put no fire under: and I will dress the other bullock, and lay it on wood, and put no fire under:

24. And call ye on the name of your gods, and I will call on the name of the Lord: and the God that answereth by fire, let him be God. And all the people answered and said, It is well spoken.

36. And it came to pass at the time of the offering of the evening sacrifice, that Elijah the prophet came near, and said, Lord God of Abraham, Isaac, and of Israel, let it be known this day that thou art God in Israel, and that I am thy servant, and that I have done all these things at thy word.

37. Hear me, O Lord, hear me, that this people may know that thou art the Lord God, and that thou hast turned their heart back again.

38. Then the fire of the Lord fell and consumed the burnt-sacrifice, and the wood, and the stones, and the dust, and licked up the water that was in the trench.

39. And when all the people saw it, they fell on their faces: and they said, The Lord, he is the God; the Lord, he is the God.

DICTIONARY

Ahab—1 Kings 18:17—Eighth king of Israel, who married Jezebel, a fanatical worshiper of Baal and his female consort Astarte. Her father had been a priest of Astarte, a fact which likely explains her pagan zeal.

Elijah (ee-LIE-jah)—1 Kings 18:17—The outstanding prophet of the ninth century who was raised by God to fight the encroachment of Tyrian Baalism that was being fostered by Jezebel.

Baalim—1 Kings 18:18—This is the plural form of the word and denotes the various forms in which Baal was worshiped in different localities.

groves—1 Kings 18:19—The Hebrew should not have been translated, but like Baal, just translated directly into English, as Asherah. This was the female goddess who was the consort of Baal.

Jezebel (JEZ-uh-bell)—1 Kings 18:19—Daughter of Ethbaal, king of the Zidonians, and queen of Ahab, king of Israel. She had been brought up as a zealous worshiper of Baal.

Mount Carmel—1 Kings 18:20—A prominent mountain which today extends into modern Haifa. It stretches southeast for about thirteen miles. The events of today's lesson probably took place on the southeastern end.

bullocks—1 Kings 18:23—Young bull oxen or steer.

evening sacrifice—1 Kings 18:36—The Hebrew word indicates "meal offering," which consisted of fine flour, oil, salt, and frankincense. It probably corresponds to the daily afternoon sacrifice (Exodus 29:38-41) offered in the sanctuary. It was offered at 3:00 p.m.

LESSON OUTLINE

I. COMMUNICATING GOD'S MESSAGE
  A. Commanded by the Lord
  B. Met by Obadiah
  C. Heard by Ahab
II. CHALLENGING SPIRITUAL WICKEDNESS
  A. God's Plan
  B. The King's Compliance
  C. The Prophet's Challenge
III. CONQUERING BY GOD'S POWER
  A. Fruitless Efforts
  B. Vindication of Jehovah
  C. Removal of Divine Judgment

LESSON EXPOSITION

INTRODUCTION

From the earliest stages of salvation history, the **prophet** performed an essential but almost invariably thankless role. Noah, "the preacher of righteousness," appeared first in the role of prophet—both **forthtelling** and **foretelling** as he proclaimed God's requirements and warned of God's judgment. Since the office of prophet—from Noah onward—normally entailed a **predictive** function, an obvious test of authenticity was built into the prophetic role—the occurrence or nonoccurrence of that which was predicted.

The prophet appeared when religious or political offices (or both) were failing to function according to divine commands and when the populace was therefore drifting away from propriety of worship and from holiness of conduct. A simple roll call of some of the prophets of Judah and Israel will illustrate this point: Noah, Moses, Samuel, Elijah, Elisha, Jonah, Isaiah, Jeremiah, Hosea, Malachi. In the case not only of each member of this list but also of every other prophet of God, an improperly directed people must receive leadership, and an erring people must be warned. Hence, God raised up courageous men who were willing to speak and act fearlessly and to stand unbendingly against enormous pressures from constituted but evil authority.

Elijah the Tishbite exemplified eminently well the prophetic function. Born and reared in the isolated forests of Gilead, he developed strength of character and independence of spirit. Those qualities, joined with deep spiritual sensitivity, made him useful to God in a role unique during his age—that of divine spokesman in a time of rampant apostasy and gross immorality. When God spoke, he listened, then strode forth unhesitatingly to relay the divine message or to perform the divinely commanded act.

This fearless servant of Jehovah ministered both to the nation in general and to particular persons. He sustained the widow of Zarephath and brought restoration of life to her son. He nurtured the sons of the prophets (and particularly the young Elisha, his designated successor). He also pronounced divine judgment upon both king and kingdom and thereby made himself feared and hated by the heinous Ahab and Jezebel. But his zeal also made him beloved and honored by the Lord himself, who finally terminated Elijah's earthly existence by translating him to glory in a chariot of fire.

The occasion of the present lesson found Elijah performing that prophetic role of both pronouncer and agent of divine judgment upon an apostate kingdom. In 1 Kings 17:1, Elijah declared to King Ahab: "As the Lord, the God of Israel, lives, whom I serve, there will be neither dew nor rain in the next few years except at my word" **(New International Version)**. Following this statement, drought and famine immediately ensued—as authentication of the prophet, vindication of the Lord, and judgment upon evil. During this three-and-one-half-year period (Luke 4:25), God miraculously sustained Elijah, first by means of ravens at the brook Cherith and later, after the brook had dried up, by multiplying the meal and oil of the widow of Zarephath. Meanwhile, both king and peasant in Israel languished, as the water sources dried up, the land became parched, and vegetation withered.

I. COMMUNICATING GOD'S MESSAGE (1 Kings 18:1-18)

A. Commanded by the Lord (vv. 1, 2)

The drought and famine continued for a sufficiently long period to remove any idea of chance occurrence from the minds of either king or people. This act of divine judgment, begun at the word of God through His spokesman Elijah, must also terminate by means of divine pronouncement through the prophet. No reasonable doubt could then remain as to the reason for its occurrence and the agency of its institution and termination. Thereby, the omnipotence of Jehovah would become apparent, the authenticity of the message and the character of Elijah would receive sure confirmation, and God's purpose of judgment upon an evil leadership and a teeter-tottering people would stand as an obvious fact.

The mercy of the Lord also stands evident.

The land was now languishing. The water sources were virtually dried up, except in a few locations such as on Mount Carmel. The production of food had become impossible, and any food supplies still existing must soon be entirely depleted. Widespread starvation would inevitably result. Before this ultimate result of the expression of divine displeasure ensued, the Lord commanded Elijah to confront the wicked Ahab once again. Unhesitatingly, this entirely dedicated servant of Jehovah obeyed—and with great risk to life and limb; for Ahab had likely convinced himself that Elijah was the source of all his troubles, and the king might exact dire vengeance on the prophet. Nonetheless, Elijah went seeking for the king.

Samaria was now the capital of the northern kingdom. Jeroboam had established Shechem as capital but had soon relocated it at the more easily defensible Tirzah. The wicked but strong Omri, father of Ahab, had built Samaria to serve as his capital, and it so remained until the destruction of the northern kingdom in 723 B.C. Now, however, Samaria was besieged not by an invading army but by famine. The king himself was reduced to the humiliating role of wandering about the land on foot, searching for that rare spring of water which would preserve the lives of his horses and mules.

B. Met by Obadiah (vv. 3-14)

At this point, the eighteenth chapter of 1 Kings introduces an explanatory parenthesis. Obadiah served as an administrative assistant whose particular duties entailed oversight of the palace in Samaria. This courageous and devout adherent of the true religion had served his evil master faithfully—except when such service conflicted with his first allegiance to Jehovah God. Obadiah had kept one hundred prophets from the wrath of Jezebel by hiding them in a cave and sustaining them there. Since Obadiah had charge over the food budget for the royal palace, he apparently had fed the prophets of the Lord out of the royal kitchen. Had king or queen discovered this act of disloyalty to themselves but of fidelity to God, Obadiah must have forfeited his life. This man's entire allegiance to God therefore cannot be questioned.

Obadiah had now set out with King Ahab to search for some rare spring yet flowing—the servant eventually taking one direction and the king another. The servant of the king suddenly came upon a most startling sight.

Elijah the prophet came into view. Obadiah showed both respect and fear. First, he bowed deeply before the prophet, an indication of the reverence in which he held this man of God. One notes that Elijah had neither social rank nor recognized temporal function to give him status; only his demonstrated standing with the Lord God could afford him any honor. It is a sign of Obadiah's true spiritual mettle that he recognized, as his royal master refused to do, Elijah's divinely sanctioned prophetic role.

Obadiah stood in fear once Elijah had given him the message for Ahab, although that message was completely straightforward, consisting in the Hebrew of only two words, which translated are, "Behold, Elijah." Obadiah, however, felt panic concerning the possibility that, while he went to inform his master, Elijah would be secreted away by divine agency and he, in turn, would face the fury of King Ahab. This fear probably arose from rumors regarding the supernatural watch-care over Elijah and from Obadiah's knowledge of Ahab's hatred of the prophet and exhaustive search for him, not only throughout Israel but also in foreign countries.

Obadiah, justifiably, reminded the prophet of his faithfulness to the Lord, even at the risk of his own life, as if to say, "I don't deserve such treatment from the spokesman of the Lord whom I serve." Obadiah, while unquestionably righteous, was rather unperceptive spiritually. Otherwise, he would have known that God would never behave so treacherously as he was imagining, nor would He authorize His servant to do so. Although the continuation of the mortal life of a believer in the true God must never be his highest consideration (as Obadiah had already proved himself to know), God values that life and certainly will terminate it only when that believer's earthly usefulness has ended and his readiness for the eternal dimension is complete. However, the believer himself is able to cause its termination through disobedience (as Obadiah seemed not to understand so well).

In any case, Elijah now would confront Ahab, and Obadiah must so inform the king.

Can the obedient Christian today rest in the assurance that his **dying** as well as his **living** is in the hands of his Maker and Lord?

C. Heard by Ahab (vv. 15-18)

The forthrightness of the prophet is both refreshing and astonishing. Elijah at this point could not predict the response of the king. He knew only what he must do. Such a singleminded bent toward obedience to God is born of deep self-knowledge and utter spiritual dedication. Even among the prophets of the Old Testament the degree of Elijah's dedication was not always approached; in fact, we have studied only recently of the fatal disobedience of the unnamed man of God who had been used mightily of God only hours before to warn Jeroboam of impending divine judgment (1 Kings 13:11-32).

The Christian believer who begins to approach Elijah's totality of trust and commitment thereby renders himself the instrument of Deity, totally pliable and therefore greatly usable by God. Such utter surrender will not necessarily lead to spectacular ministry, as in the case of Elijah, but it will inevitably result in employment of the dedicated individual in the highest service he could know on earth —doing the bidding of his Maker. The blind seventeenth-century poet John Milton expressed this idea masterfully:

When I consider how my light is spent
  Ere half my days, in this dark world and
    wide,
  And that one talent which is death to hide,
  Lodged with me useless, though my soul
    more bent
To serve therewith my Maker, and present
  My true account, lest he returning chide;
  "Doth God exact day-labour, light denied?"
I fondly ask; but Patience to prevent
  That murmur, soon replies, "God doth not
    need
  Either man's work or his own gifts; who best
  Bear his mild yoke, they serve him best.
    His state
Is kingly. Thousands at his bidding speed
  And post o'er land and ocean without rest:
  They also serve who only stand and wait.

Obadiah, well aware of King Ahab's rage against Elijah, informed the king of the prophet's intention to meet with him. The king complied. Indeed, Ahab may have intended to imprison or execute Elijah, but as the drought wore on and famine ensued, the king's need for Elijah's aid must have come to supersede his impulse for vengeance. A calm meeting was possible despite the hatred yet seething within the breast of the wicked ruler.

17. And it came to pass, when Ahab

saw Elijah, that Ahab said unto him, Art thou he that troubleth Israel?

18. And he answered, I have not troubled Israel; but thou, and thy father's house, in that ye have forsaken the commandments of the Lord, and thou hast followed Baalim.

The depth of rebellion and the resulting spiritual darkness of the king are apparent here. Ahab refused to see any relationship between his own behavior and the divine judgment his kingdom was experiencing. He instead revealed his complete reversal of values and total lack of perceptiveness as to the proper scale of spiritual values.

That immutable divine law enunciated centuries later by Paul the Apostle in Galatians 6:7 has functioned since the creation of man and certainly applies in our present Bible context: "Whatsoever a man soweth, that shall he also reap." The result of good or bad actions may appear during one's lifetime and be evident to all. It may appear only in eternity, or it may appear on earth as a direct result of divine agency. But the moral law will not be abridged or circumvented. Ahab's lack of spiritual awareness may not have been **immediately** willful, but he had willed to sin. His grave sins had destroyed any spiritual awareness possible to him.

In fact, Ahab and his heinous wife Jezebel were the chief troublers of Israel. They had continued to lead God's people ever downward, they had fostered idolatry, and they had defied basic laws of ethics and morality. In contrast, Elijah was the mere instrument of Deity, communicating or acting out God's commands at His direct bidding. As conspicuous role models for the kingdom, Ahab and Jezebel were directly responsible for the almost total lapse of the Israelites into the worship of Baal and Ashtoreth. They were also responsible for the immorality which accompanied this worship.

Furthermore, the king and his queen must take chief responsibility for the present suffering of their subjects since they had led the nation into the moral and spiritual state which produced the divine judgment. Hence, Ahab truly had "troubled Israel." The prophet also included the "house" of Ahab in his indictment. This might refer to both the king's ancestry (the ruling house) and to the members of the present royal household.

> Does plunging into evil behavior often produce spiritual blindness?

II. CHALLENGING SPIRITUAL WICKEDNESS
(1 Kings 18:19-24)

A. God's Plan (v. 19)

19. Now therefore send, and gather to me all Israel unto mount Carmel, and the prophets of Baal four hundred and fifty, and the prophets of the groves four hundred, which eat at Jezebel's table.

Elijah's **directive** to the king (it certainly is not couched in the terms of a **request**) was that he call a national assembly. The prophet—at the direct command of Jehovah—would direct a test to discover which "alleged deity" was truly God—Jehovah or Baal. Mount Carmel was a logical location for such a test since it earlier had been a local center of worship of Jehovah and had likely been usurped as a center of worship by the followers of Baal. Some Old Testament scholars suggest too that it was suitable because it was the location of a spring which never ceased to flow, even during the severest drought—providing thereby a source of water for Elijah's sacrifice. The prophet, moreover, instructed the king to bring all 850 false prophets—of both Baal and Ashtoreth. (The "prophets of the groves" were devotees of Baal's counterpart, Ashtoreth, the moon goddess.)

B. The King's Compliance (v. 20)

20. So Ahab sent unto all the children of Israel, and gathered the prophets together unto mount Carmel.

Ahab's compliance was the result of desperation, not of repentance. He had not the least intention of altering his lifestyle, of amending his method of rule, or of stamping out the worship of Baal and Ashtoreth. He simply wished to survive the present emergency, and, obviously, Elijah now had the upper hand. The king might well have attributed Elijah's power to magical charms or to divination rather than to the direct agency of Jehovah. Since Ahab chose not to serve Jehovah, it would have been difficult for him to acknowledge His power, and, in fact, we have no record that he ever did so, although he, begrudgingly, made use of true prophets when he must. Indeed, Ahab and Jezebel became ever more wicked after the astounding event of our present study.

C. The Prophet's Challenge (vv. 21-24)

21. And Elijah came unto all the people, and said, How long halt ye between two opinions? if the Lord be God, follow him:

but if Baal, then follow him. And the people answered him not a word.

Elijah did not address this great challenge to the intransigent king. He already knew of Ahab's subservience to his heinous queen. He was also aware of Ahab's own love of wickedness. The prophet, therefore, appealed directly to the people of Israel. The Israelites apparently yet had some inner pull toward worship of Jehovah, inasmuch as **halt** in verse 21 means a sort of teeter-tottering, first in the one direction, then in the other. The vast majority of Israelites apparently were participating in Baal worship. These same people, however, were also periodically offering sacrifices to Jehovah at the local shrines. It would seem that they were not really loyal to the true God but not yet willing to abandon those worship traditions which probably made them feel emotionally comfortable. Because of their actions they were being totally inefficacious, given their lack of exclusive dedication to the true God.

Elijah, like Joshua centuries before him (Joshua 24:15), offered to the people of Israel diametrically opposed alternatives—Jehovah, the true God, eternal Spirit, with His rigorous demands for moral and ethical purity; or Baal, the false sun-god, a fertility deity, with sensual orgies involved in his worship. "Which will you have?" challenged the great prophet. "Will it be truth or error, holiness or evil, true spiritual dedication or rank self-indulgence?" The people apparently preferred to await the outcome of the ensuing events: they remained silent. It may well be that, in their spiritual blindness, they no longer recognized the exclusive sovereignty of Jehovah. They may have come to believe, like the pagan nations surrounding them, in a multiplicity of local deities with limited spheres of influence. They were now waiting to see which god would prove supreme.

The challenge of Elijah to Israel is a perpetual challenge to people who name the name of the Lord God. To modern believers the challenge goes forth: Will we merely give lip service to Christian faith, or will we dedicate ourselves fully to Christ, becoming truly sold out to God—and without any reservations? Only by so doing can one become fully useful to God, for His work requires completely yielded instruments.

22. Then said Elijah unto the people, I, even I only, remain a prophet of the Lord; but Baal's prophets are four hundred and fifty men.

Elijah's appraisal could have been inaccurate. In 1 Kings 19:14, 18 one learns that in his time of extreme discouragement following the episode of our present lesson, Elijah expressed to God his belief that he was the only person in Israel still keeping covenant with Jehovah. He was then informed by the Lord that, to the contrary, seven thousand true believers in Jehovah yet remained. It is, then, possible that Elijah's statement on the present occasion was honest but mistaken. After all, Obadiah had hidden one hundred prophets of the true God. Had all of them subsequently fled the kingdom or been slain by Jezebel's henchmen? Possibly, but the contrary view might also be true—that Elijah's information was inaccurate and that somewhere in the kingdom other true prophets yet lived. In fact, in 1 Kings 20:13-15, shortly after the confrontation on Mount Carmel, an unnamed prophet addressed King Ahab. That prophet could have come from Judah but might also have been a native of Israel.

23. Let them therefore give us two bullocks; and let them choose one bullock for themselves, and cut it in pieces, and lay it on wood, and put no fire under: and I will dress the other bullock, and lay it on wood, and put no fire under:

24. And call ye on the name of your gods, and I will call on the name of the Lord: and the God that answereth by fire, let him be God. And all the people answered and said, It is well spoken.

Elijah posed a test: Let the true God speak for Himself, giving a sign of His existence and power. An unauthorized test of God like this one could well constitute a tempting of God and in that case might well result in further divine judgment. In the present case, however, Elijah was acting at the direct behest of Jehovah, following His precise instructions; hence, the trial by fire was a legitimate test. Elijah at this point stated his general instructions for preparations of the sacrifices, but the text provides more specific description of the preparations later in 1 Kings 18.

The particular test chosen was highly appropriate. Since Baal was the sun-god, what better test of his power could there be than to have him light the fires which would consume his own sacrifice, unaided by human agency? And, obviously, the **nature** of the test would make no difference to Jehovah since He indeed was, is, and ever shall be completely sovereign throughout His universe.

The people, moreover, acquiesced. After all, how could they refuse so obviously fair a test?

Should the Christian believer ask for "signs" from God? What about "putting out fleeces"?

III. CONQUERING BY GOD'S POWER (1 Kings 18:25-46)

A. Fruitless Efforts (vv. 25-29)

Ironically, Elijah's **authority** was already evident, for the prophets of Baal accepted Elijah's instructions totally, without any recorded protest or even comment. Elijah invited these 450 prophets of Baal to offer their sacrifice first—openly and nonsurreptitiously, not secretly lighting the sacrifice from underneath the altar, as we are told by Old Testament scholars had sometimes happened in Baal worship.

During the entire morning the false prophets continued to call upon Baal, uninterrupted by Elijah or Baal. They began to perform a peculiar ritualistic dance which involved a quaint leaping motion on one foot. At noon Elijah indulged in a bit of mockery and sarcasm (v. 27); he suggested that perhaps Baal was conversing, pursuing (in vengeance?), traveling, or sleeping—rather ungodlike activities. But they responded seriously to Elijah, crying aloud—rather pathetically by now—and lacerating their flesh with knives and lancets until blood gushed out. All day they continued without avail.

B. Vindication of Jehovah (vv. 30-40)

At the time of the evening sacrifice, Elijah called the still-assembled Israelites to him and began to repair the altar of the Lord, apparently broken down through neglect. He used twelve stones in his rebuilding of the altar, one to represent each of the twelve tribes of Israel. These stones stood as a potent symbol of the originally intended unity of the twelve tribes and of God's ultimately single purpose for those twelve tribes.

Having rebuilt the altar and dug a trench large enough to contain "two measures," or about thirteen quarts, Elijah began to prepare the sacrifice. The prophet of God followed the instructions for a burnt offering given in Leviticus 1:5-9, as far as one can ascertain from the details given in 1 Kings 18:33. During the age of the patriarchs, each follower of the true God had offered his own offerings. From the time of Moses this function had become the specialized task of the descendants of Aaron, assisted by other Levites. There were, however, no priests left in the northern kingdom (unless Elijah, as we have no reason to believe, was himself of the tribe of Levi). In any case, Elijah was the spokesman of Jehovah and acted at His direct command.

Having prepared the sacrifice, Elijah instructed that four barrels (large jars) be filled with water three times and poured upon the sacrifice. This rather large amount of water, which might have come from a nearby ever-flowing spring known to have existed on Mount Carmel, soaked the sacrifice and filled the trench. It was therefore apparent to all of the people that the sacrifice could not burn through normal means. It would also be apparent afterward that Jehovah God had been able to meet the severest possible test of His power and deity.

36. And it came to pass at the time of the offering of the evening sacrifice, that Elijah the prophet came near, and said, Lord God of Abraham, Isaac, and of Israel, let it be known this day that thou art God in Israel, and that I am thy servant, and that I have done all these things at thy word.

37. Hear me, O Lord, hear me, that this people may know that thou art the Lord God, and that thou hast turned their heart back again.

Elijah now prepared to offer his sacrifice as if it were the regular burnt offering of the evening. His prayer at this moment merits careful consideration. First, in the naming of Deity, the prayer emphasized the unchanging nature of God, for Elijah addressed the "Lord God of Abraham, Isaac, and of Israel." But in using "Lord" or "Jehovah" (or "Yahweh"), Elijah emphasized the covenant relationship established between the Lord and His people at Mount Sinai under Moses' leadership, for that name for the true God would be easily associated with that crucial event in salvation history. Elijah made several distinct requests: (1) that God vindicate Himself before the assembled Israelites, (2) that God vindicate His prophet, (3) that God reveal Himself as "the Lord God," the God of covenant, and (4) that Israel be made aware that God had "turned their heart back again," an experience which indeed must be initiated by Jehovah. This specific prayer, moreover, was granted specific answers; one can, in fact, believe that each of Elijah's four requests received an individually ascertainable answer.

38. Then the fire of the Lord fell and consumed the burnt-sacrifice, and the wood, and the stones, and the dust, and licked up the water that was in the trench.

God vindicated Himself and His prophet through supernatural fire. Ordinary fire (through lightning, for instance, as some modern scholars believe actually happened) would not have resulted in the complete consuming of the sacrifice, wood, stones, and water. The event can be viewed only as totally miraculous. And the contrast with the failure of Baal's false prophets could not be more complete. The test had been precisely devised to show that Baal, the sun-god, could not light the fire for his own sacrifice. This was surely an indication that Baal was powerless and even nonexistent, given the crucial importance of this occasion and the inability of this so-called god to vindicate his devotees.

39. And when all the people saw it, they fell on their faces: and they said, The Lord, he is the God; the Lord, he is the God.

When the assembled Israelites fell on their face in worship of Jehovah God and in renewal of covenant relationship, all of Elijah's remaining requests in his prayer before the sacrifice were thereby answered. God had vindicated Himself and His servant Elijah, proved the validity of Elijah's actions, restored the covenant relationship, and turned the heart of Israel back to Himself. What a day of triumph for God and for good!

Elijah, filled with holy zeal, now became the direct agent of God's vengeance upon the false prophets. He "had them brought down to the Kishon Valley and slaughtered there" (1 Kings 18:40, **New International Version),** most probably while the for-now helpless king looked on.

Does God still vindicate His Word today?

C. Removal of Divine Judgment (vv. 41-46)

Elijah immediately warned Ahab of the imminence of rain—without any physical evidence in the sky. Then he and his servant went quickly to the top of Mount Carmel to pray for that promised rain. Eight times he prayed before his servant reported the presence of a cloud about the size of a man's hand, rising from the sea. That was sufficient evidence for the prophet. He sent his servant to warn Ahab to start in his chariot for Jezreel before the plain near Mount Carmel became a sea of unnegotiable mud. Elijah himself, under the power of the Lord, outran the king's chariot all the way to Jezreel.

James the Apostle assured the recipients of his letter that in the Christian era, just as in Elijah's day, "the prayer of a righteous man is powerful and effective" (James 5:16, **New International Version).** God's nature has not changed and will not change; therefore, His basic requirements for relationship with Himself remain the same. The yielded heart can still commune with God, experience His peace, and obtain supernatural results from prayer.

REVIEW QUESTIONS

1. Why did Obadiah fear to relay Elijah's message to King Ahab?

2. Who had really "troubled" Israel, and how had Israel been troubled?

3. What process did the prophets of Baal futilely undergo in an attempt to receive an answer from their god?

4. How was that prayer prayed by Elijah just previous to his offering of sacrifice very precisely answered?

5. **Specifically,** how did the three-and-one-half years of drought end?

GOLDEN TEXT HOMILY

"GREATER IS HE THAT IS IN YOU, THAN HE THAT IS IN THE WORLD" (1 John 4:4).

Here is the secret of the children of God being able to overcome the powers of darkness. They are indwelt by the Holy Spirit.

When the Lord Jesus Christ returned to the glory from which He had come, He sent the Spirit of God from heaven to earth (John 15:26) to dwell in us and abide with us forever (John 14:16, 17). Our bodies have become His temple (1 Corinthians 6:19).

The Spirit of truth guides us into all truth (John 15:13, 26). We are able to overcome the spirit of this world by using the Word of God, the sword of the Spirit.

No matter how strong the enemy of our souls may seem to be, nothing can change the revealed fact that He who is in us is greater than the spirit and prince of this world (John 14:30; 1 Corinthians 2:12). When we recognize this truth and act upon it, we become more than conquerors.—**Selected**

SENTENCE SERMONS

TO SEE WHAT is right and not do it, is want of courage.
—**Confucius**

FAITH IN GOD can make us more than conquerors over the forces of wickedness.
—**Selected**

ONE EXAMPLE IS worth a thousand arguments.
—**Thomas Carlyle**

NOTHING CAN BE MORE noble or fairer than the holy ferver of true zeal.
—**Jean Baptiste Moliere**

EVANGELISTIC APPLICATION

FREEDOM TO ACCEPT OR REJECT CHRIST MEANS THAT EACH MAN DETERMINES HIS OWN DESTINY.

When the supernatural fire fell on the altar on Mount Carmel, the assembled Israelites bowed in worship of Jehovah and, at least for the time, once more acknowledged Him as Lord. King Ahab, however, gave no evidence of either remorse or spiritual renewal; in fact, his actions soon afterward revealed the continued state of wickedness of his heart. Both people and king had witnessed clearly miraculous evidences of Jehovah's power, yet the assembled people chose to serve God, and the king who should have been leading them back to God remained intransigent in his evil.

So it is today. God comes to every man with evidences of His power and of His grace. Some, softened by those divine influences, yield to the prompting of the Spirit, experience remarkable changes in lifestyle, and dedicate themselves to Christian service. Others feel identical promptings, but push those benevolent influences out of their heart and turn steadfastly in the direction of carnal pleasure. Every man inevitably makes his choice for or against commitment to Jesus Christ and thereby determines his destiny for time and eternity.

ILLUMINATING THE LESSON

Harry Shepler, a young man of whom the **Sunday School Times** tells, was in the signal service. Being ordered one morning by a sergeant to report for duty at the canteen, he refused to do so, and the sergeant threatened to report him to the officer of the day.

"All right," said Shepler, "go ahead. I did not enlist to be a bartender, but a soldier, and I will not report at the canteen."

He was duly reported to the major, who sent for him. Shepler went with trembling knees but with a steady heart, for he knew he was right. The officer said to him:

"Are you the young man who disobeyed orders this morning?"

"Yes, sir, I am."

"Why did you do it?"

"Simply because I do not believe it is right to do what I was asked to do. I enlisted to be a soldier and not a bartender."

The major arose quickly from his stool, and, extending his hand, said:

"Shepler, you are the kind of a man we want. I am glad to see a fellow who has the courage of his convictions. You are not obliged to report at the canteen."

The great need of the day is for men to have convictions founded upon the Word of God, and then be true to those convictions.
—**"Christian Victory"**

DAILY DEVOTIONAL GUIDE

M. Courage to Obey God's Law. Joshua 1: 1-9

T. Strength for God's Champion. Judges 15: 14-20

W. Courage Through Trust in the Lord. 1 Samuel 17:15-50

T. Courage to Confront With God's Claims. 1 Kings 18:1-15

F. Courage in Calling to Repentance. Matthew 3:1-10

S. Victory for the Courageous. Acts 7:54-60

July 19, 1981

Quest for Spiritual Power

Bible Background: 1 Kings 19:19-21; 2 Kings 2:1-25
Time: Around 854 B.C.
Places: Jericho, Jordan River
Supplemental References: Joel 2:28-32; Matthew 3:11; John 7:37-39; Acts 2:1-21; 10:45; 19:6; 2 Corinthians 1:20-22
Golden Text: "I pray thee, let a double portion of thy spirit be upon me" (2 Kings 2:9).
Central Truth: Obedience is the key to receiving spiritual power.
Evangelistic Emphasis: We need God's power to be effective witnesses.

PRINTED TEXT

2 Kings 2:6. And Elijah said unto him, Tarry, I pray thee, here; for the Lord hath sent me to Jordan. And he said, As the Lord liveth, and as thy soul liveth, I will not leave thee. And they two went on.

7. And fifty men of the sons of the prophets went, and stood to view afar off: and they two stood by Jordan.

8. And Elijah took his mantle, and wrapped it together, and smote the waters, and they were divided hither and thither, so that they two went over on dry ground.

9. And it came to pass, when they were gone over, that Elijah said unto Elisha, Ask what I shall do for thee, before I be taken away from thee. And Elisha said, I pray thee, let a double portion of thy spirit be upon me.

10. And he said, Thou hast asked a hard thing: nevertheless, if thou see me when I am taken from thee, it shall be so unto thee; but if not, it shall not be so.

11. And it came to pass, as they still went on, and talked, that, behold, there appeared a chariot of fire, and horses of fire, and parted them both asunder; and Elijah went up by a whirlwind into heaven.

12. And Elisha saw it, and he cried, My father, my father, the chariot of Israel, and the horsemen thereof. And he saw him no more: and he took hold of his own clothes, and rent them in two pieces.

13. He took up also the mantle of Elijah that fell from him, and went back, and stood by the bank of Jordan;

14. And he took the mantle of Elijah that fell from him, and smote the waters, and said, Where is the Lord God of Elijah? and when he also had smitten the waters, they parted hither and thither: and Elisha went over.

15. And when the sons of the prophets which were to view at Jericho saw him, they said, The spirit of Elijah doth rest on Elisha. And they came to meet him, and bowed themselves to the ground before him.

DICTIONARY

sons of the prophets—2 Kings 2:7—Not a physical relationship, but a "school" or group of students being trained by a prophet.

mantle—2 Kings 2:8—Besides the tunic (inner garment) which was worn directly on the body, the Israelites generally wore an outer garment which was loosely wrapped over the tunic. It was made of a large piece of cloth, generally of a heavier weave than the cloth of the tunic. Prophets seem to have had a mantle which would immediately identify them as to their office. It may well have been made of some animal skin as John the Baptist's "raiment of camel's hair" (Matthew 3:4).

rent them—2 Kings 2:12—A commonly used method of showing mourning and bereavement.

LESSON OUTLINE

I. GOD'S POWER SOUGHT
   A. From Gilgal to Bethel
   B. From Bethel to Jericho
   C. From Jericho to Jordan
   D. From West of Jordan to Transjordan

II. GOD'S POWER RECEIVED
   A. Translation
   B. Continuity

III. GOD'S POWER IN ACTION
   A. Parting the Waters
   B. Advising Against a Fruitless Search
   C. Healing the Waters
   D. Cursing Rebellious Youths

LESSON EXPOSITION

INTRODUCTION

Last week we studied about a mighty demonstration of divine power, a chilling act of divine judgment, and a reassuring account of divine operation upon nature in order to bring about the end of drought and famine. In every instance Elijah, an utterly dedicated servant of Jehovah ready to do His bidding on any occasion, functioned as His direct agent. After these astounding events, Jezebel served notice that within twenty-four hours Elijah would be dead. Now the prophet, master only a few hours before of king and peasant alike under the Lord's anointing, fled the wrath of the evil queen. Sustained by angels, he reached a place of safety where God provided a mighty demonstration of His power and addressed him with words of assurance and challenge (1 Kings 19:1-18).

Included in the Lord's message to Elijah was the specific directive to anoint three men for special tasks—Hazael to be king over Syria, Jehu to be king over Israel, Elisha to be his own successor. Elijah immediately found Elisha and threw his mantle about the young man's shoulders (1 Kings 19:19-21). Elisha, recognizing the spiritual meaning behind this act, immediately made all necessary preparations and set out to accompany Elijah as his personal attendant.

Throughout the remainder of his life, Elijah, in an era of apostasy and immorality, continued to function with extraordinary force as spokesman for Jehovah and as agent of divine judgment. For example, he fearlessly and unhesitatingly condemned Ahab for his murder of Naboth and his appropriation of Naboth's vineyard and prophesied that Ahab's dynasty would cease as a direct result of this heinous sin (1 Kings 21:1-29). Some time later, when Ahab's successor Ahaziah attempted to arrest Elijah, the prophet called down fire from heaven to destroy the military contingents sent after him (2 Kings 1:9-16). In the dauntless Elijah, one discovers a sensitive temperament and highly individualistic personality traits and learns thereby that God can use for His glory any human instrument sufficiently dedicated to Him. One learns that the Lord even makes potential weaknesses into extraordinary strengths.

In the present lesson we witness the homegoing of this great servant of the Lord and the final designation of Elisha as his successor. We also witness Elisha's unremitting quest for spiritual power and thereby learn some of the steps to be taken if one would have power with God today.

I. GOD'S POWER SOUGHT (2 Kings 2:1-10)

A. From Gilgal to Bethel (vv. 1-3)

Elijah was now approaching the end of his sojourn on earth. Likely, the prophet and his attendant Elisha set out on their last journey together from that **Gilgal** located near Mount Gerizim in the northern kingdom. Geographically, it is the most likely starting point since the village near the Jordan River named Gilgal would fit less plausibly into the pattern of travel of Elijah and Elisha.

Elijah informed Elisha of his intention to visit Bethel and suggested that Elisha remain at Gilgal. But Elisha was already aware of his master's imminent departure from the world (v. 3) and had determined that he would accompany the prophet until the very end. Perhaps Elijah was testing Elisha. How intent was the young prophet on continuing his master's ministry? Would he be easily dissuaded from service at Elijah's side? If so, once the elder prophet was gone, some strong temptation or severe trial would quickly pull him away from divinely ordered ministry. Hence, Elijah forced his young companion to demonstrate his mettle, to reveal his dedication. And to this first test of his mettle, Elisha responded firmly, " 'As surely as the Lord lives and as you live, I will not leave you' " (v. 2, **New International Version**).

Elijah apparently was paying a last visit to each school of the prophets. Old Testament scholars speculate (on a sound basis) that the prophet had established such training grounds and places of spiritual retreat in order to perpetuate the true religion and to continue prophetic ministry in an era of apostasy and immorality.

These young prophets knew—as a result either of divine revelation or of information previously gleaned from Elijah himself—that the aging prophet would be taken from them that very day. Whether they were aware of the **mode** of his leave-taking remains uncertain. Probably, they did not have such full knowledge of what would take place. The young prophets quartered at Bethel queried Elisha, " 'Do you know that the Lord is going to take your master from you today?' " (v. 3, **New International Version**). Elisha's reply was direct: " 'Yes, I know . . . but do not speak of it' " (v. 3, **New International Version**).

Was it that Elisha's emotion surged too strongly for him to permit light conversation about so heartrending a matter? Or did he have information he did not think appropriate for sharing with these men—despite their religious orientation and spiritual insight? We do not know the answer, of course. What is obvious, however, is Elisha's determined, disciplined spirit. Nothing would dissuade him from his journey—from his quest. No idly speculative query from companions less personally concerned than he in this last earthly mission of his master would divert Elisha's single-minded attention either from Elijah or

from his own proper seriousness of demeanor and of purpose.

There are times when ordinary conversation deflects one from that meditative cast of mind appropriate to the particular moment—on a day devoted primarily to prayer and fasting, for instance, or during the few moments before public worship. We value the person who is talking to us but wish not to have our solitude interrupted. And, indeed, if we do not provide ourselves with such untrammeled periods of concentration upon the spiritual, our spirit becomes lean, and our life becomes less useful to the Master.

B. From Bethel to Jericho (vv. 4, 5)

Soon Elijah was ready to travel further—to Jericho. And again he urged Elisha to remain where he was, this time at Bethel. Elisha's response here was identical to that of verse 2—adamantly he affirmed his intention to accompany his master. If God and Elijah were alive (the strongest affirmation imaginable), he would not leave Elijah's side. The student prophets at Jericho posed the same question to Elisha as had those at Bethel and received the same reply. Elisha was well aware of the imminence of his master's departure, but chose not to discuss the matter. After all, these were rare, precious moments, not to be lightly spent in speculative conversation about Elijah. Rather, Elisha wuld either converse with his master or else engage in that silent communion of friend with friend which occurs when words are either insufficient or else superfluous.

C. From Jericho to Jordan (vv. 6-8)

6. And Elijah said unto him, Tarry, I pray thee, here; for the Lord hath sent me to Jordan. And he said, As the Lord liveth, and as thy soul liveth, I will not leave thee. And they two went on.

Once more, the elderly prophet suggested to Elisha that he remain behind—a final test of his faithfulness, determination, and dedication. Elisha's response was unvarying; his resolve, unshakable. Elijah knew the challenges that God's spokesman would face in a society which ignored law, prophet, and God; hence he set up test after test. Elisha too comprehended the nature of the tasks ahead of him, was ready to perform them, and therefore would not be dissuaded.

During my childhood, I heard a sermon on Elisha's quest for power which has remained riveted in my mind. The minister was an elderly Free Will Baptist country preacher, a godly man who was pastoring a tiny country church which offered little financial remuneration. The method of the preacher was allegorical. He viewed the final journey of Elijah and Elisha as a series of steps toward complete salvation, leading ultimately to the "second blessing," in his view an infilling of the Holy Spirit which produced entire sanctification. But the preaching was anointed, the recounting of the narrative was graphic, and the impact on my mind and spirit was permanent.

You see, since this preacher personified in his everyday living that level of dedication which he was preaching about that Sunday morning, the power behind his words was contagious. As a result, the impact of both the sermon and the life behind it has been lasting upon that tiny boy who listened so eagerly over thirty years ago.

Maybe Elijah's impact upon Elisha was analogous. The aging prophet had profoundly influenced—in day-by-day encounter—the younger man who accompanied him. And now Elisha was intent upon receiving a generous portion of power like that which had impelled his master and made him that fearless spokesman for truth which he had again and again proved himself to be.

7. And fifty men of the sons of the prophets went, and stood to view afar off: and they two stood by Jordan.

The company of the prophets was in a state of expectancy. They knew Elijah was to be taken from them and were both curious and concerned. They, without doubt, had engaged in speculation regarding Elisha's role after his master's death. Could there also have been some discussion regarding whether Elijah's successor should come from an apprenticeship rather than schooling such as they were receiving? Likely, more than a little sheer curiosity was operating. They might simply have wished to know what would happen to two men whom they knew and with whom they often must have engaged in intercessory prayer, held discussions, and enjoyed fellowship.

Elijah and Elisha meanwhile stood on the west bank of the Jordan River, poised—Elisha wondering, but Elijah sure of what he would now do and of where he would soon go. From a distance, the company of the prophets eyed the pair expectantly.

8. And Elijah took his mantle, and wrapped it together, and smote the waters, and they were divided hither and thither, so that they two went over on dry ground.

Elijah did not pause for long. He soon rolled up his mantle ("the sheepskin cape or capote, which covered his shoulders"—**Pulpit Commentary**) and struck the waters with it. The effect of his action was immediate: the waters divided, creating a dry path in the middle. This action constituted Elijah's last miracle. For years he had functioned as God's instrument, through his mightily inspired words proclaiming the will of Jehovah and through his mighty deeds demonstrating the power behind those words. Now God was ready to reward His faithful servant by translating him to glory. But first He would give to Elisha and the sons of the prophets who looked on from a distance a very appropriate final indication of the extraordinary dedication and spiritual power of this remarkable figure who had walked among them.

Can twentieth-century Christians who are completely "sold out to God" expect to witness supernatural evidences of the activity of the Holy Spirit in their life?

D. From West of Jordan to Transjordan (vv. 9, 10)

9. And it came to pass, when they were gone over, that Elijah said unto Elisha, Ask what I shall do for thee, before I be taken away from thee. And Elisha said, I pray thee, let a double portion of thy spirit be upon me.

The two men of God now walked through the middle of a miracle as they traversed the supernaturally created thoroughfare, likely glancing from time to time at the walls of water standing on the right and on the left. Now Elisha's persistence in accompanying Elijah and ministering to him until the very end of Elijah's earthly existence would be compensated, for the young man was invited to make his request. Elijah placed no bounds upon what would be granted—that would be up to God and, probably, also dependent upon the bounds of Elisha's faith and upon his boldness in asking. The young attendant upon Elijah had proved himself a worthy recipient of divine grace and power and must now exercise his spiritual maturity and even imagination in response to Elijah's invitation.

Is it possible that many Christians lack

spiritual blessings because they, oriented toward self-control, do not even ask for divine power, or else ask timidly, faithlessly, or even unimaginatively?

Elisha responded boldly and straightforwardly; he asked for "a double portion" of Elijah's spirit. Often interpreters consider Elisha's request to be for **twice as much**. This is not really a plausible view since it would seem to imply that God's power is "stuff," like a liquid, to be measured out fortuitously and regardless of need and circumstance. Some say Elisha's ten miracles, various in kind and mode, would indicate that he had spiritual power double that of his predecessor. But, again, such would be a mechanical, even low view of the operation of God's Spirit. The Holy Spirit functions in a man's life: (1) according to his consecration, (2) according to his need, and (3) according to the will of our sovereign God. The Lord chooses vessels of blessing and makes them adequate for ministry **as He wills**, and without exception He does all things well.

Scripture suggests an answer: "He must acknowledge the son of his unloved wife as the firstborn by giving him a double share of all he has. That son is the first sign of his father's strength. The right of the firstborn belongs to him" (Deuteronomy 21:17, **New International Version**). The eldest son received a double share of his father's goods under the Mosaic Code. Might not Elisha have been asking here for the right of the firstborn? If he were granted such a right, he would serve—like Elijah before him—as chief spokesman for the Lord and as supervisor of the schools of the prophets. He would have authority beyond that of the other prophets in the nation. The entire company of the prophets, as they yielded to the Lord, would exercise anointed ministries, but Elisha would exercise the chief spiritual authority. He would have supernatural signs of divine favor to back up that authority and to authenticate his ministry.

10. And he said, Thou hast asked a hard thing: nevertheless, if thou see me when I am taken from thee, it shall be so unto thee; but if not, it shall not be so.

Likely, Elisha's request was "hard" because what he had requested lay within the **divine** prerogative. Elijah's successor must be chosen and anointed by Jehovah; hence, Elijah could only set up a mechanism through which God could indicate His final selection or rejection of Elisha. Thus the test: "If you see me when I am taken from you, it will be yours—otherwise not" **(New International Version).**

How does God designate Christians for particular ministries within the body of Christ today?

II. GOD'S POWER RECEIVED (2 Kings 2:11-13)

A. Translation (vv. 11, 12)

11. And it came to pass, as they still went on, and talked, that, behold, there appeared a chariot of fire, and horses of fire, and parted them both asunder; and Elijah went up by a whirlwind into heaven.

Seemingly, the whirlwind was the means of locomotion for the chariot of fire which conveyed Elijah to heaven. If this chariot resembled military chariots (as seems likely from Elisha's comment in verse 12), what could be more appropriate than for God's dynamic spokesman who had fought for the spiritual life of Israel to be conveyed home in a replica of a chariot of war? Thus did God's mighty warrior for truth take leave of earth without having to die and thus did he enter the abode of God (for we must assume that such is the meaning of "heaven" in this verse).

12. And Elisha saw it, and he cried, My father, my father, the chariot of Israel, and the horsemen thereof. And he saw him no more: and he took hold of his own clothes, and rent them in two pieces.

So, Elisha, with divine permission, met Elijah's requirement for his receiving of the "double portion"—he witnessed the translation of his master. Now Elisha would assume the reins of prophetic leadership, functioning as head of the schools of the prophets and as anointed spokesman for Jehovah to the apostate nation. And as God had authenticated Elijah's ministry through clearly supernatural manifestations, so would He that of Elijah's successor. Since the temperaments of the two men differed, though, God would use Elisha in perfect accord with that personality which He had allowed to be formed within him.

Elisha's emotional outcry of verse 12 might possibly refer to Elijah's mode of transportation into eternity. However, that cryptic exclamation might also (as seems more likely) refer to Elijah himself. Elisha's "father," then, would himself be "the chariot of Israel, and the horsemen thereof." The image would in this case have been **suggested (Pulpit Commentary)** by Elisha's sight of the chariot of fire but would not refer to it. The structure of the sentence seems to support this reading: "chariot" and "horsemen" appear to rename "father." Elijah had indeed been the defense of Israel. His relationship with God had allowed him to function as God's instrument as he fought for Israel's moral and spiritual integrity against the forces of godlessness operating in the highest levels of the kingdom—even in the royal palace itself.

So Elijah and Elisha were now separated— the one to continue his intimate fellowship with God in heaven itself, the other to function as God's representative on earth. Elisha's first act, once he lost sight of Elijah (for, unlike Christ's disciples after His ascension, Elisha did not stand "gazing up into heaven"), was a forceful expression of grief, entirely appropriate for the venting of extreme emotion—a tearing of his garments.

Overt expression of grief is neither unmanly nor unspiritual. The emotion of grief, although often rooted in our selfishness (since it is **our loss** we usually mourn), is an inevitable outflow of our God-given human nature, neither to be indulged in inordinately nor to be checked unnaturally. In this case, the open expression of grief surely was the outcome of a godly affection which had grown with the years of intimate fellowship. We shall see, however, that Elisha would by no means allow himself to be paralyzed into inactivity by his loss; rather, he immediately would assume his new role and begin to act accordingly.

B. Continuity (v. 13)

13. He took up also the mantle of Elijah that fell from him, and went back, and stood by the bank of Jordan.

Elisha's taking up of Elijah's mantle, inevitable though that action was, yet serves to symbolize his assumption of his master's role. The **mantle** without the **authority** would be meaningless. But Elisha had, in accordance with the divine will, met the technical condition (a **sign** purely for Elisha himself since no one else witnessed it) and knew that he was now the authorized spokesman for Jehovah. He need not hesitate to display and to use as a symbol of authority that mantle of Elijah lying before him.

Hence, his second act (after the genuine expression of homage to his departed master) was to pick up the mantle. Next, we see him poised on the east bank of the Jordan River— this time alone and this time with the mantle in his hand. He would use that sign of spiritual authority immediately, and within view of the waiting sons of the prophets who would eagerly wish to see Elisha's behavior on this occasion.

III. GOD'S POWER IN ACTION (2 Kings 2: 14-25)

A. Parting the Waters (vv. 14, 15)

14. And he took the mantle of Elijah that fell from him, and smote the waters, and said, Where is the Lord God of Elijah? and when he also had smitten the waters, they parted hither and thither: and Elisha went over.

Elisha likely had never before been employed as God's instrument in the display of the supernatural. He had instead stood at Elijah's side as Jehovah had mightily worked through him. Now, with a bold demeanor but certainly not without trepidation, he exercised his newly acquired authority.

Do Christian believers often fail to avail themselves of spiritual privileges because of their lack of understanding of spiritual authority?

Elisha's question need not be seen as arrogant; rather, the prophet was flexing his spiritual muscles, trying out his newfound role. And he discovered that the God of Elijah was indeed **his** God as well—**omnipresent, omniscient,** and, as is most relevant here, **omnipotent.** For the waters immediately parted, and the prophet crossed over to the west bank of Jordan.

How would God respond if a modern-day believer—in complete sincerity—put forth a challenge such as that of Elisha?

"There was a boy dying in one of the English counties. He had heard Whitefield, with his marvelous voice, and glowing heart, preach about the Lord Jesus Christ, and the impression never left him. While yet a child, he had to die; and as the fever flush mounted to his brow, and as the fire burned in his eye, he said, 'I should like to go to Mr.

Whitefield's God.' What a testimony! what a recommendation!" **(The Biblical Illustrator).** Elisha, similarly, invoked Elijah's God—the living God, sovereign over that universe which He had created long since and able to manipulate its forces at His will.

15. And when the sons of the prophets which were to view at Jericho saw him, they said, The spirit of Elijah doth rest on Elisha. And they came to meet him, and bowed themselves to the ground before him.

The sons of the prophets witnessed Elisha's first miracle and discerned immediately its implications: Elisha now bore that spiritual authority which Elijah previously had exercised. They therefore were ready to submit humbly to his oversight. Whether these devoted men knew it or not, "the spirit" now resting upon Elisha was more than the "spirit of Elijah"; it was in fact the Spirit of the Lord God. Elisha was acting **in** "the spirit of Elijah," however, as he now exercised similar spiritual authority.

One notes that the authority which the sons of the prophets recognized in Elisha was in fact **spiritual.** Men may try to mimic that divine anointing, they may adopt various substitutes for it, or they may try to deny its validity or its force; but its absence will readily be apparent in their lives and in their ministries, for God's work cannot be pursued successfully without the anointing of the Holy Spirit.

B. Advising Against a Fruitless Search (vv. 16-18)

The sons of the prophets did not understand that Elijah had been translated to glory; they thought his body might have been cast down upon some nearby mountain peak or into some valley close by. They therefore implored Elisha to allow a party of fifty men to search for the prophet's body. After they had asked repeatedly, Elisha relented and allowed what he knew would be a fruitless search. Actually, it was an act of doubt rather than of faith, it was backward looking rather than forward looking, and, as we know, it was foredoomed to failure.

C. Healing the Waters (vv. 19-22)

Elisha, still at Jericho (from whence he had sent out the search party for Elijah), was now approached by the men of that city concerning the quality of its water. The city was a pleasant enough location, but its water was causing disease and death and preventing the growth of food. The prophet now performed his second miracle. As a symbol of cleansing, of purification, he threw salt into the waters and then proclaimed a word of healing from the Lord. Immediately a wonderful change was evident.

D. Cursing Rebellious Youths (vv. 23-25)

Elisha's spiritual authority was challenged and, indeed, gross disrespect for his person was shown as the prophet went from Jericho to Bethel. A number of "young lads" mocked him, saying, " 'Go up, you baldhead; go up, you baldhead!' " (v. 23, **New American Standard).** Elisha's response was severe, but he did not react in pique; if he had, God would not have honored his declaration of judgment. Rather, he pronounced an act of judgment upon godless young men who were regardless of divine authority and devoid of respect for God's representatives. Forty-two of these boys were mauled by bears.

This judgment from God served as a warning to the entire populace that Jehovah still lived, even though Elijah was no longer present, and that He would not stand idly by as they mocked His messenger and defied His will. Elisha, then, had indeed proved his mettle: He was God's anointed servant, ready to do His bidding and utterly dedicated to the divine purpose for himself and for the nation of Israel.

REVIEW QUESTIONS

1. Why did Elijah repeatedly urge Elisha not to accompany him on his last journey?

2. What was the meaning of Elisha's response to the sons of the prophets?

3. What was Elijah's last miracle?

4. What was Elisha's last request of Elijah?

5. How was Elijah carried to heaven?

GOLDEN TEXT HOMILY

"I PRAY THEE, LET A DOUBLE PORTION OF THY SPIRIT BE UPON ME" (2 Kings 2:9).

Elisha had stood the test of unswerving fidelity and perseverance. Elijah paused to ask him what he desired. As Solomon, when he came to the throne of Israel, asked not for riches, honor, or a long life, but rather a wise and understanding heart, so Elisha realized his request should be limited to that which was most important for the minister of God so that he could meet the needs of the people; accordingly, he requested **a double portion** of Elijah's spirit.

C. H. Irvin reminds us that, "He who would lead and teach others must be doubly spiritual, doubly wise, doubly careful, doubly holy, doubly zealous and scrupulous for the honor and cause of Christ. The spirit of Elijah was needed then, and it is needed still. The sins of his time are the sins of our own time. There is the same immorality, the same covetousness, the same forgetfulness of God, the same absorption in the concerns and pleasures of the present world. We need more men with the spirit of Elijah, who will be faithful to God and conscience at any cost, who will rebuke sin in high places and in any place. . . . We need more men with the spirit of Elijah, to ask, Who is on the Lord's side? and to cry aloud to the faltering, weak-kneed, half-hearted Christians, How long halt ye between two opinions? If the Lord be God, follow him; but if the world be your god, follow it."

The Great God who allowed a double portion of the Spirit to fall on Elisha, is ready to respond to the pleas of all who desire spiritual power for kingdom service.—**James E. Humbertson, Editorial Director, Evangelical Commentary**, Pathway Press, Cleveland, Tennessee

SENTENCE SERMONS

OBEDIENCE IS THE key to receiving spiritual power.

—**Selected**

THERE ARE TWO world powers, the sword and the Spirit, but the Spirit has always vanquished the sword.

—**Napoleon**

I ASK NOT WEALTH, but power to take
And use the things I have aright;
Not years, but wisdom that shall make
My life a profit and delight.

—**Phobee Cary**

MY HUMAN BEST filled with the Holy Spirit makes a good motto.

—**"Sunday School Journal"**

EVANGELISTIC APPLICATION

WE NEED GOD'S POWER TO BE EFFECTIVE WITNESSES.

Elisha relentlessly quested for divine power. Nothing would dissuade him from his intention to receive that spiritual anointing which had rested upon Elijah and rendered him mighty for God. The young prophet: (1) followed closely and unremittingly, (2) requested boldly, and (3) received graciously.

Twentieth-century Christians must do no less, for our victorious living depends upon our appropriation of divine resources. To overcome the spiritual foes which surely will beset us requires the fullness of the Spirit. No Christian can be an effective witness whose life is not dedicated fully to Christ. It is as the Holy Spirit indwells us, motivates us, and brings the Word of God alive in our heart that we become able to walk with Christ, in love—living out the life of Christ as we conform to His image. Furthermore, we will be emboldened to witness as we walk daily in the Spirit. We will in fact feel impelled to share that life surging within us rather than listlessly seeking to fulfill a burdensome sense of obligation to witness. Hence, we must have the anointing of the Spirit resting upon us daily if we would be effective witnesses for Jesus Christ.

What are the steps which lead to this life in the Spirit which inspires and enables powerful witnessing? (1) We must be genuinely converted. (2) We must deliberately cultivate a spiritual lifestyle—praying, reading the Word of God, and worshiping both privately and in community with fellow believers. (3) We must be baptized in the Spirit like the disciples on the Day of Pentecost—an enduement of divine power for service. (4) Finally, we must remain yielded constantly to the Spirit's control. Having met these conditions, we will inevitably be witnesses of great power through both **what we say** and **what we are**.

ILLUMINATING THE LESSON

It costs much to obtain the power of the Spirit. It costs self-surrender and humiliation and the yielding up of the most precious things to God. It costs the perseverance of long waiting and the faith of strong trust. But when we are really in that power, we shall find this difference: whereas before it was hard for us to do the easiest things, now it is easy for us to do the hardest things. James Hervey, the friend of the Wesleys at Oxford, describes the change which took place in him through the anointing by the Spirit: that while his preaching was once like the firing of an arrow, all the speed and force thereof depending on the strength of his arm in bending the bow, now it was like firing a rifle-ball, the whole force depending upon the powder back of the ball, and needing only a finger-touch to let it off.—**A. J. Gordon**

DAILY DEVOTIONAL GUIDE

M. Persistence in Seeking God's Power. 2 Kings 2:1-5
T. Exercising the Spirit's Power. 2 Kings 2:19-22
W. God's Promised Power. Joel 2:23-32
T. Christ's Promise to Believers. John 14:18-26
F. Receiving God's Power. Acts 2:1-4, 38, 39
S. God's Power Is for Godly People. Acts 19:11-18

July 26, 1981

Showing Concern for Others

Bible Background: 2 Kings 6:24—7:20

Time: Around 885 B.C.

Place: Samaria

Supplemental References: Isaiah 59:16-21; Romans 9:1-3; 2 Corinthians 4:1-18

Golden Text: "None of us liveth to himself, and no man dieth to himself" (Romans 14:7).

Central Truth: It is a privilege and duty of believers to share the gospel with others.

Evangelistic Emphasis: The message of salvation brings good tidings to a lost soul.

PRINTED TEXT

2 Kings 6:24. And it came to pass after this, that Ben-hadad king of Syria gathered all his host, and went up, and besieged Samaria.

25. And there was a great famine in Samaria: and, behold, they besieged it, until an ass's head was sold for fourscore pieces of silver, and the fourth part of a cab of dove's dung for five pieces of silver.

7:3. And there were four leprous men at the entering in of the gate: and they said one to another, Why sit we here until we die?

4. If we say, We will enter into the city, then the famine is in the city, and we shall die there: and if we sit still here, we die also. Now therefore come, and let us fall unto the host of the Syrians: if they save us alive, we shall live; and if they kill us, we shall but die.

5. And they rose up in the twilight, to go unto the camp of the Syrians: and when they were come to the uttermost part of the camp of Syria, behold, there was no man there.

6. For the Lord had made the host of the Syrians to hear a noise of chariots, and a noise of horses, even the noise of a great host: and they said one to another, Lo, the king of Israel hath hired against us the kings of the Hittites, and the kings of the Egyptians, to come upon us.

7. Wherefore they arose and fled in the twilight, and left their tents, and their horses, and their asses, even the camp as it was, and fled for their life.

8. And when these lepers came to the uttermost part of the camp, they went into one tent, and did eat and drink, and carried thence silver, and gold, and raiment, and went and hid it; and came again, and entered into another tent, and carried thence also, and went and hid it.

9. Then they said one to another, We do not well: this day is a day of good tidings, and we hold our peace: if we tarry till the morning light, some mischief will come upon us: now therefore come, that we may go and tell the king's household.

10. So they came and called unto the porter of the city: and they told them, saying, We came to the camp of the Syrians, and, behold, there was no man there, neither voice of man, but horses tied, and asses tied, and the tents as they were.

11. And he called the porters; and they told it to the king's house within.

DICTIONARY

ass's head—2 Kings 6:25—The boniest part of an unclean animal
fourth part of a cab—2 Kings 6:25—About ten cubic inches
Hittites (HIT-tights)—2 Kings 7:6—One of the three great powers that confronted early Israel. The western part of the Fertile Cresent is now confirmed to have been the land of the Hittites.

LESSON OUTLINE

I. DISTRESSING CONDITIONS
   A. An Enemy's Siege
   B. An Extensive Famine
   C. Extreme Alternatives

II. JOYFUL DISCOVERY
   A. A Venture of Faith
   B. An Empty Camp
   C. A Bountiful Supply

III. ACTIVE CONCERN
   A. An Awakened Conscience
   B. A Shared Report

LESSON EXPOSITION

INTRODUCTION

Elisha, whose quest for spiritual power was the subject of our studies last week, again plays an important role in the lesson for today. In the former lesson the portion of God's power which he requested from Elijah was evidenced by the parting of the waters of the River Jordan when he struck the water with his mantle. The continued anointing on him is evidenced in today's lesson by the fulfillment of the prophecy he made concerning the end of the siege of Samaria and of the abundance of food for a famine-stricken city.

The background of the lesson goes back several chapters in the Book of 2 Kings. In 2 Kings 6:15-23, the account is given of a blindness the Lord inflicted on the Syrians when they surrounded the city of Dothan in an effort to capture Elisha. But in spite of this obvious intervention by Jehovah, Ben-hadad II, king of Syria, could not long withhold his ambition to reduce Israel to the status of a tributary part of his dominion. Consequently, after a period of peace, he conducted a prolonged siege of Samaria which brought about a famine in the city.

That God used Elisha to fulfill His purpose is a most inspiring backdrop to our lesson; but it is in fact the account of four leprous men—men who were willing to share the spoils of a deserted camp with the inhabitants of a famine-stricken city—that speaks to us at the human level. Their concern reveals to us that God can and will use what society might classify as unseemly vessels to accomplish His purpose. As if to abase human pride, He purposely selects human instruments which the wisdom of men would scorn.

I. DISTRESSING CONDITIONS (2 Kings 6: 24, 25; 7:3, 4)

A. An Enemy's Siege (v. 24)

24. And it came to pass after this, that Ben-hadad king of Syria gathered all his host, and went up, and besieged Samaria.

Just how long a time the words "after this" implies cannot be determined exactly. Some scholars establish 884 B.C. as the time when Hazael murdered Ben-hadad. If this date is correct, it would give some support that "after this" might refer to a period of up to one year. There are reasons to believe that a peace did exist for some time due to the influence for good exerted by Elisha.

B. An Extensive Famine (vv. 6:25—7:2)

25. And there was a great famine in Samaria: and, behold, they besieged it, until an ass's head was sold for fourscore pieces of silver, and the fourth part of a cab of dove's dung for five pieces of silver.

(2 Kings 6:26—7:2 is not included in the printed text.)

In addition to verse 25, a description of the deplorable famine in Samaria is given in verses 26-29.

The long siege by Syria had caused the money behind the walled city to become cheap; food, though, became so expensive that only the rich could eat. Even the bony head of an ass, which would not ordinarily be thought of as food, commanded a price of eighty pieces of silver—equal to about fifty dollars. Likewise, about ten cubic inches of dove's dung was sold for five pieces of silver. Indeed, so hard put were some of the people that they resorted to eating their children. One mother complained to the king that another woman failed to keep her part of an agreement between them when it came turn to eat her child.

Learning of these extreme conditions as he walked upon the wall, King Jehoram tore his royal clothes and exposed for the people to notice the sackcloth that he wore next to his skin. The wearing of sackcloth was a religious gesture which Jehoram had evidently conjured up in an effort to get help from the God of Elisha.

After viewing the extreme conditions, Jehoram vowed that he would have the head of Elisha (v. 31), which indicates that he blamed the prophet for the plight of the city.

It can only be surmised, but apparently Elisha had advised that under no conditions should the city be given up, and had promised that God would deliver it, if the people humbled themselves before Him and if they prayed for His assistance. Perhaps King Jehoram thought that he had done his part by putting on the sackcloth; but when help did not come he flew into a rage for which the prophet was to pay a penalty. However, the rage soon gave way to a better manifestation from his conscience. The king hastened after the messenger he had already dispatched to behead Elisha. He was therefore showing his intentions to prevent a murderous act which he had commanded in his rage.

Before either the first messenger or the one who was dispatched to stop him arrived, Elisha had already informed the elders who had gathered at his house of the two approaching men. Consequently he commanded the elders to shut the door against the first messenger, because he knew that on the heels of that messenger was the approach of one with a different intent.

The action of Elisha was not designed to resist the authority of the king's messenger, but was an act of prudence by which he delayed the carrying out of an unrighteous and murderous command which had been issued in a fit of anger. By his action, Elisha rendered a service to the king.

Under the direction of the Spirit of God, Elisha prophesied that the shortage of food would end the very next day. The grains usually available for food, but now unavailable at any price, would be sold at normal prices (7:1). The king's captain who had expressed disbelief was assured that he would witness the relief to the inhabitants of the city, but that he himself would not eat thereof.

C. Extreme Alternatives (7:3, 4)

3. And there were four leprous men at the entering in of the gate: and they said one to another, Why sit we here until we die?

4. If we say, We will enter into the city, then the famine is in the city, and we shall die there: and if we sit still here, we die also. Now therefore come, and let us fall unto the host of the Syrians: if they save us alive, we shall live; and if they kill us, we shall but die.

Four lepers were at the gate of the city of Samaria, separated from human society in accordance with the Law (Leviticus, chapters 13, 14). Probably they resided in a small hut erected for that purpose, just as some present-day lepers have their huts by the entrance of the Zion Gate. If their presence had been noticed by the Syrians, no attention was given to them, for their physical condition limited them from being any sort of military threat.

Ordinarily the lepers received food from the city, either through appropriations or from private charitable deeds by families and friends. However, the famine of Samaria made it necessary to cancel the rations of food. There was no help available from the Samaritans even if the lepers were to go into the city. Consequently, there was only one remaining chance for help—from the Syrians.

As the lepers pondered their condition and the limited alternatives, they reasoned that the Syrians might help them. But if the Syrians would kill them, they fully recognized that the enemy warriors would be bringing about a death that was certain to come anyhow.

Are there conditions of hopelessness that cause men to completely abandon any chance for help?

II. JOYFUL DISCOVERY (2 Kings 7:5-8)

A. A Venture by Faith (v. 5)

5. And they rose up in the twilight, to go unto the camp of the Syrians: and when they were come to the uttermost part of the camp of Syria, behold, there was no man there.

Although the lepers had calculated the risk

they would take by entering the camp of the Syrians, the time came when it was necessary to act. They rose up in the twilight and made their way to the camp of the Syrians.

It is often at the point of desperation that men will rise from their position of hopelessness to explore alternatives and find that God, in His mercy, has arranged a way of escape. In his commentary on 2 Kings, Loyal R. Ringenberg says, "Four lepers sat outside the walls of Samaria in evident silence. They had given up. When a man comes to such a condition he sometimes finds the ray of light that leads to a new beginning. There is a blind optimism which merely makes believe that everything is all right. Under the delusion, the capacity for being excited about anything is lost. Blind resignation and complacency set in and a person does little more than wait for death. The four lepers caught themselves giving up; then they bestirred themselves and found the best trickling of light possible. They followed it and came out wonderfully well. Christian optimism is justifiable on the basis of the fact that the supreme Sovereign of the world is a being of redemptive providence and mercy" **(Comments on 2 Kings).**

Name some biblical examples of divine help when a call of desperation was sounded.

B. An Empty Camp (vv. 6, 7)

6. For the Lord had made the host of the Syrians to hear a noise of chariots, and a noise of horses, even the noise of a great host: and they said one to another, Lo, the king of Israel hath hired against us the kings of the Hittites and the kings of the Egyptians, to come upon us.

7. Wherefore they arose and fled in the twilight, and left their tents, and their horses, and their asses, even the camp as it was, and fled for their life.

The last part of verse 5 indicates that the lepers found no one at the Syrian camp when they entered into its uttermost part—the part where the advanced guards would have been. God had intervened in behalf of Samaria. King Ben-hadad could go no farther than God permitted.

Consider the twofold illusion that God brought to bear on the Syrians. First, there was an auditory illusion, the mistaking of a noise for a host of warriors. Second, there was a psychological and logical illusion of supposing that what they heard must be the allied forces of Egypt and the Hittites. How the noise was produced is impossible to say. In their **Commentary on the Old Testament, Vol. 6**, Keil and Delitzsch suggest, "The miracle by which God delivered Samaria from the famine or from surrendering to the foe, consisted of an oral delusion, namely, in the fact that the besiegers thought they heard the march of hostile armies from the north and from the south. . . . Whether the noise which they heard had any objective reality, say a miracle buzzing in the air, or whether it was merely a deception of the senses produced in their ears by the Lord is uncertain; and this is a matter of no importance, since in either case it was produced miraculously at the precise time by God."

It was no very improbable supposition on the part of the Syrians that King Jehoram had called in the aid of the Hittite confederacy and that they had marched an army to his assistance. Egyptian history shows that about that date, Egypt was becoming disintegrated and that two or three distinct dynasties were sometimes ruling at the same time in different parts of the country. Hence, the term "kings of Egypt."

In their panic, the Syrians did not stop to weigh the probabilities or to think how unlikely it was that such a simultaneous attack—one from the north and one from the south—could have been arranged between powers so remote from each other. They realized that if they were to escape it was necessary to travel light and to leave during the twilight. Consequently, the Syrians left camp in a hurry. They did not even take the time to take their tents, horses, asses, or food supply.

C. A Bountiful Supply (v. 8)

8. And when these lepers came to the uttermost part of the camp, they went into one tent, and did eat and drink, and carried thence silver, and gold, and raiment, and went and hid it; and came again, and entered into another tent, and carried thence also, and went and hid it.

We do not know exactly how the lepers interpreted the fact of the empty camp and the abundance of food. We do know that it was natural for the starving men to pounce upon the food in an effort to satisfy their need. They ate and drank until they were filled.

The lepers' attention was also drawn to the silver, gold, and raiment that was left by the Syrians. They gathered the precious treasures from one tent and then another and went and hid them. In his commentary on 2 Kings, G. Rawlinson reminds us that the presence of precious jewelry and trappings was not unusual in military camps. "Orientals, as well as those of the Western world, carried with them vast quantities of precious metals in the shape of gold and silver vases, goblets, dishes, chains, and trappings. . . . When the camp of Mardonius at Plataea fell into the hands of the Greeks, there were found in it 'many tents richly adorned with furniture of gold and silver, many couches covered with plates of the same, and many golden bowls, goblets, and other drinking vessels. On the carriage were bags of gold and silver kettles; and the bodies of the slain furnished bracelets and chains, not to mention embroidered apparel.' The camp of the Syrians would scarcely have been so richly provided; but it still contained, no doubt, a very large amount of valuable plunder" **(Pulpit Commentary, Vol. 5).**

The lepers had no right by military standards to pick up the spoil. It belonged to the nation, and it was probably the king's right to apportion it. The lepers were undoubtedly aware of this condition. Consequently, they had to conceal the treasures that they gathered.

Would the lepers have citizenship rights?

III. ACTIVE CONCERN (2 Kings 7:9-11)

A. An Awakened Conscience (v. 9)

9. Then they said one to another, We do not well: this day is a day of good tidings, and we hold our peace: if we tarry till the morning light, some mischief will come upon us: now therefore come, that we may go and tell the king's household.

After feasting on the food left by the Syrians, and after gathering some of the spoil, the lepers experienced an awakening of conscience. Perhaps it was a somewhat tardy recognition of what their duty required of them. Keil and Delitzsch quote Grotius, "For it is the duty of citizens to make known things relating to public safety" **(Commentary on the Old Testament, Vol. 6).**

Reflecting on the obligation imposed upon them by the knowledge of the good news, the lepers began experiencing some self-reproach for their silence. They were convinced that some retribution would fall on them if they continued in their silence. Some commentators translate the phrase "guilt will find us," "we shall incur blame," "we shall be accused of wrongdoing."

The Hebrew word *'awon* is a comprehensive word which includes not only the "iniquity" itself, but also the consequences. In Genesis 4:13, the English rendering is given as "punishment." In fact, the prophets were always insistent that sin could not be separated from its consequences, so much so that the same word can be used for both **(The Interpreter's Bible).**

Alexander MacLaren adds a present-day application to the thought of mute Christians when he reflects on the silence of the lepers. "These four men had some superstitious idea that mischief might come upon them in the darkness. But they expressed a truth when they said, 'If we be silent, some punishment will find us.' . . . Be sure of this, that convictions unspoken, like plants grown in a cellar, will get very white in the stems and will bear no fruit. A religion which is dumb will very soon tend to lose its possession of truth and if you carry that great gift hid away in your heart it will be like locking up some singing bird in a box. When you come to open it, the bird will be dead. There shall stand in that last day, humble workers before the Throne who will say, 'Behold, I and the children whom Thou hast given me.' And there will stand some before the throne, solitary and lonesome" **(Expositions of Holy Scripture, Vol. 2).**

With pricked conscience, the lepers resolved to announce the joyful event in the king's household (the king's court—the medium through which the king was normally approached). So they set out on the journey to announce to a famine-stricken city the good news of a bountiful supply of food.

What evangelistic message do you receive from the words of the lepers, "We do not well: this day is a day of good tidings, and we hold our peace"?

B. A Shared Report (vv. 10, 11)

10. So they came and called unto the porter of the city: and they told them, saying, We came to the camp of the Syrians, and, behold, there was no man there, neither voice of man, but horses tied, and asses tied, and the tents as they were.

11. And he called the porters; and they told it to the king's house within.

The word **porter** ("gateman") is used collectively. This is evident from the words which follow, "they told them." The lepers gave a report of the status of the camp as they found it—no men in the camp, but horses, asses, tents, and food.

King Jehoram received the news but was suspicious of it. He suspected that the Syrians had gone away from the camp with the thought that the hungry Samaritans would storm the camp, then they, the Syrians, would return and capture them. In verses 13-15 the account is given of the return of the king's messengers with confirmation that his suspicion was groundless. Consequently, the people swarmed into the abandoned Syrian camp and obtained the food they desperately needed.

Elisha's prediction concerning conditions of relief and the death of the king's captain was fulfilled. The captain, appointed to keep order in the gate where the corn was sold, saw the wonderful fall of prices within twenty-four hours which Elisha had prophesied; but he did not "eat thereof." He didn't obtain any benefit from the sudden plenty, since he perished before he could profit by it. "For the people trode upon him in the gate, and he died" (v. 20).

Are famine conditions always a punishment from God because of waywardness of leaders? Explain.

REVIEW QUESTIONS

1. What actions had been taken by Benhadad to bring about the famine conditions?
2. What value did money have during the famine?
3. What part did the four lepers play in finding food?
4. What had happened to the Syrian army?
5. What spiritual applications do you draw from this lesson?

GOLDEN TEXT HOMILY

"NONE OF US LIVETH TO HIMSELF, AND NO MAN DIETH TO HIMSELF" (Romans 14:7).

In essence, Paul is dealing with the subject of ownership. Man is not a self contained individual. All that he is and all that he will become is lived in the eyes of God. We are owned by and live a life in relation to Christ.

Man also lives his life in relation to others. The increased physical contact we will experience over the next decade will be intensified. By the end of this century the world's population will have exceeded six and one-half billion. The whole world is our neighbor; and all of it is reachable in mere hours by flight. Man finds himself bound more closely with the masses around him. Nothing man does affects only himself. Rather, everything man does has consequences which affect others. Isolation is simply not possible; not from fellow men or from God.

The individual tends to question his own personal worth and lose his sense of identity. God's care for ones personal needs is applicable to all. The search for identity and personal worth is answered by the Christian concept that we are God's creation owned by God. Whether we live or die we belong to the Lord. Christ is forever present in our life. Do our actions tell others that Christ owns us?
—**Tom L. Murray, Assistant to the President, Southwestern College, Oklahoma City, Oklahoma**

SENTENCE SERMONS

IT IS A PRIVILEGE and duty of believers to share the gospel with others.
—**Selected**

BLESSED ARE THE HAPPINESS makers; blessed are they that remove friction, that make the course of life smooth and the converse of men gentle.
—**Henry Ward Beecher**

"BEAR YE ONE another's burdens and so fulfill the law of Christ."
—**James (4:17)**

THERE IS NO EXERCISE better for the heart than reaching down and lifting people up.
—**John Andrew Holmer**

EVANGELISTIC APPLICATION

THE MESSAGE OF SALVATION BRINGS GOOD TIDINGS TO A LOST SOUL.

Matthew Henry once wrote, "The individual is required under pain of being stunted and enfeebled in his own development if he disobeys, to carry others along with him in his march toward perfection." Anywhere and everywhere the possession of advantage, of means of happiness, imposes the obligation to share with those who lack it, else mischief comes upon one. No greater obligation rests on the Christian family than that of sharing the good news of redemption with lost and searching humanity.

The story of the four lepers at the gate of Samaria is one of the great missionary scriptures of the Bible. For all of us this is a day of good tidings—the glad tidings of great joy announced by the Christmas angels, which are not for us only but for all the people. This is the burden of Mary A. Thomson's poetry:

> . . . how many thousands still are lying
> Bound in the darksome prison house of sin,
> With none to tell them of the Savior's dying,
> Or of the life he died for them to win.

Are we failing to publish glad tidings? Then mischief will come upon us. If we have received this unspeakable gift, the unsearchable riches of Christ, into our own lives, then it must be upon pain of moral deterioration if we do not have the passion to make this truth prevail.—**Excerpts from the "Interpreter's Bible"**

ILLUMINATING THE LESSON

Is anybody happier
  Because you passed his way?
Does anyone remember
  That you spoke to him today?
This day is almost over,
  And its toiling time is through;
Is there anyone to utter now,
  A friendly word for you?
Can you say tonight in passing,
  With the day that slipped so fast,
That you helped a single person,
  Of the many that you passed?
Is a single heart rejoicing,
  Over what you did or said?
Does one whose hopes were fading
  Now with courage look ahead?
Did you waste the day, or lose it?
Was it well or poorly spent?
Did you leave a trail of kindness,
Or a scar of discontent?

—**Anonymous**

DAILY DEVOTIONAL GUIDE

M. Facing Desperate Conditions. 2 Kings 6: 26-30

T. Doubting a Glorious Report. 2 Kings 7: 12-20

W. Realizing an Obligation. Romans 1:7-17

T. Revealing an Endless Concern. Romans 9:1-5

F. Joyful Sharing. 2 Corinthians 9:6-15

S. Expressing Concern With Love. 1 John 3:16-24

August 2, 1981

Principles of Success

Bible Background: 2 Chronicles 19:1—20:37

Time: Around 853 B.C.

Place: Samaria

Supplemental References: Habakkuk 3:1-19; Matthew 16:24-27; Revelation 3:21

Golden Text: "Believe in the Lord your God, so shall ye be established; believe his prophets, so shall ye prosper" (2 Chronicles 20:20).

Central Truth: Living close to God brings an assurance of His help during times of adversity.

Evangelistic Emphasis: When people turn to the Lord He will deliver them from sin.

PRINTED TEXT

2 Chronicles 20:14. Then upon Jahaziel the son of Zechariah, the son of Benaiah, the son of Jeiel, the son of Mattaniah, a Levite of the sons of Asaph, came the Spirit of the Lord in the midst of the congregation;

15. And he said, Hearken ye, all Judah, and ye inhabitants of Jerusalem, and thou king Jehoshaphat, Thus saith the Lord unto you, Be not afraid nor dismayed by reason of this great multitude; for the battle is not your's, but God's.

16. To morrow go ye down against them: Behold, they come up by the cliff of Ziz; and ye shall find them at the end of the brook, before the wilderness of Jeruel.

17. Ye shall not need to fight in this battle: set yourselves, stand ye still, and see the salvation of the Lord with you, O Judah and Jerusalem: fear not, nor be dismayed; to morrow go out against them: for the Lord will be with you.

18. And Jehoshaphat bowed his head with his face to the ground: and all Judah and the inhabitants of Jerusalem fell before the Lord, worshipping the Lord.

19. And the Levites, of the children of the Kohathites, and of the children of the Korhites, stood up to praise the Lord God of Israel with a loud voice on high.

20. And they rose early in the morning, and went forth into the wilderness of Tekoa: and as they went forth, Jehoshaphat stood and said, Hear me, O Judah, and ye inhabitants of Jerusalem; Believe in the Lord your God, so shall ye be established; believe his prophets, so shall ye prosper.

21. And when he had consulted with the people, he appointed singers unto the Lord, and that should praise the beauty of holiness, as they went out before the army, and to say, Praise the Lord; for his mercy endureth for ever.

22. And when they began to sing and to praise, the Lord set ambushments against the children of Ammon, Moab, and mount Seir, which were come against Judah; and they were smitten.

23. For the children of Ammon and Moab stood up against the inhabitants of mount Seir, utterly to slay and destroy them: and when they had made an end of the inhabitants of Seir, every one helped to destroy another.

DICTIONARY

Jahaziel (ja-HAY-zee-el)—2 Chronicles 20:14—In the time of peril he was led by the Holy Spirit to announce a victory when defeat seemed certain.
Zechariah (zek-uh-RYE-uh)—2 Chronicles 20:14—A common Hebrew name, twenty-eight of which are given in biblical listings. This one is the father of Jahaziel.
Benaiah (bee-NAY-yah)—2 Chronicles 20:14—Father of Zechariah mentioned in the lesson.
Jehoshaphat (jee-HOSH-uh-fat)—2 Chronicles 20:15—One of the ablest rulers of Judah. He reigned from about 873 to 849 B.C.
cliff of Ziz . . . wilderness of Jeruel (jee-ROO-el)—2 Chronicles 20:16—The exact location of these places is unknown, but they are close to the city of En-gedi (v. 2) which is on the edge of the Dead Sea about midway between the northern and southern ends of that body of water.

LESSON OUTLINE

I. SEEKING GOD
   A. An Enemy's Approach
   B. A Leader's Response
   C. A Prayer for Help
II. TRUSTING GOD
   A. Families in Prayer
   B. Downfall of Enemy Foretold
III. PRAISING GOD
   A. Gratitude Expressed
   B. The Enemy Defeated
   C. The Triumphant Return

LESSON EXPOSITION

INTRODUCTION

In the lesson for today our attention is turned to King Jehoshaphat, son of Asa and fourth in lineal descent from Solomon. The twenty-five-year reign of Jehoshaphat (872-848 B.C.) was one of the most encouraging and hopeful eras in the religious history of Judah.

In the early years of his reign Jehoshaphat revived the policies of religious reform which had been so effective in the first part of Asa's kingship. Since Jehoshaphat was thirty-five years old when he began to reign, he, during his childhood, very likely had come under the influence of Judah's great religious leaders.

His program of reform was well organized. Five princes who were accompanied by nine principal Levites and two priests were sent throughout Judah to teach the Law. Besides this, the high places and the groves were removed so that the people would not be diverted to them. Instead of seeking the idol Baal, as the people probably had done during the last two decades of Asa's reign, Jehoshaphat and the people turned to God.

The revived interest and worship of Jehovah had a wholesome effect on the surrounding nations as well as on Judah. When Jehoshaphat fenced and fortified some of his cities, the Philistines and Arabs were discouraged from making any attacks on Judah. Rather, they developed a practice of bringing tribute and gifts to King Jehoshaphat. This providential favor and support prompted him to build throughout his territory store cities and fortresses staffed with military units. In addition to the military units throughout the land, he had five army commanders in the city of Jerusalem. Consequently, under the reign of Jehosphaphat, the southern kingdom prospered both religiously and politically. "And the fear of the Lord fell upon all the kingdoms of the lands that were round about Judah, so that they made no war against Jehoshaphat" (2 Chronicles 17:10).

In the course of years, Jehoshaphat's oldest son Jehoram was married to Athaliah, Ahab's daughter by Jezebel. Perhaps Jehoshaphat thought this union of the two kingdoms a good policy in that it might result in the union of the two kingdoms under his own posterity. But this step displeased God, was extremely hurtful to Jehoshaphat, and offered a mischievous example to his subjects.

It appears that at least ten years passed between verses 1 and 2 of 2 Chronicles 18. The year was about 853 B.C. Ahab had participated in the battle of Karkar in alliance with the Syrians in an attempt to curb the advance of the Assyrians. Soon after this battle, Ahab invited Jehoshaphat to Samaria where he entertained the king of Judah in a most sumptuous manner. It was later revealed that he had a motive behind his gesture. Ahab had contemplated the recovery of Ramoth-gilead which Benhadad the Syrian king had not returned to him in accordance with the treaty of Aphek. Consequently, Ahab decided to go to battle and invited Jehoshaphat to join forces with him. King Jehoshaphat agreed to join in the battle, but insisted on securing the services and advice of a true prophet. Micaiah, the prophet, predicted that Ahab would be killed in battle. Upon hearing this, Ahab disguised himself. However, he was fatally wounded by a stray arrow and Jehoshaphat narrowly escaped before returning to Jerusalem in peace.

Boldly, Jehu confronted Jehoshaphat with words from the Lord that his fraternization with Israel's Ahab and the royal family was displeasing, and that judgment was certain to follow. In contrast to his father Asa, Jehoshaphat accepted the rebuke and went personally throughout Judah from Beersheba to Ephraim to encourage the people to turn to God.

Shortly after this Judah was confronted with a terrifying invasion from the southeast. A messenger reported that a great multitude of Ammonites and Moabites was coming up against them from the land of Edom, south of the Dead Sea. It is at this point during the reign of Jehoshaphat that our lesson begins today.

I. SEEKING GOD (2 Chronicles 20:1-12)

A. An Enemy's Approach (vv. 1, 2)

It often happened in the Old Testament that, after a genuine revival, one or more of the surrounding nations took the occasion to attempt an invasion and conquest of the Israelites. In some cases it was an obvious means of bringing judgment on the people of God for their resolve to depend on the hand of flesh. The account in today's lesson of the approaching invasion by the Moabites and the Ammonites along with other allies coincides with the pattern of troubles after a period of revival.

The invaders were made up of at least three groups of soldiers: (1) The children of Moab, descendants of Lot and his elder daughter. Their territory lay east of Jordan and the Dead Sea. (2) The children of Ammon, likewise descendants of Lot. They originally occupied the same region as their kinsmen, the Moabites, but were eventually obliged to retreat eastward where they remained in the mountains. (3) The "Ammonites." Probably the Mennites, or Maonites—a tribe whose headquarters was the city of Maon, in the neighborhood of Petra to the east of Wady Musa. They are afterwards described as inhabitants of Mount Seir (vv. 22, 23).

As the invading forces made their way northward, they attracted attention and their movement was announced to Jehoshaphat. Just how many soldiers was meant by the term "a great multitude" is unknown, but it is reasonable to believe it was a great host of soldiers, otherwise it would not have prompted the fear that settled on Jehoshaphat.

B. A Leader's Response (v. 3)

King Jehoshaphat responded to the message about the invading forces in three ways: (1) by manifesting fear, which is a logical and reasonable response in the presence of danger; (2) by engaging in personal seeking of God, perhaps in terms of his own motives or shortcomings; and (3) by proclaiming a fast throughout all Judah.

The human disposition is to place confidence and trust in the arms of flesh, in human wisdom, in strength, and in ability first, rather than in God. Only as a last resort will we take the problem to the Lord and seek His counsel. Based on human logic and numerical strength, Jehoshaphat and the nation faced almost certain and overwhelming defeat. But Jehoshaphat had seen many times what God was able to do for his nation.

How important is past experience in developing faith?

C. A Prayer for Help (vv. 4-12)

In hours of crisis it is a source of strength to be able to recall previous experiences of God's help. King Jehoshaphat called upon the God of his fathers and rehearsed past experiences of deliverance as the people of Judah gathered to hear their leader. This was taking place in the "new court"—the outer or greater court of the Temple which Solomon had built. It is here called the "new court" probably because is had been restored or extended under Jehoshaphat or Asa. The king recalled and quoted from his great-great-grandfather Solomon's prayer on the occasion when that hallowed spot—the Temple—had been dedicated.

The prayer which Jehoshaphat directed to Jehovah consisted of a short presentation of the circumstances. The God of their fathers had given the land to His people for an everlasting possession, and they had not provoked the Ammonites, Moabites, and Edomites to fall upon them. On these two facts Jehoshaphat rested his petition for help: in respect to the first, calling to mind the divine promise to hear the prayers offered up to God in the Temple (v. 9); and in reference to the second, laying emphasis upon the inability of Israel to fight against so numerous an army (v. 12). Adam Clark says of Jehoshaphat's prayer of 2 Chronicles 20:5-12: "The foremost fact in Jehoshaphat's mind was not the magnitude of the harassing army which flanked the southern border of Judah. Rather it was the matchless greatness of the Lord God. He acknowledged the One whom he addressed as the God of his fathers, on the one hand, but as the God of heaven on the other hand. He recognized Him as supreme in sovereignty over all the kingdoms of the heathens. He expressed the confidence that none can withstand the power and might which are in God's hand" (**Clark's Commentary**).

The king and his people faced the kind of dilemma that every man faces more than once in a life—"Neither know we what to do" (v. 12). But Jehoshaphat also had recourse to the solution just as a recourse is open to every true servant of God—"Our eyes are upon thee" (v. 12).

Discuss the value of national unity and corporate prayer.

The biographies of many national leaders reveal the dependence that was placed on prayer. Abraham Lincoln called America to prayer during the Civil War; the Battle of Gettysburg, a major turning point, soon followed. In 1918, Memorial Day was a day of prayer; by mid-July the German advance was halted. In World War II, the British Army was trapped at Dunkirk. England prayed and an unusual fog protected a startling rescue. Mary, Queen of Scots, once declared that she feared the prayer of John Knox more than any army of ten thousand men. Prayer is still a nation's greatest power.

II. TRUSTING GOD (2 Chronicles 20:13-17)

A. Families in Prayer (v. 13)

13. And all Judah stood before the Lord, with their little ones, their wives, and their children.

Following the devout leadership and example of Jehoshaphat, husbands, wives, and children stood before the Lord with their king. Philip C. Barker says, "If the whole narrative called for one more touch, it has it in the graphic presentation of verse 13, 'their little ones'" (**Pulpit Commentary**). The Hebrew word used here is expressive of the quick, tripping steps of the young and the women.

It must have been a great comfort to Jehoshaphat to view the combined expression of family units engaged in prayer and worship. Nations and civilizations vary with the family, and the family with nations and civilizations. But where leadership and the family unit are engaged in common desires under the rule of Jehovah, there is a strength that cannot be conquered.

B. Downfall of Enemy Foretold (vv. 14-17)

14. Then upon Jahaziel the son of Zechariah, the son of Benaiah, the son of Jeiel, the son of Mattaniah, a Levite of the sons of Asaph, came the Spirit of the Lord in the midst of the congregation;

15. And he said, Hearken ye, all Judah, and ye inhabitants of Jerusalem, and thou king Jehoshaphat, Thus saith the Lord unto you, Be not afraid nor dismayed by reason of this great multitude; for the battle is not your's, but God's.

16. To morrow go ye down against them: Behold, they come up by the cliff of Ziz; and ye shall find them at the end of the brook, before the wilderness of Jeruel.

In the midst of the assembly, the Spirit of the Lord came upon Jahaziel with a message of prophecy and revelation as God's answer to the national petition of Jehoshaphat and the people of Judah. Jahaziel's descent is traced back for five generations to the Levite Mattaniah of the sons of Asaph. His being of the "sons of Asaph" may connect him with the prominence of singing which is given later.

In verse 15 we see the straightforward message which Jahaziel bore from the Lord. The message was to the nation as well as to the king since the prayer was on the part of all the people. God's words to Judah and King Jehoshaphat were ones of comfort and encouragement which gave assurance that He had accepted the problem as His as the king and his people manifested faith. In commenting on the phrase "the battle is not your's, but God's," Oliver G. Wilson says, "Every lover of truth is fighting a battle. Often we are made to feel that the way is all uphill and the outcome most uncertain. When the conflict is set, if we would raise this scripture as a battle cry the thunder of the enemy's artillery would not be so disconcerting. . . . It is not great numbers, nor modern equipment, nor brilliant plans that giveth the victory, it is God—the God that reigneth.

"Since the battle is the Lord's and since the ordering of the battle is His sole responsibility, neither honor nor prestige nor praise should come to me. The battle is His—the glory shall also be His" **(The Wesleyan Methodist)**.

Verse 16 gives proof of God's revelation through the message by Jahaziel: "To morrow go ye down against them: Behold, they come up by the cliff of Ziz; and ye shall find them at the end of the brook, before the wilderness of Jeruel." The instructions were specific, the directions clear. At this point, the enemy itself probably did not know its direct course of attack.

The "ascent of Ziz" **(The Amplified Bible)** is described by Robinson to be a fearful pass. "The path winds up in zigzags, often at the steepest gradient which horses could ascend, and runs partly along projecting walls of rock on the perpendicular face of the cliff, and then down the heaps of debris which are almost as steep. When one looks back at this part from below, it seems quite impossible that there could be any pathway; but by skillful windings the path has been carried down without any unconquerable difficulties, so that even loaded camels often go up and down" **(Commentary on the Old Testament,** by Keil and Delitzsch). Whether it was this pass that was used by the enemy is uncertain. Josephus tends to support the idea that it was. Although it was a difficult path to travel, it might have been part of the strategy of the Lord to cause the invaders to get caught in such a difficult territory.

17. Ye shall not need to fight in this battle: set yourselves, stand ye still, and see the salvation of the Lord with you, O Judah and Jerusalem: fear not, nor be dismayed; to morrow go out against them: for the Lord will be with you.

The concluding words of the Lord's message to Judah through His servant Jahaziel were freighted with comfort and instructions—they would not even have to fight in this battle.

The instructions given and at once accepted were as unlike those of ordinary warfare as is the whole incident, for there was to be no sword drawn or blow struck. The action would be merely to take their position and "stand . . . still, and see the salvation of the Lord." With that assurance of victory, Jehoshaphat and the people of Judah must have slept with a calm restfulness as they awaited the next morning when they would go out to observe the action of the Lord against their foes.

In reflecting on this verse, Alexander MacLaren poses a question and suggests a course of action for us. "May we not take the message of Jahaziel as one to ourselves in the midst of our many conflicts both in the outward life and in the inward life. If we have truly grasped God's hands, and are fighting for what is accordant with His will, we have a right to feel that 'the battle is not ours but Gods' and to be sure that therefore we shall conquer. . . . Even in the struggles of outward life, and much more in those of our spiritual nature, every man who watches his own career will many a time have to recognize God's hand, unaided by any act of his own, striking for him and giving him victory; and in the spiritual life every Christian man knows that his best moments have come from the initiation of the Holy Spirit who 'bloweth where He listeth.' How often we have been surprised by God's help; how often we have been quickened by God's inbreathed Spirit, and have been taught that the passivity of faith draws to us greater blessings than the activity of effort. 'They also serve who only stand and wait,' and they also conquer who in quietness and confidence keep themselves still and let God work for them and in them.

"The first great blessing of trust in God is that we may be at peace on the eve of battle, and the second is that in every battle it is, in truth, not we that fight, but God who fights for and in us" **(Expositions of Holy Scripture).**

Can you recall happenings in your own life when God gave you the assurance of victory in the face of depressing problems?

III. PRAISING GOD (2 Chronicles 20:18-30)

A. Gratitude Expressed (vv. 18, 19)

18. And Jehoshaphat bowed his head with his face to the ground: and all Judah

and the inhabitants of Jerusalem fell before the Lord, worshipping the Lord.

19. And the Levites, of the children of the Kohathites, and of the children of the Korhites, stood up to praise the Lord God of Israel with a loud voice on high.

The infinite relief to the mind of Jehoshaphat and his people found a fitting expression of gratitude and adoration to the God who had made their problem His problem. They bowed their heads with faces to the ground, while the Levites of the Kohathites and Korhites stood up to praise the Lord God of Israel with a loud voice.

Sir Moses Montetifiore, the Hebrew philanthropist, had as a motto for his family, "Think and Thank." In the old Anglo-Saxon language **thankfulness** means "thinkfulness." Thinking of all God's goodness draws forth gratitude. "Gratitude to God," says Charles Simmons, "should be as habitual as the reception of mercies is constant, as ardent as the number of them is great, as devout as the riches of divine grace and goodness is incomprehensible" (**The Encyclopedia of Religious Quotations**).

B. The Enemy Defeated (vv. 20-24)

20. And they rose early in the morning, and went forth into the wilderness of Tekoa: and as they went forth, Jehoshaphat stood and said, Hear me, O Judah, and ye inhabitants of Jerusalem; Believe in the Lord your God, so shall ye be established; believe his prophets, so shall ye prosper.

(For additional exposition on verse 20, see the Golden Text.)

The next morning the assembled men of Judah, in accordance with the words of the prophet, marched to the wilderness of Tekoa, not less than ten miles away. Jehoshaphat's own faith and zeal perhaps made him nervously anxious that his people should not fall behind him and fall short of their duty and the grandeur of the occasion. Consequently, he exhorted them to faith in God's message and in His promise to deliver them.

21. And when he had consulted with the people, he appointed singers unto the Lord, and that should praise the beauty of holiness, as they went out before the army, and to say, Praise the Lord; for his mercy endureth for ever.

Here is faith in God demonstrated. Jehoshaphat so literally trusted the word of God by the Prophet Jahaziel that he placed the singers at the front end of the procession before the army to lead the people forth to the enemy with praise to God upon their lips.

It is undoubtedly their refrain "for his mercy endureth forever" that is sounded throughout the Psalms and especially that of Psalm 136, where the phrase concludes each verse.

"Anybody can sing the 'Te Deum' when the battle is over," says H. P. Hughes. "The difference between an ordinary man of war and a Christian is this: a Christian shouts before the victory, because he knows it is sure to come" (**The Preacher's Homiletical Commentary**).

In 1632 A.D., when Gustaf Adolph of Sweden faced Wallenstein who had brought the Austrian forces to bring Northern Europe back to the Roman Church, 20,000 Swedes joined their king in singing, "A mighty fortress is our God," and gained a mighty victory.

22. And when they began to sing and to praise, the Lord set ambushments against the children of Ammon, Moab, and mount Seir, which were come against Judah; and they were smitten.

23. For the children of Ammon and Moab stood up against the inhabitants of mount Seir, utterly to slay and destroy them: and when they had made an end of the inhabitants of Seir, every one helped to destroy another.

The passage indicates that God moved to deliver the moment that Judah and the inhabitants of Jerusalem began to thank Him for doing so. When faith took God at His word and began to praise Him for doing what He had promised, then He honored that faith by an affirmative response.

The secret of the disruption to the invaders lay in the use of ambushments. The word **ambushment** denotes "liers in wait" or "men lying in wait." Who these men were cannot be determined with certainty. Some of the older commentators think it refers to powers, angels sent by God, who are called insidiators, because of the work they had to do in the army of the hostile peoples. However, Keil suggests: "Most probably earthly liers in wait are meant, who unexpectedly rushed forth from their ambush upon the hostile army, and raised a panic terror among them; so that . . . the Ammonites and Moabites first turned their weapons against the inhabitants of Mount Seir, and after they had exterminated them, began to exterminate each other. But the ambush cannot have been composed of men of Judah because they were . . . not to fight [vv. 15, 17], but only to behold the deliverance wrought by the Lord. Probably it was liers in wait of the Seirites, greedy of spoil, who from an ambush made an attack upon the Ammonites and Moabites, and by the divine leading put the attack in such fear and confusion, that they turned furiously upon the inhabitants of Mount Seir, who marched with them, and then fell to fighting with each other; just as, in Judges 7:22, the Midianites were, under divine influence, so terrified by the unexpected attack of the small band led by Gideon, that they turned their swords against and mutually destroyed each other" (**Commentary on the Old Testament**).

24. And when Judah came toward the watch tower in the wilderness, they looked unto the multitude, and, behold, they were dead bodies fallen to the earth, and none escaped.

It is scarcely likely that a constructed watch-tower is intended here, but rather a high or elevated position on the ground where a view of a large group of persons could be realized. Judah and its army and heralding singers could now see in new significance that thing said by Jahaziel in verse 16, "You will find them at the end of the ravine before the wilderness of Jeruel" (**The Amplified Bible**).

C. The Triumphant Return (vv. 25-30)

(Verses 25-30 are not included in the printed text.)

Delivered from foes and fears, Judah began gathering the booty which was so plentiful that it took them three days to gather the treasures. Then they concluded the campaign with a worthy expression of praise to the Lord. Perhaps in the cliff country of the wilderness of Judah, the victors gathered and there in the valley of Berachah "blessed the Lord."

"Here we have in vivid form," says MacLaren, "the truth that all our struggles and fightings may end in a valley of blessing, which will ring with the praise of the God who fights for us. If we begin our warfare with an appeal to God, and with prayerful acknowledgment of our own impotence, we shall end it with thankful acknowledgment that 'we are more than conquerors through Him that loved us.' Our choral songs of praise will echo through the true Valley of Blessing, where no sound of enemies shall ever break the settled stillness and the host of the redeemed, like that army of Judah, shall bear 'psalteries and harps and trumpets, and shall need spear and sword no more at all for ever' " (**Expositions of Holy Scripture**).

REVIEW QUESTIONS

1. What was the national crisis that caused Jehoshaphat to seek the Lord?

2. Discuss fear as an occasion for seeking the Lord.

3. How extensive was Jehoshaphat's effort to turn his people back to God?

4. Who was Jahaziel? What was his message?

5. In what sense is praise an element of victory?

GOLDEN TEXT HOMILY

"BELIEVE IN THE LORD YOUR GOD, SO SHALL YE BE ESTABLISHED; BELIEVE HIS PROPHETS, SO SHALL YE PROSPER" (2 Chronicles 20:20).

The exhortation in the text, which is Jehoshaphat's final word to his army before they went out to witness the destruction of the enemy, has in the original Hebrew a beauty and emphasis that is impossible to preserve in translation. There is a play on words which cannot be reproduced in another language, although the sentiment of it may be explained. The two expressions for **believing** and **being established** are two varying forms of the same root word which might be translated as follows: "Hold fast by the Lord your God, and you will be held fast"; or, "Stay yourself on Him and you will be stable."

If we note this connection of the two clauses we come to the general principle which lies here—that the true source of steadfastness in character and conduct, of victory over temptation, and of standing fast in slippery places, is simple reliance, or to use the New Testament word **faith**. Believe and ye shall be established. Put out your hand and clasp Him, and He puts out His hand and steadies you. But all the steadfastness and strength come from the mighty hand that is outstretched, not from the tremulous one that grasps it.

In the same breath in which Jehoshaphat exhorted his people to "believe in the Lord," he also said, "Believe his prophets, so shall ye prosper." The immediate reference is to the man Jahaziel who the day before had assured them of victory. But the wider truth suggested is that the only way to get to God is through the Word that speaks of Him, and which has come from the lips either of prophets or of the Son who has spoken more and more sweetly and clearly than all the prophets put together. If we are to believe God, we must believe the prophets that tell of Him.

Immediately after exhorting the people to "hold fast to your God" and "holding fast to the words of the prophets, Jehoshaphat appointed singers to chant praise and gratitude to the Lord, for faith was convinced of the victory. Instead of the Ark, the Levites headed the army, singing of the beauty of holiness and the steadfast love of their God. Such is the faith that triumphs—holding fast and singing praises."—Excerpts from **Expositions of Holy Scripture**

SENTENCE SERMONS

LIVING CLOSE TO GOD brings an assurance of His help during times of adversity.
—**Selected**

WE BELITTLE GOD begging for crumbs when He is the bread of life, the manna from heaven.
—**"Notes and Quotes"**

PRAYER IS NOT to be the last resort, but the first resort.
—**"Notes and Quotes"**

PRAY WHEN THERE seems to be no way. God specializes in the impossible.
—**Selected**

EVANGELISTIC APPLICATION

WHEN PEOPLE TURN TO THE LORD HE WILL DELIVER THEM FROM SIN.

Canst Thou restore, O mighty God
　The years so long gone by?
So devastated, desolate—
　In barren waste they lie.
I started out to serve Thee, Lord,
　When youth's responsive hour
Gave promise that the seed then sown
　Would burst forth into flower.

But, oh! the barrenness of years.
　No effort of my own
Can reap a harvest from the fields
　The cankerworm hath mown.
The locust of my faithlessness
　Hath blasted and destroyed

The harvest that in course of years
　The Master had enjoyed.
Wilt Thou restore? Then, Lord, in faith
　Before Thy feet I bow,
Confess to Thee my shame and loss,
　Fulfill Thy promise now.
Thus cleansed and sanctified, made meet
　To do the humblest task;
To be well-pleasing in Thy sight,
　My Lord, is all I ask.
—**Mrs. G. Henderson**

(From **1200 Notes, Quotes, and Anecdotes,** by A. Naismith. Copyright 1962 by A. Naismith. Published by Moody Press. Used by permission.)

ILLUMINATING THE LESSON

Prayer saved the congregation of the first church ever built in Madison county from an Indian massacre.

This information was found by W. T. Cash, state librarian, in an old letter which is a part of the historical manuscripts he has collected at the state library.

Cash said the date of the incident is not given in the letter, but that it occurred between 1830, when the church was built, and 1848 when the Florida Indian war ended. The church stood in Hickstown, about five miles west of the present town of Madison. The town was named after a Seminole Indian chief, Billy Hicks, Cash said.

The Indians determined to surround the Hickstown church one Sunday when a large congregation had assembled and massacre the entire assemblage, the letter said. When the Indians had gathered close to the church they noticed the congregation was kneeling in prayer.

The Red Men then said to each other, "They are talking to the Great Spirit and He will be very angry with us if we kill them."

The letter said the Indians then slipped away quietly, but one of them captured later related to the whites how narrowly they had escaped being massacred in the Hickstown church.
—**Tampa (Florida) Tribune**

DAILY DEVOTIONAL GUIDE

M. Be Strong and Courageous. Joshua 1:1-9
T. Trust the Lord. Psalm 37:1-7
W. Follow God's Word. Psalm 119:33-40
T. Put God First. Matthew 6:25-34
F. Continue in Good Works. Galatians 6:9; Titus 2:7-14
S. Grow in the Lord. 2 Peter 3:14-18

August 9, 1981

Responding to God's Call

Bible Background: 2 Chronicles 26:1-23; Isaiah 6:1-13
Time: Around 739 B.C.
Place: Jerusalem
Supplemental References: Ezekiel 1:1-28; Revelation 1:9-18; 22:16, 17
Golden Text: "Go ye into all the world, and preach the gospel to every creature" (Mark 16:15).
Central Truth: Our response to God's call should involve humble worship and willing service.
Evangelistic Emphasis: Each Christian is called to a ministry of sharing the gospel with others.

PRINTED TEXT

Isaiah 6:1. In the year that king Uzziah died I saw also the Lord sitting upon a throne, high and lifted up, and his train filled the temple.

2. **Above it stood the seraphims: each one had six wings; with twain he covered his face, and with twain he covered his feet, and with twain he did fly.**

3. And one cried unto another, and said, Holy, holy, holy, is the Lord of hosts: the whole earth is full of his glory.

4. **And the posts of the door moved at the voice of him that cried, and the house was filled with smoke.**

5. Then said I, Woe is me! for I am undone; because I am a man of unclean lips, and I dwell in the midst of a people of unclean lips: for mine eyes have seen the King, the Lord of hosts.

6. **Then flew one of the seraphims unto me, having a live coal in his hand, which he had taken with the tongs from off the altar:**

7. And he laid it upon my mouth, and said, Lo, this hath touched thy lips; and thine iniquity is taken away, and thy sin purged.

8. **Also I heard the voice of the Lord, saying, Whom shall I send, and who will go for us? Then said I, Here am I; send me.**

9. And he said, Go, and tell this people, Hear ye indeed, but understand not; and see ye indeed, but perceive not.

10. **Make the heart of this people fat, and make their ears heavy, and shut their eyes; lest they see with their eyes, and hear with their ears, and understand with their heart, and convert, and be healed.**

11. Then said I, Lord, how long? And he answered, Until the cities be wasted without inhabitant, and the houses without man, and the land be utterly desolate.

12. **And the Lord have removed men far away, and there be a great forsaking in the midst of the land.**

13. But yet in it shall be a tenth, and it shall return, and shall be eaten: as a teil tree, and as a oak, whose substance is in them, when they cast their leaves: so the holy seed shall be the substance thereof.

DICTIONARY

Uzziah (you-ZIGH-uh)—Isaiah 6:1—The tenth king of Judah who ruled for more than fifty years. He began his reign as a co-regent with his father for about twenty-five years, ruled alone for seventeen years, and then ended his reign with his son as co-regent for ten years. For the greater part of his reign he lived in the fear of God and was a wise and active ruler.

the Lord—Isaiah 6:1—The word in Hebrew means "sovereign," "master."

his train—Isaiah 6:1—Not the train of attendants, but "the skirts of His robe."

seraphims (SER-rah-fims)—Isaiah 6:2—More correctly without the **s** since the **im** in Hebrew is plural. This is the only place in the Bible where these are mentioned as heavenly beings. They had human characteristics with six wings. **Seraph** means "burning," which would indicate that they were "on fire" or that they "burned away" sin. A creature of similar description was found reproduced on stone in Gozan, Mesopotamia, a city where Jewish captives were taken during this period.

posts of the door moved—Isaiah 6:4—A better translation is that "the foundations of the thresholds shook."

fat—Isaiah 6:10—Dull, insensitive.

teil tree—Isaiah 6:13—The terebinth tree, commonly found in stony soil and scrub. It has leaves of a reddish color.

oak—Isaiah 6:13—The oak of Tabor, the more common of the two kinds of leaf-shedding oaks found in Palestine.

LESSON OUTLINE

I. A REVELATION OF HOLINESS
   A. The Lord
   B. The Angels
   C. The House

II. A WORK OF CLEANSING
   A. The Confession
   B. The Live Coal

III. A CALL TO SERVICE
   A. The Response
   B. The Commission
   C. The Desolation
   D. The Holy Seed

LESSON EXPOSITION

INTRODUCTION

God's call comes to different people in different ways. His call sometimes comes in a very dramatic fashion. This was true in the case of Isaiah. He saw a vision and heard a voice. In his vision, he saw the Lord upon His throne and the angels of God worshiping Him. He felt the touch of the coal upon his lips. He heard the voice of God seeking him and instructing him. God's call of the Apostle Paul was equally dramatic. He saw the glory of the Lord brighter than the noonday sun. He heard the voice of the Lord inquiring of his intentions and then instructing him as to what he was to do. Finally, the Lord clearly spelled out his commission. There could be no question in Paul's mind about his mission in life.

The call of God does not always come as clearly or as dramatically as it came to Isaiah and Paul. Sometimes the Lord shows us the direction for our life through the talents and abilities He has given us. He expects us to use our energies to seek information that will help us make decisions in life. He does not want us to make stupid decisions or to avoid making any decisions until it is too late and then expect that God will somehow get us out of the mess we've gotten ourselves into. We should pray for guidance, direction, and blessing. We should believe that God will help us to make the right decisions and to move in the right direction. But we should remember that the Lord will not do for us the things that we can do for ourselves.

I. A REVELATION OF HOLINESS (Isaiah 6:1-4)

A. The Lord (v. 1)

1. In the year that king Uzziah died I saw also the Lord sitting upon a throne, high and lifted up, and his train filled the temple.

Uzziah came to the throne of Judah when he was sixteen years old and reigned for fifty-two years. His son, Jotham, succeeded him to the throne. At the time of Uzziah's death, neighboring Israel was in a state of chaos and was soon to be scattered.

As a youth, Uzziah determined to seek God and as a result he enjoyed a period of remarkable prosperity. Under his leadership the nation regained much lost territory from the enemies of God and developed the internal resources of the people. It was a highly successful reign until Uzziah allowed pride to enter his heart. Losing sight of the source of his blessings, he rebelled against God, was smitten with leprosy, and for the last period of his life lived in a lazar house.

Isaiah lived in Judah, and had known no occupant of the throne of his own people other than Uzziah. The news of Uzziah's death spread rapidly. Isaiah must have felt a sense of loss. The only throne to which he had looked for support was empty. Knowing Israel's peril, seeing Judah headed in the same direction, perceiving that chaos was everywhere, Isaiah must have had a sense of helplessness. It was in these circumstances that the prophet could say, "I saw . . . the Lord sitting upon a throne." G. Campbell Morgan comments: "Behind the empty throne, there is a throne that is never empty. Over the chaos that appalls the heart there is the God of order and government."

"The Lord God omnipotent reigneth!" This is the mainspring of Christian hope and courage. It gives us certainty that we are not fighting a losing battle. It assures us that the real pull of the universe is on the side of the man who follows after righteousness. It is a glorious truth that echoes down into the world of darkness, and shakes that world to its foundations. It is the thunderous chant of a great marching host, fair as the moon, clear as the sun, terrible as an army with banners. If God is on the throne of the universe, then evil is doomed, never has been anything but doomed, doomed from the foundation of the world. And victory belongs to the people of God.

B. The Angels (v. 2)

2. Above it stood the seraphims: each one had six wings; with twain he covered his face, and with twain he covered his feet, and with twain he did fly.

Isaiah not only saw the Lord upon a throne, high and exalted, he also saw seraphs—angelic beings—worshiping and adoring the Lord. These beautiful creatures had six wings. With one pair of wings each one covered his face. Even they could not gaze upon the dazzling brightness of Jehovah's throne. With another pair of wings each one covered his feet, or his body, or his lower parts. The seraph remembered that, though sinless, he was yet a creature, and therefore he concealed himself in token of his nothingness and unworthiness in the presence of the thrice Holy One. The middle pair of wings was used for flight. Adoration is not complete until it manifests itself in active obedience and readiness of heart for service.

These seraphs can teach us something about Christian service:

They dwell near the Lord, and so should we. If we live at a distance from God, we cannot expect His blessings. We must move in close to Him if we expect to be used by Him.

God is their center and their bliss, and so should He be ours. The psalmist wrote: "Trust in the Lord, and do good; so shalt thou dwell in the land, and verily thou shalt be fed. **Delight thyself also in the Lord**; and he shall give thee the desires of thine heart. Commit thy way unto the Lord; trust also in him; and he shall bring it to pass" (Psalm 37:3-5). Is God at the center of your life? Do you find your happiness in Him? This is the key to joyful, abundant living.

They were burning ones, and so should we be. The word **seraphim** means "burning ones." They were creatures of fire, ablaze with ardor. Jehovah, who is a consuming fire, can only fitly be served by those who are on fire, whether they are angels or men. He desires that His people be on fire with love divine. May He make us, like John the Baptist, burning and shining lights.

They devoted twice as much energy to adorations as they did to service, and so should we. With four wings, they paid homage to the King. With two wings, they carried out His wishes. We would accomplish more for God if we spent more time in spiritual preparation before we undertook a task in His service.

C. The House (vv. 3, 4)

3. And one cried unto another, and said, Holy, holy, holy, is the Lord of hosts: the whole earth is full of his glory.

4. And the posts of the door moved at the voice of him that cried, and the house was filled with smoke.

Discuss various ways God manifests Himself to the human family.

The seraphs utter a threefold cry of adoration: "Holy, holy, holy." This expression may be interpreted in several ways. Three is the biblical number which symbolizes perfection. It is also the number of persons in the Godhead. Also, this repetition of expression may point out unwearied perseverance in worship. It is as though Isaiah had said that the seraphs never cease from their melody in singing the praises of God. Certainly, the holiness of God supplies us with inexhaustible reasons for songs of praise.

The expression "the whole earth is full of his glory" may have a twofold meaning. It could refer to the fullness of the earth: the fruits, the animals, and the manifold riches with which God has supplied the earth. Through the great variety of His provisions in the world, the glory of God shines. His beautiful provisions are evidence of a father's love.

But more naturally the passage means that the glory of God is spread through every region of the earth. By including this expression Isaiah is telling the Jews that their boasting is foolish. They thought that the glory of God was nowhere to be seen but among themselves. They would keep it shut up within their own Temple. Even Simon Peter, after the Day of Pentecost, had to struggle with this concept. But Isaiah says that the glory of God is not limited to one people or to one place; it fills the whole earth.

The prophet knew that the voices he heard —the voices of the angels—were more than natural voices. So powerful were they that the doorposts and the thresholds of the building shook. In addition to this supernatural shaking, the Temple was filled with smoke. This was the common and ordinary sign which the Lord used to indicate His presence. Whenever Moses entered into the Tabernacle, smoke was diffused through it in such a manner that the people could not see either Moses or the Tabernacle (see Exodus 33:9).

This is another stage in God's plan to prepare Isaiah to recognize His presence and to respond to His message.

II. A WORK OF CLEANSING (Isaiah 6:5-7)

A. The Confession (v. 5)

5. Then said I, Woe is me! for I am undone; because I am a man of unclean lips, and I dwell in the midst of a people of unclean lips: for mine eyes have seen the King, the Lord of hosts.

Having been given a glimpse of God's glory, Isaiah sees himself as he is. He realizes that he is a mere man and that he is unworthy even to speak of God's glory. Having heard the angels worshiping God with heaven-pure lips, he sees himself as a man of unclean lips. His feeling of unworthiness is heightened by the fact that he has seen the King, the Lord of hosts. E. J. Young comments: "In these two expressions, 'the King' and 'the Lord of hosts,' there is united the thought that God is the covenant God, the King of the theocracy, as well as the fact that He is the Creator, the living and true God. It is not only that Isaiah has seen God, but it is the infinite distance between the Holy God and the sinful creature which produces this prostrating effect."

How does a vision of God affect you? Does it leave you with a sense of awe and reverence? It should produce a sense of true humility which is the only proper attitude of man toward God. Every time you worship God—whether at church on Sunday morning, or in your private devotions—His presence should bring a deepened sense of true Christian humility. The Lord is always ready to reveal Himself to those who seek after Him. He often takes the initiative in seeking. Of Him, Isaiah writes, " 'I revealed myself to those who did not ask for me; I was found by those who did not seek me. To a nation that did not call on my name, I said, "Here am I, here am I." ' " (Isaiah 65:1, **New International Version**). If God is not real to you, how earnestly have you sought after Him?

B. The Live Coal (vv. 6, 7)

6. Then flew one of the seraphims unto me, having a live coal in his hand, which he had taken with the tongs from off the altar;

7. And he laid it upon my mouth, and said, Lo, this hath touched thy lips; and thine iniquity is taken away, and thy sin purged.

Isaiah's acknowledgement of his unworthy state before God was also a prayer of repentance. Later, he could look back on this experience and write with confidence: "Let the wicked forsake his way and the evil man his thoughts. Let him turn to the Lord, and he will have mercy on him, and to our God, for he will freely pardon" (Isaiah 55:7, **New International Version**).

Now one of the seraphs responds to Isaiah's heart attitude and touches his lips with a live coal from the altar. The effect produced by this touch is that his guilt is taken away and his sin is atoned for.

What a beautiful picture we have here of the grace of God in action to remove sin. It is everlastingly wonderful that all through the Scriptures this truth is set forth: God takes away our sins. This is not easy for the human heart to understand, but it is gloriously true. It is God who cleanses and delivers. The four Gospels show how the Lord Jesus Christ spent His life doing the work of God and laid Himself on the altar as a sacrifice to do God's will. He was put to death with cruel hands and His blood was shed; but it is His blood that cleanses me from my sin. And it is God who does it. This truth is almost too grand for our mind to fathom.

The glowing coal in which the fire is still active represents Christ. He has stepped from the throne and laid Himself on the altar. As such He became the Paschal Lamb—the glowing coal. Let this coal touch the unclean lips ever so lightly, and at once all iniquity is taken away. F. C. Jennings observes: "The very word used for 'touched' forbids the thought of it being a casual, inoperative contact. The word conveys the same significance exactly as its Greek equivalent in Luke 8:45, when the Lord felt that light fingertip and asked, 'Who touched me?' In that touch there is always an effect—a communication of virtue."

Isaiah's experience was not only designed to forgive his sins, but also to make him suitable for the Lord's use. We too need this touch of infinite grace if we are going to render effective service for the Master.

In addition to what God does for us, if we are to be used of God we have a responsibility to cleanse ourselves. Paul wrote to Timothy: "In a large house there are articles not only of gold and silver, but also of wood and clay; some are for noble purposes and some for ignoble. If a man cleanses himself from the latter, he will be an instrument for noble purposes, made holy, useful to the Master and prepared to do any good work" (2 Timothy 2:20, 21; **New International Version**). Again, Paul says: "Let us cleanse ourselves from all filthiness of the flesh and spirit, perfecting holiness in the fear of God" (2 Corinthians 7:1). John adds: "And every man that hath this hope in him purifieth himself, even as he is pure" (1 John 3:3).

"Christ washes away the sin that condemns us, but we must cleanse ourselves from habits and attitudes that are unlike Him," says Charles W. Conn.

III. A CALL TO SERVICE (Isaiah 6:8-13)

A. The Response (v. 8)

8. Also I heard the voice of the Lord, saying, Whom shall I send, and who will go for us? Then said I, Here am I; send me.

In what way is the call to service an obligation on all Christians?

God has chosen to do His work through men. He could intervene directly into the affairs of men, or He could rely upon angels. But He allows men the honor of bearing His name to other men. The man whom God uses must be a volunteer, a man who is willing to do the work of God. The Lord will not force men into service. But He will gladly employ those who genuinely and wholeheartedly offer themselves to His service.

Isaiah offered his service to the Lord **freely**. He was not forced to do so. He saw the Lord; he felt His cleansing touch; and he gladly volunteered to serve Him. The prophet also offered his service to the Lord **boldly**. He did not ask the Lord what He would require of him. He was satisfied to know that God was to direct his mission. Although he did not know the nature of the mission, he knew that God would lead him aright. He placed himself as an instrument in God's hands. He was ready to go where, when, and on what errand God might determine. Such are the offers to service in which God delights. Such are the men that God can use.

Someone has suggested that this is "a chapter of autobiography. Here is disclosed the secret of the wonderful energy with which for more than half a century Isaiah prosecuted his ministry. He is the Paul of the Old Testament. Allowance being made for difference of phraseology, there is a striking resemblance between the call of Isaiah and of Paul (compare chapter 6 with Acts 9). Both sought to serve the heavenly King; and both received a commission to work, spiritual and universal beyond all conceptions of their time—the one penning the gospel of the suffering Messiah, the other vindicating the truth that the gospel is God's message to the **world**."

B. The Commission (vv. 9, 10)

9. And he said, Go, and tell this people,

Hear ye indeed, but understand not; and see ye indeed, but perceive not.

10. Make the heart of this people fat, and make their ears heavy, and shut their eyes; lest they see with their eyes, and hear with their ears, and understand with their heart, and convert, and be healed.

In the ninth verse the revelation of perpetual principles ends. After that we have the commission spoken to Isaiah concerning his own time. He was commissioned to utter a message of devastating judgment. The local, and the incidental, occupy the last section of this chapter. The essential and the eternal occupy the first part.

Of Isaiah's mission, Dean Plumptre says, "No harder task, it may be, was ever given to man. Ardent dreams of reformation and revival, the nation renewing its strength like the eagle, were scattered to the winds; and he had to face the prospect of a fruitless labor, of feeling that he did but increase the evil against which he strove. It was the very opposite mission of that to which St. Paul was sent, 'to open their eyes, and to turn them from darkness to light' " (Acts 26: 18).

One of the most painful things anyone who proclaims the truth has to come to grips with is that the gospel is a two-edged sword. It not only sheds a bright light; it also casts a deep shadow. It not only produces life; it also generates death. Its effect depends upon how it is received by the hearer.

When a greater than Moses legislates, and a wiser than Solomon speaks, the hearer has a solemn responsibility. His level of accountability is higher than that of those who received the Law from Sinai, or of those who lived under the reign of the son of David. So much more is required of him because so much more has been given. The man who hears the Word today has the written revelation of God plus the accumulated witness of Christian history for which he must answer. To reject the overwhelming evidence of truth is to place his soul in jeopardy.

The minister must proclaim the truth whether it is received or not. He must not be discouraged in his preaching just because it does not produce the results he wanted. He must be content to obey God, and to leave the consequences of his labor in the Lord's hand.

By some of the standards used today in measuring success in God's work, Isaiah would have been judged a failure. He had to declare the truth to an obstinate and rebellious people, not only for a year or two, but for more than sixty years. The only thing he had to show for his efforts was faithfulness. And God puts a premium on faithfulness. What a lesson we can learn from Isaiah. The truth must always be heard from our lips, even though there are no ears to receive it. It is enough for us that we labor faithfully for the glory of God, and that our services are acceptable to Him. The sound of our voice is never ineffectual if we are speaking the truth in love. Obedience to God always has its reward.

C. The Desolation (vv. 11, 12)

11. Then said I, Lord, how long? And he answered, Until the cities be wasted without inhabitant, and the houses without man, and the land be utterly desolate,

12. And the Lord have removed men far away, and there be a great forsaking in the midst of the land.

Isaiah inquired of the Lord as to how long the rebelliousness of the people would continue to keep them from God. His compassion caused him to ask how long this hardness of heart would continue. Could he look forward to a time when the rebellion would end and the people would begin to repent of their sin?

The answer was not encouraging. This rebellion would go on until the nation was destroyed and carried away into captivity. Unpleasant as the news was, it let Isaiah put his preaching in proper perspective. It would not immediately turn many from their sins and save the country from ruin.

The plight of the people of God is a picture of the total depravity of man. This is a truth that every person must deal with. Dr. Donald Grey Barnhouse illustrates this fact effectively in his book **Let Me Illustrate:**

"Several years ago, I motored across the continent with my family. One summer day we saw some of the beauties of the national parks in southern Utah; we drove on to the north rim of the Grand Canyon of the Colorado, arriving there after sunset. We found our rooms for the night and ate our dinner; then we walked down the path to the wall that guards the edge of this mighty chasm. There was no moon and we looked out into pitch darkness. I told my children what lay before them, but it was impossible to see anything whatsoever in the inky blackness.

Far to the south we could see the lights of the hotel on the south rim of the canyon. I told the children that between us and those lights was a distance of many miles, and that separating us from the lights was the greatest canyon in the world, going down a mile to the great river which lay hidden beneath us. I suppose that the children accepted what I said on faith, and that they formed some sort of mental picture of what I described to them, but if we had left the place and driven on, they would never have really understood what the canyon really was.

"In the morning we arose early, before sunrise, in order that to see the coming of the dawn. The canyon was still invisible beneath us, but far to the southeast we could see the great range of the San Francisco peaks. At first, they were but a faint shadow; then they became etched in outline, and soon the first rays of the invisible sun touched them. The canyon remained invisible beneath us. The line of things that we could see descended from those peaks to the rim of the canyon near us, and then to the distant rim to the south, but the depths of the canyon were still not visible. After the brilliance of the new day broke, our sight began to pick up the walls of the canyon, and little by little we were able to see farther and farther—to the very depths of the canyon.

"My own awareness of the total depravity of my being and the incapacity of my fleshly nature is a close parallel to the experience we had on the rim of the Grand Canyon. At first I was aware of the biblical statement concerning my nature just as a man might be aware of a geographer's description of the Grand Canyon. Then as time passed I stood on the brink of my own sinfulness without knowing it was there in reality. At last, I saw, not the canyon of my depravity, but the distant mountain peaks of the cross of Jesus Christ, brought to my vision by the illumination of the Holy Spirit. Only then did I begin to see the edges of the abyss that is in the human heart, and as the years have passed my sight has gone deeper and deeper into that sinful depth. I discovered from the Word of God the statistics of my depravity without having known at close range the depths of its capacity. Every Christian must come to this knowledge for himself."

D. The Holy Seed (v. 13)

13. But yet in it shall be a tenth, and it shall return, and shall be eaten: as a teil tree, and as an oak, whose substance is in them, when they cast their leaves: so the holy seed shall be the substance thereof.

This verse shines a small glitter of hope in a passage that is otherwise gloomy. When Jerusalem is carried away captive, one tenth of the people will remain in the land. And so it was. When Nebuchadnezzar "carried away all Jerusalem" (2 Kings 24:14), he left the poorest people behind "to be vinedressers and husbandmen" (2 Kings 25:12). Although the few who were left behind suffered great peril, Israel was not destroyed. A holy seed, a chosen remnant, were the substance of the children of Israel.

Isaiah is given the figure of the terebinth or turpentine tree and the oak. The terebinth is an evergreen, except that in very severe and inclement weather it loses its leaves; but even then the tree is not dead. The oak also loses its leaves, but it is not dead. The Lord is saying that the tree in winter stands naked and bare, without any sign of life, its roots buried in the hard and frozen soil, and its naked branches exposed to every blast; yet the substance is in the tree when the leaves are gone. It is still alive and it shall bud again. Likewise, Nebuchadnezzar shall cut off all the leaves of the tree of Israel—take away the inhabitants, only a tenth shall be left; still the Israel of God never shall be destroyed.

And what is true of the Israel of God is also true of the Church of God. No matter how great the assault against the Church may be, Christ has assured us that the gates of hell shall not prevail against her (see Matthew 16:18).

REVIEW QUESTIONS

1. Describe the heavenly creatures Isaiah witnessed in his vision.
2. How did Isaiah first react to the vision?
3. How did Isaiah respond to the plea, "Who will go for us?"
4. How long did God tell Isaiah that the people would refuse to hear and heed the word of God?
5. What applications for Christian living do you draw from this lesson?

GOLDEN TEXT HOMILY

"GO YE INTO ALL THE WORLD, AND PREACH THE GOSPEL TO EVERY CREATURE" (Mark 16:15).

Just a very short period of time would elapse before Jesus would return to His Father. Then

His disciples would be left to carry on His work of building the Kingdom and preparing for His return. What a tremendous work—and what seemingly little education and preparation had been made in order for the eleven men who remained faithful to Him after His death and resurrection to assume positions of leadership in the infant Church which was to be born on that eventful day in the city of Jerusalem. Jesus depended almost entirely on the power and the anointing of the Holy Spirit to complete the work of making ready the men to whom was entrusted the planting and discipling of the men and women who formed the nucleus of Christ's kingdom.

There is an old, familiar illustration which points out the faithfulness which Christ left the entire future of His Church. When He returned to heaven, one of the angels had a few moments of conversation with Him relative to His earthly ministry. The last question asked by the angel was something like this, "But, Jesus, just in case all of the Eleven do not obey Your words and some of them fail to wait and receive the Holy Ghost, what alternative plan have You set up for the building of Your kingdom?" With His brown eyes flooded with tears and a tender, loving smile on His features, He quietly replied, "Well, then, angel, I have no other plan—but none of them will fail!"

The great plan of evangelizing the world, of building the kingdom of God and keeping the gospel message clear and firm was utterly dependent on three factors—**go**—**preach**—**everywhere**. The message has not failed. The messengers have not failed. And we shall not fail as we meet the challenge of the future and continue to **go**—**preach**—**everywhere**.—**Idabeth McDole, D.D., Editor, PENTECOSTAL MESSENGER, Joplin Missouri**

SENTENCE SERMONS

THERE IS A vast difference between a person with a vision and a visionary person. The person with a vision talks little but does much. The person who is visionary talks much but does nothing.
—**Selected**

A VISION WITHOUT a task is a dream;
A task without a vision is drudgery;
A vision and a task is the hope of the world.
—**Anonymous**

RESPONSE TO GOD'S call should involve humble worship and willing service.
—**Selected**

GOD'S CALL TO service is also His assurance that grace sufficient for the task is available.
—**H. Bert Ames**

EVANGELISTIC APPLICATION

EACH CHRISTIAN IS CALLED TO A MINISTRY OF SHARING THE GOSPEL WITH OTHERS.

When we speak of a minister we usually think of a man in the pulpit. But every believer is in reality a minister. One of the major tasks of the man in the pulpit is to guide those who do not have a pulpit ministry into their area of service. Paul explained it this way: "It was he [Christ] who gave some to be apostles, some to be prophets, some to be evangelists, and some to be pastors and teachers, to prepare God's people for works of service, so that the body of Christ may be built up until we all reach unity in the faith and in the knowledge of the Son of God and become mature, attaining to the whole measure of the fullness of Christ" (Ephesians 4:11-13, **New International Version**).

One important function of the pastor-teacher is to prepare God's people to minister to others. Each believer has a responsibility to aid other believers in their quest for spiritual maturity and to introduce Christ to those who are not yet committed to Him. The church that has not yet embraced this concept is not functioning as a New Testament church.

ILLUMINATING THE LESSON

How can God give us visions when life is hurrying at a precipitate rate? I have stood in the national gallery and seen people gallop round the chamber and glance at Turner's picture in the space of five minutes. Surely we might say to such trippers, "Be still and know Turner!" Gaze quietly at one little bit of cloud or at one branch or at one wave of the sea or at one ray of the drifting moon. "Be still, and know Turner." But God has difficulty in getting us still. That is perhaps why he has sometimes employed the ministry of dreams. Men have had "visions in the night." In the daytime I have a Divine visitor in the shape of some worthy thought or noble impulse or hallowed suggestion, but I am in such feverish haste that I do not heed it and pass along. I do not "turn aside to see this great thing," and so I lose Heavenly vision. If I would know more of God, I must relax the strain and moderate the pace. I must be "still."—**J. H. Jowett**

DAILY DEVOTIONAL GUIDE

M. God's Call and Enablement. Exodus 3:1-12

T. Age No Barrier to God's Call. 1 Samuel 3:1-10

W. Called to Warn the Wicked. Ezekiel 3:16-21

T. Called to Follow Christ. Matthew 16:24-28

F. Called to Be Conquerors. Romans 8:28-39

S. The Christian's Calling. 1 Corinthians 1:26-31

August 16, 1981

Deliverance Through Prayer

Bible Background: 2 Kings 18:1—19:37; 2 Chronicles 29:1-36; 30:1-27; 31:2-10; 32:24-30
Time: Around 712 B.C.
Place: Jerusalem
Supplemental References: Matthew 6:5-15; John 15:1-7; James 5:13-18
Golden Text: "The effectual fervent prayer of a righteous man availeth much" (James 5:16).
Central Truth: Effective prayer taps the resources of an almighty God who can meet every need.
Evangelistic Emphasis: Any person who comes to God in sincere repentance will receive deliverance from sin.

PRINTED TEXT

2 Kings 19:14. And Hezekiah received the letter of the hand of the messengers, and read it: and Hezekiah went up into the house of the Lord, and spread it before the Lord.

15. And Hezekiah prayed before the Lord, and said, O Lord God of Israel, which dwellest between the cherubims, thou art the God, even thou alone, of all the kingdoms of the earth; thou hast made heaven and earth.

16. Lord, bow down thine ear, and hear: open, Lord, thine eyes, and see: and hear the words of Sennacherib, which hath sent him to reproach the living God.

17. Of a truth, Lord, the kings of Assyria have destroyed the nations and their lands,

18. And have cast their gods into the fire: for they were no gods, but the work of men's hands, wood and stone: therefore they have destroyed them.

19. Now therefore, O Lord our God, I beseech thee, save thou us out of his hand, that all the kingdoms of the earth may know that thou art the Lord God, even thou only.

20. Then Isaiah the son of Amoz sent to Hezekiah, saying, Thus saith the Lord God of Israel, That which thou hast prayed to me against Sennacherib king of Assyria I have heard.

21. This is the word that the Lord hath spoken concerning him; The virgin the daughter of Zion despised thee, and laughed thee to scorn; the daughter of Jerusalem hath shaken her head at thee.

32. Therefore thus saith the Lord concerning the king of Assyria, He shall not come into this city, nor shoot an arrow there, nor come before it with shield, nor cast a bank against it.

33. By the way that he came, by the same shall he return, and shall not come into this city, saith the Lord.

34. For I will defend this city, to save it, for mine own sake, and for my servant David's sake.

35. And it came to pass that night, that the angel of the Lord went out, and smote in the camp of the Assyrians an hundred fourscore and five thousand: and when they arose early in the morning, behold, they were all dead corpses.

36. So Sennacherib king of Assyria departed, and went and returned, and dwelt at Nineveh.

DICTIONARY

Hezekiah (hez-ah-KIGH-uh)—2 Kings 19:14—The thirteenth king of Judah after Solomon; he ruled from 729 to 696 B.C., or possibly 716 to 686 B.C. (the date is not definite). He was one of the three best kings of Judah.

letter—2 Kings 19:14—In Hebrew this word and the verb are in the plural, perhaps indicating that the document was a lengthy one and may have comprised several scrolls, of which only the main part is given in preceding verses.

cherubims (CHAIR-you-bem)—2 Kings 19:15—The **im** of the word makes it the plural of cherub; the **s** is not needed. These were composite creature-forms, a kind of religious insignia. Two facing each other were on the mercy seat of the ark. We know nothing about their shape except that they were winged.

Sennacherib (sen-NACK-ah-rib)—2 Kings 19:16—The king of Assyria, 716 to 681 B.C. (dates uncertain). He managed only eight military campaigns in his twenty-four-year reign, a small amount in comparison to the kings that preceded him. He inaugurated a period of relative peace in the Middle East.

Isaiah—Isaiah 19:20—The greatest of all the prophets of Israel: a statesman, a man of wisdom, eloquence, and literary genius, a fearless preacher of the message of the Lord. He was married and had two sons. Jewish tradition states that he was of royal descent.

Amoz—Isaiah 19:20—The father of Isaiah. Jewish tradition states that he was a brother of Amaziah, king of Judah.

Nineveh—Isaiah 19:36—Most famous city of Assyria; its capital from Sennacherib to the last king of the empire.

LESSON OUTLINE

I. FACING DIFFICULT CIRCUMSTANCES
   A. The Threat
   B. The Prophecy
   C. The Threat Renewed

II. OFFERING EARNEST PRAYER
   A. The Temple
   B. Earnest Prayer
   C. The Great Name

III. RECEIVING GOD'S ANSWER
   A. Persistence in Prayer
   B. Promise of Peace
   C. Our Defense

IV. EXPERIENCING GOD-GIVEN VICTORY
   A. Assyria Defeated
   B. Sennacherib Killed

LESSON EXPOSITION

INTRODUCTION

How important is prayer in your life? How much difference does prayer really make? If you stopped praying altogether, what impact would it have on your life?

Senator Everett Dirksen suddenly had a blur in front of his eyes. He could not read fine print and he was alarmed. He went from one physician to another and though they differed, the general suggestion seemed to be: "You should go to Johns Hopkins for one final examination. And while there have your right eye removed."

Senator Dirksen made the appointment at Johns Hopkins in Baltimore. He got on a train and prayed: "Lord, I don't ask that You heal the eye. I really don't care if You take it. But, Lord, I do want to know Your decision about my eye. I want to know what You want me to do with my eye."

After the examination was completed at Johns Hopkins, the physician said: "Now then, I want to tell you what we're going to do."

At that point Senator Dirksen looked up, interrupted him and said: "Just a moment, I will not have my right eye removed."

"You what?"

"I will not have my right eye removed. You see, I stopped and had a consultation with another doctor enroute to Baltimore."

The Johns Hopkins physician looked at him in amazement. "That's impossible, sir. What was his name?" the doctor asked.

"The Great Physician upstairs!" replied the Senator.

At that the Johns Hopkins physician looked at him, "Oh, I see. You're one of those guys!"

"Yeah, I'm one of those guys."

And to his dying day Senator Dirksen claimed that his right eye was his best eye!

Yes, there is power in prayer. The difference it can make is illustrated in today's lesson.

I. FACING DIFFICULT CIRCUMSTANCES (2 Kings 19:1-13)

A. The Threat (vv. 1-5)

(2 Kings 19:1-5 is not included in the printed text.)

Hezekiah became king of Judah when he was twenty-five years old. He reigned in Jerusalem for twenty-nine years. He did what was right in the eyes of the Lord, and he instituted reforms more widespread and drastic than had been attempted by any of his predecessors.

One of the things he did was to break into pieces the bronze snake Moses had made. The people had sunk so low that they had made this serpent an object to worship.

It was in the sixth year of Hezekiah's reign that Israel was carried away into captivity. The scripture says, "This happened because they had not obeyed the Lord their God, but had violated his covenant—all that Moses the servant of the Lord commanded. They neither listened to the commands nor carried them out" (2 Kings 18:12, **New International Version**).

In the fourteenth year of King Hezekiah's reign, Sennacherib, a most formidable foe appeared. He was the king of Assyria and he attacked all the fortified cities of Judah and captured them. In response, Hezekiah manifested a weakness unworthy of him and of the God who had so wonderfully sustained him. He offered to pay whatever Sennacherib demanded of him. The king of Assyria required of him three hundred talents (11 tons) of silver and thirty talents (1 ton) of gold. Hezekiah gave him all the silver that was found in the Temple of the Lord and in the treasuries of the royal palace. He also stripped off the gold that covered the doors and doorposts of the Temple of the Lord, and gave it to the king of Assyria.

This acquiescence did not satisfy Sennacherib. He sent his field commander, Rabshakeh, with a message for Hezekiah. He deliberately, and with every evidence of contempt, challenged the God in whom the nation of Judah had professed to put its trust. He sought to drive a wedge between Hezekiah and the people of Judah. He said to them, " 'Do not listen to Hezekiah, for he is misleading you when he says, "The Lord will deliver us." Has the god of any nation ever delivered his land from the hand of the king of Assyria?' " (2 Kings 18:32, 33; **New International Version**).

Faced with a very perilous situation, Hezekiah turned to his old and trusted friend, the Prophet Isaiah, and urged him to pray for God's people.

B. The Prophecy (vv. 6, 7)

(2 Kings 19:6, 7 is not included in the printed text.)

Isaiah sent a message of comfort from the Lord to Hezekiah. The king was assured that he did not have to fear what he had heard. The Lord regarded the blasphemy which Sennacherib had uttered as against Himself, and not against Hezekiah alone. Therefore, He put such a spirit in the king of Assyria that when he heard a certain report, he returned to his own country. There the Lord had him cut down with the sword.

These words must have encouraged Hezekiah. It is always encouraging to the believer to be reminded that the Lord is with him. He can then put his problems in proper perspective. What seemed to be an impossible situation suddenly became a very acceptable state of affairs. What a difference the Lord makes!

A small boy sailed his toy boat on a pond. The boat floated out of his reach and he appealed to a larger boy to help him. This boy, without saying a word, picked up rocks and began throwing them out near the boat. The small boy pleaded with him not to hit his boat, but the big boy kept on. Soon the small boy noticed that each stone was falling on the far side of the boat, making a wave that pushed it nearer the shore. Then he realized that the big boy was planning the fall of each stone in order to bring the boat nearer to the shore. Soon it was within reach and the owner had his boat again.

We must never forget that God plans the fall of each stone within our circumstances, and that each storm and wave is calculated by Him in order to bring us nearer to Himself.

C. The Threat Renewed (vv. 8-13)

(2 Kings 19:8-13 is not included in the printed text.)

God said that through Isaiah Sennacherib

would hear a certain report and would return to his own country. This is precisely what happened. Because of the report the king of Assyria heard, he withdrew his forces. When Rab-shakeh returned, he found that Sennacherib had diverted his attention from Israel to other quarters. The report he had received was that Tirhakah, the Cushite king of Egypt, was marching out to fight against him.

However, Sennacherib did not forget about the people of God. He sent messengers again to Hezekiah, informing him of his intentions of conquering the land. He reminded the king that other countries had been unsuccessful in stopping the Assyrian armies. Also, he attacked the god of Judah again. The gods of the other nations had not stopped him, he asserted, and neither could the Lord God Almighty.

This was a time of real testing for Hezekiah and the people of Judah. Were they to believe the prophecy of Isaiah? Was Sennacherib's withdrawal only a temporary thing? Would God fight for them? Why had the problem that appeared to have gone away returned? The believer's true allegiance is evidenced in the time of testing.

II. OFFERING EARNEST PRAYER (2 Kings 19:14-19)

A. The Temple (vv. 14, 15)

14. And Hezekiah received the letter of the hand of the messengers, and read it: and Hezekiah went up into the house of the Lord, and spread it before the Lord.

15. And Hezekiah prayed before the Lord, and said, O Lord God of Israel, which dwellest between the cherubims, thou art the God, even thou alone, of all the kingdoms of the earth; thou hast made heaven and earth.

Confronted again by the possibility of an attack from Sennacherib, Hezekiah turned to the Temple of the Lord. There he expected to find God. He had often beheld the glory of God in the house of the Lord. Troubled in soul, he longed to find the peace which a fresh encounter with God brings. Furthermore, by going to the Temple in this hour of need, Hezekiah set a worthy example before his people. They, too, would be encouraged to call upon the Lord. Then, Hezekiah's action was a public demonstration that he believed God's power was sufficient to protect them from any attack the enemy might make.

Hezekiah took the letter he received from the king of Assyria and spread it out before the Lord. He appealed to God as the God of Israel. Perhaps he wished to remind himself of Jacob's power in prayer when he uttered the name Israel, who was a prince who prevailed with God. What God had been to his forefathers, he desired Him to be now to the nation of Judah. Hezekiah also recognized that Jehovah alone was God over all the kingdoms of the earth. He who created the heaven and earth was supreme in it. No threat from an enemy camp could become a reality as long as God stood with His people. Hezekiah harbored this hope.

Is it reasonable to believe that modern day national leaders would see greater manifestations of God's power if He was petitioned?

B. Earnest Prayer (vv. 16-18)

16. Lord, bow down thine ear, and hear: open, Lord, thine eyes, and see: and hear the words of Sennacherib, which hath sent him to reproach the living God.

17. Of a truth, Lord, the kings of Assyria have destroyed the nations and their lands,

18. And have cast their gods into the fire: for they were no gods, but the work of men's hands, wood and stone: therefore they have destroyed them.

As Hezekiah sought the Lord in prayer, his earnestness was evident. He ardently craved for a divine intervention. Earnestness is the living spirit in prayer. Our prayers may have order, beauty, and eloquence, but without earnestness they are vain. To desire fervently will lead invariably to ardent expressions. Cold prayers are no prayers. James writes: "The prayer of a righteous man is powerful and effective" (James 5:16, **New International Version**). Then he illustrates: "Elijah was a man just like us. He prayed earnestly that it would not rain, and it did not rain on the land for three and a half years. Again he prayed, and the heavens gave rain, and the earth produced its crops" (James 5:17, 18; **New International Version**).

Hezekiah knew that this was no small matter that he sought from the Lord. Other nations had fallen before the armies of Assyria. He knew that their only hope was in God. No human ingenuity or might could deliver them. No gods could protect them; Jehovah alone could save Judah. In every life there arises that situation where the individual realizes his dependence upon God. In those moments, he understands how weak man is. How wonderful it is that in our hour of weakness, God's strength is manifest!

C. The Great Name (v. 19)

19. Now therefore, O Lord our God, I beseech thee, save thou us out of his hand, that all the kingdoms of the earth may know that thou art the Lord God, even thou only.

Hezekiah's appeal is couched in the honor of the Lord. Deliverance from Sennacherib would be evidence that the Lord alone is God. There are some occasions when the name of God is very closely tied with the history of His people. Sometimes in reliance upon a divine promise, a believer will be led to take a certain course of action. Now, if the Lord should not be as good as His promise, not only is the believer deceived, but also the wicked world looking on would ask, "Where is your God?"

How mightily did Moses argue with God on one occasion upon this ground! "Wherefore should the Egyptians speak, and say, For mischief did he bring them out, to slay them in the mountains, and to consume them from the face of the earth?" (Exodus 32:12). Joshua also used this argument: "O Lord God, wherefore hast thou at all brought this people over Jordan, to deliver us into the hand of the Amorites, to destroy us? . . . For the Canaanites and all the inhabitants of the land shall hear of it, and shall environ us round, and cut off our name from the earth: and what wilt thou do unto thy great name?" (Joshua 7:7, 9).

III. RECEIVING GOD'S ANSWER (2 Kings 19:20-34)

A. Persistence in Prayer (v. 20)

20. Then Isaiah the son of Amoz sent to Hezekiah, saying, Thus saith the Lord God of Israel, That which thou hast prayed to me against Sennacherib king of Assyria I have heard.

Through Isaiah, the Lord assured Hezekiah that He had heard his prayer. Every believer can be certain that God hears him when he prays. John wrote: "This is the assurance we have in approaching God: that if we ask anything according to his will, he hears us. And if we know that he hears us—whatever we ask—we know that we have what we asked of him" (1 John 5:14, 15; **New International Version**).

When Jesus taught His disciples how to pray, He emphasized the importance of persistence. He told them a story about a man who came to his friend at midnight in search of bread. A visitor had stopped at the man's house and he had nothing to set before him. But his friend would not come to his aid. He explained that the door was locked and his children were in bed so he could not help him. But Jesus said that because of the man's persistence, his friend got up and gave him as much as he needed.

Jesus then, urged His disciples to ask, seek, and knock. He assured them that their persistence in prayer would produce results. He also compared the Heavenly Father with an earthly father. If an earthly father would respond to their needs when they asked, how much more would their Heavenly Father minister to them (see Luke 11:1-13).

B. Promise of Peace (vv. 21-31)

21. This is the word that the Lord hath spoken concerning him; The virgin the daughter of Zion hath despised thee, and laughed thee to scorn; the daughter of Jerusalem hath shaken her head at thee.

(2 Kings 19:22-31 is not included in the printed text.)

In His answer to Hezekiah's prayer, God assured him that He was fully aware of the arrogance of Sennacherib. The Lord also saw that the blasphemy of the king of Assyria was directed "against the Holy One of Israel." One is reminded of the confrontation between Saul of Tarsus and the Lord of glory. Saul did not realize that his persecutions were not against the church only but against the Lord also. So Jesus could ask Saul, "Why do you persecute Me?" So it was with Sennacherib. The Lord made it clear that the battle was not with Hezekiah or with the people of Judah. The king of Assyria found himself doing battle with the King of kings.

The Lord assured Hezekiah that He would stop Sennacherib. Of Judah's enemy, He says, "Because thy rage against me and thy tumult is come up into mine ears, therefore I will put my hook in thy nose, and my bridle in thy lips, and I will turn thee back by the way by which thou camest" (2 Kings 19:28).

In addition to this, the Lord assured Hezekiah that Judah would still flourish in peace and prosperity. Someone has observed: "How great is the condescension of our God. He not only hears our prayer; He also assures us of an answer. And the answer is adequate to meet the case, turning fear into confidence, humiliation into triumph, and sorrow into joy."

C. Our Defense (vv. 32-34)

32. Therefore thus saith the Lord concerning the king of Assyria, He shall not come into this city, nor shoot an arrow there, nor come before it with shield, nor cast a bank against it.

33. By the way that he came, by the same shall he return, and shall not come into this city, saith the Lord.

34. For I will defend this city, to save it, for mine own sake, and for my servant David's sake.

The Lord said that Sennacherib would not be permitted to adopt any of the principal modes of attack followed in ancient military art in his efforts to conquer Jerusalem. The Lord declared that the king of Assyria would not enter the city, "nor approach near enough to shoot an arrow, not even from the most powerful engine which throws missiles to the greatest distance, nor shall he occupy any part of the ground before the city by a fence, a mantelet, or covering for men employed in a siege, nor cast (raise) a bank (mound) of earth, overtopping the city walls, whence he may see and command the interior of the city" (Jamieson, Fausset, Brown).

The army under Rab-shakeh marched toward Jerusalem and encamped at a little distance with a view to blockade it. They delayed siege of the city awaiting the arrival of the king and his detachment. He felt that all the combined forces of Assyria would have little difficulty in conquering the capital.

Sennacherib was so determined to conquer Judah and the neighboring countries that nothing but a divine interposition could have saved Jerusalem. God promised that He would intervene to save the city. He gave two reasons for His action. It was "for my sake," He said. That was what Hezekiah prayed for in verse 19. It was also "for the sake of David my servant." God made a promise to Solomon after Solomon had disappointed Him by his wayward living. He warned him that He would tear the kingdom away from him, but He made this condition: "Nevertheless, for the sake of David your father, I will not do it during your lifetime. I will tear it out of the hand of your son. Yet I will not tear the whole kingdom from him, but will give him one tribe for the sake of David my servant and for the sake of Jerusalem, which I have chosen" (1 Kings 11:12, 13; **New International Version**). So God was honoring His promise to Solomon when He defended Jerusalem in the days of Hezekiah. His Word is always trustworthy.

In 1815 Queen Louise, the Prussian queen, wrote a great letter about Napoleon to her father. In this letter she said: "It were a crime to say that God is with the French Emperor; but he is manifestly an instrument in the hands of the Almighty to bury out of sight the old order, for which He has no further purpose." Whether men execrate or admire Napoleon, they must all acknowledge that he broke down the barriers between men and nations, that he, like Cromwell, shook down in the dust what God had condemned. He told his soldiers that every soldier carried in his knapsack a marshal's baton. He was therefore the preacher and herald of the popular movements that have swept the world since then, sometimes for good, sometimes for evil. He preached a terrific sermon on the text that the nations that forget God shall be cast into hell. He proclaimed, unconsciously, perhaps, the supremacy of the moral order; and even by his own flaming fall, like that of the star Wormwood out of heaven, was a witness that righteousness and judgment are the habitation of God's throne. Thus we see that God uses men like Napoleon and Sennacherib to further His own purposes.

Another lesson we should learn from this passage is that God is our defense. The psalmist expresses it this way: "He who dwells in the shelter of the Most High will rest in the shadow of the Almighty. I will say of the Lord, 'He is my refuge and my fortress, my God, in whom I trust'" (Psalm 91:1, 2; **New International Version**).

This beautiful promise is conditional. It is only the person who dwells in the shelter of the Almighty who can claim the promises that follow. Too many people dart in and out of His presence and then expect to constantly receive His blessings. The Lord calls upon His people to serve Him faithfully and consistently. These are they who are continuously in the flow of His power and care.

Written large upon the pages of holy Scripture and human history is the fact that God is faithful. He is a Being upon whom we can absolutely rely. His faithfulness requires Him to keep every promise He has made. Moses wrote: "Know therefore that the Lord your God is God; he is the faithful God, keeping his covenant of love to a thousand generations of those who love him and keep his commands" (Deuteronomy 7:9, **New International Version**). In that great psalm where the Word is extolled for its many virtues, the psalmist wrote: "Your word, O Lord, is eternal; it stands firm in the heavens. Your faithfulness continues through all generations; you established the earth, and it endures" (Psalm 119:89, 90; **New International Version**).

God's protective care of David is an example of His faithfulness as our defense. " 'I have found David my servant; with my sacred oil I have anointed him. My hand will sustain him; surely my arm will strengthen him. No enemy will subject him to tribute; no wicked man will oppress him. I will crush his foes before him and strike down his adversaries. My faithful love will be with him, and through my name his horn will be exalted. I will set his hand over the sea, his right hand over the rivers. He will call out to me, "You are my Father, my God, the Rock my Savior" ' " (Psalm 89:20-26, **New International Version**).

His protective care is extended to all believers: "So then, those who suffer according to God's will should commit themselves to their faithful Creator and continue to do good" (1 Peter 4:19, **New International Version**).

IV. EXPERIENCING GOD-GIVEN VICTORY (2 Kings 19:35-37)

A. Assyria Defeated (v. 35)

35. And it came to pass that night, that the angel of the Lord went out, and smote in the camp of the Assyrians an hundred fourscore and five thousand: and when they arose early in the morning, behold, they were all dead corpses.

The Lord moved swiftly to prove that He was Jerusalem's defender. The attack described in this verse probably happened the night following the day on which Isaiah had foretold to Hezekiah the deliverance of Jerusalem. We are not told where the Assyrian army was located when this terrible catastrophe befell it. It could be that the Assyrians were scattered in different locations when the attack came: some of them near Jerusalem; others at Libnah; some on their way to Jerusalem. The smiting of 185,000 men by an angel of the Lord by no means presupposes that the whole of Sennacherib's army was concentrated at one spot. The blow could have fallen upon the Assyrians wherever they were located. The "angel of the Lord" is the same angel that smote the firstborn of Egypt (see Exodus 12:23), and inflicted the pestilence upon Israel after the numbering of the people by David (see 2 Samuel 24:15, 16). The slaying of 185,000 men in a single night is nothing short of a miracle from God.

What is a miracle? Millions of people listened to the voice of King George VI speaking in the venerable Westminster Abbey in London as he took the vows of kingship and promise to uphold the law of the realm and defend the Protestant faith. No doubt many said to another during that day, "The radio is a wonderful thing, isn't it? A miracle." But is the radio—your hearing in Pittsburgh the voice of a man speaking in Westminster Abbey in London—a miracle? No. It is something that takes place by man's using and obeying in the strictest way the laws of nature—the atmosphere, electricity, call it what you please. Many of the things that are popularly spoken of as miracles are things done in strictest obedience to physical laws.

What do you consider to be the characteristics of a miracle?

What, then, is a miracle? Here is a good definition of it: "A miracle is an event occurring in the natural world, observed by the senses, produced by divine power, without any adequate human or natural cause, the purpose of which is to reveal the will of God and to do good to man." A wonder, such as the radio or television, however little the layman may be able to explain it, is an event occurring in the natural world and observed by the senses, and produced by natural causes; whereas the miracle is without natural cause and is produced by the power of God.

B. Sennacherib Killed (vv. 36, 37)

36. So Sennacherib king of Assyria departed, and went and returned, and dwelt at Nineveh.

(2 Kings 19:37 is not included in the printed text.)

The judgment of God upon the Assyrian army compelled Sennacherib to retreat without delay, and to return to Nineveh as Isaiah had predicted. The king of Assyria broke camp and withdrew. He returned to Nineveh and stayed there. He did not undertake any fresh expedition against Judah.

One day, when Sennacherib was worshiping in the temple of his god Nisroch, two of his sons slew him and fled into the land of Ararat. Another of his sons became king in his stead. Nisroch is believed to have been the supreme deity of the Assyrians.

REVIEW QUESTIONS

1. What demands were being directed to Hezekiah by the king of Assyria?
2. What was the report Isaiah gave Hezekiah concerning the retreat of the Assyrian army?
3. What action did the Lord take against the Assyrians?
4. What did the defeated Sennacherib do after the loss of his army?
5. What applications for life in today's world do you draw from this lesson?

GOLDEN TEXT HOMILY

THE EFFECTUAL FERVENT PRAYER OF A RIGHTEOUS MAN AVAILETH MUCH (James 5:16).

Normal exposition of this verse boils down to this: prayer changes things.

From preceding verses, we know that James addressed himself to practical matters. He did not speak subjectively. He was not philosophizing. He spoke of the sick and of their healing through prayer. He spoke of the sinful and of their forgiveness through prayer. He spoke of our confessing faults one to another, of our need to pray for each other, and of organized methods by which such spiritual help is requested and administered.

James uses two qualifying phrases to set forth his concept of effective prayer.

First, prayer must be fervent: not cold, or apathetic, or halfhearted, but hot with passion and concern. This conforms with the promise of Christ: "What things soever ye desire, when ye pray, believe that ye receive them, and ye shall have them" (Mark 11:24). It is also in keeping with human experience. Burning desire and fervent prayer are Siamese twins.

Second, effective prayer must be sincere: it must be backed by decision and action. James' righteous man is more than talk. He is not necessarily saintly or beyond human frailty, but he is one who sincerely believes and who backs faith with a life of commitment.

Elijah was James' example.

Live as Elijah . . . then pray as Elijah . . . and God will answer.—**Hoyt E. Stone, Editor, Christian Education Literature, Church of God Publishing House, Cleveland, Tennessee**

SENTENCE SERMONS

EFFECTIVE PRAYER TAPS the resources of an almighty God who can meet every need.
—**Selected**

PRAYER IS NOT conquering God's reluctance, but taking hold of God's willingness.
—**Phillip Brooks**

FAITH IS DEAD to doubt, dumb to discouragement, and blind to the impossible.
—**"The Defender"**

STRONG FAITH CAN only be produced amid darkness, discouragement, and seemingly hopeless situations. Strong muscles are produced in the gymnasium of necessity.
—**A. P. Gouthey**

EVANGELISTIC APPLICATION

ANY PERSON WHO COMES TO GOD IN SINCERE REPENTANCE WILL RECEIVE DELIVERANCE FROM SIN.

The importance of the message of repentance is underscored by its place in the ministry of John the Baptist, Jesus, and the disciples. The keynote of John's preaching was "Repent, for the kingdom of heaven is near" (Matthew 3:2, **New International Version**). After Jesus identified Himself as the fulfillment of Isaiah's prophecy about the coming Messiah, it is said: "From that time on Jesus began to preach, 'Repent, for the kingdom of heaven is near' " (Matthew 4:17, **New International Version**). After his masterful sermon on the Day of Pentecost, Peter responded to the inquiry of the audience as to what they should do by saying, " 'Repent and be baptized, every one of you, in the name of Jesus Christ so that your sins may be forgiven. And you will receive the gift of the Holy Spirit' " (Acts 2:38, **New International Version**).

This is certain: if a man repents of his sin, God forgives him. John wrote: "If we confess our sins, he is faithful and just and will forgive us our sins and purify us from all unrighteousness" (1 John 1:9, **New International Version**).

ILLUMINATING THE LESSON

Some years ago it was my pleasure to listen to a gospel address by an officer of the Royal Navy who had fought in many encounters during World War I, and came through safely. He read the 91st Psalm every day while aboard ship. With the outbreak of the war he again was called to the colors. Once more his ship was in conflict with the enemy. While in the line of duty she received a bad hole in her side. That did not deter her nor her crew. In fact, the ship was in several encounters after being struck. This British officer related a most interesting fact. He said the ship's flag had on it these words, "In the care of God." Whenever the ship was in a heavy engagement, the men aboard could look up and see the old flag still "in the care of God."—**Erling C. Olson**

DAILY DEVOTIONAL GUIDE

M. Sincere Prayer. Psalm 66:16-20
T. Pattern of Prayer. Matthew 6:9-15
W. Believing Prayer. Matthew 21:18-22
T. Humble Prayer. Luke 18:9-14
F. Authoritative Prayer. John 14:10-14
S. Confident Prayer. 1 John 5:13-15

August 23, 1981

Giving Priority to God's Word

Bible Background: 2 Kings 22:1—23:30; 2 Chronicles 34:1-33
Time: Around 622 B.C.
Place: Jerusalem
Supplemental References: Deuteronomy 31:24-30; Matthew 5:17-20; 1 Timothy 4:6-16
Golden Text: "Study to shew thyself approved unto God, a workman that needeth not to be ashamed, rightly dividing the word of truth" (2 Timothy 2:15).
Central Truth: When men and nations obey God's Word, His blessing rests upon them.
Evangelistic Emphasis: The Word of God shows the sinner how he can find forgiveness and peace.

PRINTED TEXT

2 Kings 22:8. And Hilkiah the high priest said unto Shaphan the scribe, I have found the book of the law in the house of the Lord. And Hilkiah gave the book to Shaphan, and he read it.

9. And Shaphan the scribe came to the king, and brought the king word again, and said, Thy servants have gathered the money that was found in the house, and have delivered it into the hand of them that do the work, that have the oversight of the house of the Lord.

10. And Shaphan the scribe shewed the king, saying, Hilkiah the priest hath delivered me a book. And Shaphan read it before the king.

11. And it came to pass, when the king had heard the words of the book of the law, that he rent his clothes.

12. And the king commanded Hilkiah the priest, and Ahikam the son of Shaphan, and Achbor the son of Michaiah, and Shaphan the scribe, and Asahiah a servant of the king's, saying,

13. Go ye, enquire of the Lord for me, and for the people, and for all Judah, concerning the words of this book that is found: for great is the wrath of the Lord that is kindled against us, because our fathers have not hearkened unto the words of this book, to do according unto all that which is written concerning us.

14. So Hilkiah the priest, and Ahikam, and Achbor, and Shaphan, and Asahiah, went unto Huldah the prophetess, the wife of Shallum the son of Tikvah, the son of Harhas, keeper of the wardrobe; (now she dwelt in Jerusalem in the college;) and they communed with her.

15. And she said unto them, Thus saith the Lord God of Israel, Tell the man that sent you to me,

16. Thus saith the Lord, Behold, I will bring evil upon this place, and upon the inhabitants thereof, even all the words of the book which the king of Judah hath read:

17. Because they have forsaken me, and have burned incense unto other gods, that they might provoke me to anger with all the works of their hands; therefore my wrath shall be kindled against this place, and shall not be quenched.

DICTIONARY

Hilkiah (hill-KIGH-uh)—2 Kings 22:8—The high priest during the reign of Josiah; he became famous as a result of the events of today's lesson. He was very probably the same Hilkiah mentioned as the great-grandfather of Ezra (Ezra 7:1).

Shaphan (SHAY-fan)—2 Kings 22:8—The secretary-financial officer of Josiah. He and his sons figured very prominently in the affairs of the government at this time; the sons were also the friend and protector of Jeremiah during his difficult days of persecution before the fall of Judah.

the king—2 Kings 22:9—Josiah, the sixteenth king of Judah who ruled from 640 to 609 B.C.

Ahikam (uh-HIGH-cam)—2 Kings 22:12—A minister of Josiah, the sole protector of Jeremiah from death under Jehoiakim (Jeremiah 26:24); the father of Gedaliah, the last governor of Judah after the last king had been taken captive by the Babylonians.

Achbor (AHK-bore)—2 Kings 22:12—Another minister of the king.

Asahiah (aa-suh-HIGH-uh)—2 Kings 22:12—Another type of official of Josiah; he probably had different types of duties from the two mentioned before.

Huldah (HULL-dah)—2 Kings 22:14—One of the few women who filled the office of prophetess in the Bible. Her husband was a "keeper of the wardrobe," which could have been of either royal robes or priestly vestments.

LESSON OUTLINE

I. DISCOVERING GOD'S WORD
   A. A Righteous King
   B. A Noble Task
   C. A Sacred Book

II. SEEKING DIVINE COUNSEL
   A. A Quick Reaction
   B. A Sad Pronouncement
   C. A Worthy Exception

III. RESPONDING WITH OBEDIENCE
   A. A Valiant Effort
   B. A Courageous Attack
   C. A Restored Observance

LESSON EXPOSITION

INTRODUCTION

Have you discovered the Word of God? You probably own a copy of the Bible, or you may own several copies. You probably read your Bible, and you may read it systematically day after day. But, are you reading only words? Has its message come through to you? Does it vibrate with life as far as you are concerned? Have you learned how to apply its truths to your daily life?

There was a time in the history of Judah when the Word of the Lord was lost. Men no longer had access to its strengthening portions. It was a glad day for that nation when the Book of the Law was discovered in the Temple of the Lord. Because a righteous king ruled, he saw the value of the Book and immediately turned to its pages for direction. Obedience to the Word would bring the blessings of God to the nation.

What you do with the Bible is all important. As the Stagirite philosopher, Aristotle, said of his work, "This book is given for action and not for discussion," so the Scriptures are given to us for action and not for discussion. Arguments about the Bible reverberate through the centuries; vast libraries house the literature on the study of the sacred writings. But it was not for this purpose that God gave the Scriptures and that holy men of old spoke through the Holy Ghost. The Bible was given to man in order that he might have eternal life through Jesus Christ. What John said at the close of his Gospel is true of every book in the Bible: "But these are written that you may believe that Jesus is the Christ, the Son of God, and that by believing you may have life in his name" (John 20:31, **New International Version**).

I. DISCOVERING GOD'S WORD (2 Kings 22: 1-10)

A. A Righteous King (vv. 1, 2)

(2 Kings 22:1, 2 is not included in the printed text.)

When Manasseh was twelve years old he became king of Judah. Of him the Scriptures say, "He did evil in the eyes of the Lord, following the detestable practices of the nations the Lord had driven out before the Israelites" (2 Kings 21:2, **New International Version**).

By way of contrast, Josiah was eight years old when he became king of Judah. His guardians trained him in the principles and practices of piety. Of him the Word says, "He did what was right in the eyes of the

Lord and walked in all the ways of his father David, not turning aside to the right or to the left" (2 Kings 22:2, **New International Version**). So strong was the influence for good upon his life that he continued to adhere all his life, with undeviating perseverance, to the cause of God and righteousness.

Solomon recognized the wisdom of proper training early in life. He wrote: "Train a child in the way he should go, and when he is old he will not turn from it" (Proverbs 22:6, **New International Version**). One of the secrets of Timothy's great usefulness was his childhood training. Paul wrote to him: "I have been reminded of your sincere faith, which first lived in your grandmother Lois and in your mother Eunice and, I am persuaded, now lives in you also" (2 Timothy 1:5, **New International Version**). Again he wrote: "From infancy you have known the holy Scriptures, which are able to make you wise for salvation through faith in Christ Jesus" (2 Timothy 3:15, **New International Version**).

B. A Noble Task (vv. 3-7)

(2 Kings 22:3-7 is not included in the printed text.)

In his attempt to lead the people in the way of righteousness, Josiah turned his attention to the Temple of the Lord. He had already initiated reform in the nation, and now he wanted to restore the Temple to its former glory. Money had already been collected from the people and builders had been employed to do the work. Hilkiah the high priest was charged with the responsibility to ascertain what needed to be done and to oversee the project.

Care should be taken to keep the church building in good repair. The Church itself is a never-dying institution. From age to age the enemies of the gospel have proclaimed that the Church is dying, that it has lost its hold upon mankind, that before long its temples will be forsaken.

Some years ago, two noted unbelievers were passing the beautiful Corinthian-columned Madeleine Church in Paris. It was a Sabbath morning and many worshipers were coming out of the church.

One of these men remarked to the other, "God has a good many callers this morning."

"Yes," replied his companion, "but they are making their last call."

Yet that last call has never been made, and never shall be made; and until all the redeemed shall gather about the throne of the Lamb in heaven, the followers of Christ will "enter into his gates with thanksgiving, and into his courts with praise: be thankful unto him, and bless his name" (Psalm 100:4).

C. A Sacred Book (vv. 8-10)

8. And Hilkiah the high priest said unto Shaphan the scribe, I have found the book of the law in the house of the Lord. And Hilkiah gave the book to Shaphan, and he read it.

What further steps could be taken by the church and by evangelicals in general, to make people more aware of the value of the Bible?

While the Temple of the Lord was being repaired, Hilkiah the high priest found something of great value. He found the Book of the Law—the Pentateuch. It was the Temple copy which had been laid beside the Ark in the most holy place. Moses instructed the Levites thus: " 'Take this Book of the Law and place it beside the ark of the covenant of the Lord your God' " (Deuteronomy 31:26, **New International Version**).

The kings who preceded Josiah were wicked men. Under their administrations, the Temple had been profaned by idols, and the Ark also removed from its site (see 2 Chronicles 35:3). While all of this was happening, the Book of God was somehow lost, but now it was found again as the Temple was being repaired.

No greater tragedy could befall the Church than for it to lose the Bible. There are countries today where the only Scripture believers have is what they have recorded in their mind. How they yearn for access to the Word of God. In contrast to this, the Bible is readily available to people in many countries. Yet many of those who could read and study the Word neglect to do so. How sad that a treasure of such infinite worth could lay in one's home undiscovered.

9. And Shaphan the scribe came to the king, and brought the king word again, and said, Thy servants have gathered the money that was found in the house, and have delivered it into the hand of them that do the work, that have the oversight of the house of the Lord.

10. And Shaphan the scribe shewed the king, saying, Hilkiah the priest hath delivered

me a book. And Shaphan read it before the king.

When Hilkiah the high priest discovered the Word of God, he took it to Shaphan the scribe. Shaphan took the Book and read it. Then he went to the king, showed him the Book, and read to Josiah from the Book. What a beautiful illustration of the importance of sharing the Word with others. Paul instructed Timothy: "The things you have heard me say in the presence of many witnesses entrust to reliable men who will also be qualified to teach others" (2 Timothy 2:2, **New International Version**). We cannot afford to keep to ourselves the wonderful discoveries we make in the Word of God. We must share these experiences with others that they too may discover the power of the Word.

How much time do you spend in reading the Bible? Perhaps the more important question is, how do you read the Word? A young lady explained devotional reading of the Bible this way:

"Yesterday morning I received a letter from one to whom I had given my heart and devoted my life. I freely confess to you that I have read that letter five times, not because I did not understand it at the first reading, nor because I expected to commend myself to the author by frequent reading of his epistle. It was not with me a question of duty, but simply one of pleasure. I read it because I am devoted to the one who wrote it.

"To read the Bible with the same motive is to read it devotionally, and to one who reads it in that spirit it is indeed a love letter."

On one occasion Abraham Lincoln said: "I am profitably engaged in reading the Bible. Take all of this Book upon reason that you can, and the balance by faith, and you will live and die a better man." Douglas MacArthur said: "Believe me, sir, never a night goes by, be I ever so tired, but I read the Word of God before I go to bed." Dwight D. Eisenhower commented: "To read the Bible is to take a trip to a fair land where the spirit is strengthened and faith renewed." Woodrow Wilson mused: "I have a very simple thing to ask of you. I ask every man and woman in this audience that from this day on they will realize that part of the destiny of America lies in their daily perusal of this great Book."

How sad it is to discover this Book only after it is too late to search for its treasures.

Patrick Henry, near death, said: "Here is a Book, the Bible, worth more than all others that were ever printed; yet it is my misfortune never to have found time to read it."

II. SEEKING DIVINE COUNSEL (2 Kings 22: 11-20)

A. A Quick Reaction (vv. 11-13)

11. And it came to pass, when the king had heard the words of the book of the law, that he rent his clothes.

We are not told what passage Shaphan the scribe read to Josiah the king. But we are told of the king's reaction to the reading of God's Word. He tore his robes, signifying great grief and terror over what he had heard. Some scholars have suggested that the passage read to the king was a portion of Deuteronomy, chapters 28, 29, and 30. These chapters call for a renewal of the national covenant, and enumerate the curses which will befall those who violate the law of God. They make it clear that no one is exempt from the punishment such violations bring forth.

The Word of God is to be taken seriously. When God gives a promise, He means it. When He issues a warning, He will carry it out. There can be no light, flippant reading of the Bible. Its message is eternal. It deals with matters that are of the first importance in terms of the welfare of the soul of man. It is a source of hope and help to those who will apply its principles to their life. It has stood the test of time. Multiplied millions from every age can testify that its promises are true. Other millions can speak with equal authority that its warnings are not idle expressions. When unheeded, they are carried out.

12. And the king commanded Hilkiah the priest, and Ahikam the son of Shaphan, and Achbor the son of Michaiah, and Shaphan the scribe, and Asahiah a servant of the king's, saying,

13. Go ye, enquire of the Lord for me, and for the people, and for all Judah, concerning the words of this book that is found: for great is the wrath of the Lord that is kindled against us, because our fathers have not hearkened unto the words of this book, to do according unto all that which is written concerning us.

Why is it so important to place great emphasis on the Bible during periods of revival?

Josiah was so disturbed by what he heard from the Word of God that he wanted an immediate audience with the Lord. He sent some of his closest associates, men who were immediately available to him, to inquire of the Lord about the status of His people. Hilkiah was the high priest. Ahikam was a friend of Jeremiah (see Jeremiah 26:24). Achbor was a man of influence at court (see Jeremiah 26:22). Shaphan was the secretary of state. And Asahiah was an officer of the king. This select group was sent to get an answer from the Lord about the things Josiah had heard.

Josiah's concern was for himself, for his people, and for the entire kingdom—all Judah. He wanted to know what God's will was, and what God had determined concerning the king, the people, and the kingdom. He knew that the commandments which the Lord gave were not for their fathers only, but applied to them as well. If God's anger was kindled against their fathers for their disobedience, the people of Judah could expect His wrath against them for their disobedience.

Whether or not we understand everything about a command from the Lord, we can be sure that He has our best interest at heart. If we obey Him, He will prove His love to us. Sometimes He tests us as did the father of the little girl who had been given a beautiful toy. She came into his room bright-eyed and happy as could be. When the father saw the toy, he told her that she would have to throw it into the fire.

The little girl was appalled by the suggestion. For her, it was a great trial. "Now I shall not compel you to do it; I leave it to you: but you never knew Dad to ask you to do a thing that was not kind to you—I cannot tell you why: but if you can trust me, do so."

The child began to reason in her own way —"Father has always been kind to me, I suppose it is right," and she took the toy and with great effort threw it into the fire. The father said no more for some time. The next day, however, he gave her something far more beautiful which she had long desired.

"Now, my child," he said, "I did this to teach you to trust in that greater Father in heaven. Many a time in your life He will require you to give up and avoid what you cannot see the reasons for avoiding, but if you trust that Father as you have trusted me, you will always find that He wants only the best for you."

Every believer can testify that God always works in his best interest. What an incentive to obedience.

We need the attitude of the native of the Congo who prayed: "Dear Lord, You be the needle and I will be the thread. You go first, and I will follow wherever You may lead!" The Lord is looking for a people who will follow Him in just this fashion. Such persons will experience His blessings continually.

B. A Sad Pronouncement (vv. 14-17)

14. So Hilkiah the priest, and Ahikam, and Achbor, and Shaphan, and Asahiah, went unto Huldah the prophetess, the wife of Shallum the son of Tikvah, the son of Harhas, keeper of the wardrobe; (now she dwelt in Jerusalem in the college;) and they communed with her.

These ambassadors of the king went to the prophetess Huldah in search of a word from the Lord. They did not go to Zephaniah, who was probably young, nor to Jeremiah, who was probably out of town and at his house in Anathoth. Rather, they came to a prophetess who was close by and who was recognized for her prophetic gifts. She was probably a widow. She lived in Jerusalem, in the second district. Respect for her was so great that Jewish writers say that she and Jehoiada the priest (see 2 Chronicles 24:16) were the only persons not of the house of David who ever were buried in Jerusalem.

God uses the usable. In Josiah's day, women occupied a low rung on the social ladder. Yet, Huldah overcame all the obstacles a woman in her society faced, and was sought out by the king as a spokeswoman for God. The Lord will use you if you will make yourself available to Him. Whatever the obstacles are, they can be overcome. There is a place of service which you can fill. God is looking for persons who will commit themselves and their talents to Him. Given that kind of dedication, only eternity will reveal all that He will do through those persons.

15. And she said unto them, Thus saith the Lord God of Israel, Tell the man that sent you to me,

16. Thus saith the Lord, Behold, I will bring evil upon this place, and upon the inhabitants thereof, even all the words of the book which the king of Judah hath read:

The word which Huldah received from the Lord and conveyed to Josiah was not welcomed news. The message was a pronouncement of judgment upon the land of Judah and its people. The judgment would be based upon their violations of the words of the Book which the king of Judah had read.

While the Lord is a God of love and mercy, He is also a God of judgment. Whenever the law of God is broken, the judgment of God follows. Adam and Eve found this to be true. The Lord placed only one restriction upon them. He said, "Of every tree of the garden thou mayest freely eat: But of the tree of the knowledge of good and evil, thou shalt not eat of it: for in the day that thou eatest thereof thou shalt surely die" (Genesis 2:16, 17). Satan came along and suggested that God did not really mean what He had said. Eve partook of the fruit of the tree and also enticed Adam to eat. The judgment of God was swift in coming. They were expelled from the Garden. But, more importantly, they experienced spiritual death—separation from God—and later, physical death. Judgment came just as God said it would.

Like Adam and Eve, many think that judgment will not come to them. They think that they can disregard the laws of God and that punishment will not follow. His judgment may not come as swiftly as it did in the case of Adam and Eve, but it is sure and it will come. Paul wrote: "Be not deceived; God is not mocked: for whatsoever a man soweth, that shall he also reap. For he that soweth to his flesh shall of the flesh reap corruption; but he that soweth to the Spirit shall of the Spirit reap life everlasting. And let us not be weary in well doing: for in due season we shall reap, if we faint not" (Galatians 6: 7-9).

Judgment comes to nations as well as to individuals. The message of the Lord to Josiah was that judgment was coming to Judah as a nation. Collectively, the inhabitants of Judah had sinned against God. And so judgment would come upon its people collectively. Herein is a word of warning for our nation. Can we violate the laws of God and not experience His judgment? The answer is no. God will not make an exception in our case. As a nation, we must return to God. This returning must begin with the individual. Therefore each person is important in a revival of righteousness that will again bring the blessings of God to our land.

17. Because they have forsaken me, and have burned incense unto other gods, that they might provoke me to anger with all the works of their hands; therefore my wrath shall be kindled against this place, and shall not be quenched.

The accusation which the Lord brought against Judah was twofold. First, they had forsaken Him. They owed their very existence to God. It was He who delivered them from Egyptian bondage; who sustained them in the wilderness; who secured the land of Canaan for them; and who defeated the armies of their enemies. Yet they had forsaken Him. One is reminded of Demas, the companion of the Apostle Paul. Although he lived close to the presence and power of God as manifested in Paul's life, the time came when he turned aside from following after the Lord. Paul attributed Demas' demise to love for this world (see 2 Timothy 4:10). How unfortunate that any people should turn away from the Lord. Do you know anyone who was once warm to the Lord, but who is cool to Him now?

The second accusation which the Lord mentioned against Judah was that they had burned incense unto other gods. Not only had they forsaken God, they also had turned to other gods. Very specifically, the Lord had said to Israel: "I am the Lord thy God, which have brought thee out of the land of Egypt, out of the house of bondage. Thou shalt have no other gods before me" (Exodus 20:2, 3). The record of the conquest of the Christian message is: "Ye turned to God from idols to serve the living and true God" (1 Thessalonians 1:9).

When a person forsakes God and turns to idols, he provokes God to anger and incurs His wrath. Judah felt the heavy hand of God upon them because of their sin.

C. A Worthy Exception (vv. 18-20)

(2 Kings 22:18-20 is not included in the printed text.)

In the midst of His pronouncements of judgment, God displayed mercy toward Josiah, king of Judah. The Lord based His show of mercy upon Josiah's righteous and humble attitude. The king's tender heart bled when he heard of the judgments that were coming. He rent his clothes and wept before the Lord.

It is a beautiful thing to be a reed unto God's judgments, rather than an oak. The meek and gentle reed stoops, and therefore stands; the oak stands stiffly against the strongest gust, and therefore is turned up by the roots. There is great wisdom in knowing when to bend and bow and yield to the voice of the Lord.

Because of his godlike behavior, Josiah did not see the judgment of God upon Judah. The desolation and curse and evil were stayed until the king died. He was allowed to go to his grave in peace.

Josiah set a worthy example for the people of Judah. His life and actions were pleasing to the Lord. He sought to bring the nation back to God. Although his efforts failed to avert the judgment of God upon the land, they nevertheless had their impact. God is still looking for men who will lead the way in righteousness.

III. RESPONDING WITH OBEDIENCE (2 Kings 23:1-23)

A. A Valiant Effort (vv. 1-3)

(2 Kings 23:1-3 is not included in the printed text.)

Although Josiah had been assured that he would be personally exempted from the forthcoming calamity, he did everything in his power to save the people. His first move was to bring all the people together and to instruct them in the Word of the Lord. By reading the Word, he had experienced a personal revival. He hoped that the people would respond in the same manner as they heard the Word.

Josiah read to the people the covenant responsibilities that God required of them. Then he led them in making a commitment to the Lord. He promised that he would follow the Lord with all his heart and soul. The people joined with him in this commitment. Josiah is an example of a man who uses his influence for the good of others and the glory of God. We need more like him today.

B. A Courageous Attack (vv. 4-20)

(2 Kings 23:4-20 is not included in the printed text.)

Josiah intensified his campaign to wipe out idolatry in the land. According to 2 Chronicles 34:3-7, he had already begun his efforts toward reform. Then after the people joined with him in a covenant with the Lord, he sought to continue and to carry to completion his crusade to eradicate evil and to restore good. He began by destroying the idols that had been brought to the Temple of the Lord. He also did away with the idolatrous priests whom the kings of Judah had appointed. He violated the graves of the dead and burned their bones on the altar.

We must bear in mind that idolatry was the oppressive curse under which the kingdom of Judah lay crushed. As a theocratic king, he could admit no rival to Jehovah; idolatry must be utterly stamped out.

C. A Restored Observance (vv. 21-23)

(2 Kings 23:21-23 is not included in the printed text.)

In addition to his attacks on all forms of idolatrous worship, Josiah also sought to restore the observance of the Passover. It seems that this important part of the symbolic history of Israel had been neglected since the time of the judges. At least, if it had been observed, it was observed according to custom rather than according to the prescribed formula of the Law. What Josiah proposed to do was to have the Passover observed strictly according to all the Mosaic laws. Whatever had been changed or neglected in the past, he hoped to have restored to its proper order. It was an obvious attempt to do everything in his power to gain the favor of God for the people of Judah.

REVIEW QUESTIONS

1. Where was the Book of the Law found?

2. How did Josiah react when he first heard the Law read?

3. What charge did Josiah make after he had heard the Law read?

4. To whom did the delegation go to inquire of the Lord?

5. What was the message from the Lord which Huldah gave to the delegation?

GOLDEN TEXT HOMILY

"STUDY TO SHEW THYSELF APPROVED UNTO GOD, A WORKMAN THAT NEEDETH NOT TO BE ASHAMED, RIGHTLY DIVIDING THE WORD OF TRUTH" (2 Timothy 2:15).

Paul's letter to Timothy could easily be renamed "Encouragement From a Dungeon." The aged apostle described, to his close friend Timothy, the conditions of the evil world in which they lived. He realized Timothy would be ministering in a world of deception.

We experience deception in numerous

forms. It is practically impossible to become so knowledgeable of every angle of life that all deception would be readily recognizable. We know that some form of control or deception over one another is an inescapable part of human living.

Paul's encouraging words to Timothy were intended to persuade him to put out every effort to present himself to God as one who has stood the test. The spiritual "tests" are comprehensive. The lessons are to be taught from an early age through adulthood. The workman needs the proper input if he is to become effective in his world of deceivers.

The Greek word for one who has stood the test is **doKimos**. DoKimos describes anything which has been tested and purified and which is fit for service. The opposite idea would be an **adoKimastos**, which means "tested and found wanting." Timothy was to become a doKimos. Paul desired that he would become a fit weapon for the work of Christ, a workman who had no need to be ashamed.

It is extremely difficult, if not impossible, to properly distribute or divide the Word of God unless we have been purified for service. The workman is to divide the words of life, just as a father will equally divide the food at a meal so each family member receives his necessary portion.

The Greeks used the phrase "rightly divide" for the work of a mason in cutting and squaring a stone so that it fitted into its correct place in the building. So the man who has passed the necessary qualifications, found his place in the structure, and is not ashamed of the truth is ready to share his experience. He takes each section of the truth and fits it into its correct position. Each workman should desire to allow himself to become properly prepared, because he, just like Timothy, will one day be in the position of "rightly dividing the word of truth" to those God has allowed him to train.—**Wayne White, M-Div., Chaplain/US Army, Fort Hood, Texas**

SENTENCE SERMONS

THERE IS ONLY one great issue and that is to get the truths of the Bible into the hearts of the people.

—**William Gladstone**

ONE EVIDENCE of the value of the Bible is the character of those who oppose it.

—**Anonymous**

AN AFRICAN WOMAN was asked if she enjoyed reading her new Bible. She replied, "Sir, I am not reading this Book. The Book is reading me!"

—**"Bible Society Record"**

THE BIBLE HAS lost hold, but nothing has arisen to take its place. That is the gravest aspect of the matter. It was the cement with which our Western communities were built and by which they were held together.

—**H. G. Wells**

THE BIBLE seems to me like a river of light flowing through my darkness and it has kept my hope of accomplishments bright when things seemed too difficult to overcome.

—**Helen Keller**

EVANGELISTIC APPLICATION

THE WORD OF GOD SHOWS THE SINNER HOW HE CAN FIND FORGIVENESS AND PEACE.

A man serving a life sentence for murder escaped from the Oklahoma State Penitentiary. The warden, Jerome J. Waters, offered the fugitive $1,500 if he presented himself at the gate of the prison. There was a catch to the offer, however. The reward was to be earned and saved by the escapee by his working in the prison. "If he comes, we will see that he doesn't get out again. Justice must prevail," said the warden.

How different, by contrast, is the offer God makes to all fugitives from divine justice! There is no catch to His offer. His justice has been satisfied by the vicarious death of the Savior. All who present themselves to God in faith and repentance will be received, not as fugitives, but as sons of God, "justified from all things" (Acts 13:39). When we confess our sins, God forgives. With His forgiveness comes a peace that passes all understanding. Faith in Jesus Christ elevates the soul and produces a calm and serene spirit.

ILLUMINATING THE LESSON

Some years ago a little group of freethinkers in Scotland decided on a plan whereby they might show up the inaccuracies of Scripture and so cause the people to realize, as they put it, that the Bible was not really the Word of God. One member was given the task of going to Asia Minor and southern Europe and the islands of the Mediterranean, and visiting all the places mentioned by Luke in connection with Paul's journeys. It was hoped that he would be able to unearth so much information as would make evident the falsity of Luke's record, that many who had pinned their faith to the book of Acts as a part of God's inspired Word would have to give it up. The young man chosen was Sir William Ramsay. He investigated very carefully, and after the most minute examinations concluded that Luke was absolutely accurate in every particular; and he himself, once a freethinker, became a Christian, and has written some splendid books in defense of the Word of God.

—**Dr. H. A. Ironside**

DAILY DEVOTIONAL GUIDE

M. Teaching God's Word. Deuteronomy 6:1-9

T. Reading the Word. Nehemiah 8:1-12

W. Cleansing by the Word. Psalm 119:9-16

T. Quoting the Word. Matthew 4:1-11

F. Power of the Word. Hebrews 4:1-13

S. Regenerated by the Word. 1 Peter 1:13-25

August 30, 1981

Divine Discipline

Bible Background: 2 Kings 24:1—25:30; Book of Nehemiah; Jeremiah 30:1—31:34

Time: 586 B.C.

Place: Jerusalem

Supplemental References: 2 Chronicles 36:9-23; Jeremiah 39:1-10

Golden Text: "After those days, saith the Lord, I will put my law in their inward parts, and write it in their hearts; and will be their God, and they shall be my people" (Jeremiah 31:33).

Central Truth: The purpose of God's discipline is to correct disobedience and to restore fellowship with His people.

Evangelistic Emphasis: God forgives those who repent of their sin and disobedience and accepts them into His fellowship.

PRINTED TEXT

2 Kings 25:1. And it came to pass in the ninth year of his reign, in the tenth month, in the tenth day of the month, that Nebuchadnezzar king of Babylon came, he, and all his host, against Jerusalem, and pitched against it; and they built forts against it round about.

2. And the city was besieged unto the eleventh year of king Zedekiah.

3. And on the ninth day of the fourth month the famine prevailed in the city, and there was no bread for the people of the land.

4. And the city was broken up, and all the men of war fled by night by the way of the gate between two walls, which is by the king's garden: (now the Chaldees were against the city round about:) and the king went the way toward the plain.

5. And the army of the Chaldees pursued after the king, and overtook him in the plains of Jericho: and all his army were scattered from him.

6. So they took the king, and brought him up to the king of Babylon to Riblah; and they gave judgment upon him.

7. And they slew the sons of Zedekiah before his eyes, and put out the eyes of Zedekiah, and bound him with fetters of brass, and carried him to Babylon.

8. And in the fifth month, on the seventh day of the month, which is the nineteenth year of king Nebuchadnezzar king of Babylon, came Nebuzar-adan, captain of the guard, a servant of the king of Babylon, unto Jerusalem:

9. And he burnt the house of the Lord, and the king's house, and all the houses of Jerusalem, and every great man's house burnt he with fire.

10. And all the army of Chaldees, that were with the captain of the guard, brake down the walls of Jerusalem round about.

Jeremiah 30:1. The word that came to Jeremiah from the Lord, saying,

2. Thus speaketh the Lord God of Israel, saying, Write thee all the words that I have spoken unto thee in a book.

3. For, lo, the days come, saith the Lord, that I will bring again the captivity of my people Israel and Judah, saith the Lord: and I will cause them to return to the land that I gave to their fathers, and they shall possess it.

August 30, 1981

DICTIONARY

Nebuchadnezzar (neb-yoo-kud-NEZ-ur)—2 Kings 25:1—The king of the Neo-Babylonian empire who reigned from 605 to 562 B.C. It was he who carried away Judah in the 70 year Babylonian captivity.

Zedekiah (zed-ee-KI-uh)—2 Kings 25:2—The last king of Judah. He reigned only eleven years—597 to 586 B.C.

Chaldees (kal-DEES)—2 Kings 25:4—The people of Chaldea. Babylon was the capital of the country of Chaldea.

Riblah (RIB-lah)—2 Kings 25:6—The city at the head waters of the Orontes River.

Nebuzar-adan (NEB-yoo-zar-AA-dan)—2 Kings 25:8—A general in Nebuchadnezzar's army.

LESSON OUTLINE

I. RESULTS OF DISOBEDIENCE
  A. Jerusalem Sieged
  B. Jerusalem Burned
  C. Judah Exiled
II. PROMISE OF DELIVERANCE
  A. Deliverance Assured
  B. Deliverance Explained
  C. Deliverance Completed
III. DIVINE RESTORATION
  A. Remnant Returned
  B. Wall Rebuilt
  C. Sins Confessed

LESSON EXPOSITION

INTRODUCTION

One of the most beautiful tributes in Scripture is paid to Josiah: "And before him there was no king like him who turned to the Lord with all his heart and with all his soul and with all his might, according to all the law of Moses; nor did any like him arise after him" (2 Kings 23:25, **New American Standard Bible**). Unfortunately, Josiah's sons did not follow his worthy example. Of both Jehoahaz and Jehoiakim it is said: "And he did evil in the sight of the Lord" (2 Kings 23:32, 37; **New American Standard Bible**). Consequently, the Lord did not turn away from His fierce anger against Judah.

A father's devotion is not always emulated by his children. What joy it brings to a father's heart when his children follow the Lord even as he has followed Him. What pain a father experiences when his children choose to ignore his example and turn away from the Lord. Such was the case with Josiah's sons.

At this point, Nebuchadnezzar, king of Babylon, appears on the scene. He and his servants besieged Jerusalem. He took the king, Jehoiachin, his family, servants, captains, and officials captive. He stripped the Temple of the Lord and the king's house of all their treasures. He also captured all the mighty men of valor, and all the craftsmen and the smiths. The only ones he left were the poorest people of the land. He then made his uncle, Zedekiah, king. Zedekiah reigned in Jerusalem for eleven years.

Nebuchadnezzar was not a righteous king, yet God used him to carry out His judgments against Judah. The Scripture says: "For through the anger of the Lord this came about in Jerusalem and Judah until He cast them out from His presence" (2 Kings 24:20, **New American Standard Bible**). God is sovereign. He rules in the affairs of men. He can work through whomsoever He chooses to accomplish His purposes.

I. RESULTS OF DISOBEDIENCE (2 Kings 25: 1-30)

A. Jerusalem Sieged (vv. 1-7)

1. And it came to pass in the ninth year of his reign, in the tenth month, in the tenth day of the month, that Nebuchadnezzar king of Babylon came, he, and all his host, against Jerusalem, and pitched against it; and they built forts against it round about.

2. And the city was besieged unto the eleventh year of king Zedekiah.

Although Nebuchadnezzar had handpicked Zedekiah to be king in Jerusalem, Zedekiah rebelled against him. Consequently, Nebuchadnezzar brought his forces against Jerusalem. He laid siege to the city and encamped outside it. The siege continued for less than two years. Its effects were devastating.

As we shall see, the overthrow of Jerusalem was total. The city was sacked, its palaces and public buildings demolished, and its massive walls pulled down. Even the Temple

—the house of the Lord, the pride of the Hebrews, the pivot of their national history, the lament of the faithful to this day—was pillaged, dismantled, burned to the ground, and its sacred vessels and furniture broken and scattered. Unmistakably, the divine Word was fulfilled. If God pronounces judgment, His judgment is sure.

Exhibited in one of the cases in the library of the Vatican is an ancient palimpsest. Centuries ago, men had written line after line on sheets of papyrus until their work filled an entire volume. Many years later, when paper was difficult to secure, someone found the old volume and wrote a new work across the original manuscript, in lines perpendicular to the first. Today the blacker ink of the second writing is more legible, but the text underneath is still clear enough to read with ease; scholars frequently take more delight in reading the older than they do the more recent writing.

Across the pages of the Bible, God has written the eternal truths of His being, His holiness, His justice, and the certainty of His wrath against sin. Men have turned the pages sidewise and written with blacker ink the history of their doings and their philosophy. But the day will come when the acid of God's judgment will eat away the writings of man, and the original writing by which man will be judged will surface.

3. And on the ninth day of the fourth month the famine prevailed in the city, and there was no bread for the people of the land.

4. And the city was broken up, and all the men of war fled by night by the way of the gate between two walls, which is by the king's garden: (now the Chaldees were against the city round about:) and the king went the way toward the plain.

Nebuchadnezzar was so incensed by the revolt of Zedekiah that he accompanied his immense army to Jerusalem. They besieged the city for one and a half years until its inhabitants were reduced to misery and starvation. Then at midnight, in our month of July, 587 B.C., an entrance was forced into the lower city on the north side. In desperation the whole army attempted to escape even though the city was surrounded by the Babylonians. They moved out in the direction of the Jordan Valley. The king, his family, and his attendants also attempted to escape.

As we shall see, this desperate effort at deliverance failed. What a different outcome can be expected when one waits upon God for deliverance.

Missionaries at a certain Chinese mission were ordered by the British legation to leave Sanyuan because of the dangers from conflicting soldiers. "Carts were ordered, and all was ready to start the next day. Then it came over the missionaries that it would be dishonoring God to go to a place of safety, leaving their flock exposed. So a prayer meeting was held, with the result that the carts were sent away and they stayed. They were kept in peace of mind, although a robber band, a thousand strong, was marching on the city and was within twelve miles. Then came a terrific downpour of rain, such as had not been known for years, scattering the robbers and making the roads impassable."

Israel and Judah had seen the hand of God work in just such a miraculous manner many times. One of the more recent displays of His might was seen in His intervention against Sennacherib and his armies (see 2 Kings 19:35, 36). Now, without God, Judah was faced with humiliation and utter defeat.

5. And the army of the Chaldees pursued after the king, and overtook him in the plains of Jericho: and all his army were scattered from him.

6. So they took the king, and brought him up to the king of Babylon to Riblah; and they gave judgment upon him.

7. And they slew the sons of Zedekiah before his eyes, and put out the eyes of Zedekiah, and bound him with fetters of brass, and carried him to Babylon.

A fearful slaughter is pictured in this passage. King Zedekiah, his wives, children, and guards fled through an opening made in the wall only to be captured in the plains of Jericho. His army was scattered, and he and his family were forced to march to Riblah to face the angry Nebuchadnezzar. Because he violated his oath of allegiance to Babylon, Zedekiah was compelled to watch as his family and friends were murdered. Then his own eyes were put out, and he was carried in chains to Babylon.

Regardless of the severity of Zedekiah's misdeeds, the punishment meted out to him was a horrible example of the barbarity of the times. The last thing that he ever saw was the murder of his own sons. Then he was rendered forever incapable of seeing anything else by his eyes being gouged out. This was done, as one writer strongly puts it, that "his sons might be ever dying before him, and himself in their death ever miserable." The last vassal king of Judah perished in a Babylonian prison. What a sad conclusion to a many times glorious story.

A remarkable story recently appeared in a daily newspaper. An oyster fisherman opened the shell of an oyster and discovered within it a fish, three and a half inches long, alive and weakly struggling. The oyster, however, was not to be found. The fisherman was convinced that the fish had entered the open shell and had been trapped by its closing. Once inside, however, the fish proceeded to devour the oyster, but being unable to open the shell, would have died in it.

Sin sometimes enters the life through the door of a careless will. Once inside, it is most difficult to remove, and speedily makes itself master of the premises, eventually destroying the whole life. Zedekiah learned this lesson.

B. Jerusalem Burned (vv. 8-10)

8. And in the fifth month, on the seventh day of the month, which is the nineteenth year of king Nebuchadnezzar king of Babylon, came Nebuzar-adan, captain of the guard, a servant of the king of Babylon, unto Jerusalem:

9. And he burnt the house of the Lord, and the king's house, and all the houses of Jerusalem, and every great man's house burnt he with fire.

10. And all the army of the Chaldees, that were with the captain of the guard, brake down the walls of Jerusalem round about.

About one month expired between the time that Zedekiah and his armies fled from Jerusalem and the destruction of the city. Apparently the Babylonian army was waiting for directions from Nebuchadnezzar. He sent Nebuzaradan to carry out the destruction of the city.

The havoc wrought upon Jerusalem was not total but it was extensive. Every important house, including the Temple of the Lord and the royal palace, was burned down. Then the Babylonians assaulted the walls of the city and broke them down. Thus Jerusalem lay in ruins.

The magnificent buildings for which David had made such elaborate plans, and which Solomon had erected with enormous effort, and adorned with so much pomp, were ruthlessly destroyed with fire and crowbar. The Temple of the Lord had stood for 436 years. It beautified the earth and honored heaven. Now, it was reduced to a heap of ashes. Jerusalem—the wonder of all times, the paragon of nations, the glory of the earth, the favorite of heaven—was now a spectacle of desolation, a monument of ruin.

Those who were taken away captive mourned the destruction of Jerusalem by an annual fast. In later days when the Jews built a house they left one part of it unfinished, in remembrance that Jerusalem and the Temple lay desolate. At the least, they left about a yard square of the house unplastered, on which they wrote in great letters: "If I forget thee, O Jerusalem."

At one point, Jerusalem had seemed to be invincible. But when God was no longer acknowledged and worshiped within its walls, it shared the fate of many great cities, and was leveled. How we need His guardian presence!

C. Judah Exiled (vv. 11-30)

(2 Kings 25:11-30 is not included in the printed text.)

Nebuzaradan carried the majority of the people into exile. He left only the poorest of the poor to work the vineyards and fields. These were the common people, the people without property, not merely in Jerusalem, but throughout the whole land.

Not satisfied that the Temple had been burned down, the Babylonians proceeded to plunder the place. The pillars of brass, the stands, and the brazen sea were broken in pieces; it would have been difficult to carry these colossal things away without breaking them up. Along with the smaller vessels of brass, silver, and gold, these pieces were carried away.

It seems that certain Jews had taken sanctuary in the Temple. They came forth when it was set on fire. They, along with some other officials in the city, were taken to Riblah where the king had them executed.

Then Nebuchadnezzar appointed Gedaliah to be over the people he had left behind in Judah. The people were encouraged to settle down in the land, and to serve the king of Babylon They were assured that if they did so all would be well with them. But, in time, Ishmael, the son of Nethaniah, came with ten men and assassinated Gedaliah and also the men of Judah and the Babylonians who were with him at Mizpah. This action struck fear in the hearts of the people and they fled to Egypt.

This chapter concludes with the report that Jehoiachin gained favor with the king of Babylon. He was released from prison and given a seat of honor. "So Jehoiachin put aside his prison clothes and for the rest of his life ate regularly at the king's table" (2 Kings 25:29, **New International Version**). Jehoiachin represented the faded glory of Israel; and his treatment suggests a faint hope of the future restoration and elevation of his unhappy people. No doubt, the improvement in Jehoiachin's condition is to be traced to the overruling providence and grace of Him who still cherished purposes of love to the house of David. Thus the longest, weariest, darkest night comes to an end, and the long-looked-for dawn breaks at last, bringing rest, and hope, and gladness with its expanding light.

II. PROMISE OF DELIVERANCE (Jeremiah 30: 1-22)

A. Deliverance Assured (vv. 1-3)

1. The word that came to Jeremiah from the Lord, saying,

2. Thus speaketh the Lord God of Israel, saying, Write thee all the words that I have spoken unto thee in a book.

3. For, lo, the days come, saith the Lord, that I will bring again the captivity of my people Israel and Judah, saith the Lord: and I will cause them to return to the land that I gave to their fathers, and they shall possess it.

The promise of God through Jeremiah is clear and unmistakable. The people of Judah would not always be captive. God would bring them back to the land of their fathers and they would possess it again. The Lord promised to restore the fortunes of the people. In a judicial sense this meant that He would remove the sentence of imprisonment. In a broader sense it meant a restoration of the people to their primal status. It certainly meant a restoration from exile. This news was music to the ears of the people of God.

God's eye is still upon the Jews as is evidenced by this interesting account. A Jewish son came home to spend the weekend with his parents. He said to his father: "I have never believed in God before. But now, after what I have experienced in the war, I can never again doubt God's existence. In the midst of the fighting in the Negev, three divisions of Egyptian troops came to attack a point that was held by only about twenty of us. We knew that it was an absolutely impossible situation, but we decided to fight to the last man. We had hardly begun to fire at the enemy when two divisions of them turned and fled, and the third held up their hands and surrendered. Afterward, they were greatly surprised to find there were so few of us. They said to us, "Where are the others?" We replied, "What others do you mean?" The Egyptians said, "We saw others with you. Where are they?" We answered, "There were no others with us." The son ended his story by saying, "Then we knew that God had worked a miracle for us."

In what ways has God demonstrated His love in your life? Can you recount the times that He has intervened at the point of your need?

B. Deliverance Explained (vv. 4-11)

(Jeremiah 30:4-11 is not included in the printed text.)

Jeremiah gives a description of the plight of Israel in their captivity. He also prophesies about the future tragedy that will befall that nation. In both instances, the people of God are assured of God's presence. He lets them know that any punishment they face is temporary and corrective; it is not final and fatal. Ultimately, the Lord is their deliverer, and He will deliver them.

In captivity, the Israelites faced fear, pain, and terror. But their misery ushered in their deliverance—a deliverance as speedy as is the transition from a woman's labor pangs to her joy at giving birth to a child. In unmistakable terms, the Lord says, " ' "So do not fear, O Jacob my servant; do not be dismayed, O Israel," declares the Lord. "I will surely save you out of a distant place, your descendants from the land of their exile. Jacob will again have peace and security, and no one will make him afraid. I am with you and will save you," declares the Lord.' " (Jeremiah 30:10, 11; **New International Version**)

Jeremiah's message has more than a local and immediate meaning. It has future significance and universal application. Its reference to "the time of Jacob's trouble" (v. 7) refers also to the end-time struggles of the Jews. Its mention of "David their king, whom I will raise up unto them" (v. 9) speaks of the coming Messiah, even the Lord Jesus Christ. No one of David's lineage had occupied the throne since the captivity. Zerubbabel was of David's line, but he never claimed the title of king. Therefore, the Messiah must be meant in this passage. He was appointed to the throne of David (see Isaiah 9:7; Luke 1:32). He is shown as deserving equal allegiance with God. In fact, God rules His people through His Son (see John 5:22, 23, 27). Christ is the great deliverer of the Chosen People. His hand will be in their final restoration.

C. Deliverance Completed (vv. 12-20)

(Jeremiah 30:12-22 is not included in the printed text.)

The afflictions which Judah faced were the results of their sin. There was nothing that man could do to relieve their plight. Their sin had been so grievous that their hope of the punishment soon coming to an end was vain. They had no one to blame for their circumstances but themselves. Their affliction was just; it was no more than they deserved. They had no right to complain.

Sin is a powerful force and its consequences are far reaching. Little did the people of Judah realize where their rebellion against God was leading. Sin is that way. It conceals the end result from the mind of the indulger. The pain, sorrow, and heartache which inevitably follow evil practice are hidden until the person is sufficiently trapped. When it is too late, sin emerges as the vile and wicked thing it really is. Then man cannot break its bonds by himself.

What Judah could not do for herself, and what others could not do for her, the Lord said that He would do. " ' "I will restore you to health and heal your wounds," declares the Lord' " (Jeremiah 30:17, **New International Version**). When the time for deliverance came, the Lord would overwhelm their foes. He would treat the enemy as the enemy had treated His people. Judah would again become the object of His abundant grace.

What a God we serve! He is a God who punishes and corrects when it is needed, but who also loves eternally. Regardless of the extent of our faults and shortcomings His grace is able to reach us and to restore us.

The Lord assured Israel of His blessings upon every aspect of their lives. The ultimate promise He made to them, " ' "So you will be my people, and I will be your God" ' " (Jeremiah 30:22, **New International Version**). He desires to say the same to each of us.

III. DIVINE RESTORATION (Nehemiah 1:1-3; 7:1-6; 9:1-3)

A. Remnant Returned (1:1-3)

(Nehemiah 1:1-3 is not included in the printed text.)

The promise which God made to the Jewish captives was now fulfilled. After 150 years of Babylonian captivity, many of them were back in their homeland. Their return was encouraged by King Cyrus of Persia. By this time, Persia had superseded Babylon as the dominant nation. So, when Cyrus decreed the rebuilding of Jerusalem's Temple and the return of Jewish captives, about fifty thousand of them returned with Ezra and Zerubbabel.

Although many Jews survived the exile and were back in Judah, their circumstances were unfavorable. When Nehemiah inquired about them, he was told that they were " 'in great trouble and disgrace.' " Their problems were further emphasized by the statement: " 'The wall of Jerusalem is broken down, and its gates have been burned with fire' " (Nehemiah 1:3, **New International Version**).

The wall had a symbolic significance for Nehemiah and for the Jews. It symbolized security, safety, and strength. Without the wall, the city was unprotected. Night prowlers and thieves, roving bandits and wild beasts, all were meant to be shut out by these walls so common to the ancient East.

There is a spiritual wall which every believer needs. Unless we are encircled by the wall of God's grace, we are unprotected from the attacks of the enemy. Within that wall we have salvation, security, and strength.

B. Wall Rebuilt (7:1-6)

(Nehemiah 7:1-6 is not included in the printed text.)

Nehemiah exercised more than a mental concern for Jerusalem. He took steps to do something about the plight of God's people in their homeland. He went to the Persian king, Artaxerxes, and requested permission to return to Jerusalem. The king granted his request. Upon arriving in Jerusalem, Nehemiah inspected the walls of the city. Then he organized the work force that was needed to rebuild the walls. In spite of fierce opposition he persisted until the wall was complete.

After the completion of the wall, Nehemiah sought to organize the inhabitants of the city. He chose Hanani to be in charge of Jerusalem. The basis of his choice was that "he was a man of integrity and feared God more than most men do" (Nehemiah 7:2, **New International Version**).

What criteria do we employ in selecting leaders for the church? Is our standard as high as that of Nehemiah?

If every worker in God's kingdom was chosen on the basis of his integrity and his reverence for God, what a difference it would make. The work of the Lord deserves no less.

There are times when interest and concern are not enough. At such times, we must take action to correct a situation or to accomplish a certain task. Less than this is displeasing to the Lord.

C. Sins Confessed (9:1-3)

(Nehemiah 9:1-3 is not included in the printed text.)

The children of Israel gathered in the Temple to humble themselves before God through mourning and fasting. After they heard the reading of the Word of God, they confessed their own sins and the sins of their fathers. This confession of sin much resembled the confession of the faithfulness of God and the unfaithfulness of Israel in Psalm 106. We are told that they stood up or remained standing in their place and listened to the reading of the Word of God for a fourth part of the day or about three hours. Then for another fourth part of the day, the next three hours, they made confession of their sins, and worshiped the Lord their God. How they must have hungered for a better knowledge of God and of His Word. How does your longing for God compare with theirs? Do you have an insatiable thirst to drink from the crystal stream which flows from His throne?

God honored the attitude of the Jews. Their confession and their spirit of worship did not go unnoticed by Him. Likewise, every sincere confession of sin is met with a positive response from the Lord. John wrote: "If we confess our sins, he is faithful and just and will forgive us our sins and purify us from all unrighteousness" (1 John 1:9, **New International Version**).

REVIEW QUESTIONS

1. By what action did Zedekiah become king of Judah?

2. What caused Nebuchadnezzar, king of Babylon, to impose a siege on the city of Jerusalem?

3. What did the Chaldeans do to king Zedekiah when he was overtaken in his attempt to flee the city of Jerusalem?

4. Describe the extent of the destruction the invaders brought on the city of Jerusalem.

5. What practical applications do you draw from this lesson?

GOLDEN TEXT HOMILY

"AFTER THOSE DAYS, SAITH THE LORD, I WILL PUT MY LAW IN THEIR INWARD PARTS, AND WRITE IT IN THEIR HEARTS; AND WILL BE THEIR GOD, AND THEY SHALL BE MY PEOPLE" (Jeremiah 31:33).

Perhaps the most familiar portion of Jeremiah's preaching is this covenant passage (31:31-34), often called the cornerstone of personal religion, definitively declaring that every person is to be his own priest and prophet. J. Philip Hyatt in his book **Jeremiah: Prophet of Courage and Hope** speaks of this passage as forming the verbal basis of the division of our Bible into the Old and New Testaments and of all the ideas centering around the old covenant with Israel and the new covenant of Christianity.

This declaration of Jeremiah was to a self-righteous people who naively deluded themselves into believing that their national identification with the Mosaic Covenant was unconditional. This is to say that God's existence was to serve His people, rather than the nation's existence being to serve the purposes of God. As a consequence of this erroneous, religious predisposition, the seemingly great promise of King Josiah's religious reformation (2 Kings 22, 23) produced ineffective results indeed. This abortive attempt to cause the people of God to face the firm consequences of disobedience and respond through repentance resulted in a soul-searching experience for Jeremiah. His appeal for a fundamental reordering of the Judaic society which would exemplify an acceptance of their covenant responsibilities was in vain.

Viewing Judah's rampant spiritual and civil corruption, Jeremiah realized that the Mosaic Covenant had failed and that a new covenant would have to be written, written not on tablets of stone, but upon the hearts of the people. This new covenant would be more than an intellectual comprehension of God's existence and nature. Reminiscent of the Johannine teaching of regeneration, a person under the new covenant would have the will and ability to obey God's moral requirements as well as knowing and understanding them, a consequence of an intimate, spiritual relationship with God within which forgiveness and renewal are a continuing reality.—**Edward E. Shoupe, Chaplain, Lieutenant Colonel, United States Air Force (Retired)**

SENTENCE SERMONS

GOD ADMINISTERS DISCIPLINE to correct disobedience and to restore fellowship with His people.

—**Selected**

GOD IS MORE interested in making us what He wants us to be than giving us what we ought to have.

—**Walter L. Wilson**

DEPEND ON DIVINE displacement rather than self-discipline.

—**Dr. Robert B. Munger**

THE SAINTS OF HISTORY have been people of both self and divine discipline.

—**"Speaker's Sourcebook"**

EVANGELISTIC APPLICATION

GOD FORGIVES THOSE WHO REPENT OF THEIR SIN AND DISOBEDIENCE AND ACCEPTS THEM INTO HIS FELLOWSHIP.

Jesus told a story about a young man who became known as a prodigal son. This young man requested from his father his share of the estate. He chose to take his wealth and squander it by wild living in a distant country. Before long he had spent everything. His problems increased when a severe famine hit the country where he was staying. To relieve his misery, he finally got a job feeding pigs. Without money, without food, utterly destitute, he reassessed his lot in life. He realized his folly, and longed to return to his father's house.

Before he ever returned home, he made a confession in his own heart. He decided that when he got home he would say, " ' "Father, I have sinned against heaven and against you" ' " (Luke 15:18, **New International Version**).

How did his father respond? " 'But while he was still a long way off, his father saw him and was filled with compassion for him; he ran to his son, threw his arms around him and kissed him' " (Luke 15:20, **New International Version**).

If an earthly father responds to his son's return in this way, how much more receptive will the Heavenly Father be!

ILLUMINATING THE LESSON

A Free-thought lecturer had just delivered himself of the following sentence:—"If there is a God in heaven, why does He not paralyse this right arm or strike me dead?" when a sturdy butcher stepped to the front, saying, "My man, the Almighty does na' think it worth His while to strike you, but His servant will do it in His name." The argument and scuffle which followed brought the lecturer to the ground, and the lecture to an abrupt conclusion.

—**"Durham County Chronicle"**

If there were never so fair a garden planted, and left without a fence, its herbs and plants would soon be rooted up; so it is in the Church where discipline is wanting.

—**Cawdray**

Men think God is destroying them because he is tuning them. The violinist screws up the key till the tense cord sounds the concert-pitch; but it is not to break it, but to use it tunefully, that he stretches the string upon the musical rack.

—**Beecher**

DAILY DEVOTIONAL GUIDE

M. God's Patience. Genesis 18:22-33

T. God's Nature. Exodus 34:1-7

W. The Path of Repentance. Psalm 51:1-12

T. The Blessing of Discipline. Psalm 94:12-19

F. Counsel Concerning Discipline. Proverbs 3:1-12

S. Need for Self-discipline. 2 Peter 3:8-18